Catherine LaBerta

Computers Are Your Future

Introductory

Second Custom Edition for Brookdale Community College

Taken from:
Computers Are Your Future, Introductory, Twelfth Edition
by Catherine LaBerta

Cover Art: Courtesy of Photodisc/Getty Images.

Taken from:

Computers Are Your Future, Introductory, Twelfth Edition
by Catherine LaBerta
Copyright © 2012, 2011, 2009, 2008, 2006 by Pearson Education, Inc.
Published by Prentice Hall
Upper Saddle River, New Jersey 07458

This special edition published in cooperation with Pearson Learning Solutions.

All trademarks, service marks, registered trademarks, and registered service marks are the property of their respective owners and are used herein for identification purposes only.

Pearson Learning Solutions, 501 Boylston Street, Suite 900, Boston, MA 02116
A Pearson Education Company
www.pearsoned.com

Printed in the United States of America

1 2 3 4 5 6 7 8 9 10 V303 17 16 15 14 13 12

000200010271689953

CW

ISBN 10: 1-256-84077-7
ISBN 13: 978-1-256-84077-0

With love

to my parents, Chester and Eleanore, for their unending support; to my son, Michael, for years of laughter, challenges, and insight; to my brother, sister, and brother-in-law for help during the tough times; and to Stephanie Wall for providing me with an exceptional opportunity, one I truly enjoyed.

Acknowledgments

Thanks to the many professionals at Prentice Hall who made this book possible and assisted with questions and feedback during the writing process. Special thanks to Stephanie Wall, Executive Editor, for providing me with this wonderful opportunity, and to my project managers, Virginia Guariglia and Meghan Bisi, for keeping me on schedule and connected to the process. Thanks also to Linda Harrison, my developmental editor, for her input, guidance, patience, and incredible eye for detail throughout the development cycle, and to Amanda Roscoe for using her insight and skill to convert storyboards into the exceptional videos included in this edition. I am grateful for the friends and colleagues who, through the years, have encouraged my professional growth and energy. Finally, thanks to my family and friends, but especially my parents, Chester and Eleanore, for encouraging me when I was young, and to my son, Michael, for keeping me on my toes, providing me with input when asked, and being patient when I was writing and could not join him on the golf course. I am sure I forgot to mention someone, but in my heart I have forgotten no one. Thank you all!

Brief Contents

Contents

Preface

A Reference Tool for Today's Students

Today, students are not as "wowed" by technology as they used to be; it is part of their everyday lives. This book has been written to match what they already know with what instructors have told us they should know.

Computers Are Your Future serves as a reference tool without being overwhelming or intimidating. Today's students want a practical "what it is" and "how it works" approach to computers, with less explanation of "why." This new edition has been written with this in mind. For example, the new Spotlight about cloud computing highlights the many newer Web-based tools available that many students aren't necessarily aware of.

Computers Are Your Future, 12/e, will help you with the challenge of teaching even the most diverse class—without sacrificing quality, integrity, or choice.

The 12th edition includes the following new items:

- NEW! Videos that illustrate key concepts in each chapter are included on a CD that accompanies the book.
- NEW! You will find a Facebook page for the text with updated content.
- NEW! Fast Forward boxes in each chapter keep students up to date on emerging technologies.
- NEW! A How-to element was added in each chapter, providing students with a hands-on activity utilizing information covered in the chapter.
- New Spotlight on cloud computing covers this emerging technology.
- All new end-of-chapter assignments are included in all chapters.
- Updated statistics and screen captures are incorporated.
- In Spotlight sections, we added Key Terms, Multiple Choice questions, and 50%+ new projects.
- Added focus on collaboration, a key concept in today's world, is covered.
- Coverage of social networking has been expanded.
- Enhanced coverage of Web-based applications is included.
- The application software chapter has been revised to cover Microsoft Office 2010.
- Updated hardware coverage includes the iPad, iPhone 4, and Droid, as well as additional content on netbooks.
- The chapter on the Internet and the World Wide Web has been completely reorganized.

- Content on viruses and virus protection as well as programming has been heavily revised.
- Some topics students found challenging in previous editions, including storage, operating system functions, and the use of cache memory, have been clarified.

ABOUT THIS BOOK

Spotlight sections are essentially mini-chapters that cover the practical, as well as the innovative, in various subject areas. For example, Ethics, File Management, and Buying and Upgrading Your Home Computer System focus on the practical, whereas Web 2.0, Cloud Computing, and Digital Life cover innovation in software, hardware, and technology for the future. We've added reinforcing exercises at the end of each Spotlight, and most of them are new in this edition.

Teamwork exercises are included as an end-of-chapter activity to reinforce chapter concepts by requiring students to work in teams to conduct research and interviews and to create group papers and presentations.

Green Tech Tips provide eco-friendly solutions to living and working with technology. These range from actions students can apply on their own to those that are initiated by companies in an effort to preserve the environment.

Ethics boxes offer an ethical perspective on decisions and situations that involve computers and technology. They raise "what if"-type questions in a "What would you do format?" to prompt thoughtful discussion and debate on complicated issues.

New **Fast Forward** boxes address emerging technologies relevant to each chapter. Adding these boxes enabled us to eliminate the Spotlight on Emerging Technologies found in previous editions, and allows for more coverage of these topics throughout the book.

The new **How-to** feature provides students with hands-on opportunities to use the information covered in the chapter.

INSTRUCTOR'S RESOURCE CENTER CD-ROM

The Pearson Prentice Hall Instructor's Resource Center on CD-ROM includes the tools you expect from a Prentice Hall Computer Concepts text, such as these:

- Teaching Notes
- Solutions to all questions and exercises from the book and Web site
- Customizable PowerPoint slide presentations for each chapter
- Sample syllabus
- Assignments

- Discussion questions
- Internet exercises
- Web resources
- Key terms
- An image library of all of the figures from the text
- Test bank

TESTGEN SOFTWARE

TestGen is a test generator that lets you view and easily edit test bank questions, transfer them to tests, and print the tests in a variety of formats best suited to your teaching situation. Powerful search and sort functions enable you to easily locate questions and arrange them in the order you prefer.

TOOLS FOR ONLINE LEARNING

myitlab *Computers Are Your Future* content is now included in my**it**lab's Content Library. This enables instructors to make learning tools such as PowerPoint presentations and end-of-chapter quizzes available to students, as well as to deliver performance-based testing on Microsoft Office applications and objective testing on both computer concepts and office applications.

Companion Web Site This text is accompanied by a companion Web site at **www.pearsonhighered.com/ cayf**. This site offers an interactive study guide, downloadable supplements, additional Internet exercises, Web resource links such as Careers in IT and crossword puzzles.

CourseCompass CourseCompass, available at **www.coursecompass.com**, is a dynamic, interactive online course-management tool powered exclusively for Pearson Education by Blackboard. This exciting product allows you to teach market-leading Pearson Education content in an easy-to-use, customizable format.

Blackboard Prentice Hall's abundant online content, combined with Blackboard's popular tools and interface, results in robust Web-based courses that are easy to implement, manage, and use—taking your courses to new heights in student interaction and learning.

WebCT Course-management tools within WebCT, available at **www.pearsonhighered.com/webct**, include page tracking, progress tracking, class and student management, a grade book, communication tools, a calendar, reporting tools, and more.

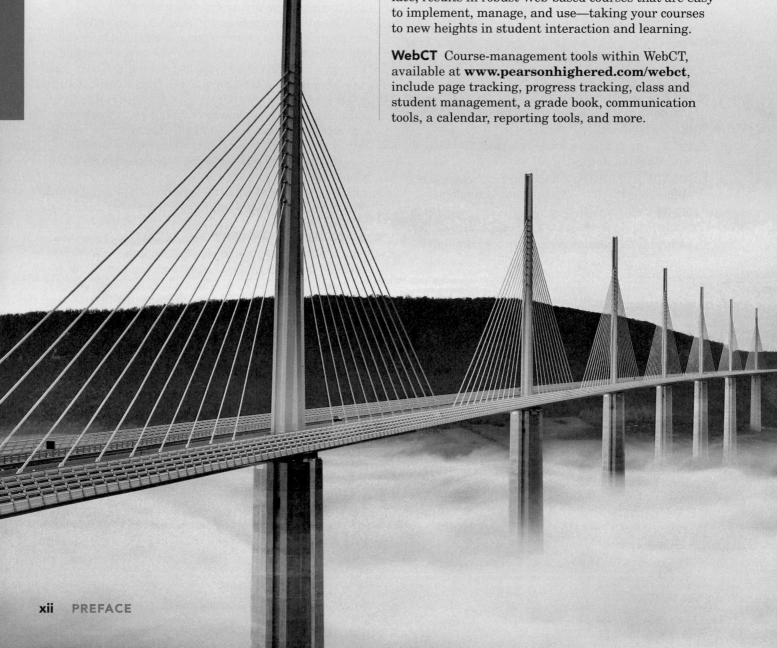

About the Author

Catherine LaBerta is currently an adjunct professor with SUNY at Buffalo and Canisius College, an independent contractor that provides application and technical training for the Western New York Work Force Development Institute, and a former Professor of Computer Science/Mathematics at Erie Community College in Buffalo, NY. She teaches courses that range from an introduction to computers to programming in C++ and Web development. Originally a math major, LaBerta took additional courses in computers and programming and found another field that clicked for her. She enjoys the constant changes in the computer and related fields because they force her to keep up and constantly learn. Not a total bookworm, LaBerta loves skiing (with Purgatory, CO, being a favorite spot) and boating (especially schooner trips off the coast of Maine) and will always be working on that golf game.

Visual Walkthrough

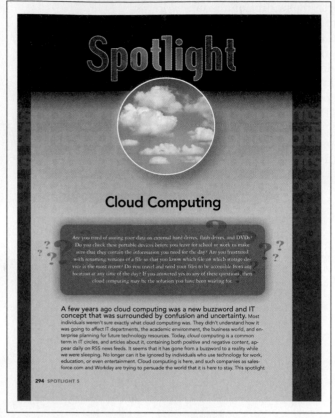

Cloud Computing

Are you tired of storing your data on external hard drives, flash drives, and DVDs? Do you check these portable devices before you leave for school or work to make sure that they contain the information you need for the day? Are you frustrated with renaming versions of a file so that you know which file on which storage device is the most recent? Do you travel and need your files to be accessible from any location at any time of the day? If you answered yes to any of these questions, then cloud computing may be the solution you have been waiting for.

A few years ago cloud computing was a new buzzword and IT concept that was surrounded by confusion and uncertainty. Most individuals weren't sure exactly what cloud computing was. They didn't understand how it was going to affect IT departments, the academic environment, the business world, and enterprise planning for future technology resources. Today, cloud computing is a common term in IT circles, and articles about it, containing both positive and negative content, appear daily on RSS news feeds. It seems that it has gone from a buzzword to a reality while we were sleeping. No longer can it be ignored by individuals who use technology for work, education, or even entertainment. Cloud computing is here, and such companies as salesforce.com and Workday are trying to persuade the world that it is here to stay. This spotlight

294 SPOTLIGHT 5

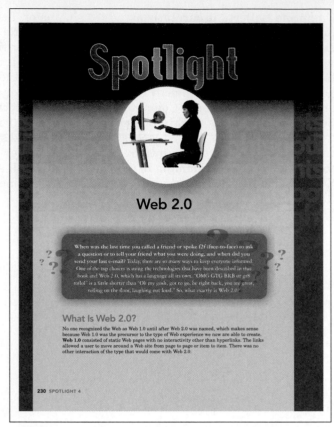

Web 2.0

When was the last time you called a friend or spoke f2f (face-to-face) to ask a question or to tell your friend what you were doing, and when did you send your last e-mail? Today, there are so many ways to keep everyone informed. One of the top choices is using the technologies that have been described in this book! Web 2.0, which has a language all its own. "OMG GTG BRB ur gr8 rotlol" is a little shorter than "Oh my gosh, got to go, be right back, you are great, rolling on the floor, laughing out loud." So, what exactly is Web 2.0?

What Is Web 2.0?
No one recognized the Web as Web 1.0 until after Web 2.0 was named, which makes sense because Web 1.0 was the precursor to the type of Web experience we now are able to create. **Web 1.0** consisted of static Web pages with no interactivity other than hyperlinks. The links allowed a user to move around a Web site from page to page or item to item. There was no other interaction of the type that would come with Web 2.0.

230 SPOTLIGHT 4

Spotlight sections highlight important ideas about computer-related topics and provide in-depth, useful information to take your learning to the next level.

ETHICS

USB DEVICES AND CONFIDENTIAL DATA
USB flash drives are incredibly popular, but many experts worry that they pose a great security risk. Some companies are so concerned about corporate espionage that they disable USB ports to prevent the unauthorized copying of data. Even so, many people carry a lot of critical or personal data on their USB flash drives. What are the implications if the device is lost? Should USB drive manufacturers be required to provide a means of securing these devices or some type of registration process? With such processes in place, a lost device could be returned to the manufacturer and matched to the owner. What actions should individuals take to safeguard their data? Is hooking a USB flash drive to your backpack or keychain a very good idea? If you found a USB flash drive and did not know who it belonged to, what would you do? What should you do?

Ethics Boxes highlight ethical issues for students to think about.

More than 700 million inkjet and laser toner cartridges are sold every year. What happens when they are empty? Although many organizations and retail stores have recycling programs, every second nearly eight used cartridges are thrown away in the United States—approximately 875 million pounds of environmental waste each year! So what can you do? Take advantage of your local recycling program. Some programs even pay you for your old cartridges because they can be recycled and sold again. Keeping them out of the waste stream reduces toxicity levels and saves landfill space. Besides, half a gallon of oil is saved for every toner cartridge you recycle! ●

Green Tech Tips share ways to be aware of the effects of technology on our earth.

FAST FORWARD

COURTROOMS OF THE FUTURE
Are you familiar with the sayings: "Seeing is believing," and "A picture is worth a thousand words"? If these words of wisdom are placed in the content of a courtroom, they gain even more strength. Now, add the ability to use technology to magnify voices, provide testimony from a witness confined to a hospital bed via webcam, obtain a translator through videoconferencing, and reproduce the scene and figures to provide a reenactment of the event digitally. Yes, it sounds like an episode from your favorite crime investigation show. But this is no television episode. With jurors traditionally having information organized for them in bulleted lists, slide shows, and presented in visual images.

Fast Forward boxes address emerging technologies relevant to each chapter.

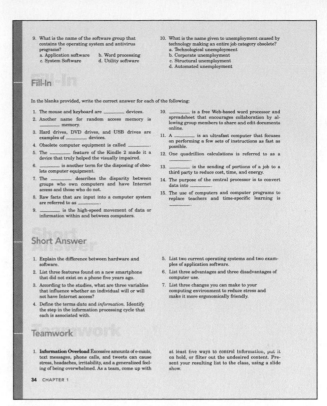

End-of-Chapter Material includes updated multiple-choice, matching, fill-in, and short-answer questions, identification, teamwork, as well as Web research projects so students can prepare for tests.

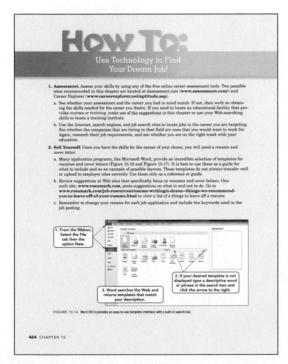

The **How To** activity in each chapter has students do some sort of hands-on exercise (such as creating something or choosing the appropriate technology) in which they apply what they learned in the chapter and demonstrate understanding.

NEW videos accompany the text, illustrating a key concept covered in each chapter.

Introductory

COMPUTERS
Are Your Future

chapter 1

Computers and You

Chapter Objectives

1 Define the word *computer* and name the four basic operations that a computer performs. (p. 7)

2 Describe the two main components of a computer system: hardware and software. (p. 7)

3 Provide examples of hardware devices that handle input, processing, output, and storage tasks. (p. 9)

4 Give an example of the information processing cycle in action. (p. 12)

5 Discuss the two major categories and the various types of computers. (p. 13)

6 Explain the advantages and disadvantages of computer use. (p. 21)

7 Recognize the ethical and societal impacts of computer use. (p. 25)

8 Discuss how computers affect employment. (p. 26)

9 List ways to be a responsible computer user. (p. 28)

So you have a cell phone in your hand and an iPod in your pocket and consider yourself a technologically savvy individual. But have you taken the time to look back and understand how the developments in technology have affected your family, friends, and way of life? Likewise, do you daydream of a future where you and your family members use communication devices with embedded translation capabilities, visit virtual reality vacation centers, and use solar- and wind-powered phone chargers?

The more you work with computers, the deeper and richer your understanding of computers and technology will become; eventually you will grow to be confident in your abilities. As your confidence and knowledge expand, you will become more adept in your use of computers and better prepared for the changes computer technology brings. No one is insulated from the impact that computers have or will continue to have on daily life.

This text provides information and insight into technology—its uses, assets, and drawbacks—related careers, and the knowledge and skill set required to make informed decisions about technology in all areas of your life. When you understand these concepts, you'll be better able to

- Decide whether to purchase new equipment or upgrade specific components.
- Judge the likely impact of computer innovations on your personal and business activities.
- Be aware of the different types of computing systems, their capabilities, and the businesses that they best compliment.
- Select the best applications for the information that you are processing or presenting.
- Keep abreast with and maintain a balance between the increase in mobile and portable computing and your privacy.
- Make career choices that use the technology skills you have acquired.
- Sort through the difficult ethical, moral, and societal challenges that computer use brings. ■

Check out f Facebook for our latest updates

www.facebook.com

Computers: Yesterday, Today, and Tomorrow

Computers have become so integral to our daily lives that it's difficult to think of a time without them. There are millions of individuals that wake up and turn on their computer every day in hundreds of cities across all nations. This increase in computer popularity has also caused an increase in its diversity of applications. Think about it, how many technology based applications or devices do you use in one day? How many of these applications or devices did not exist 10 years ago? How many will be extinct 10 years from now? Look over the list of computer applications and devices below; how many have you used or encountered?

- Word-processor—an application that automatically checks spelling and grammar in a document
- Internet—a connected system of computers that enables users to obtain information quicker than from a library and perform such communication activities as video conferencing
- Online Banking— the ability to use the Internet to open a new account, transfer your own money from one account to another, or pay a mortgage, all from the comfort of your own home
- Online classes— classes offered using applications such as Blackboard and Angel via the Internet that enable students and teachers to communicate outside of the physical classroom
- GPS systems—computing devices that are either portable or embedded within the dashboard of many vehicles and provide driving directions from your current location to the entered destination as well as help you locate restaurants, gas stations, and fast food chains, even the phone number for your favorite pizza place
- ATM machines—devices that can connect to the database of banking institutions to allow a customer to withdraw and deposit funds without entering the brick and mortar structure of the bank itself
- Mobile phones—the telecommunication favorites of most individuals today, replacing landline twisted pair technology and offering additional features such as calculators, calendars, and even Internet connectivity
- Weather prediction—the use of supercomputers and satellite connections to determine weather patterns and predict the location and strength of a weather event

> "The real power of the use of computers . . . **relate** the tasks, **understand** the technology used to perform them, use that technology to **collect** information, **share** that information with others locally and globally, and then singularly or collectively **use** the information to make **decisions.** "

I am sure that you can add a few additional devices and applications to this list that you use personally on a daily basis. But you get the point.

Computers are used at home, at work, and in school; they're embedded into our cars, phones, and cameras. You use them daily to perform the tasks listed above; but your future isn't about just performing single, unrelated tasks. The real power of the use of computers comes when you begin to relate the tasks, understand the technology used to perform them, use that technology to collect information, share that information with others locally and globally, and then singularly or collectively use the information to make decisions. Let's look back at the events that led up to our current technology state and then forward to the preparation you will need in order to capitalize on future technological advancements.

A Brief Look Back

A look at the past can help clarify the present and direct the future. Think about the changes that have occurred as a result of technological innovation during the past several decades. When nations were

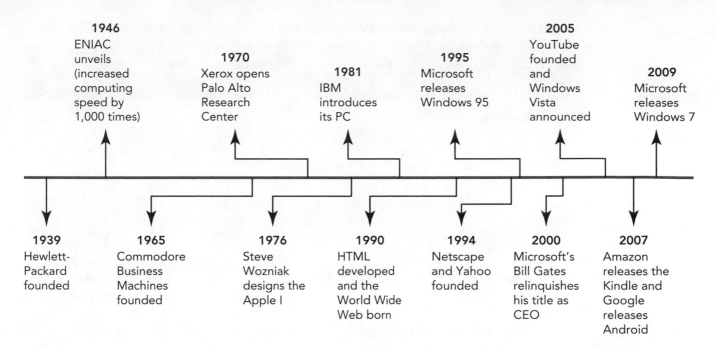

1946
ENIAC unveils (increased computing speed by 1,000 times)

1970
Xerox opens Palo Alto Research Center

1981
IBM introduces its PC

1995
Microsoft releases Windows 95

2005
YouTube founded and Windows Vista announced

2009
Microsoft releases Windows 7

1939
Hewlett-Packard founded

1965
Commodore Business Machines founded

1976
Steve Wozniak designs the Apple I

1990
HTML developed and the World Wide Web born

1994
Netscape and Yahoo founded

2000
Microsoft's Bill Gates relinquishes his title as CEO

2007
Amazon releases the Kindle and Google releases Android

FIGURE 1.1 This timeline focuses on a few of the critical events that occurred in the computer development lifecycle and provided the foundation for the devices that we use today.

attempting something as complex as sending a person to the moon, there were no telephone answering machines, no cell phones, no handheld calculators, and no personal computers. People wrote letters by hand or with a typewriter, kept track of numbers and data in ledgers, and communicated in person or over the telephone. Those telephones were physically connected: Cordless handsets didn't come onto the market until the late 1970s, and cell phones followed in the 1980s.

In the 1980s only the U.S. government, colleges, and universities were able to access the Internet (including e-mail); cell phones were just coming into use; and fax machines were the fastest way for most businesses to share documents across distances. The World Wide Web would not become viable until 1993. Today millions of people use the Internet daily in both their professional and personal lives. Cell phones and personal digital assistants seem to be a necessary part of everyday life; GPS units guide travelers to their destinations; and retail e-commerce, which didn't begin until 1995 and had sales of $32.0 billion in the third quarter of

2009, is projected to grow to $203 billion by 2013.

For a look back in time, view Figure 1.1, a compressed computer history timeline, or go to **www.computerhope.com/history/** for a year-by-year breakdown of computer developments and advances. For those interested in the development of the Apple, you can view a timeline at **http:// en.wikipedia.org/wiki/History_ of_Apple** that displays the progress of Apple from 1976 to the present.

FIGURE 1.2 Computers were once considered tools for programmers and technical developers. Today they, and the devices they are embedded within, are part of most jobs and our daily life.

A Glance at the Present

Today it's becoming difficult to find an activity that doesn't involve computers, technology, and sharing information (Figure 1.2). It would be advantageous to learn all you can about computers and become comfortable with application programs, the Internet, and the World Wide Web. You'll need computer and Internet skills to succeed in almost any occupational area. Studies consistently show that workers with such skills are in demand and earn salaries significantly above the median personal

FIGURE 1.3 Salaries of Workers in Computer and Computer-Related Jobs

Categories	Salary Ranges		
	High ($/yr.)	Low ($/yr.)	Average ($/yr.)
Computer operations	$220,000	$23,000	$59,000
Database systems	$120,000	$30,000	$67,000
E-commerce/Internet	$175,000	$37,000	$79,000
Executive level	$250,000	$69,000	$118,000
Hardware	$100,000	$30,000	$56,000
Help desk	$110,000	$23,000	$44,000
Networking	$333,000	$22,000	$69,000
New media	$65,000	$32,000	$43,000
Project management	$130,000	$34,000	$83,000
Technical writing	$77,000	$45,000	$59,000
UNIX	$108,000	$50,000	$79,000
Windows development	$101,000	$40,000	$69,000
Wireless systems	$95,000	$46,000	$66,000

This is a selection of common job types; the original survey had 2,145 positions listed.
Average salary of all positions in the original survey: $70,000 per year.

income level of approximately $30,000 (Figure 1.3). Check out **www.cis.udel. edu/jobs/market** for information about the future of the computer science job market and links to related sites. Another site, **www.ticker.computerjobs. com/content/ticker.aspx**, lists computer-related jobs and their average salaries.

An Insight into the Future

Isolated skills won't be enough to keep you connected or job-ready in the future. To be a fully functioning member of the computerized world of tomorrow, you need to understand the concepts that underlie computer and Internet technologies, such as the distinction between hardware and software, and how to manage the excessive amount of files that are created each day, insure the privacy of data as it makes its way across a variety of new technologies, and perform a continual evaluation of your skills to determine the need for re-education and fine tuning.

As computers and the Internet play an increasingly direct and noticeable role in our personal lives, understanding the difference between their appropriate and inappropriate use becomes increasingly difficult. Should you shop on the Internet on company or school time? Are the photos you share with friends on social networking sites like Facebook or MySpace

going to turn up when you least expect or cause an employer to disqualify your application because of your Web content? Is your credit card information, Social Security number, or personal communication safe from intrusion or misuse? In the past the only way to shop during work or school was to leave the premises; employers had to call a reference to find personal information about an applicant; and the only time you needed to worry about losing your personal information was if your wallet or mail had been stolen!

You also need to know enough to the correct types of technology to use in your personal and professional lives (Figure 1.4). Use the questions below as a starting point to evaluate your technology needs.

- How much power and speed do you need for everyday tasks?
- What will a more powerful and faster computer, smartphone, or iPad enable you to do better?
- What types of technology tools do you need (as opposed to want)?
- Will you need advanced training?

The more you understand about computers and become familiar with how they work, the less mysterious they seem and the easier they are to use. Like driving a car or riding a bike, the more you practice and use the equipment, the more comfortable you will be and the better able you will be to adjust to future models and variations. Let's start by describing the machine that's at the center of what you need to know.

Computer Fundamentals

Learning computer and Internet concepts is partly about learning new terms and the connection between them. So let's start with the most basic terms.

Understanding the Computer: Basic Definitions

A **computer** is an electronic device that performs four basic operations: input, processing, output, and storage (Figure 1.5). Together these four operations are called the **information processing cycle**.

- **Input** is the action of receiving data—raw facts like a user's login ID number.
- **Processing** is the manipulation done on the input by a program (instructions), to convert the input (data) into information (data converted into a meaningful form). An example of processing could be aligning a letter's return address in a Word document, averaging a column of grades by following a formula that has been entered in an Excel worksheet, or searching a database to confirm a login ID number.
- **Output** is the actual displaying of the information, the processed data. This would be displaying the shifted return address in the Word document, placing the average below the column of grades in the Excel worksheet, or confirming the entry of a valid ID.
- **Storage** is saving the information for later use.

Because these operations depend on one another, the information processing cycle (sometimes abbreviated as the IPOS cycle) is always performed in this sequence.

You'll often hear the term *computer system,* which is normally shortened to *system.* This term is more inclusive than *computer.* A **computer system** is a collection of related components that have been designed to work together to meet

Desktop

Mac

Notebook

Netbook

iPad

Smartphone

FIGURE 1.4 Being familiar with the latest technology tools will help you become more confident in your abilities to select the correct technology based on need and usability, not advertising hype.

the needs of the user. These components can be placed in two major categories: hardware and software. A computer system's **hardware** includes all the physical components of the computer and its related devices. The components include the **system unit**: the base unit of the computer made up of the plastic or metal enclosure, the motherboard, and the integrated peripherals. The **motherboard** is the circuit board that connects the central processing unit(s) anchored on the board and other system components. **Integrated peripherals** are the devices embedded

| Input data: login ID | Computer processes login ID to confirm identity | If ID is valid— output welcome to user | Store the ID of user and time of login on the hard disk |

FIGURE 1.5 The information processing cycle is the path data takes from input through output.

within the system unit case and generally include the power supply, cooling fans, memory, CD drive, DVD drive, and internal hard drive. Besides the system unit, the hardware also includes the **peripheral devices**: components located outside the system unit housing that are connected physically or wirelessly to the system unit and motherboard. Examples include keyboards, mice, monitors, speakers, external webcams, external modems, and external storage devices (Figure 1.6).

A computer system's hardware needs programs to function. A **program** is a set of instructions that tells the hardware how to perform an operation on the input data in the processing phase of the information processing cycle. **Software**, a more inclusive term, is the collection of programs, and the associated documentation, that directs the operation of the computer to complete a desired end result. Software can be divided into two categories: system software and application software.

System software is the collection of programs written and configured to provide the infrastructure, basic services, and hardware control that let other programs function properly. The most important and well-recognized type of system software is the computer's **operating system (OS)**, which integrates and controls the computer's internal functions and provides the connectivity for the user to interact with

the computer's hardware. Common operating systems include Microsoft Windows 7, Microsoft Vista, Microsoft Windows XP, Linux, and Mac OS X Snow Leopard. Consumers may get frustrated with the frequency with which new versions of operating systems are released, but operating systems are actually updated to improve performance and accommodate new hardware devices. The most current operating systems are Windows 7, released by Microsoft in July 2009, and Mac OS X Snow Leopard, released by Apple in August 2009. Besides operating systems, other examples of system software include system utility programs that aid in system maintenance, such as backup programs, cleanup tools, and antivirus software.

Application software can be thought of as sitting on top of the operating system. The programs that are integrated to create application software provide instructions that direct the computer's hardware to perform a task for the user. For example the programs to spell check, grammar check, locate synonyms, and insert a header or footer are combined with many other such programs to create a word processing application. Typical examples of application software include word processing, spreadsheet, database, presentation, e-mail, Web browser, and communication software.

Webcam

System unit

Monitor

CD or DVD drive

Media card reader

USB ports

Keyboard

Speakers

Mouse

Sound connections

Cable or DSL modem

Network interface card

Printer

Headset with microphone

FIGURE 1.6 Get to know your system. A typical computer system includes these hardware components.

To better understand how computer system components are interrelated, you might compare a computer system to an aquarium. The computer hardware is like the fish tank, the operating system is like the water, and the software applications are like the fish (Figure 1.7). You wouldn't put fish in an empty aquarium. Fish can't survive without water, just as software applications can't function without an operating system to support them. And without the water and fish, an aquarium is an empty box—just as computer hardware isn't much use without an operating system and applications.

Now that we know the basic terms, let's take a closer look at the operations in the information processing cycle (input, processing, output, and storage) and at the hardware devices involved in each step.

Input: Getting Data into the Computer

During input, the computer receives data. The term **data** refers to raw facts, which can be made up of words, numbers, images, sounds, or a combination of these.

Input devices enable you to enter data into the computer for processing. The most common input devices are the keyboard and mouse (Figure 1.8). Microphones, scanners, and devices such as digital cameras and camcorders offer other ways of getting different types of data into the computer.

FIGURE 1.7 A computer system can be compared to an aquarium.

Hardware = fish tank

Operating system = water

Software applications = fish

Processing: Transforming Data into Information

Processing transforms data into information. **Information** is data that has been consolidated and organized in a way that people can use. During processing, the computer's processing circuitry (Figure 1.9), called the **central processing unit (CPU)** or **microprocessor** (or just **processor** for short), is directed by the software in use to perform operations on the input data. The CPU is located within the system unit and is a component on the motherboard.

Even though the CPU is often referred to as the "brain" of the computer, computers don't really think. They are capable of performing only repetitive processing actions organized into an **algorithm**—a series of steps that results in the solution to a problem. After an algorithm is tested for accuracy, it is coded into a language that the computer hardware understands and becomes the program or software that the system uses to solve that problem.

Because the CPU needs to juggle multiple input and output requests at the same time, it uses high-speed memory chips to store program instructions and data so it can move between requests quickly. Memory is essential to the smooth operation of the CPU. A typical computer contains several types of memory on the motherboard; the most important of these is **random access memory (RAM)**, which temporarily stores the programs and data with which the CPU is interacting. RAM is also referred to as primary memory or temporary memory. The second name comes from the fact that it does not retain any content when power is interrupted or turned off.

FIGURE 1.9 The CPU (microprocessor or processor) is the component on the motherboard that performs operations on the data to convert it to information.

FIGURE 1.8 Because the mouse and keyboard are the two most common input devices, several variations are available.

Output: Displaying Information

Output commonly is dispensed through **output devices**, like monitors, printers, and speakers that enable people to see, hear, and—with some newer inventions—feel the results of processing operations (Figure 1.10).

Storage: Holding Programs and Data for Future Use

The storage operation makes use of **storage devices**, hardware that embeds programs and data onto **storage media**, like CDs and DVDs, which retain the programs and data even when power is disrupted or turned off. Storage devices, also referred to as **sec-ondary storage**, can be both integrated and external peripherals (see Figure 1.11), depending on whether the information being stored is to remain within the current system or must be portable and transferable to another system, notebook, or computing device. The internal hard disk holds all the programs, system and application

FIGURE 1.10 Most users view the output of computer-related work either on the monitor screen or hard copy that has been printed.

Internal hard drive　　　**External hard drive**

FIGURE 1.11 Hard drives can store very large quantities of data, making them the media of choice for activities that generate large files like movies, pictures, and backups.

software, and data that are intended to remain within that computer system. This storage device is usually an integrated peripheral that is mounted inside the system unit's enclosure and not visible to the user. However, for individuals who require a lot of graphic and multimedia data to be portable, or those that want to back up critical data, hard disks can also be purchased as nonintegrated peripherals and connected to the system unit through USB cables. These external storage devices can be colorful, fit into an average sized eyeglass case, and are economical, costing approximately $100 for 500GB of storage. For some, data portability is necessary. Due to smaller file sizes, an external hard drive may not always be needed. For this type of convenience, individuals usually make use of CDs, DVDs, media cards, or USB flash drives (Figure 1.12).

These portable devices have replaced the floppy disk drive and zip drive that might be found in some older systems. Devices like these, now obsolete, are often referred to as **legacy technology**. The popular **USB flash drive** is the average user's choice of portable storage today. It is about the size of an adult's thumb; can hold up to 64 GB of data (approximately 180 CDs), although a larger 256 GB one is available only in the United Kingdom and Europe; uses solid-state technology; conveniently plugs into a computer's USB port; and is easy to use, rewritable, and inexpensive. If you have never used a flash drive, go to **http://usb-flash-drive-review.toptenreviews.com/usb-flash-drive-c180-video-1.html** and view the very brief and easy-to-understand video. Visit **www1.pacific.edu/comp25/reading/1-InfoProcessingCycle.html** to find out more about the information processing cycle.

Communications: Moving Data

Communications, the high-speed movement of data or information within and between computers, has become more important due to our increasingly global and mobile society. Such needs as getting data from your computer to the server hosting your Web site or from a school computer to the one at your house have taken communications technology from the back office and communications department at work to your own desk at home. To communicate, computers have to be connected to a network by a **communications device**, which is a hardware component that moves data into and out of a computer. Two or more connected computers are called a **network**. The primary reason to create a network is to share data, information, input/output devices, and other resources. If sharing is easy, individuals will collaborate more, distribute information more freely, increase their knowledge,

FIGURE 1.12 Popular external inexpensive storage devices include CD and DVD drives, media card readers that are used with flash memory cards, and flash drives that connect though a USB port.

CD & DVD drives　　　**Media card reader**　　　**Flash drive**

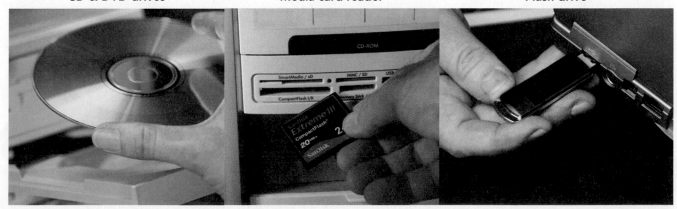

expand their scope of reasoning, become more global, and make better individual and group decisions.

Most computers are equipped with a **modem** (short for modulator/demodulator), a communications device that converts data from one form into another. It enables the computer, a digital device, to access data through nondigital media, such as telephone lines, cable, satellite, and cellular connections. Many computers have internal modems that can be used for dial-up Internet access over a standard telephone line. External modems are used for high-speed access to the Internet via cable, DSL, or satellite.

Another important component, a **network interface card (NIC)**, is a hardware element located in the system unit that houses the electronic components used to connect a computer to a network. Many computers already have a NIC integrated into the motherboard, but external NICs can be plugged into a USB port or inserted into a specially designed slot. NICs can connect to wired or wireless networks.

Now that you have had a brief introduction to hardware and software and know their purpose and location in a typical computer system, let's look at an example of how the computer uses the basic functions of input, processing, output, and storage.

The Information Processing Cycle in Action

Even if you haven't wondered what goes on behind the scenes when you use a computer, the following example illustrates your role and the computer's role in each step of the information-processing cycle (Figure 1.13):

- *Input:* You're writing a research paper for a class. You know it has misspellings and grammatical errors, but you keep typing because you can run your word processing program's spell-checker at any time to help correct the errors. In this example, your entire word-processed document is the input.

- *Processing:* A spell checker is a program that uses the computer's ability to quickly perform simple processing operations to construct a list of all of the words in your document. It then compares yours words against a huge list of correctly spelled words. If you've used a word that isn't in this internal dictionary, the program puts that word into a list of apparent misspellings.

  Note that the computer isn't really "checking spelling" when it performs this operation. The computer can't check your spelling because it doesn't possess the intelligence to do so. All it can do is tell you which words you've used do not appear in the dictionary

FIGURE 1.13 The Information Processing Cycle in Action

Your role:	Your role:	Computer's role:	Your role:
Enter word-processed document.	Start spell-checker program.	Display list of misspelled words.	Save corrected document.

Computer's role:	Computer's role:	Your role:	Computer's role:
Receive document.	Spell-checker program compares words in document to built-in dictionary.	Accept or reject suggested misspelled words.	Store final document to disk or drive.

Input → Processing → Output → Storage

list. Ultimately, only you can decide whether a given word is misspelled.

- *Output:* The result of the processing operation is a list of apparent misspellings. The word *apparent* is important here because the program doesn't actually know whether a word is misspelled. It can tell you only that a word isn't in its massive, built-in dictionary. But many correctly spelled words, such as proper nouns and technical terms, aren't likely to be found in the computer's dictionary. For this reason, the program won't make any changes without asking you to confirm them.

- *Storage:* After you've corrected the spelling in your document, you save or store the revised document to the integrated hard disk or an external portable storage device.

In summary, computers transform data (here a document full of misspellings) into information (a document that is free of misspellings).

Up to this point, we've been talking about computers in a general sense. Let's be more specific and examine the various types of computers, their components, and the tasks that they are built to perform.

Types of Computers

Computers come in all sizes, from large to small. For discussion, it is convenient to divide them into two categories: computers for individuals and computers for organizations. Computers for individuals are designed for one user at a time. They process and store smaller amounts of data and programs, such as a research paper, household budget, or a personal Web page. In contrast, computers for organizations are designed to meet the needs of many people concurrently. They process and store large amounts of data and more complex programs, such as the database of all students on campus or a school's entire Web site. Computers are further subcategorized by power (their processing speed) and purpose (the tasks they perform).

> " Computers for **individuals** are designed for one **user** at a time . . . . computers for **organizations** are design to meet the needs of **many** people concurrently. "

Computers for Individuals

A **personal computer (PC)**, also called a **microcomputer**, is designed to meet the computing needs of an individual or, when connected to a network, can be used by a contributor in a collaborative project. The two most commonly used types of personal computers are Apple's Macintosh (Mac) systems and the more numerous IBM-compatible systems, which are made by manufacturers such as Dell, Gateway, Sony, Hewlett-Packard (HP), and many others. These PCs are called *IBM-compatible* because the first such computer was made by IBM. The acronym *PC*, although originally used to refer to all personal computers, has become more closely aligned with IBM-compatible personal computers, while Apple has coined the term *Mac*. Although PC sales have exceeded those of the Mac, the Mac has a loyal following and has been increasing in popularity. Statistics on the use of the Safari browser, used primarily on Apple systems, indicate a continuous increase in its use from 2007 to 2009. Apple advocates point to this statistic as an indication of an increase in Apple system sales. Go to **www.w3schools.com/browsers/browsers_stats.asp** and decide for yourself.

Personal computers are subcategorized by size, power, and function. They include the larger units like the **desktop** and **all-in-one computer** systems down to the more portable styles like the **notebook**, **subnotebook**, and **tablet PC**. The table in Figure 1.14 displays such features as size, use, and price of these popular categories of computers used by individuals.

With the trend to smaller size, wireless connectivity, and a greater focus on communication, many individuals are finding a less powerful, less expensive device is meeting their needs. These devices include **netbooks**, **handheld computers**, **personal digital assistants (PDAs)**, **smartphones**, the **iPad**, and dedicated devices like the **Kindle DX**, an **e-book reader**. For the consumer, it is becoming harder to make choices because every manufacturer offers new features or applications. Figure 1.15 categorizes handheld computing devices, outlines their features, and gives an approximate price range.

FIGURE 1.14 Computers for Individual Use

Category	Size	Application	Cost	Image
Desktop Manufacturers: Dell, Gateway, Sony, Hewlett-Packard, Apple	Consists of a system unit approximately the size of a printer with an independent monitor and keyboard.	Home or office environment	$300 to $5,000 depending on customized features	
All-in-one Manufacturers: Apple iMac (trend leader), Lenovo, Hewlett-Packard, Dell, Sony	Combines the system unit and monitor into one.	Home or office environment, good for small cubicles or apartments	$300 to $5,000 depending on customized features	
Notebook (laptop) Manufacturers: Dell, Sony, Gateway	The size of a spiral bound notebook. Fits into a briefcase or backpack.	Designed for portability, popular with students and business people that travel.	$300 to $5,000	
Subnotebook Manufacturers: Apple, Dell, Sony, and Asus	Omits components as CDs or DVDs, weigh 3 pounds or less, approximately 1 inch thick but still runs a full operating system	Used by individuals that like full application features but not all the peripherals devices.	$200 to $500	
Tablet PC (convertible notebook) Manufacturers: Hewlett-Packard, Fujitsu, Lenovo, Dell	The size of a notebook with a screen that swivels and lies flat over the keyboard. A stylus can be used to handwrite input that is then converted to digital text by handwriting recognition software.	Designed for portability, and ease of note taking. Used by sales persons and others that need to input data quickly.	$300 to $5,000	

FIGURE 1.15 Handheld Computers for Individual Use

Category	Size	Application	Cost	Image
Netbook Manufacturer: Acer, Asus, Dell, HP, and Lenovo	Between 5 and 15 inches in size and weighs 2 to 3 pounds	Primary use is Web browsing and e-mail. Because netbooks usually do not have large hard drives, they are great for cloud computing, an online service that provides applications and document storage remotely instead of on the user's hard drive.	$150 to $400	
iPad Manufacturer: Apple	Dimensions are 7.47 inches wide by 9.56 inches high and a depth of 0.5 inches, weight is 1.5 to 1.6 pounds	The iPad can download and read e-books; surf the Internet; play movies, TV shows, and other media; make calls; send instant messages/texts; take still photos or video; edit photos and videos; run off battery power for a full day; connect to a TV and play media; and sync its media with a computer.	$500	
Handheld computers or personal digital assistants Manufacturers: Asus, Dell, HP, Palm, and Sony	Fits in the palm of your hand or the pocket of your jeans	Designed for portability, these devices usually use a stylus or virtual keyboard, one that appears on the touch screen, to manage contacts, use e-mail, and schedule appointments.	$200 to $400	
Smartphone Manufacturers: Apple iPhone, BlackBerry Curve, HP iPAQ, Motorola Droid, Palm Pre, and Treo Pro	Fits in the palm of your hand or the pocket of your jeans	Designed to use as a mobile phone with Web access. With the added features and downloadable applications, the line between the smartphone and handheld computers has become blurred.	$100 to $300	
Dedicated Devices Example: Kindle DX Reader by Amazon, the Nook by Barnes and Noble, and the Sony Reader	Dimensions are approximately 7.2 inches wide by 10.4 inches high, depth of 0.4 inches, and weight of 1.1 pounds	Dedicated to a specific activity. The Kindle DX Reader is an e-book reader (electronic book reader) designed to download, display, and read books obtained through an e-bookstore (an electronic book store accessed via the Internet where books are purchased online and downloaded to a Kindle reader, smartphone, iPad, netbook or other connected device for the purchaser to read).	$299 to $400	

larger entities need more storage capacity for databases and files that contain customer and employee information.

Professional workstations (Figure 1.16) are high-end desktop computers with system units designed for technical or scientific applications, requiring exceptionally powerful processing and output capabilities. Used by engineers, architects, circuit designers, financial analysts, game developers, and other professionals, they are often connected to a network and are equipped with more powerful CPUs, extra RAM, additional graphics power, and multitasking capabilities. For these reasons they are more expensive than desktop PCs. Manufacturers include HP, Dell, and Lenovo.

Servers (Figure 1.17) are computers that range in size from a personal computer to a four-drawer file cabinet.

FIGURE 1.17 Servers contain software that enables them to provide services to users connected to the server through a network. Depending on the configuration, they can range in cost from a couple of thousand to tens of thousands of dollars.

FIGURE 1.16
Workstations can be mistaken for a desktop due to their similar size; however, the engineering and mathematical applications that they are designed to handle require high-end components that usually place it in the $2,000 to several thousand dollar price range.

Computers for Organizations

Organizations or corporations usually need computing systems that are capable of performing transactions faster than those done on a computer designed for individual or small business use. Additionally, these

They are equipped with the hardware and software to make programs and data available to people who are connected via a network. They are not designed for individual use and are typically centralized or operated from one location. Users connect to a network on **clients**, which can be desktops, notebooks, workstations, or **terminals** (primarily input/output devices consisting of keyboards and video displays, used as an inexpensive means to connect to a server). A **fat client** accesses the server but does most data processing in its own system; a **thin client** relies on the server for its processing ability. This use of client computers and a centralized server is called a **client/server network**. Servers play an important role in today's businesses and can be as small as a personal computer or as large as a computer that runs a banking institution with millions of clients. These larger units are typically housed in a secure, temperature-regulated environment to protect them from deliberate or accidental damage. The top three server manufacturers are HP, Dell, and IBM.

mainframe to handle airline reservations, or a bank might manage customer accounts on such a system. Mainframes are usually stored in special secure rooms that have a controlled climate. They are manufactured by firms such as IBM, Fujitsu, and Amdahl.

Supercomputers (Figure 1.20) are ultrafast systems that process large amounts of scientific data, often to search for underlying patterns. A supercomputer can be a single computer or a series of computers working in parallel as a single computer. Like mainframes, they are stored in special, secure rooms that have a controlled climate. The main difference between a supercomputer and a mainframe is that a supercomputer focuses on performing a few sets of instruction as fast as possible, whereas a mainframe executes many instructions concurrently.

FIGURE 1.18 Minicomputers or midrange servers like the IBM AS/400 (iSeries) and HP 300 Alpha family have a wide price range. Although units start as low as $25,000, they can easily exceed $500,000.

Minicomputers or **midrange servers** (Figure 1.18) are midsized servers approximately the size of one or several four-drawer file cabinets with the hardware and software to handle the computing needs of 4 to approximately 200 client computers in a smaller cor-poration or organization. In size and capability, minicomputers fall between workstations and mainframes; but as these markets have evolved and work-stations have become more powerful and main-frames less expensive, the demand for mini-computers has decreased. Minicomputers are manufactured by IBM and HP.

Mainframes or **enterprise servers** (Figure 1.19) are powerful servers that are part of a networked system designed to handle hundreds of thousands of clients at the same time. They are usually used in large corporations or government agencies that handle a high volume of data and can fill an entire wall of an average room. For example, an airline might use a

The TOP500 list (**www.top500.org**) tracks the most powerful computer systems worldwide. As of November 2009, ORNL's Jaguar, located at the Department of Energy's Oak Ridge Leadership Computing Facility, recorded a 1.75 petaflops per second performance speed. Jaguar surpassed the prior leader, IBM Roadrunner, located at the Department of Energy's Los Alamos National Laboratory, which recorded a 1.04 petaflops per second performance speed. One **petaflop** is the equivalent of one quadrillion calculations per second. In a more understandable comparison, that is the same as 150,000 calculations for every human being on the planet per second.

Visit **www.unm.edu/~tbeach/ terms/types.html** to learn more about the various types of computers. Now that you know about the variety of computers available, let's look at how their use affects you as an individual and society in general.

FIGURE 1.20 Supercomputers can perform mathematical calculations at lightning speed and are used in such fields as weather prediction and space travel. The price of these room-sized systems usually runs several million dollars.

FIGURE 1.19 Mainframes or enterprise servers connect thousands of clients concurrently, are used by large organizations and government agencies, and can cost from several thousand to millions of dollars.

Computers, Society, and You

Computers help us be more productive and creative, reducing the amount of time spent on tedious tasks. A good example of this is using a word processing program to create a term paper. The program being used provides spelling and grammar assistance, often automatically, as well as formatting suggestions and easy options to include graphics. Without a computer, the student would need dictionaries and encyclopedias, not to mention style guides and other special resources, along with extra time to gather and go through all of these sources.

Computers let us collect, organize, evaluate, and communicate information. Although computers are merely tools, requiring humans to write the programs and set up the data, we can use them for a variety of common activities to ease our daily lives. Rather than going to the mall to buy the latest movie on DVD, you can now purchase it or even view it online. To organize your music or movie collection before computers, you would have had to physically sort through and arrange it on your shelf. A computer makes it possible to organize your entire collection and sort it in a variety of ways, including by title, artist, release date, or genre, making it simple to reorganize and update your collection. And there's no need to wait for movie reviews to come out in the newspaper—just go online to find the latest reviews from critics and other moviegoers, or watch the trailer yourself. You can select your favorite movie, use your smartphone to locate a nearby theater, make dinner reservations before the show, and even display driving directions. To invite or inform family and friends of your plans, simply use a digital method of social networking and post the information to your Facebook page, blog, Web page, or send out a tweet. The amount of time we save during a day by using computers or computer-related devices is phenomenal.

A computer, with the appropriate software, can perform various tasks on all types of data. That is a major reason for the remarkable penetration of computers into almost every occupational area and into 80 percent of U.S. households in 2008 (a significant increase from 49 percent in 2001 and 2002). So, four out of every five households in the United States have a computer. Although computers seem to be everywhere, computers and the Internet aren't readily accessible in some segments of society. Computers and the Internet possess the ability to cut across all educational, racial, and economic boundaries; but there are still inequities.

The Digital Divide

The more educated you are and the more income you make, the more likely you are to own a computer and have Internet access. Figure 1.21 displays the results of the Nielsen report comparing income and home Internet access though the third quarter of 2008. The chart clearly highlights the income discrepancy with respect to Internet connectivity. This same report also identified the East South Central region (Alabama, Mississippi, Tennessee, and Kentucky) of the United States as the geographic region with the highest number of households (26%) having no Internet access. Further, a study by Pew Internet and American Life Project in December 2008 showed that approximately one-third of people in the United States have a bachelor's degree, and 95 percent of college-educated individuals use the Internet; but only 53 percent of people with a high school education do.

FIGURE 1.21 The digital divide is often thought of as the difference in computer and Internet use between the have and have-not nations. This Nelson report actually highlights the digital divide that exists over Internet use within the United States.

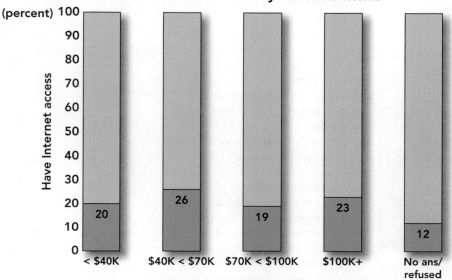

U.S. Internet access by household income

(percent)

Have Internet access

| < $40K | $40K < $70K | $70K < $100K | $100K+ | No ans/refused |
| 20 | 26 | 19 | 23 | 12 |

Annual income

Age, race, and income are also factors in U.S. computer use. The December 2009 Pew Internet and American Life Project indicated that only 38 percent of adults 65 and older use the Internet, compared with 70 percent of 50- to 64-year-olds, 81 percent of 30- to 49-year-olds, and 93 percent of 18- to 29-year-olds. Another Pew report in the same year substantiated that 80 percent of whites, 72 percent of African Americans, and only 61 percent of the Hispanics have Internet use. This disparity in computer ownership and Internet access, known as the **digital divide**, isn't limited to the United States. Similar statistics exist for other countries, indicating that this is a global problem. Studies of the expansion or reduction of the digital divide are contradictory; however, government and educational programs are working to bridge this gap by attempting to provide computer access for all (Figure 1.22).

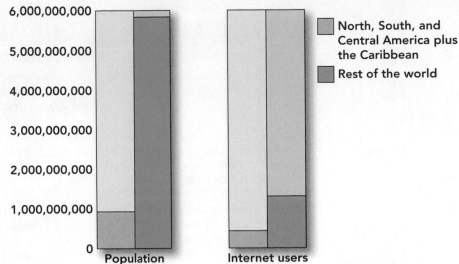

Source of data: Internet World Stats

FIGURE 1.22 Almost 50 percent of the populations of North America, South America, Central America, and the Caribbean have Internet connectivity, while only 20 percent of the rest of the world enjoys that technology.

Social Networking

Some of the uses of computers, such as social networking, seem to be more for communication or entertainment than for information or learning. It would be a mistake to dismiss these types of sites or applications as child's play. Results from statistics provided by a Forrester Research Report can be seen in Figure 1.23 These summarizations substantiate that the contact between adults on these sites and the amount of information being shared daily is real, on the rise, and reaching a population demographic that is staggering. One of the most basic forms of this interaction is **instant messaging (IM)**, a free, real-time connection between two or more parties that uses a buddy list to identify and restrict the contacts a person wishes to communicate with.

The use of online **social network sites** such as Facebook, MySpace, LinkedIn, and Twitter is increasing rapidly. These are sites that individuals are invited or allowed to join and support such tools as instant messaging and e-mail among members. **Facebook**, the largest of

FIGURE 1.23 The Use of Social Network Sites by Adults

Statistics	Related Sites
A third of adults post at least once a week to a social site.	A social site can be Facebook, MySpace, Twitter, as well as eHarmony, Match.com, and Yahoo singles.
A quarter of adults publish a blog and upload video/audio they created.	The most recognized video broadcasting site is YouTube. Blogs created by individuals contain entries that resemble journal entries.
Nearly 60% of adults maintain a profile on a social networking site.	The most popular social networking sites are Facebook and Twitter.
Approximately 70% read blogs, tweets, and watch UGC (user-generated content) videos.	Blogs can be located on almost any Web page and on any topic. Radio and TV stations as well as political sites are popular for hosting blogs to collect opinions. UGC videos can be posted on individually created Web pages or, for viewing by a larger audience, YouTube.

FIGURE 1.24 Making the Social Network Work for Businesses

Action	Purpose
Encourage supervisors and colleagues to investigate the Web presence of competitors.	To size up the competition, their manner of presentation on a social network site, the type of offers and interaction they provide for the customer.
Sharpen leadership knowledge of some of the high profile sites and learn the language of their users. Create a page in Facebook or become a follower of a favorite coach or actor on Twitter.	To get the feel of the social environment and learn its language, and interface. Being comfortable is a prerequisite for launching a business site.
Poll customers and analyze their responses. Use a variety of options to connect with target audiences or promote different product lines.	To determine the type of customer involved in the social networking world. This will determine the tone the business decides to project on its page and the type of offers that are posted.
Once the decision is made to create a Web presence for the business, assign the task of maintaining it to an individual that understands the technology. Old or inaccurate information will have a negative effect on business.	To maintain consistency and currency of layout, design, and content in order make the customer comfortable.

such social networking sites, allows anyone over the age of 13 with a valid e-mail account, residing in a country where it has not been banned, to become a Facebook user. Often users will join groups set up by region, job, interest, or school and communicate with group members. Adult Internet users who have profiles on online social network sites have more than quadrupled in the past four years—from 8 percent in 2005 to 35 percent in 2008, according to the Pew Internet and American Life Project December 2008 report. Mark Brooks, a social network and online dating analyst, suggests that these sites are locations where individuals are looking for friends. Sites dedicated to matchmaking offer more anonymity, but social networking sites offer an environment that allows someone to look at a friend's postings, follow their social interaction with others, and allow for a more insightful view of a members personality and behavior.

Twitter, the newest phenomenon, is a free, real-time social messaging utility that allows postings of up to 140 characters. The exchanges are short and usually in a question-and-answer mode. People need merely look up the Twitter accounts of their friends and indicate that they want to become a follower and view their Twitter posts, which are called **tweets**.

From a business point of view, using these social networking sites can enable a business to reach individuals standard advertising media might miss and provide much more exposure than any commercial or single Web site posting. Most organizations and companies are looking to increase their Web presence. What better way than to use a social networking site? The suggestions in Figure 1.24 offer a starting point to evaluate the Web presence of a business and the target population it is trying to reach. It also provides suggestions on making necessary adjustments. For many businesses, it might be time to make the jump to a more dynamic Web presence that includes social networking sites. When each Twitter account holder has an average following of 126 users, the amount of information that is dispersed in seconds through this portal alone is phenomenal. Think about how quickly a happy customer can spread the word.

Collaborative Work

Computers also help us work, teach, and learn together. Computers facilitate collaboration with others to solve problems. For instance, computers are increasingly part of law enforcement activities. They facilitate quick and efficient communication between jurisdictions, enable law enforcement officials to browse criminal databases like the Automated Fingerprint Identification System (AFIS) (Figure 1.25), and allow pertinent data to be shared nationally and globally. Additionally, as cybercrime becomes a bigger concern, police are using the Internet and **computer forensics**, a branch of forensic science that deals with legal evidence found on computers, to find and apprehend these criminals.

Collaboration software, the collection of programs that help people share ideas, create documents, and conduct meetings, regardless of location or time zone, are making their move into the academic and business worlds. Whether you're an employee of a multinational firm developing a new product with a group of colleagues located halfway around the globe or a student enrolled in a distance learning course, computers and their facilitation of collaboration play a big part in making these tasks possible.

The need to stay connected to complete group projects and research has caused a rise in the use of online applications that advance collaboration. **Google Docs**, a free Web-based word processor and spreadsheet, allows project members to share and edit documents online. A **wiki** is a collection of Web pages designed to let anyone with access contribute or modify content. Wikis are often used to create collaborative or community Web sites. The collaborative encyclopedia Wikipedia is one of the best-known wikis. **Google Groups** is a free service provided by Google to help users connect, share information, and communicate effectively over the Internet. Its current version allows group members to collaborate on shared Web pages; set group pictures, colors, and styles; upload and share individually created work; and learn more about other members in the group. After the project is finalized, you can use your own computer to print, store, and present the finished product.

Even though computers offer us many advantages and communication options, the responsible computer user should also be aware of the disadvantages of computer use.

Advantages and Disadvantages of Using Computers

It seems that for every positive effect an invention provides there is a negative effect.

FIGURE 1.25 The ability to convert a fingerprint into a digital image and send it over the Internet to other law enforcement agencies enables comparisons to be made quicker and a suspect apprehended faster.

That is also true for computers. A computer system provides certain advantages to its users, such as speed, memory for work in progress, storage for access later, hardware reliability, and accuracy. However, with these advantages come some disadvantages (Figure 1.26), including information overload, the expense of computer equipment, data inaccuracy, and an increasing dependence on unreliable software.

Speed is one of the greatest advantages of a computer. It can perform, in a minute, calculations or tasks that would take a human days. In fact, people are generating so much information via computers today that they often succumb to **information overload**: a feeling of anxiety and incapacity experienced when people are presented with more information than they can handle. According to research from the firm Basex, which chose information overload as its 2008 problem of the year, constant e-mail messages, phone calls, text messages, and tweets across the U.S. workforce resulted in $650 billion of lost productivity in a single year. That is an estimate of up to eight hours a week per worker. Some see this connectivity as an annoyance. However, young people do not seem as irritated at the multitasking demands of technology. They listen to music while reading, IM friends while typing a paper, tweet constantly, and do not seem annoyed. It remains to be seen whether this ability to handle information overload will produce a future workforce that is better able to handle an overfilled Inbox.

FIGURE 1.26 Advantages and Disadvantages of Computer Use

Advantages	Disadvantages
Speed	Information overload
Memory	Cost
Storage	Data inaccuracy
Hardware reliability and accuracy	Software unreliability

Cost is another drawback that must be weighed against computer performance. A computer's performance is enhanced by the amount of random access memory the system possesses. Random access memory (RAM) is high-speed, temporary memory that holds all programs and data currently in use; in other words, it holds our work in progress. The processor accesses programs and data in RAM quickly. The faster the processor receives the data, the faster it returns results. Once we are done with it, the information in RAM must be placed on a storage device so we can retrieve it later. Depending on the quantity of data you process and the number of files you save, you may need to purchase additional RAM and storage devices.

Purchasing more RAM or additional storage can be costly. Most computers are equipped with just enough RAM and storage to hold an average amount of programs and data. If you use many high-end applications, you may experience a slowdown when moving between graphics, see a pause in a long video, or receive a message that one of your storage units is full. If that happens, you need to investigate the reason for the slowdown and may need to purchase more RAM or storage. High-end users or intense gamers may also find that when new applications are installed on an older machine, the computer might not have enough CPU power to keep up with the new software speed and graphics. This might require upgrading the CPU or purchasing a new system. Investigate the benefits and drawbacks of either decision on a case-by-case basis.

Hardware reliability and accuracy are two more advantages of computers. Computers show up at school or work every day and almost always respond when turned on. If given a calculation to do several times, they consistently output the same result. A computer can transcribe your speech with an accuracy of 95 percent or more, which is better than most people's typing accuracy. In fact, almost all "computer errors" are actually caused by flaws in software or errors in the data supplied by people. Some more interactive programs allow the user to correct an error and save the correction. This enables the program to automatically fix future occurrences of that error.

Along with computers' strengths and weaknesses, consider some additional points in your quest to become a respon-sible user.

FAST FORWARD ▶▶

COURTROOMS OF THE FUTURE

Are you familiar with the sayings: "Seeing is believing," and "A picture is worth a thousand words"? If these words of wisdom are placed in the content of a courtroom, they gain even more strength. Now, add the ability to use technology to magnify voices, provide testimony from a witness confined to a hospital bed via webcam, obtain a translator through videoconferencing, and reproduce the scene and figures to provide a reenactment of the event digitally. Yes, it sounds like an episode from your favorite crime investigation show. But this is no television episode. With jurors traditionally having information organized for them in bulleted lists, slide shows, and presented in visual images, the atmosphere of the conventional courtroom, which is based on oral delivery and inaccurate sequencing of information, can be confusing. In the future, expect more visual aids in the courtroom to help jurors organize the data. Headsets will be provided so that jurors may replay parts of the testimony, or they may put on 3D goggles to review a video clip or simulation or revisit the actual scene of the crime. From any angle, this will look like a TV episode of today. Attorneys of the future will have to combine their legal and technical skills to not only present the information, but also present it in a manner that best suits their objective.

Become Comfortable with Hardware

Some people feel threatened by computers because they fear that computers are too complicated. But without humans, computers have no intelligence at all. They process simple repetitive operations. Remember, without a person and a program to tell it what to do, the computer is no more frightening—or useful—than an empty fish tank.

One way to get comfortable with your computer is to learn how to care for it. Read any instructions that accompany your purchase and remember that dust, moisture, static electricity, and magnetic interference may affect your system's performance. Additionally, keeping cords and devices in places that do not interfere with the traffic pattern of the room will avoid unnecessary accidents and make your work environment safe and comfortable. Does your work area look like the one in Figure 1.27?

To maintain a safe working environment for you and your hardware, heed the following advice:

FIGURE 1.27 A messy computer environment is an unsafe and unproductive one.

- Use a surge protector and avoid plugging too many devices into the same electrical outlet.
- Place computer equipment in a secure position so it won't fall or cause accidents.
- Leave plenty of space around computer equipment for sufficient air circulation to prevent overheating.
- Make sure computer cables, cords, and wires are fastened securely and not strung haphazardly or left lying where you could trip over them or where they could cause a fire.
- Keep the computer area free of food and liquids, as one spill can cause the loss of weeks of work.

Now that you know how to create a safe computing environment, it is equally important to understand how to avoid eye, back, and wrist strain that can occur from long periods of use. Healthy computing habits combined with ergonomic devices and proper positioning and arrangement of equipment and lighting can make all the difference in your computing environment and physical health.

Ergonomics is the field of study that is concerned with the fit between people, their equipment, and their work. It takes into account worker limitations and capabilities in attempting to ensure that the tasks, equipment, and overall environment suit each worker (Figure 1.28). The most common injuries related to prolonged computer use occur to the wrist and back. Prolonged keyboard use can cause **carpal tunnel syndrome** (also known as cumulative trauma disorder or repetitive strain injury), which is caused by repeated motions that damage sensitive nerves in the hands, wrists, and arms. Sometimes these injuries are so serious that they require surgery. To help prevent these problems, ergonomic keyboards, such as the Microsoft Natural Keyboard, have been designed to keep your wrists flat, reducing (but not eliminating) your chance of an injury (Figure 1.29). Because of the back strain sitting at a computer causes, many hotel chains try to attract business travelers by promoting their ergonomic desk chairs

FIGURE 1.28 Keys to an Ergonomically Correct Work Station

Viewing distance 18–24"

Viewing angle

Wrists straight

90°

Lumbar support for lower back

Seat back angle 90°

90° Knee angle

Adjustable seat height

23"–28"

Feet on floor; footrest for shorter people

FIGURE 1.29 A typist using an ergonomic keyboard is taking an extra precaution and also using wrist guards designed to reduce the damage to nerves in the wrist, arms, and hands.

(Figure 1.30) along with high-speed Internet access. Go to **http://ergo.human. cornell.edu** to view a list of links that include videos and worksheets that provide information to help you make healthy ergonomic decisions.

In addition to using properly designed equipment, you can promote a safe and comfortable computer environment by following the tips below.

- Position the top of your monitor at eye level.
- Tilt the monitor back 10 to 20 degrees and keep it no closer than 20 inches from your eyes.
- Try to keep your wrists flat; use a wrist rest if necessary.
- Rest your eyes frequently by focusing on an object 20 or more feet away.
- Stand and stretch periodically.

If you purchase devices that fit your body, treat the physical components of your computer with respect, and monitor your work health habits, you will get the most return for your money and promote a healthy work and life style. For guidance, a workspace planner is provided at **www.ergotron. com/tabid/305/language/en-US/ default.aspx**.

Recognize the Risks of Using Flawed Software

Computer hardware can be amazingly reliable, but software is another matter. Most programs contain some errors or **bugs**, as they are called. Many programs contain millions of lines of code (Figure 1.31). In general, each line of program code tells the computer to perform an action, such as adding two numbers or comparing them.

FIGURE 1.30 The multi-positioning chair, made from breathable fabric, and a well-positioned head rest should help alleviate neck and lower back stress.

Consider this: The program that allows you to withdraw cash from an ATM contains only 90,000 lines of code. But when you file your taxes, the Internal Revenue Service (IRS) program that calculates your refund contains 1,000 times that—100 million lines of code!

With so many lines of code, bugs are inevitable—and they are almost impossible to eradicate completely. On average, commercial programs contain between 1 and 7 errors for every 1,000 lines of code. This means that an ATM is likely to have approximately 360 errors in its code, and the IRS program code might have over 400 hundred thousand errors. Fortunately, most errors simply cause programs to run slowly or to perform unnecessary tasks; but some errors cause miscalculations or other inconveniences, such as your computer becoming nonresponsive. According to IBM's annual X-Force and Trend Risk Report for 2009, the overall number of bugs in software decreased, but bugs in document readers and multimedia applications saw a 50 percent increase.

These are ample reasons why it's not a good idea to put off writing a paper, especially if you plan to embed a multimedia component, until the night before your assignment is due. Bugs in a word processing program aren't usually life threatening, but computers are increasingly being used in mission-critical and safety-critical systems. Mission-critical systems are essential to

FIGURE 1.31 Code Length for Key Programs

Program	Lines of Programming Code
Bank ATM	90,000
Air traffic control	900,000
Microsoft Windows 2000	35 million
Microsoft Windows Vista	50 million
Microsoft Office XP	35 million (estimated)
Internal Revenue Service (IRS)	100 million (all programs)

an organization's viability, such as a company's computerized cash register system. If the system goes down, the organization can't function—and the result is often an expensive fiasco. A safety-critical system is one on which human lives depend, such as an air traffic control system or a computerized signaling system used by high-speed commuter trains (Figure 1.32). When these systems fail, human lives are at stake. Safety-critical systems are designed to much higher quality standards and have backup systems that kick in if the main computer goes down. For a specific case, do an Internet search on "F-22 software problems."

FIGURE 1.32 Subway and train systems, like the Intercity Express (ICE) in Cologne, Germany, along with air traffic control, defense, and security systems are run by safety-critical software. Code for such systems must be of the highest standards and bug-free.

Take Ethics Seriously

One disturbing thing about computers is what some people do with them. *Ethics* is the behavior associated with your moral beliefs. You have learned what is right and wrong from your parents, teachers, and spiritual leaders. By this stage of your life, you should know which behaviors fall into which category. However, people's use of computers and the Internet has created ethical situations that we might not have otherwise encountered. **Computer ethics**, a branch of philosophy that continues to evolve, deals with computer-related moral dilemmas and defines ethical principles for computer use.

How many people do you know who have "borrowed" software, downloaded movies from the Web, shared music files with friends, or illegally burned copies of music CDs? If you ask around, you'll find that you're surrounded by people who don't think it's wrong to steal digital data. They view **digital piracy**, the unauthorized reproduction and distribution of computer-based media, differently from photocopying a book or taking a DVD from a store without paying. In reality, these forms of theft are similar. Current statistics show that global losses due to digital piracy amount to more than $40 billion annually, with a 30 percent decrease in sales in the music industry alone from 2004 to 2009. This is not just a loss of products, but jobs, retail business, and collected tax dollars. The Business Software Alliance reports that reducing U.S. piracy rates by just 10 percent over the next four years could create more than 32,000 new jobs, generate $6.7 billion in tax revenues, and result in $40 billion in economic growth. The Anti-Counterfeiting Trade Agreement is an international assault on software piracy and trademark violations. The chief players in this agreement include the United States, South Korea, Japan, Australia, Canada, and members of the European Union. With the Internet rapidly becoming the leader in dispersing all forms of media, governments cannot ignore piracy.

Responsible computing requires that you understand the advantages and disadvantages of using a computer as well as the potential harm from computer misuse. There are daily reports about the misuse of computerized data. Names and e-mail addresses are distributed freely without permission or regard for privacy. Viruses are launched against unsuspecting victims. Credit card information is stolen and fraudulently used. Children and women are stalked. Pornography abounds. Illegitimate copies of software are installed every day. Research papers are bought and sold over the Internet. Homework assignments are copied and then modified to look like original work. The Internet is a hotbed of illicit and sometimes illegal content. Computers are very powerful tools. They can magnify many positive aspects of our lives but can also highlight negative aspects, including unethical behavior.

Societal Impacts of Computer Use

Computers and the Internet are here to stay, and they have improved the quality of our lives and society as a whole. Almost everyone has been affected by computers and the Internet. Although most people are able-bodied, consider the effect of technologies that support and provide opportunities to the disabled and the disadvantaged (Figure 1.33).

With the integration of individuals with special needs into the regular classrooms and workforce environments, schools and employers must provide computer access and the devices needed to facilitate that access for special needs students and employees. Here are just some of the developments to provide adaptive technologies.

FIGURE 1.33
Continued innovation in computers, software, and related technologies help individuals with myriad disabilities. Shown here, the Alternative Computer Control System (ACCS) manufactured by Gravitonus is designed to provide computer access for severely motor-impaired individuals.

- Your school must, in order to meet the requirements of the Americans with Disabilities Act of 1990, provide computer access to people with disabilities. Special speech recognition software is needed to help people with vision impairments use computers. Input and output devices designed for the physically disabled can be installed, or existing devices can be modified, to accommodate users with hearing or motor impairments.

- Amazon released its **Kindle 2** in 2009. This e-book reader allows the user to scroll though pages of a book, enlarge text size, purchase materials through an e-book store, and make use of the text-to-speech function. This text-to-speech feature initially caused some copyright issues as books that are read usually receive additional royalties. Amazon tried to recall the Kindle 2, but protests from individuals and agencies that represent the disabled were effective and royalty agreements were worked out.

- Other computer controlled devices that help those with physical disabilities lead more independent lives include treadmills, muscle stimulators, and video game therapy.

- The blue-sky research division of the Defense Advance Projects Research Agency (DARPA) is developing a "neurally" controlled artificial limb that will restore full motor and sensory capability to people who have had their arms amputated. This prosthesis will be controlled, feel, look, and perform like a natural arm.

Students can use computers to take advantage of inexpensive training and learning opportunities.

- **E-learning** is the use of computers and computer programs to replace teachers and the time–place specificity of learning.

- Libraries have improved their computer-related resources, and most have Internet connectivity.

- Online classes make use of specially developed software to provide an interface for students to interact with the instructor in a secure and private environment from the comfort of their own homes.

- Internet cafés and workforce agencies provide access to the Internet for social purposes or to enable access to research and employment sites.

- You can find online training, templates for all types of documents, and instruction on how to do just about anything.

The Effect of Computers on Employment

Although computers are creating new job opportunities, they're also shifting labor demand toward skilled workers—particularly those who are computer proficient. As a result, these skilled workers are in greater demand and earn higher wages.

Computer skills have never been more important to a person's future. A recent ad from an IT (information technology) staffing firm in Providence, Rhode Island, announced that the company would host its first Rhode Island Young Information Technology Happy Hour. Free food would be provided during the event and free drink tickets given to individuals who signed up to attend before the event. Anyone signing up to attend on the Web site and completing a short survey would also be entered for a chance to win a free Asus Eee mini-laptop computer; registrants had to be present at the event to win. This ad shows the extremes that staffing agencies will go to in hopes of attracting IT and computer-knowledgeable professionals.

As we've pointed out, computers help people complete their work; however, advanced technology can also free people from occupations with hazardous working conditions and ones with repetitive tasks, making workflow safer and more efficient—and increasing productivity. The result is that fewer workers may be required to perform a task, and certain jobs may be eradicated. **Automation**, the replacement of human workers by machines and computer-guided robots, is taking over many manufacturing jobs that people once held (Figure 1.34).

Robots might play a more important role in the future. The robot named ASIMO (Advance Step in Innovative Mobility) is the result of more than two decades of experimentation by Honda engineers (Figure 1.35). It has human-like flexibility and endless possibilities. Visitors to the Disneyland park in Anaheim, California, can see ASIMO in action at the Honda ASIMO theater in the Innoventions attractions. ASIMO is still a work in progress.

On a larger scale, more than 1 million robots are in use worldwide, mostly in Japan, although the United States ranks second. Contrary to popular opinion, fewer than half of the robots used in the United States are found in automotive plants. The rest are used in industries such as health care and in locations such as warehouses, laboratories, and energy plants.

The government of South Korea has promised to invest 1 trillion won (about $750 million) in that country's robotics industry in an attempt to accelerate its growth. The goal is to help the global robotics market grow to more than $30 billion by 2013 and to help Korean companies take as much as 10 percent of that market, according to the Director General for Emerging Technologies. This will make Korea one of the top three producers of robotic products by 2013 and the leading producer by 2018.

Globalization of jobs is another effect of technology on employment. No longer is a product made and sold in the same country. More often, pieces of a product are produced in several countries, assembled into sub-units, and shipped to another location where the subunits are pulled together into the finished product. The term **outsourcing**, the subcontracting of portions of a job to a third party to reduce cost, time, and energy, has become closely related to globalization. Outsourcing is blamed for eliminating as many as 12,000 to 15,000 jobs monthly, with the total amount of lost outsourced jobs predicted to reach

FIGURE 1.34 Computer-guided robots are taking over many manufacturing jobs that people once held.

FIGURE 1.35 Asimo is a humanoid robot that stands 4 feet 3 inches and weighs 114 pounds. It can walk and run on two feet at rates of up to 4.3 miles per hour.

3.3 million by 2015. Some studies argue that increased productivity is an associate cause of job loss. Increasing U.S. productivity by as little as 1 percent can eliminate up to 1.3 million jobs a year. **Structural unemployment** results when advancing technology makes an entire job category obsolete. Structural unemployment differs from the normal economic cycles of layoffs and rehires. People who lose jobs because of structural unemployment are not going to get them back. Their only option is to retrain themselves to work in other careers.

Consider this: Half of all the jobs that will be available in 10 years don't exist today. So, who will survive—and flourish—in a computer-driven economy? The answer is simple: The survivors will be people who understand technology, know that education is a lifelong process, and adapt quickly to change.

Being a Responsible Computer User

You use a computer and the Internet; have a smartphone; and send e-mail, text messages, and tweets throughout the day. All of this seems okay within your own personal space; but how does your usage affect others in your school, office, family, community, and the environment? For starters, don't hog public computer resources. If you are using a computer and Internet connection at a library or in a wireless hot spot, don't download or upload large files; be considerate of others who might be sharing the connection. Recycle paper and printer cartridges to help protect the environment. Don't talk on your phone or text message while driving; many states have enacted laws against using handheld devices while operating a vehicle and impose stringent fines. Be aware of the people near you in the theater; they paid for tickets to watch the show—not to hear your phone or conversation or see your screen light up with a text message.

Another concern is how to dispose of obsolete computer equipment, also called **e-waste**. More than 100 million computers, monitors, and TVs become obsolete each year, and these numbers keep growing. In the first quarter of 2008, 294.3 million mobile phone units were sold, a 13.6 percent increase over the first quarter of 2007. Because monitors, batteries, and other

electronic components contain hazardous materials, they can't just be thrown in the trash. Unfortunately, only 12.5 percent of this e-waste is properly recycled. At least 24 states either have passed or are considering laws regarding e-waste disposal (Figure 1.36). Responsible users look for computer and electronics equipment disposal and recycling companies in their area or check state and federal Web sites, such as the Environmental Protection Agency site (**www.epa.gov**), for tips on computer disposal.

Private companies are stepping up recycling services. Dell has initiated a program that will recycle anyone's PC, regardless of manufacturer. HP will recycle any manufacturer's computer hardware or printer cartridges and has also set up battery recycling programs in many computer stores. Gateway gives you cash for your old technology; if your product has zero value, Gateway will pay for shipping it and will recycle it free of charge. For more information, go to **www.gateway.com/about/corp_responsibility/env_options.php**.

Another way to solve the disposal problem and give back to your community is by donating old computer equipment to

FIGURE 1.36
Responsible computer users and manufacturers recycle old computers, printers, monitors, batteries, and other types of e-waste.

local charities that could refurbish it to help new users learn the basics. Perhaps you might consider donating a little of your time to help too.

Being a responsible technology user also means being aware of how computers and Internet use can affect your own well-being and personal relationships. Researchers at Carnegie Mellon University were surprised to find that people who spent even a few hours a week on the Internet experienced higher levels of depression and loneliness than those who did not. These people interacted with other Internet users online, but this interaction seems to have been much shallower than time spent with friends and family. The result? According to the researchers, Internet use leads to unhealthy social isolation and is a deadened, mechanized experience that is lacking in human emotion. Interestingly, other studies show just the opposite; these studies demonstrate that there is no difference in socialization between those who use the Internet and those who do not. Who is right? It will take years of research to know. But for now, keep in mind that computer and Internet overuse may promote unhealthy behaviors.

Staying Informed About Changing Technology

It is important to stay informed about software and hardware advances in technology. Upgrading the application software on your computer helps you enjoy the most current features the software manufacturer offers. Upgrading your antivirus application helps prevent the latest computer viruses from infecting and harming your system. (A *virus* is a malicious program that enters your computer with or without your permission.) Some viruses are harmless; others slow down performance; and still others delete programs and files. Viruses wreak havoc on computers every day. By knowing all you can about the latest viruses and how they're spread, you can keep your computer from getting infected.

The steady advance of computer hardware has created faster processors, cheaper storage devices, and lighter, thinner, vision-friendly monitors. For the user, this means that next month's computer will be more powerful than this month's computer and will probably cost less. You can stay informed about the latest technology by reading periodicals, visiting Web sites such as CNET (**www.cnet.com**), subscribing to print and online newsletters and publications, and reading technology columns in your local newspaper. Learning about computers and technology will help you be a better consumer, a more productive student and employee, and, in general, a more responsible computer user.

How To:

Choose between a Mac and a PC?

Mac and PC users have been battling it out for years. Each side is entrenched in its beliefs and loyalty. As a potential buyer, it it critical to investigate all possibilities before making a purchase and not let habit or marketing sway your decision. The logical comparison of components, intended use, the opinion of current users, and cost should weigh in on your final evaluation. Each user has to determine his or her budget and purpose, review the features of each type of computer, and make an educated decision. Use the following chart to help you make the decision about whether you would prefer a Mac or a PC.

▶ PC					
COST	**SETUP**	**HARDWARE**	**OPERATING SYSTEM**	**SECURITY AND STABILITY**	**APPLICATIONS**
Usually **less expensive** initially, but might require more hardware to run advanced programs.	Usually requires **some configuration** with external devices.	Intel processor.	Vista and Windows 7 both have **over 5 versions** from which to choose, each with different options. The key here is **familiarity**. A lot of individuals have used previous versions of a PC operating system and feel more comfortable with it.	PCs are **subject to viruses** and will require the purchase of additional antivirus software.	Most (95%) of the world uses PCs. So to share files in the **business world,** a PC is the better choice. A PC is **better suited for gaming,** but a special gaming machine is probably better for the serious gamer.
▶ MAC					
More expensive out of the box, but comes with more hardware and rarely needs any upgrades.	Little to **no set up** required.	Intel processor.	The Mac OS has only **one version** and an extremely appealing and graphic interface.	The Mac is **more stable** and has seldom been compromised by a virus.	Mac is more used in the **graphics community**. Microsoft makes applications for the Mac but does not upgrade them as frequently as they do for the PC. Mac is **better suited for working with graphics,** photo editing, and video creating.

Chapter Summary

Computers and You

- A computer system is a collection of related components that have been designed to perform the information processing cycle: input, processing, output, and storage.
- A system includes both hardware—the physical components such as the system unit, keyboard, monitor, and speakers—and software—the programs that run on it.
- In a typical computer system, a keyboard and a mouse provide input capabilities. Processing is done by the microprocessor (CPU) on programs and data held in RAM (random access memory). You see the results (output) on a monitor or printer, and a hard disk is typically used for long-term storage.
- A computer is an electronic device that performs four operations; input, processing output, and storage. These four operations, performed in sequential order, are called the information processing cycle.
- There are two major categories of computers: computers for individuals and those for organizations. Types of computers for individuals include personal computers (PCs), desktop computers, all-in-one computers, notebooks, subnotebooks, tablet PCs, and handheld computers (such as PDAs and smartphones). Types of computers for organizations include professional workstations, servers, minicomputers, mainframes, and supercomputers.
- Computers have advantages and disadvantages. Some advantages include speed, memory, storage, hardware reliability, accuracy, and assistance to those with disabilities. Disadvantages include information overload, expense, data inaccuracy, unreliable software, viruses, software piracy, identity theft, loss of jobs to automation, and health problems due to improperly fitting equipment and poorly arranged work environments.
- The use of social networking sites such as Facebook, MySpace, LinkedIn, and Twitter is growing daily. Such sites provide a method of connectivity that is inexpensive (most often free), available 24/7, and globally accessible. Businesses have realized the power of such sites and have become users to analyze their customers and keep an eye on competitors.
- Computers are creating new job opportunities, shifting labor demand toward skilled workers, helping people complete their work; freeing workers from occupations with hazardous working conditions, making workflow safer and more efficient, and increasing productivity.
- Being a responsible computer user means respecting others when using technology, recycling computer hardware, sharing public computing resources, being aware of computer and Internet overuse, and staying informed about changing technology and its effect on the environment.

Key Terms and Concepts

Identification

Label each device as input, output, processing, or storage.

1. _____

5. _____

2. _____

6. _____

3. _____

7. _____

4. _____

8. _____

Matching

Match each key term in the left column with the most accurate definition in the right column:

_____ 1. random access memory

_____ 2. netbook

_____ 3. program

_____ 4. tablet PC

_____ 5. CPU

_____ 6. operating system

_____ 7. ergonomics

_____ 8. instant messaging

_____ 9. application software

_____ 10. information overload

_____ 11. network interface card

_____ 12. digital piracy

_____ 13. Facebook

_____ 14. all-in-one computer

_____ 15. Twitter

a. Referred to as the brain of the computer

b. A social network used for lengthy communication with friends

c. A computer system in which the system unit and monitor are combined to reduce the space needed to hold the system

d. A hardware component of a computer system that contains the electronics to connect the computer to the network

e. A free real-time connection that makes use of a buddy list

f. A convertible notebook that can be used in two different configurations and accepts handwritten input

g. Unauthorized reproduction and distribution of computer-based media

h. A set of instructions that tells a computer how to perform a process

i. Anxiety experienced when individuals are presented with more information than they can handle

j. High-speed temporary memory that holds programs and data in use

k. A social network site designed for short messages that do not exceed 140 characters

l. The collection of programs that provides the infrastructure for other programs to function properly

m. A portable, lightweight computer equipped with wireless technology and used primarily to browse the Web and access e-mail

n. A collection of programs that together perform a task for the user

o. The matching of computer components to fit an individual's posture and body design

Multiple Choice

Circle the correct choice for each of the following:

1. Which of the following is *not* an output device?
   a. Monitor
   b. Printer
   c. Disk drive
   d. Speaker

2. Which of the following is *not* an example of a social network?
   a. Twitter
   b. Google Docs
   c. Facebook
   d. MySpace

3. What part of the system unit processes the input data?
   a. Read-alone memory
   b. CPU
   c. Random access memory
   d. NIC

4. What component of a computer is *not* located in the system unit?
   a. RAM
   b. Flash drive
   c. CPU
   d. Hard drive

5. Which is an example of an e-book reader?
   a. Wiki
   b. NIC
   c. Tweet
   d. Kindle DX

6. What is the replacement of human workers by machines and computer-guided robots called?
   a. Outsourcing
   b. Automation
   c. Digital piracy
   d. Structural unemployment

7. What is the name of the board within the system unit that connects the CPU and other system components?
   a. Motherboard
   b. Processing board
   c. NIC board
   d. Information board

8. Which of the following computers is designed for portability or use while traveling?
   a. All-in-one
   b. Notebook
   c. Desktop
   d. Workstation

9. What is the name of the software group that contains the operating system and antivirus programs?
   a. Application software   b. Word processing
   c. System Software   d. Utility software

10. What is the name given to unemployment caused by technology making an entire job category obsolete?
   a. Technological unemployment
   b. Corporate unemployment
   c. Structural unemployment
   d. Automated unemployment

Fill-In

In the blanks provided, write the correct answer for each of the following:

1. The mouse and keyboard are _____ devices.

2. Another name for random access memory is _____ memory.

3. Hard drives, DVD drives, and USB drives are examples of _____ devices.

4. Obsolete computer equipment is called _____.

5. The _____ feature of the Kindle 2 made it a device that truly helped the visually impaired.

6. _____ is another term for the disposing of obsolete computer equipment.

7. The _____ describes the disparity between groups who own computers and have Internet access and those who do not.

8. Raw facts that are input into a computer system are referred to as _____.

9. _____ is the high-speed movement of data or information within and between computers.

10. _____ is a free Web-based word processor and spreadsheet that encourages collaboration by allowing group members to share and edit documents online.

11. A _____ is an ultrafast computer that focuses on performing a few sets of instructions as fast as possible.

12. One quadrillion calculations is referred to as a _____.

13. _____ is the sending of portions of a job to a third party to reduce cost, time, and energy.

14. The purpose of the central processor is to convert data into _____.

15. The use of computers and computer programs to replace teachers and time-specific learning is _____.

Short Answer

1. Explain the difference between hardware and software.

2. List three features found on a new smartphone that did not exist on a phone five years ago.

3. According to the studies, what are three variables that influence whether an individual will or will not have Internet access?

4. Define the terms *data* and *information*. Identify the step in the information processing cycle that each is associated with.

5. List two current operating systems and two examples of application software.

6. List three advantages and three disadvantages of computer use.

7. List three changes you can make to your computing environment to reduce stress and make it more ergonomically friendly.

Teamwork

1. **Information Overload** Excessive amounts of e-mails, text messages, phone calls, and tweets can cause stress, headaches, irritability, and a generalized feeling of being overwhelmed. As a team, come up with at least five ways to control information, put it on hold, or filter out the undesired content. Present your resulting list to the class, using a slide show.

2. **"I am a Mac, and I am a PC"** As a team, use a search engine to locate and review at least three of the "I am a Mac, and I am a PC" commercials. These are 30-second commercials that praise the features of the Mac while mocking the PC. Cite the commercials viewed. Create a new 30-second commercial that will reverse the ad: Have the commercial support the PC while mocking the Mac. Your team will have to research both systems to find a PC asset that the Mac lacks. Rehearse your commercial and present it to the class.

3. **Netbook or iPad—You Decide** As a team, determine whether you would purchase a netbook or an iPad. Use the Internet or contact a local vendor and compare the prices for similarly equipped units. Based on your needs and finances, prepare a report to present to the class explaining which device you would buy and give reasons that support your decision.

4. **Ergonomics** As a team, use a search engine and locate at least three Web sites that contain information about the ergonomics of setting up computer stations.

Prepare a report that covers the following items. First, define the term *ergonomics,* and then list at least five items that should be ergonomically designed in a computer station for the user's health and comfort. For at least three of these five items, find two retailers that sell such ergonomic products. Describe the products, explain how they will ergonomically correct or prevent a problem, and note how much the devices cost. Be sure to cite your resources.

5. **Social Networks** As a team create a survey of at least 10 questions on social networking. Your questions should try to find out the social networking site to which each respondent belongs, the number of times in a week the individual visits that site, and the number of friends or followers the individual has for starters. Additionally, the age and gender of the individual might give you some more insight into trends. Give the survey to 30 people from a variety of backgrounds. Regroup and, using a spreadsheet, summarize your survey data, citing any trends that your collected data exposed.

On the Web

1. **Green Computers** Go to **www.worldchanging. com/archives/004350.html** and use Google (**www. google.com**) or another search engine to locate sources of information about green computers. List at least three green computer features and their components. Then use the Internet to locate three manufacturers of green computers. State the name of each computer, its price, and the green features that each system possesses. Present this information in a one- or two-page, double-spaced report. Be sure to cite your references.

2. **Trends in Education** Using either your school or another in your community, collect information from the online course catalog on the number of classes that are traditional or seated classes, how many are hybrids (a combination of seated and online meetings), and how many are purely online. Interview a few students and ask about the type of classes they have taken and their opinion of the three different class structures. Then interview several instructors and get their opinions. Collect all of your course data, state the percentage of courses that fall into each category, and summarize your student and instructor replies. Present your results in a slide presentation.

3. **Input Hardware Trends** Use your favorite search engine to locate information on the Luxeed dynamic Pixel LED keyboard, virtual laser keyboards, and the new touch screen on the iPad. In a one–page, double-spaced paper summarize your findings. Include the

new or unusual features of each device, a summary of any online reviews that you could locate, and your opinion of each input device.

4. **Ethics** Use your favorite search engine and locate the "Ten Commandments of Computer Ethics" published by the Computer Ethics Institute. Read each one, and in a one-page paper indicate at least three commandments with which you agree and three with which you disagree. Give logical and historical reasons for your statement. You might want to reference the Bill of Rights or other historical documents to support your stance. Cite your references and present your reasons in a one- or two-page, double-spaced paper.

5. **Employment** Use your favorite search engine to locate computer-related jobs in your area. Make a list of the positions, the type of required computer skill required, and, if possible, the level of education needed for the position and the salary range. Using a word processor, make a table of your results. Determine whether there is an employment trend in your region. Do you or any of you family members qualify for any of the jobs located? Does your school offer the courses or degrees to meet the demands of your local job market? Submit your table and summary comments in a one-page, double-spaced word processed report.

Spotlight

Ethics

What's the difference between ethical and unethical behavior? Is it possible for an action to be unethical but still legal? You might not realize it, but in some way you probably face this question daily, especially when you use computers and, more specifically, the Internet. Have you downloaded any music recently, ripped any CDs lately, or copied music from a friend? Did you pay for that music? Have you watched a DVD movie or played a video game this weekend? Was the DVD or game a legally purchased copy? Perhaps you've posted a nasty comment about someone on a discussion board or sent an anonymous nasty e-mail that caused someone undo stress. These are some of the behaviors at school, home, or on the job to consider in the scope of ethical behavior.

Ethics is often described as knowing the difference between right and wrong, based on approved standards of social and professional behavior, and choosing to do what is right.

In other words, we *choose* to behave in an ethical way so we can live with our conscience. Ethics is not about whether we'll get caught but more about our ability to live with the decision we make.

This spotlight examines some of the most common issues in computer ethics, including ethical dilemmas, in which the difference between right and wrong is not so easy to discern. We look at ethical principles that can serve as guides for making decisions that might be difficult or in an unfamiliar area. Additionally, we consider the significance of a code of conduct. Ethical standards are provided to act as guides for computer users, professionals, and organizations. Finally we look at unethical behavior that is also illegal.

Ethical choices are often personal and are made with great consideration and thought by the individual making the choice. Hopefully, some of the insights in this chapter will help serve as a basic steering guide or reference points to alleviate some of the uncertainty surrounding making ethical decisions even when they are difficult.

Computer Ethics for Computer Users

It isn't always easy to determine the right thing to do. Even when you know what's right, it isn't always easy to act on it. Peer pressure is a tremendous force. Why should you be the one to do the right thing when you believe everyone else is getting away with using copied software and music files?

Computers cause new ethical dilemmas by pushing people into making decisions in unprecedented situations (Figure 1A). **Computer ethics** is the use of basic ethical principles to help you make the right decisions in your daily computer use. Ethical principles help you think through your options.

FIGURE 1A Computers present new ethical dilemmas where individuals must choose among paths they are unfamiliar with.

ETHICAL PRINCIPLES

An **ethical principle** defines the standards that promote trust, fairness, good behavior, and kindness. These principles are used as justification for considering an act or a rule to be morally right or wrong. Over the centuries, philosophers have come up with many ethical principles. For many people, it's disconcerting to find that these principles sometimes conflict. An ethical principle is only a tool that you can use to think through a difficult situation. In the end, you must make your choice and live with the consequences.

The Belmont Report from the U.S. Department of Health, Education, and Welfare shows three of the most useful ethical principles:

- *An act is ethical if, were everyone to act the same way, society as a whole would benefit.*

- *An act is ethical if it treats people as an end in themselves rather than as a means to an end.*
- *An act is ethical if impartial observers would judge that it is fair to all parties concerned.*

If you still find yourself in an ethical dilemma related to computer use even after careful consideration of these ethical principles, talk to people you trust. They might be able to provide insight into the dilemma that you face, pointing out factors that you might have not considered, helping you to make the correct ethical decision. Make sure you have all the facts. Think through alternative courses of action based on the different principles. Would you be proud if your parents knew what you had done? What if your actions were mentioned in an article on the front page of your local newspaper? Can you live with your conscience? Remember, always strive to find a solution you can be proud of and live with.

FOLLOWING YOUR SCHOOL'S CODE OF CONDUCT

When you use a computer, one of the things you will have to determine is who owns the data, programs, and Internet access you enjoy. If you own your computer system and its software, the work you create is clearly yours, and you are solely responsible for it. However, when you use a computer at school or at work, it is possible that the work you create there might be considered the property of the school or business. In short, you have greater responsibility and less control over content ownership when you use somebody else's system than when you use your own.

Sometimes this question isn't just an ethical one but a legal one as well. How companies and schools enforce computer usage rules tends to vary. So where can you, the college computer user, find guidance when dealing with ethical and legal dilemmas? Your college or place of employment probably has its own code of conduct or **acceptable use policy** for computer users. You can usually find this policy on your organization's Web site (Figure 1B), in a college or employee handbook, or included in an employment contract that you have been asked to sign. You might call the help desk at your computing center and ask for the Web site address of the policy or request a physical copy of it. Read the policy carefully and follow the rules.

Common to most acceptable-use policies are such guidelines as these:

- **Respect yourself.** If you obtain an account and password to use the campus computer system, don't give your password to others. They could do something that gets you in trouble. In addition, don't say or do anything on the Internet that could reflect

FIGURE 1B Many organizations and schools publish their computer and network use (or acceptable use) policy on their Web site.

poorly on you, even if you think no one will ever find out. Internet content has a way of resurfacing.

- **Respect others.** Obviously, you shouldn't use a computer to threaten or harass anyone. You should also avoid using more than your share of computing resources, such as disk space. If you publish a Web page on your college's computers, remember that your page's content affects the college's public image.
- **Respect academic integrity.** Always give credit for text you've copied from the Internet. Obtain permission before you copy pictures. Don't copy or distribute software unless the license specifically states you have permission to do so.

Classroom computer etiquette is increasingly becoming an academic issue. Within their course syllabi, instructors are providing clear guidelines for the use of computers and portable devices, such as cell phones, in a classroom. Such statements may look like the excerpt below and even tie improper use to a grade reduction.

Appropriate Classroom Laptop Use . . . Although having a laptop [or other portable device] in class opens up new learning possibilities for students, sometimes students utilize it in ways that are inappropriate. Please refrain from instant messaging, e-mailing, surfing the Internet, playing games, writing papers, doing homework, etc., during class time. Acceptable uses include taking notes, following along with the instructor on PowerPoint, with demonstrations, and other whole-class activities, as well as working on assigned in-class activities, projects, and discussions that require laptop use. It is easy for your laptop [or portable device] to become a distraction to you and to those around you. Inappropriate uses will be noted and may affect your final grade.

TEN COMMANDMENTS FOR COMPUTER ETHICS

The Computer Ethics Institute of the Brookings Institution, located in Washington, DC, has developed the following "Ten Commandments for Computer Ethics" for computer users, programmers, and system designers. Many businesses, academic institutions, and organizations post or refer to these principles:

1. Thou shalt not use a computer to harm other people.
2. Thou shalt not interfere with other people's computer work.
3. Thou shalt not snoop around in other people's computer files.
4. Thou shalt not use a computer to steal.
5. Thou shalt not use a computer to bear false witness.
6. Thou shalt not copy or use proprietary software for which you have not paid.
7. Thou shalt not use other people's computer resources without authorization or proper compensation.
8. Thou shalt not appropriate other people's intellectual output.
9. Thou shalt think about the social consequences of the program you are writing or the system you are designing.
10. Thou shalt always use a computer in ways that ensure consideration and respect for your fellow humans.

NETIQUETTE

General principles such as the "Ten Commandments for Computer Ethics" are useful for overall guidance, but they don't provide specific help for the special situations you'll run into online—such as how to behave properly in chat rooms or while playing an online game (Figure 1C). As a result, computer and Internet users have developed a lengthy series of specific behavior guidelines called **netiquette** for the various Internet services available

FIGURE 1C Netiquette refers to guidelines for behaving properly in online interactions.

(such as e-mail, mailing lists, social networking sites, discussion forums, and online role-playing games) that provide specific pointers on how to show respect for others—and for yourself—while you're online. A document posted by the Responsible Use of the Network Working Group (RUN) of the Internet Engineering Task Force at **www.dtcc.edu/cs/rfc1855.html** provides detailed netiquette guides for online activities that effect one-to-one and one-to-many communications.

A consolidation of rules from the site above and **www.albion.com/netiquette** as well as other Internet sources are categorized and summarized below.

- **Discussion forums.** Before posting to a discussion forum, review the forum and various topics to see what kinds of questions are welcomed and how to participate meaningfully. If the forum has a FAQ (frequently asked questions) document posted on the Web, be sure to read it before posting to the forum; your question may already have been answered in the FAQ. Post your message under the appropriate topic or start a new topic if necessary. Your post should be helpful or ask a legitimate question. Bear in mind that some people using the discussion forum may not speak English as their native language, so don't belittle people for spelling errors. Don't post inflammatory messages; never post in anger. If you agree with something, don't post a message that says "Me too"—you're just wasting everyone's time. Posting ads for your own business or soliciting answers to obvious homework questions is usually frowned on.

- **E-mail.** Check your e-mail daily and respond promptly to the messages you've been sent. Download or delete messages after you've read them so that you don't exceed your disk-usage quota. Remember that e-mail isn't private; you should never send a message that contains anything you wouldn't want others to read. Always speak of others professionally and courteously; e-mail is easily forwarded, and the person you're describing may eventually see the message. Check your computer frequently for viruses that can propagate via e-mail messages. Keep your messages short and to the point; focus on one subject per message. Don't type in all capital letters; this comes across as SHOUTING. Spell check your e-mail as you would any other written correspondence, especially in professional settings. Watch out for sarcasm and humor in e-mail; it often fails to come across as a joke. Requesting a return receipt may be an acceptable academic policy to verify the submission of an assignment, but in some situations it might be considered an invasion of privacy.

- **Instant messages (IM) and text messages.** IM and text messages are ideal for brief conversa-

tions; but complex or lengthy discussions may be better handled in person, by e-mail, or by phone. IM can be easily misinterpreted because tone is difficult to convey. Never share bad news or a major announcement in a text message or send an IM while you are angry or upset. Don't assume that everyone knows what IM acronyms such as BRB (be right back) and LOL (laughing out loud) mean. Be mindful that some smartphone plans still charge for text messages. Also, remember to set away messages and use other status messages wisely.

- **Chat rooms.** Only visit chat rooms that are appropriate for your age and follow the rules and regulations of the chat. If you are unsure of the protocols, contact the administrator or host of the chat room. Say hello when you enter the room, and take some time to review the conversation currently taking place before jumping in. Avoid entering personal information, and respect other chatters. Foul language may get you expelled or permanently banned from the room. Some rooms allow you to put a chatter on ignore status if you are being bothered by that person. This type of behavior should be immediately reported to the administrator or chat room host.

> "Remember that **e-mail** isn't private; you should **never** send a **message** that contains anything you wouldn't **want** others **to read**"

Netiquette is important in the classroom. According to an article published in *The Journal of Higher Education*, several colleges have offered guidelines and suggestions for curbing misuse of computers in class and have set netiquette standards, like turning off the computer's volume before class begins.

In addition to respectful use of Internet services, playing computer games is another area in which you might face ethical dilemmas.

COMPUTER GAMES: TOO MUCH VIOLENCE?

Computer gaming isn't universally admired, but statistics support that it is universally on the increase. Sixty-five percent of households in the United States have at least one member who plays video games. Seventeen billion hours have been logged on Xbox Live by some 20 million players; this is roughly two hours for every person on the planet. To further support this growth, recent statistics estimate online gaming revenue at $15 billion. How is this related to ethics? Approximately 94 percent of the video games fall into the fantasy category and include such titles as *Halo*, *World of Warcraft*, and *Call of Duty: Modern Warfare*. These games emphasize strategy development and team play, but they also emphasize violent behaviors. Parents and politicians are concerned that children who play these games may be learning aggressive behaviors that will prove dysfunctional in real life.

Fears concerning the impact of violent computer games were heightened by the Columbine High School tragedy in 1999, in which two Littleton, Colorado, teenagers opened fire on teachers and fellow students before committing suicide. Subsequently, investigators learned that the boys had been great fans of splatter games such as *Doom* and *Quake* and may have patterned their massacre after their gaming experiences. In 2009, there was a school shooting in Germany that left 15 dead. A neighbor and childhood friend of the shooter was quoted as saying, "He [the shooter] was fascinated by video games; he used to play a shooting game called *Tactical Ops* and he used to watch horror films like *Alien* and *Predator*."

Still, psychologists disagree on the effect of violent computer games. Some point out that they're little more than an extension of the World War II "combat" games children used to play on street corners before television—and the computer—came along. Others claim that violent video games provide an outlet for aggression that might otherwise materialize in homes and schools.

One thing is for certain: Computer games are becoming more violent. In the past few years, the video game industry has released a slew of new titles that offer a more streamlined gaming experience, particularly when a player is connected to the Internet in multiplayer mode—and of course, much more realistic portrayals of violent acts (Figure 1D).

So who is responsible? Is it the software manufacturers who create the programs? Is it the consumers who purchase and use the programs? More importantly, is there anything you can do about it? Refer back to the "Ten Commandments for Computer Ethics," especially numbers 9 and 10. Think about the personality of the person you are purchasing a game for or inviting to play a game. If the content of the game seems to be inappropriate, select a different game or activity. With regard to minors, parents certainly have a responsibility over what their children do, but what about you—do you make "good" decisions when it comes to your own exposure to violence?

Now that you know about the ethical issues individuals face, let's take a look at how organizations deal with computer ethics.

Computer Ethics for Organizations

Every day, newspapers carry stories about people getting into trouble by using their computers to conduct personal business while they're at work. In many cases, the offenders use company computers to

FIGURE 1D Some computer games are both engrossing and violent.

browse the Web, make personal travel plans, send personal e-mail on company time, or to commit crimes such as cyberstalking or distributing pornography. The use of a company computer for non-business-related tasks is generally prohibited. Such policies are typically included in the company's acceptable use policy.

However, those are rules set by the company to control individuals' behavior while at work. What ethical responsibilities do the companies themselves have to their employees, customers, and the general public? A business or organization needs to protect its data from loss, damage, error, and misuse. Each business entity needs to have business continuity and disaster recovery plans in place to prevent and respond to security breaches or other malfunctions that occur.

Protecting data from loss or change is often simply a matter of following proper backup procedures. **Backup procedures** involve making copies of data files to protect against data loss, change, or damage from natural or other disasters. Without backup procedures, an organization may place its customers' information at risk. Moreover, it is unethical not to keep regular backups, because the loss of the company's data could negatively impact the stakeholders in the business (Figure 1E). What would happen to a bank, for example, if it lost all of its data and didn't have any backups? As our dependency on information increases, our tolerance for lost data is decreasing. It is this dependency that has led to the use of **continuous backups**, programs that automatically create a backup when a change in a system or a data file occurs.

Data errors can and do occur. It is the ethical responsibility of any organization that deals with data to ensure that its data is as correct as possible. Data that hasn't been properly maintained can have serious effects on the individual or associated organization.

Data misuse occurs when an employee or company fails to keep data confidential. A breach of confidentiality occurs when an employee looks up data about a person in a database and uses that information for something other than what was intended. For example, U.S. government workers accessed the passport files for 2008 presidential candidates John McCain, Barack Obama, and Hillary Clinton, in addition to more than 100 celebrities. Such actions are grounds for termination.

Companies may punish employees for looking up customer data, but many of them think nothing of

FIGURE 1E A backup system can help protect a business's information assets and enable the business to continue to operate as usual. A computer tape library is one way to store backed-up files.

considered the most innovative and far reaching. According to the ACM general moral imperatives, a computing professional

1. Contributes to society and human well-being
2. Avoids harm to others
3. Is honest and trustworthy
4. Is fair and takes action not to discriminate on the basis of race, sex, religion, age, disability, or national origin
5. Honors property rights, including copyrights and patents
6. Gives proper credit when using the intellectual property of others
7. Respects the right of other individuals to privacy
8. Honors confidentiality.

Like other codes of conduct, the ACM code places public safety and well-being at the top of the list.

CODE OF CONDUCT FOR THE INSTITUTE FOR CERTIFICATION OF COMPUTING PROFESSIONALS

Other organizations also have codes of conduct or define elements of good practice for professionals. The Institute for Certification of Computing Professionals is one such organization. It prides itself on the establishment of professional standards for those who work with computers. According to the organization, the essential elements related to conduct that identify a professional activity are as follows:

- A high standard of skill and knowledge
- A confidential relationship with people served
- Public reliance upon the standards of conduct and established practice
- The observance of an ethical code

SAFETY FIRST

Computer professionals create products that affect many people and may even expose them to risk of personal injury or death. Increasingly, computers and computer programs figure prominently in safety-critical systems, including transportation monitoring (such as with air traffic control) and patient monitoring in hospitals (Figure 1F).

Consider the following situation. An airplane pilot flying in poor visibility uses a computer, called an autopilot, to guide the plane. The air traffic control system also relies on computers. The plane crashes. The investigation discloses minor bugs in both computer programs. If the plane's computer had been dealing with a person in the tower rather than a computer or if the air

selling it to third parties. A mail-order company, for example, can gain needed revenue by selling customer lists to firms marketing related products. Privacy advocates believe that it's unethical to divulge customer data without first asking the customer's permission. These advocates are working to pass tougher privacy laws so the matter would become a legal concern, not an ethical one.

As an employee, what can you do to stop companies from misusing data or to protect your customers' privacy? Often, there's no clear-cut solution. If you believe that the way a company is conducting business poses a danger to the public or appears to be illegal, you can report the company to regulatory agencies or the press, an action called whistle-blowing. But what if your whistle-blowing causes your company to shut down, putting not only you but also all of your coworkers out of work? As this example illustrates, codes of ethics don't solve every ethical problem, and innocent individuals may suffer as a result of an ethical action; however, ethical principles at least provide solid guidance for most situations.

Computer Ethics for Computer Professionals

No profession can stay in business for long without a rigorous (and enforced) code of professional ethics. That's why many different types of professionals subscribe to ethical **codes of conduct**. These codes are developed by professional associations, such as the Association for Computing Machinery (ACM).

THE ACM CODE OF CONDUCT

Of all the computing associations' codes of conduct, the one developed by the ACM (**www.acm.org**) is

FIGURE 1F Patient monitoring in hospitals helps to create a safer environment, with audio warnings and information automatically transmitted to a central, monitoring station.

traffic control program had been interacting with a human pilot, the crash would not have occurred. Where does the liability lie for the loss of life and property?

Experienced programmers know that programs of any size have bugs. Most complex programs have so many possible combinations of conditions that it isn't feasible to test for every combination. In some cases, the tests would take years; in other cases, no one could think of all the possible conditions. Because bugs are inevitable and programmers can't predict all the different ways programs interact with their environment, most computer experts believe that it's wrong to single out programmers for blame.

Software companies are at fault if they fail to test and document their products. In addition, the organization that buys the software may share part of the blame if it fails to train personnel to use the system properly.

At the center of every computer code of ethics is the underlying intention of computer professionals to develop, maintain, upgrade, and evaluate programs and devices to preserve and protect human life and to avoid harm or injury. If the public is to trust computer professionals, those professionals must have the ethics needed to protect our safety and welfare—even if doing so means that the professional or the company he or she works for suffers financially.

Unlike the ethical dilemmas we've discussed up to now, right and wrong are more easily defined when it comes to matters of the law.

It's Not Just Unethical, It's Illegal Too

Some unethical actions are also illegal and have serious consequences. Let's start with something that gets many college students into serious trouble: plagiarism.

PLAGIARISM

Imagine the following scenario. It's 4 AM, and you have a paper due for your 9 AM class. While searching for sources on the Internet, you find a Web site with an essay on your topic. What's wrong with downloading the text, reworking it a bit, and handing it in? Plenty.

The use of someone else's intellectual property (their ideas or written work) is called **plagiarism**. Plagiarism predates computers; in fact, it has been practiced for thousands of years. But, computers—and especially the Internet—make the temptation and ease of plagiarizing even greater. It's not only very easy to copy and paste from the Internet but some sites are actually set up specifically to sell college-level papers to the lazy or desperate. The sites selling the papers aren't guilty of plagiarism, but you are if you turn in the work as your own.

Plagiarism is a serious offense. How serious? At some colleges, even a first offense can get you thrown out of school. You might think it's rare for plagiarizers to be caught, but the truth is that college instructors are often able to detect plagiarism in students' papers without much effort. The tip-off can be a change in the sophistication of phraseology, writing that is a little too polished, or errors in spelling and grammar that are identical in two or more papers. Software programs such as Turnitin are available that can scan text and then compare it against a library of known phrases (Figure 1G). If a paper has one or more recognizable phrases, it is marked for closer inspection. Furthermore, even if your actions are not discovered now, someone could find out later, and the evidence could void your degree and even damage your career.

The more well-known you are, the more you're at risk of your plagiarism being uncovered. Take noted historian and Pulitzer Prize–winning author Doris Kearns Goodwin, for example. In 2002, she was accused of plagiarizing part of her best-selling 1987 book, *The Fitzgeralds and the Kennedys*. Although she claimed her plagiarizing was inadvertent and due to inadequate research methods, she suffered a significant decline in credibility and even felt obligated to leave her position at the PBS news program *NewsHour with Jim Lehrer*. It took 15 years for Goodwin's plagiarism to come to light.

Plagiarism is both unethical and illegal: The unethical part is the dishonesty of passing someone else's work off as your own. The illegal part is taking the material without permission. Plagiarizing copyrighted material is called **copyright infringement**, and you can be sued and may have to pay damages in addition to compensating your victim for any financial losses due to your theft of the material. Trademarks, products, and patented processes are also protected. If you're tempted to copy anything from the Web, bear

FIGURE 1G Turnitin is one of the popular software packages used by professors at colleges and universities to identify instances of plagiarism.

in mind that the United States is a signatory to international copyright regulations, which specify that an original author does not need to include an explicit copyright notice to be protected under the law.

Does this mean you can't use the Internet source you found? No, you can use or refer to your source, but you must follow certain citation guidelines. In academic writing, you can make use of someone else's effort if you use your own words and give credit where credit is due. If you use a phrase or a few sentences from the source, use quotation marks. Attach a bibliography and list the source. For Internet sources, you should list the Web site's address (or Uniform Resource Locator [URL]), the date the article was published (if available), the date and time you accessed the site, the name of the article, and the author's name. You can usually find a link at the bottom of a Web site's home page that outlines the owner's copyright policy. If not, there is usually a "contact us" link that you can use to contact the owner. You cannot assume that it is legal to copy content from a Web site just because you cannot find a disclaimer. Starting with Microsoft Office 2007, adding citations to a research paper became even easier. One of the features of the software is a tool to help you organize and input the correct reference information in a variety of different referencing styles.

You'll often hear people use the term **fair use** to justify illegal copying. The fair use doctrine justifies *limited* uses of copyrighted material without payment to or permission from the copyright holder. This means that a *brief* selection from a copyrighted work may be excerpted for the purposes of commentary, parody, news reporting, research, and education. Such excerpts are short—generally, no more than 5 percent of the original work—and they shouldn't compromise the commercial value of the work. Of course, you must still cite the source. In general, the reproduction of an entire work is rarely justifiable by means of the fair use doctrine.

As a responsible computer user, you should be concerned not only about wrongly using someone else's words but also about the correctness of the content you create yourself. The written word carries a lot of power. Publishing words that are untrue about a business or individual could be crossing into dangerous, and illegal, territory.

LIBEL

The power of computers, with their ease of uploading, publishing, and reaching a huge group of viewers in seconds, has also caused an increase in cases of libel. In the United States, **libel** is the publication, in written or faxed form, of a false statement that injures someone's business or personal reputation. A plaintiff who sues for libel must prove that a false statement caused injury and demonstrate some type of resulting damage. This could include being shunned by friends and associates or the inability to obtain work because potential employers believed the false accusations. Some states allow a jury to assess damages based generally on harm to the person's reputation. It is in your best interest to ensure that any electronic publication statement you make about an individual or a corporation is truthful.

SOFTWARE PIRACY

Here's another common situation. You need to have Microsoft Office 2007 for your computer class. A friend gives you a copy that she got from her mom's office. You've just installed that copy on your computer. Have you done something wrong? Yes, of course you have! In fact, so has your friend. It is illegal for her to have a copy of the software from her mom's office in the first place.

Just like written works, most computer software (including computer games) is copyrighted, which means that you can't make copies for other people without infringing on the software's copyright. Such infringements are called **software piracy** and are a federal offense in the United States (Figure 1H).

How serious is software piracy? The information technology industry loses billions of dollars a year because of piracy. If you're caught pirating software, you may be charged with a felony. If you're convicted of a felony, you could spend time in jail, lose the right to vote, and ruin your chances for a successful career.

When you purchase commercial software, you're really purchasing a **software license**, which generally grants you the right to make backups of the program disks and install the software. You need to read the license agreement to determine how many machines you can install the software on. You are not allowed to provide the program to others or modify the program's function. A blank sample of a software license can be

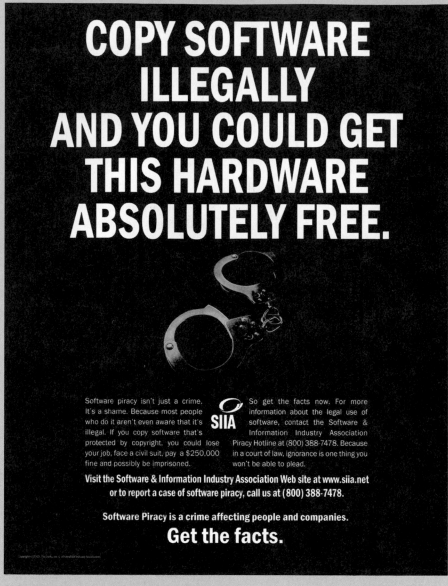

FIGURE 1H The Software & Information Industry Association (SIIA) is trying to raise consciousness about software piracy.

found at **www.lawsmart.com/documents/software_license.shtml**. Note that this is a sample, and reading it is *not* a substitute for examining the software license for each program you purchase.

Free programs that users can copy or modify without restriction are called **public domain software**. However, don't assume that a program is public domain unless you see a note (often in the form of a Read Me text file) that explicitly identifies the file as being copyright free.

Unlike public domain software, you can't copy or modify **shareware** programs without permission from the owner. You can usually find the owner and licensing information by accessing the Help menu or by locating and reading a Read Me file that is usually placed in the same directory as the program. You may, however, freely copy trial or evaluation versions of shareware programs. When the evaluation period expires, you must pay a **registration fee** or delete the software from your computer.

Other programs qualify under the provisions of the Free Software Foundation's **General Public License (GPL)**, which specifies that anyone may freely copy, use, and modify the software, but no one can sell it for profit.

Organizations with many computers (including colleges) also have to be concerned about software piracy. A **site license** is a contract with the software publisher that allows an organization to use multiple copies of the software at a reduced price per unit. Taking copies outside the organization usually violates the contract. However, check the license agreement. Some organizations negotiate the agreement to allow employees to load the software on their home computers as well, as long as only one copy is in use at any one time and the programs are used for academic and noncommercial tasks.

Software manufacturers are working very hard to develop **copyright protection schemes** to thwart the illegal use of their programs. Increasingly, software is becoming **machine dependent**. This means that the program captures a machine ID during the installation process and writes that ID back to the software company's server during a mandatory online registration process. If you attempt to install the program on another machine, the code will be checked and the installation will terminate unless your license allows multiple installations. Microsoft checks your computer for a valid copy of its software before it will permit you to make updates, access templates, or download other add-ons.

How can you tell whether you're guilty of software piracy? All of the following actions are illegal:

- *Continuing to use a shareware program past the evaluation version's expiration date without paying the registration fee.*
- *Violating the terms of a software license, even if you've paid for the program. For example, if you have copies of the same program on your desktop and notebook computers but the license allows only one installation, you are in violation of the license.*
- *Making copies of site-licensed programs that you use at work or school and installing them on your home computer (unless expressly allowed through the license).*

- *Giving or selling copies of commercial software to others.*
- *Incorporating all or part of a GPL program in a commercial program that you offer for sale.*

Do you have pirated programs on your computer? The police aren't likely to storm into your home or dorm room and take you away kicking and screaming. Most software piracy prosecutions target individuals who are trying to distribute or sell infringing copies, or companies that have illegally made multiple copies for their employees. If you have any pirated software, you should remove those programs from your computer right away. In the future, consider whether your actions constitute software piracy before the software is installed on your computer. If you still don't see the need to delete pirated software from your computer, consider this: It's very, very wise to become accustomed to a zero-tolerance approach to pirated software. If you're caught with an infringing program at work, you could lose your job. A company can't risk retaining employees who expose the firm to prosecution. There are software auditing applications that a school or company can purchase to monitor software usage.

Some software sold on auction sites and installed on systems created by build-it-yourself computer vendors may be unlicensed (and therefore illegal) software. Ask for the product registration key and the original CDs or DVDs for any products purchased online or pre-installed on a system. A **product registration key** is a unique alphanumeric code specific to that particular copy of the program. It is necessary to enter this key after installation in order to validate its authenticity and activate the program. The key may be necessary later to download upgrades, patches, or templates.

The Business Software Alliance (BSA) helps combat software piracy by educating the public and businesses about the legal and safety issues regarding commercial software use. You can even fill out a confidential form on their Web site at **https://reporting.bsa.org/usa** to report incidences of piracy. By doing so, you could be eligible for a $1 million reward.

FILE SHARING: MUSIC, MOVIES, AND MORE

You may have heard that it's okay to download a copyrighted MP3 file as long as you keep it for no longer than 24 hours, but that's false. If you upload music copied from a CD you've paid for, you are violating the law. You can't justify spreading a band's copyrighted music around by saying it's "free advertising;" if the group wants advertising, they'll arrange it themselves (Figure 1I). Moreover, don't fall into the trap of thinking that sharing MP3s is legal as long as you don't charge any money for them. Anytime you're taking royalties away from copyright holders, it's illegal.

Several years ago eschoolnews.com reported that more than 400 students were slated to be sued for allegedly using Internet2, a network of academic, business, government, and not-for-profit organizations, for music and movie piracy. The situation has not improved significantly. A 2008 survey found that the average digital music player contains 842 illegally copied songs. Although many people seem to believe that illegal file sharing is okay because so many others are doing it, the entertainment industry is fighting back. Ohio State University recently led the nation in music piracy—its students received more than 2,300 warning letters about pirated music in just one school year. A report by the Institution for Policy Innovation (IPI) indicates that not only is the copyright holder of the pirated digital product injured, but so are all citizens and taxpayers. As a result of global and U.S. piracy, the report states:

- The U.S. economy losses $12.5 billion annually.
- Approximately 71,000 jobs are lost in the United States in both the recording industry and related fields.
- U.S. workers lose $2.7 billion in annual earnings.
- U.S. federal, state, and local governments lose $422 million in annual tax revenue.

More recently, a 2009 report estimated 9 million pirated e-book copies were downloaded, representing nearly $3 billion in lost revenue. However, in April 2010, the U.S. Government Accountability Office issued a report on the economic effects of counterfeit and pirated goods. This statement concluded that after reviewing data from both government and outside sources, it was "difficult, if not impossible, to quantify economy-wide impacts." The reason for this statement is cited as being the inability to accurately detect and account for pirated activity due to the illegal and undetectable nature of piracy itself, and that prior statistics assumed that the obtaining of a pirated copy implied

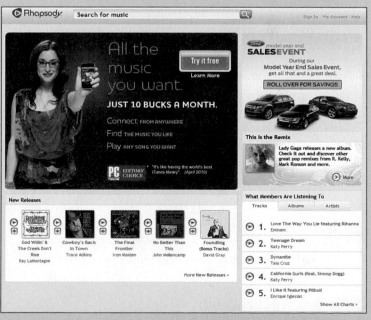

FIGURE 1I Sites such as Rhapsody offer fans the opportunity to play music, not download it, by connecting to their Web site for a price of $10 a month.

the loss of sale of a legitimate copy, again an assumption that is unsubstantiated. Statistics can always be argued and slanted to support one's favored opinion. However, any illegal or counterfeit copy of any product is a source of lost income in any economy. The size of the loss can be debated—but not the loss itself.

Students can face fines or even jail time for copyright infringement, but schools may also be penalized. Some colleges are taking steps to reduce their liability, such as limiting bandwidth and providing students with free, legal download service.

Key Terms and Concepts

Multiple Choice

1. Which action is *not* behavior that illustrates academic integrity?
   a. Citing the reference to a source of information that you copied from the Internet or a printed source
   b. Sharing licensed software without permission
   c. Obtaining permission before using an image obtained from the Internet or other source
   d. Using only your allotted share of computer resources

2. In which Internet interaction should the participant check the frequently asked questions document (FAQ) prior to posting his or her own question?
   a. E-mail
   b. Chat room
   c. Discussion forum
   d. Instant messaging

3. _____ is/are basic ethical principles or guidelines that can be used to help you make the right decisions in your daily computer use.
   a. Computer ethics
   b. Netiquette
   c. Code of conduct
   d. Acceptable use policy

4. What term refers to the act of using someone else's intellectual property as if it were your own?
   a. Acceptable use policy
   b. Piracy
   c. Libel
   d. Plagiarism

5. What defines the standards that promote trust, fairness, good behavior, and kindness, and is used as justification for considering an act or a rule to be morally right or wrong?
   a. Code of conduct
   b. Acceptable use policy
   c. Netiquette
   d. Ethical principle

6. Which is a true statement about ethics?
   a. Ethics is concerned about getting caught.
   b. Some unethical actions are legal.
   c. Ethical actions are evaluated by the consequences they produce, not their innate value of right or wrong.
   d. Peer pressure is not a factor in ethical behavior.

7. What is the term for publishing of a false statement that injures someone's business or personal reputation?
   a. Piracy
   b. Libel
   c. Plagiarism
   d. Whistle-blowing

8. Which action is considered illegal?
   a. Uploading music from a CD that you paid for
   b. Downloading a copyrighted MP3 file and listening to it for only 24 hours, then deleting it
   c. Sharing MP3s with others as long as you do not charge a fee for the music
   d. All of the above

9. What is the lengthy series of specific behavior guidelines developed for computer and Internet users in general?
   a. Netiquette
   b. "Ten Commandments for Computer Ethics"
   c. Code of conduct
   d. Acceptable use policy

10. The use of no more than 5 percent of a copyrighted document, without payment or permission, is called _____.
    a. Piracy
    b. Copyright infringement
    c. Fair use
    d. Plagiarism

Spotlight Exercises

1. Obtain the acceptable use policy provided by your school. Have you ever seen this policy without actively searching for it? If so, where did you see it for the first time? In a one-page, double-spaced report created in a word processing program, summarize the policy. Cite the statements that you think are the most aggressive and those that you believe are overkill or unnecessary. Overall, do you feel that the statement is being upheld by the student body, or is there a need for more enforcement?

2. Go to **www.ibackup.com** and view the demonstration located on the home page. In a PowerPoint presentation of at least five slides, provide a brief description of the various backup services that this site offers. Identify the services that are suitable for your home system and which ones might be suitable for the servers at your school. From what you discovered about this online company, would you make use of this service? Provide justification for your decision.

3. The disagreement between online auctions and software companies over who is responsible for the sale of pirated software is a constant debate. Using the Internet and your favorite browser, locate at least three policy statements regarding liability from online auction or other Web sites that sell software. Do these statements state who is responsible for the sale of a pirated product? Is any advice given to help the buyer determine whether a product is authentic? Do these statements indicate that you can obtain a refund or offer to act as an arbitrator between you and the seller if the product you receive cannot be authenticated? Present your statements of liability and answer to the questions above in a one-page, double-spaced report created in a word processing program.

4. Create a survey consisting of descriptions of several scenarios that could occur in an academic situation that requires the involved individual to make an ethical decision. For example, a student leaves the computer lab and forgets to logoff: If you were the next individual to sit at that computer, what action would you perform? Present at least five scenarios in your survey and administer it to 25 students at your school. Summarize the survey results and determine whether in these five situations the surveyed individuals responded more often in an ethical or an unethical manner. In a three- to five-minute presentation, describe your scenarios to the class and summarize the survey results.

5. With technology becoming more portable, popular, and embedded into social settings, computer ethics becomes even more important. Develop a list of five additional commandments for computer ethics that can be applied specifically to portable computing devices. Present your five commandments and the reasons for your choices in a one-page, double-spaced report created with a word processing program.

6. You downloaded the beta version of a software program over three months ago. The beta was good for a 90-day period that has now expired. You continue to get e-mails stating that your trial period has expired for this product and that you can purchase the final release version by going to a specified Web site. You ignore the e-mails and continue to use the expired beta version. Now every time you try to open the program, you are presented with several pop-ups warning you that you are using an expired and unauthenticated copy. You also notice that it is taking longer to load the program and that after 10 minutes of use the program automatically closes. Analyze the ethical issue of using an expired copy of a program. Do you feel it is right to continue using the program when the trial period has expired? Would you be more inclined to purchase the program if the trial program self-destructed on the expiration date instead of slowly deteriorating? Is it ethical for the manufacturer to slowly undermine your work with this gradual product degeneration? Present your opinions on the ethical issues concerning software offered for trial periods in a one-page, double-spaced report created in a word processing program.

chapter 2

Inside the System Unit

You feel empowered, full of technological information and ready to make that big new computer purchase. You go online, browse a few popular manufacturer sites, and quickly recognize that there is a gap in what you thought was your flawless knowledge. Questions start to come to mind. How much RAM is enough? What is cache? Do I need a separate video card? How many USB ports should my system have? What type of processor do I need? You finally ask yourself the most important question: Do I really know enough to make this purchase?

No one wants to make you nervous about your purchase; but when the price of a new computer ranges from $300 to $1,000, you might want to take a closer look at the details. There is a difference in talking about computers with your friends over lunch and having a conversation with a salesperson or someone with more expertise. With your friends, the conversation centers on the visible and most used components of a computer, the monitor, keyboard, USB ports, and network capability. You don't need to be a technology whiz to purchase a computer, but more information on the internal components will shed light on the ability of the system to meet your price and performance needs.

In this chapter we provide insight into the hardware components of a computer system and the way they work including:

- How computers represent data
- How the components inside the system unit process data to create information
- How to make intelligent decisions when buying a computer system, upgrading a system, or just talking about technology ■

How Computers Represent Data

Computers need data to work with, but that data must be represented in a specific way for the computer's hardware to accept and understand it. When you type on a keyboard and the information appears on the monitor, the information passes from the input device to the output device in a manner that is probably not what you expect. The letter Z is not passed inside your system looking anything like a Z; it is represented by units of information called bits. A **bit** is a single circuit that either contains a current or does not. The **binary digits** of 0 and 1 are used as a means of representing the off/on state of a computer switch, or bit. In the Off state, current is not flowing through the switch and is represented by the digit 0. In the On state, current is flowing through the switch and is represented by the digit 1. The bit is the smallest piece of data a computer can process. Remember that the use of 1 and 0 are for human representation; it is the current that is actually flowing through the circuitry of the computer that the system understands (Figure 2.1).

FIGURE 2.1 A bit has two states: Current (On represented by 1) and No Current (Off represented by 0).

Binary Digit	0	1
Bit (circuitry)	○ no current	● current
Status	Off	On

Representing Data as Bits and Bytes

You are familiar with the decimal system of numbers, which consist of 10 digits (0, 1, 2, 3, 4, 5, 6, 7, 8, 9). Computers do not use the decimal system to represent numbers or characters. Rather, computers use a series of circuits whose pattern of off/on current is converted into strings of binary digits called **binary numbers** (Figure 2.2).

To grasp this idea, it might help to think of a bit as acting like a light switch. Both a light switch and a bit have the same two states, off and on. If a computer system used one bit (or one switch) to transfer data, your keyboard would have only two keys: a key with the number 0 and a key with the number 1. If the switch were off, that would represent the fact

FIGURE 2.2 Common Keyboard Characters and Their Equivalent Binary Number Representation

Keyboard Character	Binary Number Representation
R	01010010
S	01010011
T	01010100
L	01001100
N	01001110
E	01000101

that you pressed 0; if the switch were on, it would represent you pressing the 1 key. If your system had two light switches, you would have four possibilities and thus a keyboard with four keys representing the four options: both switches on, both switches off, the first switch on and the second switch off, or the first switch off and the second switch on. Three switches allow eight possibilities, and so on. The number of possible combinations of on/off patterns is calculated by the formula 2^n, where n is the number of switches. So, how many switches (bits) are needed to represent an entire keyboard, which can contain from 128 to 256 different characters, including all the letters of the alphabet (both uppercase and lowercase), the numbers 0 through 9, and punctuation marks? The answer is somewhere between 7 and 8 because $2^7 = 128$ and $2^8 = 256$ (Figure 2.3).

FIGURE 2.3 Number of Bits versus Number of Possibilities

Number of Bits	Number of Possibilities
1	$2^1 = 2$
2	$2^2 = 4$
3	$2^3 = 8$
4	$2^4 = 16$
5	$2^5 = 32$
6	$2^6 = 64$
7	$2^7 = 128$
8	$2^8 = 256$

A **byte** is a group of eight bits and is the method of representing one character of data, such as the essential numbers (0–9), the basic letters of the alphabet like the character Z (uppercase and lowercase), and the most common punctuation symbols. For this reason, you can use the byte as a baseline unit to express the amount of information a computer's storage device can hold. Because it takes eight bits (on/off switches) to make a byte, and eight bits result in 256 possible on/off combinations, you'll see the number 8 and multiples of 8 appearing behind the scenes in many computer functions, applications, and references to storage capacity. For example, a typical college essay contains 250 words per page, and each word contains (on average) 5.5 characters. Therefore, the page contains approximately 1,375 characters. In other words, you need about 1,375 bytes of storage to save one page of a college paper.

For clarity, the terms *bit* and *byte* are used to present different types of information. Whereas bytes are used to express storage capacity, bits (1s and 0s) are commonly used for measuring the data transfer rate of computer communications devices such as modems. To describe rapid data transfer rates, the measurement units **kilobits per second (Kbps)**, **megabits per second (Mbps)**, and **gigabits per second (Gbps)** are used. These respectively correspond (roughly) to 1 thousand, 1 million, and 1 billion bits per second. Remember that these terms refer to *bits* per second, not *bytes* per second (Figure 2.4).

Bytes are commonly used to measure data storage. The measurements—**kilobyte (KB)** for one thousand bytes, **megabyte (MB)** for one million bytes, **gigabyte (GB)** for one billion bytes, and **terabyte (TB)** for one trillion bytes—describe the amount of data a computer is managing either in RAM memory or in longer-term storage (hard disk, CD, DVD, or USB drive). Figure 2.5 shows these units and the *approximate* value of text data for each. For these units the equivalents of a thousand, a million, and so on, are not exact; rounding numbers has become acceptable. For example, a kilobyte is actually 1,024 bytes.

As the uses of computers escalate and the amount of information we use and save increases, storage devices have had to expand their capacity. Originally, storage units held kilobytes and megabytes of data. Today most devices express their capacity in gigabytes and terabytes. In anticipation of a continued increase in data use and storage, terms already exist for representing even

FIGURE 2.4 Units of Data Transfer Rates

Unit	Abbreviation	Transfer Rate	Text Equivalent
Kilobits per second	Kbps	1 thousand bits per second	125 characters
Megabits per second	Mbps	1 million bits per second	125 pages
Gigabits per second	Gbps	1 billion bits per second	125,000 pages

FIGURE 2.5 Current Units of Data Storage

Unit	Abbreviation	Storage Amount	Text Equivalent
Byte	B	8 bits	1 character
Kilobyte	KB	1 thousand bytes	1 page
Megabyte	MB	1 million bytes	1,000 pages
Gigabyte	GB	1 billion bytes	1,000 books
Terabyte	TB	1 trillion bytes	1 million books

larger units. A **petabyte** is 1 quadrillion bytes; an **exabyte** is 1 quintillion bytes; a **zettabyte** is 1 sextillion bytes; and a **yottabyte** is 1 septillion bytes (Figure 2.6).

FIGURE 2.6 Larger Units of Data Storage

Unit	Abbreviation	Storage Amount	Text Equivalent
Petabyte	PB	1 quadrillion bytes	1 billion books
Exabyte	EB	1 quintillion bytes	7,500 libraries the size of the Library of Congress
Zettabyte	ZB	1 sextillion bytes	Not able to estimate
Yottabyte	YB	1 septillion bytes	Not able to estimate

Hexadecimal: An Alternate Representation for Binary Numbers

Binary numbers are difficult to work with because many digits are required to represent even a small number. For example, when you enter the decimal number 14 into your computer, the binary number representation uses four bits or switches, and 14 is represented as 1110.

When computer programmers need to look at the data that is passing through a

FIGURE 2.7 Decimal, Binary, and Hexadecimal Numbers

Decimal Number	0	1	2	3	4	5	6	7	8	9	10	11	12	13	14	15
Binary Number	0000	0001	0010	0011	0100	0101	0110	0111	1000	1001	1010	1011	1100	1101	1110	1111
Hexadecimal Number	0	1	2	3	4	5	6	7	8	9	A	B	C	D	E	F

computer system, often to locate an error in a program, they frequently convert the binary numbers the system displays into **hexadecimal numbers** (**hex** for short). The hexadecimal number system uses the numbers 0 through 9 and the letters A through F to represent a binary string. These digits and letters are referred to as the *base 16 characters*. For example, the decimal number 100 is represented as the lengthy binary number 01100100 and then quickly translated to 64 in hex notation. Each single hex digit represents four binary digits, making it a shorter, faster, and more compact representation of a binary number (Figure 2.7). You can convert among decimal, binary, and hex by using the converter at **http://easycalculation.com/decimal-converter.php**. To learn the procedure to convert between decimal, binary, and hexadecimal through manual arithmetic go to **www.mindspring.com/~jimvb/binary.htm**.

Representing Very Large and Very Small Numbers

To represent and process numbers with fractional parts (such as 1.25) or numbers that are extremely large (in the billions and trillions), computers use **floating point standard**. The term *floating point* suggests how this notation system works: There is no fixed number of digits before or after the decimal point (thus the word *float*), so the computer can work with very large and very small numbers. Floating point standard, set by the Institute of Electrical and Electronics Engineers (IEEE), requires special processing circuitry, which is generally provided by the floating-point unit (FPU). Modern computers integrate one or more FPUs with the CPU (processor or microprocessor), but in older computers the FPU was sometimes a separate chip called the *math coprocessor*.

So, how does floating point standard convert very small or very large numbers into binary representation? The IEEE single precision floating point standard representation requires the use of 32 bits, which may be represented as numbers from 0 to 31, left to right. The first bit is the sign bit, S; the next eight bits are the exponent bits, E; and the final 23 bits are the fraction, F. So what does the decimal number +6.5 look like in floating point standard? For the answer and an explanation, refer to Figure 2.8. The

FIGURE 2.8 Bit Layout for Floating Point Standard and the Number +6.5

Sign	Exponent	Fraction
S	EEEEEEEE	FFFFFFFFFFFFFFFFFFFFFFF
IEEE Single Precision Floating Point Standard Bit Layout		
0	1 8	9 31
+6.5 Represented in Single Precision Floating Point Standard		
0	10000001	10100000000000000000000
An **Off** bit stands for a **positive** number.	This binary number is decimal 129. However, the exponent for the base number of 2 is calculated by taking this number, 129, and subtracting 127, for an actual exponent of 2.	This last component is actually the binary number 1.101, which in decimal form is 1.625.
+1	2^2	1.625
So, the actual conversion calculation is $+1 * 2^2 * 1.625 = +1 * 4 * 1.625 = +6.5$		

purpose of this example is not to make you a binary converter expert but rather to demonstrate the complexity of the conversions that take place inside the system unit.

We know that computers process not only numeric data but also character data. Because we communicate with spoken and written text, let's look next at the processing of the character data that composes our daily interactions.

Representing Characters: Character Code

Character code uses an algorithm as a bridge between the computer's bit patterns and the letters, numbers, and symbols on our keyboards called **characters** that we're accustomed to using. Depending on your system, the conversion from computer code to actual keyboard characters is accomplished by using one of three different character coding formats: ASCII, EBCDIC, or Unicode.

The most widely used character code is **ASCII** (pronounced "ask-ee"), the **American Standard Code for Information Interchange**, which is used in minicomputers, personal computers, and computers that make information available over the Internet. ASCII uses seven bits and can thus represent 128 ($2^7 = 128$) different characters (see Figure 2.9). A variation of ASCII code, called **Extended ASCII** (see Figure 2.10), uses eight bits and allows 128 additional characters, like the fractions ½; and ¼; and logical symbols such as ≥, for a total of 256 ($2^8 = 256$). In

both systems the first 128 codes represent the same characters. The code order for ASCII starts with the lowest codes representing punctuation marks and numbers, followed by more punctuation marks, uppercase letters, more punctuation marks, and finally lowercase letters. Go to **www.asciitable.com** to view the complete ASCII and Extended ASCII listings.

IBM mainframe computers and some midrange systems use a different eight-bit code system, **EBCDIC** (pronounced "ebb-see-dic"), **Extended Binary Coded Decimal Interchange Code**. EBCDIC code is ordered using a low-to-high sequence starting with punctuation, lowercase letters, uppercase letters, and then numbers.

Although ASCII and EBCDIC provide enough bits to represent all characters used in the English language and some foreign language symbols, neither has enough binary combinations for some Eastern languages and historic symbols that exceed 256 characters. Because computers make international communication and business transactions possible, a new coding system—**Unicode**—is becoming popular. Unicode uses 16 bits, can represent over 65,000 characters, and can symbolize all the world's written languages. The first 128 codes in the Unicode system represent the same characters as the first 128 in the ASCII system.

When discussing numbers and alphabetical characters, it is important to remember that all data being transmitted through a computer system is represented by bits or circuit notation. A fingerprint, picture, or company logo is also converted

FIGURE 2.9 Sample of a Section of ASCII Code

Character	ASCII Code	Character	ASCII Code	Character	ASCII Code
!	00100001	E	01000101	e	01100101
#	00100011	P	01010000	p	01110000
$	00100100	A	01000001	a	01100001
space	00100000	Y	01011001	y	01111001

FIGURE 2.10 Pay $6.50! Written in Extended ASCII Code

P	a	y	space	$	6.50	!
01010000	01100001	01111001	00100000	00100100	0 10000001 10100000000000000000000	00100001

by appropriate programs into patterns of binary digits (Figure 2.11).

Now that you understand bits, bytes, and how computers represent data, it is important to understand their connection to the rest of the system. Let's take a closer look at the system unit, its components, and how these concepts will come into play.

Introducing the System Unit

FIGURE 2.11 The Automated fingerprint identification system (AFIS) smoothes and converts fingerprints to binary code.

The **system unit** is a boxlike case that comes in a variety of shapes and sizes, and houses the computer's main hardware components (Figure 2.12). The system unit is actually more than just a case: It provides a sturdy frame for mounting internal components, including storage devices, a power supply, a fan, and connectors for input and output devices; it protects those components from physical damage; and it keeps them cool. A good case also provides room for system upgrades, such as additional disk drives.

System units come in a variety of styles. In some desktop computing systems, the system unit is a separate metal or plastic box. Originally, these cases were horizontal and were positioned on top of a desk, often with a monitor sitting on top—thus the name "desktop." To minimize the space it occupied, the case needed a small **footprint**, which is the amount of space used by the device. However, a small case didn't allow enough room for add-on components. The **tower case**, a system unit case designed to sit on the floor next to a desk, provided the solution. The tower case has a vertical configuration, being tall and deep. A smaller version of the tower that has less internal room for components is called a **minitower case**.

In a notebook computer or a personal digital assistant (PDA), the system unit contains all the computer's components, including input components, such as a keyboard, and output components, such as the display. Some desktop computers, such as Apple's iMac, contain the display within the system unit, making them all-in-one systems. To ensure access identification and security, biometric authentication devices like fingerprint readers, retina scanners,

FIGURE 2.12 Every kind of computer has a system unit: all-in-one, notebook, smartphone, and desktop.

All-in-one system unit

Notebook system unit

Desktop system unit

Smartphone system unit

FIGURE 2.13 This fingerprint reader is one of several devices that provide biometric authentication.

and face recognition systems are embedded into some individual system units (Figure 2.13).

System units also vary in their form factor. A **form factor** is a specification for how internal components, such as the motherboard, are mounted inside the system unit. Let's take a look!

Inside the System Unit

Most computer users don't need to and don't want to open their system units; they receive their computers in ready-to-use packages. However, if you ever need to open your system unit, remember that the computer's components are sensitive to static electricity. If you touch certain components while you're charged with static electricity, you could damage them.

To avoid this disaster, always disconnect the power cord before opening your computer's case, and discharge your personal static electricity by touching something that's well grounded or by wearing a grounding bracelet. A **grounding bracelet** is a bracelet that has a cord attached to a grounded object. If it's one of those low-humidity days when you're getting shocked every time you touch a doorknob, don't work on your computer's internal components.

The basic components you would see if you were to open a system unit include such items as the motherboard, power supply, cooling fan, internal speakers, internal drive bays, external drive bays, and various expansion cards, regardless of the manufacturer or type of computer (see Figures 2.14 and 2.15).

An overview of these basic components will help you to identify and clarify the purpose of each.

- *Motherboard:* The motherboard is the large circuit board located within your system unit to which all other components are connected. It specifically contains a chip referred to as the computer's central processing unit (CPU). You'll learn more about the motherboard and the CPU later in this chapter; for now remember that the CPU, referred to as the "brain" of the computer, is the central component of the computer; all other components (such as disk drives, monitors, and printers) exist only to bridge the gap between the user and the CPU.

FIGURE 2.14 The Location of the Components of the System Unit on a Tower

Power supply

Cooling fan

Memory cards

Expansion card

Expansion slot

Motherboard

External drive bay

Internal drive bay

Internal speaker (not present)

Power supply

Notebook motherboard

Processor

Cooling fan

FIGURE 2.15 The Location of the Components of the System Unit in a Notebook

- *Power supply:* A computer's power supply transforms the alternating current (AC) from standard wall outlets into the direct current (DC) needed for the computer's operation. It also steps the voltage down to the low level required by the motherboard. Power supplies are rated according to their peak output in watts. A 350-watt power supply is adequate for most desktop systems, but 500 watts provide sufficient voltage if you plan to add many additional components. If it is ever necessary to replace a power supply on a desktop computer, seek the help of a professional. You can replace your own power supply on a notebook because it is usually outside of the box and part of the component that plugs into the wall. However, be sure to replace the power supply with an identical component, preferably from the same manufacturer. This assures that the amperage and voltage are within your system limitations and eliminates the possibility of damaging the battery or other components.

- *Cooling fan:* The computer's components can be damaged if heat accumulates within the system unit. A **cooling fan** keeps the system unit cool. The fan often is part of the power supply, although many systems include auxiliary fans to provide additional cooling.

- *Internal speaker:* The computer's **internal speaker** is useful only for the beeps you hear when the computer starts up or encounters an error. Current computers include sound cards and external speakers for better-quality sound.

- *Drive bays:* **Drive bays** accommodate the computer's disk drives, such as the hard disk drive, CD or DVD drive, and portable drives. Internal drive bays are used for hard disks that are permanently contained in the system unit; therefore, they do not enable outside access. External drive bays mount drives that are accessible from the outside (a necessity if you need to insert and remove a CD from the drive). External drive bays vary in size to accommodate different media devices. Current systems offer 5.25-inch external drive bays to accommodate CD or DVD drives.

- *Expansion slots:* The system unit also contains **expansion slots**, which are receptacles that accept additional circuit boards or expansion cards. **Expansion cards**, also referred to as **expansion boards**, **adapter cards**, or **adapters**, contain the circuitry for peripherals that are not normally included as standard equipment. Examples of expansion cards are additional memory modules, enhanced sound cards, modem cards, network interface cards (NICs), video cards, and on some systems' wireless network cards (Figure 2.16).

Now that you have an overview of the internal components of the system unit, let's look more closely at the most important component: the computer's motherboard.

What's on the Motherboard?

The **motherboard** is a large flat piece of plastic or fiberglass that contains thousands of electrical circuits etched onto the board's surface. The circuits connect numerous plug-in receptacles that accommodate the computer's most important components (such as the CPU and RAM). The motherboard provides the centralized physical and electrical connectivity to

Memory module
(RAM)

Modem card

Network
interface card

Sound card

Video card

enable communication among these critical components. Most of the components on the motherboard are integrated circuits. An **integrated circuit (IC)**, also called a **chip**, carries an electric current and contains millions of transistors. To view a short video about how chips are created, go to **www97.intel. com/en/TheJourneyInside/ ExploreTheCurriculum/EC_ Microprocessors/MPLesson4**.

FIGURE 2.16 Expansion cards enable you to enhance and customize your system to meet your own personal needs.

A **transistor** is an electronic switch (or gate) that controls the flow of electrical signals through the circuit. Transistors are made out of layers of special material, called a **semiconductor**, that either conducts electrical current or blocks its passage through the circuit. Semiconductor material, like silicone, produces the off and on impulses that enable the binary representation of characters within the system unit. A computer uses such electronic switches to route data in different ways, according to the software's instructions. Encased in black plastic blocks or enclosures, most integrated circuits or chips fit specially designed receptacles or slots on the motherboard's surface. What do these chips do? Let's look at some of the most important components you'll see on the motherboard: the CPU (or microprocessor), the system clock, the chipset, input/output buses, and memory (Figure 2.17).

Heat sink and fan

Memory (RAM)

CPU

Power supply

Video card

DVD burner

Expansion slots

Motherboard

Hard drive

FIGURE 2.17 This typical PC motherboard shows the system unit's main components and where they would be located or connected on the motherboard.

The CPU: The Microprocessor

When you're ready to buy a computer and determine whether it will meet your computing needs, you will need to understand the capabilities and limitations of current microprocessors. No single element of a computer determines its overall performance as much as the CPU.

The **central processing unit (CPU)** is a **microprocessor** (or **processor** for short)—an integrated circuit chip that is capable of processing electronic signals. It interprets and carries out software instructions by processing data and controlling the rest of the computer's components. Many electronic and mechanical devices we use daily, such as smartphones, calculators, automobile engines, and industrial and medical equipment, contain **embedded processors**. These processors are designed and programmed to perform only the tasks intended to be done by that device.

CPUs (microprocessors) that are within a computer system unit are incredibly complex devices. They must be able to perform many different functions, depending on the program running at the time.

Processor Slots and Sockets

An integrated circuit of incredible complexity, a CPU plugs into a motherboard in much the same way that other integrated circuits do—through a series of pins that extend out from the bottom of the chip. However, only special slots and sockets can accommodate CPUs. Part of the reason for this is that CPUs are larger and have more pins than most other chips. In addition, CPUs generate so much heat that they could destroy themselves or other system components. The CPU is generally covered by a **heat sink**, a heat-dissipating component that drains heat from the chip. To accomplish this, the heat sink may contain a small auxiliary cooling fan. The latest high-end CPUs include

> " No **single element** of a **computer** determines its **overall performance as much as** the CPU. "

their own built-in refrigeration systems to keep these speedy processors cool.

The Instruction Set

Every processor can perform a fixed set of operations, such as retrieving a character from the computer's memory or comparing two numbers to see which is larger. Each of these operations has a unique number, called an *instruction*. A processor's list of instructions is called its **instruction set**. Because each type of processor has a unique instruction set, programs devised for one type of CPU won't necessarily run on another. For example, a program written for an Intel chip may not run on a Motorola chip. A program that can run on a given computer is said to be compatible with that computer's processor. If a program is compatible, it's said to be a **native application** for a given processor design.

The Machine Cycle

A CPU contains two subcomponents: the control unit and the arithmetic logic unit. Both components play a part in the four-step process called the **processing** or **machine cycle**. The **control unit**, under the direction of an embedded program, switches from one stage to the next and performs the action of that stage. The four steps of the machine cycle are:

- *Fetch:* Retrieves the next program instruction from the computer's RAM or cache memory.
- *Decode:* Takes the fetched instruction and translates it into a form that the control unit understands.
- *Execute:* Performs the requested instruction using the **arithmetic logic unit (ALU)** to perform **arithmetic operations**, which include addition, subtraction, multiplication, and division, and **logical operations**, which involve the comparison of two or more data items. Arithmetic operations return a numeric value, whereas logical operations return a value of true or false.

- *Store:* Stores the results in an internal register (a location on the CPU) or in RAM.

Registers are temporary storage areas located within the microprocessor. Even though the word *store* is used when describing their function, they are not considered as part of memory and act more as digital scratch pads. There are different types of registers, depending on their function. Some accept, hold, and transfer instructions or data, and others perform arithmetic or logical comparisons at high speed. The importance of registers lies in the fact that they work extremely fast, actually at the same speed as the CPU they are embedded within.

These four steps of the machine cycle, or processing cycle, are grouped into two phases: the **instruction cycle** (fetch and decode) and the **execution cycle** (execute and store). Today's microprocessors can go through this entire four-step process billions of times per second (Figure 2.18).

Microprocessor Performance

The number of transistors available has a huge effect on the performance of a processor. The more transistors and the closer they are in proximity to each other, the faster the processing speed. The data bus width and word size, clock speed, operations per microprocessor cycle, use of parallel processing, and type of chip are also factors that contribute to microprocessor performance.

Data Bus Width and Word Size The **data bus** is a set of parallel wires that acts as an electronic highway on which data travels between computer components. It is the medium by which the entire system communicates with the CPU. More technically, the bus is a pathway for the electronic impulses that form bytes. The more lanes this highway has, the faster data can travel. Data bus width is measured in bits (8, 16, 32, or 64).

The width of a CPU's data bus partly determines its **word size**, or the maximum number of bits the CPU can process at once. Data bus width also affects the CPU's overall speed: A CPU with a 32-bit data bus can shuffle data twice as fast as a CPU with a 16-bit data bus. The terms *8-bit CPU, 16-bit CPU, 32-bit CPU,* and *64-bit CPU* indicate the maximum number of bits a CPU can handle at a time.

A CPU's word size is important because it determines which operating systems the CPU can use and which software it can run.

FIGURE 2.18 The four steps of the machine cycle are the same in all systems, from personal computers to mainframes. What differs is the speed at which the cycle is performed.

FIGURE 2.19 Word Size Capacity (in Bits) of Popular Operating Systems

Operating System	Word Size	When Used
Windows 95/98/NT/2000/XP	32	Past (but still used)
Windows Vista (all editions except Starter)	64	Current
Windows 7	64	Current
Linux	64	Current
Mac OS X Snow Leopard (with Velocity Engine chip)	64	Current

Figure 2.19 lists the word size requirements of current operating systems.

Today's PC market consists of older 32-bit CPUs that run 32-bit operating systems and the more commonplace 64-bit CPUs that run 64-bit operating systems. Intel's 64-bit Itanium processor, introduced in 2001, brought 64-bit computing to the PC market for the first time. Linux was the first OS to use the 64-bit technology in 2001. In 2003 Apple released a 64-bit version of Mac OS X, and in 2005 Microsoft released Windows XP Professional ×64. The current Windows operating systems, Windows Vista and Windows 7, are available in both 32-bit and 64-bit versions, while the Mac OS X Snow Leopard comes in one version that runs both 32-bit and 64-bit applications. Visit **http://windows.microsoft.com/en-US/windows7/32-bit-and-64-bit-Windows-frequently-asked-questions** to obtain information that will help you decide whether a 32-bit or 64-bit operating system is adequate for your needs.

Clock Speed Within a computer, events happen at a pace controlled by a tiny electronic "drummer" on the motherboard: The **system clock** is an electronic circuit that generates rapid pulses to synchronize the computer's internal activities, including the movement from one stage of the machine cycle to another. These electrical pulses are measured in **gigahertz (GHz)**, or billions of cycles per second, and are referred to as a processor's **clock speed**. Any new computer will have a clock speed of 3 GHz or higher; a 3-GHz processor is capable of processing 3 billion cycles in 1 second. In general, the higher the clock speed of the processor, the faster the computer. For editorial reviews of the latest products, such as the fastest processors, memory, graphics chips, and more, go to **www.geek.com/articles/chips**.

Operations per Cycle The number of *operations* per clock tick (one pulse of the system clock) also affects microprocessor performance. You might think that a CPU can't perform more than one instruction per clock tick (Figure 2.20), but thanks to new technologies, that's no longer the case. **Superscalar architecture** refers to the design of any CPU that can execute more than one instruction per clock cycle; today's fastest CPUs use superscalar architectures. Superscalar architectures often use a process called **pipelining**, a technique that feeds a new instruction into the CPU at every step of the processing cycle so that four or more instructions are worked on simultaneously.

Processing cycle without pipelining

Instruction 1 completed

Instruction 1

Instruction 2 enters fetch phase

Instruction 2

Clock ticks 1 2 3 4 5 6 7 8

One processing cycle completed

Legend: Fetch, Decode, Execute, Store

Pipelining resembles an auto assembly line in which more than one car is being worked on at once. Before the first instruction is finished, the next one is started (Figure 2.21). If the CPU needs the results of a completed instruction to process the next one, that condition is called **data dependency**. It can cause a pipeline stall in which the assembly line is held up until the results are known. To cope with this problem, advanced CPUs use a technique called **speculative execution**, in which the processor executes and temporarily stores the next instruction in case it proves useful. CPUs also use a technique called **branch prediction**, in which the processor tries to predict what will happen (with a surprisingly high degree of accuracy).

Parallel Processing Another way to improve CPU performance is by using **parallel processing**, a technique that uses more than one processor to execute a program. It usually is found on systems that run programs that perform a lot of computations, such as simulations or graphic processing software. These

processors can be located within one system, on the same motherboard, or on independent systems networked with sophisticated distributed processing software (Figure 2.22). The idea is to speed up the execution of a program by dividing the program into multiple fragments that can execute simultaneously, each on its own processor. In theory, a program should execute faster in a system making use of parallel processing. In reality, it is difficult to divide a program into segments in a way that one segment does not interfere or need to wait for the result generated by another. Parallel processing should not be confused with **multitasking**, a process by which the CPU gives the user the illusion of performing instructions from multiple programs at once when in reality the CPU is rapidly switching between the programs and instructions. Most computers have one CPU, but some have several. Today multi-core processors are becoming the norm.

Multi-Core Processing The newest computers being sold are equipped with dual-core and quad-core processors. These

STUDENT VIDEO

Processing cycle with pipelining

Instruction 1

Instruction 2

Instruction 3

Instruction 4

Clock ticks 1 2 3 4 5 6 7 8

One processing cycle completed

Legend: Fetch, Decode, Execute, Store

FIGURE 2.22 Because the processor is the most expensive system unit component, a system with more than one processor, capable of parallel processing, is costly.

processors attempt to correct the slowdown that occurs in the processing cycle when the CPU needs to access instructions and data from RAM or a hard disk. In dual-core and quad-core processors, access time is reduced and overall processing time improved because each core handles incoming streams of data or instructions at the same time. This behavior reinforces the concept that two hands are better than one. AMD and Intel offer multi-core 64-bit processors. For a dual-core or quad-core processor to be used to full capacity, your system must use a compatible operating system and specifically designed application software. When the operating system and application software are not designed to make use of the multiple cores of the processor, only one core will be recognized, and the processor will never work to its full potential.

Popular Microprocessors

The most commonly used microprocessors are those found in IBM-compatible computers and Macs. Most PCs are powered by chips produced by Intel and AMD. Figure 2.23 shows how popular microprocessors for PCs have improved since the days of the first PC.

In 2010 Intel released the Core i7 Extreme Edition microprocessor with a clock speed of 3.30 GHz (Figure 2.24). Since 2003 Intel has been concentrating on producing processors that are suited to certain computing needs—such as the Centrino processor for mobile computing

GREEN *tech tips*

Did you know that keeping computers turned on all the time drains the community power supply, stresses the computers' internal components, and wastes energy? The Environmental Protection Agency (EPA), technology manufacturers, and nonprofit organizations are working on ways to keep you connected 24/7 with reduced environmental consequences. If you purchase a computer with the EPA's Energy Star Logo, it can go to sleep during intervals of inactivity, thus boosting its energy efficiency.

Are you and your friends aware of the fact that U.S. college students could save over 2.3 billion kilowatt hours of electricity per year by enabling power-saving features on their desktop PCs? That is a saving of over $200 million in energy costs and a 1.8 million–ton reduction in CO_2 emissions—an equivalent of taking 350,000 cars off the road. So, power down when not using your electrical devices, and do your share! ●

and the Core Extreme family of processors for multimedia and gaming. Intel now rates its processors not only by cycles per second, but also by features such as

FIGURE 2.23 The Evolution of Intel Microprocessors

Year	Chip	Bus Width	Clock Speed	Transistors
1971	4004	4 bits	108 KHz	2,300
1993	Pentium	32 bits	Up to 66 MHz	3.1 million
2000	Pentium 4	32 bits	Up to 2 GHz	42 million
2006	Core Duo	32 bits	Up to 2 GHz	151 million
2007	Core 2 Quad	64 bits	Up to 2.4 GHz	582 million
2008	Core 2 Extreme, Quad Processor	64 bits	3.2 GHz	820 million
2010	Core i7 Extreme Edition	64 bits	3.3 GHz	732 Million

architecture, cache, and bus type. The rating, then, represents the power and usefulness of the processor—not just the clock speed. Visit **http://download. intel.com/pressroom/kits/ IntelProcessorHistory.pdf** to view a detailed timeline of the history of Intel processors.

Normally faster is better; however, the cost of microprocessor speed can keep it out of reach. When deciding on a processor, list the activities you plan to use your system for over the next few years. Then match the processor capabilities to those activities. For example, the Intel Celeron is a processor geared to users who perform basic tasks such as word processing, Web surfing, and listening to and buying music. The Intel Pentium Core 2 and Core i7 family of processors are geared toward advanced applications such as gaming, video editing, and advanced digital photography. The Intel Atom is specifically designed for handheld and mobile Internet devices.

After you match your needs with the processors that can manage them, you can address the processor's speed. For most users an increase of 0.4 GHz in speed would not perceptibly change performance, but it would make a noticeable difference in cost. For articles, videos, forums, and charts that provide detailed information about a large variety of processors and other hardware elements, go to **www. tomshardware.com/cpu**.

For years Motorola Corporation and IBM made the chips for Apple computers, producing the 68000 series and the PowerPC series. Apple gave its own name to the PowerPC chips: Motorola's 750 was the same chip as Apple's G3, Motorola's 7400 was the G4, and the 64-bit IBM chip was the G5. In January 2006, Apple began transitioning to Intel processors for the Mac, with all new Macs using Intel processors by August of that year.

FIGURE 2.24 New multi-core processors, like the Intel Core i7, require software written to use all of the cores for them to function at their peak.

The Chipset and the Input/Output Bus

Another important motherboard component is the **chipset**, which is a collection of chips that work together to provide the switching circuitry needed by the microprocessor to move data throughout the computer. One of the jobs handled by the chipset is linking the microprocessor's system bus with the computer's input/output buses.

An **input/output (I/O) bus** refers specifically to the pathway that extends beyond the microprocessor to communicate with input and output devices. Typically, an I/O bus contains expansion slots to accommodate plug-in expansion cards.

Today's PCs use the **PCI (peripheral component interconnect) bus,** a slower bus that connects devices like hard drives and sound cards to the faster microprocessor system bus. Many motherboards still contain an industry standard architecture (ISA) bus and have one or two ISA slots available. The accelerated graphics port (AGP) is a bus designed for video and graphics display.

The microprocessor is just one of several chips on the computer's motherboard. Among the others are those that provide the computer with various types of memory.

RECYCLING—THE PROS, CONS, AND RESPONSIBILITY

People are becoming more aware of the need to make decisions that will result in less pollution and fewer environmental hazards, and thus produce a greener, healthier environment. Recycling instead of disposing of old computer equipment has become a popular topic of environmentally concerned individuals. But who should be covering the cost of recycling? Where does the estimated 400,000 tons of annual e-waste end up? If e-waste is shipped overseas, does this solve the problem or just move it? And is it ethical to ship our wastes to less developed areas? For every plus there is a minus, and that applies to the issue of recycling e-waste as well.

So, where do you stand? Are you willing to take the time to shop around before you purchase to locate products that have a higher energy efficiency rating and are free of toxic materials? Are you willing to pay 10 to 15 percent more for such products? If there is a cost to recycle your devices, are you willing to pay? Will you support a bill to create e-waste recycling plants in your community?

Everyone dreams of a greener and healthier environment, but when the question of who will shoulder the burden of that dream is asked, corporations, individuals, and governments all seem to look elsewhere. Reach into your own conscious and review your stand on the burden of recycling. What can you do to make a difference? Become an active part of the solution!

Pros of Recycling	Cons of Recycling
There is a reduction of hazardous waste entering the environment.	Through the process of reclaiming some of the e-waste elements, other harmful byproducts can be released into the environment.
Some materials in e-waste, such as tin, silicone, and iron, can be reused.	Some businesses are shipping older computers and less environmentally friendly ones to underdeveloped nations. These nations have weaker restrictions on e-waste. So, what seems like recycling is really delayed dumping.
With less e-waste being disposed of, landfills around the world will fill up more slowly.	The cost to recycle effectively is high, and the question of who is to pay for recycling services remains unanswered.

Memory

Memory refers to the chips, located on the motherboard or within the CPU, that retain instructions and data to be accessed by the CPU. As a program is running, the instructions and data are loaded from a permanent storage device, such as a hard drive, into these memory chips. Once transferred, the other components of the system access this information only from its memory location and not the permanent storage device. The main reason for what appears as a double set of information is that the access time from memory is significantly less than the access time from a storage device like a hard drive. Access from memory improves overall system performance. As you'll see in this section, the computer's motherboard contains several different types of memory, each optimized for its intended use.

RAM

The large, rectangular memory modules housed on the computer's motherboard contain the computer's **random access memory (RAM)**. RAM is volatile memory, which means it is not permanent and its contents are erased when the computer's power is switched off. The purpose of RAM is to

- Receive and hold program instructions and data while being used by the system.
- Provide those instructions and data to the CPU when needed.
- Hold the results of the CPU's processing until an instruction is received to

transfer it to a printer or permanent storage device.

Why is it called *random access memory*? RAM is called *random access* because any storage location can be accessed directly without having to go from the first location to the last in sequential order. Perhaps it should have been called *nonsequential memory*, because RAM access is hardly random. RAM is organized and controlled in a way that can be compared to post office boxes (Figure 2.25). Each location has a **memory address** (in binary form) that enables the location to be found and the content within to be accessed directly. IBM preferred the term *direct access storage*. Note that other forms of storage such as the hard disk and CD-ROM are also accessed directly or randomly (meaning out of sequential order), but the term *random access* is never applied to these forms of storage.

Of the various types of RAM available, today's newest and fastest PCs contain either DDR2-SDRAM (double-data-rate two synchronous dynamic RAM) or DDR3-SDRAM. RAM appears today in the form of **memory modules** or **memory cards**. A memory module is actually a small circuit board that holds several RAM chips and fits into special slots on the motherboard. Today RAM modules are usually **dual inline memory modules (DIMM)** that have a 168-pin connector and a 64-bit data transfer rate. Their predecessor, **single inline memory modules (SIMM)**, used a 72-pin connector and a 32-bit data transfer rate. Remember that any type of RAM must have a constant power supply or it loses its contents. RAM is not permanent storage!

How much RAM does a computer need? In general, the more memory a system has,

the better. Windows Vista and Mac OS X theoretically require only 512 MB of RAM, but neither system functions well with so little. For today's Microsoft Windows, Linux, and Macintosh operating systems, 1 GB of RAM is a practical working minimum.

Windows 7 touts a new reduced **memory footprint**, the amount of RAM the program uses while it operates. In the past, each successive Windows OS required larger amounts of system resources like RAM. The fact that Windows 7 is bucking that trend is giving people hope that OS RAM requirements might stabilize.

Operating systems frequently use **virtual memory** in addition to RAM. With virtual memory, the computer looks at RAM to identify data that has not been used recently and copies this data onto the hard disk. This frees up space in RAM to load a new application or increase the space needed by a program currently in use. The computer uses virtual memory when RAM gets full (which can easily happen if you run several programs at once). Accessing data on a disk drive is much slower than using RAM, so when virtual memory kicks in, the computer may seem to slow to a crawl. To avoid using virtual memory, choose a system with at least 2 GB of RAM. Many new systems are being advertised with 3 to 4 GB of RAM. If you have a system and need to increase the amount of RAM, visit **www.crucial.com.** This Web site provides you with a three-step advisor to guide you to the correct memory purchase:

- *Step 1:* Select a manufacturer.
- *Step 2:* Select a product line.
- *Step 3:* Select a model.

FIGURE 2.25 The addressing scheme used to identify RAM locations makes storage and retrieval fast and easy.

1001 1002 1003 1004
1005 1006 1007 1008
1009 1010 1011 1012
Data
1013 1014 1015 1016

If you are unsure of any of the requested information, you can allow the Web site to scan your system and, within its ability, determine the appropriate type of RAM you should add.

Cache Memory

RAM is fast, but it isn't fast enough to support the processing speeds of today's superfast microprocessors, such as the Intel Core i7 Extreme Edition or the AMD Phenom X4. These microprocessors use cache memory to function at maximum speed. **Cache memory** is a small unit of ultrafast memory built into or near the processor that stores frequently or recently accessed program instructions and data. Cache (pronounced "cash") memory is much faster than RAM, but it's also more expensive. Although the amount of cache that comes on a system is relatively small compared with RAM, 2GB to 4 GB, cache memory greatly improves the computer system's overall performance because the CPU retrieves data more quickly from cache than from RAM.

Cache is identified by its location relative to the CPU. There can be three levels of cache in a system.

- **Level 1 (L1) cache**, also called **primary cache**, is a unit of 4 KB to 16 KB of ultrafast memory included in the microprocessor chip that runs at approximately 10 **nanoseconds**. A nanosecond is one-billionth of a second. Primary cache is the fastest memory.
- **Level 2 (L2) cache**, also called **secondary cache**, is a unit of up to 512 KB of ultrafast memory that can be located within the microprocessor, but further from the registers than Level 1 cache, or on a separate cache chip located

on the motherboard very close to the microprocessor. It runs at 20 to 30 nanoseconds.

- **Level 3 (L3) cache**, is found on some systems with newer microprocessors, like Intel's Xeon processor, that are located in some servers and workstations. It is located outside of the processor on a separate cache chip on the motherboard very close to the microprocessor.

Keeping the Level 2 and Level 3 cache as close as possible to the microprocessor improves overall system performance (Figure 2.26).

Now that you know the different levels of cache and where they can be located, how is the information in them accessed? There is a sequence that the CPU (microprocessor) follows when looking for an instruction or data. The sequence goes like this: If the next instruction or data to be fetched is not already in a register, the CPU (microprocessor) attempts to locate that instruction in Level 1 cache. If it is not located in Level 1 cache, the CPU checks Level 2 cache; and if the instruction is not in Level 2 cache, then it checks Level 3 cache, if any Level 3 cache exists on the system. If the command is not already loaded into one of the cache chips, then the CPU must make the longer and slower trip and check RAM.

Because cache is part of the microprocessor or the motherboard, it cannot be upgraded. For this reason, it is important to check the amount of the various levels of cache on a system when you purchase a computer.

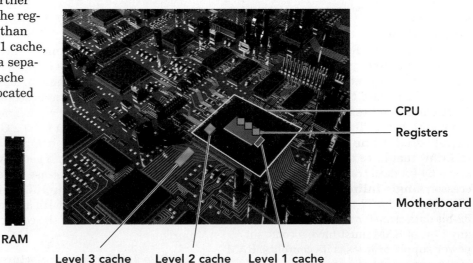

RAM

Level 3 cache   Level 2 cache   Level 1 cache

CPU

Registers

Motherboard

FIGURE 2.26 The close proximity of cache to the CPU is one reason why accessing information from cache is quicker than from RAM.

ROM and Other Types of Memory on the Motherboard

If everything in RAM is erased when the power is turned off, how does the computer start up again? The answer is **read-only memory (ROM)**, a type of nonvolatile memory in which instructions are prerecorded and not erased when the system is shut down. Listed here are some of the programs stored in ROM:

- **BIOS,** the **basic input/output system**—the first code run when a system is powered on. It checks and initializes such devices as the keyboard, display screens, and disk drives. Many modern systems have flash BIOS, which means that the BIOS is stored on flash memory chips and can be updated if needed.
- **Bootstrap Loader**—a program that locates and loads the operating system into RAM.
- **CMOS** or **complementary metal-oxide semiconductor**—controls a variety of actions including starting the power-on self test and verifying that other components of the system are functioning correctly. Many settings can be altered in the CMOS configuration screen, available by pressing certain keys during the boot process. This screen contains information about the components of the system, for example, the hard drive type and size, and should only be altered by an experienced user. CMOS is often mistaken for the BIOS.
- **POST,** also called the **power-on self test**—a program that is run when the system is started. It checks the circuitry and RAM, marking any locations that are defective so that they do not get used.

ROM has evolved over the decades from read-only memory that cannot be changed to variations that can be programmed and re-programmed.

- **PROM**—programmable read-only memory that can be written on only once, but requires a special writing device. It cannot be erased and reused. It is used to hold startup programs that are bug free and are never meant to be changed.
- **EPROM**—electrically programmable read-only memory is erasable PROM that can be reused many times. Erasure is accomplished using a UV (ultraviolet) light source that shines

through a quartz erasing window in the EPROM package. It is used primarily by programmers in the development process of programs so that errors can be corrected.

- **EEPROM**—electrically erasable programmable read-only memory that can be rewritten many times while the chip is in the computer. EEPROM is erased one byte at a time, using an electric field instead of an UV light source, eliminating the need for an erasing window. It is used in the development process to allow for the quick correction or editing of programs being tested.

- **Flash EPROM**—similar to an EEPROM except that flash EPROMs are erased in blocks, whereas regular EEPROMs erase one byte at a time. This is the type of chip that currently holds the BIOS so that it can be altered by the user during the boot process by holding down certain keys. Again, changes should be made with care only by an experienced user.

The following sections explore what can be found on the outside of the system unit of a typical desktop computer.

What's on the Outside of the Box?

You'll find the following features on the outside of a typical desktop computer's system unit:

- The front panel with various buttons and lights
- The power switch

FIGURE 2.28 The connectors on the outside of a system unit enable you to connect peripherals such as a printer, keyboard, or mouse.

FireWire
PS/2 (keyboard)
USB
DVI (LCD monitor)
FireWire
Audio jacks

PS/2 (mouse)
Ethernet (network)
S-video (television)
VGA (monitor)

- Connectors and ports for plugging in keyboards, mice, monitors, and other peripheral devices

On the front panel of some system units, you'll find a **drive activity light**, which indicates your hard disk is accessing data, and a **power-on light**, which indicates whether the power is on.

The power switch is usually on the front of the system unit. In earlier days it was placed on the back of the unit because of fears that users would accidentally press it and inadvertently shut down their systems. Computers don't handle sudden power losses well. For example, a power outage could scramble the data on your hard drive, corrupting files and making them inaccessible the next time you try to use them. Likewise, just turning off your computer instead of shutting it down properly can leave the system unstable and possibly unable to restart. You should always follow the appropriate shutdown procedure to shut off your computer.

If your computer freezes or won't respond to any key or mouse commands, first try pressing the Ctrl, Alt, and Del keys simultaneously to activate the Windows Task Manager. The dialog box the Task Manager opens allows the user to force the closing of a nonresponsive program. Using this should be a last resort because using the Ctrl, Alt, Del action will cause any unsaved work to be lost.

Connectors and Ports

A **connector** is a physical receptacle located on the system unit or an expansion card that is visible on the outside of the unit. Each connector is designed for a specific type of plug. Plugs are sometimes secured by **thumbscrews**—small screws that are usually attached to the plug and are used to secure the plug to the system unit or expansion card extender to prevent an accidental disconnect. Expansion cards are plug-in adapters that fit into slots on the motherboard and connect the computer with various peripherals. The connectors on these cards are located on extender pieces that are visible through slots on the outside of the system and are described as being *male* (those with external pins) or *female* (those with receptacles for external pins).

Figure 2.28 summarizes the connectors you may find on the computer's case. Most of these connectors are on the back of the case, but on notebook computers (Figure 2.29) it's now common to find several on the front or

Right side (15-inch and 17-inch)

Security port   USB 2.0   FireWire   FireWire   Gigabit   Dual-link
                            400   800   ethernet   DVI

(IEEE 1394)   (IEEE 1394 b)

Left side (15-inch)

MagSafe   USB 2.0   Audio in   Audio   ExpressCard/34
port   out

FIGURE 2.29 The location of connectors on a notebook may vary. Many are located on the sides, and some might even appear on the front.

side, providing easier access for many different peripheral devices.

It's important to remember that a connector isn't the same thing as a port. A **port** is an electronically defined pathway or interface for getting information into and out of the computer. A connector is a physical device—a plug-in. A port is an interface—the matching of input and output flows. A port almost always uses a connector, but a connector isn't always a port. For example, a telephone jack is just a connector—not a port. To function, a port must be linked to a specific receptacle. This linking is done by the computer system's start-up and configuration software located in ROM memory. For more information about connectors and ports, their location on the system unit, and the devices that connect to each, go to **www.howstuffworks.com** and type "**connectors and ports**" in the search box located near the top of the screen.

The following section uses *port* as if it were synonymous with *connector*, in line with everyday usage; however, keep the distinction in mind. Let's look next at the types of ports found on the exterior of a typical computer system's case.

USB Ports

USB (universal serial bus) ports can connect a variety of devices, including keyboards, mice, printers, and digital cameras, and were designed to replace older parallel and serial ports. A single USB port can connect up to 127 peripheral devices, eliminating the need for special ports that work only with specific devices (Figure 2.30).

Although introduced in 1995, USB ports didn't become widespread until the 1998 release of the best-selling iMac. The current standard, USB 2.0 (high-speed USB), replaced USB 1.1 and was released in April 2000. USB 2.0 is fully compatible with USB 1.1 products, cables, and connectors.

USB 2.0 ports use an external bus standard that supports data transfer rates of 480 Mbps (480 million bits per second) between the computer and its peripheral devices; they do not transfer data between devices within the system. Some advantages include hot swapping and support for plug-and-play. **Hot swapping** is the ability to connect and disconnect devices without shutting down your computer. This is convenient when you're using portable devices that you want to disconnect often, such as a digital camera. **Plug-and-play (PnP)** refers to a set of standards, jointly developed by Intel Corporation and Microsoft, which enable a computer to automatically detect the brand, model, and characteristics of a device when you plug it in and configure the system accordingly.

Computer manufacturers have been installing increasing numbers of USB ports because of their convenience and versatility; many systems now have six or more. Ports on the back of a computer are typically used for peripherals that won't be

FIGURE 2.30 USB ports and connectors will be the standard for years to come. Because of their universal connectivity, they are replacing expansion boards for some devices.

FIGURE 2.31 If your computer needs more USB ports, a USB hub can expand your options.

removed often, like a printer or keyboard, whereas front ports are ideal for syncing a handheld device or MP3 player. If your computer doesn't have enough USB ports, it is possible to obtain a **USB hub**—a device that plugs into an existing USB port and contains four or more additional ports (Figure 2.31).

Up next on the horizon is USB 3.0, known as *SuperSpeed USB*. USB 3.0 is expected to use a fiber optic link to attain a data transfer rate of 4.8 Gbps—up to 10 times faster than USB 2.0. Additionally, USB 3.0 will be compatible with older versions, providing the same benefits while consuming less power.

1394 Ports (FireWire)

In 1995 Apple introduced **FireWire**, an interface Apple created and standardized as the IEEE 1394 High Performance Serial Bus specification. It is also known as Sony i.Link or IEEE 1394, the official name for the standard. FireWire is similar to USB in that it offers a high-speed connection for dozens of peripheral devices (up to 63 of them). It is especially well suited for transmitting digital video and audio data (Figure 2.32).

On non-Apple systems a FireWire port is called a **1394 port**, after the international standard that defines it. Like USB, FireWire enables hot swapping and PnP. However, it is more expensive than USB and is used only for certain high-speed peripherals, such as digital video cameras,

FIGURE 2.32 FireWire cables are used with FireWire ports to transmit digital video or audio files at high rates of speed.

that need greater throughput (data transfer capacity) than USB provides.

FireWire 400 has a data transfer rate of 400 Mbps; FireWire 800 offers 800 Mbps. The next generation, FireWire S3200, is expected to transfer data at 3.2 Gbps. Although some experts consider FireWire technologically superior to USB, the popularity and affordability of USB 2.0, coupled with the promise of an even faster USB interface in the future, lead most to believe that the 1394 FireWire standard may fade away.

Video Connectors

Most computers use a video adapter (also called a video card) to generate the output that is displayed on the computer's screen or monitor. On the back of the adapter you'll find a standard **VGA (video graphics array) connector**, a 15-pin male connector that works with standard monitor cables. VGA connectors transmit analog video signals and are used for legacy technology cathode ray tube (CRT) monitors.

Many liquid crystal display (LCD) monitors can receive analog or digital video signals. A **DVI (digital visual interface) port** lets LCD monitors use digital signals. However, unless you have a keen eye or are doing professional video editing, the difference between analog and digital signals may not be noticeable.

On some computers the video circuitry is built into the motherboard. This type of video circuitry is called **onboard video**. On such systems the video connector is on the back of the system unit case.

Additional Ports and Connectors

You may find the following additional ports and connectors on the exterior of a computer's case or on one of the computer's expansion cards:

- *Telephone connector:* The typical modem interface, a telephone connector (called RJ-11), is a standard modular telephone jack that will work with an ordinary telephone cord.
- *Network connector:* Provided with networking adapters, the network connector (called an RJ-45 or Ethernet port) looks like a standard telephone jack but is bigger and capable of much faster data transfer.
- *PC card slots:* Notebook computers provide one or more PC card slots for plugging in PC cards or ExpressCards.

Like USB devices, these cards can be inserted or removed while the computer is running.

- *Sound card connectors:* PCs equipped with sound cards (adapters that provide stereo sound and sound synthesis), as well as Macs with built-in sound, offer two or more sound connectors. These connectors, also called jacks, accept the same stereo miniplug used by portable CD players. Most sound cards provide four connectors: Mic (microphone input), Line In (accepts input from other audio devices), Line Out (sends output to other audio devices), and Speaker (sends output to external speakers).

- *Game card:* Game cards provide connectors for high-speed access to the CPU and RAM for graphics-intensive interaction.

- *TV/sound capture board connectors:* If your computer is equipped with TV and video capabilities, you'll see additional connectors that look like those found on a television monitor. These include a connector for a coaxial cable, which can be connected to a video camera or cable TV system.

- *ExpressCard:* This is the newest standard for the PC card, originally known as the PCMCIA card (short for Personal Computer Memory Card International Association). Mostly designed for and used in notebook computers, the ExpressCard can also be found in desktops. The **ExpressCard** is a credit card–sized adapter that fits into a designated slot to provide expanded capabilities such as wireless communication, additional memory, multimedia, or security features.

Some legacy ports are being replaced by technologies like **SATA (serial advance technology attachment)**. The Serial ATA International Organization (SATA IO) is responsible for developing, managing, and pushing the adoption of the serial ATA specifications. Users of the SATA interface benefit from greater speed, simpler upgradable storage devices, and easier configuration. The interface greatly increases the data transfer rate between the motherboard and storage devices like hard drives and optical drives.

Legacy Technology

Legacy technology is an older technology, device, or application that is being

Legacy Technologies	
Connector	Use
Serial	Dial-up modems, mice, scanners, or printers
Parallel	Printers, external storage devices, or scanners
PS/2	Mice and keyboards
SCSI	Scanners, zip drives, and external hard drives

FIGURE 2.33 Legacy Technologies

phased out in favor of new advances in technology. Although legacy technology may still work, it may not be available on newer computer systems. The following types of ports are all considered legacy technology (Figure 2.33).

- **Serial ports** were one of the earliest types of ports and were often used with dial-up modems to achieve two-way communication. Although they are still in use on servers, many new computers no longer include serial ports, opting to use USB ports instead.

- **Parallel ports** were commonly used to connect a PC to a printer but have been replaced by USB ports and Ethernet ports.

- **PS/2 ports** were typically used for mice and keyboards, but were not interchangeable. Today most mice and keyboards connect via USB connectors.

- **SCSIs** (pronounced "scuzzy"; short for **small computer system interface ports**) were a type of parallel interface that enabled users to connect up to 15 SCSI-compatible devices, such as printers, scanners, and digital cameras, in a daisy-chain series.

These legacy ports are becoming obsolete because newer ports, such as USB, FireWire, and SATA, provide greater flexibility and faster data transfer rates.

Select System Unit Components for a New Computer System

► **Use this checklist of components within the system unit to keep your purchase in line with your needs.**

1. **Uses**

   a. What will you use your system for? ☐ Work ☐ Personal ☐ Gaming

   b. What is more important to you? ☐ Speed ☐ Memory

2. **Portability**

   a. Do you need to take your system with you? ☐ Yes ☐ No

   b. Do you need to have Internet access? ☐ Yes ☐ No

   c. If you answer yes to part b, indicate whether you will you need an ☐ Ethernet connector network interface card or ☐ wireless network interface card

3. **Processor Speed**

   a. What is the processor speed of your current system? _____

   b. Do you need a system with a processor that runs faster? ☐ Yes ☐ No

   If yes, why? _____

4. **Processor Type**

   a. What is the processor type of your current system? _____

   b. Do you need a dual- or quad-core processor? ☐ Yes ☐ No

   If yes, why? _____

5. **Memory Usage**

   a. What is the amount of RAM in your current system? _____

   b. Do you need a system with more RAM? ☐ Yes ☐ No

   If yes, why? _____

6. **Cache Types and Amount**

   a. What types of cache is in your current system? ☐ L1 ☐ L2 ☐ L3

   b. Do you need a system with more cache? ☐ Yes ☐ No

   If yes, why? _____

Chapter Summary

Inside the System Unit

- The basic unit of information in a computer is the bit—a single circuit whose electrical state is represented by the binary digits—0 or 1. A sequence of eight bits, called a *byte*, is sufficient to represent the basic letters, numbers, and punctuation marks of most languages.

- Bits are used to describe data transfer rates, whereas bytes describe storage capacity. Common transfer rates are kilobits per second (Kbps) megabits per second (Mbps), and gigabits per second (Gbps). These respectively correspond (roughly) to 1 thousand, 1 million, and 1 billion bits per second. Common storage units are kilobyte (KB), megabyte (MB), gigabyte (GB), and terabyte (TB). The respective sizes of these units are 1 thousand, 1 million, 1 billion, and 1 trillion characters.

- The system unit contains the motherboard, memory, circuits, power supply, cooling fan(s), internal speakers, drive bays for storage devices, and expansion cards.

- The computer's motherboard contains the microprocessor, the system clock, the chipset, memory modules, and expansion slots.

- The computer's central processing unit (CPU) processes data in a four-step machine cycle using two components: the control unit and the arithmetic logic unit (ALU). The control unit follows a program's instructions and manages four basic operations: fetch, decode, execute, and store. The ALU performs arithmetic and logical operations.

- The performance of the microprocessor is determined by number of transistors, their proximity to each other, processing speed, the data bus width and word size, clock speed, operations performed per microprocessing cycle, the use of parallel processing, and the type of chip.

- The computer's main memory, random access memory (RAM), holds programs, data, and instructions currently in use for quick access by the processor. Level 1, Level 2, and Level 3 cache, physically positioned within or close to the CPU, operate at speeds faster than RAM and keep frequently accessed data available to the processor. Read-only memory (ROM) holds prerecorded start-up operating instructions.

- A variety of ports and connectors enable peripheral devices, such as USB drives, external hard drives, digital cameras, and iPods, to function effectively.

Key Terms and Concepts

Identification

Label each hardware component.

1. _____

3. _____

2. _____

4. _____

5. _____

7. _____

6. _____

8. _____

Matching

Match each key term in the left column with the most accurate definition in the right column:

_____ 1. ASCII

_____ 2. gigabyte

_____ 3. ROM

_____ 4. register

_____ 5. multitasking

_____ 6. virtual memory

_____ 7. parallel processing

_____ 8. RAM

_____ 9. megabyte

_____ 10. Extended ASCII

_____ 11. pipelining

_____ 12. memory footprint

_____ 13. terabyte

_____ 14. Unicode

_____ 15. cache

a. A character coding system that uses eight bits and can represent 256 characters.

b. Temporary storage, located on the motherboard, used to hold programs and data currently in use

c. A small unit of very high-speed memory that works closely with the microprocessor and is either located in the microprocessor or in close proximity

d. A unit of storage capacity that refers to 1 million characters

e. Memory that is not volatile and contains start-up instructions

f. A character coding system that uses seven bits and can represent 128 characters

g. The amount of memory that a program uses while running

h. A unit of storage capacity that refers to 1 trillion characters

i. A technique that feeds a new instruction into the CPU at every step of the processing cycle

j. A character coding system that uses 16 bits and can represent 65,000 characters.

k. A unit of storage capacity that refers to 1 billion characters

l. The use of more than one processor to execute program instructions

m. The rapid switching between programs and instructions in use

n. A high-speed temporary storage location that runs at the same speed as the central processing unit it is embedded within

o. Temporary use of the hard drive to hold programs and data in use

Multiple Choice

Circle the correct choice for each of the following:

1. What is the term used to refer to the ability to connect and disconnect devices without shutting down a system?
   a. Hot swapping   b. Memory footprint
   c. PnP   d. Parallel processing

2. What is the smallest unit of information a computer can work with?
   a. Megabyte   b. Kilobyte
   c. Byte   d. Bit

3. Which of the following is listed in order from largest to smallest?
   a. MB, GB, TB, KB   b. GB, MB, TB, KB
   c. TB, GB, MB, KB   d. KB, MB, GB, TB

4. Which of the following can be added by an expansion card?
   a. Cache   b. RAM
   c. Registers   d. ROM

5. Which step of the machine cycle retrieves the next program instruction from memory?
   a. Fetch   b. Decode
   c. Execute   d. Store

6. Which of the following is an example of a binary number?
   a. AF   b. 0002
   c. 0101   d. 08A

7. Which number describes a computer's word size?
   a. 30   b. 64
   c. 60   d. 4

8. What is plug-and-play (PnP)?
   a. A multifunctional port that allows the connection of various peripherals
   b. A feature that automatically detects new compatible peripherals connected to a system
   c. Hard drive storage that is used as RAM when RAM is filled
   d. The name of a new CPU for systems used by gamers

9. Which component of the CPU is responsible for performing addition, subtraction, multiplication, and division?
   a. L1 cache   b. L2 cache
   c. ALU   d. Control unit

10. What is the freeway of parallel connections that allows internal and external components of the system unit to communicate?
    a. CPU   b. Port
    c. Connector   d. Bus

Fill-In

In the blanks provided, write the correct answer for each of the following:

1. If your computer freezes and won't respond, press the three keys _____ simultaneously to access the Windows Task Manager.

2. A(n) _____ processor is placed within a device and is designed and programmed to perform only the tasks done by that device.

3. Current is converted from alternating (AC) to direct (DC) by the _____ located within the system unit.

4. _____ is a situation in which the CPU needs the results of a previous instruction to process another one.

5. The _____ step of the machine cycle translates an instruction into a form that the processor can understand.

6. The two subcomponents of the CPU are the _____ and the _____.

7. _____ is the maximum number of bits a CPU can process at once.

8. Video circuitry built into the motherboard is called _____.

9. The network connector called RJ-45 that looks like a standard phone jack but is bigger and capable of faster data transfer is also called a(n) _____ port.

10. The execution portion of the machine cycle contains the _____ and _____ steps.

11. The _____ numbering system uses the digits 0 through 9 and the characters A through F.

12. _____ is a type of ROM that is erased in blocks and currently holds a system's BIOS.

13. The number _____ is the binary representation for a circuit that contains current.

14. The instruction portion of the machine cycle contains the _____ and _____ steps.

15. The two types of operations performed by the ALU are _____ and _____ operations.

Short Answer

1. List the four operations of the processing cycle and provide a brief description of their function.

2. What are the differences between pipelining, multitasking, and parallel processing?

3. Place the following hardware in order from the one with the fastest access speed to the one with the slowest access speed: Level 2 cache, Level 1 cache, RAM, registers, hard disk. Indicate the reason for the differences in their access speeds.

4. What is the difference between Level 1, Level 2, and Level 3 cache? Why is it important to have some amount of cache on a system today?

5. List the two subcomponents of the CPU and explain the function of each.

Teamwork

1. **Dream Machine** For this exercise your team will use the information in this chapter and your computing needs and desires to come up with the technical specs and price for your dream computer. Include the name and details of the processor you select, the amount of RAM, the type and amount of cache, and the type of video and sound card you want installed. Additionally, cite the purposes for which your team members intend to use the system. Use an Excel spreadsheet to display each component, its technical specs, and its associated price. Provide a total for the dream system. Below the technical specs, include the list of purposes that the team proposed in ranked order from the use that most members cited to the one that was cited the least.

2. **Design a New Computer Lab** As a team, use a word processing program to create a questionnaire with options for possible computer systems to be placed in a hypothetical new computer lab on campus. Use the hardware and system information in this chapter to help create the checklist on the questionnaire. Distribute the questionnaire to at least 30 students on campus. Collect the data and, using prices from local vendors or Internet retail sites, generate a spreadsheet. The spreadsheet should list the most popular components chosen by the survey participants and their cost from at least two different vendors. Use the cost of the least expensive units to estimate the cost for 20 units. If time allows, add to the spreadsheet the cost of 20 desks and 20 chairs for a more comprehensive lab cost estimate. Turn in the questionnaire distributed, the responses to the questionnaire, the spreadsheet with the cost comparisons of at least two vendors, and your final lab estimate.

3. **Step into the Game** Your team is to research three of the newest and most popular gaming systems. Research the components within each system. Your team members will probably be surprised to find out that the internal components of these systems are similar to a desktop or notebook computer. Make a comparison chart of the three units in an Excel spreadsheet. Include the type of central processor (CPU), the type of gaming processor (GPU), the amount of RAM, the type of audio processors, and the number of controller ports. Come up with a list of the games that your team would use on each system. Then, as a team, rank the units as 1, 2, or 3, with 1 being the unit most desired and 3 being the unit least desired. State the reasons for your ranking.

4. **Let Your Imagination Soar** As a team, make a list of the features that you would want in a desktop, notebook, or netbook of the future. Include such features as processor speed, monitor size or shape, input devices, output devices, the size and shape of the system unit, and any green features that you want it to include. You might search the Internet for some creative ideas. After all ideas have been discussed, as a team, select the best five to eight ideas and present them to the class in a PowerPoint slide show. If you used the Internet, identify your source and include a picture, if one is available. If any members can draw an image of your own future idea or concept, include those images also.

5. **Buy New or Upgrade?** Whether to buy a new computer or upgrade is a question that every computer owner faces at some time. Your team members should locate several references on this topic. Make a list of some of the behaviors that a computer can exhibit that might indicate that the system is old or malfunctioning. In a one-page, double-spaced report, use your list of behaviors to support a decision to buy a new system or to simply upgrade a current one. Remember to cite your references.

On the Web

1. **All Aboard the Motherboard** Go to **http://videos.howstuffworks.com/howstuffworks/23-computer-tour-video.htm** and watch the video about the components found on the motherboard. In a one-page, double-spaced report, describe the seven components on the motherboard that the video reviews. In addition, detail five additional pieces of information that the video covers that are not discussed in this chapter.

2. **Let the Games Begin!** Computer gaming has created a use for computer systems that demands more speed and graphic capabilities than are available from most systems in a business environment. Go to **www.cyberpowerpc.com**. On the menu across the top of the page, select the Intel desktop and AMD desktop options. From each of these two choices, additional choices appear. Select an option under each that contains the word *gamer*. After reviewing several gaming systems, pick two from Intel and two from AMD. In a spreadsheet or table, list the following information: name of each system, price, CPU name and speed, amount of RAM, name and number of video cards, size of hard drive, and any additional fans or cooling systems. When you have researched all four systems, indicate the one you favor and the reasons for your choice.

3. **Code Converter** Use your favorite search engine to locate a Web site that displays the "ASCII code binary table." Use that table to code the message here into binary form. Once it's converted, use the converter calculator in the chapter, or any other such calculator located on the Web, to convert the binary code into hexadecimal.

   Message to convert: Less is more!

4. **The Base of Mobility** In mobile devices, the brain or processor is one of the most important components. Use your favorite search engine to locate information about processors for mobile devices. Locate several Web sites that either give you information about the new AMD processors or direct you to articles about this topic. In a one-page, double-spaced report, provide information about the competition in this mobile market. Who are the key players? Which devices use which processors? What are the capabilities of competing processors? Remember to cite your Web references.

5. **Recycle, Recycle, Recycle** With the emphasis today on reusability, recycling, and a greener environment, it should not surprise you that the disposal of computing devices has become a great concern. Using the Internet and your favorite Web browser, research the recycling and disposal options available to a user when getting rid of an aging computing device. Indicate the cost of recycling, if any, and whether the owner of the device, the manufacturer, or the recycling source pays the cost. Present your options in a PowerPoint slide show. Remember to include the reasons for recycling, the cost and who pays it, and the possible recycling options.

Spotlight

File Management

You've just finished your term paper—where should you save it? You never know when you may need a writing sample for a graduate school or job application, so you'll want to keep it someplace safe. The secret to finding what you're looking for in the future is good file management now. Managing computer files is an essential skill for any computer user. Are your skills honed? Do you understand how to save and back up your files effectively?

Once you learn the basics, file management is intuitive. You can think of managing computer files as being similar to the way you organize and store paper files and folders in a file cabinet (Figure 2A). You start with a storage device (the filing cabinet), divide it into definable sections (folders), and then fill the sections with specific items (documents) that fit the defined sections. Most people tend to organize the things in their lives, and the organizational principles used are the same ones used when managing computer files.

The Big Picture: Files, Folders, and Paths

A **file** is a named unit of related data stored in a computer system. The data and the programs installed on your computer are stored in files. Files store Word documents, music, photo images, Excel spreadsheets, applications, and a variety of other digital compilations.

Every file that is stored has certain properties. A **property** is a setting that provides information such as the file's date of creation, its size, and the date it was last modified.

You use **folders** (also called **directories**) to organize groups of files that have something in common. Many folders have **subfolders**—folders within folders—that enable you to organize your files even further. For example, you might create a folder called "Classes," and then create subfolders for each school course and then subfolders within each course for each assignment.

All of the files and folders you create must reside on a storage device called a **drive**. The primary storage devices on desktop computers are the hard drive, the CD and DVD drives, the external hard drives, and USB flash drives. Older computers may also have a floppy disk drive. On PCs, these storage devices are designated by drive letters. A **drive letter** is simply a letter of the alphabet followed by a colon and a backslash character. If your computer has a floppy disk drive, it is typically referred to as A:\. The hard drive is generally referred to as C:\. The CD or DVD drive might be labeled drive D (D:\), and other drives are often labeled sequentially, so a USB flash drive might be labeled drive E (E:\). On the Mac, drives are not labeled with letters. You'll see them as icons appearing on your screen.

FIGURE 2A   You can organize files on your computer the same way you would organize documents in a filing cabinet.

For the computer to access a particular file, it needs to know the path it should take to get to the file. A **path** is the sequence of directories that the computer must follow to locate a file. A typical path might look like this:

C:\Classes\ Expository Writing 201\Homework #1\ Homework#1_draft1.docx

In Figure 2B, the C:\ in the path indicates that the file is located on the C:\ drive. The **top-level folder**, "Classes," contains, as the name indicates, things that have to do with classes. The subfolder named "Expository Writing 201" is the subfolder for your writing class and contains two subfolders, one for each homework assignment. The file at the end of the path, "Homework#1_draft1.docx," is the first draft of your first homework assignment. The .docx extension indicates that the file is a Microsoft Word 2007 or 2010 document. We'll

FIGURE 2B   The drive and folder structure is often referred to as a "tree" structure. The drive letters can be pictured as roots, the folders as branches, and the files as leaves.

Computer
— Drive A: \
— Drive C: \
  — Programs
    — Windows
    — Office 2010
    — AntiVirus
  — Classes
    — Math 211
    — Biology 201
    — Expository Writing 201
      — Homework #1
        — Homework#1_draft1.docx
        — Homework#1_draft2.docx
      — Homework #2
— Drive D: \
  — My music
    — Favorites
    — Albums

discuss file names in greater depth shortly. Figure 2B illustrates what a hierarchical drive, folder, and file structure might look like.

FILE-NAMING CONVENTIONS

To save a file, you need to know where you're going to store it—in other words, on which storage device and in which folder. In addition, each file needs a specific file name. The **file name** is the name that the storage device uses to identify each unique file, so the name must differ from all other file names used within the same folder or directory. You may use the same name for different files, but they must exist on different drives or in different folders. Be careful to include enough detail in naming a file so that you will be able to recognize the file name when you need the file later. The name you use when you create a file is usually very obvious to you at the time—but the name may elude you when you try to remember it in the future.

Every file name on a PC has two parts that are separated by a period (read as "dot"). The first part, the part you're probably most familiar with, is called the **name**. The second part is called the **extension**, an addition to the file name, typically three to five characters in length. In a file called "Homework#1_draft1.docx," Homework#1_draft1 is the name and .docx is the extension; together they make up the file name.

Typically, an extension is used to identify the type of data that the file contains (or the format it is stored in). Sometimes it indicates the application used to create the file. In Microsoft Office, each application automatically assigns an extension to a file when you save it for the first time. For example, Microsoft Word 2010 automatically assigns the .docx extension. Workbooks created in Microsoft Excel 2010 use the .xlsx extension. When naming files, you never need to be concerned about typing in an extension, because all programs attach their extension to the file name by default.

Program files, also called application files, usually use the .exe extension, which stands for executable. The term *executable* is used because when you use an application, you execute, or run, the file. Figure 2C lists several of the most commonly used extensions and their file types. Note that when using Mac OS, extensions are not needed because Macintosh files contain a code representing the name of the application that created the file. However, it is generally recommended that Mac users add the appropriate extension to their file names so that they can more easily exchange them with PC users and avoid conversion problems.

In Microsoft Windows 7, you can use up to 260 characters in a file name, including spaces. However, this length restriction includes the entire file path name; therefore, file names actually need to be shorter than 260 characters to be valid. Windows file names cannot include any of the following characters: forward slash (/), backslash (\), greater than sign (>), less than sign (<), asterisk (*), question mark (?), quotation mark ("), pipe symbol (|), colon (:), or semicolon (;). In Mac OS and Windows XP, you can use up to 255 characters in a filename, including spaces, and all characters except the colon. Although you can use a large number of characters to create a file name, it is still best to keep file names concise and meaningful. Longer file names may be subject to automatic truncation (shortening), which can create file management difficulties.

Now that you understand the basics of paths, folders, and file naming conventions, let's turn our attention to the business of managing files.

Managing Files

Files can be managed in two ways: (1) with a file management utility such as Windows Explorer or (2) from within the programs that create them. In the following sections, we'll explore both methods.

FILE MANAGEMENT UTILITIES

Microsoft Windows uses the Windows Explorer program for file management. There are a number of ways that you can launch this program. The Start, All Programs, Accessories menu sequence is one method. Another method is to click Start and select one of the options shown on the top right side of the Start menu to view the contents of a specific folder

FIGURE 2C Commonly Used File Name Extensions

Extension	File Type
.exe	Program or application
.docx	Microsoft Word 2007 and 2010
.xlsx	Microsoft Excel 2007 and 2010
.pptx	Microsoft PowerPoint 2007 and 2010
.accdb	Microsoft Access 2007 and 2010
.pdf	Adobe Acrobat
.txt	ASCII text
.htm or .html	Web pages
.rtf	Files in rich text format
.jpeg or .jpg	Picture or image format

FIGURE 2D The Start menu provides various options for viewing commonly accessed files and programs.

(Figure 2D). The Start menu can also be used to access the Computer folder, which lets you view the disk drives and other hardware connected to your computer (Figure 2E).

The Windows Explorer program in Windows 7 has a number of features that make file management

easier and more versatile. Windows Explorer provides navigation buttons, an address bar, a search box, and a toolbar at the top of the window. The main body of the window is split into two panes—a navigation pane and a content pane—and a detail pane is often displayed at the bottom of the window (Figure 2F). The **navigation pane** on the left allows you to navigate directly to specific folders listed in the Favorites area or access a prior search that you have saved by clicking on a desired folder. You can also add a shortcut to a frequently used folder by dragging the folder into the Favorite Links area of the navigation pane.

The **details pane** at the bottom of the window provides a thumbnail view and information about the selected file or folder. The details vary depending on the object that has been selected. Users can edit many of these items. Just click the item you wish to change, revise it, and press the Save button.

The right pane, or **content pane**, sometimes called a **file list**, displays subfolders and files located within the selected folder. You can view the contents of the right pane in several ways. Eight different view options are accessible from the View menu or from the Change your view button on the Standard toolbar. You can click the Change your view button to cycle through the choices or click the dropdown arrow next to the button to make a selection. The Tiles view and various icon views are particularly helpful if you're searching through pictures and photographs, because they show you a small copy of the images you have in the folder—before you open them. The List view simply lists the names of the files, whereas the Details view offers you information regarding file size, file type, and the

FIGURE 2E The Computer window provides quick access to information about the disk drives and other hardware that are connected to your computer.

FIGURE 2F Windows Explorer is a useful and versatile file-management tool.

Content pane

Navigation pane

Details pane

date a file was last modified. There are additional optional headings available to further customize the Details view.

The column headings at the top of the file list can be used to change how the files are organized—if you use the Details view. New column headings can be added by right-clicking a heading and selecting one or more options from the shortcut menu. You can also delete column headings by selecting the heading that is checked to remove the checkmark. As in previous versions of Windows Explorer, it is possible to sort the contents of a folder, but users can now also group, stack, and filter the items displayed in the right pane.

To sort, simply click a column heading; click the column heading a second time to reverse the sort order. A sorted column displays a small triangle in the column heading; the direction of the triangle indicates whether the column has been sorted in ascending or descending order. If a folder contains subfolders and files, the subfolders are sorted separately from the files.

To access the group options, click the dropdown arrow beside the column heading to reveal the submenu. The group option arranges files and folders within specified groups, depending on the column heading you've selected. You can select how you want to group files and folders (Figure 2G). It is possible to

Ways to group files

Content pane/ File list

FIGURE 2G The dropdown list on the Type heading provides a way to group files by type.

display only the files created by a specific application (Figure 2H).

The **address bar (breadcrumb bar)** has also been updated. It is now possible to use it for breadcrumb navigation. The address bar displays the route you've taken to get to the current location. It may or may not correspond with a file's path name. To view the actual path name, click the folder icon on the left side of the address bar. The breadcrumbs can be used to easily move from one location to another—simply click the dropdown arrow to reveal a list of destinations (Figure 2I).

Locating Files and Folders Despite your best efforts, it's possible to forget where you've saved a

file. The **Search box** in Windows Explorer can make locating a lost file less painful. Select one of the four default Libraries, such as Documents and begin typing a search term in the box. As you type, Windows Explorer searches the contents of the selected folder and subfolders, immediately filtering the view to display any files that match the search term. Windows Explorer searches file names, file properties, and file contents for the search term. If the search returns too many results, or you need to create a more complex search, the Advanced Search feature can help.

If you can't locate the file or folder by using Search, you can customize your search in the Search Documents window by adding a filter

FIGURE 2I The address bar lets users navigate by breadcrumbs. Click the dropdown arrow to reveal a list of possible destinations.

FIGURE 2J You can add a search filter or, if you do not see the file you need, you can search other locations.

a number of commonly used folders, such as Documents, Pictures, and Music, displayed in the right pane. If you prefer to create your folder on a removable storage device, instead choose Computer from the Start menu and double-click the storage device you wish to use.

Step 2. Select a folder, such as My Documents, and double-click it. While pointing to the right pane, right-click and choose "New" and then "Folder" from the short-cut menus to create a folder within the selected folder. In other words, if you have selected the Documents library, the new folder will be placed at the top level. See Figure 2K for an example of a new folder that has been created within the Documents library.

(Figure 2J). If you find that you are often searching for the same files, click the Save Search button on the toolbar. Assign a name for your search and, by default, the results will be stored in the Searches folder. Searches are **dynamic**, which means that the next time you open a saved search, the results are automatically refreshed—new files are added and files that no longer meet the search criteria are not included.

You can repeat this process as many times as is necessary to create your desired folder structure. For example, if you're taking three classes, you might want to create three separate subfolders with the appropriate class names under a top-level folder called "Classes." That way, you'll know exactly where to save a file each time you create one, and you'll

Creating Folders Another way to manage your files effectively is to create a **folder structure** or **directory structure** (the terms *folder* and *directory* are synonymous) —an organized set of folders in which to save your files. The process of creating a folder structure is accomplished in two steps:

Step 1. Decide on which drive, such as a USB flash drive, hard drive, or CD drive, you will create your folder. To create a folder on your computer's hard disk drive, click the Start menu and select your personal folder—typically, this folder will use your name and will appear at the top of the Start menu. Windows Explorer will open with

> New folder added and placed in alphabetical order

FIGURE 2K The New folder was created within the Documents library in the Documents folder on the hard disk drive.

avoid having a cluttered and disorganized storage space.

Of course, creating a well-organized folder structure requires that you add, rename, and move folders as your needs change. For example, if you add a class to your schedule, you'll want to create a new subfolder in your top-level "Classes" folder. Next term, you'll create new subfolders for each of your classes.

One Windows method that is effective for managing, modifying, and creating folders, subfolders, and files is the use of the right-click mouse action. Right-clicking within the right pane of Windows Explorer, in a blank space, will cause a pop-up context-sensitive menu to appear. Right-clicking on a folder or file will provide a menu with different choices.

Transferring Files When you've created a useful folder structure, you're ready to transfer files and folders that already exist. Whether you're working with files or folders, the same rules apply. Files and folders can be transferred in two ways: You can copy them or you can move them. The easiest way to accomplish these tasks is to *right-drag* the files you want to transfer to the new location. Press the right mouse button and drag to new location. When you release the right mouse button, a context-sensitive menu appears, allowing you to choose the result of your right-drag. The choices on this menu are Copy Here, Move Here, Create Shortcuts Here, and Cancel.

- Copying creates a duplicate file at the new location and leaves the existing file as is.
- Moving is similar to cutting and pasting; the file is moved from its original location to the new location.
- Creating a shortcut leaves the original file in place and creates a pointer that will take you to the file for which you've created the shortcut. This action is handy for files that you access often.

If you *left-drag* a file *within the same drive*, the file is automatically moved to the new location on the drive. Left-dragging by pressing the left mouse button and dragging the file *between drives* creates a copy of the file in the new location.

Right-clicking a file invokes a context-sensitive menu that enables you to choose among many common tasks, such as copying, deleting, and renaming files and creating shortcuts (Figure 2L). You may also use the toolbar to accomplish these and other file management tasks.

FIGURE 2L The context menu that appears when you right-click provides you with a shortcut to common tasks.

Backing Up You can create a backup copy of your files in several ways. The first, and easiest, way is to create intermediate copies as you work. You can do this by saving your original file, and then using the Save As sequence to save the original file with changes every 15 or 20 minutes. Name your intermediate copies by appending a number or letter to the file name. For example, "Writing121_homework.docx" would become "Writing121_homework1.docx," then "Writing121_homework2.docx," and so forth. After saving, close the new intermediate file and reopen the original file you saved to continue working.

Additionally, you can use the Windows Explorer program to drag a copy of your file to a USB flash drive or CD/DVD drive. Backing up files to the same drive that the original copy is on risks losing both copies in a disk failure or other disaster, so you should always use a remote or portable medium for your backups.

A third way to be sure that you don't lose your work is to use backup software that is specifically designed to back up files.

Getting Help If you need help when working within the Windows Explorer program, click the Get help button on the right side of the toolbar and then type "managing files" into the Search box of the Windows

Help and Support dialog box. This will bring up a variety of links to topics that will help you to further understand file management practices.

MANAGING FILES FROM WITHIN PROGRAMS

As mentioned earlier, all software applications use program-specific file name extensions. The advantage of using a default file extension is that both you and your computer will be able to easily associate the file with the program with which it was created. By using appropriate extensions, you can double-click a file in a file management utility such as Windows Explorer and the program used to create the file will be launched.

You can use an application to open a file or use a file to launch the application that created it. Let's say you create a document in Microsoft Word. You give the file the name "Letter_Home," and Word 2010 assigns the extension ".docx" by default. Later, you use Windows Explorer to locate the file and then double-click the file name. The file will open in Word. Alternately, you could launch Word and then click the *File* tab and choose *Open* to locate the file and open it. The Open dialog box includes a button that allows you to decide which files to display—there are a number of options to choose from. Selecting *All Files* from the dropdown list will display all files in the current location, no matter what the file type might be. Choosing *All Word Documents* displays files created in any version of Microsoft Word along with macros and templates, whereas selecting Word Documents will show only Word 2007 and 2010 files.

Choosing the *File, Open* menu sequence in many programs, or clicking the *File* tab and then choosing *Open* in Microsoft Office 2007 and 2010 applications, also enables you to manage files. There are icons for creating new folders and for changing the current view, and there is an icon called Organize that enables you to copy, rename, and create shortcuts to files. Pointing to a file and pressing the right mouse button within the Open menu also invokes a file management menu with various tasks.

SAVING FILES

Saving refers to the process of transferring a file from the computer's temporary memory, or RAM, to a permanent storage device, such as a hard disk. In Microsoft Office, documents are saved by default to a folder called Documents unless you specify another folder from within the *Organize this folder's contents* button and then selecting *Properties*, and then the *Location* tab. For Office 2010 applications, you can do this from within the program's Word *Options* menu, which can be found by clicking the *File* tab (Figure 2M). A critical decision you'll make when managing files is whether to use the Save or Save As command to save files.

Save or Save As? Many computer users never figure out the difference between Save and Save As. It is actually quite simple. When you choose the Save command under the File tab, the program takes what you've created or modified in memory and writes over, or replaces, it to the same storage device and folder, with the same file name that it had when it was opened in the application. When you first save a file, the initial Save menu sequence always invokes the

FIGURE 2M To change the default location for saved files in Microsoft Office 2010, click the File tab, then click Options, and then click Save to access the dialog box.

Save As dialog box, because the drive, path, and file name must be designated the first time a file is saved. You can select any folder by using the navigate pane. However, when you're working with a previously saved file, you need to be more careful. The Save command doesn't allow you to designate a different drive, folder, or file name; it simply replaces what is stored with the contents of memory.

The Save As command, however, brings up a dialog box that offers all of the choices you had when you first saved a file. You may choose a different drive or a different folder or a different file name. Modifying the file name is a good way to save various versions of your work, just in case something happens to what is in memory and you need to go back to a previous version.

Once you've successfully saved a file, you can always save another copy elsewhere by using the Save As command, which enables you to save the file using a new location, a new file name, or both. You might also use the Save As command to save a copy of your finished work on a USB flash drive, CD, or DVD or in an alternate folder as backup, just in case something happens to your original work. Once you use Save As, all subsequent saves of that file will now be saved in that location.

Managing E-mail

Many e-mail users quickly become overwhelmed by the number of messages they receive. It's not unusual to get dozens, or even hundreds, of messages every day. You can handle the deluge by organizing your messages into folders.

Most e-mail programs enable you to create your own mail folders. For example, you could create folders for each of the classes you're taking. In each folder, you can store mail from the teacher as well as from other students in the same class. You could create another folder to store mail from your family. In many e-mail programs you can create a rule to send e-mail to a specific folder or send an auto reply.

If you're trying to find a message in a lengthy message list, remember that you can sort the mail in different ways. By default, your e-mail program probably sorts mail in the order the messages were received. You can also sort by sender or recipient; some programs give you more ways to sort. With Microsoft Outlook you can quickly sort messages by clicking one of the buttons at the top of the message list. For example, to sort messages by date, click the Received button. Click it again to sort the list in the opposite order.

Still can't find a message or your e-mail program does not allow you to sort messages? Most e-mail programs provide a Find or Search command, which enables you to search for information in the message header. The best programs enable you to search for text in the message body as well. To search for a message within Outlook, enter a search term in the Search box. Results begin to display as soon as you begin typing.

A Few Last Reminders

Good file management is the hallmark of a competent computer user. File management should not be an intimidating or frustrating task. Computers are tremendously complex and powerful devices, but the principles of managing your work are simple. Plan and construct folder structures that make sense to you. Name your files in such a way that you can easily find them. Always begin at the beginning. If something doesn't work, go back to when it did. Read the manual. Follow directions carefully. Make backup copies of your work. And if all else fails, don't be afraid to ask for help.

Key Terms

Multiple Choice

Circle the correct choice for each of the following:

1. The default extension for Microsoft Word 2010 is:
   a. .pptx.
   b. .xlsx.
   c. .accdb.
   d. .docx.

2. A file name has two parts, the name and the
   _____.
   a. extension
   b. directory
   c. path
   d. letter

3. Another name for folder is _____.
   a. director
   b. directory
   c. file
   d. link

4. In Microsoft Windows 7, you can use up to _____ characters in a file name.
   a. unlimited
   b. 260
   c. 255
   d. 525

5. The file management utility that comes with Microsoft Windows 7 is called:
   a. Windows Internet.
   b. Internet Explorer.
   c. Windows Explorer.
   d. Windows Folders.

6. To locate a file or folder you can use the _____.
   a. Search box
   b. Where is it box
   c. Dynamic search
   d. Main folder

7. To invoke a context sensitive menu, you _____.
   a. right-click
   b. double-click
   c. left-click
   d. roll over the item

8. The Navigation pane on the left allows you to _____.
   a. navigate to the search box
   b. navigate directly to specific folder
   c. navigate directly to specific files
   d. navigate to the Internet

9. There are _____ different view options from the Change your view button.
   a. six
   b. seven
   c. eight
   d. nine

10. Which of the following does not leave a file in its original location.
    a. Copying
    b. Moving
    c. Saving As
    d. Creating a Shortcut

Spotlight Exercises

1. Launch Windows Explorer. Select a folder from the navigation pane. Sort the contents in the content pane, using the column headings. Sort it several different ways. Add or remove a few columns from the content pane. Write a brief paper that answers the following questions. Why is sorting beneficial? Which sort would you use most often? Why? List the sorts you tried and how you would use them. Why are some columns more beneficial than others? Which columns did you find more useful?

2. In this exercise, you will use the Windows Explorer program to use the group, stack, and filter options. Select a folder from the navigation pane. Using the dropdown arrow next to the sorted column, choose one of the options. Experiment with how it works and how it can be used. Repeat for the other options available. Write a one-page paper on the different options and how they can be used to help you in your courses.

3. Being able to locate your files and folders is very important. To locate files and folders we create a folder (directory) structure. In this exercise, you will use the Windows Explorer program to build a folder structure within the Documents folder. Create a top-level folder named with your name that contains three subfolders and then right-drag two or more files from some other source into one of the three subfolders (make sure you copy these files and do not move them). Click the new folder that has your name and then double-click on the subfolder that contains the files. Note the extensions on the files or the file names. Click in the Search Documents box and type in either the extension or file name. Once the list appears, press the *Print Screen* key that is at the top of the right side of your keyboard. Open a Microsoft Word document and press *Ctrl+v*. Type your name below the picture on your screen and follow your instructor's instructions to send it to him or her. When you are finished with all your exercises, you may want to delete the new folder structure you created if it is not on your personal computer.

4. Open your e-mail program. Create a new folder using the File, New, Folder menu sequence (in Outlook—other mail readers will have a similar method but may call folders something different, for example Gmail calls them labels). For the folder or label name, use the name and year of the term you are in now, such as Fall_2012. Open your new folder and create a folder/label for each of your classes. Now practice dragging messages back and forth between your Inbox folder and your new folders. Feel free to delete these folders/labels when you are through; make sure any e-mails in the folders can be deleted, or drag them back to their original locations. Write a paragraph describing your experience.

5. It is a very frustrating day when you go to open the term paper you spent hours creating and either it is not there or the content is incorrect. One way to help prevent this situation is to make backups of your files. Open Microsoft Word and create a short document stating why you should do backups. Save the file with the name "backup1.docx." You can use the folder structure you created earlier. After the file has been saved, make some changes to the document. Use Save As to save the document with the name "backup2.docx." Reopen backup1.docx. Make a few more changes to the document, explaining what you did. Save the document one more time as "backup3.docx." Be prepared to hand in your work.

6. Create a simple folder structure on your hard drive that consists of three folders named "draft_1," "draft_2," and "draft_3." Using the documents from Exercise 5 or others you may have on your computer, practice moving and copying the files to different folders. Use a flash drive to copy and move files. Write a short paper on the benefits of moving and copying files. When and why would you move a file? When and why would you copy a file?

chapter 4

System Software

Whatever happened to simple? When it comes to operating systems it seems that the names are as confusing as the products: Windows 95, Windows 98, Windows XP, Windows Vista, Windows 7—and don't forget Tiger, Leopard, and Snow Leopard. A little confused? Well, you're not alone. Besides wondering what the numbers and names stand for, you may have several other questions about operating systems. Which one is on my home computer, notebook, and smartphone? If different, are they all compatible? When is it necessary to upgrade an operating system, and how do I do it? How many more versions will there be? What is the difference between operating system software and application software?

This chapter will reveal answers to these questions while providing insight into the power and purpose of operating systems in use today.

Without software—the set of instructions that tells the computer what to do—a computer is just an expensive collection of wires and components. **System software** includes all the programs that provide the infrastructure and hardware control needed for a computer, its peripheral devices, and other programs to function smoothly. Although some system software works behind the scenes, some requires your guidance and control.

System software is often confused with application software—programs that assist user productivity such as writing a college essay or creating a presentation. System software has two major components: (1) the operating system and (2) system utilities that provide various maintenance functions. This chapter explains

- The difference between the operating system and system utilities, along with the functions each are responsible for

- Different operating systems, their newest versions, and their identifying features

- Utilities that every user should be familiar with, how to access them, and some of the settings that might help facilitate their use

- Some basic troubleshooting techniques in case of system software malfunction

Learning how to use an operating system and system utilities is the first step you should take toward mastering any computer system and ensuring a safe and enjoyable computing experience. ■

Check out **f** Facebook for our latest updates

www.facebook.com

The Operating System

The **operating system (OS)** is a set of programs designed to manage the resources of a computer. Its primary functions include

- Starting the computer and transferring files from the storage device to RAM memory
- Managing programs that are active and on the desktop and taskbar or running in the background
- Managing memory (RAM) to optimize its use
- Coordinating tasks including the communication between input and output devices and programs
- Providing a user interface to allow for easy and seamless communication with the user

The primary reason that a computer needs an operating system is to coordinate the interactions of its hardware components with each other as well as to coordinate their interaction with application software. The OS is most often located on a hard disk, although it can be stored and loaded from a USB drive, CD, or DVD. On some small handheld computers and smartphones, it is held on a memory chip within the system unit.

You can think of the OS as a traffic officer standing at a busy intersection (Figure 4.1). Imagine the traffic at a downtown New York City intersection at rush hour, and you'll have a good idea of what it's like inside a computer. Bits of information are whizzing around at incredible speeds, sent this way and that by the OS, the electronic equivalent of a harried traffic officer. Impatient peripherals and programs are honking electronic "horns," trying to get the officer's attention. As if the scene weren't chaotic enough, the "mayor" (the user) wants to come through right now. Just like a traffic officer, the computer's OS, standing at the intersection of the computer's hardware, application programs, and user, keeps traffic running smoothly.

Now that you have a visual of the importance and amount of control that the operating system has on your computer, notebook, or smartphone, let's examine the five functions of an OS more closely.

Starting the Computer

The first function of the operating system is to start the computer. When you start a computer, it loads the OS into the computer's RAM (remote access memory). To **load**

FIGURE 4.1 The operating system works at the intersection of application software, the user, and the computer's hardware.

Manages the computer system's hardware and peripheral devices

Provides a way for the user to interact with the computer

The operating system

Manages the memory and storage

Manages the processor

Provides a consistent means for software applications to work with the CPU means to transfer something from a storage device, such as the hard disk, to memory. RAM is a form of volatile memory. **Volatile memory** is storage that is very fast but that is erased when the power goes off. RAM is located on the motherboard and holds all programs in use and all documents in progress. The process of loading the OS to memory is called **booting**. This term has been used in computing circles since the very early days. It comes from an old saying that people can pull themselves up by their boot straps or, in other words, get started on their own. With a **cold boot**, you start a computer that has not yet been turned on. With a **warm boot**, you restart a computer that is already on. Warm boots, or **restarts** as they are currently called, are often necessary after installing new software or after an application crashes or stops working. In a PC you can restart a computer running a Windows OS by following these steps (Figure 4.2):

1. Click the Start button in Windows Vista and Windows 7.
2. Click on the right arrow located to the right of the lock button in Vista and to the right of the Shut down button in Windows 7.
3. Select Restart.

On a Mac press the Control + Command + Eject keys to restart the computer with the option to save changes in open documents. Use Control + Command + Power button to restart without the option to save changes in open documents. On either system, when the unit refuses to respond, attempt a warm boot or restart before using the Power off button on the system unit.

With both types of booting, the computer copies the kernel along with other essential portions of the OS from the hard disk into the computer's memory, where it remains while the computer is powered on and functioning. The **kernel** is the central part of the OS that consists of the instructions that control the actions the OS uses most frequently, for example,

1. Start button

2. Right arrow

3. Restart

FIGURE 4.2 In a newer OS like Windows 7, using the Restart option from the Start button is the preferred way of restarting a nonresponsive system.

starting applications and managing hardware devices and memory. The kernel resides in RAM at all times, so it must be kept as small as possible. Less frequently used portions of the OS are stored on the hard disk and retrieved as needed. Such portions are called *nonresident* because they do not reside in memory.

The booting of a system, whether it is a cold or warm boot, is a step-by-step process (Figure 4.3):

1. Activate the basic input/output system (BIOS)
2. Perform the power-on-self-test (POST)
3. Load the operating system into RAM
4. Configure and customize settings
5. Load needed system utilities
6. Authenticate the user

The following sections discuss each of these boot-up steps in detail.

Step 1: Activate the BIOS and Setup Program When you first turn on or reset a PC, electricity flows from the power supply through the system. When the CPU receives the signal that the power level is sufficient for the system to run, the CPU will

FIGURE 4.3 The Six Sequential Steps Involved in Starting a Computer

1. Locate and activate BIOS.
2. Initiate POST.
3. Load OS.
4. Configure and customize the system.
5. Load system utilities.
6. Authenticate user.

Leaving a computer running when it's not in use is wasteful. By default, a computer running Windows Vista and Windows 7 will go into Sleep mode after a period of inactivity, saving its owner $70 or more in annual energy costs. There are three energy settings you can adjust in Windows 7 to help conserve energy.

- Use **Sleep mode** to transfer the current state of your computer to RAM, turn off all unneeded functions, and place the system in a low-power state. Returning from Sleep mode is faster than returning from Hibernate due to the state of the computer being held in memory.

- Choose **Hibernate mode** to save battery power. Used primarily in notebooks, this mode puts your open documents and programs on your hard disk and then actually turns off your computer. When you restart your system, it is returned to the state prior to hibernation. All windows and programs that were open are restored automatically.

- If you are using a desktop, **Hybrid sleep** may be the option for you. This mode is a combination of sleep and Hibernate mode and puts open documents and programs in both RAM and on your hard disk, and then places the system in a low-power state so you can quickly resume your work. If power is suddenly terminated, the Hibernate portion of this mode guarantees that your work can be restored. Hybrid sleep is usually turned on by default on most desktops.

To access the settings for Sleep and Hibernate modes in either Windows 7 or Windows Vista, click the Start button and select the Control Panel option from the menu on the far right. Then find the power options, which are located in the System and Security category in Windows 7 and the System and Maintenance category in Windows Vista (Figure 4.4).

FIGURE 4.4 The On battery options should be 5 minutes or less to conserve battery life on a notebook computer.

In Windows 7, to place your system in Sleep or Hibernate mode, click the Start button and from the arrow to the right of the Shut down button select either Sleep or Hibernate (Figure 4.5). You can also put your computer into Sleep mode from the Start button by clicking the icon of the Power button. To wake your system, press the Power button on your system unit.

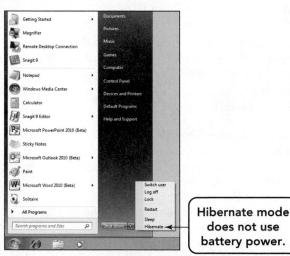

Hibernate mode does not use battery power.

FIGURE 4.5 In Windows 7, Hibernate and Sleep are easily activated from the Start menu.

If you are purchasing a new system, go one step further and purchase an Energy Star–qualified computer and monitor. New efficiency specifications mean that these products save energy while in use, not just while in Sleep mode. ●

start executing. The CPU can be said to have amnesia at this time; it has absolutely nothing at all in memory to execute or work on. So the processor makers have written programs, activated during this stage of start-up, to direct the CPU to the same place in the system, the BIOS ROM, for the start of the system's BIOS boot program. The **BIOS (basic input/output system)** is the part of the system software that provides the computer with the descriptions of the equipment that your system contains, typically the CPU, hard disk, RAM, and video component—equipment not usually replaced by the user. The operating system then uses the BIOS data to control those devices. Other external devices, such as jump drives and speakers, which are frequently replaced by a user, are not run by BIOS, but are controlled and accessed by the operating system. The BIOS is encoded, or permanently written, in the computer's ROM. **ROM**, or **read-only memory**, is **nonvolatile memory**—memory that is not easily edited and keeps its content even when the system powers off. It's these features that guarantee the reliability and reusability of the programs stored there. After the BIOS is located, you may briefly see the BIOS screen, a text-only screen that provides information about BIOS-controlled devices (Figure 4.6).

While the BIOS information is visible, you can access the computer's setup program by pressing a special key, such as Del or F8. (During the boot process, you'll see an on-screen message indicating which key to press to access the setup program.) If your system displays a logo instead of the BIOS access information, press the Esc or Tab key while the logo is showing to enter the setup program. The **setup program** includes settings that control the computer's hardware. Entering this program is not easy and you should *not* alter or change *any* of these settings without understanding the purpose of each setting and the problems that can arise from incorrect entries. Making an incorrect change to a BIOS device will cause the system not to boot.

Step 2: Initiate the Power-On Self-Test
After the BIOS instructions are loaded into memory, a series of tests are conducted to make sure that the computer and associated peripherals are operating correctly.

Collectively, these tests are known as the **power-on self-test (POST)**. Among the components tested are the computer's main memory (RAM), the keyboard, mouse, disk drives, and the hard disk. If any of the power-on self-tests fail, you'll hear a beep, see an on-screen error message, and the computer will stop. You often can correct such problems by making sure that components, such as keyboards, are plugged in securely.

However, some failures are so serious that the computer cannot display an error message; instead, it sounds a certain number of beeps. If this happens, it's time to call for technical support. To help the technician repair the computer, write down any error messages you see and try to remember how many beeps you heard.

CPU manufacturer, type, and speed

FIGURE 4.6 This BIOS screen is for a system with an Intel Core i7 CPU running at 2666 MHz.

Step 3: Load the Operating System
Once the power-on self-test is successfully completed, the BIOS initiates a search for the operating system. Options (or settings) in the setup program determine where the BIOS looks for the OS. If multiple possible locations exist (such as an optical drive, a floppy drive, or a hard disk), the settings also specify the search order. If no OS is found in the first location, the BIOS moves on to the next location.

On most PCs, the BIOS first looks for the OS on the computer's hard disk. When the BIOS finds the OS, it loads the OS's kernel into memory. At that point, the OS takes control of the computer and begins loading system configuration information.

Step 4: Configure the System
In Microsoft Windows, configuration information about installed peripherals and software is stored in a database called the **registry**. The registry also contains information about your system configuration choices, such as

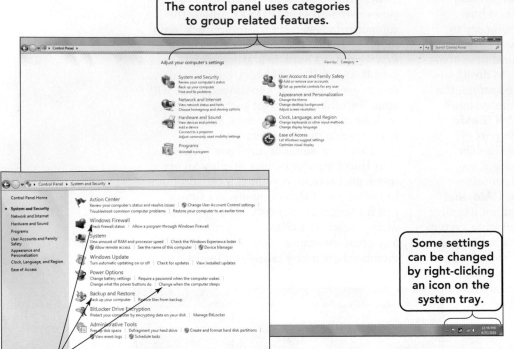

The control panel uses categories to group related features.

Key system settings can be set from the System and Security category.

Some settings can be changed by right-clicking an icon on the system tray.

FIGURE 4.7 Many options for managing and customizing your computer system can be found on the Control Panel under one of the eight main categories.

background graphics and mouse settings.

Once the operating system's kernel has been loaded, it checks the system's configuration to determine which drivers and other utility programs are needed. A **driver** is a utility program that contains instructions to make a peripheral device addressable or usable by an OS. If a peripheral device that is already installed on the system requires a driver to operate, that peripheral's driver will be installed and loaded automatically. If the driver is missing or has become corrupted, you may be prompted to insert a CD or download the needed driver from the manufacturer's Web site.

Windows and Mac operating systems are equipped with **plug-and-play (PnP)** capabilities, which automatically detect new PnP-compatible peripherals that you might have installed while the power was switched off, load the necessary drivers, and check for conflicts with other devices. Peripheral devices equipped with PnP features identify themselves to the OS and require no action on the part of the user.

Step 5: Load System Utilities After the operating system has detected and configured all of the system's hardware, it loads system utilities such as speaker volume control, antivirus software, and power management options. In Microsoft Windows, you can view available custom configuration choices by right-clicking the

icon of the feature you want to reconfigure located in the system tray (located on the right side of the Windows taskbar) or through the Control Panel located on the Start menu (Figure 4.7).

Step 6: Authenticate a User When the operating system finishes loading, you may see a request for a user name and password. Through this process, called **authentication** (or **login**), you verify that you are indeed the person who is authorized to use the computer.

Today, most consumer-oriented operating systems, such as Microsoft Windows and Mac OS, require or highly recommend that you supply a user name and password to use the computer. A **profile**, a record of a specific user's preferences for the desktop theme, icons, and menu styles, is associated with a user name. If you set up a profile for yourself, your preferences will appear on the screen after you log on. You can enable other users to create profiles that are associated with their user names and passwords so that when they log in they'll see their preferences without disturbing yours. It is always wise to create an Administrator account to manage installing and uninstalling software, operating system devices, and resetting forgotten passwords. The Administrator account should be password protected with only one or two trusted users having access.

On multiuser computer systems such as in a university lab or a corporate office environment, you must have an account to access a computer. Your **account** consists of your user name, password, and storage space, which is called a *user folder* or *user directory*. The account is usually created by a server/computer administrator, who is a person responsible for managing the accounts.

Now that the OS is loaded and running, let's look at another important task that the OS handles: managing applications.

Managing Applications

The operating system function that most dramatically affects overall quality of the system is the ability to run and manage applications. When you start an application, the CPU loads the application from storage into RAM. In the early days of personal computing, **single-tasking operating systems** could run only one application at a time, which was often inconvenient. To switch between applications, you had to quit one application before you could start the second.

Today, multitasking operating systems are the norm. **Multitasking operating systems** enable more than one application to run at the same time. With multitasking operating systems, the computer may not actually run two applications at once, but switches between them as needed. For example, a user might be running two applications, such as Word and Excel, simultaneously. From the user's perspective, one application (the **foreground application**) is active, whereas the other (the **background application**) appears inactive, as indicated by its appearance on the desktop (Figure 4.8).

A clear measure of the operating system's stability is the technique it uses to handle multitasking. If one of the running applications invades another's memory space, one or both of the applications will become unstable or, at the extreme, crash.

Most current operating systems use a more recent, improved type of multitasking called **preemptive multitasking**, an environment in which programs do not run from start to finish but are interrupted or suspended in order to start or continue to run another task. In this system each task receives a recurring slice of time from the CPU. Depending on the operating system, the time slice may be the same for all programs or it may be adjustable to meet a program's hardware and user demands. When one task uses its time slice or is

interrupted by a task of higher priority, the task is suspended and the other started. This method of multitasking ensures that all applications have fair access to the CPU and prevents one program from monopolizing it at the expense of the others. Even if one program becomes unstable or stops working, the OS and other applications will continue to run. Although you may lose unsaved work in the application that fails to respond, chances are good that everything else will be fine.

Now that you understand how the OS manages individual and multiple applications, let's take a look at how it manages RAM, its primary memory.

Managing Memory

If the operating system had to constantly access program instructions from their storage location on your computer's hard disk, programs would run very slowly. A **buffer**, an area that temporarily holds data and instructions, is needed to make the processing of instructions more fluid. Computers use RAM, a temporary storage medium, to function as this buffer. The computer's OS is responsible for managing this memory. The OS gives each running program and some devices their own portion of RAM and attempts to keep the

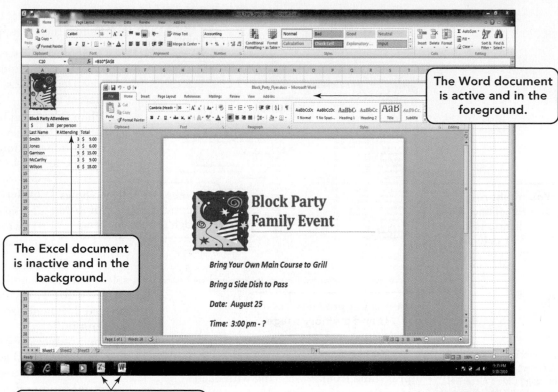

The Word document is active and in the foreground.

The Excel document is inactive and in the background.

An icon appears on the taskbar for each open application.

FIGURE 4.8 Today multitasking operating systems are the norm, and most users keep more than one application open at a time. The taskbar displays an icon for each open program.

Select the Processes tab to view a list of processes running.

You might recognize the Excel and Word applications in the first column.

The memory column shows the current amount of RAM each process is using.

The status bar provides details on CPU and memory usage.

FIGURE 4.9 Access the Windows Task Manager by pressing Ctrl + Alt + Del and selecting the Start Task Manager option. Details on all processes running are displayed along with total CPU usage.

FIGURE 4.10 The print icon on the system tray provides fast access to the print queue. If the printer is on a network, you might need administrator rights to access and delete documents in the queue.

programs from interfering with each other's use of memory (Figure 4.9).

A print buffer is a good example. Have you ever given the command to print three documents of reasonable length, one right after another? While the printer is printing the first document, the second and third documents are being held in the print buffer. The documents wait in the buffer until the spooling program, a program that monitors the print jobs in the buffer and the busy state of the printer, indicates that the printer is available. The second document will then move from the buffer to the printer. This process continues until the print buffer is empty. Have you ever wondered why turning off the printer to stop the printing of a document doesn't work? Well, stopping the printer does not erase the print buffer. When you turn the printer on again, the documents in the print buffer continue to print. So, how do you stop

documents in the print buffer from printing? Follow the steps listed below:

1. Once a print instruction is given, a print icon will appear on the system tray. Double-click the print icon on the system tray.
2. When the dialog box opens, a window in which the user can supply additional information, you will see the queue, a list of names of the documents in the print buffer.
3. Select the document you want to erase from the queue.

From the menu in this dialog box, select Document and then Cancel (Figure 4.10). This will remove the selected document from the queue and the print buffer.

Today's operating systems can make the computer's RAM seem larger than it really is. This trick is accomplished by means of **virtual memory**, a method of using a portion of the computer's hard disk as an extension of RAM. In virtual memory, program instructions and data are divided into units of fixed size called **pages**. If memory is full, the OS starts storing copies of pages in a hard disk file called the **swap file**. This file is not an application but a temporary storage space for bits and bytes that the OS will access as you do your work. When the pages are needed, they are copied back into RAM (Figure 4.11). The transferring of files from the hard disk to RAM and back is called **paging**.

Although virtual memory enables users to work with more memory than the amount of RAM installed on the computer, excessive paging is called **thrashing** and slows down the system. Accessing data from a hard disk is much slower than accessing it from RAM. For this reason, adding more RAM to your computer is often the best way to improve its performance. With sufficient RAM, the OS makes minimal use of virtual memory.

Instead of using the hard drive for virtual memory, Windows Vista and Windows 7 come with Windows ReadyBoost, a feature that allows for the allocation of space on removable memory devices that can be used to increase the size of RAM memory. ReadyBoost performance is better than hard disk virtual memory because accessing files on flash memory (USB flash drives and secure digital SD memory cards) is quicker than accessing

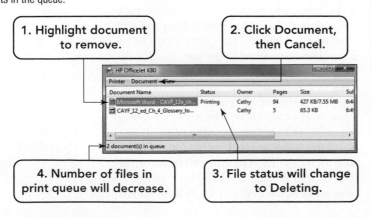

1. Highlight document to remove.

2. Click Document, then Cancel.

4. Number of files in print queue will decrease.

3. File status will change to Deleting.

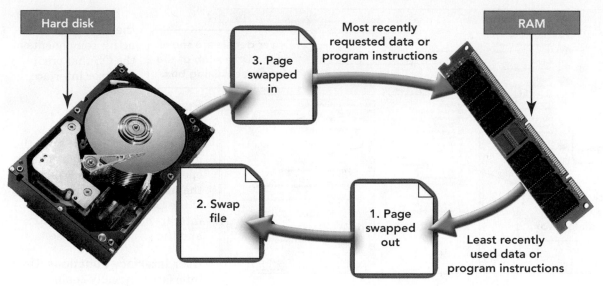

Hard disk

3. Page swapped in

Most recently requested data or program instructions

RAM

2. Swap file

1. Page swapped out

Least recently used data or program instructions

information on a hard drive. To allocate flash memory, follow these steps (Figure 4.12):

1. Insert a flash device into your system. The operating system checks to see whether the device can perform fast enough to work with Windows Ready-Boost. If it can, an additional option, Speed up my system, will appear at the bottom of the AutoPlay menu.

2. From the AutoPlay menu, select Speed up my system (usually the last option).

3. If your device is ReadyBoost-compatible, the next dialog box should open with the ReadyBoost tab active. Select the radio button option to Use this device and set the amount of space you want to allocate for memory use. In Windows 7 there is no upper limit on the amount that can be allocated. If your flash media does not have the option to make use of ReadyBoost, the ReadyBoost tab will indicate that the device is not compatible.

4. Click Apply and then click OK.

Once the computer's OS is running and managing applications and memory, its next responsibility is to be able to coordinate activities from accepting data and commands to representing the results of processing operations.

Coordinating Tasks

How does your computer "know" that you want it to do something? How does it

show you the results of its work? Another operating system function is coordinating tasks involving input and output devices, as well as enabling communication with these devices and the programs in use.

Most operating systems come with drivers for popular input and output devices. Device drivers are programs that contain specific instructions to allow a particular brand and model of input or output device to function properly. The driver enables communication between the OS and the input and output devices connected to a computer system. Printers, scanners, monitors, speakers, and the mouse all have drivers (Figure 4.13). Hardware manufacturers usually update their drivers when they develop a new operating system. You can also obtain updated drivers yourself from the manufacturer's Web site if they are not already included with the OS. When you change devices, the Windows operating system provides a feature called Windows Update that can automatically detect new hardware and install the required driver in less than one minute. Windows Update also

FIGURE 4.11 Only a portion of RAM is allocated to virtual memory. A user can increase this amount; however, a better solution would be to purchase more RAM.

FIGURE 4.12 It is fairly easy to set up ReadyBoost to enhance your virtual memory.

1. From the AutoPlay menu, select Speed up my system.

2. On the ReadyBoost tab, select Use this device.

3. Set the amount of space.

1. Select Device Manager.

2. Double-click the device name to open its Properties dialog box.

3. Driver details are shown on the Driver tab of the Properties dialog box.

FIGURE 4.13 The Device Manager is accessible from the Hardware and Sound option in the Control Panel and provides information on the devices connected to your computer and the drivers they are using.

handles the retrieval and installation of new drivers as they are needed. But new drivers aren't always needed. If your device is working properly, you may not need to upgrade the driver. A good rule of thumb is: If it's not broken, don't fix it.

Hardware, such as input and output devices, as well as software can generate **interrupts**, signals that inform the OS that an event has occurred and is in need of immediate attention. For hardware, this can be the user pressing a key, the mouse moving to a new position, or a notice that a document is waiting to print. A software event that generates an interrupt would be an attempt to divide by zero. This operation is undefined and throws the system into an interrupt to prevent the processor from attempting something that cannot be done. Software interrupts are handled mostly by the processor, whereas hardware interrupts are handled by the OS. Our discussion will focus on hardware interrupts.

The OS provides **interrupt handlers**, also called **interrupt service routines**, which are miniprograms that immediately respond when an interrupt occurs. The type of response or action the handler initiates depends on the type and source of the interrupt. On a busy system, multiple interrupts can occur at the same time. Remember the traffic officer analogy at the beginning of this chapter. In the case of multiple interrupts, the responses are held in RAM in an **interrupt vector table** and are processed, by the operating system, starting with the one having the highest priority rating to the one with the lowest. The actual interrupting of an event by an interrupt signal is called an **interrupt request (IRQ)**.

Now let's explore the visual and interactive components of the OS that create the user interface.

Providing the User Interface

From the user's perspective, the most important function of an operating system is providing the **user interface**, the part of the OS that facilitates your interaction with the computer and the programs you use.

User Interface Functions User interfaces typically enable you to do the following:

- Start (launch) application programs.
- Manage storage devices, such as hard disks, optical drives, and USB drives, and organize files. The interface provides options to copy files from one storage device to another, rename files, and delete files.
- Shut down the computer safely by following an orderly shutdown procedure.

Types of User Interfaces The three types of user interfaces are graphical, menu driven, and command-line interfaces (Figure 4.14).

By far the most popular user interface, a **graphical user interface** (**GUI**; pronounced "goo-ee"), uses graphics and the point-and-click technology of the mouse to make the operating system and programs easier to use. On most of today's computers, GUIs are used to engage the user through the **desktop**, the screen image that appears after the OS finishes loading into memory (RAM). A typical desktop on most personal computers can be divided into three regions (Figure 4.15):

- The left side of the desktop is where the Start button and icons appear. **Icons** are small images that represent computer resources such as programs, data files, and network connections.
- The right side of the desktop is where an invisible 1-inch vertical strip called the **sidebar** is positioned. In the sidebar the user can place and arrange **gadgets**, applications that appear as active icons that are

Graphical interface

Menu-driven
interface

Command-line-driven interface

FIGURE 4.14 Examples of graphical, menu-driven, and command-line Interfaces. Most handheld devices today, for example, GPS systems and smartphones, make use of the graphical interface.

constantly running to keep you updated on weather changes, stock prices, and current events, to name a few. This feature was not available in operating systems prior to Vista.

• The center of the desktop is where the programs you open will appear in a window structure. Windows can be re-sized and rearranged so that multiple ones can be cascaded or tiled and viewed on the screen at the same time

Windows—center

Sidebar—right side

Icons—left side

Gadgets

Start menu—left side

Start button

Programs in use

Control Panel Option

Taskbar

System tray

FIGURE 4.15 Remember that the desktop has a left, center, and right region, with certain icons appearing in each region.

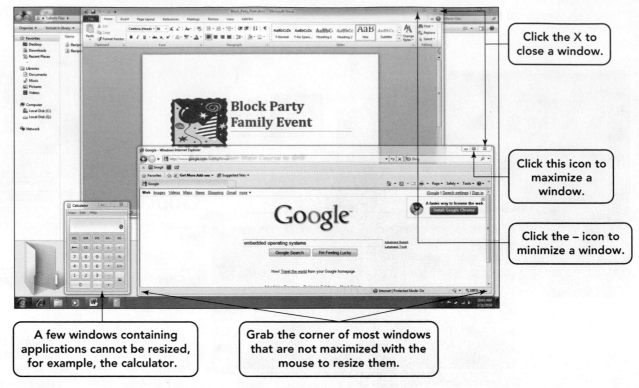

Click the X to close a window.

Click this icon to maximize a window.

Click the – icon to minimize a window.

A few windows containing applications cannot be resized, for example, the calculator.

Grab the corner of most windows that are not maximized with the mouse to resize them.

FIGURE 4.16 Most users have a preference for the arrangement of open windows and use the maximize, minimize, and resize features of a window to create a unique layout.

(Figure 4.16). Windows can also be maximized to take up the entire desktop. In maximized form they will cover your icons and gadgets.

The desktop image can change with the OS or OS version, and certain components of it can be customized by the user to create a personal look. The use of the

Appearance and Personalization option located in the Control Panel is one way for a user to make changes in the desktop appearance, while other features, such as gadgets, can be added and deleted by right-clicking in the sidebar (Figure 4.17).

Menu-driven user interfaces enable you to avoid memorizing key words

FIGURE 4.17 You can set desktop options from the Control Panel or by right-clicking the sidebar.

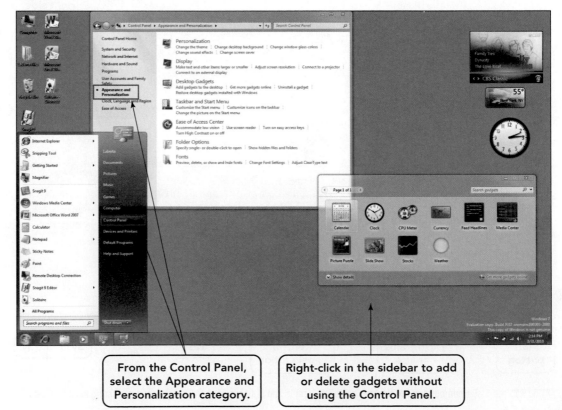

From the Control Panel, select the Appearance and Personalization category.

Right-click in the sidebar to add or delete gadgets without using the Control Panel.

(such as *copy* and *paste*) and syntax (a set of rules for entering commands). On-screen, text-based menus show all the options available at a given point. With most systems, you select an option with the arrow keys and then press Enter, click the desired option with the mouse, or strike a designated keyboard letter.

So what type of interface is used in Windows 7 and Vista? Are they systems that use a GUI or menu-driven user interface? If you have used one or both of these operating systems, then you know that they are actually a combination of both. It is very difficult to place an icon for every option somewhere on the main window of any program. Often the icons for the most frequently used options are visible on the Ribbon or toolbar. The less frequently used features can be accessed though menus or dialog boxes that were opened by selecting a menu option or clicking an icon.

Command-line user interfaces require you to type commands using keywords that tell the OS what to do (such as *Format* or *Copy*) one line at a time. You must observe complicated rules of syntax that specify exactly what you can type in a given place. For example, the following command copies a file from the hard disk drive C to a removable USB drive identified as drive F:

```
copy C:\myfile.txt F:\myfile.txt
```

Command-line user interfaces aren't popular with most users because they require memorization, and it's easy to make a typing mistake. Although the commands are usually very simple, such as *Copy* and *Paste*, others are more cryptic. However, some experienced users actually prefer command-line interfaces because they can operate the computer quickly after memorizing the keywords and syntax.

Now that you've seen how the OS makes itself available to you, let's explore the most popular OSs in depth.

Exploring Popular Operating Systems

We will look at the three categories of operating systems: **stand-alone operating systems** that are used by single users, **server operating systems** used in client/server network environments, and **embedded operating systems** that are

FIGURE 4.18 Operating Systems by Category

Category	Name
Stand-alone	DOS—developed for original IBM PC Windows 3.X, Windows 95, Windows 98, Windows 2000 Professional, Windows ME, Windows XP, Windows Vista, Windows 7 MAC OS X UNIX Linux
Server	Windows NT Server, Windows 2000 Server, Windows Server 2003, Windows Server 2008 UNIX Linux Novell Netware Solaris Red Hat Enterprise Server
Embedded	Windows CE (variations are Windows Mobile, Pocket PC) iPhone OS Palm OS BlackBerry OS Embedded Linux Google Android Symbian OS

found on ROM chips in the portable or dedicated devices we use today (Figure 4.18). Although your choice of operating system might be limited by the computing device you own and the network you are using, you should know how the various systems have evolved and their strengths and weaknesses.

Stand-Alone Operating Systems

A stand-alone operating system works on a desktop computer, notebook, or any portable computing device. The name *stand-alone* comes from the fact that it does not need to be connected to any other system or computer in order to run. Almost all of the operating systems in this class (category) have been enhanced with enough networking capabilities and connectivity options to allow them to manage a home or small business network. The keyword here is *small*.

Microsoft Windows Microsoft Windows is by far the most popular group of operating systems. Over the years, it has gone through several iterations and is now considered *the* operating system of

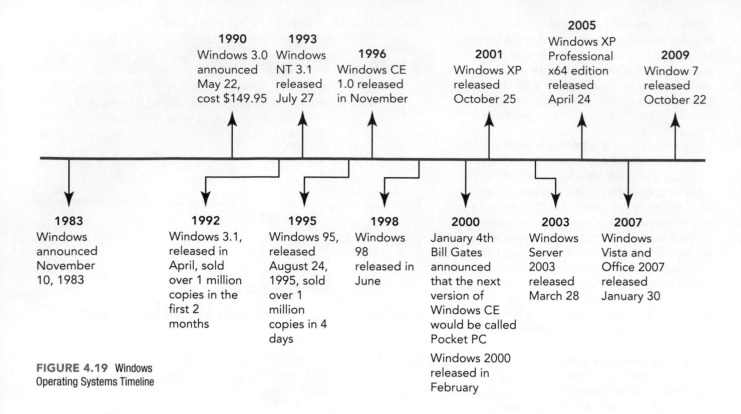

1990
Windows 3.0 announced May 22, cost $149.95

1993
Windows NT 3.1 released July 27

1996
Windows CE 1.0 released in November

2001
Windows XP released October 25

2005
Windows XP Professional x64 edition released April 24

2009
Window 7 released October 22

1983
Windows announced November 10, 1983

1992
Windows 3.1, released in April, sold over 1 million copies in the first 2 months

1995
Windows 95, released August 24, 1995, sold over 1 million copies in 4 days

1998
Windows 98 released in June

2000
January 4th Bill Gates announced that the next version of Windows CE would be called Pocket PC

Windows 2000 released in February

2003
Windows Server 2003 released March 28

2007
Windows Vista and Office 2007 released January 30

FIGURE 4.19 Windows Operating Systems Timeline

PCs worldwide. Figure 4.19 is a compressed timeline highlighting some key developments in the Windows OS over the years. A very detailed timeline is available at **www.computerhope.com/history/windows.htm**. When you purchase a computer, it usually comes with an OS already installed. Microsoft has agreements with the major computer manufacturers to provide Windows on almost all of the personal computers that are made today. Some manufacturers offer a choice of operating systems, but Windows is expected to remain the standard for years to come.

Microsoft Windows 7, the latest version of the Microsoft Windows operating system, was released in late 2009 and is available in six different versions: Starter, Home Basic, Home Premium, Professional, Enterprise, and Ultimate (Figure 4.20). All versions of Windows 7 promise to be more efficient than its predecessor, performing equally or better on the same hardware, and claim to have resolved the compatibility issues that existed between applications.

Windows 7 includes several new features to make using a PC notebook easier. See Figure 4.21 for an overview of four of these features. Test them out and decide for yourself whether they make your notebook computing experience more enjoyable and somewhat faster.

Released to the general public in January 2007, **Microsoft Windows Vista** replaced the popular Windows XP operating system and is designed for home and professional use. Vista is available in five different versions—Basic, Home Premium, Business, Ultimate, and Enterprise. Vista introduced features such as translucent windows, three-dimensional animation, and live taskbar thumbnails—just hover the mouse over a button on the taskbar to get a preview of its contents. Vista also addressed the growing popularity of mobile computing. Previously, tablet PCs required the Windows XP Tablet PC Edition OS, but Vista supported tablet PCs and other mobile devices through the Windows Mobility Center. This OS differentiated itself from previous Windows releases by its improved search features and networking tools, integrated speech recognition capabilities, and new multimedia tools such as gadgets.

MAC OS

The original Macintosh operating system, called **Mac OS**, released in 1984, was the first OS to bring the GUI to the world. Although Apple eventually lost market share to Microsoft, it has a diehard fan base. Many prefer the Mac OS for its stability and ease of use, although the

FIGURE 4.20 Windows 7 Editions

Edition	Features
Windows 7 Starter	Designed for small notebook computers, this edition was originally known as "the one that would not let you run more than three applications at a time." The decision on the limit of three was reversed, and the final version can run just about any Windows task. When multitasking, it is recommended that you avoid high-resource tasks like watching a DVD. This edition must be preinstalled on notebooks and is not available for individual purchase.
Windows 7 Home Basic	This is the other "nonpremium" edition available only in emerging markets (not in the United States, Canada, Europe, and other developed nations). It is more graphically interesting than Starter but lacks premium features like Windows Media Center.
Windows 7 Home Premium	This is the entry-level edition for most average consumers. It has the full Aero interface (translucent design, subtle animation, and additional colors) and Windows Media Center.
Windows 7 Professional	This is the preferred edition for businesses and advanced home users. It builds on Home Premium and runs a remote desktop server, encrypts files, and makes network folders available offline.
Windows 7 Enterprise	Enterprise and Ultimate editions have most of the same features, but the Enterprise edition is geared to enterprise users and is available through volume licensing.
Windows 7 Ultimate	The Ultimate edition is for the high-end user, gamer, and multimedia professionals. It includes BitLocker disk encryption, which now works on USB flash drives.

interfaces of Macs and PCs are becoming very similar (Figure 4.22). Operating systems for the MAC were numbered as Mac OS 8, Mac OS 9, and Mac OS X (X for the Roman numeral 10). Newer versions of Mac OS X have, in addition to their numeric identification, been given names associated with large cats. Mac OS v10.0 is called Cheetah and Mac OS v10.6 is labeled Snow Leopard.

FIGURE 4.21 Windows 7 Features That Make Using a Notebook PC Simple

Feature	Description
Jump list	A list activated by right-clicking an icon on the taskbar or the Start menu. The options in the list are specific to the icon clicked. By selecting an option in the jump list, the user instantly gets the result.
Pin	A method of attaching your favorite program anywhere on the taskbar by dragging it from the desktop to the taskbar. Removing it from the taskbar is done by dragging it off the taskbar.
Snap	A quick (and fun) new way to resize open windows by dragging them to the edges of your screen.
Windows Search	A feature activated by simply typing a description of what you want to locate in the search box located at the bottom of the Start menu. The results will be a list of relevant documents, pictures, music, and e-mail that match your entered description. Because most users store data on several devices, Windows 7 is designed to search external hard drives, networked PCs, and libraries (a Windows 7 feature that groups related files together regardless of their storage location).

The menu bar contains commands and tasks for the current application.

The System Preferences panel is similar to the Windows Control Panel.

The Dock, similar to the Windows taskbar, provides access to frequently used applications and those currently in use.

The dashboard icon is used to access widgets, similar to the gadgets stored on the sidebar in Windows 7.

FIGURE 4.22 Today the Mac OS X interface and Windows 7 are very similar.

For a detailed explanation on what Mac OS X is, go to **www.apple.com/macosx/what-is-macosx/**.

Mac OS X Snow Leopard, the current version of Mac OS X released in August 2009, has a smaller memory footprint (taking up to 50 percent less RAM than the previous version). It includes a more responsive and snappier Finder, a Put Back option to return deleted items to their original location, more reliable ejection of external drives, faster shut down and wake up, four new fonts, 80 percent faster Time Machine backup, increased Airport signal strength for wireless networks, and built-in support for Microsoft Exchange Server 2007. For a detailed review of the features incorporated into Snow Leopard, visit **www.apple.com/macosx/refinements/enhancements-refinements.html**.

UNIX

Developed at AT&T's Bell Laboratories in 1969, UNIX is a pioneering operating system that continues to define what an OS should do and how it should work. **UNIX** (pronounced "you-nix") was the first OS written in the C language. It is a free OS installed primarily on workstations and features preemptive multitasking.

If UNIX is so great, why didn't it take over the computer world? One reason is the lack of compatibility among the many different versions of UNIX. Another reason is that it's difficult to use. UNIX defaults to a command-line user interface, which is challenging for new computer users. An online tutorial on UNIX is available at **www.ee.surrey.ac.uk/Teaching/Unix**.

In the past few years, a number of GUI interfaces have been developed for UNIX, improving its usability (Figure 4.23). Did you know that the Mac OS X is based on UNIX?

Linux

In 1991, Finnish university student Linus Torvalds introduced **Linux**, his new freeware operating system for personal computers (Figure 4.24). He hoped Linux would offer users a free alternative to UNIX. Linux has since been further developed by thousands of programmers, who have willingly donated their time to make sure that Linux is a very good version of UNIX. The community approach to Linux has made it a marvel of the computer world and has made Torvalds a folk legend.

Linux is **open source software**, meaning that its source code (the code of the program itself) is available for all to see and use. Unlike most other commercial software, which hide the program's code and prohibit users from analyzing it to see how the program was written, users of open source software are invited to scrutinize the source code for errors and to share their discoveries with the software's publisher. Experience shows that this approach is often a very effective measure against software defects.

What makes Linux so attractive? Two things: It's powerful and it's free. Linux brings many features similar to those found in commercial versions of UNIX, including multitasking, virtual memory, Internet support, and a GUI, to the PC.

FIGURE 4.24 Ubuntu version 9.10, also referred to as Karmic Koala, is a popular version of Linux that features a Windows-like GUI interface and includes programs such as a media player, image editor, and the Firefox Web browser.

Although Linux is powerful and free, there are some versions that are proprietary or are available for a fee. Because Linux isn't a commercial product with a single stable company behind it, many corporate chief information officers shy away from its adoption. When someone needs technical support, they have to find a Web site such as **www.redhat.com** or someone who knows more about Linux than they do—this is not the same as calling technical support when your Mac OS X or Windows 7 operating system ceases to operate. Linux is gaining acceptance, especially for use with Web servers. One main drawback to using Linux was its inability to run Microsoft Office applications. Recently, through the development of proprietary software as VMWare and WINE, this is becoming less of a problem.

The beauty of Linux, and its development model, is that it doesn't run on any particular type of computer: It runs on them all. Linux has been translated to run on systems as small as iPods and as large as homegrown supercomputers. For the latest in Linux news and developments, visit Linux Today at **www.linuxtoday. com**. Linux beginners can get assistance at **www.justlinux.com** and at **www. linux.org**.

ETHICS

The inequity in computer equipment and computer-related knowledge between developed, developing, and underdeveloped nations always brings economic, educational, and ethical issues to the foreground. Whose responsibility is it to bridge this gap? The One Laptop per Child (OLPC) initiative is trying to bring equity in access to computers to these diverse populations by focusing on the child. The idea was founded by Nicholas Negroponte and others associated with MIT Media Lab in conjunction with several corporate partners, such as Google, AMD, and Red Hat. The goal of the initiative is to provide low-cost, low-power, rugged, and connected notebook computers to the world's poorest children. The aim is to encourage self-discovery, collaboration, and self-empowered learning.

OLPC and Red Hat have jointly developed Sugar, the OLPC Linux operating system, which is based on Red Hat's open source operating system called Fedora (actually named for the type of hat that is the logo for Red Hat products). This operating system focuses on activities rather than the applications. Figure 4.25 illustrates the first image a child will see when the system boots. It is symbolic of a man (represented by an O on top of the letter X) surrounded by other symbols that stand for home, friends, and community.

Although support is strong, there are still some obstacles, for example, getting Internet to some of the remote and poorer regions. Those who don't support the project say that without Internet accessibility in the poorest regions, the computers given to the children won't close the digital divide. Instead, they will increase the toxic waste from discarded computers that either don't work or are in need of repairs.

What do you think? Is the initiative something that should continue despite the problems? Is it truly the answer to the problem? Or do the dangers to the environment outweigh the potential benefits?

FIGURE 4.25 The Notebook Provided to Children through the One Laptop per Child Initiative

PC Versus Mac Versus Linux

Traditionally, computer users have had two major platforms to choose from. A **platform** is determined by the combination of microprocessor chip and operating system used by a distinct type of computer, such as a Mac or a PC. Previously, Macs used a Motorola or IBM chip and the Mac OS, and PCs have used an Intel or AMD chip and the Windows OS. Macs have since switched to Intel chips, which has blurred the platform lines a bit because they can now run the Windows OS too. Depending on which OS is loaded on a computer, it is simply referred to as a Mac or a PC. As the Linux OS becomes more popular, some people may want to consider a third alternative.

The debate over which platform is best has raged for years, and if market power is anything, PCs are winning by a landslide. But Apple hangs in there with its slew of adherents who choose to "think different." What's the difference between the platforms? Although you'd never know from listening to people who love or hate Macs, there's really not much difference, at least not in terms of power. Still, the debate goes on.

On the one side, Mac lovers say their machines are easier to set up and use. Macs come with everything you need built right in—simply plug them in and you're on your way. Mac lovers also point out that Apple has developed some incredibly advanced technology. (Even PC users will agree to that.)

It's not just the system and the software Mac users love. Most Macophiles love their one-button mice as well as their many shortcut keys. In addition, certain professions, especially creative fields such as graphic design, rely almost exclusively on Macs.

Linux offers another option. Linux can be installed on a Mac or a PC, and because it is open source software, cost isn't an issue. Security is another benefit. Few types of malware are targeted at Linux machines. Experts disagree on whether this is due to the security of the Linux OS or the fact that there are so few systems that hackers can't create the chain reaction they can easily muster using Windows. The casual user cites the lack of structured computer support and the level of computer knowledge required to set up a Linux system as the main deterrent.

However, PCs still dominate, and the race isn't even close. PCs claim the largest chunk of the marketplace and are the choice of corporate America. They tend to be cheaper in terms of both their hardware and software, with a much larger selection of software products to choose from than their Mac or Linux counterparts. In recent years, Apple, through its humorous "I am a Mac, I am a PC" commercials, has tried to woo PC users by playing on the idea that Macs are easier to use. However, software products developed for Windows greatly outnumber those written for Macs, one reason PCs have led the marketplace. But now that Mac OS X can run Windows, Mac users are able to run existing Windows software. Unfortunately, as Apple moves into the PC market with its recent innovations, it may make itself more vulnerable to the viruses that have been, until now, mostly a PC headache. In any case, both Macs and Linux have a long way to go to catch PCs—and few experts see that happening any time soon. It is only fair to mention that, although slow to catch on in the PC market, the growth of Linux in the area of server installations has been exponential.

For a look at a humorous spin on the familiar "I am a Mac, I am a PC" commercial that includes the arrival of Linux, watch the clip at **www.youtube.com/watch?v=cldeHjFig_c**. Figure 4.26 illustrates differences in the use of the big three as of March 2010.

The cost of software and frequent upgrades is a source of concern for all users, regardless of the platform they are using. Open source software seems to be a viable solution for this problem; however, some warning is needed. Arguments can be presented to support the fact that although the software is free, you pay for quality support or the courses to learn to support the OS yourself.

Operating System Usage

1% 2%
5%
92%

- Windows
- Mac
- Linux
- Other

FIGURE 4.26 Windows operating systems dominate the market, with Mac OS X and Linux quite a distance behind.

Server Operating Systems

Server operating systems are designed for network use. Normally they are complete operating systems with a file and task manager. Additional features like a Web server, directory services, and a messaging system may also be included.

Microsoft Windows Server 2008 An upgrade to Microsoft Windows Server 2003, **Microsoft Windows Server 2008** is a sophisticated operating system specifically designed to support client/server computing systems in a corporate environment. Servers are special computers used to manage various resources on a network, including printers and other devices, file storage, and Web sites. Windows Server 2008 shares many similarities in architecture and functionality with Windows Vista because the underlying code is closely related. Benefits include the following:

- **Security.** New technologies help prevent unauthorized access to corporate networks, data, and user accounts.
- **Web server.** Enhanced capabilities are available for developing and hosting Web applications and services.
- **Administration.** All configuration and maintenance is done through the command-line interface or through remote administration.
- **Virtualization.** Multiple servers can be consolidated as separate virtual machines on a single physical server, and multiple operating systems can run in parallel.

Other Server Operating Systems Other server operating systems that you might hear mentioned are listed below:

- UNIX and Linux are also categorized in the stand-alone section. They are actually referred to as multipurpose operating systems because they fall into both categories.
- Netware by Novell is a client/server system that manages concurrent requests from clients and provides the security needed in a multiuser environment.
- Solaris, a version of UNIX developed by Sun Microsystems, is designed for networks using e-commerce applications. It is known for its scalibility—ability to expand, an essential feature when handling e-commerce apps.
- Mac OS X Server, by Apple, can be used with an unlimited number of users and is suitable for big companies and IT departments as well as small businesses and retail stores.

Embedded Operating Systems

Embedded operating systems are specialized operating systems designed for specific applications. They are usually very compact and efficient. They also eliminate many features that nonembedded computer operating systems provide because the specialized application has no need for them. PDAs, cell phones, point-of-sale devices, VCRs, industrial robot controls, and even modern toasters that control the temperature based on bread type and the settings for the attached egg poacher, are examples of devices that contain embedded systems (Figure 4.27). Some of the more common embedded operating systems that are installed on our handheld devices are Microsoft Windows Mobile, Windows CE, Palm OS, Symbian OS, Android, and iPhone OS.

Microsoft Windows Mobile Designed for smartphones and PDAs, **Microsoft Windows Mobile** provides a user interface

FIGURE 4.27
Embedded operating systems can be found in devices that we use every day. How many more devices can you come up with?

Automobiles that display the fuel and energy use   **All smartphones**   **Programmable thermostats**

THE BIONIC EYE

Researchers at Bionic Vision Australia (BVA) have produced a prototype of a bionic eye implant that could bring limited vision to the blind by 2013. With the Australian government contributing $40 million to the research, the timeframe and continual improvements on the prototype look promising. Here's how the system works:

- A camera is mounted on top of a pair of glasses.
- The images are sent to a small processor housed in a unit about the size of a cell phone and carried by the individual.
- The processor, with the help of an embedded operating system, sends a condensed image to the chip directly implanted onto the retina.

- The chip stimulates the visual neurons that, in turn, send rough images to the brain for processing.

The challenge in the bionic eye is not to get the signals to the brain—that has been accomplished—but to improve the resolution and detail of that signal (Figure 4.28). The implication for visually impaired individuals is beyond anything ever hoped for. What are some of the possible applications for those of us with sight? Think about having text magnified without a magnifying glass, shading your eyes from bright light without having to wear sunglasses, and mom actually having eyes in the back of her head. Although the immediate excitement is site for the blind, who can't help but take that glimpse into the future!

1. Camera on glasses views image.
2. Signals are sent to handheld device.
3. Processed information is sent back to glasses and wirelessly. transmitted to receiver under surface of eye.
4. Receiver sends information to electrodes in retinal implant.
5. Electrodes stimulate retina to send information to brain.

FIGURE 4.28 This is only one of several variations of a bionic eye implant currently under development.

for simplified versions of Windows programs, such as Microsoft's own Office applications. Users can create documents on the go and then transfer them to a desktop computer for further processing and printing. Personal information management tools, such as a calendar and address book, along with an e-mail client and a Web browser are also included (Figure 4.29). Windows Mobile supports handwriting recognition and voice recording. Users can

quickly synchronize their mobile devices with corresponding programs on their desktop computers.

Windows CE One of the early embedded operating systems, **Windows CE** was first introduced in 1996, with a significant upgrade made available in 1997. It consists of a low overhead device driver and built-in power manager. Windows CE is used by consumer electronic devices like handheld PCs, video game players, and digital cameras, and by industrial products like barcode readers.

Palm OS The **Palm OS** was initially developed by Palm Inc. for personal digital assistants (PDAs) in 1996. It was designed for use with a touch screen using graphical user interfaces and comes with a suite of personal information management applications. The most current versions power smartphones like the Palm Pixi that runs on the Palm webOS platform and responds to a multitouch screen and natural gestures (Figure 4.30).

Symbian OS An open industry standard operating system for data-enabled mobile phones, **Symbian OS** continues to power devices at the lower end of the smartphone price spectrum because of its reasonable cost, ample suppliers of add-on devices, and the operating system's reduced demand on the processor and memory. The open industry standard guarantees that the OS must be freely and publicly available (e.g., from a stable Web site) under royalty-free terms at reasonable cost.

Android Google released the latest version of its operating system for mobile devices, **Android** 1.6 in late 2009. The updated OS adds support for CDMA (Code

FIGURE 4.29 Although Windows Mobile can look slightly different depending upon the phone vendor, it still brings Windows functionality to mobile devices.

Division Multiple Access) and more screen resolutions. Supporting CDMA will allow operators, such as Verizon, to add Android phones to their portfolios. Android phones use a touch-screen scroll system that allows you to scroll to the left and right, creating the same three divisions (left, center, and right) on your portable device that you have on a computer monitor. The marketplace is filled with applications from a simple coin toss to games that were played on the Sega systems of 17 years ago. The view and On-screen Keyboard changes from vertical to horizontal automatically when the phone changes position. Some interesting statistics from January 2010 indicate that iPhone and Android users, between the ages of 25 and 34, spend an average of 79 minutes a day on apps, while an iPod Touch user spends over 100 minutes. The average cost of an app on both systems is around $8. A little different statistic is that more males use Android system, 73 percent, than iPhones, 57 percent.

iPhone OS The iPhone sports the **iPhone OS** (Figure 4.31). Its current version 3.1 offers such features as these:

- Genius Mixes—automatically generated music mixes based on what types of music are already in your library
- Genius Recommendations—suggestions for apps based on the apps you have already downloaded
- Saving video from mail and MMS (multimedia message service) directly into Camera Roll
- Save as New Clip option—allows you to keep your original video and save the new version when trimming a video on the iPhone 3Gs.

Open Source Software

The open source model is revolutionizing the software world. Because the basic code is free, you can find pieces of it running iPods, supercomputers, smartphones, and many other computer systems. Need Linux in Hungarian, Thai, or Zulu? Don't

FIGURE 4.30 The Palm webOS, used on mobile devices like the Palm Pixi, offers quick access icons for e-mail and contacts along with a full set of menus to set preferences and access photos and text messages.

worry: Volunteers have translated versions of Linux into dozens of languages, giving computer users of all types—individuals, government organizations, and research groups—a free alternative to buying traditional operating systems. You can even download free open source programs for applications such as word processing and database management.

Although Linux remains free, adapting it to the needs of corporations and other large-scale users has become big business. For example, IBM will customize Linux for corporate customers; Red Hat offers a Linux version, as well as consulting, development, and training services to Linux users. With assistance and

FIGURE 4.31 The MMS in the iPhone allows for images, videos, and contact information to be included in the message.

customization so readily available (for a fee), it's not surprising that Linux's popularity with large-scale users is growing.

Linux has always been more popular in the server market than in the desktop market. There are, however, signs that this may be changing. France's police force, the National Gendarmerie, has switched 70,000 desktop computers from Windows to Linux and low-cost computers like the OLPC XO, Everex CloudBook, Classmate PC, and the Asus Eee PC are being offered with the choice of Linux OS. Linux is also making inroads in mobile computing, with Motorola expecting to offer Linux on 60 percent of their phones within the next few years. Other devices, such as TiVo and Amazon Kindle, also use Linux-based operating systems.

No matter what operating system you or your company are running, you need to work with associated programs, called utilities, that help maintain the smooth operability of your system.

System Utilities: Housekeeping Tools

Providing a necessary addition to an operating system, **system utilities** (also called **utility programs**) are programs that work in tandem with the operating system and perform services that keep the computer system running smoothly. Sometimes these programs are included in the OS; sometimes you must purchase them from other software vendors. System utility programs are considered essential to the effective management of a computer system. They include programs that perform such tasks as these:

- Backing up system and application files
- Providing antivirus protection
- Searching for and managing files
- Scanning and defragmenting disks and files
- Compressing files so that they take up less space on storage media

System utilities

FIGURE 4.32 Some utilities run only when selected; others can be programmed to run on a regular schedule.

- Providing additional accessibility utilities to meet the needs of individuals with special needs

You can access these utilities by opening the Start menu, selecting All Programs, then selecting Accessories, and from the Accessories submenu selecting System Tools (Figure 4.32).

Backup Software

An essential part of safe, efficient computer usage, **backup software** copies data from the computer's hard disk to backup devices, such as flash drives, CDs, DVDs, an external hard drive, or an online storage location. Should the hard disk fail, you can recover your data from the backup disk (Figure 4.33).

Backup software can run a **full backup**, which includes all files and data on the entire hard disk, or an incremental backup. In an **incremental backup**, the backup software copies only those files that have been created or changed since the last backup occurred. In this way, the backup disk always contains an up-to-date copy of all data. Full backups should be made at least once each month. Incremental backups should also be made on a regular basis. In a business environment, that can be as frequently as one or more times a day.

Drive imaging software creates a mirror image of the entire hard disk—including the OS and applications, as well as all files and data. In the event of a hard disk or computer system failure, the drive image can be used to restore the system. This avoids the individual reinstallation of each program and can save an incredible amount of time.

Even if you don't have backup software, you can still make backup copies of your important files: Just copy them to an alternative storage device. Don't ever rely on a hard disk to keep the only copies of your work. Backups should be stored away from the computer system, usually in a different building that can withstand natural disasters and is located in a geologically stable region so that in the event of a fire or flood, they don't suffer the system's fate.

Windows 7 includes a backup utility that you can access from the System and Security category of the Control Panel by clicking Backup and Restore Center. The Complete PC Backup option will create an exact image of your computer—backing up all files and data, plus the OS and applications. Basic Backup is available on all versions of Windows 7, but the option to back up to a home or network drive is only available on the Professional, Enterprise, and Ultimate editions. Although many people know that backing up their files is important, most forget. Relying on the Automatic Backup option solves that problem with

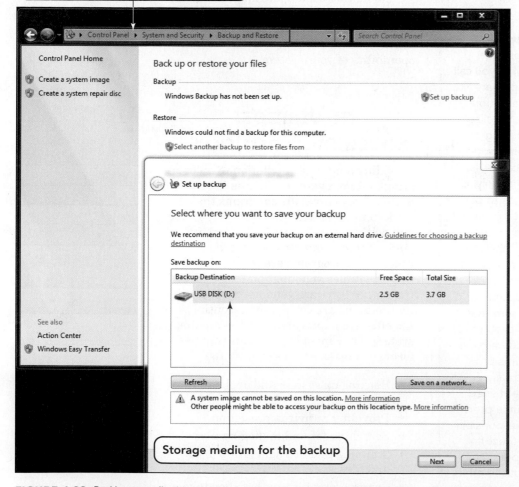

Location of Backup and Restore utility

Storage medium for the backup

FIGURE 4.33 Backing up applications and data is an important part of maintaining a viable system. Using the automatic backup feature in Windows 7 will guarantee that backups are performed on a regular schedule.

the inclusion of the File Backup Scheduling Wizard. Choose the time and backup location you prefer and Windows 7 will do the rest! You can also obtain stand-alone backup or imaging software from local or online retailers, or check for user reviews and find free utility programs on sites like Download.com (**www.download.com**).

Antivirus Software

Antivirus software protects a computer from computer viruses. Such software uses a pattern-matching technique that examines all of the files on a disk, looking for telltale virus code "signatures." One limitation of such programs is that they can detect only those viruses whose signatures are in their databases, and there are plenty of those. As of this writing, one antivirus program, Webroot, scans for nearly 2 million viruses and adds more each day. Most antivirus programs enable you to automatically update the software. However, new viruses appear every day. If your system becomes infected by a virus that's not in the system's database, it may not be detected. Because of this shortcoming, many antivirus programs now include programs that monitor system functions to detect abnormal behavior and stop the destructive activities of unknown viruses before they start.

An antivirus software review conducted in 2009 by TopTenREVIEWS, an independent evaluation company, ranked these as the top five preferred antivirus programs:

1. BitDefender Antivirus
2. Kaspersky Anti-virus
3. Webroot AntiVirus with SpySweeper
4. Norton AntiVirus
5. ESET Nod32 Antivirus

All five programs provide users with frequent updates for the term of a license. Licenses are typically issued for a year. Additionally, many ISPs now offer free antivirus protection and other security tools to help keep their customers safe online.

Some viruses do their damage immediately, whereas others hide on your hard disk waiting for a trigger before doing their

work. Regardless of when they do their damage, viruses spread quickly and can affect thousands, even millions, of users in a short time if the malware can locate targeted hosts. Some argue that the resistance to viruses is more a function of market share and concentration than security advances. This might be true; however, it takes only one nasty virus to cause you a lot of grief. So, install and use antivirus software to avoid hours of aggravation and data loss.

Searching for and Managing Files

Another important system utility is the **file manager**, a program that helps you organize and manage the data stored on your disk. The file manager enables you to perform various operations on the files and folders created on your computer's storage devices. You can use file managers to make copies of your files, manage how and where they are stored, and delete unwanted files. Windows 7 and Vista use Explorer, Mac OS X uses Finder, and Linux has various file management utilities. Explorer has been enhanced considerably in the latest Window operating systems and includes many new features (Figure 4.34).

On a large hard disk with thousands of files, the task of finding a needed file can be time-consuming and frustrating

FIGURE 4.34 A file manager, such as Windows Explorer, enables you to organize your files and folders.

Content of the current folder appears on the right side of the screen.

Breadcrumbs in the Address bar show the path to your current location.

Content can be sorted or filtered by using the column headings.

The Navigation pane, on the left side of the window, displays folders and drives.

The Details pane displays specifics on the selected file.

if you try to do it manually. For this reason, most operating systems include a **search utility**, which enables you to search an entire hard disk or any indexed network storage device for a file. In Microsoft Windows, Instant Search is integrated into every Explorer window, and you can query for files in a number

dialog box to access the utilities. The Mac OS X scanning utility is called Disk Utility. You can find commercial products that perform this function, but the one that comes with your operating system is usually adequate and best suited for managing your hard disk.

A physical problem that a scanning program might detect involves an irregularity on the disk's surface that results in a **bad sector**, a portion of the disk that is unable to store data reliably. The scanning program can fix the problem by locking out the bad sector so that it's no longer used.

Logical problems are usually caused by a power outage that occurs before the

> Enter the description of your search into the Search box located at the bottom of the Start menu.

> The Save Search tool can save frequently used searches.

> Search results begin to appear as soon as you start to type.

> In the Search Results window, your search string appears in the upper right corner.

FIGURE 4.35
Windows Instant Search tool is part of the Explorer window. It searches file names, file properties, and text within files, using the search terms you provide.

of ways, including by name, date, and size (Figure 4.35). The Spotlight utility in the Mac OS performs similar tasks.

Scanning and Defragmenting Disks

A **disk scanning program**, or error checking program, can detect and resolve a number of physical and logical problems that may occur when your computer stores files on a disk. The error-checking and defragmenting utilities in Windows are found by clicking the Computer option in the Start menu, then right-clicking the drive to be checked and choosing Properties. Select the Tools tab in the Properties

computer is able to finish writing data to the disk. In this situation, the system is unable to place an end of file marker (eof), and there is some confusion as to where the file actually terminates. Logical errors are more complex to correct than physical ones.

A **disk cleanup utility** differs from a disk scanning program in that it doesn't rectify any problems. Instead, it improves system performance and increases storage space by removing files that you no longer need. Without your knowledge, some programs create temporary files on the hard drive to perform actions that improve their performance. These files are automatically removed when the program is properly

STUDENT VIDEO

Fragmented files on disk

Defragmented files on disk

FIGURE 4.36 The defragmentation process repositions the sectors of a file into adjacent locations.

reorganize data on the disk so that file pieces are reassembled as one chunk of disk space (decreasing disk search time), storage is made more efficient (by clustering files into structures more efficiently searched), and the time needed to access files decreased (Figure 4.36). Scanning and defragmentation utilities should be run anywhere from once every three or four months for the light computer user to as much as once every three to four weeks for the power user.

File Compression Utilities

Most downloadable software is compressed. A **file compression utility** exchanges programs and data efficiently by reducing the size of a file by as much as 80 percent without harming the data (Figure 4.37). Most file compression utilities work by searching the file for frequently repeated but lengthy data patterns and then substituting short codes for these patterns. Compression enables faster downloads, but you must decompress a file after downloading it. When the file is decompressed, the utility restores the lengthier pattern where each short code is encountered. Both compressed and decompressed files can be saved and opened on a computer system, but a file needs to be decompressed prior to use if changes that are made to that file are to be saved.

Most compression utilities also can create archives. An **archive** is a single file that contains two or more files stored in a compressed format. Archives are handy for storage as well as file-exchange purposes because as many as several hundred separate files can be stored in a single, easily handled unit. The most basic archiving

closed. A power outage can cause these files to remain on your hard drive and waste valuable storage space. A disk cleanup utility will search for and delete these unusable files along with any files in the Recycle Bin.

As you use a computer, it creates and erases files on the hard disk. The result is that the disk soon becomes a patchwork of files, with portions of files scattered here and there. This slows disk access because the system must look in several locations to find all of a file's segments. A disk with data scattered around in this way is referred to as being **fragmented**. A fragmented disk isn't dangerous—the locations of all the data are known, thanks to the operating system's tracking mechanisms—but periodic maintenance is required to restore the disk's performance. **Disk defragmentation programs** are utility programs used to

FIGURE 4.37
A compressed file is saved to the same folder as the original file, but with a different icon and file type.

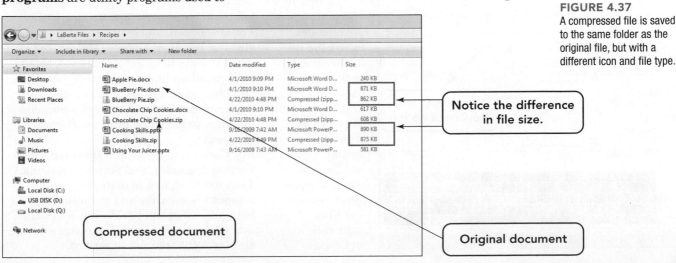

Notice the difference in file size.

Compressed document

Original document

FIGURE 4.38 The On-Screen Keyboard, along with other accessibility utilities, makes computer use easier for many individuals.

programs sequentially attach or pack files into the archive, including some additional information about each file, for example, the name and lengths of each original file, so that proper reconstruction or unpacking is possible. To edit and save the changes to any file in the archived packet, the packet must first be restored to its original format.

To compress, or zip, a file in Windows 7 or Vista, right-click it and choose Send To Compressed (zipped) Folder. This creates a new zipped file with the same file name. There are several ways to decompress, or unzip, a zipped file. One way is to double-click the file and use the Extract all files button. Another way is to right-click the zipped file and choose Extract All.

Accessibility Utilities

Accessibility utilities are utilities designed to make computing easier for individuals with special needs. Windows 7 includes the following utilities, which are accessible from the Control Panel in the Ease of Access category:

- Magnifier—A feature that magnifies a portion of the screen to make reading easier for the visually impaired
- On-Screen Keyboard—A feature used by clicking or hovering over the keys on the screen with a pointing device (Figure 4.38)
- Speech Recognition—A program that allows you to use your voice to control your system and dictate documents
- Narrator—A very basic speech program that reads everything on the screen.

Additional features can be activated through the Ease of Access category in the Control Panel.

System Update

Because the world of computers is rapidly changing, Microsoft provides an operating system update service called **Windows Update** that is meant to keep your operating system up to date with fixes (service patches) or protections against external environment changes. If you are using Windows 7, you can ensure that your OS is current by opening the Control Panel's System and Security category, clicking Windows Update, and setting Windows Update to automatically download and install updates at a time of your choosing (Figure 4.39). You can also get more information at Microsoft's Security at Home page (**www.microsoft.com/protect**).

Updates may include service packs, version upgrades, and security updates. They are designed to maintain your computer's security and reliability and to help protect against malicious software and exploits. Mac users have access to a similar software update service.

Path to the Ease of Access Center

Start On-Screen Keyboard option

Choose how Windows can install updates

When your computer is online, Windows can automatically check for important updates and install them using these settings. When new updates are available, you can also install them before shutting down the computer.

How does automatic updating help me?

Important updates

☑ Install updates automatically (recommended)

Uploads can be set to occur automatically.

Install new updates: Every day ▼ at 3:00 AM ▼

Recommended updates

☑ Give me recommended updates the same way I receive important updates

Who can install updates

☑ Allow all users to install updates on this computer ◄

Rights can be restricted.

Software notifications

☐ Notify me when new featured programs and updates are available

How to get updates for other Microsoft products

☑ Use Microsoft Update

You will receive updates for Windows and other products from Microsoft Update.

Note: Windows Update might update itself automatically first when checking for other updates. Read our privacy statement online.

FIGURE 4.39 Setting the appropriate Windows Update options ensures your system will receive the latest software patches and antivirus protection and that it is optimized for the best performance.

Besides system utilities, there are additional ways to safeguard your data or take care of operating problems.

Troubleshooting

Almost every user of a computer system experiences trouble from time to time. The trouble can stem from an error in the boot cycle, the failure of a command to work in a running program, or the addition of hardware or software. Before you panic, review the problems and possible causes below for some practical tips that might help get you through the crisis.

- If your computer fails to start normally, you may be able to get it running by inserting a **boot disk** (also called an **emergency disk**). The boot disk is a storage device, like a USB drive, CD, DVD, or network device, that in case of an emergency or boot failure can load a reduced version of the OS that can be used for troubleshooting purposes. Sometimes the boot disk comes with a new computer, but often you need to create it yourself. Consult the documentation that came with your computer or choose Help and Support from the Windows Start menu to learn about this process.

- Improperly shutting down your system may cause trouble on restarting. When you've finished using the computer, be sure to shut it down properly. Don't just switch off the power without going through the full shutdown procedure. In Microsoft Windows 7, click Start and then click the Shut Down button. In Windows Vista, click

start, then click the arrow to the right of the Lock button, and click Shut Down. In Mac OS, choose Shut Down from the Apple menu. If you switch the power off without shutting down, the operating system may fail to write certain system files to the hard disk. File fragments that result from improper shutdown could result in permanent damage to the OS or to personal files.

- In Microsoft Windows, configuration problems, issues with new equipment communicating with other devices, can occur after adding a new peripheral device such as an external hard drive or new printer to your system. Some of these additions may cause conflicts that could interfere in the boot cycle. Conflicts can often be resolved by starting the computer in Windows **Safe Mode**, an operating mode in which Windows loads a minimal set of drivers that are known to function correctly. Within safe mode, you can use the Control Panel to determine which devices are causing the problem. You access safe mode by pressing the F8 key repeatedly during the start-up process (before the Windows splash screen with the logo appears). Safe Mode will reset or report any conflicting programs or device drivers. Once the reset is complete, shut down the system, boot up normally, and then correct any conflicts that were not reset in safe mode (Figure 4.40).

FIGURE 4.40 An error during the boot process may cause your system to open in Safe mode, where some settings may be adjusted. To exit Safe Mode, shut down your computer and then restart the system.

Desktop wallpaper image missing

Icons not in their usual spot on the desktop

Safe Mode displayed in corners of screen

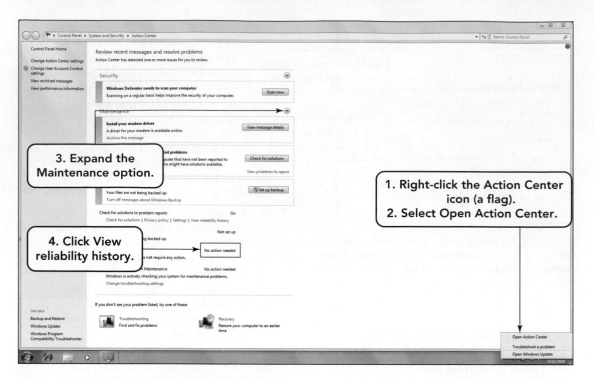

FIGURE 4.41 The Action Center icon is a flag located on the system tray.

* System slowdown can sometimes occur because something has changed gradually over time to cause performance to degrade or there has been an addition made in hardware or software to the system. The Windows operating system has a tool to help diagnose these problems—the

FIGURE 4.42 Each different symbol on the graph represents a different type of activity. An *x* represents an improper shut down, whereas an *i* indicates that a system update occurred.

Reliability and Performance Monitor. With this feature you can check to see when your system's performance began to degrade and get details about individual events that might have caused the problem. The best way to ensure that your system runs optimally is never to change more than one thing at a time. That way, if the system has problems, you can undo your last action or installation and see whether the problem goes away. Follow these steps to access this tool in Windows 7.

1. Right-click the *Action Center* icon in the system tray (the icon is a flag) (Figure 4.41).
2. From the window that opens choose *Open Action Center*.
3. Expand the Maintenance category by clicking the arrow to its right.
4. Click the *View reliability history* option.
5. Windows 7 will display the stability of your system in graphical form (Figure 4.42).

* Help and Support, just a click away on your own computer, is sometimes the best place to look for troubleshooting guidance. Microsoft Windows includes a Help and Support utility. You can explore its contents by clicking the *Start* button and then clicking *Help and Support*. The

Windows Help and Support Center includes several ways to manage and maintain your computer.

- Additional troubleshooting help is available for both PCs and Macs on the Web. Some offer free advice and user forums, whereas others, such as Ask Dr. Tech, offer support packages for a price. Type **troubleshooting** into your favorite search engine or visit sites such as **www.macfixit.com** or **www.askdrtech.com** to find out more.

How To:

Adjust the Settings for Sleep, Hibernate, and Hybrid Power Modes

Be careful when you increase the amount of time your computer waits before activating any of these power-saving modes on a battery-powered PC. A loss of data may occur if you make the delay time too long and the battery goes dead. The purpose of changing these settings is to optimize your power usage, keeping in mind your work habits and battery strength.

1. Open the Start menu and select the *Control Panel*. From the Control Panel options, select *System and Security* and then select *Power Options* (Figure 4.43).

FIGURE 4.43 Changes to power settings are done through the System and Security option of the Control Panel.

2. Under Select a power plan, to the left of the Balanced (Recommended) option, select *Change plan settings*. If you do not see the word *Balanced*, your manufacturer may have edited this option and replaced it with a more identifying phrase, such as *HP Recommended*.

3. In the Change settings for the plan screen, select *Change advanced power settings* (Figure 4.44).

FIGURE 4.44 The advanced power settings make it possible to change settings for specific behaviors such as Sleep and Hibernate.

4. In the Power Options dialog box, there are three settings:

- **Expand the Sleep and Sleep after options.** Set the time for On battery and Plugged in settings based on whether you are using a notebook or desktop system and the time length of inactivity that would trigger the system to enter Sleep mode (Figure 4.45). The interval of inactivity for a notebook (On battery) should be less than 15 minutes to conserve battery power. On a plugged in

FIGURE 4.45 Each option in the dialog box can be expanded, and additional features set by the user.

system, like a desktop, usually 30 minutes is tops, but that is up to the individual. Entering Sleep or Hibernate mode too frequently can be very annoying and frustrating. Monitor your habits and set the interval accordingly.

- **Expand the Hibernate after option.** Set the time for On battery and Plugged in settings again based on whether you are using a notebook or desktop system and the length of inactivity that would trigger the system to enter Hibernate mode. Remember that Hibernate mode saves your open programs and data on the hard disk and totally powers down your system. If you are very energy conscientious, then you might choose this setting over Sleep. However, due to the total power down, returning from Hibernate mode takes longer than returning from Sleep mode.

- **Expand the Allow hybrid sleep option.** The settings for Sleep and Hibernate should be set before this step because Hybrid will activate sleep first, and then, if no activity occurs, it moves your system into Hibernate. Here your only choices are On or Off for both On battery and Plugged in settings.

5. Click *OK* to save changes. Close the Control Panel.

6. Test your system and make sure that the delays work.

Chapter Summary

System Software

- System software has two major components: (1) the operating system (OS) and (2) system utilities. The OS coordinates the various functions of the computer's hardware and provides support for running application software. System utilities provide such features as backup, defragmenting, and file compression.

- An operating system acts as an interface between the user and the computer's hardware. Its five basic functions are starting the computer, managing applications, managing memory, coordinating tasks, and providing a means of communicating with the user.

- A computer needs an operating system to coordinate the interaction of hardware components with each other as well as with application software.

- When you start or restart a computer, it reloads the operating system into the computer's memory. A computer goes through six steps at start-up: loading the BIOS, performing the power-on self-test, loading the OS, configuring the system, loading system utilities, and authenticating users.

- The three major types of user interfaces are graphical user interfaces (GUIs), menu-driven user interfaces, and command-line user interfaces. Most users prefer to use graphical user interfaces, which makes use of small images called icons to identfy linked programs. The next most popular type of interface is the menu-driven interface, in which you open programs and selecte options by clicking on a selection in an on-screen menu. Command-line interfaces are hardly ever used anymore because they require the memorization of keywords and punctuation that must be typed on a text line. Such commands are executed when you press the Enter key.

- Operating systems can be placed in three categories: stand-alone, server, and embedded. A stand-alone system does not need to be connected to any other system or computer in order to run.

- A server system, on the other hand, is designed to work in a network with other units and peripherals. Embedded operating systems are not designed for general purposes but for the specific conditions and actions of the device that they are embedded within.

- The major strength of Windows is that it has dominated the market for more than 15 years and is installed and maintained on more than 90 percent of the personal computers in the world. The major strength of OS X is that it has been modified and upgraded for more than 20 years and is the most stable graphical OS. The biggest weakness of Windows is that Microsoft continues to bring new versions to market before all of the bugs and security holes have been resolved. The main disadvantage of OS X is that it is used on only approximately 8 percent of the computers in the world and thus does not support as many applications as Windows does.

- Essential system utilities include backup software, antivirus software, a file manager, search tools, file compression utilities, disk scanning programs, disk defragmentation programs, and access utilities for those with special needs. Additionally, features like Windows Update keep your OS up to date with fixes (service patches) or protections against external environment changes. These features are also available for a Mac in the Mac OS X Toolbox (or Utilities folder).

- An incremental backup creates a duplicate copy of files that have changed or have been created since the last backup. A full backup duplicates all of the files and data on a hard disk. Each individual or business needs to set a schedule for the time and tye of backup to be performed. This can be automated through such utilities as Windows Update.

- Be aware of problems with your system and attempt to troubleshoot them at the onset. Make use of such features as Help and Support, Safe Mode, and the Action Center to help correct the problem.

Key Terms and Concepts

Identification

Label each interface item with its name.

1. _____

2. _____

3. _____

4. _____

5. _____

6. _____

7. _____

8. _____

Matching

Match each key term in the left column with the most accurate definition in the right column.

_____ 1. cold boot

_____ 2. load

_____ 3. warm boot

_____ 4. menu driven

_____ 5. graphical user interface (GUI)

_____ 6. interrupt

_____ 7. thrashing

_____ 8. sidebar

_____ 9. page

_____ 10. icon

_____ 11. kernel

_____ 12. platform

_____ 13. gadget

_____ 14. command-line

_____ 15. profile

a. A term used to describe excessive paging

b. A method of interacting with a program or OS by selecting choices from on-screen, text-based options

c. A record of a specific user's preferences for the desktop theme, icons, and menu styles

d. A method of interacting with a program or OS by typing instructions one line at a time, using correct syntax

e. The central part of the operating system that resides in RAM

f. The process of transferring a file from storage to memory

g. A small image that represents a computer resource

h. Starting a computer that is not already on

i. The combination of the processor and operating system

j. A fixed size unit of data used to swap content between RAM and virtual memory

k. Starting a computer that is already on

l. The far right side of the screen in Windows 7, in which gadgets can be positioned

m. The use of small images to activate choices, making a program or OS easier to use

n. A signal from a device to the operating system to inform it that an event has occurred

o. An application that appears as an active icon on the far right side of the desktop

Multiple Choice

Circle the correct choice for each of the following:

1. Which OS is *not* designed for smartphones and PDAs?
   a. Android
   b. Symbian
   c. Mac OS X
   d. Windows Mobile

2. What utility program reduces a file size by as much as 80 percent by substituting short codes for lengthy data patterns?
   a. Defragmentation
   b. Compression
   c. Interrupt
   d. Cleanup

3. Which of the following is an OS function?
   a. Creating letters
   b. Managing memory
   c. Defragmenting a disk
   d. Writing e-mail

4. Windows ReadyBoost allows a _____ to be used for virtual memory.
   a. hard disk
   b. CD
   c. flash drive
   d. DVD

5. Virtual memory is used when:
   a. booting fails.
   b. an IRQ conflict occurs.
   c. RAM is full.
   d. a power-on self-test fails.

6. Which test makes sure the computer and its peripherals are working correctly during the start-up process?
   a. BIOS
   b. POST
   c. Upgrade
   d. ReadyBoost

7. Which device is *not* managed by BIOS?
   a. Hard drive
   b. CPU
   c. Jump drive
   d. RAM

8. Which system utility creates duplicates of the files and programs on a system?
   a. Compression
   b. Defragmentation
   c. Backup
   d. Driver

9. Utilities that make computer use easier, especially for individuals with special needs are categorized as
   a. encryption utilities.
   b. supplemental utilities.
   c. accessibility utilities.
   d. system software.

10. Which power-saving mode places a copy of your system's state on the hard drive and shuts off the system?
    a. Sleep   b. Hibernate
    c. Power down   d. Screen saver

Fill-In

In the blanks provided, write the correct answer for each of the following:

1. _____ automatically installs fixes and upgrades service patches to maintain a computer's security and reliability.

2. When troubleshooting a system, one strategy is to boot your system in _____, an operating mode in which only a minimum number of drivers that are known to function correctly are loaded.

3. The _____ is a utility program that repositions file sectors in adjacent locations on a hard disk.

4. Linux makes its source code available for everyone to see and use. This is an example of _____ software.

5. A device _____ is a program that enables communication between the operating system and a peripheral device.

6. A disk with data scattered and empty locations where files have been deleted is said to be _____.

7. A copy of all the files and data on an entire hard disk is called a(n) _____.

8. The _____, or login, process verifies that the user is authorized to use the computer.

9. BIOS information is stored in nonvolatile memory called _____.

10. An area of RAM used to temporarily hold information when printing multiple files is a print _____.

11. _____ is the name of the most current Windows operating system for a PC.

12. Windows Explorer and Mac Finder are both examples of a(n) _____ utility.

13. _____ is the name of the most current Mac operating system.

14. _____ is a feature that allows compatible devices to be automatically detected.

15. _____ is the feature in Windows 7 and Vista that allows the user to use a flash device as virtual memory.

Short Answer

1. Briefly describe the three types of user interfaces. Indicate which are in use today, and provide an example.

2. Explain the Sleep, Hibernate, and Hybrid power options and the type of computer user they best suit.

3. What is virtual memory and how does it improve system performance?

4. Explain which devices in a system are controlled by the BIOS and which are controlled by the operating system.

5. Identify three of the accessibility utilities included with Windows 7. State the purpose of each and how it improves computing for those with special needs.

Teamwork

1. **Operating Systems** Your team is to research three of the operating systems presented in this chapter. In a table created in Microsoft Word or Excel, compare the basic functions performed by each. What future improvements in each OS can you envision or do you see as essential? If you have used several versions of the same OS, what improvements have been incorporated into new versions? Present your comparison table and answers to the questions above in a one-page, double-spaced paper.

2. **Find a Solution** You turn on your computer and enter your user name and password. The system indicates that the password is invalid. You try again and receive the same error message. As a team, come up with at least three possible explanations for the invalid password message and how they might be resolved. Present your troubleshooting results and suggestions for fixes in a slide show of at least five slides.

3. **Windows vs. Mac OS X vs. Linux with Some Added Humor** Review the humorous spin on the familiar "I am a Mac, I am a PC" commercial that includes the arrival of Linux at **www.youtube.com/watch?v=cldeHjFig_c**. As a team, research the difference between these three systems. Create a short commercial, under 90 seconds, that actually provides some information (and humor) to the viewer on the strengths, differences, or shortcomings of each. Cite your references in a Word document.

4. **Using System Tools** As a team, research some of the system tools found in the System Tools folder located in the Accessories option of the Start menu. Split into groups of two or three. Each group should select two tools that were not covered in detail in this chapter. Investigate the purpose of the tool and any options that will need to be set for it to work correctly. What will be the effect of using this tool on your system? Then try to use the tool yourself and evaluate its performance and results. Regroup and, as a team, combine your information into a one- to two-page, double-spaced report.

5. **Buying a Smartphone** You and your teammates are to consider the purchase of a smartphone. Split into groups and visit local mobile device stores. What companies manufacture smartphones? What operating system and applications are installed on the phones that you are researching? Obtain literature and try out several models. Specifically, try out the operating system. What OS and version of that OS does each use? How does this OS compare with those on desktop and notebook computers? How does it differ? With regard to the OS, what phone would you recommend and why? Collate your findings and present a summary in a one-page, double-spaced paper.

On the Web

1. **Examine Deep Freeze** Many educational institutions and lab settings are installing a program on their computers called Deep Freeze. Research this product and in a one-page, double-spaced paper, explain how this program produces a safer computer experience for individuals that have to work in a multiuser environment. What does this program do to protect the operating system and system utilities from change?

2. **Antivirus Programs** In this exercise, use your favorite browser to obtain information on the five top antivirus software programs listed in this chapter. In a Word document, make a list of at least 10 features that all five have in common. Below this list make another list that identifies one feature unique to each one. Then locate the home page of two of the popular antivirus applications. In your Word document include the following additional information:

   - The name of the program and URL of each home page

   - The operating systems each antivirus program works with.

   - List the current versions and suggested retail prices of each.

   - Locate free or evaluation versions, if any exist.

   From your research, would you purchase one of these products? Explain why or why not.

3. **Windows 7 versus Mac OS X Snow Leopard** Using the Internet and a search engine of your choice, research the features of each of the two top operating systems, Windows 7 and Mac OS X Snow

Leopard. In a Word table or Excel spreadsheet, list the features and make a chart that clearly displays which features each OS supports. Indicate the various versions of each system and the cost of each.

4. **Smartphone Accessibility Utilities** In this chapter the accessibility utilities of Windows 7 were reviewed. Smartphones service a very large and general population and contain embedded operating systems that have limitations that single-user operating systems don't have to worry about. Use the Internet and research the accessibility utilities available on smartphones and other mobile devices. Come up with at least five utilities that make using a device easier and less frustrating. Indicate the device and operating system each utility is associated with. Can you come up with any suggestions for additional utilities that would make using a smartphone and its features easier? Use Word and present your research and suggestions in a one-page, double-spaced paper.

5. **Oh Where, Oh Where Can Linux Be?** In the ethics section of this chapter, we discuss the One Laptop Per Child initiative. The laptops for this movement run an operating system called Sugar, a derivative of Linux. Use the Internet and locate at least 10 other devices that are running the Linux operating system, or a variation of Linux. List the devices and any additional information on the Linux system it is running in a Word document.

Spotlight

Buying and Upgrading Your Computer System

You are in the market to purchase a computer. There are several questions that should be going through your head before running off to the local retail store or online site. What will the system be used for? Will it need to run applications or just access the Internet? Will an internal CD or DVD player be required? How much RAM and processing power is necessary? What operating system will best suit your needs and demands? Is portability essential? How much are you willing to spend?

By having your own PC, you can type term papers, create slide presentations, and in many cases use the high-speed wireless network all over campus. Many schools encourage students to purchase a computer before they arrive on campus. Even though schools still provide computer labs, with your own computer you can work when you want and, in the case of notebooks and netbooks, where you want. Buying a computer doesn't have to be intimidating! This spotlight will guide you step by step through the process of buying your own computer. Read on to learn how to choose the equipment you'll need, at the best prices on today's market.

Getting Started the Right Way

There's a right way and a wrong way to select a computer system. The right way involves understanding the terminology and the relative value of computer system components. You then determine your software needs and choose the computer that runs this software in the most robust way. What's the wrong way? Buying a computer system based only on price, being influenced by sales hype, or purchasing a system you know nothing about. First, we'll discuss how to select the best type of computer for your needs.

Notebook, Netbook, or Desktop?

Deciding whether to buy a notebook (also referred to as a laptop), a netbook, or a desktop computer is often one of the hardest decisions you'll have to make when considering which computer to buy (Figure 3A). Today's notebook computers rival the power of desktop machines. The best of them are truly awesome machines, with big (17-inch or larger) displays, fast processors, plenty of memory, and lots of hard drive space. An average notebook with a 17-inch monitor has the dimensions 16.38″ (W) × 10.83″ (D) × 1.25″ (H) and weighs 7.5 lbs. Netbooks are lighter and smaller than notebooks; with a screen size of up to 11 inches and a weight less than half the weight of a 17-inch laptop, a netbook is easier to carry. Netbooks have a substantially longer battery life than a notebook. They also have lower power consumption due to absence of an optical drive and a smaller screen. A netbook with 2 GB of RAM and a 250 GB hard drive is 10.55 inches (L) × 6.9 inches (D) × 0.9–1.11 inches (H) and weights 2.7 lbs.

The main advantages of a notebook computer are portability and size. Because notebooks are portable, you can take them to class in a specially designed

FIGURE 3B   Notebook computer bags come in a variety of sizes and styles designed to protect your computer and hold your work.

carrying case (Figure 3B). In class, a notebook fits easily on your desk so you can type notes. As you're probably well aware, campus housing or shared rental units often have a limited amount of desk space, which makes notebooks even more appealing. Although desktops are not as portable as notebooks and netbooks, they can have more processing speed and more RAM. This makes them quite powerful. They can also have a larger internal hard drive.

On the downside, notebook computers cost more than comparable desktop models. You should also consider that notebooks are easily lost or stolen. Moreover, if your notebook goes missing, your precious data will go along with it. For that reason alone, it is crucial to

FIGURE 3A   Which one is right for you? Notebook? Netbook? Desktop?

backup your data at least every week. Here are some interesting facts on notebook theft:

- The FBI reported that over 1.5 million notebooks were stolen in the United States alone in 2009.
- Every second of the day 2.85 notebooks are stolen in the United States.
- Notebook theft doubled over the past year.
- Over 85 percent of notebook theft is an insider job.
- Notebook theft is one of the top three computer crimes, along with virus creation and hacking.
- Approximately 81 percent of U.S. firms lost notebooks with sensitive data in the past year.

Thieves also target college campuses, making safety another important factor when considering a notebook.

Netbooks are even smaller, making them easier to carry with you. The downside to them is they do not have internal CD/DVD drives, and they have smaller hard drives, less processing power, and memory. Still, if you want something very portable to take to class, a netbook might be the answer. If you want to listen to music, view a DVD, or install software, you will need an external device or to be connected to a network.

A desktop computer tends to be less expensive than a notebook computer of similar specification. Desktop computers are easier to upgrade and have internal slots for expansion cards and additional hard drives. Faulty accessories and components, such as a monitor or keyboard, are easier to replace on a desktop system.

In the end, the decision most often hinges on convenience versus expense. It's a good idea to speak with friends, family, and instructors about their experiences with different computers. Additionally, many computer sites like **www.pcmag.com** or **www.cnet.com** regularly review and rate products from many different manufacturers. Besides choosing a notebook or desktop model, another decision you'll need to make is which platform you want to work on: Mac or PC?

MAC or PC?

There are two main computer system platforms: Windows (PC) and Mac (Figure 3C). If you ask around, you'll find that some users prefer the Mac, whereas others prefer Windows. Each thinks their platform is the best, and rarely do they cross platforms. How do you know which platform is best for you?

Today's top-of-the-line Macs and PCs are virtually indistinguishable in terms of features and performance. In January 2010, the market share for Macs was only about 10.9 percent. Apple's relative share of the market grew by 29.4 percent in 2009, while Windows lost 3.8 percent. This has been attributed to Macs now using Intel processors and being capable of running the Microsoft Windows operating system and Windows-based software. So how do you decide? First, you need to know some of the differences between Macs and PCs that can become major issues for some people.

One difference between Macs and PCs is software availability. More than 87 percent of the computers in use today are PCs, and developers are more inclined to develop software for the broadest market. The most noticeable gap is within the gaming software industry, which is primarily Windows based. With the advent of VM (virtual machine) software, which is an application in the host operating system that synthesizes or virtualizes a hardware environment for the guest OS, you can create a virtual Windows PC on your MAC and run Windows based-software. Some examples of VM for the Mac are Parallels, Parallels Desktop, Virtual Machine, Virtualbox, VMware, VMware Fusion, and Windows on Mac OS X. Although game play is possible, performance will not be the same as running the application with the Windows operating system because the resources are being shared.

Some software publishers have discontinued some of their Mac products altogether. For example, Autodesk, publisher of the top-selling computer-aided design (CAD) program AutoCAD, dropped its sluggish-selling Mac version to focus on its Windows products, but it still produces other applications for Macs. Even software publishers that continue to support the Mac typically bring out the Mac versions later and may not include as many features. However, many of the most popular software packages, including Microsoft Office, are available for Macs as well as PCs. For

FIGURE 3C PCs are most frequently found on the desktops of engineers and businesspeople. Macs have a strong niche market in artistic fields, such as music, graphic design, and illustration.

example, Microsoft Office 2010 was released in Spring 2010, Microsoft Office for Mac 2011, based on the Office 2010 release, is scheduled for release in late fall 2010. Microsoft Office file formats are compatible between the Mac and the PC. You can also choose to run Windows on your Mac using VM software. If you do, you will be able to use Windows-based software too. This, however, adds to the cost of the system because you have to purchase VM software.

In the past, file compatibility between Macs and PCs was a problem, but that's no longer true. Not only can users easily share files between Macs and PCs, they can attach both types of computers to a network and share printers, Internet access, and other resources.

So does software availability really make a difference? If you're planning to use your computer only for basic applications, such as word processing, spreadsheets, databases, presentation graphics, e-mail, and Web browsing, the Mac-versus-PC issue really isn't important. Because many of the formats are compatible (particularly if you use Microsoft Office or Google Docs), you can often move files from the PC to the Mac and back again using a flash drive. Excellent software for all of these important applications is available for both platforms. Look down the road. What if you declare a major a couple of years from now, only to find that your professors want you to use special-purpose programs that run on the platform that you don't have?

Thus, when deciding whether to buy a PC or a Mac, it's important that you anticipate your future software needs. Find out which programs students in your major field of study are using, as well as which programs are used by graduates working in the career you're planning to pursue. To find out what type of computer is preferred by people working in your chosen career, interview appropriate professionals. PCs figure prominently on the desktops of engineers and businesspeople. The classic stereotype is that the successful artist has a Mac, but her accountant uses a PC. However, like all stereotypes, this is not always the case. For example, you might think that scientists would use PCs, but that's not necessarily true. In the "wet" sciences (chemistry and biology), Macs have many adherents, because these sciences involve visual representation, an area in which Macs excel.

If you're on a budget, consider cost too. Although the price gap is narrowing, Macs and Mac peripherals and software are somewhat more expensive than comparable PC equipment. Macs used to be easier to set up and use, but thanks to improvements in Microsoft Windows, Macs and PCs are now about even. To assist you with your decision, try out different computers,

keyboards, and monitors at a store location. With the introduction of Apple stores, you have the opportunity to see and work with a Mac before you purchase it.

Now that you've determined whether your computer will be a Mac or a PC, we'll discuss how to select the right hardware.

Choosing the Right Hardware

You'll need to understand and evaluate the following hardware components when buying your computer:

- Processors
- Memory
- Hard disks
- Internal and external drives
- Monitors and video cards
- Printers
- Speakers and sound cards
- Modems and network cards
- Keyboards and mice
- Uninterruptible power supplies
- Notebook cooling pads

The following sections examine each of these components.

PROCESSORS

One of the most important choices you'll make when buying a computer is the microprocessor (also known as the processor or CPU). This decision may seem overwhelming. Not only do you have to compare brands—Intel versus AMD—and each brand's models, you also have to consider features such as clock speed, number of cores, and power consumption. With the advent of multicore processing, a processor's performance isn't defined solely by its clock speed (typically measured in GHz). In most modern applications, a dual-core CPU can outperform a single-core CPU, even if the single-core has a higher clock speed. Using this reasoning, you might think that a quad-core CPU would be even better, but many applications are unable to take advantage of the quad-core's power. Using a quad-core processor for ordinary computer tasks such as word processing and surfing the Internet is a bit like taking a Formula One racecar around the block to the minimarket! Visit the Intel (**www.intel.com**) and AMD (**www.amd.com**) sites to compare the different types of processors each company manufactures. Many sites, such as PassMark Software (**www.cpubenchmark.net**), rigorously test processors. Known as benchmarking, these tests provide a good way to compare overall processor performance results (Figure 3D). Keep these results in mind as

> " . . . when **deciding** whether to **buy** a PC or Mac, it's **important** that you **anticipate** your future software needs. "

Intel Core i7 930 @ 2.80 GHz	Average CPU mark
Description: Intel® Core™ i7-930 processor (8M cache, 2.80 GHz, 4.80 GT/s Intel® QPI)	**5825**
CPU first benchmarked: 2010-02-19	
CPUmark/$Price: 20.09 **Overall rank:** 25	
Last price change: $289.99 USD (2010-08-26)	Samples: 1508

CPU mark relative to top 10 common CPUs
29/August/2010 - Higher results represent better performance

Intel Core i7 930 @ 2.80 GHz	5,825
Intel Core i7 920 @ 2.67 GHz	5,568
Intel Core i7 860 @ 2.80 GHz	5,529
AMD Phenom II X6 1055T	5,157
Intel Core2 Quad Q9650 @ 3.00 GHz	4,589
Intel Core2 Quad Q9550 @ 2.83 GHz	4,352
AMD Phenom II X4 965	4,259
Intel Core i5 750 @ 2.67 GHz	4,209
Intel core2 Quad Q9450 @ 2.66 GHz	4,020
AMD Phenom II X4 955	3,934
Copyright passmark 2010	

CPU value (CPU mark/$Price)
29/August/2010 - Higher results represent better value

AMD Phenom II X4 955	26.23
AMD Phenom II X6 1055T	25.79
AMD Phenom II X4 965	25.66
Intel Core i5 750 @ 2.67 GHz	21.59
Intel Core i7 920 @ 2.67 GHz	20.62
Intel Core i7 930 @ 2.80 GHz	20.09

FIGURE 3D PassMark Software (**www.cpubenchmark.net**) provides benchmark test results for more than 300 CPU models and updates its results daily. The first graph shows the relative performance of the CPU compared to the 10 other common CPUs in terms of PassMark CPUmark. The second graph shows the value for money, in terms of the CPUmark per dollar.

you compare computer systems. Each system will have its strengths and weaknesses; however, the processor is the brain of the machine and often dictates the robustness of the rest of the components. It's important that the processor be a good match for the rest of the system. You don't want to put a high-performance processor on a low-end machine or use an underperforming processor on a high-end system.

When researching different processors, keep in mind that you'll pay a premium if you buy the newest, most powerful processor available. One approach is to buy the second-best processor on the market. That way you'll get plenty of processing power without paying a premium for being the first to have the most. You only need enough processing power to handle the work or play you intend to accomplish. If you're a heavy game user, you may need a lot of processing power, but if you plan to use your computer only to surf the Web, play audio files, access social networking sites, and communicate using e-mail and instant messaging, a mid-speed processor should suit your needs just fine.

MEMORY

The next item to consider when buying a computer is how much memory you need. Two important issues are the amount of RAM (random access memory) and whether the system has cache memory.

RAM To maximize your computer's performance, you should seriously consider purchasing as much RAM as you can. You need to check the operating system's requirements and any applications you will be running. If you are purchasing a new computer and a new operating system is being released, you will want to make sure your computer's RAM can handle the requirements or, better yet, the recommendation for RAM, especially if you plan to use a virtual environment or play games. The operating system and applications use RAM for temporary storage. Increasing the amount of available memory allows the CPU to process more instructions and permits more applications to be run simultaneously. Computers with sufficient amounts of RAM are quicker and more responsive than computers with inadequate amounts.

When purchasing a new computer, ask whether the memory can be upgraded and what the maximum amount of memory is for the system. You never know what your future use will demand. You may find that

you already own a perfectly good system that just needs more memory to be effective and efficient.

Secondary Cache When researching cache memory, keep in mind that systems with cache memory tend to be faster than systems without it. **Secondary cache**, also known as L2 cache, provides an additional location for memory storage that can be quickly accessed by the processor. It may be located on the processor's architecture or very close to it. If a CPU already includes L2 cache, another level, known as L3 cache, may be located close to the processor on the motherboard.

HARD DISKS

A common mistake made by first-time buyers is underestimating the amount of disk storage they'll need. Today, a 500 GB hard drive may sound like quite a lot, but you won't believe how easy it is to fill it up. (For example, 500 high-resolution photos take up approximately 1 GB of storage.) A good rule of thumb is never to use more than 75 percent of available disk space. Many entry-level systems on the market today come with a hard drive that store anywhere from 160 GB to more than 1 TB. Yes, that's correct—1 trillion bytes! Storage has become very inexpensive, so purchase as much as you can.

INTERNAL AND EXTERNAL DRIVES

A **drive** is a connected storage device. Drives can be internal (installed within the system unit) or external (attached to the system unit by a cable connected to a port). For instance, to install new software from a DVD or CD, you'll need a drive that is capable of reading these discs. Although it is possible to have individual DVD and CD drives installed internally or attached as stand-alone devices, most new computers include a combination DVD±RW/CD-RW drive (Figure 3E) that is capable of reading

FIGURE 3E DVD drives are used for recording and playing high-definition video and storing large quantities of data.

and writing both DVDs and CDs. Not only will you be able to read CDs, you'll also be able to view movies on DVDs and save files to either storage medium.

The latest optical disc format is Blu-ray Disc (BD), which was developed to enable recording and viewing of high-definition video. Blu-ray also enables you to store large amounts of data. Up to 25 GB of data can be stored on a single-layer disc, and up to 50 GB can be stored on a dual-layer disc. BD drives are now affordable for PCs. Blu-ray has become more popular as high-definition material becomes more prevalent.

Flash drives, also known as thumb drives or USB drives, are an excellent supplement to your hard drive. They come in many different sizes from 512 MB to 64 GB and higher. You can also purchase external hard drives that can be as big as 2 TB. These drives are great for backing up your system or storing your digital photos and videos—and, of course, for your classwork.

MONITORS AND VIDEO CARDS

Monitors are categorized by the technology used to generate images, the colors they display, their screen size, and additional performance characteristics.

In the past few years, as LCD (liquid crystal display) monitor pricing has dropped, CRT (cathode ray tube) monitors have become obsolete and are now considered legacy technology. LCD monitors have become popular because they consume less electricity, have a slimmer design, and weigh less than older CRT monitors weigh. LCD monitors are sometimes referred to as flat-screen or flat-panel monitors because they are very thin, usually no more than 2 inches deep, and they are getting thinner. The flat screen also causes less distortion, resulting in decreased eyestrain— which is critical for people who spend long stretches of time working on a computer.

The quality and resolution of the display you see on your monitor is determined by the computer's **video card**. Display standards vary depending on whether you have a standard monitor with a 4:3 aspect ratio or a widescreen monitor with a 16:10 aspect ratio. **Aspect ratios** are determined by dividing a monitor's width by its height. Standard 17- and 19-inch monitors typically use **Super Extended Graphics Array (SXGA)** with a resolution of 1280 × 1024. Widescreen standards include **Widescreen Extended Graphics Array plus (WXGA+)** for 19-inch monitors with a 1440 × 900 resolution, **Widescreen Super Extended Graphics Array plus (WSXGA+)** for 20-inch monitors with a 1680 × 1050 resolution, and **Widescreen Ultra Extended Graphics Array (WUXGA)** for 24-inch monitors with a 1920 × 1200 resolution. The

higher the resolution, the more memory required. Generally, video cards made before 2006 are unable to support widescreen monitors and standard monitors larger than 19 inches.

To increase performance speed, video data is transferred directly from the video graphics card to the motherboard. The interface used by the graphics card is determined by the motherboard. Older systems used the **Accelerated Graphics Port (AGP)** interface; however, AGP is being phased out in favor of the faster **PCI Express** (Peripheral Component Interconnect Express) and **PCI Express Base 2.1** interface (which is the most current as of this writing). PCI Express 2.1 supports a large proportion of the management, support, and troubleshooting systems. However, the speed is the same as PCI Express 2.0. The data and transfer rate improve with each version. Most current video cards from manufacturers like ATI and NVIDIA use PCI Express (Figure 3F).

Monitors are available in different sizes. You can purchase anything from a 17-inch to a 29-inch monitor. Some monitors are over 30 inches, but the larger the monitor, the higher the cost. The industry standard for desktop monitors ranges from 19 to 22 inches, and the typical notebook computer screen measures 15.4 to 17 inches. If you plan to do any desktop publishing or CAD work, you may want to upgrade to a 24-inch monitor.

FIGURE 3F   Current video graphics cards use PCI Express Base 2.1 technology for improved performance.

The monitor's dot pitch is also an important factor. **Dot pitch** (also called **aperture grill**) is the distance between the dots (pixels) on a CRT monitor. The lower the dot pitch, the closer the dots are to each other— and the sharper the image produced. Don't buy a monitor with a dot pitch larger than 0.28 mm—the smaller the dot pitch, the better your display. Many computer systems can now use your LCD or plasma TV as a monitor.

PRINTERS

Printers fall into four basic categories: color inkjet printers, monochrome laser printers, color laser printers, and multifunction devices that fax and scan as well as print. The difference in print quality between inkjets and laser printers is virtually indistinguishable. Color inkjets and monochrome laser printers are popular and affordable choices for college students. However, the pricing for color lasers and multifunction devices is becoming more competitive, making these viable options too. There are still impact printers that are used for multipart forms.

You should also consider the cost of supplies such as ink or toner for your printer. Toner for laser printers is often more expensive than the ink used by inkjet printers, but it also lasts longer. When shopping for a new printer, be sure to research a printer's cost per page, not just the purchase price.

Speed matters, too. The slowest laser printers are faster than the fastest inkjet printers, and the slowest inkjet printers operate at a glacial pace. High-end monochrome laser printers can print as many as 200 ppm (pages per minute). Still, the best inkjet printers for home use churn out black-and-white pages at a peppy pace—as many as 35 ppm. High-end inkjet printers can print 120 ppm. If you go the inkjet route, look for a printer that can print at least 15 ppm. In addition, look for the ability to print on both sides of the paper (duplexing). You too can help save our environment.

If you have a notebook, you may not want to be encumbered by wires. One option is a wireless printer. It can be across the room from you and still print. The speed of wireless printers is about the same as for their wired relatives. You also have the option of choosing a laserjet, inkjet, or multifunction printer.

Stay with a major brand name, and you'll be served well. It's always a good idea to purchase an extra print cartridge and stash it away with 30 or 40 sheets of paper. This way, Murphy's Law won't catch you at 2 AM trying to finish an assignment without ink or paper.

SPEAKERS AND SOUND CARDS

To take full advantage of the Internet's multimedia capabilities, you will need speakers and a sound card. The sound card is built into the motherboard; however, you'll need external speakers to hear high-quality stereo sound. For the richest sound, equip your system with a subwoofer, which realistically reproduces bass notes.

Be aware that many computers, especially the lowest-priced systems, come with low-end speakers. If sound matters a lot to you—and it does to many college students—consider upgrading to a higher-quality, name-brand speaker system.

If you are taking your notebook to class or have a roommate, be considerate and purchase a good set of headphones.

NETWORK CARDS

If you plan to log on to the campus network, you'll need a **network interface card (NIC)**, consider wired or wireless or both. A NIC is a hardware device that handles the interface to a computer network and allows a network-capable device to access that network. Check with your campus computer center to find out how to connect to your school's system and what kind of network card you need. Most colleges run 100-Mbps (100Base-T) Ethernet networks, but some require you to get a 1000-Mbps (1000Base-T) network card.

Macs and PCs have built-in support for Ethernet networks. If you have purchased a computer without a wireless NIC, you can buy one and install it in your PC, or you can purchase a USB wireless NIC.

KEYBOARDS AND MICE

Most computers come with standard keyboards. If you use your computer keyboard a lot and you're worried about carpal tunnel syndrome, consider upgrading to an ergonomic keyboard, such as the Microsoft Natural Keyboard.

Most systems also come with a basic mouse, but you can ask for an upgrade. With Windows PCs, there's good reason to do so, thanks to the improved mouse support built into the Windows operating system. Any mouse that supports Microsoft's IntelliMouse standard includes a wheel that enables you to scroll through documents with ease. Wheel mice also include programmable buttons to tailor your mouse usage to the software application you're using (Figure 3G).

FIGURE 3G An ergonomic keyboard (left) may be for you if you have pain when typing on a standard keyboard. A wheel mouse (right) includes a scrolling wheel and programmable buttons.

There is also an option for using a wireless mouse and keyboard with your desktop system. Many of the new notebooks use Bluetooth for the mouse and external keyboards.

To choose a good keyboard and mouse, go to a local store that sells computers and try some out. The button placement and action vary from model to model. You'll be using these input devices a lot, so be sure to make an informed decision.

UNINTERRUPTIBLE POWER SUPPLIES

"I'm sorry I don't have my paper. I finished it, and then a power outage wiped out my work." If this excuse sounds familiar, you may want to purchase an **uninterruptible power supply (UPS)**, a device that provides power to a computer system for a short time if electrical power is lost (Figure 3H). With the comparatively low price of today's UPSs—you can get one with surge protection for less than $200—consider buying one for your campus computer, especially if you experience frequent power outages where you live or work. A UPS gives you enough time to save your work and shut down your computer properly until the power is back on. Many UPS devices act as surge protectors to help against power spikes and may have multiple outlets so you can protect more than one piece of computer equipment.

NOTEBOOK COOLING PADS

Due to the amount of processing and memory in today's notebooks, they run very hot. To safeguard your notebook, it is wise to purchase a cooling pad (Figure 3I). The prices vary depending on the features you select. Some are adjustable to variable heights, some have extra USB ports, some have multiple fans, some are plastic, and some are aluminum. It doesn't matter which one you get, but it is strongly recommended that you get one. They are lightweight and can add years to the life of your notebook. Check to see whether your notebook has vents on the bottom. If it does, a cooling pad will be beneficial. Even though notebooks are often called laptops, do not place notebooks with vents on the bottom on your lap. It will block the cooling ability of the internal fan.

A few other items you might consider are a backup system and locks for your desktop and notebook. Now that you know what to look for when choosing hardware for your computer system, let's examine the

FIGURE 3H A UPS device can easily justify its purchase price by saving your data in an unexpected power outage.

FIGURE 3I A Cooling Pad for Notebooks

decisions you need to make about what model you want and where you want to buy it.

Shopping Wisely

When you buy a computer, it's important to shop wisely. Should you buy a top-of-the-line model or a bargain-bin special? Is it better to buy at a local store or through a mail-order company? What about refurbished or used computers or a name brand versus a generic PC? Let's take a look at some of these issues.

TOP-OF-THE-LINE MODELS VERSUS BARGAIN-BIN SPECIALS

A good argument for getting the best system you can afford is that you don't want it to become obsolete before you graduate. Inexpensive systems often cut corners by using less powerful CPUs, providing the bare minimum of RAM, and including an operating system with fewer features and capabilities. For example, if the word *home* is part of the name of your operating system, it may not be as robust as what you might need for your studies; however, it will be great for writing papers and sending e-mail. In your senior year, do you want to spend time upgrading your hardware and software when you should be focusing on your studies? In addition, every time you open the computer's cover and change something, you risk damaging one of the internal components.

The most important consideration is the type of software you plan to run. If you'll be using basic applications such as word processing, you don't need the most powerful computer available. In this situation, a bargain-bin special may be okay, as long as you exercise caution when making such a purchase. But what if you decide to declare a major in mechanical engineering? You might want to run a CAD package, which demands a fast system with lots of memory. In that case, you'd be better off paying extra to get the memory you need up front, rather than settling for a bargain-bin special that may end up being inadequate later.

LOCAL STORES VERSUS MAIL-ORDER AND ONLINE COMPANIES

Whether you're looking for a Windows PC or a Mac, you need to consider whether to purchase your system locally or from a mail-order or online company. If you buy locally, you can resolve problems quickly by going back to the store (Figure 3J). With a system from a mail-order or online company, you'll have to call the company's technical support line.

If you are considering ordering through the mail or online, look for companies that have been in business a long time—particularly those that offer a no-questions-asked return policy for the first 30 days. Without such a policy, you could be stuck with a lemon that even the manufacturer won't be able to repair. Be aware that the lowest price isn't always the best deal—particularly if the item isn't in stock and will take weeks to reach you. Also, don't forget about shipping and handling charges, which could add considerably to the price of a system purchased online or through the mail.

In addition, make sure you're not comparing apples and oranges. Some quoted prices include accessories such as monitors and keyboards; others do not. To establish a level playing field for comparison, use the shopping comparison worksheet in Figure 3K. For the system's actual price, get a quote that includes all of the accessories you want, such as a printer, a monitor, and a UPS.

You should also consider warranties and service agreements. Most computers come with a one-year warranty for parts and service. Some companies offer service agreements for varying lengths of time that will cover anything that goes wrong with your system—for a price. In the vast majority of cases, a computer will fail within the first few weeks or months. You should feel comfortable with the amount of coverage you have during the first year. Be aware, though, that extra warranty coverage and service contracts can add significantly to the cost of your system. You may also want to check to see where repairs need to be completed. Do you have to take the system back to where you purchased it? Do you have to mail it back to the manufacturer? Will a service technician come to your house or dorm? What happens if a component goes bad? Do you have to replace it yourself or take it into a shop? These are all things to consider when purchasing a computer and extended warranty.

FIGURE 3J If you buy a computer at a local retail store, you can evaluate different models and speak with a salesperson to obtain additional information.

BUYING USED OR REFURBISHED

What about buying a used system? It's risky. If you're buying from an individual, chances are the system is priced too high. People just can't believe how quickly computers lose their value. They think their systems are worth a lot more than they actually are. Try finding some ads for used computers in your local newspaper and then see how much it would cost to buy the same system new, right now, if it's still on the market. Chances are the new system is cheaper than the used one.

A number of computer manufacturers and reputable businesses refurbish and upgrade systems for resale. National chains such as TigerDirect.com or Newegg.com have standards to ensure that their systems are "as good as new" when you make a purchase. As always, check out the storefront and stay away from establishments that don't look or feel right. In addition, and most important, your refurbished machine should come with a warranty and should include software that has a valid license.

NAME-BRAND VERSUS GENERIC PCS

Name-brand PC manufacturers, such as HP (Hewlett-Packard), Dell, and Acer, offer high-quality systems at competitive prices. You can buy some of these systems from retail or mail-order stores, but some systems are available only by directly contacting the vendor.

If you're buying extended warranty protection that includes on-site service, make sure the on-site service really is available where you live; you may find out that the service is available only in major metropolitan areas. Make sure you get 24-hour technical support; sometimes your problems don't occur between 8 AM and 5 PM.

If something breaks down, you might have only one repair option: Go back to the manufacturer. After the warranty has expired, you may end up paying a premium price for parts and repairs. Fortunately, this is becoming less of an issue. Almost all of today's name-brand computers run well right out of the box, and in-service failure rates are declining.

What about generic PCs? In most cities, you'll find local computer stores that assemble their own systems using off-the-shelf components. These systems are

Shopping Comparison Worksheet

VENDOR _____   Date _____

    Brand Name _____

    Model _____

    Real Price _____ (including selected components)

PROCESSOR

    Brand _____

    Model _____

    Speed _____ MHz

RAM

    Type _____

    Amount _____ MB

HARD DRIVE

    Capacity _____ GB   Seek time _____ ns

    Speed _____ rpm   Interface _____

MONITOR

    Size _____ x _____ pixels   Dot pitch _____ mm

VIDEO CARD

    Memory _____ MB   Max. resolution _____ x _____ pixels

    Accelerated? .... ☐ yes ☐ no

REMOVABLE DRIVE

    Type _____

    Location .... ☐ internal ☐ external

DVD DRIVE

    Speed _____

DVD BURNER

    Included? .... ☐ yes ☐ no

BLU-RAY DISC DRIVE

    Included? .... ☐ yes ☐ no

SPEAKERS

    Included? .... ☐ yes ☐ no

    Upgraded? .... ☐ yes ☐ no

SUBWOOFER

    Included? .... ☐ yes ☐ no

NETWORK CARD

    Included? .... ☐ yes ☐ no

    Wireless? .... ☐ yes ☐ no

    Speed (100/1000)_____

KEYBOARD

    Upgraded? .... ☐ yes ☐ no

    External for notebook? .... ☐ yes ☐ no

    Wireless? .... ☐ yes ☐ no

    Model _____

MOUSE

    Included? .... ☐ yes ☐ no

    Wireless? .... ☐ yes ☐ no

    Upgraded? .... ☐ yes ☐ no

UPS

    Included? .... ☐ yes ☐ no

SOFTWARE

_____

_____

WARRANTY _____

    Service location _____

    Typical service turnaround time _____

FIGURE 3K   Shopping Comparison Worksheet

often just as fast (and just as reliable) as name-brand systems. You save because you don't pay for the name-brand company's marketing and distribution costs. Because of their smaller client base, the staff at local computer stores has a better chance of knowing their customers personally and thus may provide more personalized service. Their phones are not nearly as busy, and if something goes wrong with your computer, you won't have to ship it halfway across the country. Ask the technician about his or her training background and experience. Another thing to consider is that the industry's profit margin is razor thin; if the local company goes bankrupt, your warranty may not mean much.

What if you don't need an entire new computer system, but just want to improve your current system's performance? That's when you should consider upgrading.

Upgrading Your System

You may want to upgrade your system for a variety of reasons. You may have purchased new software that requires more memory to run properly. You may decide to add a game controller. You could decide that a new monitor and printer will enhance your computing experience. Many computer owners improve their system's performance and utility by adding new hardware, such as RAM, sound cards, and additional memory. This section discusses the two most common hardware upgrades: adding expansion boards and adding memory.

Some upgrades, such as upgrading the hard drive, can be accomplished by using an external device. Some thumb drives or flash drives can be used to supplement the RAM on your computer. However, many enhancements require more invasive actions. Before you decide to upgrade your computer on your own, be aware that doing so may violate your computer's warranty. Read the warranty to find out. You may need to take your computer to an authorized service center to get an upgrade. Although it can be relatively simple to install new components, it can be risky. If you have a notebook or a netbook, you may want to take your computer to a trained technician. Upgrading a notebook is more expensive than upgrading a desktop and is not an easy task. It is not recommended that you attempt this yourself. If you aren't absolutely certain of what you're doing—don't do it! If you have some knowledge, it may be more feasible for you to add, remove, or change components. But proceed with care! Also, before you start any upgrade, consider whether it may

> " **Before** you **decide** to upgrade your **computer on your own**, be aware that doing so may **violate** your **computer's warranty**. Read the warranty to find out. "

be more cost-effective to purchase a new computer than to upgrade your existing one.

REMOVING THE COVER

If you have a desktop computer, begin upgrading your computer by unplugging the power cord and removing all the cables attached to the back of the system unit. Make a note of which cable went where so that you can plug the cables back in correctly. With most systems, you can remove the cover by removing the screws on the back of the case. If you don't know how to remove the cover, consult your computer manual. Keep the screws in a cup or bowl so they'll be handy when you reassemble the computer.

ADDING EXPANSION BOARDS

To add an expansion board to your system, identify the correct type of expansion slot (PCI [Peripheral Component Interconnect], PCI Express, or AGP [Accelerated Graphics Port]) and unscrew the metal insert that blocks the slot's access hole. Save the screw, but discard the insert. Gently but firmly press the board into the slot. Don't try to force it, though, and stop pressing if the motherboard flexes. If the motherboard flexes, it is not properly supported, and you should take your computer to the dealer to have it inspected. When you've pressed the new expansion board fully into place, screw it down using the screw you removed from the metal insert. Before replacing the cover, carefully check that the board is fully inserted.

UPGRADING MEMORY

Many users find that their systems run faster when they add more memory. With additional memory, it's less likely that the operating system will need to use virtual memory, which slows the computer down. To successfully upgrade your computer's memory, visit a leading memory site like Kingston (**www.kingston.com**) or Crucial (**www.crucial.com**). There are several different kinds of memory, but only one type will work with your computer. Both of these sites include tools to help you determine what type of memory your computer requires. Crucial also includes a system scanner that will tell you how much memory is currently installed in your computer. Both sites will tell you the maximum amount of memory your system can use, what type of memory is compatible with your system, and whether you need to buy the memory modules singly or in pairs. You can purchase the specified memory directly from the site or use this information to check pricing and shop around. Following are some of the types of memory that your computer might use: Apple, DDR

FIGURE 3L SDRAM Chip Showing Both Sides

RAM, DDR-Dual Channel, DDR-Laptop , Memory, DDR2 RAM, DDR2-Dual Channel, DDR2-Laptop Memory, DDR3 RAM, DDR3 Tri-Channel, ECC Memory, and SDRAM (Figure 3L).

When you purchase memory modules, a knowledgeable salesperson might help you determine which type of module you need and how much memory you can install. In many cases, the salesperson doesn't know any more about installing memory than you do. Before you install memory modules, be aware that memory chips are easily destroyed by static electricity. Do not attempt to install memory chips without grounding yourself. You can do this by wearing a **grounding strap**, a wrist-attached device that grounds your body so that you can't zap the chips. Remember, don't try to force the memory modules into their receptacles; they're supposed to snap in gently. If they won't go in, you don't have the module aligned correctly or you may have the wrong type of module.

REPLACING THE COVER

When you have checked your work and you're satisfied that the new hardware is correctly installed, replace the cover and screw it down firmly. Replace the cables and then restart your system. If you added PnP (Plug and Play) devices, you'll see on-screen instructions that will help you configure your computer to use your new hardware.

If you're thinking about upgrading your system or if you want to understand what a particular component does, the Internet is a great resource. Sites like CNET (**www.cnet.com**) and PCMag.com (**www .pcmag.com**) can be used to learn about the newest products and read expert reviews. Other sites like HowStuffWorks (**www.howstuffworks.com**) can provide details and explanations for various components. Using a search engine for specific questions can also turn up valuable information.

Whether your computer system is brand new or merely upgraded, you need to know how to properly maintain your system's components.

Caring for Your Computer System

After your computer is running smoothly, chances are it will run flawlessly for years if you take a few precautions:

- Equip your system with a surge protector, a device that will protect all system components from power surges caused by lightning or other power irregularities (Figure 3M). Remember a power strip is not necessarily a surge protector. Most surge protectors come with a guarantee. APC, one of the largest makers of UPSs and surge protectors, has a lifetime Equipment Protection Policy on most of its equipment.

FIGURE 3M Surge protectors prevent costly damage to delicate circuitry and components.

- Consider purchasing a UPS. These devices protect your system if the computer loses power by providing time to save your work and shut down your computer properly before you lose power.
- Don't plug your dorm refrigerator into the same outlet as your computer. A refrigerator can cause fluctuations in power, and a consistent power supply is critical to the performance and longevity of your computer.
- There should be sufficient air circulation around the components. Don't block air intake grilles by pushing them flush against walls or other barriers. Heat and humidity can harm your equipment. Your computer should not be in direct sunlight or too close to a source of moisture.
- Before connecting or disconnecting any cables, make sure your computer is turned off.
- Cables shouldn't be stretched or mashed by furniture. If your cables become damaged, your peripherals and computer might not communicate effectively.

- Clean your computer and printer with a damp, soft, lint-free cloth.
- To clean your monitor, use a soft, lint-free cloth and gently wipe the surface clean. If the monitor is very dirty, unplug it—and wipe it with a cloth slightly dampened with distilled water. Never apply any liquids directly to the surface, and don't apply too much pressure.
- Avoid eating or drinking near your computer. Crumbs can gum up your mouse or keyboard, and spilled liquids (even small amounts) can ruin an entire system.
- To clean your keyboard, disconnect it from the system unit, turn it upside down, and gently shake out any dust or crumbs. You can also use cans of compressed air to clear dust or crumbs from underneath the keys. Vacuums specially designed for keyboards also are on the market. Never use a regular vacuum cleaner on your keyboard. The suction is too strong and may damage the keys.
- To keep your hard disk running smoothly, run a disk defragmentation program regularly. This program ensures that related data is stored as a unit, increasing retrieval speed.
- Get antivirus and antispyware software and run it frequently. Don't install and run any software or open any file that you receive from anyone until you check it for viruses and spyware. Be sure to update your antivirus and antispyware software. They won't be beneficial to you if you do not keep them updated.

Some Final Advice

Conducting research before you buy a computer is fairly painless and very powerful. To prepare for buying a computer, peruse newspaper and magazine ads listing computer systems for sale. Another great source is the Web, which makes side-by-side comparison easy. For instance, typing **"PC comparison shopping"** (without the quotes) into the Google search engine returns close to 772,000 links, and the Bing search engine returns 12 million links. It's also a good idea to visit a comparison site, such as CNET, PCMag.com, Yahoo!, AOL, or PCWorld. To research particular computer manufacturers (such as Apple, Dell, Sony, Toshiba, Lenovo, Gateway, and so on), simply type the manufacturer's name in the address bar of your Web browser and add the .com extension or use your favorite search engine. Use as many resources as you can when you shop for a computer, and then remember that no matter how happy or unhappy you are with your end purchase, you'll most likely be doing it all again within three to five years.

Key Terms and Concepts

Multiple Choice

1. The device that will allow you to save your data if the power goes out is called a(n) _____.
   a. UPS
   b. surge protector
   c. memory card
   d. expansion card

2. Processor speed is measured in _____.
   a. megabits
   b. bytes
   c. hertzbytes
   d. gigahertz

3. Which of the following is a major consideration when purchasing a computer?
   a. Software to be used
   b. Sound system
   c. Monitor size
   d. Color

4. The hard drive size should:
   a. be just enough for your application installations.
   b. not even be considered.
   c. be larger than anticipated.
   d. be the lowest priority.

5. In order to avoid loss of data, you should do all of the following *except* _____.
   a. get a UPS
   b. backup your data
   c. protect your computer from theft
   d. leave your computer unattended

6. Blu-ray discs can store _____ GB of data on a dual-layer disc.
   a. 50
   b. 100
   c. 150
   d. 200

7. A printer that can scan, fax, and print is called a(n) _____ printer.
   a. inkjet
   b. laser
   c. impact
   d. multifunction

8. If you own a Mac and need to run Windows-based software you can do this by installing software that will create a(n) _____.
   a. imaginary PC
   b. virtual machine
   c. image of a PC
   d. terminal machine

9. _____ is *not* an interface that is used for video cards.
   a. AGP
   b. TSA
   c. PCI
   d. PCI Express

10. To take care of the monitor, you want to keep it clean by _____.
    a. using a damp cloth to clean it
    b. spraying cleaner on it and then wiping it down
    c. putting it in the sink to clean it
    d. making sure it is on when you clean it

Spotlight Exercises

1. Have you considered purchasing a used or refurbished computer? You can purchase a computer from a company or from an individual. What are some of the advantages and disadvantages of purchasing a used or refurbished computer from a company or individual? Visit **www.tigerdirect.com** or **www.newegg.com** and search for refurbished computers. Select a specific notebook computer. Identify the computer, its specifications, and its cost. Where would you search to buy a used notebook computer from an individual? Write a short paper on where you would purchase the computer and its specifications. The paper should show that you understand at least six terms from the Spotlight as they apply to purchasing a used computer.

2. You need to upgrade your computer because the new computer game you just purchased needs more RAM than you have in your system. Go to **www.crucial.com** or **www.kingston.com** and see how much RAM your computer has and how much more you can add. Once you determine how much RAM you need to add to max out your system, go shopping for that specific configuration on three Web sites, including the one you used to obtain the information. Use your word processor or spreadsheet program to create a table of the costs. Remember to add the shipping cost if that is not included in the purchase price.

3. Write a one- to two-page paper on the proper care and maintenance of a computer. Explain why each of the items is important.

4. Create a comparison chart on the differences, advantages, and disadvantages of desktop, netbook, and notebook computers. Explain in a one-page paper which computer you would purchase and why.

5. Go to a computer retailer or manufacturer's Web site where you can select the components you want in a computer. Build the computer and price it. Make sure to include any tax and shipping charges. Take those specifications, go into a local store that sells computers, and see if you can match the components. What is the price of the computer in the store? Don't forget to include tax. Do a comparison of the two systems.

6. It is important to know what is in your computer if you plan to upgrade or purchase a new computer. Windows provides a utility to check your computer. System Information is the utility that shows the hardware that is in your system, regardless of whether it is a notebook or desktop. Use the *Start, All Programs, Accessories, System Tools* menu sequence to access the System Information utility. If you use Control Panel in the classic view and select *System,* you will get an experience rating and suggestions of how to improve performance by selecting the *Windows Experience Index*. Write a short paper that includes a table with the values for the following components: the operating system, processor, total physical memory, available physical memory, total virtual memory, and available virtual memory. Using what you learned in the sections on processing, memory, and RAM, is your system current with today's standards? Should you upgrade your computer? Why or why not?

Spotlight

Web 2.0

When was the last time you called a friend or spoke f2f (face-to-face) to ask a question or to tell your friend what you were doing, and when did you send your last e-mail? Today, there are so many ways to keep everyone informed. One of the top choices is using the technologies that have been described in this book and Web 2.0, which has a language all its own. "OMG GTG BRB ur gr8 roflol" is a little shorter than "Oh my gosh, got to go, be right back, you are great, rolling on the floor, laughing out loud." So, what exactly is Web 2.0?

What Is Web 2.0?

No one recognized the Web as Web 1.0 until after Web 2.0 was named, which makes sense because Web 1.0 was the precursor to the type of Web experience we now are able to create. **Web 1.0** consisted of static Web pages with no interactivity other than hyperlinks. The links allowed a user to move around a Web site from page to page or item to item. There was no other interaction of the type that would come with Web 2.0.

WEB 1.0

Web 1.0 has the following characteristics:

- **Web 1.0 sites are static.** They contain information that might be useful, but there's no reason for a visitor to return to the site later. An example might be a personal Web page that gives information about the site's owner, but never changes. A Web 2.0 version might be a blog or MySpace account that owners can frequently update.

- **Web 1.0 sites aren't interactive.** Visitors can only visit these sites; they can't impact or contribute to the sites. Most organizations have profile pages that visitors can look at but not impact or alter, whereas a wiki allows anyone to visit and make changes.

- **Web 1.0 applications are proprietary.** Under the Web 1.0 philosophy, companies develop software applications that users can download, but they can't see how the application works or change it. A Web 2.0 application is an open source program, which means the source code for the program is freely available. Users can see how the application works and make modifications or even build new applications based on earlier programs. For example, Netscape Navigator was a proprietary Web browser of the Web 1.0 era. Firefox follows the Web 2.0 philosophy and provides developers with all the tools they need to create new Firefox applications.

WEB 2.0

There are so many definitions of Web 2.0; it could make your head spin. **Web 2.0** is a set of techniques that collectively provide an upgraded presentation and usefulness for the World Wide Web.

The term *Web 2.0* was coined by Tim O'Reilly. His philosophy of Web 2.0 included these ideas:

- Using the Web as an applications platform
- Democratizing the Web
- Employing new methods to distribute information

Because Web 2.0 has so many meanings, many people refer to it by the particular facet they are using, for example, social networking. The Web 2.0 toolbox includes such applications as:

- Blogs and vlogs
- Wikis
- Podcasts and vodcasts
- Social networking
- Photosharing
- Communication
- Collaboration
- Content sharing

Let's take a look at how we use those Web 2.0 technologies.

Blogs and Vlogs

Many of us were taught to keep journals. At one point, they were very private. Some of us even kept them under lock and key hidden somewhere in our rooms. Today, many people want to share the thoughts they write. To share with the most readers at any time, the media of choice is the World Wide Web.

WHY BLOG?

The journals people create on the Web are called **blogs** (short for **Web log**). The Merriam-Webster dictionary defines a *blog* "as a Web site that contains an online personal journal with reflections, comments, and often hyperlinks provided by the writer." If you want to create a blog, you can access many free sites that provide helpful instructions and tutorials to guide you as you set up your blog. One of the most popular is **www. blogger.com** (Figure 4A). Another is iGoogle (**http:// googleblog.blogspot.com/**). If you don't like one of these, just search for free blogging sites and you'll find over 270,000,000 possibilities. Hopefully, there will be one that works for you.

FIGURE 4A Blogger is one of the more popular blogging Web sites.

Today we are all concerned about identity theft and privacy. We'll discuss the issues related to Web 2.0 and security more throughout this spotlight. The Web 2.0 tools can be safe if you take the necessary precautions. With regard to blogs, you may want to share your thoughts with friends, but not strangers. If so, you can restrict who has access to your blog by protecting it with a password and privacy settings.

If you don't want to blog, but want to see what others have written, you can locate a blog on just about any subject in any language. Google has a blog search engine. Visit **http://blogsearch.google.com** and you can search for a blog by subject. If you go to the advanced search on blogsearch, you can search by author and date. While using blogsearch and the advanced search capability, select the *Filter using safe search* option, and you can screen for sites that contain explicit sexual content and delete them from your search results. If you are taking this course online or have access to your school's Learning Management System, there may be a blog component that will permit you to create a blog for your classmates.

WHY VLOG?

When written blogs are just not enough, some journalers turn to video logs. A **vlog** (short for **video log**) is a series of personal reflective videos that are usually created simply by talking to a webcam and uploading the video. Many vloggers post their vlogs on YouTube, even though the video postings can only be 10 minutes long and up to 2GB in size. The stoutest vloggers update their vlogs daily. If you are reporting from a conference or are a personality, you might update your vlog on a regular basis.

There aren't as many sites for posting your vlog as there are blogging sites. The one that turns up at the top of this list is **www.freevlog.org/**. Depending on the site you use to post your vlog, you can password protect it, which is really a good idea. Just remember that what you post is out there for the world to view. If you only want to view vlogs, use the same Google blog search to search for vlogs.

Wikis

Wiki, which means "quick" in Hawaiian, was created by Ward Cunningham in 1995. A **wiki** is an online information source that allows anyone to edit, delete, or modify content that has been added to the Web site. Wikis are said to be self-correcting—if you add content that is incorrect, someone will correct it for you. Although wikis are a good source for information, they should not be a primary source for research or academic assignments because they are not always created by content experts and there may be errors in the text. They can, however, be used for confirmation of other sources.

There are many sites that have wikis. Wikipedia is one of the popular Web sites for information. It lists itself as the free encyclopedia. You can visit the site (**www.wikipedia.com**) and search on terms to gain insight into a variety of different topics. Even though it is a free site, it is important to cite your source if you use information you find on Wikipedia. If you'd like to participate in the community that keeps Wikipedia updated, you have to create an account. Once you have an account, you can correct the entries you find.

To create your own wiki, **www.wikispaces.com** has different levels of space for business, higher education, nonprofit organizations, and K–12 education. You can create an account, then start working on your wiki. PBworks.com is another popular wiki site. You can make your wiki private or public by assigning who can see or edit it.

You can edit a wiki in several different ways. You can use plain text editing, which we are all familiar with, or simple markup language, which is a variation of hypertext markup language. Figure 4B is an example of input and output using markup language.

FIGURE 4B Editing a Wiki Using HTML

HTML Text	Rendered Output

`<p>"Take some more`
`<a href="/wiki/Tea"`
`title="Tea">tea</a>,"`
`the March Hare said`
`to Alice, very`
`earnestly.</p>`
	"Take some more tea," the March Hare said to Alice, very earnestly.

`<p>"I've had nothing`
`yet," Alice replied`
`in an offended tone:`
`"so I can't take`
`more."</p>`
	"I've had nothing yet," Alice replied in an offended tone: "so I can't take more."

`<p>"You mean you`
`can't take`
`<i>less</i>," said`
`the Hatter: "it's`
`very easy to take`
`<i>more</i> than`
`nothing."</p>`
	"You mean you can't take *less*," said the Hatter: "it's very easy to take *more* than nothing."

CoffeeCup (Figure 4C) is an HTML wiki software. This software gives you a sophisticated way to do HTML editing using a graphic user interface (GUI). You can preview the text before it is posted. Of course, you don't *have* to edit a wiki; you can just read it. Many wikis are private to small groups, such as a class.

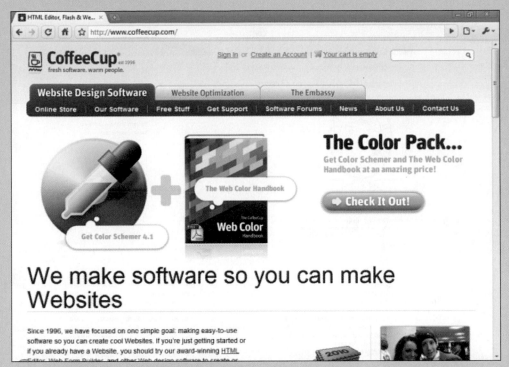

FIGURE 4C   CoffeeCup is a free software download.

Podcasts and Vodcasts

Do you like to listen to lectures while working out? Do you want to watch the world's funniest commercials on your time schedule, not when they are scheduled on TV? If so, consider a podcast or a vodcast.

PODCASTS

A **podcast** is a blend of the words *iPod* and *broadcast*. It has come to mean a program (music or talk) that is made available in digital format for automatic download over the Internet. Although, podcasts were originally for Apple's iPod, you can listen to them on other media players. You can also download podcasts to a computer and upload them to a handheld device such as an iPod or MP3 player.

There are many sources for podcasts in many different subjects. One of the premier sources of podcasts is iTunes. Most podcasts are free; others have nominal charges. Want to listen to a book? Try **www.openculture.com/ 2006/10/audio_book_podc.html** or **http://librivox.org** (Figure 4D). In additon to iTunes (**www.itunes.com**), which you have to download before you can see the available podcasts, **www.podcastdirectory. com** and **www.podcastalley. com** are two sites where you can get a directory of podcasts on a variety of subjects.

To create your own podcast you can use software such as Audacity, which is available as a free download at **http://audacity. sourceforge.net/ download**. You will also need a microphone that will work with your computer to record the podcast. Once completed, you can save and upload your own podcasts to the podcast directory sites, but you must be a registered user to do so.

VODCASTS

A **vodcast** or **video podcast** is a term used for the on-line delivery of a video clip on demand. Over the past few years, creating such videos has become very popular.

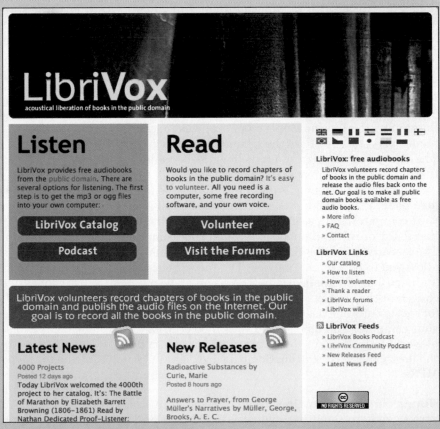

FIGURE 4D   LibriVox Home Page

YouTube YouTube (**www.youtube.com**) is a popular video-sharing Web site at which users can upload vodcasts and vlogs. As previously mentioned, you are limited to the size and length of the video or vlog you can upload, and you must be registered to upload videos, but anybody can watch them. The site warns users that they must have permission before they can upload any material that has been copyrighted. An excellent video on YouTube, created by mwesch and entitled *Information R/evolution,* explores the changes in the way we find, store, create, critique, and share information (**www. youtube.com/watch? v=-4CV05HyAbM**). This video was created as a conversation starter. Watch it and see what you think!

FIGURE 4E   Harvard University is one of many colleges that post podcasts or coursework on iTunes.

You can locate short videos on a multitude of topics on YouTube. Do you like to watch mints explode in carbonated beverages? If so, you can find about 27,000 videos on the site. YouTube is also being used by colleges and universities as a recruiting tool.

iTunes iTunes is another source of short videos. Yes, iTunes is a proprietary digital media player application used for playing and organizing digital music and video files, but it is also an interface you can use to manage the files on Apple's popular iPod digital media players as well as the iPhone and iTouch. The iTunes application must be downloaded and installed.

In addition to using iTunes on your devices to download podcasts and vodcasts, you can also install it on your computer and use it to manage your playlist. Or just listen or watch the videos through your computer. There are versions for Windows and Macs. iTunes will allow you to play music, movies, TV shows, podcasts, audio books, and applications. These can all be purchased at the iTunes store. There is a nominal charge for most, but some are free. You can create a playlist on your computer and upload it to your iPod or MP3 player. You just need to be aware of which type of device the downloads will play on. Some devices play only MP3s.

iTunes Higher Education Need to relisten to a lecture to pick up something you missed? Many professors also use iTunes as a place to post lecture supplements and other pertinent information for their courses. Similarly, some colleges and universities have set up a virtual campus in iTunes. These include some of the Ivy League schools (Figure 4E). Such campuswide storehouses of course content were very popular in 2008. Many schools have set up in-house access through their own Learning Management Systems and have not updated their virtual iTunes campus in years. Others colleges, however, are still actively using iTunes as their primary site. There may be a page on your school's Web site that provides access to a number of podcasts.

Social Networking

Social networking is a group of individuals creating a community. Social networking sites include Facebook, MySpace, LinkedIn, Twitter, Ning, and Digg, to name a few. Social networking provides a way for you to share pictures, what you are doing, and some of your thoughts with friends and family. And, it is relatively easy to share your common interests with people around the world. Rather than call or e-mail each person, all you have to do is post once, and all your friends can see what you wrote.

However, social networking is not without risks. Due to the popularity of social networking sites, there have been breaches in security. In June 2010, a threat called Clickjacking occurred. The attack allowed malicious Web site publishers to control the links that visitors can click on Facebook. Identity theft is also an issue with respect to safety on social networking sites because of the amount of information available at these sites. Features that invite user participation—messages, invitations, photos, open platform applications, and so on—are often the avenues less scrupulous individuals use to gain access to private information. This is especially true in the case of Facebook because of its popularity and the amount of information some people include. The problems plaguing social network security and privacy issues, for now, can only be resolved if users take a more careful approach to what and how much they share. Facebook has been in the news about changing privacy settings. It is important that, as a user, you constantly check to make sure the settings are where you set them.

Network World Panorama, a group from *Network World* magazine that interviews industry experts, presented a podcast on how social networks can help recruiters in their search for quality employees. The podcast references how companies can benefit by looking at sites like Facebook and Twitter in order to find the best possible employee. It stresses that potential employees should use their social networking sites and skills to find out more about companies to help them land jobs. The following sections list several of the most popular social networking sites.

SECOND LIFE

Second Life defines itself as a free online virtual world imagined and created by its residents. From the moment you enter Second Life, you'll discover a fast-growing digital world filled with people, entertainment, experiences, and opportunity. Philip Rosedale founded Linden Lab in 1999. He created a revolutionary new form of shared

experience (Figure 4F). It provides a venue where individuals jointly inhabit a 3D landscape and build the world around them. The monetary unit is called Linden dollars. You can use these dollars in the virtual world in the same way that you use "real" dollars in the "real world," to purchase goods and services. Many businesses

FIGURE 4F The possibilities in Second Life are endless. Get set to enjoy the ride and meet some interesting people (avatars) along the way.

and schools have purchased land and built a virtual complex where you can learn about their products or attend classes. If you are studying Edgar Allen Poe, you can go and visit his house. Second Life has its own blog and wiki. Second Life was featured on an episode of CSI: NY in Season 4, Episode 5: "Down the Rabbit Hole."

To get started, go to **http://secondlife.com/** and download the software to build your avatar. An **avatar** is a virtual representation of the player in a game, in this case, Second Life. Creating a basic avatar is free. If you don't like the standard choices, however, you can purchase hair and clothes using Linden dollars. Don't have any Linden dollars? You can use your credit card to buy some. Once you have chosen your name and are logged in, there is an excellent tutorial to get you flying. Then visit the virtual world.

FACEBOOK

The Facebook mission is "Giving people the power to share and make the world more open and connected." There are over 500 million people signed up on Facebook—you, movie stars, rock groups, the President, and me, just to name a few. President Barack Obama embraced Facebook during his run for office. He uses it now for town hall meetings. You can visit the White House page to join discussions. People are using Facebook (**www.facebook.com**) to stay updated on what's happening around them and share with the people in their lives.

Facebook has limitless possibilities. You can join groups, start groups, become a fan, start a fan club, get updates, send updates, and connect with friends you haven't seen in a while or those you see every day. You can upload photos, share your position or political thoughts, or let folks know just how you feel at the moment. You can play games and share the score, or play games against your friends, or find your horoscope, or what kind of sandwich you are in a Facebook quiz.

Remember, however, on this social networking site and others, be sure to protect your personal information. Don't post those party pictures or anything else that may present you in a less than favorable light. Some potential employers are looking at these social networking sites. And, in any instance, keep in mind that the more information you post, the more help you give to identity thieves.

TWITTER

Twitter (**www.twitter.com**) is a service for friends, family, and coworkers to communicate and stay connected through the exchange of quick, frequent answers to one simple question: What are you doing? With Twitter, you can stay hyperconnected to your friends and always know what they're doing. On the other hand, you can stop following them any time. You can even set quiet times on Twitter so you're not interrupted. Twitter puts you in control and becomes a modern antidote to information overload. Well, that is how it was; now Twitter is just one more information source to manage. You can follow your favorite person or movie star. Among the notables listed you can follow are Oprah, Tony Hawk, and the latest movie or album. Check **http://celebwitter.com** for a more complete listing. There have been unofficial contests about who can get the most followers. Ashton Kutcher challenged CNN to a Twitter popularity contest—and won. The potential is staggering. You can tweet from your mobile device or your computer. Staying connected is what it's all about (Figure 4G).

FLICKR

Flickr (**www.flickr.com**) is an online service that allows users to store and share photos. It is a way to get

FIGURE 4G Sign up for Twitter. It doesn't cost anything and will keep you connected.

your photos and videos to the people who matter to you. You can:

- Upload from your desktop, send by e-mail, or use your camera phone.
- Edit to get rid of red eye, crop a photo, or get creative with fonts and effects!
- Organize your photos by setting up collections, sets, and tags.
- Share photos and videos using group and privacy controls.
- Map where your photos and videos were taken.
- See photos and videos taken near you.
- Make stuff such as cards, photo books, framed prints, DVDs, and so on.
- Send photos to a vendor for printing and pickup
- Keep in touch by getting updates from family and friends.

MYSPACE

MySpace (**www.myspace.com**) permits users to view profiles, connect with others, blog, rank music, and much more! MySpace is the application that started the big push to social networking. When you set up your page, you can change the wallpaper, layout, and add music. Many sites specialize in writing the scripts you can use to change your background or make other design-related changes. Just search on "MySpace backgrounds" in any search engine. Use MySpace to find friends and classmates, meet new people, listen to free music and build playlists, share photos, and watch videos (Figure 4H). You can also blog and join forums. MySpace is not as popular as it once was and is losing marketshare. In 2010, there were only 18 million members. As previously mentioned, one big advantage to MySpace is the ability to customize.

LINKEDIN

Professionals use LinkedIn (**www.linkedin.com**) as a social networking site to exchange information, ideas, and opportunities. According to the LinkedIn Public Relations Office, as of August 2010, LinkedIn had more than 75 million registered users, spanning more than 200 countries and territories worldwide. On this site, your network consists of your connections, your connections' connections, and the people those connections know, linking you to a vast number of qualified professionals and experts. Through your network you can:

- Manage the information that's publicly available about you as a professional.
- Find and be introduced to potential clients, service providers, and subject experts who come recommended.
- Create and collaborate on projects, gather data, share files, and solve problems.
- Find potential business partners with whom to collaborate.
- Be invited by others to become involved in a business venture.
- Gain new insights from discussions with like-minded professionals in private group settings.
- Discover inside connections that can help you land jobs and close deals.
- Post and distribute job listings to find the best talent for your company.
- Start discussions and dialogues on topics of interest or questions you have.

Many employers are using this site to help screen potential employees. It is a way to interface in a professional manner.

NING

Ning (**www.ning.com**) allows you to create and join new social networks related to your interests and passions. This is a paid subscription. You can try it

FIGURE 4H   Find your friends on MySpace.

for a 30-day risk-free trial. If Facebook and MySpace are not enough for you, you can have your own social network. With over 2 million social networks created and more than 43 million registered members, millions of people everyday are coming together across Ning Networks to explore and express their interests, discover new passions, and meet new people around shared pursuits.

Ning also enables artists, brands, and organizations to simplify and control their online presence with their own unique social network that beautifully integrates with other social media services while providing the most direct, unique, and lucrative relationship with fans, consumers, and members.

DIGG

Digg is a place for people to discover and share content from anywhere on the Web. A disclosure on the Digg site (**www.digg.com**) states, "The person who associated a work with this document has dedicated this work to the Commons by waiving all of his or her rights to the work under copyright law and all related or neighboring legal rights he or she had in the work, to the extent allowable by law." This means that you no longer have ownership to what you post here. It can be copied and used anywhere without your permission. As with most social networking sites, you can link Digg with Facebook and Twitter.

RSS FEEDS

In the good old days, when you needed updates on information, you looked it up. Today, it looks you up. **RSS (Really Simple Syndication** or **Rich Site Summary**) will publish information to you and let you know when Web content has been updated or news events are taking place. Does this symbol look familiar to you? You have seen it on numerous Web sites. You click on this icon to select the feed you want. Once you request a feed, it can be sent to your computer, personal digital assistant (PDA), or any mobile device that has Web access. Want to find out what RSS feeds are available to you? Go to your favorite search engine and search for "RSS feed directory." In a recent search, over 100,000,000 were listed (Figure 4I).

As with any Web 2.0 application, security can be an

issue with RSS. There are two principal approaches for hackers to take advantage of RSS. In the first situation, the feed owner is malicious and injects malicious code into the feed directly. That's not the most popular way RSS feeds are hacked. The more common approach is for a hacker to inject an attack into an RSS feed instead of defacing a Web site. In such a scenario, the attacker would then "own" all of the site's subscribers. So, before you sign up for an RSS feed, make sure you know where your feeds are coming from. Check source Web sites for authenticity. Request RSS feeds only from Web sites with which you are familiar. Check the copyright information or learn more about the company to see whether they are who they say they are.

Instant Messaging

Instant messaging (IM) is a quick way of chatting with your buddies. There are several popular IM software packages you can download. AOL Instant Messenger (AIM) **www.aim.com**, Microsoft's Live Messenger **www.download.live.com/messenger**, and Yahoo! **http://messenger.yahoo.com/** are just a few. If you are mobile, most IMs have Web versions or mobile versions. Using IM, you never have to be too far from your buddies. The problem is that not all your friends may be on the same IM network, and individual IM networks don't play well together. If you have friends on different IM networks, there are a few programs that allow you to aggregate your buddies into one list. To use them, you also need to be a member of that platform. Two examples are Trillian (**www. trillian.com**) and Gaim (**www.gaim.com**). Many social networking sites have their own chat features. For example, you can have a live chat with your

FIGURE 4I RSS feeds from several sites can be combined into one viewable location by aggregators like Google Reader.

FIGURE 4J Chatting online.

friends on Facebook or while you're playing an online game.

Instant messaging has become so popular that many colleges and universities have IM for various departments: Admissions, Registration, and even Counseling. Some businesses and software applications have live help (chat) to assist you rather than making you look up a response or send an e-mail to explain a problem. It's a great way to provide customer service in the digital world.

When you are chatting with someone, you have to do a lot of typing. So, maybe you'd like to chat by voice. Add a webcam, microphone, and speakers to your system along with a service such as Skype (**www. skype.com**), and you can talk your way through a conversation (Figure 4J). Chatting is a **synchronous communication** activity, where you and your buddy are both online at the time and have a coherent conversation. Texting, however, is **asynchronous communication**—you are not necessarily both online at the same time. And only one of you can send a message at a time.

Texting

Court reporters have a language all their own. Gregg shorthand is a language all its own. Well, so is texting. Usually accomplished using a mobile phone, **texting** provides quick communication. Texting has been extended to include messages containing image, video, and sound content. Messages are referred to as *text messages* or *texts*.

Most texts are person-to-person, but many schools have automated systems for alerts or weather closings. Advertisers and service providers may use texting for promotions. Internet Service Providers (ISPs) have plans for texting or charge a fee for each text message you send or receive.

Because texting is usually done on a small keyboard and because they are short messages, typing full words is not efficient. Instead, text messages have their own language. Having trouble translating? Try the Lingo2word Web site (**www.lingo2word.com/ translate.php**). This Web site allows you to translate Lingo to plain English or from plain English to lingo.

Figure 4K is a short list of some of the favorite text abbreviations:

FIGURE 4K Favorite Text Abbreviations

Lingo Expression	English Translation
@TEOTD	at the end of the day
ur gr8	you are great
Adip	another day in paradise
ILU	I love you
JAS	just a second
TTFN	ta-ta for now
np	no problem
BFF	best friend forever

You can locate a full list if you search the Web.

SEXTING

Sexting is a combination of sex and texting—the sending of sexually explicit messages or photos electronically, primarily between cell phones. In 2009, *ABC News* did a story about the consequences of sexting. Several students who thought the sexually explicit message was just for each other were shocked when they discovered the message had been shared. A 17-year-old was arrested for child pornography after he uploaded pictures of his 16-year-old girlfriend online. Reuter's News Service published an article in 2009 entitled "Safe 'Sexting?' No Such Thing, Teens Warned." The article states, "In the United States, a survey last fall (2008) found one in five teenagers said they had sent or posted online nude or semi-nude pictures of themselves and 39 percent said they had sent or posted sexually suggestive messages, according to the National Campaign to Prevent Teen and Unplanned Pregnancy."

Several states have proposed legislation to prevent sexting. The legislation is designed to help young Internet users avoid sex predators, bullies, stalkers, and other dangerous contacts while interacting with friends through electronic devices. Sexting and related behaviors are also receiving attention at the federal level. The Web site for The National Conference of State Legislatures (**www.ncsl.org/**) shows legislation that has been passed by several states.

Once compromising photos are transmitted, they will never go away. Once something has been put into cyberspace, it is there forever. Just because it has been deleted from your phone doesn't mean it has been deleted from your service provider's servers or their backups. Those photos can (and sometimes do) come back to haunt those whose pictures were taken and those who transmitted them. So, stay away from questionable practices and practice safe texting.

SAFE TEXTING

WiredSafety (**www.wiredsafety.org/**), the world's largest Internet safety, help, and education resource, is a great source for information and resources on protecting yourself and others online. It provides guidance on creating a safe online presence, protecting yourself against cybercrime, and understanding cyberlaw.

Texting while driving is an international issue, and according to an article in the TimesOnline, it is more dangerous than driving under the influence of alcohol or drugs (Figure 4L). The reaction times for texters deteriorated by 35 percent, whereas the performance of those who drank alcohol at the legal limit decreased by only 12 percent. These statistics are not presented to suggest that you drink and drive. Rather, they suggest that you pay attention to the road. Avoid texting when you are:

- In motion: walking, running, jogging, riding a bike, skateboarding, skiing
- Sitting alone in a remote public place (where you could be surprised, robbed, or attacked by someone coming up behind you.
- Walking in crowds (where someone could come up behind you and either attack you or grab your purse or wallet)
- Driving

FIGURE 4L Texting and driving are a dangerous combination. Don't mix them!

Here are three more ways to make sure texting doesn't send you to the hospital:

- Always put your phone in an easily accessible place.
- If you need to text right away, stop what you're doing or pull off the road.
- Turn off your phone when you're doing something that requires your full attention.

Texting safely is not just avoiding texting while you are moving; it also includes protecting yourself. To guard yourself, don't send text messages to people you don't know. If you receive a text from a stranger, don't even open it. Delete it immediately. In addition, don't give out any personal information in a text message. Following these guidelines will start you on the road to safe texting.

Tagging

A **tag** is any user-generated word or phrase that helps organize Web content and label it in a more human way. You use tags when you want someone to find your Web page or blog. In Web development, they are called *metatags*. Using tags can bring your Web site to the top of the list when people are searching for specific content. For example, if you want someone to locate your blog on the latest way to fold napkins, you might use the tags: napkins, folding, napkin folding, and napkin folding techniques. This will help insure that your blog will show up on the list. In another meaning of the word, you may have been tagged in a photo posted on Facebook. Someone picks a photo and assigns names to the people or objects in the photo. Sometimes it is a real photo of your group and sometimes, for the novelty, it is a gag photo. You might see a lamppost tagged with the name of a friend. To tag a photo on Facebook, click on a person's face in the photo and then select their name in the box that pops up. If their name is not already in the box, you can provide it. Repeat this process for everyone in the photo. If you need to tag yourself, select "me."

A note about tagging: When you tag a friend in a photo, that photo will appear in their profile. If they don't want the photo in their profile, they can simply click "remove" next to their name. There are many Web sites where you can find group pictures and photos you can use for this purpose. Just remember turnabout is fair play.

Collaboration Tools

Web 2.0 has opened up a new world for online collaboration. **Collaboration tools** help you work in partnership with team members online. Working on a project is hard enough, but what happens when you need to share a document or idea? These tools provide a way to work together without having to physically meet. Virtual worlds are everywhere. There are many different types of collaboration tools. Some are free and some have a cost associated with them. Some are for a specific type of application such as project management, and some are a suite of applications.

One of the first of its kind is Google Apps, a suite that combines Gmail, Google Docs, Google Calendar, and other Web applications. Google hosts it all, providing space on its servers for you to save documents and collaborate. You can edit your documents from any device in the world as long as it has Internet access and can access Google Apps. Many companies and colleges are switching or have switched to these applications. For personal use, Google Apps includes:

- Gmail—Send and receive fast, searchable e-mail with less spam.
- Google Talk—IM and call your friends through your computer.
- Google Calendar—Organize your schedule and share events with friends.
- Google Docs—Share online documents, presentations, and spreadsheets.
- Google Sites—Create websites and secure group wikis.

Google Docs is a free, Web-based word processor, spreadsheet, presentation, and form application offered by Google (**http://docs.google.com**). This URL for Google Docs has information and a tour you can take to see how these applications can help you collaborate. Google Docs allows users to create and edit documents online while collaborating in real time with other users. You can create, edit, and upload the documents quickly. One handy feature is that you can import your existing documents, spreadsheets, and presentations, or create new ones from scratch. Many of the popular document extensions are accepted. With this software, you can access and edit your files from anywhere; all you need is a Web browser. Your documents, spreadsheets, and presentations are stored securely online. The collaboration feature is that you can share changes in real-time and invite people to view your documents and make changes together, at the same time.

Microsoft Office Web Apps are available on Sky Drive through Windows Live. You can get started for free at **http://office.microsoft.com/en-us/web-apps/**. If you have a Windows Live password you can log right in; if not, you can create an account. Office Apps online provides all the applications with which you are familiar: Word, Excel, PowerPoint, Hotmail, and MSN, to name a few. In addition to One Note, there is also a Bing search tool. Microsoft Office 2010 has what it calls the Backstage area. Clicking on it brings up all the controls for saving, sharing, printing, and so on.

Web 2.0 in the Classroom

Web 2.0 has many uses in the classroom. Forums and discussion boards are very, very useful. There has been some debate about the differences between these tools, but the commonality wins. They differ from a blog or a wiki in that forums and discussion boards are threaded discussions in which someone asks a question or expresses an idea and others can add their thoughts or answers. Discussion boards are common on Learning Management Systems such as ANGEL or Blackboard, where the class meets in a virtual classroom instead of face-to-face. Some are formal discussions started by the professor; some are informal and are started by a classmate.

Forums and discussion boards can be monitored or unmonitored. When you post a comment to an article on a Web site, you may not see it posted until it has been cleared for content. If you have a hobby, you will probably be able to find a forum on that topic. Having a problem with something, such as your car not starting? You can find a forum on that. You name it, and there is most likely a forum on that topic. To locate a forum or discussion board directory, use your favorite search engine. If you were working on a team project and you sent an e-mail to each member, you would receive individual responses. Then you would have to take the time to put it all together. If you had taken advantage of a discussion board, all the responses would be in one place, where each of the team members can immediately read and respond to what the other members had to say.

Collaboration is very important in courses that have you doing team projects. You can use many tools for this. Podcasts on iTunes, videos on YouTube, and Web searches are all very relevant to today's classroom. To locate podcasts that can be used in the classroom, check the section on podcasts. And don't forget blogs and wikis. Some professors are even exploring using Twitter in the classroom. They believe it has

> " Web 2.0 has opened up a new world for online collaboration. Collaboration tools help you work in partnership with team members online. "

made the student and the classroom more productive; some disagree and have banned all computer and mobile access in the classroom.

The use of digital devices in the classroom is something that will be debated for years. Remember netiquette is applicable in the classroom. It is rude to have someone clicking keys while a serious discussion is going on, as is the sound you hear when you receive an IM. If you need to listen to something that is on your computer, be courteous and use headphones. Web 2.0 can enhance a classroom or subject, but be careful not to make it the only way you communicate in the classroom.

When the search engines online are not enough, along comes Rollyo. Do you have a group of Web sites that are your favorites? Or a set of online resources that you use frequently to answer homework or reference questions? Well, Rollyo (**www.rollyo.com**) may be the tool for you. Rollyo allows you to create your own search tool for the just the Web sites you know and trust. It is a perfect application to help with your research papers.

Web 2.0 in Business

An article in *PC World* magazine states that more and more employers are checking social networking sites of potential employees. Careerbuilder.com has researched this and noted that although 24 percent of employers had hired a staff member based on his or her social-networking profile, 33 percent had also decided *not* to make a job offer after reviewing the content on a profile. Use of drugs or drinking and the posting of photographs deemed inappropriate or provocative were identified as the most popular reasons why employers eliminated a candidate after viewing his or her social networking profile. So, be careful what you post on your social networking sites. Having a proper profile on Facebook or MySpace can be beneficial in your job search, as can having a professional LinkedIn page.

Similarly, many businesses are embracing Web 2.0 technologies for their Web sites. Consider Amazon.com. When you visit a book page on Amazon.com, a list of prices for that book on other sites pops up. This shows you, the buyer, other options.

Did you ever wonder who is looking at where you are traveling on the Internet? Those top five lists you do on Facebook—who really reads them? According to *Network World* magazine, LivingSocial, the company behind the application that lets you create the lists, is

> " ... although **24 percent** of **employers** had hired a staff member **based on** his or her **social-networking-profile**, 33 percent had also decided *not* to make a **job offer** after reviewing the **content** on a **profile**. "

selling your Top 5 data to major entertainment outfits. When asked what LivingSocial does with all the data they collect from the Top 5 applications on Facebook, the CEO of LivingSocial said, "We go to marketers and say, 'Here are a couple million people into music, and here are a couple million into movies.' We're working with *American Idol,* Green Day, TNT, a lot of large brands." So not only are you sharing your Top 5 movies and books with your friends, you are potentially sharing that data with producers, rock bands, TV stations, and who knows what else. Businesses love this stuff and use the information in formulating marketing strategies.

Safety and Privacy

Here are some tips for safe social networking to help you have a good experience. After all, participating in online social networking sites leaves a trail of personal information that can make stealing your identity a whole lot easier.

- Beware of giving out too much information. You never want to share your Social Security number (including just the last four digits), your birth date, home address, or phone number. Protect all your passwords, PINs, bank account numbers, and credit card information.
- Use the privacy options. Don't let people who you do not know see your information.
- Don't trust, just verify. Verify the page belongs to who it says it does. For URLs and domain names, you can do this by going to **www.whois.com** and doing a WHOIS lookup. That will tell you who owns a domain name.
- Control comments. You can set comments so they can't be left anonymously. However, this will not stop people from using false names. Therefore, you may not want comments to post until you approve them.
- Avoid sharing personal details accidentally. Be careful about what information you list.
- Search yourself. It is a good idea to search your name on several search engines and to check your profile as others see it on the social networking sites.
- Don't violate your school or company's social networking policies. Be aware of the acceptable use policies (AUP) of your school or company, and follow them.
- Learn how Web sites can use your information. Read the privacy statement.
- Don't play the popularity content. There is no race to see who has the most friends. Do not invite strangers into your networks.

- Create smaller social networks. You may be better served by creating a smaller, more personal network using Ning.

Web 2.0 is an exciting concept. Use it, but be careful about abusing it. Protect yourself from fraud and you will be able to enjoy the benefits. So, what's next?

Web 3.0?

Some experts believe the next generation of the Web, **Web 3.0**, will make tasks like your search for movies and food faster and easier. Many of these experts believe that the Web 3.0 browser will act like a personal assistant, learning what you are interested in as you browse. The more you use the Web, the more your browser learns about you and the less specific you'll need to be with your questions. You'll be able to sit back and let the Internet do all the work for you.

Some experts insist that the trend that could help the development of Web 3.0 is the **mashup**, which combines two or more applications into a single application. As an example, programs that allow users to review restaurants and at the same time locate them with Google Maps are mashups. Some Internet experts believe that in Web 3.0, creating mashups will be so easy anyone should be able to do it.

Smartphones provide many of these search functions. Just use the movie app and you can discover movies and showtimes at the local theater. The Web is with us all the time through our smartphones. Now more than ever, we are keeping in touch with friends and family. Many of us have added them to our social networks. Just remember, when you post that you are going to the Bahamas for Spring Break, everyone on your social network knows. Who knows who might say something to someone whom you would rather not know that you are away and where you are.

Key Terms and Concepts

Multiple Choice

Circle the correct choice for each of the following.

1. The information in a wiki can _____.
   a. be accepted as the truth
   b. be updated by anyone
   c. be updated only by experts
   d. never be updated

2. Instant messaging is _____.
   a. synchronous communication
   b. asynchronous communication
   c. always secure
   d. only available on computers

3. Which of the following is *not* an example of a Web 2.0 application?
   a. Netscape Navigator   b. YouTube
   c. Facebook   d. Blogger

4. If a blog has a high amount of traffic, which of the following statements is true?
   a. The blog earns a lot of revenue.
   b. The blog has a lot of readers.
   c. The blog's author posts multiple blog entries on a daily basis.
   d. The blog contains a number of links to other sites.

5. Which of the following can be used to notify you when a blog or Web site has posted new content?
   a. blog
   b. wiki
   c. SRS feed
   d. RSS feed

6. It is dangerous to text your friends while _____.
   a. you are sitting in your room
   b. you are driving a car
   c. you are a passenger in a car
   d. you are in class

7. Which of the following is an example of a social network designed for professionals?
   a. LinkedIn
   b. MySpace
   c. Twitter
   d. Facebook

8. Which of the following sites can be used to create your own social network?
   a. Facebook
   b. YouTube
   c. LinkedIn
   d. Ning

9. Podcasts that contain videos are sometimes referred to as _____.
   a. video casts
   b. vodcasts
   c. audio casts
   d. broadcasts

10. The term Web 2.0 can best be defined as
    a. a set of techniques that collectively provide an upgraded presentation and usefulness for the World Wide Web.
    b. the term used to describe the new programming language used to create content for the Web.
    c. the term that venture capitalists use to describe the World Wide Web.
    d. an expression that describes technology used to promote and create dotcom businesses.

Spotlight Exercises

1. With your instructor's permission, set up a classroom discussion board. Use it to discuss Web 3.0 and how you believe it can be used in the business world. Send the link to your instructor so he or she can follow the discussion. Write a one-page paper on the advantages and disadvantages of discussion boards.

2. In small groups of three or four, create a Google Site page for your group. Each person in the classroom should set up an ID. Everyone should be invited to join each group. Take time to post to the page and share ideas. Add an event, chat with a classmate. Write a one-page paper on how you could use Google Sites in all your classes. How did you like the opportunity to set up your own social network?

3. To gain experience in setting up a community, create a blog on one of the blogging sites about the impact smartphones are having and share the address with the class. If you created a Google Sites page, use it to share the address. Write a one-page paper detailing your blogging experience. What did you like and/or dislike? Be sure to comment on two of your classmates' blogs.

4. Set up a Windows Live account. Then access Microsoft Office Web Apps. Create a simple document about the advantages to using an online application to create documents. Share it with your classmates and your instructor.

5. If you do not have an account on Second Life, set one up. Go through the tutorial on how to use Second Life. Communicate with one of your classmates through the chat. Write a one- to two-page paper on your experience. Did you like the site? Did you find it easy to manipulate your avatar? Will you go back and do some more exploring. What are some of the benefits and drawbacks of Second Life? Include a screen capture of your avatar in your paper.

6. With RSS feeds becoming more popular, create and share your feeds. Create a free online Bloglines account (**www.bloglines.com**) for yourself and subscribe to at least 10 newsfeeds to your reader using Bloglines tutorial steps 1 through 3 for instructions. You can search for the tutorial on Google videos. Once you have created your account, subscribe to several of your classmates' feeds. This is as easy as typing the blog URL into the subscribe field in Bloglines. Try it—it's easy! Then try adding a few other types of news feeds from news sources.

chapter

6

The Internet and the World Wide Web

Chapter Objectives

1 Define the Internet, and explain how it works. (p. 248)

2 Describe methods for accessing the Internet. (p. 251)

3 Differentiate between the Internet and the World Wide Web and describe the elements that enable Web content to be displayed. (p. 254)

4 Describe several methods of finding information on the Web including the use of a URL, surfing, conducting searches, and sharing with other Web users through RSS feeds, blogs, wikis, and podcasts. (p. 261)

5 Identify features to look for when evaluating a Web site or its content. (p. 269)

6 List the most popular Internet services and explain what they do. (p. 272)

7 Describe the three types of e-commerce. (p. 278)

8 List the rules of netiquette. (p. 283)

9 List safe surfing procedures, and identify hazards of the Web. (p. 283)

It seems that being connected 24/7 has become a necessity in our world and that the Internet is no longer just for fun, but for work, social contact, education, and everyday information. You know how to use the Internet, but do you know how to use it effectively? How would you rate your search skills? How do you know whether the information from a Web source is reputable? Are you a potential victim of cybercrime? Is the site you are about to provide with your credit card number a secure site?

The Internet has created a shift in communication methods by providing a medium that allows interactivity. With the Internet, individuals can create information as well as consume it. Perhaps that is its real appeal, the ability to speak and be heard around the world, which is propelling its use to regions and populations isolated from media in the past.

The Internet offers many benefits and is ripe with pitfalls for those who don't understand it and the responsibilities that go along with Internet usage. This chapter is your guide to understanding the Internet and using it safely for personal, educational, and business purposes. Key concepts include those listed here:

- How the Internet works and how you connect to it
- The difference between the Web and Internet
- An overview of the different browsers
- The parts of a Web address
- Tools and strategies to streamline your Internet searches
- Key Internet services such as e-mail, chats, instant messaging, social networking, online discussions, and electronic mailing lists
- Different types of e-commerce
- Good online behavior and safe surfing techniques ■

What Is the Internet and How Does It Work?

The **Internet**, also called the **Net**, is a global computer network made up of thousands of privately and publicly owned computers and networks that grew and interlinked, over time, into one giant network. In short, the Internet is a network of networks.

This idea of connecting computers of different designs and over distant locations started in the 1960s with the U.S. Department of Defense and project called ARPANET (Advanced Research Projects Agency Network). The purpose of the project was to create a form of secure communication for military and scientific purposes and to create a method for transferring such communications between computers. The outcome of the project was a network that consisted of four computers located at The University of California at Los Angeles, the University of California at Santa Barbara, the University of Utah, and Stanford Research Institute. In turn, each of these four nodes connected hundreds of other computers to the network. The Internet is the offspring of the ARPANET project. To learn more about the history of the Internet, go to **www.isoc.org/internet/history/brief. shtml**, a page posted by The Internet Society, an organization for professionals who are interested in supporting the technical development of the Internet.

Today, the Internet is composed of more than 750 million hosts. A **host** is a computer that has two-way access to other computers; it can receive requests and reply to those requests. These hosts are interconnected and geographically spread out over the world. Figure 6.1 provides a simplified image of a single network that is set up to provide its users with access to the Internet and any of its hosts. A study done by the Internet Systems Consortium substantiates the astronomical growth of the Internet by citing an increase of over 208 million hosts between 2008 and 2010.

The Internet has come a long way since its inception as a communication and file-exchange network for government agencies; scientific research; and, later, academic institutions. Today it has become a medium for discovering and exploring information, marketing products, shopping, taking classes, and socializing (Figure 6.2). Through a combination of surveys done by comScore, Inc., a global leader in measuring the digital world, the global Internet audience (defined as users ages 15 and older) as of December 2009, using home and work computers, was approaching 2 billion unique visitors. With these numbers constantly on the rise, the leap to three billion users is expected to come quickly.

But technology is not equally distributed, and Internet access and usage is no different. Countries or regions in which over 70 percent of the population has Internet access include the United States, Canada, Japan, United Kingdom, South Korea, and Spain. Countries in which less than 40 percent of the populate has Internet access include China, India, Brazil, Mexico, and the Philippines. The bar graph in Figure 6.3 makes this inequity even more apparent.

Now that you know what the Internet is and a little about how it started, let's explore how it works and how it is used.

How the Internet Works

The unique feature about the Internet is that nobody owns it. It is best thought of as the granddaddy of networks in which

FIGURE 6.1 Both wired and wireless technologies are used to connect to the Internet.

every connected computer can exchange data with any other computer on the network. The term **cyberspace** is often used when talking about the Internet. It's an appropriate term because it captures the concept of the intangible, nonphysical territory that the Internet encompasses. The networks that make up the Internet are not maintained by one company or organization. Instead, the Internet is maintained by a conglomerate of volunteers across the world. Some governing bodies restrict control and/or provide equipment. But the majority of network servers and connectivity equipment are provided by universities, telecommunications companies, businesses, corporations, and services that sell Internet access. It really is amazing that it all works!

Architecture

The **Internet backbone**, the main high-speed routes through which data travels, are maintained by **network service providers (NSPs)** such as AT&T, NCI, Sprint, BBN, and UUNET. The equipment of these providers is linked at **network access points (NAPs)** so that data may, for example, begin its journey on a segment maintained by AT&T but cross over to a Sprint segment in order to reach its destination. Between your computer or business network and the Internet backbone are **routers**, specialized devices that connect networks, locate the best path of transmission, and ensure that your data reaches its destination (Figure 6.4). Visit **www.internet2.edu/about/** for information on a nonprofit consortium of universities, government agencies, and computer and telecommunication companies in over 50 countries that develop and deploy advanced networking applications and technologies.

Interoperability

The Internet does more than merely allow the free exchange of data among millions of computers; it provides the ability for computers to exchange data

Social network
www.facebook.com

Entertainment
www.apple.com/itunes/store

FIGURE 6.2 The Internet, with applications in education, entertainment, marketing, and social networking, is the fastest and most universal form of mass media ever developed.

Source: www.internetworldstats.com/stats.htm

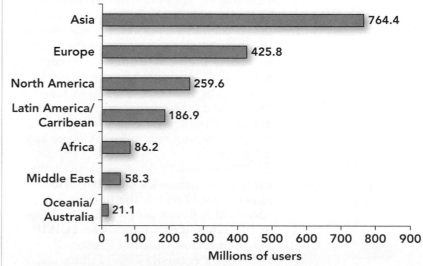

FIGURE 6.3 Internet Users by Geographic Region

FIGURE 6.4 The Path Data Takes from Your Computer to the Internet

regardless of the brand, model, or operating system the computers are running. This feature is called **interoperability**. This remarkable characteristic of the Internet comes into play every time you use the network. When you access the Internet using a Mac, for example, you contact a variety of machines that may include other Macs, Windows PCs, UNIX machines, and even mainframe computers. You don't know what type of computer you're accessing and it doesn't make any difference.

The Internet's interoperability helps explain the network's popularity. No network could match the Internet's success if it forced people to use just one or two types of computers. The **TCP/IP (Transmission Control Protocol/ Internet Protocol)** suite of protocols, which supply the standard methods of

packaging and transmitting information on the Internet are responsible for enabling interoperability (see Figure 6.5). When you obtain direct access to the Internet, usually through an Internet access provider, your computer is provided with a copy of the TCP/IP programs just as is every other computer that is connected to the Internet. The TCP/IP suite employs a two-layer communication design. The TCP layer, **Transmission Control Protocol**, manages the assembling of a message or file into smaller packets that are transmitted over the Internet and then received by a TCP layer on the destination computer that reassembles the packets into the original message. The lower layer, the **Internet Protocol (IP)**, handles the address part of each packet so that it gets to the right destination.

Now that you've learned about how the Internet works, the next section explores how you go about getting online.

Accessing the Internet: Going Online

When you access the Internet, it is referred to as *going online.* You usually do not connect directly to the Internet backbone. Instead, you usually connect to an Internet access provider that in turn connects you to the backbone via some type of wired or wireless connection.

Internet Access Providers

Internet access providers are companies or businesses that provide access to via Internet free, for a fixed monthly charge, or for an itemized per use fee.

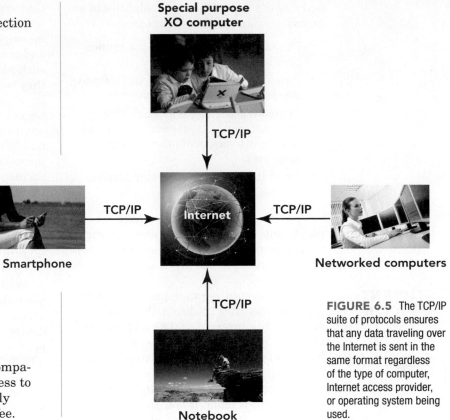

FIGURE 6.5 The TCP/IP suite of protocols ensures that any data traveling over the Internet is sent in the same format regardless of the type of computer, Internet access provider, or operating system being used.

It is easy to think of the Internet as just something out there, an intangible, having no effect on our physical world. In reality, 2009 estimates indicate that Internet data centers worldwide consumed 2 percent of global electricity production. Most of the energy was to power forced-air cooling systems in the data centers. One data center operator compared the heat emitted from a rack of servers in a data center to the amount of heat emitted by a 7-foot stack of toaster ovens. The energy to cool such centers undoubtedly did not come from green sources and cost $30 billion (U.S.).

Another way to cool the data centers is under development, with a working model named Aquasar expected to be completed in 2010. This new idea is to use water, not air, to cool the computing environment. Water cooled to 60–70°C (158°F), cool enough to keep the processing chips below their maximum heat of 85°C (185°F), will be pumped through tiny channels in the computer systems of the data centers and will absorb heat from the metal along the way. The working model, developed by IBM Zurich and the Swiss Federal Institute of Technology Zurich (ETH), will be located on the ETH campus. In this prototype, the water used to absorb the heat from the computer systems will release that heat into the building and then recirculate to cool the computer system. It is estimated that this system will reduce the carbon footprint of the ETH campus by 85 percent and save up to 30 tons of carbon emissions a year. For more information, go to **www.youtube.com/watch?v= FbGyAXsLzIc** to view a video on this new cooling concept. ●

Some of the roles and responsibilities of an access provider are listed here:

- Providing and maintaining a connection to the Internet
- Supporting the hardware and software needed to service that connection
- Protecting their site and network from external threats such as viruses, hacker attacks, and other illegal activities
- Providing 24-hour customer service and technical support

Access providers fall into three categories: Internet service providers, online service providers, and wireless Internet service providers. Let's look at the features of each.

STUDENT VIDEO

An **Internet service provider (ISP)** is a company that traditionally provided access to the Internet and no additional services. Today these providers have added features to make them a one-stop source for Internet services. There are both local and national ISPs, each having varied services and pricing. If you are looking for an Internet service provider, you might want to start with "The List" (**www.thelist.com**). This is a buyer's guide to ISPs and can be searched by area or country.

An **online service provider (OSP)** is a for-profit firm that provides a proprietary network and offers special services that are available only to subscribers. Members may participate in instant messaging, chat rooms, and discussions, and take advantage of fee-based content, such as magazines and newspapers. When they began, online services provided a large amount of content that was accessible only by those who subscribed to that online service, whereas ISPs predominantly served to provide access to the Internet and generally provided little, if any, exclusive content of their own. The distinction between these two services has become less defined as OSPs today offer Internet access and ISPs offer more user services. Popular OSPs are MSN and AOL (Figure 6.6).

A **wireless Internet service provider** can be a local or national company that provides wireless Internet access to computers and other mobile devices, such as notebooks and smartphones. Some familiar providers are AT&T, T-Mobile, and Verizon Wireless. Requirements for a wireless connection include a portable device, an internal wireless adapter or a USB port for connecting an external adapter, and a wireless Internet access plan from a provider. Wireless connectivity for portable devices in your home or office is usually provided through a wireless router located in close proximity and connected to your provider. A **hot spot** is usually a public location like an airport, college campus, or coffee shop that provides Internet access for devices fitted with the wireless technology listed above. Some hot spots allow free access; others charge a nominal fee. When using a connection at a hotspot, always turn on your system's firewall and avoid accessing private information because transmissions at these locations are usually not encrypted and are susceptible to detection by others. For a list of free Internet access locations by state go to **www.wififreespot.com**.

To access the Internet backbone, access providers distribute software that runs on users' computers to enable the connection. Essentially, the provider acts

FIGURE 6.6 Internet access providers, such as MSN, AT&T, and Comcast, provide Internet access and extra features to meet the needs of both individual and business subscribers.

as an access ramp to an expressway; in this case, the expressway is the Internet backbone. These various providers usually charge a monthly fee for Internet access, again like the fee you pay to use some expressways, but you can sometimes obtain free trial accounts for a certain number of days or hours.

Now that the difference between access providers has been covered, let's move on to the various types of physical connections that can be used to gain entry to the Internet.

Connection Options

In addition to obtaining an Internet account, you have to decide how you will access the Internet (Figure 6.7). Be aware that the speed of access advertised by an access provider is often a maximum. Few users actually find their usage reaching these advertised numbers. Your access choices typically include the following options:

- **Dial-up access.** If you are searching for an affordable connection solution and speed is not a high priority, then a dial-up provider will likely meet your needs. A dial-up connection does not require any special hardware; it uses your existing phone jack and dial-up modem configurations.

The downside of this type of access is the speed; it is the slowest of all Internet services. Many people use a dial-up connection as a backup for their existing broadband service.

- **Digital subscriber line (DSL).** A DSL connection offers faster access speeds than dial-up, while making use of ordinary phone lines with the addition of a special external modem. One drawback of DSL is that service doesn't extend more than a few miles from a telephone switching station or central office (CO). Although this distance is being extended, DSL service may be unavailable in some rural areas.
- **Cable access.** Many cable TV companies provide permanent online connections and offer high-speed Internet access, comparable to—and sometimes surpassing—DSL speeds. No phone line is needed, but a cable modem is required.
- **Satellite access.** If your geographical area has been overlooked by DSL and cable providers, go outside. If you have a clear view of the sky, then you can most likely get high-speed satellite Internet service! The connection to your high-speed satellite service is comprised of both indoor and outdoor equipment. Outside,

FIGURE 6.7 Types of Internet Access

Type	Price Range per Month	Speed of Access (receiving data)	Advantages	Disadvantages
Dial-up	$5 to $20	Slow: 56 kilobits per second (Kbps)	Availability Low user cost	Slow speed
DSL	$10 to $30	Average: 1.5 megabits per second (Mbps) Maximum: 7+ Mbps	Speed Reliability	Availability High user cost
Cable	$30 to $60	Average: 3 Mbps Maximum: 30+ Mbps	Speed Reliability	Availability High user cost
Satellite	$60 to $100	Average: 700 Kbps Maximum: 1.5 Mbps	Availability Speed	High user cost Reliability
Fiber-optic service	$40 to $140	Average: 15 Mbps Maximum: 50+ Mbps	Speed	Availability High user cost

there is an antenna and electronics to transmit and receive data, along with a connection to a small, unobtrusive dish. This equipment connects to an indoor receive unit (IRU) and indoor transmit unit (ITU) that connect to your computer through a simple USB connector. Satellite is more costly than cable or DSL, but if you live in a rural area, it might be a viable alternative to dial-up.

- **Fiber-optic service.** Fiber-optic lines running directly to the home provide users with an incredibly fast Internet connection, easily surpassing other methods. With more than 1.5 million customers (with a goal of 3 to 4 million by 2010) in at least 16 states, **fiber-optic service** is rapidly becoming a challenger to DSL and cable providers, especially in the suburbs. However, this service is still unavailable in many cities and rural areas and is usually offered by a limited number of providers. No modem is needed, but fiber-optic cable may have to be run to and within your home.

If you don't need a constant, daily Internet connection, some businesses offer special leased lines for companies, educational institutions, and large organizations. Internet access is attained through the organization's network and is usually free to the users because the company or institution pays the bill.

Now that you understand the various ways to connect to the Internet, let's differentiate the Internet from its most popular entity, the World Wide Web.

FIGURE 6.8 The Internet provides the infrastructure used to transport the ideas, queries, and information available on the World Wide Web to and from users.

The Internet and the Web: What's the Difference?

What's the difference between saying, "I'm on the Internet" versus "I'm on the Web"? Although many people talk as if the Internet and the Web were the same thing, they are not. Recall, the Internet is a network of hardware (computers, cables, and routers) through which any computer can directly access other computers and exchange data. The **World Wide Web** (or **Web** or **WWW**) is a portion of the Internet that contains billions of documents. So, the Internet is the physical connection of millions of networks, like an interstate, whereas the Web *uses* the Internet as its transport mechanism to distribute its collection of documents, called Web pages. The Web uses the Internet architecture in the same way cars and trucks use an interstate—to move goods and people (Figure 6.8).

Who owns or controls the Web? As with the Internet, no one owns the Web. Both involve thousands of publicly and privately owned computers and networks, all of which agree to follow certain standards and guidelines and share resources on the network. Standards and guidelines related to all aspects of the Web are published by the World Wide Web Consortium (W3C), an international organization based in Cambridge, Massachusetts. Visit **www.w3.org** to review the mission of the W3C, a list of its 332 members, and various Internet standards (Figure 6.9).

Besides the W3C, many other organizations contribute to the development of different aspects of the Internet and Web. Figure 6.10 provides a list of some of the more established and recognized organizations and a brief description of their missions.

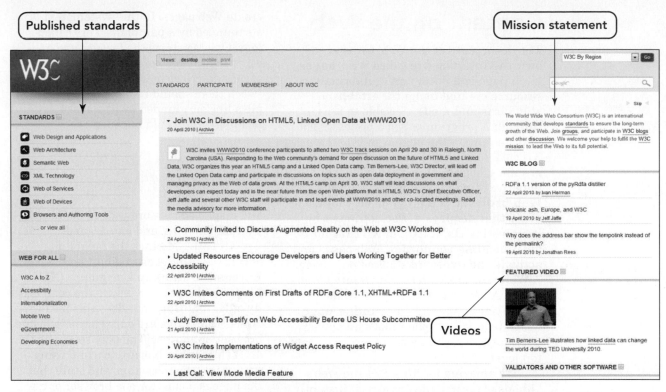

FIGURE 6.9 The W3C has members from all over the world that participate in the development of vendor-neutral standards for the Web.

FIGURE 6.10 Internet and Web Management Organizations

Name	Purpose
ICANN—Internet Corporation for Assigned Names and Numbers **www.icann.org**	Nonprofit, international organization responsible for coordinating the Internet's Domain Name System and assigning IP addresses.
IETF—Internet Engineering Task Force **www.ietf.org**	International community of information technology (IT) professionals, including network designers, operators, vendors, and researchers, responsible for developing Internet standards, best current practices, and informational documents.
ISOC—Internet Society **www.isoc.org**	Nonprofit, international association consisting of over 80 organizations and 28,000 individual members, formed to provide leadership in Internet-related standards, education, and policy for the benefit of people throughout the world.
IAB—Internet Architecture Board **www.iab.org**	Advisory body to the ISOC, this international committee of the IETF is comprised of 13 volunteers from the IT community who oversee the development of Internet architecture, protocols, procedures, and standards.
IRTF—Internet Research Task Force **www.irtf.org**	A task force of individual contributors from the research community working together in small, long-term research groups that report to the IAB and explore important topics related to the evolution of the Internet.
Network Solutions **www.networksolutions.com**	Organization responsible for managing the central domain name database.

Content on the Web

The documents of the Web, transported over the Internet, are called **Web pages**. Each page is a document or information resource created using the established standards and made viewable to a user through a program called a browser. The information on the page is in HTML or XHTML format and can include text, graphics, sound, animation, video, and hypertext links to other Web pages. A **Web browser** is a program on your computer that displays a Web document by interpreting the HTML or XHTML format, enabling you to view Web pages and activate the hyperlinks placed on a page. A **Web site** is a collection of related Web pages. A Web site typically contains a **home page** (also called an **index page**), which is a default page that's displayed automatically when you enter a site at its top level.

It's amazing to think that the Web's billions of documents are almost instantly accessible by means of the computer sitting on your desk. Tens of thousands of new Web pages appear every day. The Web has increased appeal due to its graphical richness, made possible by the integration of text and images.

In the following section, you'll learn how all of these pieces work together to make a Web page, starting with the concept of hypertext.

The Hypertext Concept

Hypertext is a system in which objects (text, pictures, music, programs, and so on) can be creatively linked to each other. It works by means of **hyperlinks** (also called **links**), elements in an electronic document that act as the connector to another place in the same document or to an entirely different document. Typically, you click on the hyperlink to bring another object into view. Hyperlinks are an important ingredient of the World Wide Web (Figure 6.11).

This system of hypertext is created by a special code called **Hypertext Markup Language (HTML)** or **Extensible Hypertext Markup Language (XHTML)**. HTML is a language that uses a tag system of code to create Web pages. In this system, text is surrounded by a pair of markers called *tags*. One tag starts the feature and another indicates where it is to stop. This pair of tags describes how the text located between them should be displayed. For example a line surrounded by h1 (level 1 heading) tags would be coded as:

```
<h1>Welcome to Computers Are
Your Future</h1>
```

and displayed by a browser as boldfaced, a larger font size, and left aligned.

XHTML combines the flexibility of HTML with the extensibility of **Extensible Markup Language (XML)**, a language designed to reduce the complexity of HTML. But what does this mean? Some HTML tags are only viewable in one browser or another. The only solutions that an HTML writer has are to avoid using those tags, use those tags and state that the page is meant for one browser or another, or write multiple pages and direct readers to the appropriate pages. With XHTML, however, if you need to define a tag for clarity across different browsers or create a new markup tag, you simply define the tag in an XHTML module and use it in your page as you would any other HTML tag. The browser interpreting the page reads the definition of the tag and presents it as defined. This feature makes a page truly compatible with all browsers.

FIGURE 6.11 Hyperlinks, often displayed in blue characters and underlined, are perfect for tutorial Web sites. The user just clicks a hyperlink to view a Web page on a specific topic.

As stated earlier, the agency responsible for standardizing HTML and XHTML is the World Wide Web Consortium (W3C).

In addition to being a global hypertext system, the Web is a distributed hypermedia system. A **distributed hypermedia system** is a network-based content development system that uses multimedia resources, such as sound, video, and text, as a means of navigation or illustration. In this system, the responsibility for creating content is distributed among many people. The current generation of the Web, known as **Web 2.0**, takes this concept further by providing even more opportunities for individuals to collaborate, interact with one another, and create new content by using applications such as blogs, wikis, and podcasts. The more people who create content, the easier information creation and dissemination will become. For example, if you are researching the White House, you might link to **www.whitehouse.gov** for an overview of the current events taking place. From there you can click one of several hyperlinks (links) that will take you to additional Web pages, like Photo and Videos, Briefing Room, and Issues, which zero in on the details of that topic. Notice in Figure 6.12 that the arrows go in both directions. This is because the Web pages included in a Web site usually provide links to related pages, links that return you to the previous page, and almost always a link back to the home page. These crosslinks provide easy navigation and reduce backtracking.

The Web's distribution of content does have some drawbacks:

- Not all links work. There's no guarantee that the Web page's author will keep the page updated or active. The author can delete it or move it at any time without notice. For this reason, **dead links** (also called **broken links**), which are links to documents that have disappeared, are common on the Web.

- No individual or organization validates information posted on the Web. When

FIGURE 6.12 In hypertext documents, links can take you further into a site for more information or take you back to revisit a Web page you have already viewed.

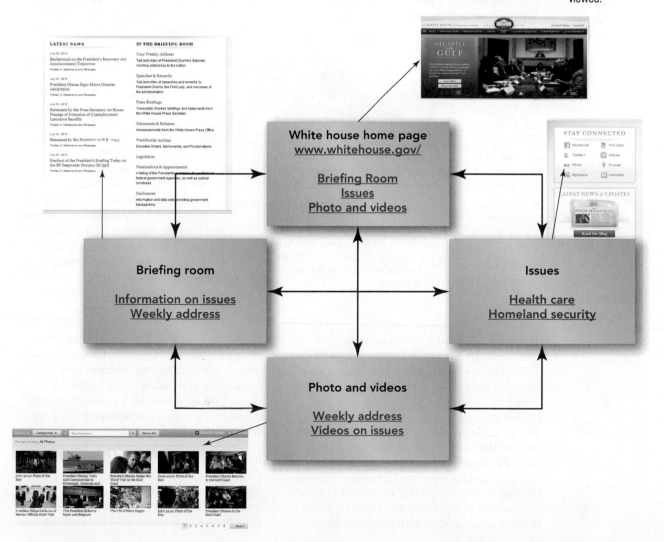

you create a hyperlink to a Web site you didn't create, investigate the credentials of the source and the accuracy of the content. This is critical to the integrity of your own Web site or Web page.

- Basic Web pages are not expensive to create or host. This has lead to the proliferation of Web content or information overload. This overload works both ways: The presenter can supply too much data, more than what is necessary to substantiate a point; and the researcher can get caught up in the search, becoming saturated with content and sidebars and losing focus.

Now that you understand hypertext and its use in providing a quick jump to Web content, let's discuss Web browsers and Web servers, items that enable us to view Web pages and make use of hyperlinks.

Viewing Content: Web Browsers

The first graphical Web browser, Mosaic, was released in 1993 and is credited with launching the Web on the road to popularity. Developed by the National Center for Supercomputing Applications at the University of Illinois, Mosaic was followed by two commercial products, Netscape Navigator and Microsoft Internet Explorer (IE). Initially, Netscape was extremely successful, but it eventually lost ground to Internet Explorer. The last version of Netscape was released in 2008. However, Mozilla Firefox, a new browser built using the Netscape model, began to challenge the popularity of Internet Explorer in 2004. As of April 2010, statistics showed IE with 54 percent of the market share and Firefox with 33 percent.

Google has recently joined the Internet browser competition full force with a very impressive entry, Chrome. Google Chrome takes a unique approach to browsing the

Source: http://gs.statcounter.com/

FIGURE 6.13 Although Internet Explorer still dominates the browser market, Firefox has captured a larger piece of the pie, and Google Chrome has made a good showing in its infancy.

Web by making complex features easy to use. In Google Chrome, every time you open a new tab, you'll see a visual sampling of your most visited sites, most used search engines, recently bookmarked pages, and closed tabs. You can drag tabs out of the browser to create new windows, gather multiple tabs into one window, or re-arrange them. Every tab you use is run independently in the browser; so if one application crashes, it won't take anything else down. Even bookmarking is easy: Just click the star icon at the left edge of the address bar and you're done.

Another browser, Opera, originated as a research project in 1994. Within a year, it branched out into an independent company named Opera Software ASA. Today Opera is a high-quality product for navigating the Internet that is compatible with a wide range of operating systems.

Previously available exclusively for Mac users, Safari is now available for PCs as well. Safari provides the Mac look and feel in the Internet environment. It is lightweight, nonobtrusive, and enables tabbed browsing, spell checking for all fields, and snapback—a temporary marker that allows a user to return to a Web page even after he or she has wandered off the beaten path. Safari competes with the top browsers but lacks some features like parental and antiphishing controls. Figure 6.13 displays the current market percentages for the top 5 browsers. Visit **http://internet-browser-review.toptenreviews.com/** for more detail on the individual features each browser offers.

All five browser programs are opened the same way and use similar features, such as tabbed browsing, navigation buttons, a search box, an address toolbar, and a status bar, as shown in Figure 6.14. When you first launch a browser, it may default to a preset home page from your ISP or the publisher of the browser software. You can either keep this as your home page, which will be displayed each time you start your browser, or you can change the browser's default home page, also referred to as customizing your browser. You can find the default home page settings in Internet Explorer under the Tools, Internet Options menu (Figure 6.15).

It is the browser that interprets and displays the content of a Web page and makes hyperlinks active. In short, browsers are meant to work with Web pages. Sometimes you need to upgrade your browser to the latest version so that you can fully enjoy the features of a Web site.

New Web page creation software is being developed all the time, and eventually older browsers don't have the capability of displaying the newest features or animations. Browsers use **plug-ins**, which are additional software programs, located on the user's computer, that extend the ability of the browser, usually to enable multimedia features. If a Web site requires a plug-in to function or be viewed properly, a pop-up message will appear in newer browsers, indicating which plug-in is needed, with an option to install the plug-in or cancel the installation. There are many kinds of plug-ins, but most Web surfers are probably familiar with one or more of those listed here:

- Acrobat Reader—allows pdf files to be read, navigated, and printed within a browser window.
- Adobe Flash Player—provides the interface to view Flash scripts, which create animation and sound and are embedded with a Web page, through a browser window.
- Adobe Shockwave Player—is used for interactive games, multimedia, graphics, and streaming audio and video.
- Apple QuickTime—enables movies, animation, music, and virtual reality worlds to be viewed within a browser window.
- Real Player—is used for streaming audio, video, movies, and live video broadcasts.
- Windows Media Player—enables MP3 and WAV files, movies, live audio, and live video broadcasts.

Another feature that browsers share is the ability to cache, or store, Web page files and graphics on a computer's hard drive. When you browse a Web page for the first time, the page is actually stored on your hard drive in a storage space referred to as **browser**

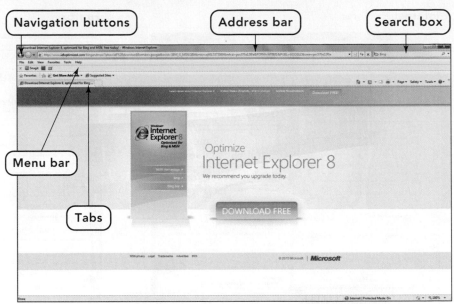

Navigation buttons

Address bar

Search box

Menu bar

Tabs

FIGURE 6.14 The major browsers have similar features.

cache. If the user attempts to retrieve the page again, the browser does not head back out on the Internet, but instead retrieves the page from the browser's cache. This eliminates excessive roundtrips to the server, brings the page up more quickly on the user's system, and greatly reduces Internet traffic. However, if you are visiting a news provider's Web site that is constantly updating current stories, browser cache might not seem like such a good idea. You really don't want to view old news. This problem has been solved by including HTTP directives, called freshness indicators, at the beginning of Web pages, images, and included scripts, that specify how long the page or item is considered fresh. If you retrieve the page within the allotted time, the page is retrieved from the browser's cache; otherwise the roundtrip is made back to the originating server and a new page is returned to the user. Because a browser's cache is not

FIGURE 6.15 You can change your default home page in your browser.

1. Click Tools and then Internet Options (IE), or click Tools and then Options (Firefox).

2. Click the General tab (IE) or click the Main option (Firefox).

3. Add a URL.

4. Click OK.

Internet Explorer

1. From the menu, select Tools, then options.

2. Click the General tab, then, click Delete.

3. Check the box to the left of Temporary Internet Files.

Firefox

1. From the menu, select Tools, then Clear Recent History.

2. Select the time range to clear.

3. Select the history element to clear (cache).

FIGURE 6.16 Clearing cache on a shared system can provide a small measure of privacy.

deleted when a user logs off or a system is shut down, it is a good idea to clear the cache after every browser session, especially on shared systems. Figure 6.16 provides the steps to clear the cache in the Internet Explorer and Firefox browsers.

Storing Content: Web Servers

Web sites and their associated images and scripts are housed on **Web servers**, a computer running special software that enables it to respond to requests for information or accept inputted information.

FAST FORWARD ▶▶

Video-on-demand (VOD), being delivered wirelessly over the Internet, is creating network slowdowns and congestion. There was a 63 percent increase in VOD users in the fourth quarter of 2009. Due to the increased demand for this service, its large swings in bandwidth, and excessive demands on a server, VOD can affect the performance of not only the video customer but also network applications. To accommodate this form of transmission, wireless networks need higher frequencies and wider bandwidth. Electrical engineers from the University of California, San Diego (UCSD), are working on developing technologies for the network of the future. The key to creating higher frequencies and wider bandwidth is advances in silicon-based circuits that operate at millimeter and microwave frequencies. Research at the university is focused on advanced radio-frequency CMOS chips, planar antennas, and system-level design that will increase data transfer 10 to 100 times, yet maintain the same energy consumption. Lawrence Larson, who leads the Radio Frequency Integrated Circuit (RFIC) group, captures the potential of the new technology by comparing the current connection and transport ability between your smartphone and tower to a straw. He claims that this technology under development will be the equivalent of replacing the straw with a fire hose. This analogy provides a good visual for the projected increased bandwidths and speed that research promises.

Millions of Web servers are located all over the world. When you click a hyperlink on a Web page, you either request information from a server (a list of sweatshirts available in size medium) or ask the server to accept your information (your order for three size medium sweatshirts in blue). Your browser sends a message to a Web server, asking the server to retrieve or accept the information. The server either sends the requested information or a confirmation that the sent information was received back to the initiating browser through the Internet. If the file isn't found, the server sends an error message.

Finding Information on the Web

With the millions of Web pages that make up the World Wide Web, how do you locate the ones that contain the information you want? Moving around the Web can feel like walking though a room with no lights; you're not sure where you are going and hope to bump into something you recognize. Although this method might lead you to the information you are looking for, there are more efficient and less frustrating methods to locate content on the Web. Let's look at of few of these techniques.

Web Addresses

To locate a resource on the Web, you have to know how to find the Web server on which it resides. Every host, computer, server, device, and application that communicates over the Internet is assigned an **Internet Protocol address (IP address)**, a numerical identification and logical address that is assigned to devices participating in a computer network. The IP address consists of four groups of numbers, separated by periods. The value in each group ranges from 0 to 255. As an example, 64.12.245.203 is the IP address for the AOL Web site.

IP addresses are either static or dynamic. A static IP address never changes. It's the type used by most major Web sites. A dynamic IP address is automatically assigned to a computer when you log on to a network. Internet service providers (ISPs) are assigned dynamic IP addresses that they, in turn, dispense to their customers. Although this numeric system works well

for computers, it doesn't work as well for people. You could type the numeric address into your browser, but most of us find that it's much easier to use a URL. A **URL (Uniform Resource Locator)** is a string of characters that precisely identifies an Internet resource's type and location. It is much easier to access the AOL Web site by typing the URL, **www.aol.com**, than it is to remember 64.12.245.203.

At times, keying in a URL can seem tedious. A complete URL actually has four distinct parts: protocol, domain name, path, and resource/filename. Each component provides a piece of data needed to locate the site (Figure 6.17).

Protocol The first part of a complete URL specifies the **Hypertext Transfer Protocol (HTTP)**, the Internet standard that supports the exchange of information on the Web. The protocol name is followed

FIGURE 6.17 A complete URL has four parts: protocol, domain name, path, and resource/ filename. This is the URL for the Pearson student support and contact page.

by a colon and two forward slash marks (//). You can generally omit the http:// protocol designation when you're typing the URL of a Web page, because the browser assumes that you are browsing an unsecured hypertext Web page. For example, you can access **http://www. pearsonhighered.com/cayf** by typing **www.pearsonhighered.com/cayf**. Most browsers can also access information using other protocols such as FTP (File Transfer Protocol), used to transfer files from one computer on the Internet to another; POP (Post Office Protocol), used to receive e-mail; and HTTPS (Hypertext Transfer Protocol Secure), used when the content being transferred requires encryption and a secure identification of the server (as is required for financial transactions).

Domain Name The second part of a complete URL specifies the Web site's **domain name**, which correlates to the Web server's IP address. The domain name has two parts: a host name and a top-level domain name. Some domain names also include a prefix, the most common of which is "www." The **host name** is usually the name of the group or institution hosting the site. The **top-level domain (TLD) name** is the extension (such as .com or .edu) following the host name and indicates the type of group or institution to which the site belongs. This two-part identifier is referred to as the **Domain Name System (DNS)**. It links domain names with their corresponding numerical IP addresses, functioning like a phone book for the Internet. The Domain Name System enables users to type an address that includes letters as well as numbers, for example *pearsonhighered.com* instead of 165.193.140.24, its IP numerical address. Through a process called **domain name registration**, individuals and organizations register a *unique* domain name with a service organization, such as InterNIC, and are assigned a *unique* Internet address (IP address) that will be associated with that domain name. You can use your favorite search engine to search for domain name registrars to find other sites that provide this service.

Domain names can tell you a great deal about where a computer is located. For Web sites hosted in the United States, top-level domain names (the *last* part of the domain name) indicate the type of organization to which the Web site belongs (Figure 6.18). Outside the United States, the top-level domain indicates the name of the country from which the Web site is published or of which the owner is a citizen, such as .ca (Canada), .uk (United Kingdom), and .jp (Japan). For more information on domain names visit the Internet Corporation for Assigned Names and Numbers (ICANN) at **www.icann.org**.

Path The third part of a complete URL specifies the location of the document on the server. It contains the document's location on the computer, including the names of subfolders (if any). In the example in Figure 6.17, the path to the student contact page on the Web server at **www.pearsonhighered. com** is "student."

Resource/Filename The last part of a complete URL gives the file name of the resource you're accessing. A resource is a file, such as an HTML file, a sound file, a video file, or a graphics file. The resource's extension (the part of the file name after the period) indicates the type of resource it is. For example, HTML documents have the .html or .htm extension.

Many URLs don't include a resource name because they reference the server's default home page. If no resource name is specified, the browser looks for a file named *default* or *index*—a default page that's displayed automatically when you enter the site at its top level. If it finds such a file, it loads it automatically. For example, **www.microsoft.com/windows** displays the default Microsoft Windows home page. Other URLs omit both the path name and the resource name. These URLs reference the Web site's home page. For example, although entering **www.microsoft.com** into a browser's address bar displays Microsoft's home page, its actual URL is **http://www.microsoft. com/en/us/default.aspx**.

Surfing the Web

Once you've subscribed and connected to an Internet service provider and downloaded and opened a browser, you are ready to surf the Web. To access a Web page, you can do any of the following, as illustrated in Figure 6.19:

- **Type a URL in the Address bar.** You don't need to type http://. Watch for spelling errors, and don't insert spaces.
- **Click a tab in the browser window.** Both major browsers, IE and Firefox, offer **tabbed browsing**, which enables a user to have several Web pages open at once and switch quickly between them. You can customize your home page by adding tabs for sites that you frequently access. The tabs are not visible in Figure 6.19 because the History list is extended.
- **Click a hyperlink.** Hyperlinks are usually underlined, but sometimes they're embedded in graphics or highlighted in other ways, such as with shading or colors. Most browsers indicate the presence of a hyperlink by changing the on-screen pointer to a hand shape when it is over a hyperlink.

FIGURE 6.18 Common Top-Level Domain Names

Top-Level Domain Name	Used By
.biz	Businesses
.com	Commercial sites
.edu	Educational institutions
.gov	Government agencies
.info	Information
.mil	Military
.name	Individuals
.net	Network organizations (such as ISPs)
.org	Nonprofit organizations

- **Use the History list.** The **History list** is a list of previously visited Web pages. It is accessed in Internet Explorer by clicking the arrow to the right of the address bar and in Firefox by selecting the History option on the menu bar. Both browsers then display a drop-down list from which the user can select a Web page.

- **Make use of the Favorites or Bookmarks feature.** This feature, called Favorites in IE and Bookmarks in Firefox, is located on the menu bar. When selected, you can mark a Web page that you visit frequently. To return to that page later, simply click the Favorite or Bookmarks option and select the Web page name from the drop-down list. Favorites can be grouped into categories.

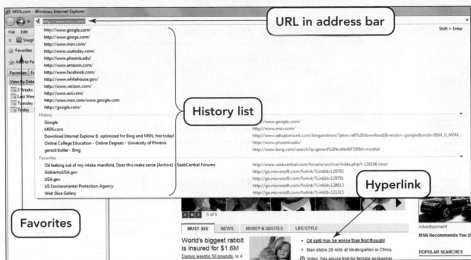

FIGURE 6.19 There are many ways to access a typical Web page.

Uploading and Downloading After you have browsed the Web and accessed various Web pages, you may want to try downloading or uploading data. With **downloading**, a document or file is transferred from another computer to your computer, as in downloading music from iTunes. Your computer is the destination; the other computer is the source. With **uploading**, you transfer files from your computer to another computer, as you do when you upload a video you created to Youtube. In uploading, your computer is the source and the other computer is the destination. Most students download and upload files when using a Web-based course management system, such as Blackboard, Angel, or MyITLab. These teaching systems allow an instructor and student to interact in classes delivered entirely online or to complement a face-to-face teaching situation. Students download course notes or application files to their own computers. When a student completes an assignment, he or she uploads the completed assignment to a drop box for the instructor to grade.

No matter how familiar you are with the source, you should exercise caution when downloading files of unknown origin from the Web. If you download software from a site that doesn't inspect files using up-to-date antivirus software, you could infect your computer with a virus. Most Internet users believe that it's safe to download software from Web sites maintained by software companies or files

created with popular software. However, be aware that some viruses are spread in the data files of popular programs, such as Microsoft Word or Excel. Be sure to use an antivirus program to check any software or data files that you download. Now that you understand the basics of the Internet and Web, let's examine how to conduct research on the Web.

Sharing Information

Sometimes the best way to get information online is from an individual or agency that is also online and communicating or contributing through an online feed, conversation, or Web posting.

Really Simple Syndication One of the current ways to keep abreast of updates on news, weather, and sports in our fast-moving and informative world is through the use of **Really Simple Syndication (RSS)**. Once a user sets up a connection to a Web site that has an RSS feed, he or she will receive constant updates over the Internet from that site without any further involvement. The URL or Web page that allows its up-to-date information to be published on another Web site is said to have an RSS feed or is referred to as being *syndicated*.

So how does RSS work? A Web page that displays constantly changing data maintains a list of RSS feeds. Individuals interested in getting updated information from locations on the list can, through an RSS file, select sources from the list and receive the updated information on their own Web page. There are hundreds of Web sites that provide RSS feeds, for example, the *New York Times*, the BBC, Reuters, and many blogs. If your site will be updating several feeds, you can use an RSS aggregator. An **aggregator**

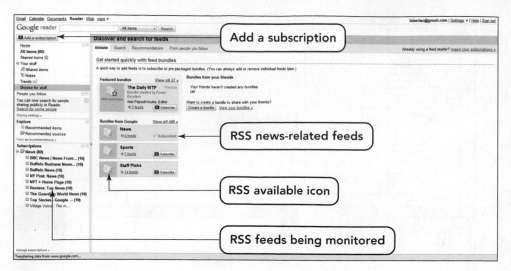

FIGURE 6.20 Google Reader is a free aggregator that can be set up by going to www.google.com/reader/view/.

is a program that remembers your subscription list, checks each site on a regular basis, alerts you if new information has been published, and organizes the results for you. Many RSS aggregators are available through your browser. Some are even integrated into your e-mail, and others are stand-alone applications (Figure 6.20).

Wikis Want to share information fast through the Web, for either personal or professional reasons? A wiki, a blog, or a podcast might be just what you need. A **wiki** (short for *wiki-wiki*, the Hawaiian word for "fast") is a simple Web page on which any visitor can post text or images, read previous posts, change posted information, and track earlier changes. No elaborate coding needed—just click to post, click to refresh the page, and you're done. If a visitor changes what you've posted and you don't like the change, just click to revert to an earlier version. Information referenced from a wiki should be verified through another source because wiki entries can be made by anyone and the content is not always verified. Next time you're online, surf over to **www.wikimusicguide.com**, an open-content music guide. Fans can create new pages, share information about their favorite songs or artists, and edit the entries others have created.

Wikis can be public or restricted to specific members. In addition to their use in the entertainment industry, this information-sharing option is being used by business and educational institutions to reduce e-mail and increase collaboration.

Blogs Another way to share information online is via a **blog** (short for Weblog). A blog is the Internet equivalent of a journal or diary. Bloggers post their thoughts and opinions, along with photos or links to interesting Web sites, for the entire world to see. Over 1 million blogs are posted on the Web. Some are meant for family and friends; some offer running commentary on politics and other timely topics; and others are written by employees about their jobs, interview hints, and various other subjects. Many Microsoft blogs have loyal followings because of their insightful observations and technical know-how. If you are interested in finding out about the Microsoft interview process check out **http://microsoftjobsblog.com/blog/**. Here blogs are posted from individuals that have been interviewed and include everything from sample categories of questions to advice on how to dress (Figure 6.21). Visit **www.blogsearchengine.com** to search for blogs by subject and for FAQs about blogging. If you are interested in creating a blog, **www.blogger.com/start** is a great place to get started.

Podcasts If you'd rather get your information in an audio or video format, podcasts may be just what you need! Despite the name, and its link to music, **podcasts** have evolved from containing just sound

FIGURE 6.21 Blogs like this one from individuals who have gone through the Microsoft job interview process can provide valuable hints and advice.

to including any kind of audio as well as images and video. Podcasts files are released periodically by means of Web syndication, a delivery method that makes use of **podcatchers** (applications such as Apple Inc.'s iTunes or Nullsoft's Winamp) that can automatically identify and retrieve new files in a given series and make them available through a centrally maintained Web site.

You can listen to podcasts on your computer or on an MP3 player. You can go to sites that provide podcasts or sign up for one using an RSS feed. Imagine taking a physics class at Massachusetts Institute of Technology or catching the radio interview with your favorite musician that you missed last week. Podcasts can make it happen. Check the Podcast Directory at **http://podcast.com** and hear what's new!

Through the simplicity of wikis, blogs, and podcasts, the Web has been expanded into a means of interactive communication.

Using Hyperlinks to Surf the Web

Although browsing or surfing the Web is easy and fun, it falls short as a means of information research. When you are looking for specific and reliable data, you need to employ more targeted methods.

Using hyperlinks on a reliable Web page could be a start. The URL of the link might provide you with some of the desired data. In general, starting this way usually has the user clicking link after link, searching for information that they never find.

Some Web sites offer a **subject guide**, a list of subject-related categories such as

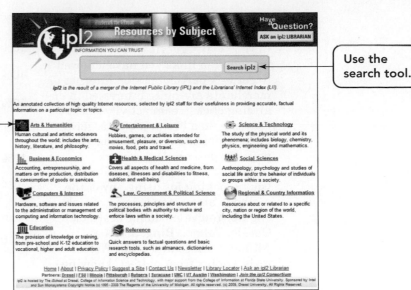

Select a category.

Use the search tool.

business, news, or trends that, when selected, displays a page of more related links (Figure 6.22). These guides don't try to include every Web page on the World Wide Web, but they offer a selection of high-quality pages that represent some of the more useful Web pages in a given category. If you're just beginning your search for information, a subject guide is an excellent place to start.

A **portal** is a Web page that acts as a gateway to a lot of diverse sources and presents those sources in an organized way. It enables a user to locate fast-breaking news, local weather, stock quotes, sports scores, and e-mail with the click of a mouse. Portal sites usually use indexes and lists of links to provide a jumping-off point for your search. Sites such as MSNBC, AOL, iGoogle, and Yahoo! are examples of portals (Figure 6.23).

FIGURE 6.22 Subject guides can help you find the information you seek quickly.

FIGURE 6.23 Portals usually make use of RSS to provide the viewer with the most update news and sporting events.

Access to e-mail is provided.

Appearance may be customized.

Favorite categories can be edited.

A side effect of your search method is the clickstream you leave in your wake. A **clickstream** is the trail of Web links you have followed to get to a particular site. Internet merchants are quite interested in analyzing clickstream activity so that they can do a better job of targeting advertisements and tailoring Web pages to potential customers.

If you can't find the information you're looking for using any of the methods above, try using a search engine. You've no doubt heard of Google, Yahoo!, Bing, and Ask. Although these and other Web search tools are far from perfect, knowing how to use them effectively (and knowing their limitations) can greatly increase your chances of finding the information you want.

Search engine returns can be extensive and broad in scope. A user has to be familiar with techniques that can be used to zero in on specific search content. Let's look at these techniques and strategies in more detail.

Using Search Engines

Using search engines is more complex than using the other methods of locating information on the Web. **Search engines** make use of databases of the Web pages they've indexed. To add pages to their databases, search engines make use of computer programs, referred to as **spiders**, to roam the World Wide Web via the Internet, visit sites and databases, and keep the search engine's database of Web pages up to date. Also known as *crawlers, knowledge bots,* or *knowbots,* they obtain new pages, update known pages, and delete obsolete ones. Most large

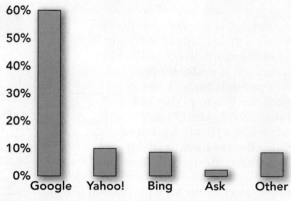

Source: www.seoconsultants.com/search-engines/

FIGURE 6.24 Google gets approximately 76 billion searches a month of the 113 billion searches completed on all search engines.

search engines operate several spiders all the time. Even so, the Web is so enormous that it can take six months to cover the content, resulting in a certain degree of "outdatedness." This outdatedness results in **link rot**, hyperlinks that no longer work and Web pages that have been removed or restructured. Such links can make a Web search frustrating and tedious.

Internet users seem to have their favorite search engine; however, Google is definitely at the top of the list. Figure 6.24 displays April 2010 statistics on the four core search engines. As the chart illustrates, Google use far exceeded any of the others, with Yahoo! a distant second.

Feel like you're stuck in a rut? Not all search engines use the same strategy to locate Web content. Try using a different search engine. Visit sites like Mahalo (**www.mahalo.com**), Dogpile (**www. dogpile.com**), Find-Sounds (**www. findsounds.com**), SurfWax (**www. surfwax.com**), or BlogPulse (**www. blogpulse.com**) and see what you find (Figure 6.25)!

To use a search engine, type one or more words that describe the subject

FIGURE 6.25 Search Engine Comparisons

Web Search Engine	Strategy Used to Obtain Results
Mahalo	Serves as a human-powered search engine and knowledge-sharing service.
Dogpile	Accumulates search results from leading search engines to present the best results in one easy-to-find place
FindSounds	Focuses on locating sound effects and musical instrument samples
SurfWax	Makes use of a patent pending spiraling matrix design to search, sort, and extract information in a simple natural interface
BlogPulse	Uses machine learning and natural language to provide a search engine that focuses on blogs

you're looking for into the search text box and click *Search* (or press *Enter*). Generally, it's a good idea to type several words (four or five) rather than just one or two. If you use only one or two words, the Web search will produce far more results than you can use.

Why do search engines sometimes produce unsatisfactory results? The problem lies in the ambiguity of the English language. Suppose you're searching for information on the Great Wall of China. You'll find some information on the ancient Chinese defensive installation, but you may also get the menu of the Great Wall of China, a Chinese restaurant; information on the Great Wall hotel in Beijing; and the lyrics of "Great Wall of China," a song by Billy Joel.

Specialized Search Engines Full Web search engines generally don't index specialized information such as names and addresses, job advertisements, quotations, or newspaper articles. To find such information, you need to use **specialized search engines**. Examples of such specialized search engines include Indeed, a database of more than 1 million jobs, and Infoplease, which contains the full text of an encyclopedia and an almanac (Figure 6.26).

You can save the results of your searches—the Web pages you visit by following the results links of a search engine—to your hard drive by using your

browser's File, Save As menu sequence. If you don't want or need the entire Web page, you can right-click the various elements of the page and choose from a variety of options (Save Target As, Save Picture As, Print Target, Print Picture, E-mail Picture). You can also use your mouse and cursor to highlight and then copy text on a Web page for pasting into a word-processing file or other document. The benefit of saving a Web page offline, to your own storage device, is that you can view that page later without connecting to the Internet. This is easily accomplished by opening your browser and then choosing the File, Open menu sequence. Simply browse through your folders and files to locate the Web page file and then open it.

Some Web sites have their own site search engines. You will often find this feature on the site's home page. It is usually a clearly marked box into which you type the keywords you are looking for. Some home pages will have a Search icon or button that will take you to the site's search page.

For the socially conscious Web searcher, there are search sites that will make donations to your favorite charity. Check out **www.goodsearch.com** and begin to donate to the charity of your choice.

Search Basics

By learning a few search techniques, you can greatly increase the accuracy of your Web searches. **Search operators**, which are symbols or words used for advanced searches, can be helpful. Most search engines include a link for advanced searches or provide search tips to explain which search operators you can use. Although specific methods may vary, some or all of the following techniques will work with most search engines.

Wildcards Many search engines enable you to use wildcards. **Wildcards** are symbols such as * and ? that take the place of zero or more characters in the position in which they are used. The use of wildcards, also called **truncation symbols**, to search for various word endings and spellings simultaneously is a technique called **truncation**.

Wildcards help you improve the accuracy of your searches and are

Search an entire site or specific resource.

Tabs act as reference tools.

Read current news and topics.

FIGURE 6.26 Specialized search engines, like Infoplease, provide access to selected reference tools and resources.

useful if you are unsure of the exact spelling of a word. Wildcards may be handled differently, depending upon the search engine used. So the search term *bank** might return *bank, banks, banking, bankruptcy, bank account,* and so forth.

Phrase Searches Another way to improve the accuracy of your searches is through **phrase searching**, which is generally performed by typing a phrase within quotation marks. This tells the search engine to retrieve only those documents that contain the exact phrase (rather than some or all of the words anywhere in the document).

Inclusion and Exclusion Operators
With many search engines, you can improve search performance by specifying an **inclusion operator**, which is generally a plus (+) sign. This operator states that you only want a page retrieved if it contains the specified word. By listing several key terms with this search operator, you can zero in on pages that only contain one or more of the essential terms. If the list of retrieved documents contains many items that you don't want, you can use the **exclusion operator**, which is generally a minus (−) sign. You can exclude the undesired term by prefacing it with the exclusion operator (Figure 6.27).

Boolean Searches

Some search engines enable you to perform Boolean searches. **Boolean searches** use logical operators (AND, OR, and NOT) to link the words you're

FIGURE 6.27 Improving Your Search Results with Search Operators

Operator/Symbol	Example	Result
Inclusion/Plus sign (+)	CD + Radiohead	Web pages that contain all search terms listed, in any order. In this case, pages would include *both* the word **CD** *and* the word **RADIOHEAD**.
Exclusion/Minus sign (−)	CD + Radiohead − eBay	Web pages that contain all included search terms listed, but not the excluded term. In this case, pages would include *both* the word **CD** *and* the word **RADIOHEAD** but *not* the word **EBAY**.
Wildcards (*)	CD*	Web pages that include variations of the search term or additional words. For example, pages could include the terms **CD**, **CDs**, **CD Ripping**, **CD Files**, etc.
Quotation Marks (" ")	"Radiohead Just Push Play CD"	Web pages that contain the exact phrase in the order listed.

FIGURE 6.28 Using Boolean Search Terms to Fine-Tune Your Search

Terms	Examples	Result
AND	CD **AND** Radiohead	Returns the same result as using the plus sign (+)
OR	CD **OR** Radiohead	Web pages that include either or both of the search terms listed, usually providing a large number of hits. For this example, results would include *either* the word **CD** *or* the word **RADIOHEAD** or *both*.
NOT	CD **AND** Radiohead **NOT** eBay	Returns the same results as using the minus sign (−)
Parenthesis ( )	(CD **OR** MP3 **OR** Record) **AND** Radiohead	Search terms in parenthesis are located first, using the search operator provided. In this case, results would include pages that included any combination of **CD**, **MP3**, or **RECORD** *and* the word **RADIOHEAD**

searching for (Figure 6.28). By using Boolean operators, you can gain more precise control over your searches. Let's look at a few examples.

The AND, OR, and NOT Operators

When used to link two search words, the AND operator tells the search engine to return only those documents that contain both words (just as the plus sign does). You can use the AND operator to narrow your search so that it retrieves fewer documents.

If your search retrieves too few documents, try the OR operator. This may be helpful when a topic has several common synonyms, such as car, auto, automobile, and vehicle. Using the OR operator usually retrieves a larger quantity of documents.

To exclude unwanted documents, use the NOT operator. This operator tells the search engine to omit any documents containing the word preceded by NOT (just as the minus sign does).

Using Parentheses

Many search engines that support Boolean operators allow you to use parentheses, a process called **nesting**. When you nest an expression, the search engine evaluates the expression from left to right and searches for the content within the parentheses first. Such expressions enable you to conduct a search

with unmatched accuracy. To learn more about search engines, their specialized capabilities, and specific examples go to **www.internettutorials.net/**.

Using Information from the Web

After you've found information on the Web, you'll need to evaluate it critically. Anyone can publish information on the Web; many Web pages are not subject to the fact-checking standards of newspapers or magazines, let alone the peer-review process that safeguards the quality of scholarly and scientific publications. Although you can find excellent and reliable information on the Web, you can also find pages that are biased or blatantly incorrect.

Critically Evaluating Web Pages

As you're evaluating a Web page for possible use or reference, read with a critical eye and consider the issues raised here:

- Who is the *author* of this page? Is the author affiliated with a recognized institution, such as a university or a well-known company? Is there any evidence that the author is qualified and possesses credentials with respect to this topic?

- Does the author *reference* his or her sources? If so, do they appear to be from recognized and respected publications?

- Who is the Web page *affiliated* with? Who pays for this page? The association between the page server, sponsor, and author should be above board. The hosting organization should not be able to exert influence over the information on the site.

- Is the language *objective* and dispassionate, or is it strident and argumentative? Is it written in a form and level that suits the target population?

- What is the *purpose* of this page? Is the author trying to sell something or promote a biased idea? Who would profit if this page's information were accepted as true? Does the site include links to external information, or does it reference only itself?

- Does the information appear to be *accurate*? Is the page free of sweeping generalizations or other signs of shoddy thinking? Do you see many misspellings or grammatical errors that would indicate a poor educational background?

- Is this page *current*? The information should be up to date.

In the next section, you will explore the practical applications of Web research to both the work and school environments.

Using the Web for Schoolwork

Finding information on the Web can help you as a consumer. But how can it help you as a student? The following sections provide some helpful hints.

Authoritative Online Sources Many respected magazines and journals have established Web sites where you can search back issues, giving you the best of both worlds—the power and convenience of the Internet, plus material that is more reliable than the average Web page.

Locating Material in Published Works Remember that the Web is only one of several sources you can and should use for research. Many high-level research tools can be found in your institution's library. Additionally, librarians are trained research professionals who are there to assist you. As institutions have begun to offer distance-learning courses, student access to library materials has become a critical issue. To meet the needs of distance-learning students, many college libraries now provide online access to their services. You can almost certainly access and search your library's inventory of books and can often order them online. The library's search engine will allow you to search books (and sometimes articles) by author, title, or key term. Your library may also provide access to valuable search tools such as EBSCOhost, LexisNexis, and other professional databases. Sometimes you can access these online materials from off campus as well as on campus. Materials may be accessible only to faculty and students, or they may also be available to the general public. Check your library's home page to find out what Internet services are available.

ETHICS

The Internet and Web have produced an environment that makes accessing information from the comfort of your home or favorite coffee shop effortless. Locating the information is simple—and so is borrowing it and embedding it into your own work. By simply using copy and paste or right-clicking and selecting the *Save Image As* option, information, pictures, and data found on Web pages can be lifted from their source and inserted into another document or Web page under development. Copyright violations and infringements often occur with material that is available online, especially when it is re-used without permission. Make sure you understand your rights and responsibilities. Visit the Electronic Frontier Foundation (**www.eff.org**), a civil liberties group that defends your rights in the digital world, or the U.S. Copyright Office (**www.copyright.gov**) for more information on the ethical use of material you find on the Internet.

FIGURE 6.29 Google Scholar uses the power of Google to search scholarly literature and provide high-quality results for academic research.

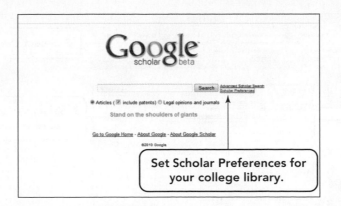

Set Scholar Preferences for your college library.

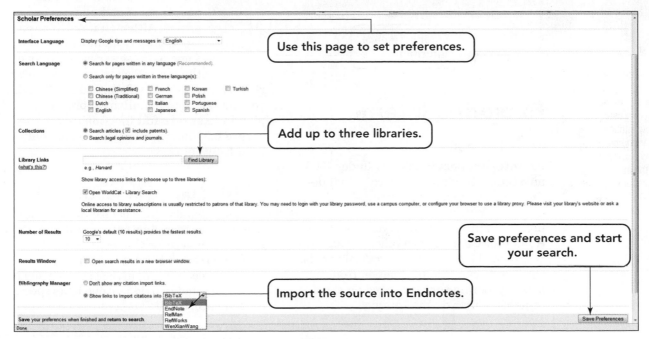

Use this page to set preferences.

Add up to three libraries.

Save preferences and start your search.

Import the source into Endnotes.

Also, visit Google Scholar (**http://scholar.google.com**) to search for scholarly literature from many academic disciplines. You can use the advanced search methods covered in this chapter and even personalize your searches to have Google Scholar indicate when materials are held by your local library. Google Scholar can help you locate peer-reviewed papers, theses, books, abstracts, and articles from academic publishers and professional sources (Figure 6.29).

Citing Online and Offline References

Including citations in your work is an important way to honor copyright and avoid accusations of plagiarism. Because citing Internet-based sources is not the same as citing traditional references, visit University of California Berkeley's General Guides site at **www.lib.berkeley.edu/**

Help/guides.html to learn how to properly cite online and electronic resources. You should know how to cite Web sites, e-mail messages, and online databases. When citing electronic resources, it is important to include the date the site was last accessed. Even more than the written and published sites, electronic sites are time sensitive.

Application developers like Microsoft have begun to include reference options within their current word processing programs. Such features prompt the user to input the necessary information into a template that the application then formats into the style the user selects, usually APA or MLA for college papers (Figure 6.30)

Now that you're familiar with how to evaluate information on the Web, let's look at some of the Internet's most useful services.

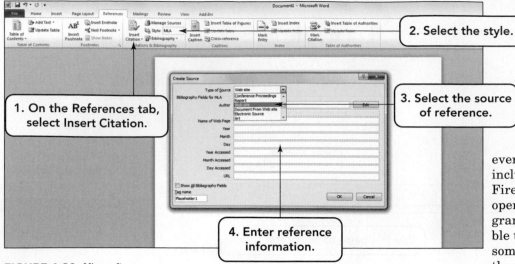

1. On the References tab, select Insert Citation.

2. Select the style.

3. Select the source of reference.

4. Enter reference information.

FIGURE 6.30 Microsoft Word 2010 includes a References tab on the Ribbon where a user can add new citations, footnotes, endnotes, or bibliography references, with all of the appropriate formatting required by the selected style.

Exploring Internet Services

An **Internet service** is best understood as a set of standards (protocols) that define how two types of programs—a client, such as a Web browser that runs on the user's computer, and a server—can communicate with each other through the Internet. By using the service's protocols, the client requests information from a server program that is located on some other computer on the Internet.

At one time, some browsers, such as Netscape Navigator and the Mozilla Suite, were distributed as software suites that included client programs to handle e-mail, newsgroups, and chat services, as well as browsing. However, most current browsers, including Internet Explorer, Firefox, and Safari (for Macs), operate as stand-alone programs. Although it's still possible to obtain client software for some of these services, many of them are Web based and don't require any special software to use, but you may need to install an appropriate plug-in to ensure full functionality. Figure 6.31 lists a selection of commonly used Internet services.

E-Mail: Staying in Touch

The most popular Internet service is e-mail. **E-mail** (short for **electronic mail**) is a software application that enables you to send and receive messages via networks. E-mail has become an indispensable tool for businesses and individuals due to its speed, convenience, and its ability to be saved and

FIGURE 6.31 Commonly Used Internet Services

Service	Client	Web-Based	Comments
E-mail			
AOL Mail	X	X	Available with AOL Desktop installation or as Web-based service
Google Mail		X	
Microsoft Outlook	X		Part of the Microsoft Office suite
Instant Message			
AOL AIM	X	X	Available with AOL Desktop installation or as a Web-based service
Google Talk	X	X	Available for download or as Web-based service
Yahoo! Messenger		X	
Windows Live Messenger		X	Formerly MSN Messenger

Include attachments.

Use formatting tools to enhance message.

Create folders to organize e-mail.

Check spelling.

retrieved. However, for immediacy, text messaging is preferred. Both of these communications tools have become media of choice for interpersonal written communication, far outpacing the postal system.

When you receive an e-mail, you can reply to the message, forward it to someone else, store it for later action, or delete it. In addition to writing the text message, you can format the text, check spelling, organize your e-mail into folders, and include an e-mail attachment (Figure 6.32). An **e-mail attachment** can be any type of computer file—document, photo, audio, or video—that is included

with an e-mail message. If you receive an e-mail message containing an attachment, your e-mail program displays a distinctive icon, such as a paper clip, to notify you. E-mail usually arrives at the destination server in a few seconds. It is then stored on the server until the recipient logs on to the server and downloads the message.

To send an e-mail, you need to know the recipient's e-mail address. An **e-mail address** is a unique cyberspace identity for a particular recipient that follows the form myname@somedomain.com. The components of an e-mail address are the user

FIGURE 6.32 E-mail can be saved and used to provide a record of past communications.

GREEN tech tips

The use of electronic communication methods can help us reduce the environmental effect of keeping in touch. Let's start with some facts:

- The average worker uses 10,000 sheets of copy paper a year. A large financial service company reported that they could save $700,000 a year if all copies were double-sided.

- The United States, which has less than 5 percent of the world's population, consumes 30 percent of the world's paper.

- Just under 50 percent of wood pulp goes to the production of paper. Reducing paper production would help reduce greenhouse gases. As an example, the greenhouse emission to create 40 reams of paper is equivalent to 1.5 acres of pine forest absorbing carbon for a year.

- It takes more than 1.5 cups of water to make one sheet of paper.

So in short, less is better. What can an average user do to help this environmental movement? Start by thinking before you print or copy. Ask yourself whether you really need a paper copy. If you do, how many do you need? Use the Print preview option of your application before printing. This eliminates printing a version with errors and having to reprint it. Change the setting on your printer to print double-sided by default (if it has that capability). Fit more on one page by changing margin and font size. And remember to recycle discarded paper.

These options may seem like small steps, but if individuals all over the world incorporate them into a daily practice, these small actions can spread and create a lasting environmental effect. ●

The Internet and the World Wide Web **273**

name or other identifier, the name of the domain that is hosting the e-mail service, and the top-level domain that identifies the provider's type of institution. For instance, you can send mail to the president of the United States at the e-mail address president@whitehouse.gov. In this instance, the user name is "president," the domain is "whitehouse," and the top-level domain is ".gov" (for government). You can often tell quite a bit about someone just by seeing his or her e-mail address!

If you normally send e-mails to the same group of individuals frequently, you might consider creating a distribution list. A distribution list is a grouping of individuals in your contacts that you want to receive the same e-mails. Instead of listing each recipient individually in the "To" section of a new e-mail you select the precreated distribution list. Everyone in that list will receive the e-mail.

E-mail has many benefits:

- It is inexpensive, fast, and easy to access.
- It enables collaboration.
- It creates an electronic paper trail.
- It saves paper.

The benefits of e-mail are tempered by some potential problems that you should be aware of. Sometimes e-mail systems fail to properly send or receive mail.

Attachments may not be delivered or they may be blocked by e-mail system administrators as potentially unsafe. Messages can become corrupted and may not display properly. Sometimes, if you don't regularly check your mail, your Inbox may overflow, which causes messages received past the overflow point to be bounced out of the box and never delivered.

Perhaps the worst thing that can happen with e-mail is that you hastily send a message that you later wished you hadn't, or you use the Reply All or Forward feature to send inappropriate or irrelevant messages that can embarrass you or that inconvenience the receiver.

Spam: Can It Be Stopped?

Many e-mail users receive unsolicited e-mail advertising called **spam**. In fact, according to a report released in May 2009

from the security vendor Symantec, 90.4 percent of all e-mail (1 out of every 1.1 e-mails) is spam. This mail is sent by spammers, businesses or individuals that specialize in sending such mail. Spammers believe that they're doing only what direct-marketing mail firms do: sending legitimate advertising. But they don't acknowledge a crucial difference between unsolicited postal advertising and spam. With postal advertising, the advertiser pays for the postage. With spam, the recipient pays the postage in the form of lost time and productivity for individuals and businesses. A 2009 study estimated that the total cost of combined consumer and corporate spam in the United States was $108.8 billion annually. Some $92.2 billion of that cost comes from lost productivity and the balance from the cost of administering and purchasing preventative services and programs.

Most Internet users detest spam but feel helpless to prevent it. For businesses, spam is a costly nuisance. It's not unusual for a massive amount of spam messages to overwhelm mail servers, resulting in impaired service for legitimate, paying customers.

In most cases, little or nothing of worth is being peddled: pornographic Web sites, get-rich-quick scams, bogus stock deals, rip-off work-at-home schemes, health and diet scams, and merchandise of questionable quality. Some spam can contain **malware**, malicious software, that places a computer in the spammer's control. This type of software can wreak havoc on a user's system by deleting files and directory entries; it can also act as **spyware**, gathering data from a user's system without the user knowing it. This can include anything from the Web pages a user visits to personal information, such as credit card numbers.

Can you filter out spam? You can try. It's often possible to set up a spam or bulk mail folder in your e-mail account. Check your mail options for how to enable this service (Figure 6.33). A word of caution on using such filters: Sometimes filters can misroute messages. Check your trash and spam folders periodically to be sure

> "Attachments may **not** be delivered or they may be **blocked** by e-mail system administrators as potentially unsafe."

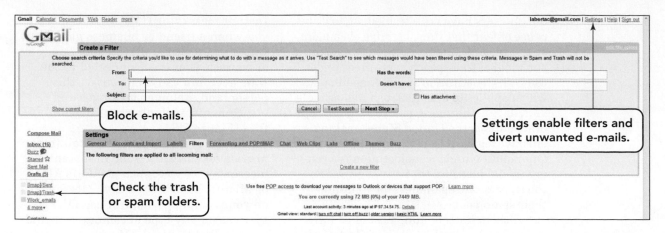

Block e-mails.

Settings enable filters and divert unwanted e-mails.

Check the trash or spam folders.

FIGURE 6.33 Check your e-mail account's mail settings to set spam filters.

important messages haven't been directed to the wrong folders.

Spam can originate from a new account, which is almost immediately closed down after the service provider receives hundreds of thousands of outraged complaints. The spammer just moves on to a new account. A more modern way to send spam is through a **botnet**, a set of computers infected with a malicious program that places the computers under the control of a **bot herder**. Vulnerable systems are ones without current security patches or antispam protection. Once infected, a machine becomes one of many zombies in a botnet and responds to commands given by the bot herder.

Some of the steps you can take to prevent spam include the following:

- Avoid posting your e-mail address in any public place.
- Don't open e-mail from a source that you do not recognize.
- Deactivate the preview option in your e-mail. The preview option automatically triggers the opening of the e-mail.
- Don't reply to spam or request to be removed from a spammer's mailing list.
- Modify your e-mail account to disable graphics.
- Get involved in reporting incidents of spam to help others and stop the source of the problem.
- Make sure that security patches on your system are current.

Increasingly, state and federal legislatures are attempting to pass laws against spam. Bills have been introduced in Congress, and the Senate's CAN-SPAM Act of 2003 is aimed at deceptive e-mails,

unsolicited pornography, and marketing. The Direct Marketing Association (DMA), an advocacy group for both online and off-line direct marketers, counters that the appropriate solution is an opt-out system, in which spam recipients request that the sender of spam remove their names from the mailing list—but that's just what

ETHICS

With the widespread use of electronic communication, most offices today are equipped with Internet access. Many employers make new employees sign Internet usage clauses that limit the use of the company Internet connection to business-related tasks. How does the employer know whether an employee used the Internet to conduct personal business? One simple method is for the employer to check the browser's history feature. A second might be to review security cameras that have your monitor screen in the range of view. A third is by purchasing a program that allows eavesdropping on Internet use that can be used by a network administrator from a remote location to drop in on an Internet session of an employee.

By signing the Internet usage clause, the employee does agree to the company's policy of Internet use, but does that give the employer the right to use any methods of surveillance without notifying the employee? Some of these methods monitor more than Internet use. At what point are the rights of the individual violated for the good of the company?

e-mail users have been trained not to do because of fear that they'll receive even more spam. In addition, efforts to outlaw spam run afoul of free-speech guarantees under the U.S. Constitution's First Amendment, which applies to businesses as well as individuals. Furthermore, many spammers operate outside the United States, making effective legislation even more difficult. One solution under consideration is a congressional measure that would give ISPs the right to sue spammers for violating their spam policies.

Although it's no fun, most of us have learned to live with spam by following the simple rule: If you don't know who sent it—don't open it! For more information and tips on how to avoid spam, recent

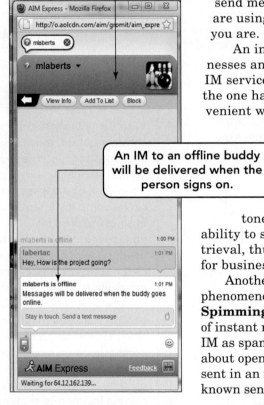

Once a buddy is selected, the message window opens.

Buddies displays contacts available to chat.

Offline Buddies are not currently available.

An IM to an offline buddy will be delivered when the person signs on.

FIGURE 6.34 Instant messaging is a popular way for Internet users to exchange near real-time messages.

law enforcement actions against deceptive commercial e-mail and spammers, and a location to file a complaint, check out the Federal Trade Commission's spam site at **www.ftc.gov/spam**.

Instant Messaging: E-Mail Made Faster

What's faster than e-mail and more convenient than picking up the phone?

Instant messaging (IM) systems alert you when a friend or business associate who also uses the IM system (a buddy or contact) is online (connected to the Internet). You can then contact this person and exchange messages and attachments, including multimedia files (Figure 6.34).

To use IM, you need to install instant messenger software from an instant messenger service, such as AOL's AIM or Microsoft's Windows Live Messenger, on your computer. You can use IM systems on any type of computer, including handhelds. Many IM services also give you access to information such as daily news, stock prices, sports scores, and the weather, and you can keep track of your appointments. There is no standard IM protocol, which means that you can send messages only to people who are using the same IM service that you are.

An increasing number of businesses and institutions are trying out IM services, with mixed results. On the one hand, IM is a novel and convenient way to communicate. On the other hand, voice communication is faster and richer. Other drawbacks to instant messaging include the misinterpretation of the tone of the message and the inability to save an IM for later retrieval, thus posing some legal issues for businesses and corporations.

Another threat to the use of IM is a phenomenon known as spimming. **Spimming** is spam that targets users of instant messaging. Spimming is to IM as spam is to e-mail. Be very careful about opening files or clicking on a link sent in an instant message by an unknown sender.

Internet Relay Chat: Text Chatting in Real Time

Internet relay chat (IRC) is an Internet service that enables you to join chat groups, called **channels**, and participate in real-time, text-based conversations. Popular in the early days of the Internet, IRC has been replaced by tools like IM. Today it is mostly the province of specialized communities, such as gamers or programmers.

FIGURE 6.35 Social networking sites, like Ning.com, that allow users to create their own social network communities are becoming popular with political candidates and business entrepreneurs.

Social Networking: Helping People Connect

Social networking is a way to build expanding online communities. On a social networking site like Facebook or MySpace, you can create an online profile, invite friends and acquaintances to join your network, and invite their friends to join too. Some sites, like LinkedIn, are used by business professionals to expand their network of business contacts. Tired of Facebook or MySpace? Why not start your own social network? Ning (**www.ning.com**) is a site that encourages people to start their own social networking community (Figure 6.35). Artists, hobbyists, educators, athletes—the list continues to grow. Find a community to join or start your own!

Many privacy and security concerns surround the use and access of social networking sites. Statistics from a Pew Internet 2008 report support this concern, citing that 73 percent of American teens who participated in the survey indicated that they use social networking Web sites. This is a significant increase over statistics from 2007 and fuels the concern over security and the need to educate teens on the use and possible repercussion of postings placed on such sites. Once posted, pictures and content are easily shared and distributed to others, sometimes with detrimental effects. Users should give thought to the information they publicly display and consider the possible consequences. If you are searching for employment, make sure that your social networking site is not offensive. Employers are researching candidates' Facebook or MySpace sites to gain insight into a potential employee's personality and behavior.

Usenet: Joining Online Discussions

Usenet is a worldwide computer-based discussion system accessible through the Internet. It consists of thousands of topically named **newsgroups**, which are discussion groups devoted to a single topic. A newsgroup typically requires participants to use a program called a news reader. Each newsgroup contains articles that users have posted for all to see. Users can respond to specific articles by posting follow-up articles. Over time, a discussion thread develops as people reply to the replies. A **thread** is a series of articles that offer a continuing commentary on the same specific subject.

Usenet newsgroups are organized into the following main categories:

- **Standard newsgroups.** You're most likely to find rewarding, high-quality discussions in the standard newsgroups (also called world newsgroups). Figure 6.36 lists the standard newsgroup subcategories.
- **Alt newsgroups.** The alt category is much more freewheeling. Anyone can create an alt newsgroup (which explains why so many of them have silly or offensive names).
- **Biz newsgroups.** These newsgroups are devoted to the commercial uses of the Internet.

The easiest way to access Usenet is through Google Groups (**http://groups.google.com**).

You can read and post messages, but be careful what you post on Usenet. When you post an article, you're publishing in the public domain. Sometimes articles are stored for long periods in Web-accessible archives.

FIGURE 6.36 Standard Newsgroup Subcategories

Subcategory Name	Description of Topics Covered
Comp	Everything related to computers and computer networks, including applications, compression, databases, multimedia, and programming
Misc	Subjects that do not fit in other standard newsgroup hierarchies, including activism, books, business, consumer issues, health, investing, jobs, and law
Sci	The sciences and social sciences, including anthropology, archaeology, chemistry, economics, math, physics, and statistics
Soc	Social issues, including adoption, college-related issues, feminism, human rights, and world cultures
Talk	Debate on controversial subjects, including abortion, atheism, euthanasia, gun control, and religion
News	Usenet itself, including announcements and materials for new users
Rec	All aspects of recreation, including aviation, backcountry sports, bicycles, boats, gardening, and scouting

A **message board** is similar to a newsgroup, but it is easier to use and does not require a newsreader. Many colleges and universities have switched to message boards for this reason.

Electronic Mailing Lists

Electronic mailing lists of e-mail addresses are similar in many ways to newsgroups and forums, but they automatically broadcast messages to all individuals on a mailing list. Because the messages are transmitted as e-mail, only individuals who are subscribers to the mailing list receive and view the messages. Some colleges and universities host electronic mailing lists. Eric Thomas developed the first electronic mailing list program, Listserv, in 1986 for BITNET. The most common freeware version of an electronic mailing list manager program is Majordomo.

VoIP

VoIP (Voice over Internet Protocol) allows a user to speak to others over a broadband Internet connection instead of traditional analog phone line. What do you need to use VoIP? This form of communication requires a broadband Internet connection, a VoIP service provider, and a normal telephone with a VoIP adapter or a computer with supporting software. Calls to others using the same service are usually free, whereas calls to those using other services can vary. Many businesses are using VoIP services, like Skype, to reduce their communication bills and operating expenses.

File Transfer Protocol: Transferring Files

File Transfer Protocol (FTP) is one way that files can be transferred over the Internet, and it is especially useful for transferring files that are too large to send by e-mail. Although you can use special FTP client software, such as WS_FTP Home, you can also transfer files to and from an FTP server simply by using your browser or Windows Explorer. FTP can transfer two types of files: ASCII (text files) and binary (program files, graphics, or documents saved in proprietary file formats).

In most cases, you need a user name and a password to access an FTP server. However, with **anonymous FTP**, files are publicly available for downloading. A word of warning: Due to the lack of security on an anonymous FTP site, do not use it to send sensitive information such as financial account numbers and passwords. FTP sites are structured hierarchically—that is, they use a folder and file structure similar to that used on your own computer. Depending on how you access the site, downloadable files may appear as hyperlinks. Just click the link to download the file. If you access the site using Windows Explorer, you can use the same file management techniques you use to organize your own files.

FTP is also used to upload Web pages from your computer to the ISP or hosting service's Web server, making your Web site available to other Internet users.

E-Commerce

A large portion of Internet traffic and Web sites are associated with e-commerce. **Commerce** is the selling of goods or services with the expectation of making a reasonable profit. **E-commerce (electronic commerce)** is the use of networks or the Internet to carry out business of any type. Many **e-tailers** (Web-based retailers) hope that while you are surfing the Web, you will stop and make a purchase. Online merchants sell books, CDs, clothes, and just about anything else you might want to buy. If you've ever made a purchase online, you're one of millions engaging in e-commerce.

E-commerce supports many types of traditional business transactions, including buying, selling, renting, borrowing, and lending. E-commerce isn't new; companies have used networks to do business with suppliers for years. What is new is that, thanks to the Internet and inexpensive PCs, e-commerce has become accessible to anyone with an Internet connection and a Web browser.

The U.S. Census Bureau reported that total retail e-commerce sales for the fourth quarter of 2009 was $42.0 billion, an increase of 34.1 percent from the third quarter of 2009. For the fourth quarter of 2009, e-commerce sales accounted for 4.3 percent of total sales (Figure 6.37). There are three types of e-commerce: business-to-business (B2B), consumer-to-consumer (C2C), and business-to-consumer (B2C).

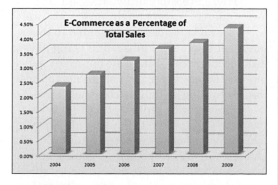

FIGURE 6.37 Statistics from the U.S. Census Bureau substantiate that e-commerce has been on the rise.

Business-to-Business E-Commerce (B2B)

When a business uses the Internet to provide another business with the materials, services, and/or supplies it needs to conduct its operations, they are engaging in **business-to-business (B2B) e-commerce**. Even though you might not personally engage in B2B, you'll probably recognize many of the industries and companies that do, for example, companies in the health care, aerospace and defense, real estate, automotive, and construction industries, and familiar computer and software companies such as Dell, IBM, and Microsoft.

In addition, many traditional and online retailers have special B2B units. For instance, the popular office supplies chain Staples has a B2B division that operates the Web site **www.staplesadvantage.com** for mid-size and Fortune 1000 companies. The Staples Contract division has experienced double-digit growth for the last seven years and launched the office supply industry's first online B2B catalog in 2007.

Unlike B2B, you may have engaged in the next type of e-commerce: consumer-to-consumer.

Consumer-to-Consumer E-Commerce (C2C)

The online exchange or trade of goods, services, or information between individual consumers is **consumer-to-consumer (C2C) e-commerce**. Often C2C e-commerce involves the use of an intermediate site, such as the popular online auction destination eBay. eBay has more than 89.5 million active users. The value of goods sold through eBay's online marketplaces, excluding autos, rose 24 percent in the fourth quarter of 2009 to $13.37 billion from $10.80 billion in the same quarter of 2008, with 58 percent of marketplace revenue from outside the U.S. (Figure 6.38). Other C2C sites include craigslist and Amazon Marketplace.

Business-to-Consumer E-Commerce (B2C)

When a business uses the Internet to supply consumers with services, information, or products, they are engaging in **business-to-consumer (B2C) e-commerce**. B2C is essentially the same as shopping at a physical store—you have a need or want, and the online marketplace offers products and solutions. The primary difference is that

FIGURE 6.38 eBay is the most well-known C2C trading site. However, its competitors like Craig's List and Amazon Marketplace are also popular.

B2C e-commerce is not place or time specific, which means that you don't have to be in any particular place at any particular time to participate. This freedom of time and place enables you to shop whenever you wish and to choose from more products and services than could ever be assembled in any one physical location.

Online Shopping

The trend is for more Web users to purchase merchandise online. In addition, many more people use the Web to research purchases from brick-and-mortar stores.

Getting Good Deals Online Have you ever tried to comparison shop on the Web? After surfing at 10 different sites (or more!), it can be daunting to keep track of where you saw the best price on that new digital camera you want. You might want to turn to shopping portals such as PriceGrabber.com, Shopzilla, NexTag, and others. These sites help you conduct price and product comparisons. They also offer reviews on just about any product you can imagine (Figure 6.39). You can search and sort by brand, price range, or product rating. To save even more, you can also

FIGURE 6.39 Shopping comparison sites can help users locate items, compare prices, view consumer feedback, and buy products.

check sites that offer coupons and rebates, such as The Bargainist and eCoupons.

The Dot-Com Phenomenon

Much e-commerce occurs in the *dot-com world,* the universe of Web sites with the suffix *.com* appended to their names. This unique world has been in existence only since 1995. Before 1995, companies were not able to sell over the Internet. But in 1995, the government eliminated all taxpayer funding of the Internet and

opened it up to commercial development. The period between 1995 and 2000 is referred to as the *dot-com boom.* As the dot-com crash of 2000 made painfully clear, not every online business is able to succeed.

Amazon.com is a dot-com company that has held its ground and become profitable. Amazon quickly discovered that books are a commodity well suited for online trade, but it didn't stop there. Its offerings have grown to include music, videos, groceries, tools, jewelry, and clothing. Amazon entices buyers to access, shop, and complete their sales online by offering professional and peer product reviews; author, artist, and subject matching; and book excerpts and music samples. Shoppers can choose from a variety of shipping options and track their purchases.

There are some drawbacks to B2C e-commerce. Buyers might miss speaking with a real sales clerk, being able to touch and feel the merchandise, and being able to take it home the same day, but many sellers are adopting creative solutions to these issues by offering online chats with live customer service representatives, various ways to view products, and a wide array of shipping options. One of the hallmarks of a successful online business is good customer service. Customers are reassured by sites that clearly post their contact information, offer pages of frequently asked questions, and respond quickly to customer inquiries.

Building Your Own Online Business

One of the tremendous advantages of B2C e-commerce is the low capital investment needed to start an online business. For less than $50, a person can open a Web storefront and start selling products online. In contrast, a brick-and-mortar business requires land, a building, utilities, display shelving, and salespeople. A Web-based storefront requires only an ISP, a Web site, and the ability to ship goods or services to customers.

The first thing you need to do when starting any business is to develop a business plan (Figure 6.40). You must decide what products to offer, determine your target market, and select how many items you plan to sell and at what price. Who will pay for shipping? Will there be service provided after the sale? Who are your competitors? What profit margin do you expect to achieve?

All businesses need to have a name, and an online business is no different, except that the online business's name is almost always the same as its Web site or domain name. So, after you've completed your business plan, you will need to shop for a domain name and a Web hosting service. Many Web hosting companies, such as 1&1 (**www.1and1. com**), offer domain name search and registration services as part of their package. You will most likely want a name with a .com extension. Try to pick a name that will be easy for your customers to remember.

You may also wish to employ an electronic shopping cart. This

FIGURE 6.40 Sites such as Bplans.com can help get your small business plan off to a good start.

feature is much like the physical shopping cart you'd use at a grocery store. It remembers your customer's order items and provides the results to the summary order page. Your Web site should project a professional image and be structured to meet your customers' needs to encourage their confidence in your product or service. Go to GoodPractices (**www.goodpractices.com**) for some Web site development guidelines.

You will also need to make arrangements for Web hosting, if you haven't already done so. Web hosting services provide server space, make your site available to the public, and offer site management utilities such as preprogrammed shopping cart services. There are thousands of Web hosting companies. Many Web hosting services offer templates and other tools to make it simple to build a professional-looking site. Sites such as 1&1, GoDaddy, and Yahoo! offer a variety of pricing plans for personal and commercial sites. Expect to pay a start-up fee as well as a monthly amount that is usually based on a one-year contract.

You can ensure that your site gets listed with search engines by visiting each engine's Web site (**www.google.com**, **www.yahoo.com**, **www.msn.com**, and so on) and searching for "submitting my site."

Provide the information requested, and then when someone searches for keywords that match your site, it will be one of the sites that are provided in the search results answer screen.

To operate a business, you need a way to receive payments. Just like in a traditional retail business, perhaps the best option may be to take credit cards. You should be aware that there are many costs involved with setting up and maintaining a credit card acceptance account—but the benefits may well outweigh the costs. Customers are comfortable using their credit cards online, and many feel more secure knowing that the credit card company is there in case of a dispute or fraudulent use (Figure 6.41).

One common method to accept credit cards is to use a PayPal merchant account. PayPal also acts as a secure intermediary, offering users the ability to make payments from their bank account, credit card, or PayPal account without revealing their personal financial

FIGURE 6.41 For online purchases, merchants prefer if customers use an electronic alternative like PayPal but customers may feel more secure using a credit card that provides dispute mediation and protection from fraud.

FIGURE 6.42 Sites such as Travelocity (www.travelocity.com) are popular because they help travelers find the cheapest fares and reservations available.

information to the seller. PayPal manages more than 40 million accounts worldwide. Transaction fees range from 2 to 3 percent, and there is a per-transaction fee of about 30 cents per transaction.

Other Areas of E-Commerce Growth

Making travel reservations is an area of e-commerce experiencing rapid growth. Sites such as Travelocity, Expedia, and CheapTickets enable leisure travelers to book flights, hotels, and car rentals online, as well as find the cheapest fares based on their trip parameters (Figure 6.42). Most travel sites provide e-tickets so that you can quickly check in at airport terminals by using small self-service kiosks.

Another rapidly growing online activity is banking. Access to your banking accounts enables you to use a Web browser to check account balances, balance your checkbook, transfer funds, and even pay bills online (Figure 6.43). In fact, 40 million Americans used online banking services by the end of 2005. The use of online banking is expected to grow by 55 percent by the end of 2011. By that time, some 76 percent of Americans (72 million households) will be using online banking services. Currently, banks that offer online banking gain a competitive advantage over those that do not because most customers now consider it a necessary and expected service, like ATMs. What else is in it for banks? Plenty. Online banking helps banks cut down on the expenses of maintaining bank

branches and paying tellers and also allows them to provide advanced levels of electronic customer service.

The sale of stock through the Internet has only been possible since 1996; however, online stock trading now accounts for one out of every six stock trades, easily making it the fastest-growing application in B2C e-commerce. Offering secure connections through the customer's Web browser, online stock trading sites enable investors to buy and sell stocks online without the aid of a broker.

The attraction of online stock trading can be summed up in one word: cost. Fees paid to traditional, full-service brokerages can add up. But the most aggressive e-traders have cut the charges to $10 per trade or less. E-traders, such as E*TRADE and Ameritrade, can offer such low prices because the trading is automatic—no human broker is involved.

Nonretail online services have spiked in activity in the last few years. These activities include dating services; credit reports; health and medical advice; news, weather, and sports information; real estate listings (for homes and apartments); and insurance products. These sites offer various levels of access and services for members and nonmembers. Some services, such as insurance quotes, up-to-the-minute news reports, and severe weather alerts, are free. You can also post dating profiles or receive diet and other health-related profiles as well as trial passes for sports subscriptions.

FIGURE 6.43 Online banking enables customers to access their accounts, balance checkbooks, and even pay bills online.

Rules of Netiquette

Along with the privilege of using the Internet comes the responsibility of using it correctly and not causing harm to others. Courtesy is as important in the online world as it is in reality.

Netiquette, short for Internet etiquette, is the code for acceptable behavior and manners while on the Internet. The basic rule is this: Talk to others the same way you would want them to talk to you. Some more specific, useful rules of netiquette for e-mail, chat rooms, instant messaging, and message boards include the following:

- Keep the message short.
- Avoid sarcasm or the use of phrases or words that could offend the reader.
- Read the message before sending or posting it, correcting spelling and grammar mistakes.
- Do not type in all capital letters as it means that you are yelling.
- Avoid sending a **flame**. Such messages express an opinion without holding back any emotion and are frequently seen as being confrontational and argumentative.

When you follow the rules of netiquette, you put your best foot forward and make a good impression. The other side of using the Internet is protecting yourself from those that are out to deceive or harm you. Let's look at some safe surfing suggestions to protect you from this dark side of technology.

Safe Surfing

Safe surfing seems to be a constant topic of discussion. Just as many hazards exist online as there are in the real world. The added online element is that individuals are difficult to recognize due to the anonymity the Internet provides.

Safe Surfing Guidelines

By taking some simple precautions you can make your Internet experience an enjoyable and safe activity.

- Never give out identifying information.
- Never respond to suggestive messages.
- Never open e-mail from an unknown source.
- Never allow a child to make arrangements for a face-to-face meeting alone, for any reason, without being accompanied by an adult.
- Remember individuals online may not be who they seem.
- Set reasonable rules and guidelines for computer use by children.
- Make using the computer a family activity.

Additional online hazards to avoid include malware; identity theft; threats to you and your family; and unscrupulous vendors.

Avoiding Malware

Malware refers to software programs designed and written to damage a computer system. Examples of malware events range from deleting files on a hard drive or removing directory information to gathering data from a user's system that can include Web sites the user visited and account numbers or passwords that were keyed in. It is unfortunate that there are individuals out there with malicious intent, but there are—and you must be prepared. You can keep your system free of malware by installing antivirus and antispyware utilities on your computer. These utility programs will seek and destroy the malware programs they find on your computer.

> "More than **half a million** people find themselves **victims** of identity theft each year. . . . And, **nothing** is more **difficult** than restoring your credit after an **identity theft** has **destroyed** your credit rating."

Protecting Your Identity

More than half a million people find themselves victims of identity theft each year. Nothing is more frustrating than having to spend the time and energy to clean up the mess created by a loss of identification. And, nothing is more difficult than restoring your credit after an identity theft has destroyed your credit rating.

There are steps you can take to greatly reduce the risk of having your identity stolen or a portion of it pilfered. Try to avoid shoulder-surfers; these are individuals who stand close enough to see PIN numbers keyed in by users at ATMs and phone booths. When shopping with an e-merchant for the first time, look for the secure Web site features before entering any personal or credit card information. These features usually include one or several of the items in the following list:

- *https://* in the address of the site instead of the usual *http://*. The added "s" stands for "secure site" and means that the data is encrypted all the way from your computer to the computer that receives it. No other computer will be able to read your input as it passes along the Internet.
- A site seal provided by a security vendor, such as VeriSign, GeoTrust, or SSL.com
- A locked padlock symbol somewhere on the Web site that, when double-clicked, displays details of the site's security (make sure that the logo is not just an image and a fake)
- The logo from other site-security entities, such as Verified by Visa
- A message box that notifies you when you are leaving (or entering) a secure site

In addition to these visible identifiers, check out any feedback provided by previous purchasers or any comments by the Better Business Bureau. Shop only on Web sites that enable you to view their privacy policy. Make it a habit to print out privacy policies, warranties, price guarantees, and other important information. Most importantly, *never* include any financial account numbers or passwords in an e-mail or respond in any way to spam. And be sure to change the passwords on your accounts frequently.

Simply being watchful and careful with your personal information, completing transactions only on validated Web sites, and knowing the signs of a secure site will help you use the Web to its full potential safely.

Protecting Children in Cyberspace

With statistics supporting the use of social networks, chat rooms, and other forms of anonymous communication by minors, there have been some creative protective responses to insulate youth from cyberstalkers, cyberbullies, and other online predators. A couple in Fanwood, New Jersey, contacted CyberAngels (**www.cyberangels.org**), a volunteer organization of thousands of Internet users worldwide, after their computer-addicted 13-year-old daughter ran away from home. The group's purpose: to protect children in cyberspace.

CyberAngels was founded in 1995 by Curtis Sliwa, who also started the Guardian Angels (the volunteer organization whose members wear red berets as they patrol inner-city streets). Today, CyberAngels volunteers scour the Internet for online predators, cyberstalkers, and child pornographers, and they've been responsible for a number of arrests. Their Web site and newsletter provide many useful articles about practical safety measures to keep you and your loved ones safe and has brought their Children's Internet Safety Program to thousands of schoolchildren across the United States. So, what about the New Jersey couple? Their daughter is home and safe thanks to the CyberAngels, who successfully used their network to identify the child's online contact.

The Internet can be a dangerous place for young children and older ones too! **Cyberbullying** occurs when one individual targets another for some form of torment or abuse through digital tools. The term used to apply to children acting against other children. However, the recent suicide death of a teen in Missouri due to cyberbullying by a parent who masqueraded as another youth has shed light on the intensity of this problem. Online stalkers and sexual predators haunt social networking sites. **Cyberstalkers** use e-mail, instant messaging, chat rooms, pagers, cell phones, or other forms of information technology to make repeated, credible threats of violence against another individual or family

" **[Never]** include any **financial account numbers** or passwords in an **e-mail** or **respond** in any way to spam. "

member of an individual. To learn more about how to protect yourself or the children in your household, visit Stop Cyberbullying (**www.stopcyberbullying.org**), SocialSafety.org (**www. socialsafety.org**), and the Family Online Safety Institute (**http://fosi.org/icra/**).

Speaking with children about Internet safety practices, being aware of where and when they surf, and knowing who their cyberfriends are should be a top priority. Concerned parents can implement the parental controls that are provided by their ISPs or included in safety and security software. Web site blocking and content-filtering software and monitoring programs like Net Nanny (**www.netnanny.com**), and bsecure (**www.bsecure.com**) can add another level of security (Figure 6.44).

After covering the personal uses for the Internet and addressing its benefits and drawbacks, let's change the focus to the Internet user conducting business.

Avoiding E-Commerce Hazards

Although there are many benefits to engaging in e-commerce, it also entails risks. These risks include identity theft, personal information exposure, money loss, and being ripped off by unscrupulous charlatans. To protect yourself, carefully create user names and passwords, particularly at sites where you must pay for goods or services. It is also wise to avoid e-commerce with little-known companies, at least until you've taken the opportunity to check their legitimacy. Checking shopping portals or other review sites to locate feedback from other users or conducting an online search combining the company's name with keywords such as *problem*, *fraud*, or *scam* can help you be better informed.

Even though you are most likely protected from monetary losses by your credit

FIGURE 6.44 Content-filtering software like Net Nanny are extending parental control from notebooks and desktop system to mobile devices.

card company, you should always be careful when giving out your credit card information—and do so only on secure sites. Never share credit card numbers, account numbers, user name, or password information with others, even if you receive an e-mail requesting that information from what seems to be a legitimate source.

Sometimes you will find that the seller is a person just like you—that the seller doesn't have the ability to take credit cards and that he or she has set up an account with an online transaction processing system such as PayPal. It is the seller who decides which vendor to use for the payment. For instance, if you see the PayPal logo on an eBay auction item site, it means that you can use PayPal as a payment option. In fact, sometimes this is the only option available. The PayPal Web site even offers a tool to help you manage your buying experience. The PayPal AuctionFinder searches eBay for items you've recently won and prefills your payment form with details taken straight from the item listing. With AuctionFinder, you can eliminate errors and pay for your items instantly. Always use extra care and caution whenever you conduct financial transactions on the Internet.

Use the Favorites Feature of the
Internet Explorer (IE) Browser

The Favorites menu located on the menu bar in the IE browser window allows you to insert a Web page into the Favorites list, making it easier to access later by not having to retype the URL in the address bar. Once you make a page a Favorite, all you have to do is click the name and the Web page will display in the browser window.

In this section, we cover how to perform two actions with respect to managing your Favorites:

- Adding a Web page to the Favorites list
- Organizing your Favorite list into folders

To add a Web page to the Favorites list:

1. Enter the URL of the page you want to access in the browser's address bar.

   After the page appears, click *Favorites* on the menu bar.

2. From the drop-down menu that appears, select *Add to Favorites* (Figure 6.45).

3. In the Add a Favorite dialog box you can do these things:

   a. Name the page you are inserting into the Favorites list or use the default.

   b. Create a new folder and place the current page into that folder.

   c. Place the page into a folder that already exists by clicking the arrow to the right of the *Create in* option.

4. After selecting your option, click *Add*. The current page is now an entry in your Favorites list.

You can organize your Favorites list into folders while you are adding the page as described above or after pages have been placed in the Favorites list.

To organize your Favorites list after Web pages have been added:

1. Click *Favorites* on the menu bar.

2. Select the *Organize Favorites* option.

FIGURE 6.45 Select the *Add to Favorites* option to open the Add a Favorite dialog box.

3. In the Organize Favorites dialog box that appears, you have four choices: New Folder, Move, Rename, or Delete (Figure 6.46).

- Select *New Folder* to create and name a new folder.
- Highlight a Favorites entry and then select *Move*. A dialog box will open and ask you to select the location to which you want to move the entry.
- Select *Rename*, with an entry highlighted, and rename that entry in the top section of the dialog box.
- Select *Delete*, with an entry highlighted, to remove the entry from the Favorites list.

FIGURE 6.46 Your Favorites list can get very long. Adding folders will organize the list and make it easier to locate a site.

Chapter Summary

The Internet and the World Wide Web

- The Internet is the network of networks that, because of its interoperability, allows connected computers to exchange data regardless of model, brand, or operating system. Interoperability is made possible by the use of TCP/IP (Transmission Control Protocol/Internet Protocol) suite of protocols, the standard methods of packaging and transmitting information on the Internet.

- Users access the Internet by way of an Internet access provider. Access providers fall into three categories: Internet service provider (ISP), online service provider, and a wireless Internet service provider. A user connects to the access provider by way of a telephone modem, a digital service line (DSL), a cable modem, a satellite, or a fiber-optic cable.

- Whereas the Internet is a global computer network that connects millions of smaller networks, the World Wide Web is a global system of billions of hypertext documents, called Web pages. These documents use hyperlinks to connect to each other and the Internet as a transport mechanism. Web pages are displayed though a combination of elements, including hyperlinks to jump from one Web page to another, a browser to interpret the HTML tags and display the Web document, including enabling of hyperlinks, and a Web server that stores the Web pages and retrieves them when a request is made by a browser.

- Information on the Web can be located by entering the URL (Web address) in the address bar of the browser, general surfing, using searches with search operators to get more specific results, and using sites and technology that allow the sharing of information with other Web users, such as RSS feeds, blogs, and wikis. Search expressions can include search operators (+, −, *) or Boolean search terms (AND, OR, NOT) to narrow down the list of results.

- Features of a reliable Web source include an author with credentials, the affiliation of the Web site with the host, the objectivity of the material presented, the overall purpose of the site, and the accuracy and currency of the information.

- Popular Internet services include e-mail and instant messaging (IM) for sending messages, Internet relay chat (IRC) for text chatting, chat rooms, social networking sites for online communities, discussion groups, newsgroups, VoIP, message boards, and File Transfer Protocol (FTP) for file exchange, and e-commerce.

- There are three types of e-commerce, business-to-business (B2B), consumer-to-consumer (C2C), and business-to-consumer (B2C).

- When using the Web, be courteous and respect the rules of netiquette.

- Follow safe surfing guidelines, avoid malware, change your passwords frequently, never enter your account number unless you are on a secured site, watch the computer usage of your children, and install software to protect your children from cyberstalkers, cyberbullies, and undesirable Web sites. When conducting online business, be aware of security indicators on Web sites conducting e-commerce, and perform transactions only with secured sites.

Key Terms and Concepts

Identification

Label each item.

1. _____

2. _____

3. _____

4. _____

5. _____

6. _____

Matching

Match each key term in the left column with the most accurate definition in the right column.

_____ 1. hot spot

_____ 2. uploading

_____ 3. interoperability

_____ 4. portal

_____ 5. hyperlink

_____ 6. router

_____ 7. home page

_____ 8. clickstream

_____ 9. downloading

_____ 10. dead link

_____ 11. RSS

_____ 12. subject guide

_____ 13. browser

_____ 14. plug-in

_____ 15. link rot

a. Transferring a document or file from another computer to your computer

b. An element in an electronic document that acts as the connector to another place in the same document or to an entirely different document

c. The set of Web links that indicates the trail a user followed to reach a Web page

d. A method of providing constant information updates over the Internet without any user involvement

e. A public location, like an airport, college campus, or coffee shop, that provides Internet access for devices fitted with wireless technology

f. A list of subject-related categories that, when selected, displays a page of more related links

g. Additional software programs that extend the multimedia ability of a browser

h. Links to documents on the Web that have disappeared

i. Transferring a document or file from your computer to another computer

j. A program on the user's computer that interprets HTML or XHTML forms, enabling the user to view Web pages

k. A Web page that acts as a gateway to diverse sources presented in an organized way

l. Outdatedness due to the delay in accumulating data and updating a search engine's database

m. Specialized devices that connect networks, locate the best path of transmission, and ensure that your data reaches its destination

n. The default page that is automatically displayed when you enter a site at its top level

o. Describes the Internet's ability to work with computers and applications of different brands and models, through the use of a common protocol

Multiple Choice

Circle the correct choice for each of the following:

1. Which of the following is *not* a search operator?
   a. −
   b. +
   c. !
   d. *

2. Which of the following is an example of a valid IP address?
   a. 12.256.56.78
   b. 38.155.400.56
   c. 45.254.77.125
   d. 266.54.77.89

3. Which of the following is *not* a top-level domain name?
   a. .edu
   b. .car
   c. .net
   d. .gov

4. RSS feeds can be grouped together through the use of a(n) _____ program.
   a. browser
   b. aggregator
   c. syndication
   d. plug-in

5. Which Internet service is plagued by spam?
   a. Instant messaging
   b. E-mail
   c. VoIP
   d. Chat rooms

6. What does the appearance of a VeriSign logo on a Web site indicate?
   a. The site is a commercial site.
   b. The site has been recently updated.
   c. The site is hosted in the United States.
   d. The site is secure.

7. What term refers to the act of abusing or tormenting an individual through digital methods?
   a. Cyberbullying
   b. Cyberstalking
   c. E-tailing
   d. Flaming

8. Which is *not* a method of e-commerce?
   a. B2B   b. C2C
   c. C2B   d. B2C

9. What is the name of spam that targets users of instant messaging?
   a. Spimming
   b. Botnet
   c. Spyware
   d. Beacon

10. A(n) _____ is a Web page on which any visitor can post text or images, read previous posts, change earlier posts, and track changes.
    a. blog
    b. wiki
    c. newsgroup
    d. electronic mailing list

Fill-In

In the blanks provided, write the correct answer for each of the following.

1. _____ is a search technique that makes use of wildcards to locate words with various endings.

2. _____ is the next generation of the Web that provides increased opportunities for collaboration.

3. _____ is a unique numerical identifier for each computer or device connected to the Internet.

4. A(n) _____ is the equivalent of an Internet diary or journal.

5. A(n) _____ is a program that travels the Web and populates the database of a search engine.

6. _____ is unsolicited e-mail.

7. A(n) _____ provides individuals and businesses with access to the Internet via phone, DSL, cable, satellite, or fiber-optic lines, for a fee.

8. A(n) _____ is a series of articles that offer a continuing commentary on the same subject.

9. _____ is a worldwide computer-based discussion system accessible through the Internet.

10. E-bay is an example of a(n) _____ e-commerce site.

11. A(n) _____ is an angry or critical response to a violation of netiquette.

12. _____ is a type of spam that collects data from a user's system without his or her knowledge.

13. _____ is the online exchange or trade of goods, services, or information between two businesses.

14. A _____ is a method of sharing information over the Internet in audio, image, or video format.

15. A(n) _____ is a Web-based retailer.

Short Answer

1. Explain the difference between the Internet and the Web.

2. List the three types of access providers and give a brief description of each.

3. List three drawbacks of distributing content over the Web.

4. What is Real Simple Syndication (RSS)?

5. List the characteristics that help to evaluate the credibility of content on Web pages.

Teamwork

1. **Security Vendors** As a team, research at least three security certificate vendors. Provide a brief description of each and describe the logo that each is identified by. Then locate at least 10 Web sites that display one of the logos that you described. Present your vendor's descriptions, logos, and the 10 associated Web sites in a PowerPoint presentation. Remember to cite your references and include the full URL of your Web site examples.

2. **Evaluating Web content** Break into groups of two or three. Each group should locate a Web site with information on a topic being covered in class or another topic approved by the instructor. Evaluate the site based on the criteria listed in this chapter. Using your word processor, create a table to display your findings. List the criteria in column 1 and your evaluation in column 2. Using the reference feature of your word processor, create end notes and reference the Web sites used. Present your evaluations in a one- to two-page word processing document.

3. **Using a Search Engine** As a team, evaluate each of the search statements below and describe the result that each will achieve. Use **www.internettutorials.net** for help with symbols you might not understand. Then create the search string to meet the specified change. Take a screen capture of the results from each search. Complete the table that follows and turn in the completed table and the screen capture from each one of the five searches.

   To create a screen capture, first press *PrtScrn* on the keyboard while the search result is on the screen. Open the Word file you plan to submit for this question. Position the cursor in the location where you want the capture to appear, and from the contextual menu in the Word window select *Edit*, then select *Paste*. The PrintScrn image captured earlier will appear in the Word document. Then save and print the document.

4. **Web-Based Course Management Systems** Most colleges and universities use some sort of Web-based course management system to provide online classes or an additional resource for face-to-face classes. Evaluate the effectiveness of the course management system at your school by breaking into two groups. Have one group create a survey and distribute it to students that are using the system. Have the other group create a survey and distribute it to faculty that are using the system. The survey should contain 8 to 10 questions and focus on the type of materials that are posted on the system, the amount of time respondents use or access the system on a weekly basis, their opinion of the effectiveness of this media for learning, and the integrity of the learning that takes place in this environment. Distribute the survey to at least 10 students and 10 faculty members. As a team, collect and summarize the results. Present your summary and analysis of the data in a PowerPoint presentation.

5. **Digital Communication** As a team, create a survey to evaluate the digital communication preferences of students at your school. Include questions on the type of devices they use (smartphones, notebooks, desktops), the type of media they use (blogs, wikis, e-mail, text messaging, course management system), the amount they pay for the service (if they pay), the frequency of use, and some general questions like the gender and class level (freshman, sophomore, junior, or senior). Distribute the survey to at least 20 students on campus. Collect and analyze the responses. As a team, draw usage conclusions from the data collected. Use a PowerPoint presentation to present a summary of your results and the conclusions your team drew from the data.

Search String	Purpose	Change to Be Made	Search String with Change
Sports + Hockey		exclude the Sabres	
"Absence makes the heart grow fonder"		include Shakespeare	
logo sports		include baseball	
clothing + LLBean + women		remove women and add men	
Go Green + US		remove US and add clothing	

On the Web

1. **Blogging for Beginners** Go to **www.blogger.com/start** and create a blog that you will add content to daily for a week. The blog content is to be about your experience in using a blogging site, the features of the site that you like or don't like, and an evaluation of the whole experience. Invite some of your classmates to participate in the blog. Your blog will be your report, so make it detailed and professional. Provide your instructor with the blog address so he/she can follow the postings. Remember the blog and its content will be considered as your submitted assignment.

2. **Using an Aggregator** Use a search engine to locate free aggregators. Review a few aggregators and select one to use in this exercise. Aggregator sites usually have categories like news and sports that contain several Web sites having RSS feeds. Select a category and then view the individual subscriptions that are available. Use the *Add* option to subscribe to a feed, and include a few of your own preferred Web sites (ESPN, USA Today) with RSS feeds in the subscription list. When they appear, locate the manage subscription option and organize the ones you added by placing them into existing categories or by creating a new separate category. Delete a few of the ones that are in the category you chose. Check out some of the other features of the aggregator. There is usually an option to return to a home page, some way to track your reading trends, and even a way to share your reader with others. After using the program for a while, review your experience. In a one-page, double-spaced paper, describe the aggregator site you chose and explain why you chose that site. Also discuss how easy (or difficult) the site was to use, the amount of feeds you received, and whether or not you would use such a program. Include any other observations and bits of advice for another user. Remember to cite your references.

3. **Plug-ins: Are They Cool or Irritating** Go to **www.coolhomepages.com/** or **www.ebizmba.com/articles/best-flash-sites** to view Web sites that make use of Flash animation. Select and view three sites. Did you have to download a plug-in, or did you already have the necessary one on your system? Are the displayed graphics of high quality and does the animation enhance the site? How long was the load time? If the site had a Flash introduction, would you like the opportunity to skip the intro?

Evaluate the three sites you viewed. Answer the previously listed questions and provide any other thoughts about your Flash experience in a one-page, double-spaced paper. Remember to cite the URL of each site.

4. **Internet Ethics** The one area of Internet use that seems to cause more controversy than others is downloading music. For some reason, the consensus is not as clear-cut on the legality of this behavior. Users compare downloading music to lending a CD to a friend. Producers and artists consider it theft. Using a search engine, identify at least two Web sites that facilitate music downloads. Review their policy, legal statements, and agreements. Who is liable if the sharing done on their site is found to be illegal? Are there any fees to subscribe to or use the site? In what country is the site being hosted? Attempt to locate statistics on the number of music downloads and the loss of revenue to the music and related industries related to downloading music files. In a PowerPoint presentation, review your findings for these and other related issues that you come across in your research. Suggest any viable solutions that you see as a compromise to this ongoing controversy. Remember to cite your references.

5. **Create Your Own Avatar** With all of the methods of animation that appear on the Internet, let's try one that is relatively new, an avatar. These talking images can be embedded within e-mails, Facebook pages, blogs, and Web sites. Using a search engine, locate a reputable Web site that allows you to create and publish you own avatar for free (**www.voki.com** is just one suggestion). Some sites offer avatars of comic book characters, television personalities, and individuals from history. Locate a site and create and customize your avatar. Most sites allow you to choose an image and then change the features of that image. Once you have your avatar's appearance completed, you will need to add the words that you want the avatar to say. This can be done by recording the words yourself with a microphone, typing them into a text box, or uploading an audio file. If you are not using your own voice, you can select the voice to speak your content. Make the content of your recording focus on your experience with this method of communication. When your avatar is complete, publish it and send an e-mail to your instructor that includes the avatar.

Spotlight

Cloud Computing

Are you tired of storing your data on external hard drives, flash drives, and DVDs? Do you check these portable devices before you leave for school or work to make sure that they contain the information you need for the day? Are you frustrated with renaming versions of a file so that you know which file on which storage device is the most recent? Do you travel and need your files to be accessible from any location at any time of the day? If you answered yes to any of these questions, then cloud computing may be the solution you have been waiting for.

A few years ago cloud computing was a new buzzword and IT concept that was surrounded by confusion and uncertainty. Most individuals weren't sure exactly what cloud computing was. They didn't understand how it was going to affect IT departments, the academic environment, the business world, and enterprise planning for future technology resources. Today, *cloud computing* is a common term in IT circles, and articles about it, containing both positive and negative content, appear daily on RSS news feeds. It seems that it has gone from a buzzword to a reality while we were sleeping. No longer can it be ignored by individuals who use technology for work, education, or even entertainment. Cloud computing is here, and such companies as salesforce.com and Workday are trying to persuade the world that it is here to stay. This spotlight clarifies what cloud computing is, focusing on its essential characteristics, service categories, and deployment models, and pointing out both its positive and negative features. We'll also look at statistics that support cloud computing's predicted continuing growth.

What Is Cloud Computing?

The cloud has been a familiar image or symbol for the Internet for sometime; however, connecting it with the word *computing* has caused some confusion and created a blurry image. **Cloud computing**, according to the Computer Security Division of the National Institute of Standards and Technology, "is a model for enabling convenient, on-demand network access to a shared pool of configurable computing resources that can be rapidly provisioned and released with minimal management effort or service provider interaction. This cloud model promotes availability and is composed of five general characteristics: on-demand self-service, broad network access, resource pooling, rapid elasticity, and measured service" (Figure 5A).

That is quite a comprehensive definition. Let's start to break it down by first examining each of the listed general characteristics.

- **On-demand self-service.** The customer or subscriber, without the need to contact or interact with a human from the cloud provider (self-service), can increase or decrease computing requirements as needed (on-demand). Computing requirements can include such necessities as server use, network storage, and software applications.

- **Broad network access.** This is the most significant component of cloud computing. The services offered by a provider must be accessible over a network, from any location, and on any standardized platform, including mobile phones and PDAs. This means that the hardware and software that you use to perform tasks on your local computer are actually on someone else's system, the provider's. You access them through a network—for a fee. The Internet, the only network that provides this scope of capability, is the core of cloud computing and is associated with the cloud image that is a part of every cloud computing illustration.

- **Resource pooling.** This characteristic refers to the provider's ability to pool services to accommodate their use by multiple subscribers at the same time. These resources are assigned when a subscriber signs on and are dynamically reassigned as demands by other subscribers occur. The subscriber (user or client) is unaware of the location of the resources he or she is using or any reassignment taking place. In cloud computing, the user gets the programs and hardware support that he or she needs, and the provider (cloud owner) gets paid. In a cloud computing environment, the burden of work is on the cloud provider to maintain, upgrade, and administer the hosts (servers) that constitute their cloud.

- **Rapid elasticity.** This term refers to the ability of a subscriber to increase computing resources in spike or peak times without having to worry about overloading a system or having to purchase additional hardware for a minimal amount of high-performance need. The size and capacity of a cloud provider allow the subscriber to scale up or down as needed and pay for only the time and amount of services used.

- **Measured service.** The cloud provider must meter usage to use this information for billing, but more importantly, to analyze usage and respond appropriately. Predictions for changes and upgrades for a cloud provider are developed primarily from the data obtained from its usage meters. If it intends to keep subscribers, it must expand, reallocate, and change in a manner that meets its subscribers' needs.

FIGURE 5A The main component of cloud computing is the Internet, the broad network that acts as a delivery vehicle used to transport services from a provider to a subscriber.

In general, hosting computers (servers) and subscribers (clients) are the main components of cloud computing—just as they are in a traditional client/server network. So what distinguishes cloud computing from a traditional client/server network? There are three major differences:

- In cloud computing, the delivery of the services from the provider to a subscriber must be over the Internet.

- The services provided over the cloud by a provider are scalable; they can be increased or decreased as the needs of an individual subscriber or company change. Services are typically offered and billed by the minute or hour.

- The services provided are managed completely by the cloud provider, the owner or manager of the host. The client or subscriber of the service does not have to worry about having a specific computer or operating system, or a certain processor or amount of RAM, and does not need to purchase software upgrades or download service patches. The subscribed services are not on the individual's computer or system. They are on the provider's hosts and are maintained by that provider and simply accessed by the subscriber.

Now that the main characteristics of cloud computing have been covered, let's investigate the three primary categories into which all cloud computing can be divided.

Cloud Computing Service Categories

The features offered by a cloud computing provider to a subscriber can be divided into three categories or models, depending on whether the services are hardware based, software based, or allow for application and interface development. The three main models of cloud computing services are: Infrastructure-as-a-Service (IaaS), Platform-as-a-Service (PaaS), and Software-as-a-Service (SaaS). Lets examine the focus of each.

INFRASTRUCTURE-AS-A-SERVICE (IAAS)

The category of cloud services that refers to the outsourcing of hardware, the equipment used to sustain the operations of a company or enterprise, is **Infrastructure-as-a-Service (IaaS)**. Because IaaS encompasses storage devices, actual servers, and network components it is also referred to as **Hardware-as-a-Service (HaaS)**. Providers of IaaS, such as Cloud.com, VMware, and Citrix, offer subscribers an offsite virtual datacenter as part of their information technology (IT) environment. This movement of the IT infrastructure from in-house to off premises aligns itself with the view that owning and operating a datacenter is no longer cost-effective (Figure 5B).

Through the use of virtualization and grids, IaaS is able to provide the hardware structure and scalability needed for both small business and enterprise functions. In **virtualization**, the application and infrastructure are independent. This means that one physical machine can run several virtual machines. A **virtual machine** is not an actual physical machine, but a software-created segment of a hard drive that contains its own operating system and applications, which makes it behave as a separate physical machine in the eyes of the user. For a brief, humorous (yet informative) video on virtualization and cloud computing in plain English, go to **www.youtube.com/watch?v=XdBd14rjcs0&feature=player_embedded#!**

A **grid** is a combination of several computers or virtual machines that are connected over a network to make them appear and function as one single computer (Figure 5C). The use of both virtualization and grids has made it possible for Infrastructure-as-a-Service to provide virtual datacenters and enable companies to eliminate the high cost of equipment and personnel to manage such a facility; focus more on their core business objectives; pay for only the equipment they use; and as a result, reduce the overall cost of doing business. The main factors driving enterprises to use Infrastructure-as-a-Service are as follows:

- Reduced budgeted outlay for equipment and its continual upgrade and maintenance
- Fast time to market with programs and ideas because the equipment needed to run them can be added to the cloud subscription
- The reassignment of IT personnel from a focus on learning and administering new equipment, because that is now done by the provider of the service, to more business-related tasks
- The replacement of unknown costs associated with running an in-house datacenter with known, predetermined operating costs provided through set subscription rates based on the services used over a period of time

PLATFORM-AS-A-SERVICE (PAAS)

The category of cloud services that permits subscribers to have remote access to application development, interface development, database development, storage, and testing is **Platform-as-a-Service**. This is the feature that enables the creation and testing of subscriber-developed programs and interfaces, using a cloud provider's hardware and development environment. For the subscriber, this is a huge savings because the equipment

FIGURE 5B   The development of IT infrastructure over time.

FIGURE 5C Virtualization and computer grids enable a cloud provider to create a network of widely dispersed computers and make it appear to run as a traditional centralized datacenter.

and software do not have to be purchased to test a possible application or interface and the fear of crashing a system during testing is alleviated by using the provider's secure test environment. Platform-as-a-Service providers include Google App Engine, Force.com, and Oracle SaaS.

SOFTWARE-AS-A-SERVICE (SAAS)

The most widely used and widely known form of cloud computing is **Software-as-a-Service (SaaS)**. The SaaS model of cloud computing enables software to be deployed from a cloud provider, delivered over the Internet, and accessed by a subscriber through a browser. Statistics from a recent survey of SaaS users by Datamation and THINKstrategies indicate that approximately 85 percent of subscribers are satisfied with the service, 80 percent would renew their subscriptions, and 61 percent would expand services. The primary reasons to subscribe to SaaS include these:

- Limited risk
- Rapid deployment
- Fewer upfront costs, such as the expense of purchasing a server
- Increased reliability as seen in reduced downtime caused by service disruptions
- Standardized backup procedures

- Lower total cost of ownership (TCO) through reduced hardware costs, software purchases, license agreements, and personnel to run and administer the systems

There are two major categories of SaaS: consumer services and business services. **Consumer-oriented services**, like those supplied by Google Apps and Google Docs, are offered to the public either on a subscription basis or, if supported by advertisement, for no cost (Figure 5D). **Business services** are sold to enterprise and business organizations of all sizes, usually on a subscription basis. This category of SaaS services

FIGURE 5D Google Docs offers SaaS with a limited amount of storage to individual users, free of charge.

FIGURE 5E Key Factors in the High Success Rate of Software-as-a-Service

focuses on facilitating business practices, for example financial services and customer relationship management (CRM). Two of the main incentives for the success of Software-as-a-Service are the user's frustration with his or her installed applications and the maturity of technology that enables the sharing of an application by multiple users over a reliable, flexible, high-bandwidth network. Figure 5E provides a more detailed list of factors behind the success of SaaS. Providers of Software-as-a-Service include Salesforce, Oracle on demand, and Google Apps.

The categories of cloud computing help to departmentalize cloud services, but how these services are deployed adds to their security and accessibility. Let's take a closer look at the main models of cloud deployment.

Cloud Deployment Methods

The way cloud services are accessed, owned, used, and physically located determines the deployment of the cloud service (Figure 5F). There are three basic types of deployment models:

- **Private cloud.** A **private cloud** is operated for a single organization and its authorized users. The infrastructure can exist on-site or off-site and is controlled by either the organization or a contracted third party. A **community cloud** is an extension of a private cloud in which organizations with similar missions share the infrastructure to reduce cost. This variation of the private cloud disperses cost while providing a high level of

FIGURE 5F Features of Cloud Deployment Methods

Cloud Deployment	Managed by	Infrastructure Ownership	Infrastructure Location	Accessible by
Private cloud	Organization	Organization or third party	On premises or off premises	Trusted users
Public cloud	Third-party provider	Third-party provider	Off premises	Untrusted users
Hybrid cloud	Both the organization and third-party provider	Both the organization and third-party provider	Both on premises and off premises	Both trusted and untrusted users

Modified from **www.rationalsurvivability.com/blog/?p=743**

FIGURE 5G The type of cloud deployment chosen by an enterprise may be directly related to security issues.

conformity and security by allowing access only to trusted users. Google's Gov Cloud is an example of a community cloud.

- **Public cloud.** Available to the general public, large organizations, or a group of organizations, the **public cloud** offers the most risk because it is accessed by users that have not been authenticated or established as trusted. Its infrastructure is owned and operated by a cloud provider and is located off site.

- **Hybrid cloud.** The **hybrid cloud** deployment method is a combination of two or more clouds (private, community, or public) that are unique but are connected by common, standard technology that enables the sharing of applications and data. Its infrastructure can be located both on-site and off the premises, and it can be managed by both the organization and a cloud provider. Users can be trusted and untrusted.

A big difference between cloud deployment models is the concern over security. A careful needs assessment and examination of security requirements are key to making the right choices for cloud computing.

As you can see in Figure 5G, a private network operates in what can be viewed as its own private disconnected cloud. The only users are those authorized and approved by the organization that owns and manages the cloud. The entire private cloud, its services, and users are behind a firewall, a security device that is actually a combination of software and hardware that stops data from exiting a network or private cloud and filters data attempting to enter a network from the Internet or public cloud. While logged into a private network and accessing its resources, the right to use the Internet or public network may be denied.

A public cloud is the least secure deployment method because its infrastructure and resources are subscribed to from a cloud provider that operates outside of the firewall. The provider of public cloud services is responsible for the security of the data and resources that it stores and provides to subscribers. This loss of control over security is a concern of some and a relief for other public cloud users.

A hybrid cloud is a combination of both types of deployment. In a hybrid cloud model, a portion of the cloud is private and behind the firewall, whereas another portion is public and outside of the firewall. Hybrids can be used to ease the transition from a private cloud to a public cloud or to secure portions of enterprise data in the private segment while still enabling access to the wide scope of services offered by public segment.

Any attempt to implement cloud computing will include a hard look at both the pros and cons of such a decision. Let's examine that area next.

Pros and Cons of Cloud Computing

Remember that technology is always changing, so the pros and cons of cloud computing will change with new developments. Additionally, something viewed as a negative feature by one enterprise or individual can be seen as an asset by another. A closer look at the current pros and cons of cloud computing might provide some insight into the features to consider if a move to the cloud is in your future (Figure 5H).

THE PROS OF CLOUD COMPUTING

The cloud seems to present a delicate balance between benefits and risks. If subscribers are willing to manage some of the risks themselves and not rely completely on the provider, then the downside of cloud computing is less of a gamble. Let's first review the positive

Cloud Computing

Flexibility of choice and agility of services	Loss of in-house control
Availability of new and current architecture	Provider limitations lock in systems
Contained management of change	Lowered reliability
Scale/cost	Security challenges

FIGURE 5H   The Main Advantages (+) and Disadvantages (−) of Cloud Computing

features of cloud computing in the light of today's technology.

Scale and Cost A big factor in transitioning to cloud computing for many organizations is the ability to meet increasing IT demands without having to absorb the high cost of equipment. This means that offerings can be expanded on a trial basis and analyzed to determine the business assets of such an implementation without accruing the "high cost of doing business." The organization or enterprise does not have to purchase equipment, license software, and hire personnel. If the innovation were not successful, the business's losses would be confined to the increase in the cloud subscription for the hardware, software, and management activities used for the period that the services were engaged. This is the beauty of cloud computing. Services can be scaled up or back depending on need. The only cost to the organization or enterprise is a change in their subscription rate that reflects the costs for only those services used.

Encapsulated Change Management The maintenance, upgrade, or even a total change to the infrastructure of an enterprise is no longer a huge concern because cloud providers make use of a cloud operating system and virtualization. A **cloud operating system**, like Windows Azure, is specially designed to run a cloud provider's datacenter and is delivered to subscribers over the Internet or other network. Recall that virtualization is used by cloud

providers to wrap an operating system and application in a self-contained segment of a hard drive, making it appear as if it were an independent stand-alone machine. Through the use of virtualization and a cloud operating system, hardware and associated technology can be maintained, redistributed, and redirected to accommodate a subscriber's request without major reconfiguration.

Choice and Agility
Without having to make costly commitments to hardware purchases and software licensing, cloud computing enables a subscriber to deploy solutions that best suit current needs and trends. It also allows flexibility to alter those solutions if the market or corporate financial situation changes. With this ability to amend solutions to match market demands comes the additional flexibility to choose among vendors. This freedom of choice is referred to as **interoperability**, the ability of a service from one provider to work with the services of another, without any subscriber interaction. What enables interoperability is **middleware**, a broad term for software that enables interoperability by assisting the passing of data among applications. Middleware provides a smooth and safe interface between network nodes and servers (Figure 5I). The results are an improvement in overall performance and flexibility because a subscriber is not tied to one provider, an essential factor if a provider goes out of business or one of its datacenters goes down. Middleware is essential for scalability as well as interoperability in the cloud.

Next-Generation Architectures The cloud enables innovation and creativity by allowing the testing and piloting of new database structures, languages, and framework through PaaS providers. Using this service provides a safe development environment, without the developer having to purchase expensive hardware and software or worrying that the deployment of the new application might interfere or crash their in-house system. Through cloud computing, innovation and foresight in IT areas are not a threat to the bottom line or current operations. Instead, they are viewed as futuristic and inventive.

Shifting from the positive to the negative, let's examine some of the shortcomings of cloud computing.

THE CONS OF CLOUD COMPUTING

Lock-in Not all cloud providers offer interoperability or the agility of choice, so "buyer beware." If you foresee your needs changing or the need for a future application that one provider supplies and another does not, make sure that you are not locked in to your provider and can switch providers without losing your ability to access or read your data. Total interoperability within the cloud is one of the long-term goals of the "Open Cloud" movement.

FIGURE 5I Middleware is the reason that a change in provider, indicated by the dotted line, can appear seamless to a subscriber.

Reliability There is a possibility that the cloud provider will lose power, run into trouble, burn down, or simply go out of business. If any of these actions did occur and your provider did not have interoperable services, you might lose all of your data. If you believe that this could never happen, you are wrong. In mid-2009, within one week, there were power outages at several datacenters that host high-profile sites like the video site Daily motion, the credit card authorization service Authorize.net, and Microsoft's Bing Travel. Additionally, with the economy the way it is, it is not impossible that a cloud provider might have to go out of business for financial reasons. If this happens, how would you access your files? Once again "buyer beware." Read the subscription conditions carefully and look for the features that give you reliability, agility, and choice.

Lack of Control Some enterprise IT staff might be uncomfortable surrendering control over resources to someone else. Not only does cloud computing surrender control to a perfect stranger, but that stranger is someone somewhere in the cloud that in-house staff will probably never meet. Scheduled maintenance, upgrades, and backups are no longer done on the premises by employees but by the provider. Administrative tasks like adding users, deleting users, and altering access rights may be done either by the subscriber's IT staff or the provider. Letting go of the daily maintenance of your infrastructure can be a difficult concession to make to receive the benefits that the cloud offers.

Security There are hundreds, maybe thousands, of articles on the security, or lack of security, in the cloud. Many of the security concerns are centered on the data being stored on servers owned and controlled by the cloud provider not the subscriber. The main issues are over who actually owns the data, the secure storage of Social Security numbers and credit card numbers, and compliance with **Sarbanes-Oxley (SOX)**—an act administered by the Securities and Exchange Commission (SEC) that specifies the type of records that need to be stored and how long they must be kept, but leaves the method of storage up to the business.

This concern of ownership and security is heightened when a cloud provider, sometimes called the primary cloud, makes use of composite clouds. A **composite cloud** evolves when a primary cloud provider offers services that are distributed through another cloud provider. Such services can include storage, computing power, or application hosting. This nesting of cloud services can have serious reliability and security issues. In addition to ownership and compliance issues, there is also a loss of control over security when a service is deployed to a cloud provider.

With cloud computing **risk management**, the process of analyzing exposure to risk and determining how to best handle it within the tolerance level set by the enterprise, is transferred to the cloud provider. Chief security officers (CSOs) have the problem of defining the risk tolerance of the enterprise and then matching it with the risk tolerance of a cloud provider, a task that is not easily done. Choosing a private or hybrid cloud deployment is often based on security issues, with hybrid deployment often viewed as a transition or test of the services, including security, in the public cloud. An August 2009 survey of 200 information technology (IT) professionals reported that 43 percent felt that cloud computing was less secure than performing such services in house.

Another issue that CSOs have to deal with is that moving services to a cloud provider is often viewed by IT staff members as a threat to their positions. These individuals have the power to create havoc with corporate information and operations. In the same August 2009 report, 47 percent of the 200 IT professionals felt that a shift to cloud services was perceived as a prelude to a reduction in IT personnel. This is supported by the IBM claim that a business could see up to a 50 percent reduction in IT labor costs as the result of a shift to cloud computing.

So, in the end, it usually comes to some type of compromise between cost and risk management. For those shopping for a cloud provider, I guess the best advice is to realize that not all cloud providers are created equal. Conducting due diligence is essential when transferring services to the cloud. As the old saying goes, "All that glitters is not gold." For all of the positive arguments supporting cloud computing, those that oppose the technology can list an equal number of negative arguments. However, projections seem to indicate that even with its negative features, the future is in the cloud. A look at some of the current statistics and future projections might surprise you.

The Future of Cloud Computing

Every new and emerging technology sparks articles, arguments, and documentation from supporters and opponents. Cloud computing is no different. Statistics from an IDC report published in mid-2010 support the continued growth of cloud computing, despite the concerns over security. The report cited some interesting projections:

- In 2009, cloud services were centered in the western hemisphere, with the United States receiving 70.2 percent of the revenue. However, the report predicts that by 2014, that figure will decline to 51.4 percent, with Western Europe and the Asia/Pacific regions making up the difference.
- Worldwide revenue from public IT cloud computing was $16 billion in 2009. The report projects 2014 revenue to exceed $55.5 billion.
- Cloud computing is growing at a rate that is five times greater than any traditional IT product.
- Cloud applications (Software-as-a-Service) were the main service in 2009. The 2014 projection of revenue redistribution leans toward a decrease in the importance of this service (SaaS) and an increase in Infrastructure-as-a-Service (IaaS) and Platform-as-a-Service (PaaS).

Another survey completed in 2010 by the PEW Internet & American Life Project and Elon University's Imagining the Internet Center, using a nonrandom sample of 895 Internet experts, supports the projection on migration to the cloud for applications and online storage.

Cloud computing is viewed as a means to test and distribute a new generation of killer apps, a method to penetrate global markets, and a means for smaller or medium-sized businesses to compete in the global market, because of decreased IT start-up costs.

As more and more organizations and individuals subscribed to cloud services, more and more providers appeared to compete for customers. This growth in providers led to the need for some guiding principles to provide a strategy for new cloud providers and realign those that already exist.

> " Conducting **due diligence** is **essential** when transferring **services** to **the cloud.** "

GUIDELINES FOR THE GROWTH OF AN OPEN CLOUD

The current and predicted growth of cloud computing indicate that the number of cloud providers will also increase. In March 2009, the **Open Cloud Manifesto** was published. This document provided some guides and business practices for cloud providers in an attempt to guarantee subscribers the freedom of choice, flexibility, and openness they need in order to take full advantage of the benefits of cloud computing. Some of the key principles stressed include the following:

- Cloud providers must work together and collaborate to see that the vulnerabilities and assets of the cloud are addressed.
- A provider should not lock subscribers into its platform, thus removing their freedom of choice.
- Providers should reduce repetition of standards by using those in existence and create new ones that do not repeat or reinvent those that already exist.
- Any changes to the standards should be driven by subscribers, not the needs of the provider.

Since its publication, the manifesto has over 375 supporters and is still growing. You can view the complete document at **http://opencloudmanifesto.org/**

The Effect of Cloud Computing on the Enterprise

Cloud computing affects not only the workings of the information technology divisions of an enterprise but also the way the entire enterprise views and uses its cloud computing capability. Some of the effects that will result from shifting to the cloud for infrastructure, platform, and software include the following:

- IT costs will be more directly related to value. If the IT department can utilize the cloud to maximize capacity on demand and meet the fluctuating needs of its customers, the result of decreased computing costs will result in a decrease in the cost of goods sold—and thus an increase in overall market value of the enterprise.
- IT departments will be more agile. The ability of an enterprise to select or change providers as their needs change and the "open cloud" concept solidifies will make the corporate IT infrastructure more elastic, agile, and amenable to change.

- Creating and testing new innovations with a greatly reduced capital outlay will encourage businesses to promote creativity, resulting in more changes taking place in less time.
- The need to stay current with business and customer demands and requests is pushing the cloud toward real-time switching among cloud resources. Real-time switching is the seamless moving of cloud computing workloads between private clouds and public clouds to maximize the best value available at the time.

It appears that the sky is the limit and that the future is in the clouds!

Key Terms and Concepts

Multiple Choice

1. Which is *not* one of the three main categories of cloud computing services?
   a. Infrastructure-as-a-Service (IaaS)
   b. Platform-as-a-Service (PaaS)
   c. Communication-as-a-Service (CaaS)
   d. Software-as-a-Service (SaaS)

2. Which model of cloud computing services provides the servers, storage devices, and networks for a subscriber?
   a. Infrastructure-as-a-Service (IaaS)
   b. Platform-as-a-Service (PaaS)
   c. Communication-as-a-Service (CaaS)
   d. Software-as-a-Service (SaaS)

3. Which cloud deployment model is operated solely for a single organization and its authorized users?
   a. Community cloud   b. Hybrid cloud
   c. Public cloud   d. Private cloud

4. Which cloud characteristic refers to the ability of a subscriber to increase or decrease its computing requirements as needed without having to contact a human representative of the cloud provider?
   a. Rapid elasticity
   b. On-demand self service
   c. Broad network access
   d. Resource pooling

5. Which cloud deployment model is managed by a cloud provider, has an infrastructure that is off site, and is accessible to the general public?
   a. Community cloud
   b. Hybrid cloud
   c. Public cloud
   d. Private cloud

6. In which category of SaaS services does customer relationship management (CRM) software fall?
   a. Consumer services
   b. Communication services
   c. Infrastructure services
   d. Business services

7. Which statistic correctly represents cloud computing?
   a. In 2009, Western Europe received a majority of cloud computing revenue.
   b. Global cloud computing revenue for 2009 exceeded $16 million.
   c. Cloud computing growth is five times greater than any traditional IT product
   d. In 2009, the main cloud computing service was PaaS.

8. Which is considered the most widely used cloud computing service?
   a. Infrastructure-as-a-Service (IaaS)
   b. Platform-as-a-Service (PaaS)
   c. Communication-as-a-Service (CaaS)
   d. Software-as-a-Service (SaaS)

9. Interoperability is enabled by _____.
   a. a cloud operating system
   b. middleware
   c. a community cloud
   d. a composite cloud

10. Which refers to the practice of a primary cloud provider offering services that are distributed through another cloud provider?
   a. Hybrid cloud
   b. Composite cloud
   c. Virtualization
   d. Grid computing

Spotlight Exercises

1. View the video on cloud computing at **http://commoncraft.com/cloud-computing-video**. This is a very simple and easy to understand explanation of cloud computing. Using this video as a model, develop a simple PowerPoint presentation that explains how Software-as-a-Service can be beneficial for colleges and for students. Use a common cloud provider of SaaS, for example Google Docs, to make your presentation more specific and relative. Present the slide show to the class. Follow up the presentation with a discussion on how the cloud might be a viable option for your classmates as students or future employees.

2. Interview the chief information officer (CIO) at your school or the director of information technology (IT). Inquire about the possibility of the school moving to cloud computing. Ask if such considerations were included in the long-term plan and what the financial benefit for such a move would be to the school and the students. Come up with a few of your own questions to determine the direction that the administrators of your school are considering. Using a word processor, summarize your findings in a one-page, double-spaced report.

3. Create a free account in Google Docs, a Software-as-a-Service (SaaS) provider. Try the document, spreadsheet, and presentation applications for a few days. Transfer files from your portable storage device or hard disk drive to the cloud storage provided by Google Docs. Access the files in Google Docs' cloud storage from another location. See whether a file made in any of the applications on this site can be opened by any of the comparable Microsoft office applications. After a few days, using a word processor, summarize your experience in a one-page, double-spaced report.

4. A direct result of any new IT development is an abundance of new terms, acronyms, and organizations. Cloud computing is no different. Several cloud-related terms have surfaced: intercloud, cloud broker, and mashup. Additionally, several cloud-related organizations have emerged: Open Cloud Consortium, The Cloud Security Alliance, and The Global Inter-Cloud Technology Forum. Research each term and organization. For each term, provide a clear definition. Describe the mission of each organization. Compile your information into a one-page, double-spaced document. Remember to cite your sources.

5. This spotlight highlighted the three main categories of cloud services: IaaS, PaaS, and SaaS. Many providers provide additional services like MaaS, CaaS, and SaaS. In a PowerPoint presentation, using one or more slides for each service, define and provide details of at least five services not covered in this chapter. If possible, include the names of several cloud providers that offer each service. Remember to cite your references.

6. Using the Internet, locate five cloud providers. Using a table in a word processing document or a spreadsheet, list the five providers, their associated Web sites, and the services and resources that each offers.

Wired and Wireless Communication

Chapter Objectives

1 Differentiate between *bandwidth* and *throughput*, and discuss the bandwidth needs of typical users. (p. 348)

2 Discuss how modems transform digital computer signals into analog signals and analog into digital. (p. 350)

3 List various physical and wireless transmission media and explain several transmission methods. (p. 351)

4 Explain the limitations of the public switched telephone network (PSTN) for sending and receiving computer data. (p. 358)

5 Describe digital telephony and multiplexing, including their impact on line usage. (p. 358)

6 Discuss last-mile technologies that connect users with their communication providers. (p. 359)

7 Provide examples of how digitization and convergence are blurring the boundaries that distinguish popular communications devices, including phones and computers. (p. 363)

8 Discuss various wired and wireless applications. (p. 369)

You are leaving the house for the day and grab your smartphone, Kindle 2, and notebook and walk out the door. You place your key in the cup holder and press a button on the dashboard to start your car. As your engine comes to life, the GPS system appears on the monitor embedded in the dash and your smartphone automatically connects to the Bluetooth device. This is not a sci-fi episode; it describes the connected life of a typical person today. How many of these devices do you or family members use? With wireless connectivity, are you even aware of the activity behind the scene that is enabling the communication you take for granted? Could you ever go back to using an atlas for directions, read a printed book, or rely solely on a landline phone?

Today everyone wants, or needs, to be connected. From the minute we get up to the minute we go to bed, notebooks and phones ding to notify us of incoming e-mails and text messages, we rely on automatic notices to update a program, and Global Positioning Systems to direct us to our destinations. **Connectivity**, defined broadly, refers to the ability to link various media and devices. In this chapter, we'll examine the various technologies, both wired (connected by a physical medium) and wireless (connected through the air or space), involved in creating the connectivity that enables communication. Some of the concepts covered include:

- The difference between analog and digital signals and how the conversion between them is essential to make the connection between various devices in use today
- The meaning of such terms associated with transmission as *bandwidth* and *throughput*
- The type of modems available and the associated transfer rates
- How the public switched telephone network connects global users and how last-mile technologies bring those signals to your door
- Web-enabled technologies such as VoIP, videoconferencing, faxing, and webcams
- Hints on the safe use of communication devices ▪

Check out **f** **Facebook** for our latest updates

www.facebook.com

Moving Data: Bandwidth and Modems

Communications (data communications or telecommunications) is the process of electronically sending and receiving messages between two or more computers or devices regardless of the distance between those devices. The **sending device** initiates the transmission while the **receiving device** accepts the transmission and responds. Communications can be split into two parts: the message (data, information, or an instruction) and the **communications channel** (also referred to as the **link**), the transmission media on which the message is sent from one location to the next.

Signals in the real world, like sound and light, are **analog signals**, or continuous waves that vary in strength and quality. Before these real-world signals can be used by digital equipment, like a computer, the signal passes through an analog-to-digital converter. An **analog-to-digital converter (ADC)** is simply a microchip that contains the circuitry to convert an analog signal into a digital signal. A **digital signal** is one that includes discontinuous pulses in which the presence or absence of electronic pulses is represented by 1s and 0s. In reverse, when a computer signal has to be sent out to the real world, for example as sound, the digital signal must pass through a digital-to-analog converter. A **digital-to-analog converter (DAC)** is a microchip that contains the circuitry to convert a digital signal to analog (Figure 8.1).

In communications, both analog and digital signals move data over communications channels. The conversion from analog to digital or digital to analog is normally not something a user can detect or has to be concerned with. However, if you have ever scanned an image, recorded your voice or used VoIP on your computer, or talked on a phone, you used an analog-to-digital

converter. Likewise, if you have ever listened on the phone or played back a CD, you made use of a digital-to-analog converter.

A codec, short for code-decode algorithm, is responsible for the conversion between analog and digital signals. Codecs accomplish the conversion by sampling the analog signal several thousand times per second. A common audio codec, the G.711 codec, samples the audio 64,000 times a second. It then converts each sample onto digitized data and compresses it for transmission. When the samples are reassembled, the missing pieces between the samples go undetected by the human ear. The most common codec for VoIP samples the analog signal 8,000 times a second. Because a digital signal is discrete, composed of 0s and 1s that are sampled from an analog signal, the data arrives in a much clearer format. The receiving end knows exactly how to reconstruct the data back into its original form (Figure 8.2). Digital signals also transfer much more data than analog and at much greater speeds. For instance, digital TV systems can now deliver more than 500 stations across digital cable, which allows not only more stations than analog cable, but also more features such as being able to view news stories related to a certain program.

Let's look at two features to consider when sending a message over communications channels: bandwidth and modems.

Bandwidth: How Much do You Need?

Bandwidth refers to the theoretical maximum amount of data that can be transmitted through a given communications channel at one time (usually per second). Two factors affect bandwidth: the physical characteristics of the transmission medium and the method used to represent and transmit the data. For analog signals, bandwidth is expressed in cycles per second, or hertz (Hz). For digital signals, bandwidth is expressed in bits per second

STUDENT VIDEO

FIGURE 8.1 The transmission of real-world sounds through digital communication devices requires the conversion of analog signals to digital signals for transmission and then back to analog in order to be heard by the receiving party.

Real-world analog signal — Analog-to-digital converter — 001010010 — Digital signal — Computer or device with embedded CPU — Digital signal — 001010010 — Digital-to-analog converter — Real-world analog signal

Digital sound wave

Samples of analog signal

TIME

Analog sound wave

Digital signal reassembled into an analog signal

TIME

FIGURE 8.2 Digital signals are composed by sampling an analog wave at discrete points in time. The analog wave is then approximated by these discrete measurements.

(bps). **Throughput**, often used incorrectly as a synonym for bandwidth, is the *actual* amount of data that is transmitted. It is almost always lower than bandwidth, especially with wireless communications.

Broadband refers to any transmission medium that carries several channels at once and thus transports high volumes of data at high speeds, typically greater than 1 Mbps (megabits per second, or million bits per second). Cable TV uses broadband transmission. So how much bandwidth do you need? Conventional dial-up connections to the Internet use a relatively low bandwidth of 56 Kbps (kilobits per second, or thousand bits per second) or less. Most users find this painfully slow when searching the Web. But dial-up connections are still cheaper than broadband connections, so some people sacrifice speed for low price. Through the practical comparisons provided in Figure 8.3, you should get an idea of what increased bandwidth can do for such Internet activities as streaming music or video. **Streaming** is the ability to hear or see content while it is being downloaded from a Web site instead of waiting till the download is complete.

If you are still confused, use the suggestions below as a guide:

- For normal use, from most providers, 1 Mbps offers the best balance between cost and performance.
- For e-mail and viewing Web pages but not streaming audio or video, then 256 Kbps to 512 Kbps should do.
- For gaming, a 2 Mbps connection or faster is necessary.

FIGURE 8.3 Basic Wired Internet Speeds and Abilities

Internet Connection Speed	Time to Download a 100 KB Web Page	Time to Download a 5 Minute Song in MP3 Format	Streaming Ability
56 Kbps dial-up modem	14 seconds	12 minutes 30 seconds	None
256 Kbps broadband	3 seconds	3 minutes	Low quality
512 Kbps broadband	1.6 seconds	1 minute 30 seconds	
1 Mbps broadband	0.8 seconds	41 seconds	
2 Mbps broadband	0.4 seconds	20 seconds	Medium quality
4 Mbps broadband	0.1 seconds	5 seconds	
6 Mbps broadband	instantaneous	3.5 seconds	
8 Mbps broadband or higher	instantaneous	2.5 seconds	TV quality

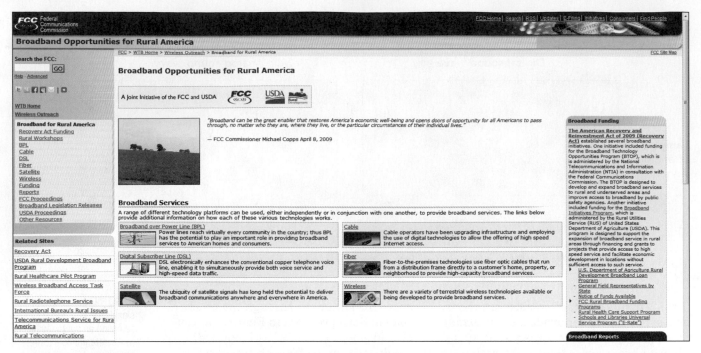

FIGURE 8.4 The options for broadband Internet services to rural locations in the United States are presented here in a cooperative effort between the Federal Communications Commission (FCC) and the Department of Agriculture (USDA) rural development.

- To share a connection between two or more computers, a minimum of a 4 Mbps connection is necessary to take advantage of music or video on demand or digital broadband Internet TV.

Broadband digital connections are now widely available in the United States. The major cable and telephone (DSL) companies added 5.4 million new subscribers in 2008, bringing the total of broadband users to 68 million. Numbers continued to rise in 2009, with broadband penetration in rural markets of 10,000 people or less up by 13 percentage points in a single year. A comparison of broadband speeds internationally in early 2010 found South Korea having the fastest home Internet service, with download speeds of 34.14 Mbps (megabits per second). The United States was ranked 26th with an average download time of 10.16 Mbps. In February of 2010, Google announced that it will test a direct-to-home fiber-optic connection with the capability of up to 1 gigabit per second. If this test becomes a reality, it will revolutionize the way we connect to the Internet and make cloud computing and other Internet-based services more appealing. Fueling the motivation to expand broadband usage is the commencement of the National Broadband Plan (**www.broadband.gov/**) developed by Congress and the Federal Communications Commission, to increase Internet access to rural America (Figure 8.4). Considering the extension of broadband

services to rural communities, the increased use of wireless devices for Internet access, and the expansion of fiber-optic services, suppliers of Internet services are facing serious challenges.

Modems: Transform Signals

The term **modem** comes from combining the words **mod**ulate and **dem**odulate. It is an appropriate compressed term because a modem is a communication device used to send and receive data from one transmission system to another. On the sending end, a modem uses a process called *modulation* to transform the computer's digital signals into signals appropriate for the transmission system bring used. On the receiving end, the process used is *demodulation,* whereby the receiving modem transforms the signal from the transmission system back into digital form that a computer can understand. For systems that use telephone lines as a transmission medium, the modulator converts the computer's digital signals into analog tones that can be conveyed through the telephone system. The demodulator receives the analog signals and converts them to digital form (Figure 8.5).

Modems are available as internal or external units. An internal modem, the most common in computer systems today, is not visible. Instead, it is located within the system unit and is powered by the system unit's power supply. An external modem, located outside of the system unit, has its

Telephone lines use analog transmission

Digital — Analog — Analog — Digital

Sender | Modem 1 | Modem 2 | Receiver

own case and power supply. For this reason, external modems are slightly more expensive. The types of modems available include analog, digital subscriber line (DSL), cable, and Integrated Services Digital Network (ISDN). Analog modems are used for dial-up connections. DSL and cable are high-speed broadband connections. ISDN modems transfer information in channels of 64 kilobits per second (Kpbs), which can be combined for higher speeds. We'll discuss integrated services digital networks in more detail later in this chapter.

The **data transfer rate**, the rate at which two modems can exchange data, is measured in bits per second and is referred to as the **bps rate**. Analog modems communicate at a maximum rate of 56 Kbps. (In practice, modems rarely achieve speeds higher than 42 Kbps.) A modem that can transfer 56 Kbps is transferring only about 7,000 bytes per second, or about five pages of text. Baud is often used incorrectly as a substitute for bps, the unit of data transfer rate. **Baud** is actually the number of signaling elements per second. At slower rates, bauds and bps may be equal, but on higher speed transmissions, more than one bit can be encoded in each signaling element. Thus a 4,800 baud rate may have a transmission rate of 9,600 bps.

Often, a single message travels over several different wired and wireless transmission media, including telephone lines, coaxial cable, fiber-optic cable, radio waves, microwaves, and satellite, before it arrives at its destination. We'll look at each of these types of wired and wireless transmission media in more detail.

Wired Transmission Media

Wired transmission media for data travel is still widely used today. Most new buildings incorporate a **wiring closet**, a central location that extends though all floors of the building in which the appropriate wiring is housed to support most types of data transfer that the individuals or companies that occupy the building might want to access (Figure 8.6). Cabling

FIGURE 8.5 A modem transforms the computer's digital signals into analog signals that can be transmitted through the telephone system. Once the transmission reaches its destination, the receiving modem converts the analog signal back to a digital signal.

Wiring closet

Server | Computer | Computer | Computer | Client-server network
Floor 3

Computer | Computer | Server | Computer | Client-server network
Floor 2

Computer | Computer | Computer | Peer-to-peer network
Floor 1

FIGURE 8.6 A wiring closet consists of cables and a location for switches and routers. It provides a central location to facilitate access for maintenance and reconfiguration.

FIGURE 8.7 A wiring closet enables an IT technician to make adjustments to several connections from one location regardless of where the devices are located.

goes through the closet to devices located throughout the building. Having one central location for all media connections facilitates the adding of new equipment or making of repairs. Figure 8.7 provides a close

up of the amount of cabling and equipment that can be crammed into single wiring closet. Now that you know where the cabling is located in a building, let's look more closely at the various forms of wired media that are essential to connect devices.

Twisted-Pair

Twisted-pair wire is a copper cable used for telephone and data communications. The term *twisted-pair* refers to the interweaving of two pairs of wires that are twisted together, a practice that provides a shield that reduces interference from electrical fields generated by electric motors, power lines, and powerful radio signals (Figure 8.8). On the plus side,

twisted-pair is an inexpensive medium. On the negative side, the bandwidth of traditional twisted-pair telephone lines is too low to simultaneously carry video, voice, and data. Twisted-pair carries data at transfer rates of less than 1 Kbps.

Key Variations of Twisted-Pair

Cat-5 cable, short for **Category 5**, is the fifth generation of twisted-pair data communication cable. Cat-5 cable contains four pairs of twisted-copper wire and

FIGURE 8.9 Cat-5e cable uses all four pairs of twisted wire and transmits data at 1,000 Mbps (1 Gbps).

supports speeds up to 100 Mbps over a maximum distance of 100 m (328 feet). However, only two of the four pairs of wires are actually used for most fast network communications. A newer variation of the Cat-5 cable, **Cat-5e**, short for **Category 5 enhanced**, uses all four wire pairs, enabling speeds up to 1,000 Mbps (1 Gbps) over a short distance. This enhanced medium is backward compatible with ordinary Cat-5 (Figure 8.9).

Cat-6, short for **Category 6**, is the sixth generation of twisted-pair cable and is backward compatible with Cat-5 and Cat-5e. It contains four pairs of copper wire like the previous

FIGURE 8.8 *Twisted-pair* refers to inexpensive copper cable that's used for telephone and data communications.

Twisted-pair cable

generation, utilizes all four pairs, supports speeds up to 1 gigabit per second (Gbps), expands available bandwidth from 100 MHz for Cat-5e to 200 MHz, and has superior immunity from external noise. Polls predict that 80 to 90 percent of new network installations will be cabled with Cat-6.

Coaxial Cable

Coaxial cable, familiar to cable TV users (Figure 8.10), consists of a center

FIGURE 8.10 In coaxial cable, data travels through the center copper wire core. The cable is connected to a coaxial wall jack.

copper wire surrounded by insulation, which is then surrounded by a layer of braided wire. Data travels through the center wire, and the braided wire provides a shield against electrical interference (Figure 8.11). Coaxial cable carries data at transfer rates of 10 Mbps. In contrast to twisted-pair, coaxial cable allows for broadband data communications. Your home is probably already wired with coaxial cable if you subscribe to a cable TV service.

Copper wire

Insulation

Copper mesh

Outside insulation

FIGURE 8.11 The copper core of a coaxial cable is shielded from interference by a braided wire shield and an external layer of rubber that provides additional insulation.

Fiber-Optic Cable

Fiber-optic cable, another broadband transmission medium, consists of thin strands of glass or plastic about the diameter of a human hair. This medium is arranged in bundles called optical cables that carry data by means of pulses of light. Fiber-optic cable (Figure 8.12) provides

FIGURE 8.12 Fiber-optic cable consists of a bundle of fiber-optic strands.

transfer rates of 10 Gbps (gigabits per second) or more. A single fiber-optic strand is composed of three parts: the core, the cladding, and the buffer coat (Figure 8.13). The core is the thin glass or plastic center through which the light travels. The cladding is the optical material surrounding the core that reflects the light back into the core. The plastic coating that protects the fiber from moisture and damage is the buffer coat. Besides increased speed, additional benefits of fiber-optic cable include these:

- Light pulses are not affected by random radiation in the environment.
- Fiber-optic lines have a significantly lower error rate.
- Fiber optics can span longer distances before needing expensive repeaters to boost the signal.

Cladding

Core

Buffer coating

FIGURE 8.13 Each fiber-optic strand has three parts.

- Security breaches in a fiber-optic line can be easily detected.
- Installation is simplified due to reduction in weight and size of fiber-optic cable as compared to coaxial cable.

Wireless Transmission Media

Unlike communications using wired transmission media such as twisted-pair, coaxial, and fiber-optic cables, wireless media don't use solid substances to transmit data. Rather, wireless media send data through air or space using infrared, radio, or microwave signals. Why would you want to use wireless media instead of cables? One instance would be in situations where cables can't be installed or the costs to do so are prohibitive. The popularity of portable computing devices has led most colleges, airports, hotels, shopping malls, and coffee shops to offer wireless access to customers. This option is usually cheaper than running wires through existing buildings. Let's investigate the wireless options of data transfer and their features.

Infrared

If you use a remote control to change television channels, you're already familiar with infrared signaling. **Infrared** is a wireless transmission medium that carries data via beams of light through the air. No wires are required, but the transmitting and receiving devices must be in line of sight or the signal is lost. When the path between the transmitting and the receiving devices is not obstructed by trees, hills, mountains, buildings, or other structures, infrared signals can work within a maximum of about 100 feet.

To use infrared technology with your computer system, you need an **IrDA port** (Figure 8.14). You may encounter an IrDA (infrared data association) port on a mobile computing device or wireless peripheral such as a PDA, digital camera, notebook, mouse,

printer, or keyboard. The most common use of the IrDA port is to transfer data from your PDA to your desktop or notebook computer or another PDA. To enable data transfer, the IrDA port on the transmitting device must be in line of sight (usually within a few feet) of the port on the receiving device. IrDA ports offer data transfer rates of 4 Mbps. With these restrictions of distance and speed, why would you want to use infrared? If you had a situation where hooking devices together with cables wasn't an option, such as with a wireless keyboard or mouse, infrared would be a good choice. On modern networks, however, IrDA is too slow to be of practical use for transferring large amounts of data.

Radio

Radio transmissions offer an alternative to infrared transmissions. You probably have experienced one type of radio transmission by listening to your favorite radio station. But you may not realize the impact that radio waves have on your daily life or on society in general. All kinds of gadgets—from cell and cordless phones to baby monitors—communicate via radio waves. Although humans cannot see or otherwise detect them, radio waves are everywhere.

With **radio transmission**, data in a variety of forms (music, voice conversations, and photos) travels through the air as radio frequency (RF) signals or radio waves via a transmitting device and a receiving device. Instead of separate transmitting and receiving devices, radio transmissions can also use a wireless transceiver, a combination transmitting–receiving device equipped with an antenna. Data transfer rates for wireless devices have the potential to reach up to 3 Mbps for cell phones and up to 250 Mbps for wireless networks.

A major disadvantage of radio transmission is susceptibility to noise and interference. One of radio's advantages is that radio signals are effective at both long range (between cities, regions, and countries) and short range (within a home or office).

FIGURE 8.14 An IrDA port allows for wireless management of external devices such as a mouse, keyboard, phone, or PDA.

WiFi WiFi is a popular wireless network technology that uses radio waves to provide high-speed Internet and network connections for home systems, notebooks, video game consoles, and other enabled wireless devices. WiFi can be based on any of the IEEE 802.11 standards and communicates through radio frequency technology, with ranges reaching 300 to 500 feet. The cornerstone of a WiFi system, like other wireless systems, is the access point that broadcasts a signal that devices equipped with wireless network adapters detect.

Bluetooth Bluetooth is a short-range radio transmission technology that has become very popular in recent years. Named after the 10th-century Danish Viking and king Harald Blatand ("Bluetooth" in English) who united Denmark and Norway, Bluetooth was first conceived by Swedish cell phone giant Ericsson (Figure 8.15). Bluetooth technology relies on a network called a piconet or a PAN (personal area network) that enables all kinds of devices—desktop computers, mobile phones, printers, pagers, PDAs, and more—within 30 feet of each other to communicate automatically and wirelessly.

How exactly does Bluetooth work? Bluetooth-enabled devices, once setup, identify each other using identification numbers that are unique to each device. When these devices are within 30 feet of each other, they automatically "find" and link to one another. You don't have to worry about being connected to Bluetooth devices that you don't want to connect to: The device requires that you confirm a connection before making it final. Up to eight Bluetooth-enabled devices can be connected in a piconet at any one time.

Unlike infrared technologies, Bluetooth doesn't require a direct line of sight to connect devices. Because the frequency used by Bluetooth devices changes often, Bluetooth devices never use the same frequency at the same time and don't interfere with each other. The new Bluetooth 3.0 standard can accommodate data transfer rates of up to 24 Mbps, up from 3 Mbps. At Bluetooth's maximum transfer capacity, you would be able to move a document easily within just a few seconds. A testimony to the popularity of the connectivity provided by Bluetooth technology is verified by industry statistics

FIGURE 8.15 Bluetooth-enabled devices make tasks, such as synchronizing your phone calendar with your computer calendar or keeping your hands free while talking on the phone, easier.

that point to the 2 billion devices that have been shipped with Bluetooth installed.

Applications using Bluetooth technology and the devices that support the technology are on the rise. In August of 2009, Bag-Claim.com, a company of RBD Consulting International, introduced a new application called Bag-Claim. This application is designed for airport and travel use. It connects a Bluetooth-enabled wireless speaker that is placed inside a suitcase. The speaker alerts the owner, through an iPhone, when the suitcase is approaching. A comparison of WiFi and Bluetooth features are listed in Figure 8.16. For more information on Bluetooth technology and a brief video on the differences between Bluetooth and WiFi, visit **www.bluetooth.com/ Bluetooth.**

Microwaves

Microwaves are electromagnetic radio waves with short frequencies that travel at speeds of 1 to 10 Mbps and are used to transmit data from a source to a receiving site. Using relay stations similar to satellite dishes (including an antenna,

FIGURE 8.16 Bluetooth versus WiFi

	Bluetooth	WiFi
Hardware requirements	A Bluetooth adapter is required on all devices connecting with each other.	A wireless adapter is required on all devices in the network. Other needs include a wireless router and/or a wireless access point.
Year of development	1994	1991
Specifications	Bluetooth SIG	IEEE 802.11
Ease of use	Simple to use, can connect up to seven devices at a time, easy to switch between devices and connect new ones	Requires the configuration of hardware and software
Primary devices	Mobile phones, mouse, and keyboards	Notebooks, desktop computers, and servers
Range	30 feet	300–500 feet
Security	More secure than WiFi because it covers a smaller radius and requires two passwords	Has same security risks as all other networks
Power consumption	Low	High

ETHICS

The use of Bluetooth signals to collect statistics on how long individuals wait in airport security lines seems to be the start of a method of collecting data that is effortless, automatic, and undetected. Two Bluetooth wireless detectors with a range of 32 feet were placed in Indianapolis International Airport in 2009. Data collected validated that 6 percent of the travelers had a Bluetooth-enabled phone, MP3 player, PDA, or other detectable device that broadcast a unique hardware number. The units were used to monitor wait times in security checkpoints on several weekends, including the weekend of the Indianapolis 500. The analysis of the data proved that the average wait time during peak travel days and times was 20 minutes and that when security was prepared for an event, the wait time was shorter.

Statistics like this can prove to be valuable when trying to improve airport security. The use of detectable devices for other types of monitoring in the future can provide enormous amounts of data and improve service. Knowing when to book a flight or which gate has the least amount of traffic when trying to enter a sporting event could be beneficial. The detectors can pick up the Bluetooth signal and monitor it, but they cannot identify the individual owner of the device or communicate with him or her.

How ethical is collecting information on the whereabouts of an individual without them knowing it? Should signs be posted indicating that the detectors are active and scanning for Bluetooth signals? Do you know how to deactivate the Bluetooth feature of a mobile device that you own? Consider the pros and cons of the data collected by such detection devices, and then consider the ethical issue of violation of privacy and nonconsensual participation. What is your ethical stance?

transceiver, and so on), microwave signals are sent from one relay station to the next. Because microwaves get weaker as they get farther away from their source, must

travel in a straight line, and cannot be obstructed by buildings, hills, and mountains, relay stations are positioned approximately every 30 miles (the line-of-sight distance to the horizon), or closer if the terrain blocks transmission. To avoid obstacles, microwave relay stations are often situated on the tops of buildings or mountains (Figure 8.17). Microwaves are used in weather monitoring, air traffic control, speed limit enforcement, and missile guidance systems.

FIGURE 8.17 Any information that can travel over a telephone or coaxial cable can be transmitted via microwave.

The advantages of microwave transmission include the elimination of a wired infrastructure, enabling cellular telephone networks and connectivity in areas where the use of physical wires is impractical or impossible, and providing security through encrypting data as it is transmitted. Disadvantages include the 30-mile line-of-sight restriction, sensitivity to electrical or magnetic interference, and costs of maintaining the multitude of relay stations it takes to transfer messages across long distances.

Satellites

Essentially microwave relay stations in space, communications satellites are positioned in geosynchronous orbit, which matches the satellite's speed to that of the Earth's rotation, and are, therefore, permanently positioned with respect to the ground below. **Satellites** transmit data by sending and receiving microwave signals to and from Earth-based stations (Figure 8.18). Devices such as handheld computers and Global Positioning System (GPS) receivers can also function as Earth-based stations.

Direct broadcast satellite (DBS) is a consumer satellite technology that uses an 18- or 21-inch reception dish to receive digital TV signals at microwave frequencies directly from geostationary satellites broadcast at a bandwidth of 12 Mbps. Increasingly, DBS operators offer Internet access as well as digital TV service, but at much lower bandwidth. A good overview of a DBS can be found at **http:// electronics.howstuffworks.com/ satellite-tv.htm**, where a video demonstrates the progression of an image from its initial capture by a camera to its reception and viewing on a home TV.

Currently, DIRECTV, a DBS operator, offers DirecWay 1-way and DirecWay 2-way Internet satellite systems. DirecWay 1-way offers high-speed broadband download via satellite link, with uploads requiring a telephone and modem. This is the inexpensive option for most broadband Internet users because downloading is used more frequently than uploading. No professional installation is required because you only receive the high-speed signal and don't transmit. DirecWay 2-way uses a high-speed satellite link both for uploading and downloading. The drawback of the 2-way system is its increased cost and the FCC's requirement that satellite dishes that both transmit and receive signals be installed professionally.

Broadband access is still not available in many rural or other low-population areas, thus many of these areas are prime candidates for DBS. If it is the only option available, something is better than nothing!

To use these various wireless transmission media, a computer system must also use a special communications device called a **network access point**, which sends and receives data between computers that contain wireless adapters. Access points are usually built into wireless routers.

So, what is it about wireless connectivity that is so interesting? Well, one answer is that wireless technology removes place-specific restrictions, that is, the need to be in a certain place to receive a service. Some forms of wireless technology allow you to be wherever you choose and still have the ability to be connected.

Now that you know more about wired and wireless media, the next section will explore the most common wired communication system: the public switched telephone network.

FIGURE 8.18
Communication satellites in space work by receiving information from one microwave station and sending it back to another at a different location on earth.

Wired Communication Via the Public Switched Telephone Network

Although many components of the conventional phone system have been enhanced, until all devices have been replaced with digital equivalents, limitations still exist.

The **public switched telephone network (PSTN)** is the global telephone system, a massive network used for data as well as voice communications, comprising various transmission media ranging from twisted-pair wire to fiber-optic cable. Some computer users derisively (and somewhat unfairly) refer to the PSTN as plain old telephone service (POTS). The derision comes from most analog telephone lines being based on standards that date back more than a century. Although a few parts of the PSTN remain based on analog communications, many sections of the system have been switched over to digital communications.

Those still using analog devices today include many homes and small business. These telephones are linked to subscriber loop carriers by means of twisted-pair wires. A **subscriber loop carrier (SLC)** is a small, waist-high curbside installation that connects as many as 96 subscribers; you've probably seen one in your neighborhood. The area served by an SLC is called the **local loop**. When the analog signal reaches the SLC, it is converted to digital form and remains that way throughout the PSTN network.

From the SLC, the digital signals are routed via high-capacity fiber-optic cables to the **local exchange switch**, a digital device capable of handling thousands of calls located in the local telephone company's central office (CO). From the local phone company's CO, the call can go anywhere in the world. It can continue on the digital portion of the PSTN's fiber-optic cables or be converted to radio waves and sent out over cellular networks (Figure 8.19).

Although analog connections still exist, **digital telephony**, a system in which the telephones and transmissions are digital, is the trend. Compared with analog devices, which are prone to noise and interference, digital phones offer noise-free transmission and high-quality audio. You might have used a digital phone at work or on campus. Typically companies and universities install their own internal digital telephone systems, called private branch exchanges (PBXs). Calls to the outside, however, must be translated into analog signals to connect to the PSTN.

Because long-distance lines must handle thousands of calls simultaneously (32 calls per second, 24 hours a day, 7 days a week in the United States), a technique called **multiplexing** is used to send more than one call over a single line. The electrical and physical characteristics of copper wire impose a limit of 24 multiplexed calls per line, whereas fiber-optic cables can carry as many as 48,384 digital voice channels simultaneously. In contrast to the analog local loop, most long-distance carriers use digital signals so that they can pack the

FIGURE 8.19 Pathways on the PSTN. In order for the signal to reach its final destination, it may travel across several different transmission medium, including a cellular network.

greatest number of calls into a single circuit.

The inability of homes or businesses to access the PSTN's high-speed fiber-optic cables, along with the bottleneck of data on the last mile of twisted-pair phone lines connecting homes and businesses, are often referred to as the **last-mile problem**. Here's why. In most areas of the United States, only the local loop is still using analog technology, because nearly all existing buildings were originally constructed with built-in twisted-pair wiring. These analog lines are vulnerable to noise and can't surpass a theoretical limit of 56 Kbps. But things are starting to change. Telephone companies are getting into other businesses (such as providing Internet connectivity) and need to deliver higher bandwidth to homes. Therefore, telephone companies are now replacing analog local loop technology with digital technology (such as FiOS). The last-mile problem might soon be solved in your neighborhood!

Last-Mile Technologies

Local loops are in the process of being upgraded, but until the upgrade is complete, phone companies and other providers offer a number of interim digital telephony technologies to bridge the gap from the Internet to a residence. This last section of the circuit is referred to as the last mile. Technologies that help bridge that gap, **last-mile technologies**, include digital telephone standards (such as ISDN and DSL) that use twisted-pair wiring, as well as high-speed wired services (such as coaxial cable and cable modems). To learn more about telephone technology from wiring a system to video conferencing and VoIP check out **http://telecom.hellodirect. com/docs/ Tutorials/ default.asp.**

Integrated Services Digital Network A standard for digital telephone and data service, **ISDN (integrated services digital network)**, offers connections ranging from 56 to 128 Kbps (basic rate ISDN) or 1.5 Mbps (primary rate ISDN), using

ordinary twisted-pair telephone lines. The cost of an ISDN line is often two to three times that of an analog phone line, but there's a payoff. With a 128-Kbps ISDN service, you get two telephone numbers with one ISDN account; you can use one for computer data and the other for voice or fax. When you're using the connection for computer data only, the system automatically uses both data channels to give you the maximum data transfer rate; if a phone call comes in, the connection automatically drops back to 64 Kbps to accommodate the incoming call. What's more, connection is nearly instantaneous. Unlike analog connections with a modem, there's no lengthy dial-in procedure and connection delay.

To connect computers to ISDN lines, you need an **ISDN adapter** (also called a **digital modem**, although it isn't actually a modem; Figure 8.20). Although ISDN has been largely supplanted by faster technologies (such as DSL and fiber optics), ISDN may be the only broadband solution in many rural areas. Keep in mind that ISDN requires that special wiring be installed from the subscriber loop carrier (SLC) to your home.

Digital Subscriber Line Another method of Internet access available in the United States is **DSL (digital subscriber line)**, also called **xDSL**. This term refers to a group of related technologies, including **ADSL (asymmetric digital subscriber line)**, **SDSL (symmetrical digital subscriber line)**, **HDSL (high bit-rate digital subscriber line)**, and **VDSL (very high bit-rate digital subscriber line)**, all forms of Internet access. DSL technologies, in general, can deliver data transfer rates of 1.54 Mbps or higher and are akin to ISDN in that they use existing

FIGURE 8.20 Various types of modems facilitate the connection between your computer and last-mile technologies.

FIGURE 8.21 The Details behind DSL Technologies

Name	Actual Name	Bandwidth	Users
ADSL	Asymmetrical digital subscriber line	Uploads at speeds of up to 640 Kbps, downloads at speeds of up to 8.1 Mbps	Frequently used with residential users in the United States.
SDSL	Symmetrical digital subscriber line	Supports data exchange rates each way, up to 3 Mbps	Popular with residents in Europe.
HDSL	High bit-rate digital subscriber line	1.544 Mbps of bandwidth each way	PBX network connections, digital loop carrier systems, interexchange point of presence (POPs), Internet servers, and private data networks.
VDSL	Very high bit-rate digital subscriber line	Uploads at speeds of up to 16 Mbps, downloads at speeds of up to 52 Mbps	VDSL is available worldwide in specific regions. Its use is growing all the time, though it's not easily found in the United States.

twisted-pair wiring. But because DSL is always on, requires no call set up time, and achieves much higher throughput than ISDN, it quickly became more popular. An overview of the technology features of each type of DSL should provide some clarification.

- **ADSL.** An ADSL modem separates an ordinary copper telephone line into three separate data channels with different capacities and speeds. The lowest capacity transmits analog voice for telephones; the second, medium capacity, uploads data to the network; and the third, highest capacity, downloads data from the network. This means that uploads are slower than downloads on an ADSL connection.

- **SDSL.** A SDSL modem splits the copper telephone line channels into three channels: telephone, upload, and download; but it does this so that the distributed bandwidth for each channel is equal. On SDSL connections, uploads and downloads occur at the same rate.

- **HDSL.** HDSL is the most mature DSL technology. It is a form of SDSL that provides T1 connections over two or three twisted-pair copper lines. Unlike most other forms of DSL, HDSL is not a typical consumer service, but it is often used for private data networks.

- **VDSL.** VDSL is the next generation DSL with super-accelerated rates of 52 Mbps for downloads and 12 Mbps for uploads. It will provide services like HDTV and Video-on-Demand along with Internet access.

For more information on the four DSL technologies, refer to Figure 8.21.

To use DSL, you need a DSL phone line and a DSL service subscription. Unlike conventional telephone service, which is available to almost any home, DSL service is limited by the distance from the CO, or telephone switching station, to your home. You also need a **DSL modem**, which is similar to a traditional telephone modem in that it modulates and demodulates analog and digital signals for transmission over communications channels. However, DSL modems use signaling methods based on broadband technology for much higher transfer speeds. DSL service is now standardized so that almost any DSL modem should work with the wiring your telephone provider uses. However, it is best to buy a DSL modem that your provider recommends. Check with your provider for a list of approved modems before purchasing one. Although DSL service is more expensive than dial-up, it is usually cheaper than other broadband access options, such as cable or fiber optics (Figure 8.22)

"DSL service is now standardized so that almost any DSL modem should work with the wiring your telephone provider uses."

Cable-Based Broadband Aside from telephone companies, the leading provider of

DSL Diagram

Public phone network

Central office

Internet service provider

Voice switch

Vendor DSL switch

ATM switch

Internet

Customer or building PBX BOX

Splitter

Telephones

DSL Modem router

Network

FIGURE 8.22 The Path of Data from an Internet Service Provider to a DSL Subscriber's Residence

broadband is your local cable TV company. Approximately 120 million homes in the United States had access to high-speed cable Internet service as of 2008 (Figure 8.23). Actual customers for this service reached 41.8 million in 2009 (Figure 8.24)

When cable and the cabling equipment were originally installed in homes, signals were designed to run in only one direction: to the home. When the Internet became popular, the cable companies invested tremendous amounts of money in equipment and cable to enable two-way communication to capture the Internet market.

For computer users, these services offer data transfer rates that exceed the speed of DSL. **Cable modems**, devices that enable computers to access the Internet by means of a cable TV connection, now deliver data at bandwidths of 1.5 to 6 Mbps or more, depending on how many subscribers are connected to a local cable segment. Bandwidth across a cable connection is shared among subscribers who are connected to the cable company in local groups. If you are lucky enough to

have subscribers in your group who don't use much bandwidth, you can experience impressive speed, up to 20 Mbps, while using the Internet. To help you decide which last-mile technology might be right for you, check out the "Cable or DSL" tutorial at **http://telecom. hellodirect. com/docs/ Tutorials/ CableVsDSL.1. 030801.asp.**

Leased Lines A **leased line**, sometimes called a dedicated line, is a connection set up by a telecommunication carrier and is usually a permanent fiber-optic or telephone connection that enables continuous, end-to-end communication between two points. Larger organizations, such as ISPs, corporations, and universities, connect using leased **T1 lines**, which are fiber-optic (or specially conditioned copper) cables that can handle 24 digitized voice channels or carry computer data at a rate of up to 1.544 Mbps. If the T1 line is being used for telephone conversations, it plugs into the users' phone system. If it is

FIGURE 8.23 In five years, high-speed Internet cable has been made accessible to an additional 30 million Americans.

(in millions)

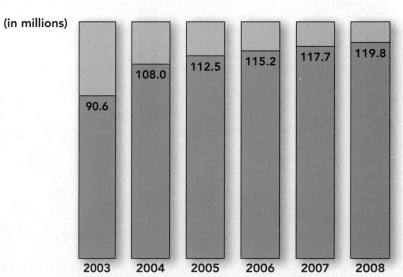

2003	2004	2005	2006	2007	2008
90.6	108.0	112.5	115.2	117.7	119.8

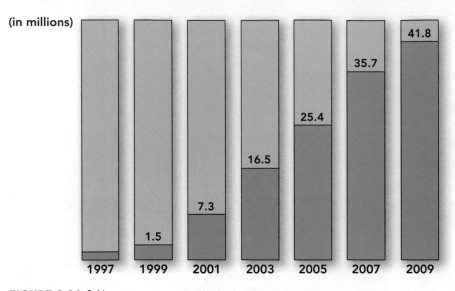

(in millions)

1997	1999	2001	2003	2005	2007	2009
	1.5	7.3	16.5	25.4	35.7	41.8

FIGURE 8.24 Cable subscribers have been on a steady increase due to its increased availability in some rural areas and more competitive pricing.

FIGURE 8.25 Often speed, price, and availability determine which method of Internet connection a user selects.

carrying data, it plugs into the network's router. The price of T1 lines ranges from $1,000 to $1,500 a month, depending on the provider, the location, and the use. Leased lines may use modems, cable modems, or other communications devices to manage the transfer of data into and out of the organization.

Other Last-Mile Technologies There are also interim technologies that make better use of existing fiber-optic cables. Fiber-optic **T2** and **T3 lines** can handle up to 44.7 Mbps of computer data. Although T3 lines can cost approximately $3,000 per month, Internet service providers, financial institutions, and large corporations that move a large amount of data find these lines critical to their operations. One T3 line is equivalent to having 28 T1 lines. Another technology, **SONET (synchronous optical network)**, is a physical layer of network technology that uses fiber-optic cable and is designed to carry large volumes of data over long distances. It is the standard for high-performance networks. The slowest SONET standard calls for data transfer rates of 52 Mbps; some higher levels enable rates of 20 Gbps or faster. SONET is widely used in North America, and a similar standard, synchronous digital hierarchy (SDH), is used in the rest of the world.

In addition to adapting twisted-pair wiring, broadband coaxial cable, and fiber-optic cable, wireless technologies are helping to solve the last-mile problem as well. Here's a look at three wireless solutions.

MMDS (multichannel multipoint distribution service, sometimes called multipoint microwave distribution system) is microwave technology that was originally slated as a wireless alternative to cable television, but now its main application is Internet access. Service providers offer MMDS Internet access within a 35-mile radius of the nearest transmission point at projected speeds of 1 Gbps. Communication with the network is through a roof-mounted disk connected with coaxial cable. The average cost is $50 per month for 2 Mbps of download speed. It is an affordable and viable option in areas where cable and DSL are not available.

MMDS will most likely be supplanted by WiMAX. **WiMAX (worldwide interoperability for microwave access)** is a wireless up-and-coming digital communication system designed to deliver high-speed access over long distances, either point to point (both sender and receiver are stationary) or through mobile access (sender or receiver is moving). WiMAX is effective for up to 30 miles for point-to-point access and 3 to 10 miles for mobile access. In mountainous areas or other places where there are obstructions, MMDS and WiMAX face challenges because they are susceptible to interference. To view a brief video on the technology behind WiMAX and an explanation of how it works, visit **www.wimax.com/education**. A general comparison of Internet connection speeds over common communication channels is displayed in Figure 8.25.

Internet Access Speed Comparison

Speed in mbps

	Basic DSL	High End DSL	Basic Cable Internet	High End Cable Internet	Fiber Optics	WiFi (3G)	WiMax (4G)
Low Range	0.34	3	4	12	15	5	7
High Range	1.5	7	6	20	50	20	

Blackberry Curve

Oqo Model 2+

FIGURE 8.26
Convergence means smaller devices do more. The Black-Berry Curve 8350i is a PDA, phone, and Internet access device all rolled into one. The OQO model 2+ is one of the world's smallest computers at 5.6 × 3.3 inches, making it easy to take your computer with you.

In the next section, we will explore the phenomenon of the coming together of these communications technologies.

Convergence: Is It a Phone or a Computer?

We've been examining technologies that carry computer data over voice lines as well as through the air. At the core of this process is **digitization**, the transformation of data such as voice, text, graphics, audio, and video into digital form. Digitization enables convergence. **Convergence** refers to the merging of disparate objects or ideas (and even people) into new combinations and efficiencies. Within the IT industry, convergence means two things: (1) the combination of various industries (computers, consumer electronics, and telecommunications) and (2) the coming together of products such as PCs and telephones.

Wireless devices are proliferating at a tremendous pace. Today, it is not unusual for your phone to double as a PDA or talk to your computer, or for your computer to be controlled by a wireless mouse or keyboard. Convergence has culminated in the transmission of data. With the advent of Internet telephony (the use of the Internet to transmit real-time voice data), all forms of information (voice, data, and video) now travel over the same network, the Internet (Figure 8.26).

Digitization also enables media convergence. Media convergence is the unification of all forms of media (including newspapers, TV, and radio). The Internet is already a major source of breaking news, rivaling such traditional sources as newspapers and television. Many telephone calls are now transmitted across the Internet using a technology known as Voice over IP (VoIP). This trend could be signaling the end of the traditional public switched telephone network.

Another threat to the PSTN is the November 2003 legislation on telephone number portability. Under this rule, people can keep their existing phone number when changing providers, whether from traditional land-based or cellular phone service. Despite the ongoing challenges of cell phones (battery life, spotty connectivity, dropped calls), more and more U.S. households are opting to disconnect their conventional landline telephones and rely solely on cellular service. As of early 2010, 25 percent of U.S. households had only cell phones, and 15 percent of those with both landline and cell phones received most of their calls on their cell. Industry professionals expect this migration away from land-based telephones to continue as the need for portability and other cell phone features, such as text messaging, become more in demand. In support of this statistic, sales of smartphones like the iPhone, Droid, and BlackBerry, which can surf the Web and provide e-mail access have been on the increase. The reason for the shift seems to the growing interest in the apps provided by the manufacturer and supported by the operating system not just the phone's operation or consistency of performance.

Why should you care about convergence? Understanding convergence will help you make more informed decisions about current and future technology purchases. This section explores some of the dimensions of computer-telephony convergence, a process of technological morphing in which previously distinct devices lose their sharply defined boundaries and blend together. As you'll see, it's creating some interesting hybrids.

Cellular Telephones

Cellular telephones are computing devices. Although cell phones started out as analog devices (**1G**, for first generation), the current generation of wireless cell phones (**4G**, for fourth generation) are all digital systems that provide high-speed access to transmit voice, text, images, and video data. Although 4G can be considered the current generation, most cell phones are still **3G** (third-generation) devices. For more information, dates, and features of

FIGURE 8.27 Cell Phone Generations

Wireless Technologies	Year	Feature
1G	1981	Analog mobile phone service allowed callers to make their own calls without operator assistance and move seamlessly from cell to cell.
2G	1991	Digital signaling decreased interference, improved reception, and provided better protection from eavesdropping. This generation also increased security features designed to discourage cell phone fraud.
3G	2001	These technologies enabled faster data transmission, greater network capacity, more advanced network services, and allowed transmission of voice, text, images, and video data.
4G (beyond 3G)	2010–2015 (estimated release)	This generation promises even higher data rates as well as real-time (streamed) formatting for voice, data, and high-quality multimedia. 4G is not currently available in all areas.

FAST FORWARD ▶▶

Convergence is moving into another arena, with Microsoft signing an agreement with Australia's leading pay TV provider, Foxtel, to stream over 30 channels to Xbox 360 consoles through Xbox LIVE. Xbox 360 owners in Australia will use their units to access Foxtel channels instead of using a set-top box with an expensive installation fee. A user will need an Xbox 360 console, Xbox LIVE gold subscription, a broadband connection with high download limits, and a Foxtel by Xbox LIVE subscription. The plan will allow access to such channels as FOX Sports, Discovery, and Nickelodeon and will provide video on demand and online chat. It should appeal to users in areas that Foxtel does not currently service and those that move frequently and want to avoid all of the reconnect fees. Microsoft has similar agreements already in Europe, France, and the United Kingdom. There is currently no comparable service in the United States. Microsoft's convergence of game consoles and pay TV is another attempt to unite features and devices to provide better services for the consumer. How long will it be until one device controls our home media needs and returning set-top boxes and paying installation charges are events of the past?

each cell phone technology generation, refer to Figure 8.27.

In 1971, AT&T built a network of transmitters that automatically repeat signals. This network of transmitters, which are called **cell sites**, broadcasts signals throughout specific, but limited, geographic areas called **cells**. When callers move from cell to cell, each new cell site automatically takes over the signal to maintain signal strength. But who or what monitors your cell phone's signal strength so that you have the best reception? That's the job of the **mobile switching center (MSC)**, and each cellular network contains several MSCs that handle communications within a group of cells (Figure 8.28). Each cell tower reports signal strength to the MSC, which then switches your signal to whatever cell tower will provide the clearest connection for your conversation.

FIGURE 8.28 When callers move from cell to cell, the mobile switching center locates the cell with the strongest signal strength and that cell automatically takes over transmission.

MSCs route calls to the gateway mobile switching center (GMSC), which in turn sends calls to their final destination. If the call is headed for a land-based phone, the GMSC sends the call to the PSTN. Otherwise, it forwards the call directly to another cellular network.

Terrain, weather, antenna position, and battery strength can all interfere and affect signal strength. However, there may be times when you've extended your antenna, recharged your battery, have clear weather, and are standing at the top of a hill—and still cannot achieve a good signal. Cell coverage is not perfect, and cellular networks have *holes* (areas in which you can't send or receive calls).

MSCs are also key players in another widely used cellular service, SMS (short messaging service), better known as text messaging and MMS (multimedia messaging service), commonly called picture messaging. As of December 2009, over 152.7 billion text messages were sent every month compared to just 18 billion in December 2006. That number has grown by 200 percent or more for each year for the last two years (Figure 8.29). Teens are the largest users of messaging. Subscribers between the ages of 13 and 17 sent and received 1,742 text messages a month in the second quarter of 2008. How do text and

multimedia messaging work? The MSC forwards the message to a messaging center for storage and then locates the other cell phone that will receive the message.

FIGURE 8.29 In 2009, an average of 152.7 billion text messages were sent per month, with a majority by users between the ages of 13 and 44.

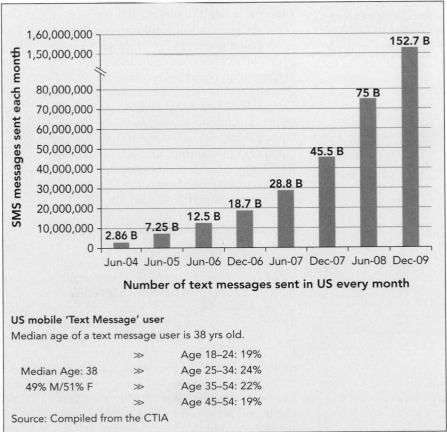

Number of text messages sent in US every month

US mobile 'Text Message' user

Median age of a text message user is 38 yrs old.

	≫	Age 18–24: 19%
Median Age: 38	≫	Age 25–34: 24%
49% M/51% F	≫	Age 35–54: 22%
	≫	Age 45–54: 19%

Source: Compiled from the CTIA

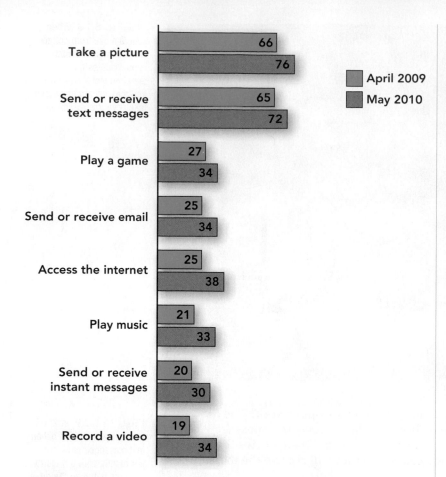

Take a picture	66 / 76
Send or receive text messages	65 / 72
Play a game	27 / 34
Send or receive email	25 / 34
Access the internet	25 / 38
Play music	21 / 33
Send or receive instant messages	20 / 30
Record a video	19 / 34

April 2009
May 2010

FIGURE 8.30 Using a cell phone to take videos and access the Internet showed the greatest percent of increase from April 2009 to May 2010.

An appropriate signal is then sent out through the cell in which the receiving phone is located to let it know it will be receiving a message. The receiving phone sends an acknowledgment to the message center when the message is received. Statistics released from the Pew Research Center Internet & American Life Project indicate that cell phone users are using their devices for much more than making calls, text messaging, and picture messaging. There has been an increase across the board in eight areas of cell phone use between April 2009 and May 2010. Figure 8.30 visually displays these increases and the variety of uses cell phones have today.

Cell phone etiquette and safety are other issues to be aware of. Many people may be irritated or concerned by others' careless use of cell phones in public places or while driving motor vehicles. A number of states have banned drivers from using handheld cell phones while operating a motor vehicle. Other agencies have policies on cellular phone use in aircraft, trains, and hospitals. Businesses may limit the use of cell phones in movie theaters and restaurants. In addition, your college or university may restrict the use of cell phones in classrooms. For a list of the top 10 cell phone etiquette rules people break go to **www.bspcn.com/2008/08/14/top-10-cell-phone-etiquette-rules-people-still-break**.

Besides cell phone etiquette and safety, burgeoning cell phone use has another societal impact. Just as with old computer equipment, you need to think about the proper disposal of your cell phone when you upgrade or damage it beyond repair. The average life of a cell phone is 18 months. Discarded cell phones produce toxic waste. When they end up in landfills, they threaten the environment through the release of arsenic, lead, cadmium, and other heavy metals that can creep into the water supply and cause cancer or birth defects. AT&T, Cingular, and many other providers, as well as indirect retailers, will accept old phones. Figure 8.31 displays the parts of a cell phone and indicates whether each component is recyclable, reusable, or hazardous. The bottom line: Recycling your old cell phone is good for the environment.

Personal Communication Service A group of related digital cellular technologies called **PCS (personal communication service)** quickly replaced most analog cellular services. PCS is also referred to as **2G**, for second-generation cellular technology, or dual-band service. Digital 2G phones made strides toward solving many of the problems that plagued analog phones. Improvements included decreasing signal interference, increasing reception, providing better protection from eavesdropping, and increasing the difficulty of committing cell phone fraud. In short, 2G design specifications enabled the manufacturers to use convergence to make the **smartphones** we enjoy today, which are handheld devices that integrate mobile phone capability, computing power, and Web access.

For millions of people, 2G made mobile computing a reality. Because 2G technology is digital, it's much more amenable to data communications than analog cellular services. It made it possible to access the Internet by means of a modem connected to an analog cellular phone, but data transfer rates were extremely low because of line noise and poor connections. Throughput of up to 384 Kbps for downloads was enabled by 2G standards.

Battery

Optical glass

Chip sets

Aluminum bezel

Flexible circuit
(contains OLED, touchscreen
antennas, chip mounts, solar array)

Recyclable

Reusable

Aluminum frame

Hazardous

FIGURE 8.31 Over 130 million cell phones are disposed of annually in the United States, with only 10 percent of that number being recycled. Globally, only 3 percent of all cell phones are recycled.

Simply throwing away a cell phone is hazardous to the environment. How you dispose of your old phone is left up to you. However, with cell phones made of mostly recyclable material (Figure 8.32) using a recycle drop off or donating it to an organization that gives them to those in need seems like the best and most environmentally sound decision. So, where can you dispose of your phone responsibly? Check out **www.nokia.com/environment/we-recycle**.

Nokia's We Recycle program will recycle your phone for no cost. With 5,000 recycle centers in 85 countries, Nokia is demonstrating corporate responsibility not only for its own product, but also for its competitors' products. Similarly, Verizon's HopeLine refurbishes or recycles old phones and uses the proceeds to help prevent domestic violence. Through this program, more than 1 million phones and more than 170,000 batteries have been disposed of properly.

Visit the Shelter Alliance (Fund Raising with Accountability) Web site at **www.shelteralliance.net/index.cfm** to learn about several cell phone recycling programs offered through this organization and its nonprofit partners. ●

Cell Phone Composition

5% other non-metals

45% plastic

20% copper

20% other metals

10% ceramics

FIGURE 8.32 The materials in your mobile phone can be used to make musical instruments, jewelry, and park benches.

Technology has marched on with the introduction of 3G technology (Figure 8.33) and the recent introduction of 4G (fourth generation) cell phones. The main benefit of 3G is that it supports much higher numbers of data and voice customers and provides higher data transfer rates (greater than 384 Kbps while walking and up to 2 Mbps while stationary). The recently released 4G offers improvements in connectivity, data transfer rates, and support for the next generation of multimedia.

So, should you dump your 2G phone and opt for a 3G? If your phone is providing you with good-quality service and the feature set is sufficient for your needs, you should probably keep it. However, if you need to regularly access the Internet, you may wish to consider upgrading to a 3G phone to take advantage of the higher data transfer rates.

FIGURE 8.33 The Nokia E90 Communicator boasts high-speed 3G mobile broadband connections for Internet browsing and file transfer.

Web-Enabled Devices

A **Web-enabled device** is any device that can connect to the Internet and display and respond to the codes in markup languages, such as HTML (Hypertext Markup Language) or XML (Extensible Markup Language), typically used to build Web pages. Web-enabled devices include PDAs, smartphones, and notebook PCs.

PDAs are fast disappearing from the market because of convergence. Many smartphones now offer all the functionality that PDAs used to offer and also act as phones. Windows Mobile and the Palm OS are popular operating systems for smartphones that were originally developed for PDAs. BlackBerry devices (which use their own operating system called RIM) continue to be a popular choice for managing enterprise business life (which includes checking e-mail, making phone calls, and accessing the Internet). BlackBerry devices actually lead the smartphone revolution as one of the first truly convergent devices.

The market for mobile operating systems has heated up, with RIM BlackBerry, Apple iPhone OS and Symbian leading the way. Windows Mobile (based on Windows CE), and Google Android are all making attempts to compete for their share of the market. Although other mobile operating systems are gaining in popularity, a study completed in February of 2009 concluded that the most secure mobile platform for business use is the BlackBerry RIM. Refer to Figure 8.34 to view the criteria used to arrive at this assessment. If you are trying to decide on which smartphone to purchase, go to **http://cellphones.about.com/od/buyersguides/qt/best_cell_phone.htm** and answer approximately 15 questions on your cell needs and wants. When you complete all questions, the site will display a list of several devices that match your needs. You probably have heard the saying that when you are opening a business it's location, location, and location that counts. With all the facts considered, when buying a cell phone it might be coverage, coverage, and coverage that are the final factors in your choice. You might have to limit your phone selection from those offered by the carrier that provides service in your region.

To work over wireless networks, Web-enabled devices require **WAP (Wireless Application Protocol)**. WAP is a standard that specifies how users can access the Web securely using pagers, smartphones, PDAs, and other wireless handheld devices. It doesn't matter which operating system your device uses because WAP is supported by all of them. However, WAP-enabled devices do require a **microbrowser**, a special

FIGURE 8.34 An assessment of operating systems, based on five areas of focus, indicate that the BlackBerry RIM OS surpasses the iPhone OS and Windows Mobile OS.

Comparative Evaluation of Mobile OS Components			
Features	BlackBerry OS	iPhone OS	Win Mobile OS
Authentication	3	1	2
Data Vaulting	3	-1	2
Reliability	3	3	2
Tamper Resistant	2	1	1
Meeting Security Validations	3	-2	1

Ranges of rankings go from a low of –2 to a high of 3.

Web browser that has all of the features of computer-based browsers but is simplified to meet handheld device limitations. These limitations include smaller screen size, smaller file sizes (due to the low memory capacities of WAP-enabled devices), and wireless networks with low bandwidth.

Now that you understand how convergence is blurring the boundaries between phone and computer devices, let's take a look at some wired and wireless applications used with these devices.

Wired and Wireless Applications

The world of wired and wireless applications is receiving more attention every day. You can't open a magazine, surf the Web, or watch TV without seeing ads for the latest wireless solutions. More and more businesses and home users are implementing these various applications to help them communicate, collaborate, and share text, graphics, audio, and video. You can sit in a classroom today and receive instant messages, e-mail, and stock quotes and even browse the Web—all from your smartphone! And it is happening at increasingly faster speeds, higher data transfer rates, and lower costs.

Internet Telephony: Real-Time Voice and Video

Internet telephony Using the Internet for real-time voice communication is commonly known as **VoIP (Voice over Internet Protocol)** or **Internet**

telephony. You can place calls via the Internet in a variety of ways, but first you'll need a computer equipped with a microphone, speakers or headphones, an Internet connection, and a telephony-enabled program such as Skype (**www.skype.com**). With Skype, you can make free calls to other similarly equipped Skype users. Stay posted as this might start to change. In May 2010 Skype announced its new iPhone app, which makes calls over the 3G network. Skype-to-Skype calls over the WiFi networks will remain free, but the company says that they will begin to charge for Skype-to-Skype calls over the 3G network by the end of 2010. Even though revenue may not be the best measure of success, a look at the graph in Figure 8.35 shows an unmistakably constant increase in Skype revenue over six consecutive quarters. The technology appears to be doing well.

What about placing a call to an ordinary telephone or cell phone? In most situations, you can't do it for free. However, VoIP service providers such as Vonage are stepping into the act by offering computer-to-phone and phone-to-phone services that use the Internet for long-distance transmission (Figure 8.36). The system is pretty

FIGURE 8.35 Between Quarter 3 and Quarter 4 of 2008, Skype revenue seemed to level out. This could be due to the economy or the fact that most users were making Skype-to-Skype free calls.

FIGURE 8.36 VoIP installation is relatively easy. The system can be configured by a novice computer user.

A phone adapter allows your computer or your existing phone to send phone calls across the Internet.

Internet — Cable/DSL modem — Vonage phone adapter — Personal computer — Telephone — FAX (optional)

You must have a broadband Internet connection to use VoIP.

simple to set up, rates are cheaper than conventional landline phones, and the quality is very good. The hottest markets for VoIP are Japan, China, and the United States.

The basic idea of Internet telephony has an enormous advantage: Because the Internet doesn't rely on switches to route messages, like the PSTN does, it's cheaper to operate. Providers can route dozens, hundreds, or even thousands of calls over the same circuit. Many conventional phone companies already send voice calls over the Internet. You may have actually experienced VoIP without even knowing it. You can try Internet telephony by using Skype (the incumbent leader), GizmoProject, PeerMe, or Jajah. Each offers free service to another computer user who has the same software installed, but most charge for connecting to a house or wireless cell phone.

Times are always changing in the world of technology. As of March 2010, Verizon and Skype have teamed up to provide free Skype-to-Skype phone calls over the Verizon voice network. With the 91 million Verizon wireless users and 600 million Skype users worldwide, that is a lot of talk. IM messages to other Skype users will also be free. Skype-to-Skype calls and IMs will not be charged against the Verizon data plan; however, a data plan is required to activate the service. Skype

mobile will only work on the Verizon's cellular voice network and not on WiFi networks in general, In addition, a BlackBerry or Android phone is needed. Video is not available as of yet, due to the limits of the devices and network. If you meet the criteria, you can simply text SKYPE to 2255 for a download link or visit **http://phones.verizonwireless. com/skypemobile.**

If you and the person you're calling have a digital video camera, you can converse through real-time videoconferencing as well. **Videoconferencing**, also called **Web conferencing**, is the use of digital video technology to transmit sound and video images to facilitate online, virtual meetings through which two or more people can have a face-to-face meeting even though they're geographically separated (Figure 8.37). Such meetings are practical, quick, and cost-effective. The many notebook computers sold today come with built-in video cameras (webcams) and Skype software to support video conferencing. However, you won't always have perfect quality; you'll hear echoes and delays in the audio, and the picture will be small, grainy, jerky, and susceptible to delays. But there are no long-distance charges (using Skype). Several vendors offer, for a price, software and packages to facilitate this online communication and improve the quality and interaction among participants. All attendees need to do is download the application to their computers or access a Web site or URL to join the group offering the meeting or presentation. To review an independent ranking of such services visit **www.webconferencing-test.com/en/webconference_ home.html.**

In addition to Internet voice and video calls, Internet telephony products support real-time conferencing with such features as a shared whiteboard, file-exchange capabilities, and text chatting. A **whiteboard**, generally shown as a separate area of the videoconferencing screen, enables participants to create a shared workspace. Participants can write or draw in this space as if they were using a physical whiteboard in a meeting. Combine this with live video

FIGURE 8.37 In a videoconference or Web conference, participants still feel personally connected to other participants, but the electronic conference eliminates the frustration, time, and cost of travel.

Webcam

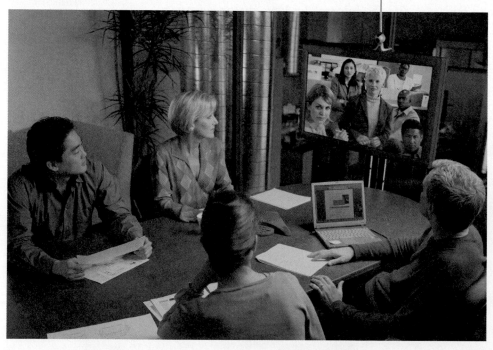

and audio and it's like being in a conference room with your group.

A **webcam** (Figure 8.38) is an inexpensive, low-resolution analog or digital video camera that is integrated into a notebook computer or designed to sit on top of a computer monitor. Sometimes an individual, company, or organization places a webcam in a public location, such as a street corner, a railway station, or a museum (Figure 8.39). Often, the camera is set up to take a snapshot of the scene every 15 minutes or so. The image is then displayed on a Web page. Some sites offer streaming cams, also called live cams, which provide more frequently updated images. Many resorts and ski areas have set up live cams so potential visitors can see weather conditions and tourist lines. Keep in mind that live cams cannot be set up to watch or spy without obtaining the proper legal documents. The consequences of posting a live cam on a social network site may come back to haunt you. To learn more about webcams and their use, and to obtain a few helpful hints, visit (**www.microsoft.com/canada/ home/styleandhome/2.3.35_ webcambasicshowdoesonework. aspx**).

If you want only to transmit voice over the Internet, and not video, you can use a dial-up modem and connection with transfer speeds of 56 Kbps. But for any high-bandwidth Internet application, such as streaming video, you need a broadband connection with transfer speeds of at least 1.5 Mbps. Network-based delivery of high-quality videoconferencing requires a bandwidth of at least 10 Mbps. Videoconferencing will be a much smoother experience for all participants with broadband's faster upload speeds.

Streaming video wasn't practical for home viewing before broadband and cheap, powerful computers became available for the home market. Now, streaming video sites such as YouTube are some of the most visited sites on the Internet. As popular as YouTube is for viewing videos,

FIGURE 8.38 If your computer lacks a webcam, you can buy one that is designed to be freestanding or placed on top of a monitor (or notebook).

it has a video length limit of 10 minutes. This means that watching a 30-minute television program will require viewing three segments. **Internet TV** refers to the ability to view television shows, videos, and movies over the Internet, for no additional cost, via download or streaming video. The benefit of this type of viewing over YouTube is that the content is provided by the original source, so copyright is not an issue, there is no limit on length, the user has a variety of selections from which to choose, and there is no time restriction on when the video has to be watched. Powerful, inexpensive computers and increased bandwidth offered by ISPs have made Internet telephony and videoconferencing affordable and practical for small businesses. And millions of Internet users watch Internet TV and employ webcams and programs such as Skype to stay in touch with friends and family—often for free (at least for now)!

FIGURE 8.39 Web cams, like those provided by the National Parks Service, provide live satellite links to many popular locations.

Faxing: Document Exchange

Facsimile transmission—or **fax** as it's popularly known—enables you to send an image of a document over a telephone line or the Internet (Figure 8.40). The sending fax machine makes a digital image of the document. Using a built-in modem, the sending fax machine converts the image into an analog representation so that it can be transmitted through the analog telephone system. The receiving fax machine converts the analog signals to digital signals, converts the digital signals to an image of the document, and then prints the image.

Some computer users use fax modems instead of fax machines. A **fax modem** is a computerized version of a stand-alone fax machine. This device and software allow your computer to do everything a fax machine can: send and receive documents, print documents, and store documents. The big difference between using a regular fax machine and using your computer as a fax machine is that the fax modem does everything in a digitized way. So, you may need a scanner to put a document into a digital format if you want to fax something that's printed or sketched on paper.

Traditional fax machines are quickly becoming obsolete. Some companies have chosen to use a spare computer as a fax server to handle incoming and outgoing faxes. Desktop software can convert e-mails to faxes and vice versa. This is referred to as fax-to-mail or mail-to-fax technology and reduces costs significantly because there is no need for a fax machine or an additional phone line. In addition, there is no extra charge for using your Internet connection to send a fax.

Faxes received in this way are usually converted to a digital file format, for example a PDF file, and attached to an e-mail, or they may be sent to a cell phone. Similarly, sent faxes are also converted to

FIGURE 8.40 Facsimile transmissions can be sent over telephone lines or the Internet through the use of fax machines or computers equipped with fax modems.

digital format before being sent over the Internet to their destinations. If the receiving fax machine is a conventional machine attached to a phone line, the fax is forwarded to the PSTN for delivery.

Because computers can send and receive faxes, it is not a far stretch of the imagination to see that sending and receiving documents will soon be accomplished by network-enabled cell phones or Web-enabled devices. One limiting feature of using this new medium for faxing is the inability to include a hard signature on the document. Although digital signatures, or soft signatures, can be embedded within an electronic document, they are not enough for some transactions especially those requiring legal signatures.

Satellite Radio, GPS, and More

Many applications use satellite technology, including air navigation, TV and radio broadcasting, paging, and videoconferencing. **Satellite radio** broadcasts radio signals to satellites orbiting more than 22,000 miles above the Earth. The satellites then transmit the signals back to a radio receiver. Unlike ground-based radio signal transmitters, satellite radio is not affected by location, distance, or obstructions. Because of their great height, satellites can transmit signals to a radio receiver wherever it might be located.

Satellite radio is a boon for folks living in areas with limited local radio stations or where regular AM/FM reception is hampered by terrain. Sirius XM Radio Inc. is one of the largest satellite radio subscriptions companies. Satellite radio can mimic your local radio broadcasting station's style, including commercials. It can provide you with more than 100 channels offering different genres, including continuous music, sports, news, and talk programs. In contrast to music programs that are offered by some cable or satellite in-home providers, satellite radio uses portable receivers that plug into your home or car stereo, so it is totally mobile and transportable to wherever you happen to want to listen. SIRIUS now offers Backseat TV, which streams live TV broadcasts to subscribers who have video receivers in their vehicles.

Total revenue for Sirius XM Radio Inc. grew by 1 percent, year over year, to $608 million, while total subscribers, currently estimated at 19 million, continued to decline, also by 1 percent, for the second quarter of 2009. The decline in subscribers is attributed to the economy and decline in auto sales, while the boost in revenue is due to an increase in monthly charges and a decrease in operating costs.

Sirius XM is battling for subscribers. Its iPhone application has been a hit with existing users of the service, but it has failed to bring in new subscribers due to its higher cost and reduced radio content. Competition from other sources like Internet radio services, for example, Pandora, which can stream music into smartphones and wireless-enabled cars such as certain Ford models, will continue to heat up as the auto industry and economy rebound.

"Most [GPS] systems are accurate to **within 109 yards**; some systems boast a **164-yard range."**

GPS Another interesting application of satellite technology is GPS. **GPS (Global Positioning System)** is a cluster of 27 Earth-orbiting satellites (24 in operation and 3 extras in case one fails). Each of these 3,000- to 4,000-pound solar-powered satellites circles the globe at an altitude of 12,000 miles, making two complete rotations every day. The orbits are arranged so that at anytime, anywhere on Earth, at least four satellites are "visible" in the sky. A GPS receiver's job is to locate four or more of these satellites, figure out the distance to each, and use this information to deduce its own location. Most systems are accurate to within 109 yards; some systems boast a 164-yard range (Figure 8.41).

A GPS receiver can be either handheld or installed in a vehicle. Navigation systems in rental cars are a typical application of GPS. OnStar is a multifaceted GPS communications system that enables drivers to talk to a service representative to obtain driving directions and information on hotels, food venues, and the like. Drivers can also use OnStar to notify the police, fire department, or ambulance

4 of 24 possible satellites

Locking into three satellites determines location in latitude and longitude.

Locking into a fourth satellite provides altitude and 3D positioning.

GPS receivers

FIGURE 8.41 GPS units lock in the signal from four satellites and use a mathematical principle called triangulation to determine the position of the receiving device in three dimensions.

service in case of an emergency. Through in-vehicle sensors, it can even detect when a car has been involved in an accident. Finally, OnStar can also aid a driver experiencing minor inconveniences, for example, by unlocking car doors should a driver accidentally lock car keys inside (Figure 8.42).

GPS units for cars have become more mobile. Many different models can be easily attached to a dashboard and moved from one vehicle to another. Some units can even convert maps from road maps to walking maps that list house numbers and specific points of interest. You can update the maps on many GPS units via the Internet. Higher priced units allow you to swap media cards to provide foreign travel maps or convert your unit into a marine GPS unit.

Other Satellite Applications Echelon is a satellite-based system operated on behalf of the five members of the UK–USA Security Agreement (Australia, Canada, New Zealand, United Kingdom, and the United States). Its mission is to intercept and process international communications passed via satellites. The system uses ground-based listening devices and up to 120 satellites to intercept messages (Figure 8.43). It combs through the huge volume of intercepted messages, looking for words and phrases such as "bomb" and "terrorist" and other information of interest to intelligence agencies.

Satellites also bring Internet access to areas that don't have a communications infrastructure. The Navajo Nation, which straddles the borders of Arizona, New Mexico, and Utah and covers a 26,000-square-mile area, faces special challenges for connecting its residents to the Internet. Approximately half the households

1. A GPS receiver in the vehicle connects to a satellite, establishes the location of the vehicle, and stores that location.

2. When an emergency feature of OnStar is activated, the unit places a call to the OnStar center and transmits the vehicle ID and GPS location.

3. The cellular call is routed to the landline phone system.

4. The call is picked up by a trained OnStar advisor.

FIGURE 8.42 OnStar makes use of a built-in GPS and cell phone system to provide assistance to drivers.

FIGURE 8.43 An Echelon Base Located in Germany

don't even have phone service, and those that do, find the quality of that service sometimes lacking. For data communications, the maximum reliable data speed is often limited to 28.8 Kbps. In addition, Internet access through a private service provider is virtually always a long-distance call.

Navajo Nation school administrators purchased a system called HughesNet, which uses a small 18-inch satellite dish to receive information from the Internet and regular telephone or data lines to send information (Figure 8.44). Because Internet use in an educational environment involves massive amounts of downloaded information, the satellite solution was ideal.

Text, Picture, and Video Messaging and More

The statistics on cell phone ownership and usage are staggering. Almost 9 out of 10 (87%) U.S. residents say they own a cell phone, and 16 percent own a PDA (personal digital assistant). An estimated 4 out of 5 teens (17 million) carry a wireless device, an increase of approximately 40 percent since 2004. Cell phones give teens (and a growing number of preteens) a sense of not only community but also freedom. Cell phone ownership is being compared with the freedom and individuality of having a driver's license.

Text, picture, and video messaging are the hot applications for mobile devices that e-mail and IM once were for computers. **Text messaging**, also called **SMS** (short message service), is similar to using your phone for instant messaging or as a receiver and transmitter for brief e-mail messages (Figure 8.45). Teens spend approximately the same amount of time texting as they do talking and no longer consider texting as an option but a necessity. In fact, 42 percent of them say that they can text blindfolded.

FIGURE 8.44
HughesNet, also used in Alaska, uses orbiting satellites to retrieve and relay information, delivering Internet access to remote locations.

2. The request is sent from the user's satellite dish to a HughesNet satellite.

3. The satellite contacts the HughesNet Network Operations Center (N.O.C.).

1. The user, from their computer, requests a Web site.

4. The N.O.C. contacts the requested Web site.

5. The Web site forwards the information back to the user through the same path.

FIGURE 8.45 Text messaging enables users to converse without bothering those nearby.

Picture and video messaging are mobile services that will transform the way we electronically interact with each other. People have sent pictures by way of FTP or as e-mail attachments for more than 10 years, but the use of the telephone for such services has exploded in recent years. Today, **picture messaging**, also referred to as **MMS** (multimedia messaging system) allows you to send full-color pictures, backgrounds, and even picture caller IDs on your cell phone. With picture messaging, your phone performs as a camera so that you can send pictures from your vacation or capture spontaneous moments and share them with others.

ETHICS

GPS devices can be extremely useful to individuals who are lost, trying to navigate through an unfamiliar neighborhood, or looking to avoid a traffic jam. But this same technology can also be viewed as an invasion of privacy. Taxi cab drivers in New York City are protesting against the installation of GPS units in all cabs citing the fear of constant surveillance. Large trucking firms are using units to keep track of drivers and inform them of alternate shorter routes or possible delays while in route. Some see the use of GPS units as a technological advance in providing knowledge and safety while reducing time and energy. Others view their use as an invasion of privacy. Do the benefits of GPS units outweigh the risk of reducing privacy?

Many people want to use their phones to take pictures instead of carrying a digital camera. In order to have your phone replace your digital camera, you have to consider the resolution of the cell phone camera, which is measured in megapixels. A megapixel is 1 million pixels, or points of light, that make up an image. For pictures that will be printed out in large format (8 × 10 inches or larger), you need a camera with a resolution of at least 4 megapixels. Otherwise, the picture will not be sharp.

Images you capture with your phone can be sent by way of e-mail attachments or as a single picture when calling or talking to someone. Note that the user on the other end needs to have a picture-enabled phone as well and that there is a charge for sending pictures or video.

One cell phone application that is more popular with parents than kids is **location awareness** (or **position awareness**). This technology uses GPS-enabled chips to pinpoint the location of a cell phone (and its user). Teens may find location awareness to be a downside of owning a cell phone because their parents can monitor their location. Teens often complain about such surveillance with statements such as "You're intruding on my privacy," "You're treading on my independence," and "I feel as though I'm always being watched." From the parents' perspective, however, they are simply keeping watch over their children in an effort to help them make better decisions.

Location awareness also has consumer and safety applications. The location-awareness feature enables your cell phone to quickly provide the location of the nearest restaurants and entertainment venues. It also can also be activated to provide your location to a police station or other emergency service if needed. Law enforcement and government officials with the right credentials can access a cell provider information on the location of a cell phone by the signal it repeatedly sends out to cell towers in its vicinity when the location feature is activated. The location feature and how it functions is dependent on the phone, provider, and service. Visit **www. ulocate.com** to learn more about location-awareness technology.

Along with all of its benefits, wireless technology also has its dark side that requires the user to be aware of evils lurking around the corner. As in the real world, predators exist and the user needs to keep a sharp eye for technology invasions.

Surfing Safely at Public Wireless Hot Spots

A wireless hot spot is easy to locate today. McDonald's, Starbucks, and many other merchants offer Internet connectivity to lure customers. But when using public hot spots, especially free ones, you need to take some extra precautions to keep you and your data safe. Here are a few issues to keep in mind at these sites: Wireless security is often not implemented on public hot spots; your shared files and directories might be accessible to others using the same wireless network; and you might be logging into a malicious network. A **malicious network** is a network set up by a hacker within the operating area of a legitimate hot spot. The hacker hopes to lure the user into the bogus network, referred to as an "evil twin," and gather sensitive information as passwords and credit card numbers.

Sounds scary, doesn't it? Well, you can't deny yourself the use of technology any more than you can deny yourself a trip to the mall for fear that something negative will happen. Here are a few precautions that you can follow to protect yourself while surfing on a public hot spot.

- Use firewalls and antivirus software.
- Ask an employee for the name of the legitimate network, to prevent connecting to an evil twin.
- Do not engage in sensitive financial transactions while connected to an unsecured hot spot.
- Select the appropriate operating system option to limit sharing of resources and discovery of your computer while connected to a public hot spot (Figure 8.46).

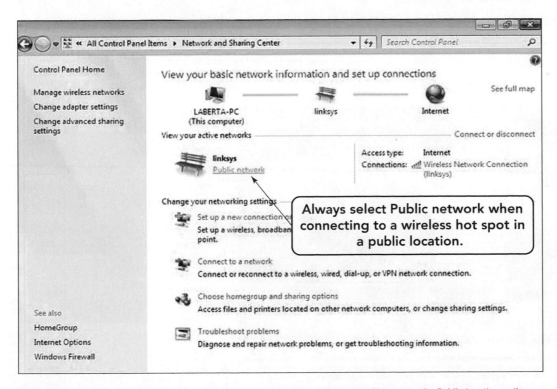

FIGURE 8.46 The screen displays the network settings available in Windows 7. Always use the Public location option when using a public wireless hot spot.

Set up and Access Skype VoIP

Make sure that you have a microphone, speakers, and headphones that are in working order and are compatible with your PC or Mac computer system. Additionally, you need an Internet connection and, if you want video calls, a webcam. This is the only equipment you will need for Skype-to-Skype VoIP, which allows communication from one computer using Skype software to another computer using Skype for no charge.

1. Download the Skype software from **www.skype.com.**

   a. Click the option to *Get Skype*.

   b. In the next window select your device type. You can select Get Skype for Windows or Get Skype on your mobile. Select *GetSkype for Windows.* This option selection will display a list of links for Windows, Mac Os X, Linux and several other operating systems (Figure 8.47).

   c. Select the Windows-based operating system for the unit on which you are installing the Skype software. Then click *Download Now*.

   d. The Skypesetup.exe file will be downloaded to the default download location on your system.

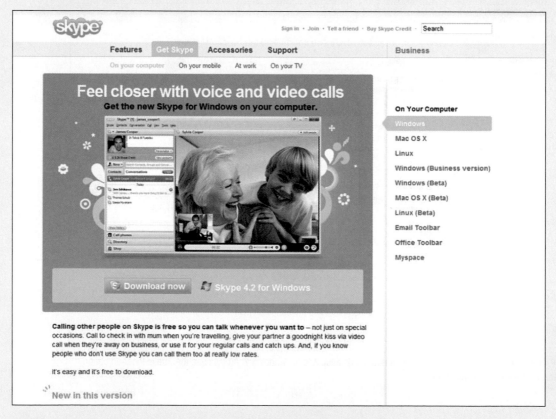

FIGURE 8.47 The Skype software download is available for most operating systems.

2. Locate the *Skypesetup.exe* file and double-click it to start the installation.

   a. Read the Warning dialog box and click *OK*.

   b. Select the language you want, and then click *Next*.

   c. Review and accept the licensing agreement. Click *Next,* and the installation will begin.

3. When the installation is complete, you can select the option to open Skype every time you start your computer. When you are done configuring your software as you would like it to appear, click *Finish* to start Skype.

4. The Skype window will open. If it doesn't, click the icon on the task tray to the left of the clock on the taskbar. If you have not used Skype before, you should click on *Don't have a Skype Name* to create your Skype name (this is the name your friends will see in their contact list) and a Personal Profile. Your Skype Personal Profile can be seen by other Skype users who will be able to search for you using this information.

5. Once you have created your Skype name and signed in, your Skype window, which includes a toolbar, will open. Skype is divided into several tabs. The main ones, the Contacts tab, Dial tab and History tab are always visible. The search option is also always available (Figure 8.48).

6. Conduct a sound test, also known as an echo test. Skype provides this facility through of the testing robot, Echo123. Simply enter **echo123** in the address bar at the bottom of Skype or add it to your contacts. When called, an automated voice recording will ask you to record a message and then play it back. If you hear your own voice clearly, Skype has been configured correctly.

7. You are now set to make Skype-to-Skype calls. Good Luck!

FIGURE 8.48 The Search option on the Skype toolbar will attempt to locate a Skype user's number if your know that user's Skype name. If it is able to find the user, it will insert that individual into your contact list.

Chapter Summary

Wired and Wireless Communication

- Bandwidth refers to the maximum data transfer capacity of a communications channel and is measured in Hertz (Hz) and bits per second (bps). To transmit text, you can get by with low bandwidth (such as a 56 Kbps connection). But for viewing multimedia on the Internet, a broadband connection of at least 1.5 Mbps is preferable. Throughput is the actual rate of data transfer. It is lower than bandwidth.

- To transmit digital data over dial-up phone lines, it's necessary to use a modem. On the sending end, the modem modulates the signal (transforms it into analog form). On the receiving end, the modem demodulates the signal (transforms it back into digital form).

- Communications require physical media, like twisted-pair wire, coaxial cable, and fiber-optic cable, or wireless media like infrared, radio, microwaves, and satellite. Additionally, WiMAX and MMDS are wireless technologies used to transmit signals over large geographic areas.

- The public switched telephone network (PSTN) is the global telephone system used for both data and voice. This system usually sends transmissons across various media ranging from twisted-pair to fiber-optic cable and makes use of a modem to convert between analog and digital signals. It is its use of analog devices that makes it prone to noise and interference and creates a bottleneck at the local loop portion of the system, reducing overall transmission time.

- Digital telephony offers noise-free transmission and high-quality audio. Many companies and universities have internal digital telephone systems; however, calls to the outside must be translated into analog signals to connect to the PSTN. Often such calls use multiplexing, in which multiple calls are carried on a single line, allowing more calls to travel over fewer lines.

- Last-mile technologies refers to the technologies, like ISDN, DSL, cable, leased lines, SONET, and WiMax, that bring data into your home or business. These technologies often rely on the services of a local broadband provider or the public switched telephone network (PSTN).

- Digitization is the transformation of data such as voice, text, graphics, audio, and video into digital form. Convergence refers to the coming together of products such as PCs and telephones. Through digitization and convergence the boundaries among such devices as smartphones, PCs, and other Web-enabled devices have become blurred because all enable digital information (voice, video, and data) to travel over wireless communication systems.

- Wired and wireless applications like VoIP; GPS systems; videoconferencing; fax transmissions; satellite radio; and text, picture, and video messaging help communicate, collaborate, entertain, and share text, graphics, audio, and video.

Key Terms and Concepts

Identification

Identify each of the following images as they apply to this chapter.

1. _____

2. _____

3. _____

4. _____

5. _____

6. _____

Matching

Match each key term in the left column with the most accurate definition in the right column.

_____ 1. whiteboard
_____ 2. sending device
_____ 3. streaming
_____ 4. WiFi
_____ 5. webcam
_____ 6. data transfer rate
_____ 7. WiMAX
_____ 8. baud
_____ 9. bandwidth
_____ 10. infrared
_____ 11. receiving device
_____ 12. convergence
_____ 13. leased line
_____ 14. throughput
_____ 15. communications

a. The actual amount of data that is sent though a specific transmission medium at one time

b. A specially conditioned telephone line that enables continuous end-to-end communication between two points

c. The maximum amount of data that can be sent though a specific transmission medium at one time

d. The rate at which two modems can exchange data

e. Accepts a transmission and responds

f. The number of signaling elements per second

g. Used to create a shared workspace for participants in a videoconference

h. The blending of industries and products

i. Initiates a transmission

j. A popular wireless network technology that uses radio waves to provide high-speed Internet and network connections

k. The process of electronically sending and receiving messages between two or more computers or devices regardless of the distance between those devices

l. A wireless transmission medium, which works within a maximum of about 100 feet, and carries data via beams of light through the air

m. A digital camera integrated into a notebook or connected to a desktop computer

n. An up-and-coming wireless digital communication system designed to deliver high-speed access over long distances

o. The ability to listen to or view content while it is being downloaded from a Web site

Multiple Choice

Circle the correct choice for each of the following:

1. What is the technology that facilitates meetings that provide voice and video of individuals in different geographical locations?
   a. Videoconferencing
   b. Piconet
   c. PAN
   d. Piggybacking

2. What communication medium must have a direct line of site between communicating devices and works within a maximum of 100 feet?
   a. WiMax
   b. Bluetooth
   c. WiFi
   d. Infrared

3. Which wireless technology makes use of short-range radio transmission to connect devices within 30 feet of each other?
   a. WiMAX
   b. Bluetooth
   c. DSL
   d. WiFi

4. GPS systems track locations by using which of the following technologies?
   a. PSTN
   b. Infrared
   c. Satellite
   d. PAN

5. Which is *not* a wired method of communication?
   a. WiFi
   b. Fiber optics
   c. Twisted-pair
   d. Cable

6. Which is an example of convergence?
   a. A smartphone
   b. The installation of fiber optics for last-mile connectivity
   c. A Global Positioning System (GPS)
   d. Converting a document to PDF format in order to be read by anyone.

7. Which communication medium uses light to transmit data?
   a. Twisted-pair
   b. Fiber optics
   c. Cable
   d. Microwave

8. Which of the following is true of VoIP (Internet telephony)?
   a. It is not quite perfected and provides poor quality.
   b. It is often cheaper than conventional phone service.
   c. It is too expensive for home use and is used primarily for business.
   d. It requires a cable modem.

9. Which is *not* an example of a wireless transmission media?
   a. Infrared   b. Microwave
   c. Satellite   d. Cable

10. When someone makes a cellular phone call to another cellular phone, which of the following eventually handles the call?
    a. Public switched telephone network (PSTN)
    b. Global Positioning System (GPS).
    c. Mobile switching center (MSC)
    d. Personal communication service (PCS)

Fill-In

In the blanks provided, write the correct answer for each of the following.

1. _____ is the transformation of data such as voice, text, graphics, audio, and video into digital form.

2. _____ is a broad term that describes the ability to link various media and devices to enhance communications and improve access to information.

3. A(n) _____ is the area serviced by a subscriber loop carrier (SLC).

4. _____ is the type of signal produced by human voice.

5. The region of coverage provided by a wireless phone network is called a(n) _____.

6. Accessing a network without permission is called _____.

7. _____ is the technique used to send more than one call over a single line.

8. On a wireless phone network, the _____ monitors the cell phone's signal strength to assure the best reception.

9. _____ is the set of standards that specifies how current wireless devices, through special Web browsers, can securely access the Web.

10. The bottleneck that occurs when data leaves high-speed cable transmission to unite with twisted-pair phone lines to connect homes and businesses is called the _____.

11. _____ uses the Internet for real-time voice communication.

12. _____ is the sending of an image of a document over a telephone line or the Internet.

13. Computers using wireless adapters use a special wireless communication device known as a(n) _____ to send and receive data.

14. A(n) _____ is a Web browser designed to meet the limitations of handheld portable devices.

15. A network set up by a hacker within the operating area of a legitimate hot spot is referred to as a(n) _____ network.

Short Answer

1. Define modem and explain the purpose of this device in the communication process.

2. List and describe three types of wired transmission media and three types of wireless transmission media.

3. Explain the difference between microwave and satellite transmissions and how the two depend on each other.

4. List three operating systems for mobile devices and provide an example of a device in which each is installed.

5. What is the difference between bandwidth and throughput?

6. Explain the last-mile problem. List the current technology being used to minimize this problem.

Teamwork

1. **Investigate the Quad Play** As a team, research the grouping of services like cell phone, TV, Internet, and landline phones into packages by local providers to offer reduced rates. The *Quad Play* is the name Verizon has given to its combination of such services. Investigate different local providers. Compare the difference between purchasing individual services versus the price of a package deal. After you complete your research, use an Excel spreadsheet to list each provider, the services it offers, and the prices of both the individual and package deals. As a team, decide whether the package deals are really a deal, and determine which provider offers the best rates. Indicate your decisions at the bottom of the spreadsheet.

2. **Cell Phone Use** As a team, using Word, develop a survey on the uses of a cell phone. Include the number of calls made in a day and the number of text and/or picture messages sent and received in a day. Inquire whether respondents are on an individual plan or a family plan, ask for an estimate of their monthly bill and whether they have Internet connectivity. Collect other general data that might shed light on your findings, such as age and gender of the user. Distribute the survey to approximately 30 individuals. Accumulate your findings in a Word table. As a team, analyze the collected data and look for patterns and trends. Include these findings in your Word document after your table. The entire report should be approximately one to two pages, double-spaced.

3. **Cell Phone Etiquette** As a team, come up with a list of 10 to 15 cell phone behaviors that a user should practice. Then rank them in order, with the first one being the practice that the group considers the most important. Present your list in a PowerPoint presentation, using one slide for each behavior, and include the reason the team placed them in that ranked position.

4. **Toys to Tools** As a team, investigate the use of cell phones in the area of education. Use your own school as an example. Inquire about courses and instructors that use cell phones or other digital technology in their classrooms. Investigate how they incorporate it into the subject matter. Use online references for additional examples and ideas. As a group, come up with a list of five ways in which cell phones (including text and picture messaging) can be helpful in learning. Present your best five in a PowerPoint presentation and indicate whether the team felt the idea was workable and how it would help or hinder learning. Remember to cite your references.

5. **Solve the Problem** You are on vacation and the house you rented has wireless network—or so it advertised. You brought your notebook, which is equipped with a wireless adaptor and connects to your wireless network at home with no problem. After you boot up, you try to access the Internet, but you receive the message that the connection is unsuccessful. Using the Internet or any other reliable reference sources, determine at least three possible causes for the problem. Present your findings in a one-page, double-spaced report. Remember to cite your references.

On the Web

1. **Green Cell Phones** Investigate the movement to control damage to the environment by reducing the toxic waste from cell phone disposal through the development of portable devices that are more environmentally friendly. Using your favorite browser, search the Internet for companies that are creating green cell phones and research the methods they are using to create them. List the companies that are leading the way, and explain exactly how they are making this change. Present your findings in one-page, double-spaced report. Remember to cite your references.

2. **Investigate HBO to GO** The convergence of TV and computers just got a boost with the addition of HBO being enabled for viewing on desktop and notebook computers. You need a television and Internet account with your local provider. And, of course, you need to be an HBO subscriber. Investigate this new level of convergence. Use online references to see how many local providers are offering

this feature, and ask other class participants whether they would make use of viewing full-length movies on their notebooks or other portable devices. Present your findings in a one-page, double-spaced report. Remember to cite your references.

3. **What Is 4G Technology?** Sprint is already advertising the benefits of its 4G network, the next generation of mobile communications devices. Using the Internet, investigate the expected data transmission rates for 4G and answer the following questions: What will 4G offer over the current 3G network? When will 4G devices be widely available? What providers are leading the way? Investigate why some feel 4G networks might bridge the digital divide. Present your findings in a one-page, double-spaced report. Remember to cite your references.

4. **Technology and Your Responsibility** GPS units have been instrumental in locating and leading to the rescue of an experienced hiker lost in the Australian desert in January 2009. On the flip side, a female lost in Death Valley National Park in California in August 2009 is blaming a GPS unit for providing her with faulty directions that led her and her son to a desolate and extremely remote region of the park. After several days, she and her son depleted their water supply. Her 11-year-old son died. She places blame on the GPS provider. Using the Internet and other reliable forms of information, research cases in which technology helped people and cases in which it has malfunctioned and caused someone to be injured or something to be damaged. When is the incident the fault of the provider and when is it the fault of the human operator? What are the limits of technology and whose responsibility is it to know those limits? What can the technology provider do to disclaim responsibility? What can the user do to validate reliability of, in the case of the Death Valley hiker, navigational instructions? Present your findings and opinions in a one-page, double-spaced report. Remember to cite your references.

5. **Location Aware Devices: Safety versus Privacy** Using the Internet and your favorite search engine, search for articles on the use of OnStar for the collection of evidence in police investigations and national security issues. Explain how the device is configured in order to listen in on car conversations that can produce incriminating evidence. Locate any court decision on whether such configuring with the OnStar device is legal and within the rights of law enforcement and federal agencies. Additionally, locate references on the benefits and drawbacks of such location-aware devices. Present your findings, court decisions, and a list of the pros and cons of such devices in a one-page, double-spaced paper. Remember to cite your references.

Spotlight

Digital Life

Can you remember when you left for the day and did not take a cell phone, notebook, or e-book reader with you? When did you last take off on a trip without the aid of some type of global positioning system (GPS)? Can you recall how you felt having to go all day without these digital devices and the communication or information they provide? For most of us, carrying our digital devices is just as important as wearing our shoes. We simply feel incomplete without them.

Multimedia is one of the reasons the Web is so popular. Simply put, **multimedia** can be defined as multisensory stimulators that stimulate our senses of sight, sound, touch, smell, or taste. For our purposes, we'll consider multimedia that stimulates the senses of sight, sound, and touch. Just a few years ago, most personal computers needed additional equipment to run multimedia applications. Today, such equipment—sound cards, CD or DVD drives, and speakers—is standard issue. However, for advanced multimedia applications, you may still need additional equipment, such as a pen-based graphics tablet, a stereo microphone, a digital camera, or a video adapter. If you enjoy playing games, you'll want a 3D video accelerator—add-on video adapter that works with your current video card. For surround sound, you'll need a sound card capable of producing the surround effect. And you'll probably want to pick up a few extra speakers and a subwoofer. If you are a movie watcher, you'll want to add a Blu-ray disk drive.

Multimedia is an integral part of computer games of all kinds, but it is also being used more and more in computer-based education (CBE), distance learning, and computer-based training (CBT). Businesses use it in multimedia presentations that are created with software programs such as PowerPoint. It's also finding its way into **information kiosks**, which are automated presentation systems used to provide information to the public or for employee training (Figure 6A).

FIGURE 6A Service kiosks that use touch-screen technology can be found in many locations.

What if you want your multimedia files to travel with you? Today, a number of portable multimedia devices are available, from MP3 players and digital cameras to Web-enabled devices such as smartphones, PDAs, e-books, and portable televisions. In this spotlight, you'll learn about a variety of multimedia devices, both mobile ones and those used with desktop computers.

Audio: MP3 Players and Voice Recorders

Unlike previous forms of push technology (products marketed by industries to consumers), such as cassette tapes and CDs, the MP3 movement has been largely fueled by music lovers' use of the Internet to compile and share libraries of digitized music files. Files are created and shared by the users—without industry involvement. An MP3 file is a compressed audio format that is usually used for music files. The term MP3 is derived from the acronym MPEG, which stands for the Motion Picture Experts Group; the 3 refers to audio layer 3.

Without losing any noticeable sound quality, the MPEG3 format reduces the size of sound files by eliminating frequencies and sounds the human ear cannot hear. A song on a typical music CD takes up approximately 32 MB. The same song in MP3 format takes only 3 MB.

MP3 works like this: A CD has a sample rate of 44,100 times per second. Each sample is two bytes in size, and separate samples are taken for the left and right speakers. Thus, the sample rate in bits per second is $44,100 \times 8$ bits per byte $\times 2$ bytes $\times 2$ channels, which is 1,411,200 bits per second. This equals a sample rate of 176,400 bytes per second $\times 180$ seconds in an average song, or roughly 32 MB per song. MPEG3 compresses the sound file by a factor of 10 to 14 by applying a compression algorithm.

You can record, store, and play MP3 files on your computer. You can legally create MP3 music files from CDs that you own, or you can purchase files from Web sites such as **www.apple.com/itunes**, **www.zune.net**, and **www.mp3.com** (Figure 6B). Windows-based PCs come with the Windows Media Player already

FIGURE 6B You can use iTunes to copy, record, and play audio files and download them to a portable MP3 player.

	Name	Time	Artist	Album	Genre
1	Don't Worry, Be Happy	4:52	Bobby McFerrin	Best of Bobby McFerrin	Vocal
2	Jump	4:02	Van Halen	The Best of Van Hale...	Rock
3	Footloose	3:43	Kenny Loggins	Yesterday, Today, T...	Rock
4	Faith	3:13	George Michael	Ladies & Gentlemen -...	Pop
5	Fruitcakes	6:57	Jimmy Buffett	Tuesdays, Thursdays...	Pop
6	Southern Cross	5:07	Jimmy Buffett	Tuesdays, Thursdays...	Pop
7	Pencil Thin Mustache	3:16	Jimmy Buffett	Tuesdays, Thursdays...	Pop
8	Trying To Reason With Hurricane ...	4:53	Jimmy Buffett	Tuesdays, Thursdays...	Pop
9	Coconut Telegraph	3:13	Jimmy Buffett	Tuesdays, Thursdays...	Pop
10	Cheeseburger In Paradise	3:07	Jimmy Buffett	Tuesdays, Thursdays...	Pop
11	Come Monday	3:43	Jimmy Buffett	Tuesdays, Thursdays...	Pop
12	Son Of A Son Of A Sailor	3:26	Jimmy Buffett	Tuesdays, Thursdays...	Pop
13	Volcano	3:37	Jimmy Buffett	Tuesdays, Thursdays...	Pop
14	Brown Eyed Girl	5:40	Jimmy Buffett	Tuesdays, Thursdays...	Pop
15	Tin Cup Chalice	3:24	Jimmy Buffett	Tuesdays, Thursdays...	Pop
16	Fins	5:07	Jimmy Buffett	Tuesdays, Thursdays...	Pop
17	One Particular Harbour	6:11	Jimmy Buffett	Tuesdays, Thursdays...	Pop
18	Margaritaville (Lost Verse)	5:35	Jimmy Buffett	Tuesdays, Thursdays...	Pop
19	Love And Luck	5:02	Jimmy Buffett	Tuesdays, Thursdays...	Pop
20	"Highway Blues"	1:34	Marc Seales, compos...	Speakin' Out	Jazz

installed. Other systems may have a different default player or you may need to download one, such as Winamp (**www.winamp.com**), from the Internet. You can find a list of the various MP3 players that are available at **www.superwarehouse.com/**.

MP3 files also can be stored on portable players. Portable players come in many shapes and sizes (Figure 6C). When purchasing an MP3 player, make sure to consider the battery life and storage capacity of the device. ZDnet.com estimates that over 286 million MP3 players will have been purchased by 2010.

FIGURE 6D   A digital voice recorder is portable and has many uses.

FIGURE 6C   You can use a portable MP3 player to take your music with you.

MP3 players have several components: a data port that is used to upload files, memory, a processor, a display screen, playback controls, an audio port for output, an amplifier, and a power supply. When you select a file to listen to on your MP3 player, the device's processor pulls the file from storage and decompresses the MP3 encoding. The decompressed bytes are converted from digital to analog, amplified, and then sent to the audio port for your enjoyment. MP3 players plug into your computer by way of a USB or FireWire port. Most players have solid-state memory, but some use a microdrive (a tiny hard drive) to store files. MP3 players are usually very small, portable, and battery powered. They range in price from less than $100 to $399 for the Apple iPod Touch with 64 GB of storage designed especially for video viewing.

You can use a digital voice recorder (Figure 6D) to record voice and sound that can later be retrieved from the device or downloaded to your computer. The device captures sound through a built-in microphone and then stores it on a memory chip. Several companies make these devices. Two things to consider when purchasing a digital voice recorder are the amount of storage offered and the price. Some of the newer phones, including the Apple iPhone and HTC Droid, also have the capability of recording voice messages, which can be stored and/or shared as an e-mail.

Visual: E-Books, Digital Cameras, and Camcorders

E-books have the potential to provide a richness that is not possible in a printed book. An **e-book** is a book that has been digitized and distributed by means of a digital storage medium (such as flash memory or a CD disc). An **e-book reader** is a device that displays e-books. E-book readers may be devices that are built solely for reading e-books or they may be PDAs, handheld devices, or other computing devices that have a processor and display screen (Figure 6E). The newest e-book readers are available in a larger size, increasing

FIGURE 6E   E-book readers share the market with PDAs and other computing devices.

the ease of reading. Some even boast an auto-rotating screen with a text-to-speech mode.

There are many companies that have e-book readers. There is an e-reader designed for children called the V.Reader by VTech (**www.vtechkids.com**). Six of the most popular e-readers are Amazon.com's Kindle 2 and Kindle DX, Sony's Daily Edition, Barnes & Noble's Nook, Plastic Logic's Que proReader, and of course Apple's iPad (Figure 6F). It is estimated that 12-month sales of the iPad will reach 7 million units, based on sales since its release in April 2010. iphonelife.com describes the iPad as a sleek tablet that looks like a cross between an iPhone and the LCD case of the MacBook Air. It measures 7.5 × 9.6 inches and is only half an inch thick. It weighs a pound and a half, has a 9.7-inch multitouch screen with 1024 × 768 resolution, and WiFi and 3G network access. The iPad has the functionality of a large iPhone without the phone.

FIGURE 6F The versatile iPad has a touch screen for easy navigating.

Someday you may read an e-book that provides background music for each page or scenario. You may find hot links on the page that will take you to pictures that support the scene. Better yet, you may find a link to a video of the scene. All of this extra material can be easily stored on a flash memory card along with the text of the story. If you don't want to purchase an e-book reader, you can download software to use your smartphone as an e-book reader! We also see schools using e-books, especially at the elementary level, when students need to carry more books than their book bag or little arms can handle. Many colleges and universities use e-books to help students defray the cost of books for their students.

DIGITAL CAMERAS

It seems as though it was just yesterday that computer technology was so difficult to use that only computer scientists were able to use it. However, today's digital technology is so easy to use that you can even digitize your family photo album!

One of the hottest products on today's consumer market is the digital camera (Figure 6G). A **digital camera** uses digital technology to store and display images instead of recording them on film. When you take a photo with a digital camera, the shot is stored in the camera until it is transferred to a computer for long-term storage or printing.

FIGURE 6G Digital cameras are among today's hottest products.

Like traditional cameras, digital cameras have a lens, a shutter, and an optical viewfinder. What sets digital cameras apart from traditional cameras is their inner workings—specifically, how an image is saved. With digital cameras, the captured image's light falls on a **charge-coupled device (CCD)**, a photosensitive computer chip that transforms light patterns into pixels (individual dots). A CCD consists of a grid made up of light-sensitive elements. Each element converts the incoming light into a voltage that is proportional to the light's brightness. The digital camera's picture quality is determined by how many elements the CCD has. Each CCD element corresponds to one pixel, or dot, on a computer display or printout; the more elements, the sharper the picture.

A 1-megapixel digital camera has a CCD consisting of at least 1 million elements; such a camera can produce a reasonably sharp snapshot-size image. With at least 2 million elements, 2-megapixel cameras can take higher-resolution pictures; you can expect to get near-photographic-quality prints at sizes of up to 5 × 7 inches with such a camera. Three- and 4-megapixel cameras can produce images that can print at sizes of 8 × 10 inches or even 11 × 14 inches. Today's 5- to 18-megapixel cameras produce high-quality photographs that can be greatly enlarged without loss of quality.

Because digital cameras do not have film, any photos you take are stored in the camera until you transfer them to a computer for long-term storage or printing. Two popular methods of storing images in the camera are **CompactFlash** and **xD Picture Cards** (Figure 6H). Both use flash memory technologies to store anywhere from 64 MB to 32 GB of image data.

About 12 MB of flash memory is the equivalent of a standard 12-exposure film roll. However, most cameras enable you to select from a variety of resolutions, so the number of shots you get will vary depending on the resolution you choose. If you need more "film," you need only carry more flash memory cards. Digital cameras enable you to preview the shots you've taken on a small LCD screen, so you can create more room on the flash memory cards by erasing pictures that you don't like.

FIGURE 6I A photo printer allows you to print your pictures at your convenience in a variety of sizes directly from your camera.

FIGURE 6H Various types of flash memory card are available in capacities of 16 MB up to 32 GB.

In most cases, you'll need to download the image data to a computer for safekeeping and printing. Most cameras are designed to connect to a computer by means of a serial or USB cable. Others can transfer data into your computer by means of an infrared port. If you're using a digital camera that stores images on flash memory cards, you can obtain a PC card that contains a flash memory card reader. This type of PC card enables the computer to read the images from the flash memory card as if it were a disk drive. Also available are stand-alone flash memory readers, which serve the same purpose. Once you've transferred the images to the computer for safekeeping and printing, you can erase the flash memory card and reuse it, just as if you had purchased a fresh roll of film.

Once the images are transferred to the computer, you can use a **photo-editing program** to enhance, edit, crop, or resize the images. Photo-editing programs also can be used to print the images to a color printer. Some specially designed printers called **photo printers** have flash memory card readers that enable you to bypass the computer completely (Figure 6I).

How good are digital cameras? With the exception of a few expensive high-end digital cameras, most digital cameras are the equivalent of the point-and-shoot 35-mm cameras that have dominated the traditional (film-based) camera market. They take pictures that are good enough for family photo albums, Web publishing, and business use (such as a real estate agent's snapshots of homes for sale); however, they are not good enough for professional photography. Some professional photographers are moving to the high-end digital cameras and are pleased with the results: flexibility, ease of use, easy-to-view photos, and cost savings.

A color printer or a photo printer can make prints from digital camera images that closely resemble the snapshots you used to get from the drugstore, but only if you choose the highest print resolution and use glossy photo paper. Getting good printout results takes time—most consumer-oriented printers will require several minutes to print an image at the printer's highest possible resolution—and can be costly when you consider the printer, ink, and special photo paper.

However, printing is only one of the distribution options that are open to you when you use a digital camera—and that's exactly why so many people love digital photography. In addition to printing snapshots for the family album, you can copy the images onto CDs or DVDs, send them to friends and family via e-mail, and even display them on the Internet using Facebook or one of the many online photo sites such as Snapfish (**www.snapfish.com**).

Point-and-shoot digital cameras are designed so that anyone can take good pictures (Figure 6J). Their features typically include automatic focus, automatic exposure, built-in automatic electronic flash with red-eye reduction, and optical zoom lenses with digital enhancement. Point-and-shoot cameras come with a built-in LCD viewfinder, so you can preview the shot to make sure it comes out right.

Single-lens reflex (SLR) digital cameras are much more expensive than point-and-shoot cameras,

FIGURE 6J Point-and-shoot cameras are designed for portability and for grabbing quick shots.

but they offer the features that professional photographers demand, such as interchangeable lenses, through-the-lens image previewing, and the ability to override the automatic focus and exposure settings (Figure 6K).

FIGURE 6K Leading camera makers feature SLR digital cameras with 15 or more megapixels.

For reviews, comparisons, and price information for digital cameras, see the Digital Camera Buyer's Guide: **www.digitalcamerareview.com/**.

DIGITAL CAMCORDERS

Just as digital cameras are revolutionizing still photography, there are indications that digital video cameras are poised to do the same for full-motion images—animations, videos, and movies.

In the past, most full-motion images were captured and stored by means of analog techniques. A video-capture board (also called a video-capture card) is a device that inputs analog video into a computer and transforms the analog video into its digital counterpart. Because a digital video file for even a short video requires a great deal of storage space, most video-capture boards are equipped to perform on-the-fly data compression to reduce file size using one of several

codecs (compression/decompression standards), such as MPEG, Apple's QuickTime, or Microsoft's AVI. Three-dimensional games have driven computer video card manufacturers to new feats of technical innovation; today's 3D video cards offer sophisticated, ultra-fast graphics processing that only a few years ago would have required a supercomputer.

Video-capture boards enable computers to display and process full-motion video—a "movie" that gives the illusion of smooth, continuous action. Like actual movies, digitized video consists of a series of still photographs called **frames** that are flashed on the screen at a rapid rate. The frame-flashing speed—the **frame rate**—indicates how successfully a given video can create the illusion of smooth, unbroken movement. A rate of at least 24 frames per second (fps) is needed to produce an illusion of smooth, continuous action. What can you "capture" with a video-capture board? You can use just about any video source, including TV broadcasts, taped video, or live video from video cameras.

With the advent of the popular Internet site YouTube, **digital video cameras** (also known as **camcorders**) have become even more popular. A digital video camera (Figure 6L) uses digital rather than analog technologies to store recorded video images. Like digital cameras, digital video cameras can connect to a computer, often by means of a USB port. Because the signal produced by a digital video camera conforms to the computer's digital method of representing data, a video-capture board is not necessary. Most digital video cameras can take still images as well as movies. Like most technologies over the years, digital video cameras have increased capabilities at a reduced price. Today, many smartphones and cell phones can take digital pictures and videos. Some mobile devices have 8 megapixel cameras and can use 32 GB memory cards.

FIGURE 6L Small, but powerful, pocket-sized camcorders provide portability, allowing you to capture HD video anytime, anywhere.

Communication and Entertainment Devices

Multimedia devices continue to transform ordinary devices and expand their capabilities. A phone is no longer just a device used to speak with another person. Many are sophisticated, wireless devices that enable you to surf the Web, send text messages, take photos, and listen to music—and you can still call your friends too!

The most notable of these is the new Apple iPhone 4. The 4 stands for the fourth generation of mobile technology, which provides enhanced capability allowing the transfer of both voice and nonvoice data, including full-motion video, high-speed Internet access, and videoconferencing.

The original iPhone was first sold in July 2007, and later that year it was named *Time* magazine's invention of the year. The iPhone 4 combines four products in one—a phone with voice control, a widescreen iPod, a camera, and an Internet device with HTML e-mail and Web browser capability. It is a small device (4.5 × 2.31 × 0.37 inches, and weighing only 4.8 ounces) yet has a 3.5-inch display screen with a screen resolution of 960 × 640 pixels. To function as a phone, it requires a broadband connection with AT&T. Additionally, it has 802.11 b/g/n and Bluetooth 2.1 wireless compatibilities. As with an iPod player, you can scroll through songs, artists, albums, and playlists; browse the music library by album artwork; and view song lyrics that have been added to the library in iTunes. The video feature enables you to watch TV shows and movies from the iTunes Store. When you connect your iPhone to your computer, you can use iTunes to synchronize the audio and video files from your computer's iTunes library to your iPhone. The iPhone 4 has a 5-megapixel autofocus camera with flash and a battery that will support up to 7 hours on the 3G network. It also has a Micro SIM rather than a Standard SIM. And Apple continues to make improvements. The iPhone 5 is expected to be released in Spring 2011.

There are several contenders to the iPhone's popularity; these include the Palm Pre, introduced on June 6, 2009, and the first to use the new Linux-based Palm operating system. This multimedia smartphone, designed and marketed by Palm, Inc., has a touch screen with an enhanced keyboard. The touch screen enables it to function as a camera phone, a portable media player, a GPS navigator, and an Internet client. It also allows the user to text message, e-mail, browse the Web, and connect to local WiFi hot spots. Having just won recognition as CNET's Best in Show, the Pre appears to be a viable competitor as of the iPhone. There are many smartphones (Figure 6M) on the market. Other contenders to the iPhone as of the summer of 2010 are the Droid, EVO 4G, and Samsung Galaxy X. The IntoMobile website (**www.intomobile.com**) lists the specs, as well as the good and bad qualities of each.

The Samsung Intercept is another smartphone. It works with fast 3G cellular networks, but it does not support WiFi. It contains GPS technology and is controlled by a multitouch interface. The Intercept is a phone, an audio and video player, and an Internet device with e-mail capability and a Web browser. It is a small device (4.4 × 2.2 × 0.6 inches, and weighing only 4.9 ounces) yet has a 3.0-inch display screen with a screen resolution of 400 × 240 pixels. To function as a phone, it requires a broadband connection with Sprint. You can get streaming media from more than 30 channels—music, videos, sporting news—streamed to your phone. The Intercept is Sprint TV enabled, which allows you to watch live TV and video-on-demand with full-motion video and sound. As with Apple's iTunes store, you can use Sprint's Music Store to download stereo-quality tracks to your wireless phone or PC. One of the newest smartphones on the market is the Droid from Motorola. It has a 3.7-inch touch-screen LCD. The slider measures 4.58 × 2.38 × 0.54 inches and weighs 6 ounces. It has an 854 × 480 resolution and uses the Android operating system. Some additional features of

FIGURE 6M A smartphone is a phone designed to make your life easier with enhanced, new capabilities featuring touch screens.

> " A **phone** is **no longer** just a device **used to speak** with **another person**. Many are **sophisticated, wireless devices** that **enable** you to surf the Web, **send text messages, take photos**, and listen to music—and **you** can **still call** your friends too! "

the Droid include the 1Ghz Snapdragon CPU, an 8-megapixel camera with dual-LED flash, 512 MB RAM, 1 GB ROM, 3G and 4G data connectivity, WiFi (b/g), GPS, microSD, an HDMI-out port, a 3.5-mm headphone jack, a front-facing camera for video calls, and a mobile hot spot feature.

DIGITAL VIDEO RECORDERS

Digital video recorders (DVRs) are similar to VCRs, but instead of using tape to store video, they use a hard disk. Hard disk storage is digital, thus the user can quickly move through video data, fast-forwarding through commercials. You can use a DVR just like a VCR or you can subscribe to a DVR-management service. One service provider, TiVo, can record up to 180 hours of your favorite shows automatically to a DVR every time they're on (Figure 6N). This way, all of your entertainment is ready for you to watch whenever you are. Just buy a DVR, activate the TiVo service, and you can enjoy television viewing your way. TiVo's competitors include UltimateTV, DirecTV, Dish Network, Arris Moxi, AT&T U-Verse, and others. Most cable and satellite companies will lease you a DVR.

FIGURE 6N You can use a DVR and a service such as TiVo to capture your favorite shows and watch them at your convenience.

COMPUTER GAMING DEVICES

Computer game consoles such as Sony's PlayStation 3 (PS3), Nintendo's Wii, and Microsoft's Xbox 360 are popular multimedia devices. You can use these devices to load and play interactive games, using a television or computer screen as the display device. You also can go online and play games against a diverse population of players. Gaming accessories are available, such as game consoles, specialized backpacks, wireless support, and cable accessory packs.

Game consoles are similar to computers. A game console has a processor, a graphics driver, an audio driver, memory, and an operating system. It reads input from a storage device, such as a CD or memory card, processes that input into sounds and animation, and then stores user input for further processing as the game progresses.

Gamers can use portable handheld game consoles such as Nintendo's DS/DSi/DSi XL to take their games with them. When Nintendo entered the home market with the introduction of the Nintendo Wii, it captivated its audience. This popular gaming device features many games for the entire family that are activity based. The Wii Fit is especially popular for the all members of the family as it combines yoga, balance, strength training, and aerobics (Figure 6O).

FIGURE 6O The Nintendo Wii brings a new level of interactivity to computer games.

According to *PC Magazine*, Microsoft was the first to enter the current console-gaming generation with its original Xbox 360, a hulk of a system that beat both Nintendo and Sony to the punch. The Xbox 360 gets more powerful every year; it is now slimmed down and souped up and has a 250-GB hard drive. Sony released the popular PlayStation Portable product line in fall 2009. Called PSP-Go, the device is touted as the smallest and mightiest of the handheld game systems. It features access to games, video, movies, and the Internet through the PlayStation Network. In 2010, Sony released its PlayStation 4 (PS4). This is in direct competition with the DSi series of handheld gaming consoles.

HEADSETS

Perhaps the ultimate multimedia device is the headset. A **headset** (also called a **head-mounted display**) is a wearable device that includes twin LCD panels. When used with special applications that generate stereo output, headsets can create the illusion that an individual is walking through a 3D environment (Figure 6P).

Gaming enthusiasts can use the **Cave Automated Virtual Environment (CAVE)** to dispense with the headsets in favor of 3D glasses. In the CAVE, the walls, ceiling, and

FIGURE 6P Headsets are essential to many computer gaming experiences.

floor display projected 3D images. More than 50 CAVEs exist. Researchers use CAVEs to study topics as diverse as the human heart and the next generation of sports cars. The CAVE is a $10 \times 10 \times 9$ foot theater made up of three rear projection screens for walls and a down projection screen for the floor.

Smart Home

Homeowners continue to embrace technology with small, clever, interesting digital devices that help the performance of the home in general while making it more eco-friendly. During spring 2009, the Museum of Science and Industry in Chicago opened an exhibit that features a smart home that is both green and wired (Figure 6Q). The exhibit portrays an environmentally responsible, modular home full of technology. Of course, the home's climate, lighting, and entertainment are controlled by touch-screen panels throughout the home. Some other interesting features are that the lights, television, and music turn off when no one is in the room; the home greets the owners when they arrive home, telling them what's been going on with the house while they were gone; the baby's room can be broadcast via cribcast on video screens in the master bedroom and on the first floor; and the home has a hibernation mode that lowers shades and turns down heat/air when residents are leaving for a day or longer—and adjustments can be made remotely via a cell phone. Many of these features may be incorporated into homes in the future.

FIGURE 6Q   Interest in smart home technologies has increased, as evidenced by the latest Museum of Science and Industry exhibit.

Although many of the items mentioned are representative of features coming in the future, there are many smart features already in our homes today. The digital photo frame is one example. It displays JPEG pictures as a slide show from a screen often measuring from 7 to 15 inches in size. Newer varieties also may display

MPEG video files and play MP3 audio files from the camera's memory card or a USB drive (Figure 6R).

FIGURE 6R   A digital photo picture frame that also projects video and audio can be used to display family pictures.

Another home digital device is the Slingbox produced by Sling Media of San Mateo, California (Figure 6S). This device is for TV streaming, allowing users to view their home's cable or satellite TV remotely from an Internet-enabled computer with a broadband Internet connection, which could be a cell phone, your iPhone, or a Droid. Hulu (**www.hulu.com**) is a Web site and app that offers streaming video of TV shows and movies. Not only can you watch these shows on your computer, you can also watch them on most smartphones.

Technology has even advanced to help pet owners know what Fido is doing while they are gone. Dogs or cats wear a specially designed digital pet camera around their necks (Figure 6T). The owner may set the camera to take pictures at various intervals, from 1 to

FIGURE 6S   A Slingbox will allow you to view video from your home cable system while you are away from home, using a remote connection, which could be supplied by your cell phone if it has broadband Internet access.

FIGURE 6T Pets wear this device around their neck so that worried owners can view what they are doing throughout the day.

15 minutes. The photos can be uploaded to a computer via a USB cable for viewing.

Homeowners continue to be more aware of conserving energy in their homes. Almost every computer sold today comes with some type of a power management utility. Ideally, computers should have the designation of ENERGY STAR (Figure 6U). This rating means the computer meets the federal standards for energy consumption as determined by the EPA (Environmental Protection Agency) and the U.S. Department of Energy. ENERGY STAR notebooks utilize about 15 watts of electricity compared to a desktop, which uses from 200–400 watts. Solar-powered computers and/or battery packs are beginning to arrive in our markets. Ideally, however, we want to move to zero waste with eco-friendly, biodegradable digital components.

FIGURE 6U Computers with the designated ENERGY STAR label indicate that the computer is built to be energy efficient.

Key Terms and Concepts

Multiple Choice

1. Multisensory stimulators are known as _____.
   a. multiaccess
   b. multimedia
   c. multitasking
   d. multidata

2. Which of the following devices will *not* store music?
   a. CD
   b. MP3 player
   c. Smartphone
   d. DVC

3. Apple's Web site for downloading music and movies is called _____.
   a. iPad
   b. iPod
   c. iTouch
   d. iTunes

4. Which device will not display an e-book?
   a. E-book reader
   b. Smartphone
   c. Computer
   d. Camcorder

5. The Web site that enables you to download movies is named _____.
   a. Hala
   b. Halo
   c. Hulu
   d. Hola

6. Smart home technology allows your home to _____.
   a. help you do your homework
   b. monitor your lights and power consumption
   c. use the most power for tasks
   d. have parties without your parents finding out

7. A Slingbox is a device that permits you to _____.
   a. stream TV shows
   b. shoot an object into the air
   c. safeguard your arm after you hurt it
   d. upload your homework

8. An Energy Star rating means _____.
   a. the computer meets the federal standards for energy consumption
   b. the computer can be used in outer space
   c. the computer uses a lot of energy
   d. the computer meets the standards to receive a star rating

9. Game consoles are similar to computers. Which of the following is not a game console?
   a. Wii
   b. PS4
   c. DSi XL
   d. PS7

10. Digitized video consists of a series of still photographs called _____.
    a. codecs
    b. frames
    c. frame rate
    d. pixels

Spotlight Exercises

1. You want to buy an MP3 player for your music collection. Research which device would be best for you. Compare four different devices. Make sure you include at least one Apple device and one smartphone. Write a one- to two-page, double-spaced paper describing the devices, which one you would choose, and why you chose that one.

2. Visit the Museum of Science and Industry at **www.msichicago.org/whats-here/exhibits/smart-home/** Investigate the smart home and its many features. Write a short paper describing five features that, in your opinion, have merit and will be incorporated into our homes within the next few years. Also, select three features of the home that may not be embraced by the home consumer. Describe them and explain why you don't feel they will be popular.

3. Use your favorite search engine and the World Wide Web to research digital cameras. How many pixels will suffice for your picture-taking needs? What is the price range for such cameras? What is the difference between optical zoom and digital zoom? How much optical zoom would be acceptable for your personal use? What is the storage medium of your chosen camera? How many pictures can you store on a 16-MB disk? How much storage capacity will you buy? What will it cost? Write a brief paper describing what you've learned.

4. Video recording has become even more popular recently due to the advent of YouTube. Many people use small, inexpensive video recorders to record and then upload their files to YouTube or another site. However, there are other reasons people want video recorders, for example, family events, business presentations, and so on. Investigate the types of digital video recorders that are available today. Choose three different recorders at three different price points. Write a short paper describing each, including the manufacturer, price, functionality, warranty, peripheral items needed, and intended audience for each.

5. Did you miss your favorite TV show because you were in class? Do you want to watch that game again? Write a one-page paper on the advantages and disadvantages of Hulu (**www.hulu.com**). Include some information on some of the classic movies and TV shows that are available to watch.

6. Create a comparison chart of the different types of e-book readers. Include a conclusion on which one you would purchase if you were to buy one or why you would not purchase an e-reader. Don't forget to include size, resolution, weight, price, and other such comparisons.

chapter

9

Privacy, Crime, and Security

Chapter Objectives

1 Understand how technological developments are eroding privacy and anonymity. (p. 402)

2 List the types of computer crime and cybercrime. (p. 413)

3 List the types of computer criminals. (p. 423)

4 Understand computer system security risks. (p. 427)

5 Describe how to protect your computer system and yourself. (p. 431)

6 Define encryption and explain how it makes online information secure. (p. 433)

7 Describe the issues the government faces when balancing the need to access encrypted data and the public's right to privacy. (p. 434)

8 Distinguish between electronic discovery and computer forensics. (p. 436)

Today, *deter*, *detect*, and *defend* are the three words associated with protecting your privacy, preventing computer related crimes, and avoiding security breaches. The first of these three, *deter*, is something all individuals can focus on and take responsibility for. How often do you change your passwords for your school login and bank account? Is your password a "strong" password? Have you altered your privacy settings and profiles on your social network site to limit what viewers can see? When you surf at public hot spots, are you aware of potential shoulder surfers? What could you do to reduce the need for detect and defend strategies?

The extensive and public nature of the Internet raises privacy issues as greater numbers of corporations and private citizens increasingly rely on the Internet as a business medium. With the recent arrival of cloud computing and its use of remote servers to hold information and data for many users, the concern for security and privacy has increased. Just as brick-and-mortar businesses in your neighborhood lock their doors at night to protect merchandise and equipment, electronic businesses employ a variety of security measures to protect their interests and your privacy from cybercriminals. In this chapter, you will explore how online connectivity can threaten your privacy, personal safety, and computer system, and you will learn how to protect yourself from online threats. Topics covered include:

- The collection of information without consent
- Ubiquitous computing and how the use of multiple devices through an omnipresent network affects security issues
- Differentiating between computer crime and cybercrime
- Some of the causes of security risks and how to protect your personal and business data
- The use of encryption to protect transmitted data
- The collection of evidence and its use to prosecute cybercriminals ■

www.facebook.com

399

Privacy in Cyberspace

Of all the social and ethical issues raised by the use of widely available Internet linked computers, threats to privacy and anonymity are among the most contentious. Government-sponsored sites, like the Identity Theft site hosted by the Federal Trade Commission (Figure 9.1) and private sites, like the Privacy Rights Clearinghouse, a nonprofit consumer information and advocacy organization (Figure 9.2), are emerging to offer practical consumer advice, display privacy alerts, and cover hot privacy issues.

Defined by U.S. Supreme Court Justice Louis Brandeis in 1928 as "the right to be left alone," **privacy** refers to an individual's ability to restrict or eliminate the collection, use, and sale of confidential personal information. Some people say that privacy isn't a concern unless you have something to hide. However, this view ignores the fact that privacy means something different to every individual, government, and corporation, and it is not just the collecting of private information that is cause for concern, but the use of this information in ways that may harm people unnecessarily. With the distinction between what is private and what is public becoming more and more blurred, some privacy advocates, like the Electronic Frontier Foundation (EFF), have developed a "Bill of Rights for Social Network Users." The principles in this bill can be applied to any individual that posts information on a server owned by someone else. The rights that the EFF proposes include the following:

- *The right to informed decision making*—Web sites should provide a clear interface that allows users to make choices about who sees their data and how it is used.
- *The right to control*—The user maintains control over the use and disclosure of his or her data. Any changes to the original agreement must be, by default, "opt-in" acceptance, as opposed to "opt-out." That distinction means that a user's data cannot be shared unless a user makes an informed decision to share it.

FIGURE 9.1 This Identity Theft site provides a link to file a complaint with the FTC and an online quiz to test your knowledge about identity theft.

FIGURE 9.2 The Privacy Rights Clearinghouse (**www.privacyrights.org/index.htm**) acts as a source of information on privacy issues to consumers, the media, and policymakers.

- *The right to leave*—The user should have the right to delete, not disable, all data or the entire account from the database. Additionally there should be data portability, that is the right of the user to transfer his/her data to another site in a usable format.

With the early 2010 security breaches in Facebook and Google Buzz, the compromise of users' data has become more public, resulting in congressional support for more security features and guarantees of privacy for users.

The Problem: Collection of Information Without Consent

Many people are willing to divulge information when asked for their consent and when they see a need for doing so. When you apply for a loan, for example, the bank can reasonably ask you to list your other creditors to determine whether you'll be able to repay your loan.

Much information is collected from public agencies, many of which are under a legal obligation to make their records available to the public upon request (public institutions of higher education, departments of motor vehicles, county clerks, tax assessors, and so on). This information finds its way into computerized databases—thousands of them—that track virtually every conceivable type of information about individuals. You are probably aware of credit reporting databases that track your credit history (Figure 9.3). Other databases include information such as your current and former addresses and employers, other names you've used (like your previous name, if you're married and use a different name now), current and former spouses, bankruptcies, lawsuits, property ownership, driver's license information, criminal records, purchasing habits, and medical prescriptions.

Most of the companies that maintain databases today claim that they sell information only to bona fide customers such as lending institutions, prospective employers, marketing firms, and licensed private

investigators. They maintain that their databases don't pose a threat to the privacy of individuals because they are highly ethical firms, have security measures in place, and would not release this information to the general public. However, no matter how secure data appears, there are always people seeking to violate that security. On January 17, 2007, TJX, a $16 billion retail conglomerate that operates 2,500 stores around the world, including T.J. Maxx, Marshall's, Home Goods, Bob's Stores, A.J. Wright, Winners, and Homesense stores, reported a security breach in its customer transaction database system. The system that was

FIGURE 9.3 Credit reporting agencies, such as Equifax, Experian, and TransUnion, collect and store data about your credit history. Everyone is entitled to one free report annually.

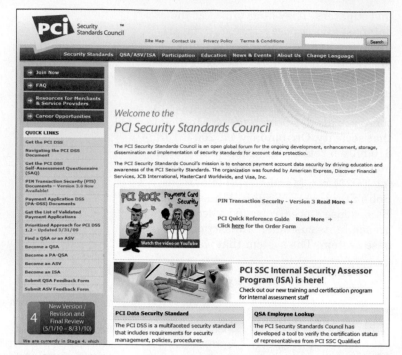

FIGURE 9.4 PCI was founded by several financial organizations, including American Express, MasterCard Worldwide, Discover Financial Services, JCB International, and Visa Inc., to develop methods to secure account data.

decode account numbers and create counterfeit credit and debit cards.

- Some of the credit card information went back to 2003, which indicated that TJX had been out of compliance with PCI standards for years. PCI (**www.pcisecuritystandards.org/index.shtml**) is a global forum for the ongoing development and implementation of security standards for account data protection (Figure 9.4).
- TJX had difficulty determining what data had been compromised and when.

With security measures in place and encryption used to guarantee privacy, the TJX case seems to indicate that no system is truly secure from modern cyberthieves.

According to privacy activists, the problem occurs after the information is compromised or sold. Before the TJX breach was even discovered, the thieves were able to steal $8 million in merchandise from Wal-Mart stores in Florida with counterfeit credit cards. The Internet has made it much easier and much cheaper for ordinary individuals to gain access to sensitive personal information, and at the same time made it easier and cheaper to distribute compromised data faster. A simple Web search for "Social Security numbers" results in a wide array of Web sites run by private investigators who offer to find someone's Social Security number for a small fee. A Google search can provide much useful information, but the personal information it can uncover can easily be misused (Figure 9.5).

compromised handled customer credit card, debit card, check, and merchandise return transactions. More than 45 million credit and debit card numbers were stolen from TJX systems over an 18-month period. It's considered to be the largest customer data breach on record. Here are some of the underlying issues with this case:

- The intruders had possession of the company's encryption key and could

Technology and Anonymity

Marketing firms, snoops, and government officials can use computers and the Internet to collect information in ways that are hidden from users. The same technology also makes it increasingly difficult for citizens to engage in anonymous speech. **Anonymity** refers to the ability to convey a message without disclosing your name or identity.

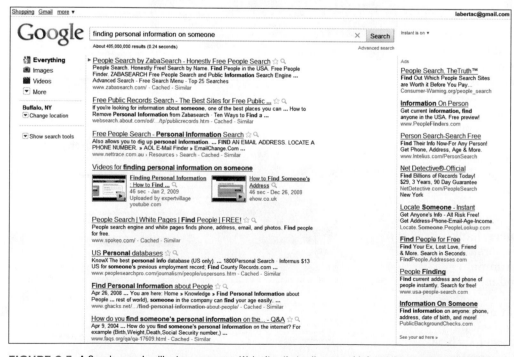

FIGURE 9.5 A Google search will return numerous Web sites that sell personal information to anyone they please. In the United States, you have little legal recourse against those who collect and sell sensitive personal information.

The security breach at TJX reached much further than just that corporation and its related stores. It had a severe financial effect on certain related agencies, like credit providers, that issued the credit cards that were compromised. These agencies had to reissue new cards and pay the fraudulent charges when they were not responsible. Some serious ethical questions surfaced from the TJX security breach. Should the agency issuing the credit card have sole responsibility for the fraudulent charges? Was it ethical for TJX to gather and keep so much information on their customers? Did TJX show due diligence in protecting customer information? Should more regulations on the storage of personal and financial information be imposed?

Anonymity is both a curse and a blessing. On one hand, it can be seen as an abuse because it frees people from accountability. On the other hand, as supported by the U.S. Supreme Court—it must be preserved in a democracy, to ensure that citizens have access to the full range of possible ideas to make decisions for themselves. Freeing authors from accountability for anonymous works, the Court argued, raises the potential that false or misleading ideas will be brought before the public, but this risk is necessary to maintain a free society.

Anonymity with respect to Internet use is necessary to protect whistleblowers. However, the right to anonymity is being challenged on an individual case basis. Recently, the Honorable Mr. Justice Eady ruled that bloggers have no right to privacy in what is essentially the public act of publishing. Eady, a high court judge in England and Wales, overturned an injunction that had prevented *The Times* from revealing the identity of Richard Norton, the detective behind the controversial NightJack blog. Additionally, a few years earlier, a judge handed a Florida sheriff a victory in his mission to suppress what he says were inflammatory postings to an Internet message board used by law enforcement. Examples of technologies that threaten online anonymity include cookies, global unique identifiers, ubiquitous computing, and radio frequency identification.

Cookies Generally downloaded into folders that hold temporary Internet files, **cookies** are small text files that are written to your computer's hard disk by many of the Web sites you visit (Figure 9.6). Cookies can be located easily by searching for the word *cookie* from the start menu. Each cookie contains a unique ID, which is assigned by the Web site on the first visit, for each user. On return visits to that Web site, the ID is used to record the visit in the Web site's database. Several cookie-related terms that a user should be familiar with are listed here:

- Temporary cookies or sessions are cookies removed from your system after you close Internet Explorer.

FIGURE 9.6 Cookies can be helpful to a user by remembering login information and passwords; but, they can also act as an informant, providing the parent site with information on the habits and purchasing tendencies of the user without the user's permission.

Cookies are text files stored in the Temporary Internet Files folder.

This text file is an example of the cookie left behind from a visit to Monster.com.

They are used to hold nonpermanent information like the contents of a shopping cart.

- Persistent cookies remain on your system after Internet Explorer is closed and hold reusable information like your login and password.
- First-party cookies come from the site you are visiting and can be temporary or persistent.
- Third-party cookies come from another Web sites' advertisements (such as pop-up or banner ads) on the Web site that you're viewing and might track your Web use for marketing purposes.

Often perceived as malicious, cookies are actually used for many useful and legitimate tasks.

- Cookies enable the Web site to obtain an actual count on the number of new and return visitors.
- They can store site preferences set by the user. When the user returns to the site, the preferences are automatically applied.
- Online retail sites use cookies to implement "shopping carts," which enable you to make selections that will stay in your cart so that you can return to the online store for more browsing and shopping.

"What troubles **piracy** advocates is the use of tracking **cookies** to gather data on Web **users'** browsing and shopping habits— **without** their consent."

Cookies, located on your hard disk, actually contain very little information. When you are on the Web site, the items you buy or the pages you are viewing are stored in the database associated with the Web page. Some users point to several problems with cookies, including these:

- Only one cookie from a Web site can be placed on a system's hard drive. When multiple users share the same computer, individual preferences for each user cannot be stored.
- Cookies can be deleted. If the cookie was holding your login ID and password, you might not remember them to log in again.
- If you use several computers, each computer will receive a new cookie

from the Web site with a different ID. As a result, the Web site will count you as a different user.

What troubles privacy advocates is the use of tracking cookies to gather data on Web users' browsing and shopping habits— without their consent. Several Internet ad networks, such as DoubleClick, use cookies to track users' browsing actions across thousands of the most popular Internet sites. When you visit a Web site that has contracted with one of these ad networks, a cookie containing a unique identification number is deposited on your computer's hard drive. This cookie tracks your browsing habits and preferences as you move among the hundreds of sites that contract with the ad network. When you visit another site, the cookie is detected, read, and matched with a profile of your previous browsing activity. On this basis, the ad network selects and displays a **banner ad** targeted to match the topic or type of products you were browsing through. A banner ad is not actually part of the Web page. Instead, it is an ad supplied separately by an ad network. The banner ad may appear at the top, side, or bottom of the page.

In response to concerns that their tracking violates Internet users' privacy, ad network companies claim that they do not link the collected information with users' names and addresses. However, current technology would enable these firms to do so—and privacy advocates fear that some of them already have. Internet ad networks such as DoubleClick can collect the following:

- Your e-mail address
- Your full name
- Your mailing address (street, city, state, and zip code)
- Your phone number
- Transactional data (names of products purchased online, details of plane ticket reservations, and search phrases used with search engines)

Internet marketing firms explain that by collecting such information, they can provide a "richer" marketing experience, one that's more closely tailored to an individual's interests. Privacy advocates reply that once collected, this information could become valuable to others. These kinds of debates ensure that cookies and the information they collect will remain on the forefront of the privacy controversy for years to come.

As a user, do you have any control over cookies? Current browsers have a setting that prevents any cookie from being placed on your hard drive. On the surface, this sounds appealing; but many Web sites will not let you browse if the cookie option is not enabled. You can also accept the cookie but set an option in your browser so that the browser informs you every time a site sends values into the cookie on your hard drive. This option allows you to accept or deny the values. The means by which you set these options differs from one browser to another. Use the help feature in your browser to locate these settings. If you are still confused about how cookies work, refer to Figure 9.7 or go to **http://computer.howstuffworks .com/cookie.htm**.

Globally Unique Identifiers

A **globally unique identifier (GUID)** is an identification number that is generated by a hardware component or a program. Privacy advocates discovered GUIDs in several popular computer components and programs, such as Intel's Pentium III chip and Microsoft's Word 97 and Excel 97. The GUIDs can be read by Web servers or embedded in various documents, identifying the computer and inadvertently making it more difficult to use the Internet anonymously. Although the use of GUIDs does not seem to be as prevalent as it was earlier this decade, a similar concept has been discovered in color laser printers. The Electronic Frontier Foundation (**www.eff.org**), a civil liberties group that defends your rights in the digital world, has reported that many color laser printers embed printer tracking dots—nearly invisible yellow dots—on every page that is printed, at the urging of the U.S. government. These dots can identify the serial number and manufacturing code of the printer, as well as the time and date the document was printed. Officially, the tracking dots are designed to track counterfeiters, but privacy advocates are concerned because there is no law to prevent this information from being used by U.S. government agencies, foreign governments, or individuals to identify materials printed and distributed by private citizens.

Companies that introduce GUIDs into their products generally conceal this information from the public. When forced to admit to using GUIDs, the firms typically remove the GUID-implanting code or enable users to opt out of their data collection systems. Advocates of online anonymity insist that these companies are missing the basic point: Users, not corporations, should determine when and how personal information is divulged to third parties.

Ubiquitous Computing

The term **ubiquitous computing** was coined by Mark Weiser in 1988, during his tenure as Chief Technologist of the Xerox Palo Alto Research Center (PARC). It refers to a trend in which individuals no longer interact with one computer at a time but instead with multiple devices connected through an omnipresent network, enabling technology to become virtually embedded and invisible in our lives. The concept is to make technology implicit, built into the things we use. The proponents of this technology hold that this type of computing will be a more natural tool and envision a system where billions of miniature, ubiquitous intercommunication devices will be spread worldwide. An example of the use of ubiquitous computing would be the automatic adjustment of an environmental

FIGURE 9.7 How a Cookie Works

2. The browser checks the local hard drive for a cookie from that URL.

3. If no cookie is located, the Web site assigns a unique ID number, records that number in its database, sends that ID back, and the browser creates the cookie.

1. Enter a URL into the address bar of a browser.

http://www.monster.com

4. If a cookie is located, the information within the cookie is sent to the Web site and the visit is recorded in the site's database.

Monster.com server and database.

setting, like heat or light, in your office or home based on the signals sent to these environmental devices by monitors built into the clothing of individuals in the setting.

Imagine your movements being tracked by an **active badge**, a small device worn by an individual that transmits a unique infrared signal every 5 to 10 seconds. Networked sensors detect these transmissions and the location of the badge and, hence, the location of its wearer, allowing e-mail, phone calls, or messages to be forwarded to wherever you are. Also imagine "electronic trails" left by you or others as they pass through the neighborhood, office, or conference. You already accept the idea of receiving e-mail anywhere; after all, that is already a feature of portable communication devices, the early ubiquitous computing tools. However, the concept of electronic trails probably made you a little uncomfortable. Proponents of ubiquitous computing say that a user can dissent and not wear a badge. Some experts argue that not being tracked, or not wearing a badge, should be the default. How do you feel about being tracked, having your movements monitored and recorded as you move about your daily routine?

Today, the closest devices to ubiquitous computing tools are digital music players, smartphones, and PCs that act as a media center for your entire home. These devices transmit data about us; they also search for data via Internet connections. Privacy can be compromised when smaller devices are lost or stolen. Most devices maintain some form of log, such as a playlist, records of incoming or outgoing calls, or a list of recently viewed media, which can be retrieved and exploited.

As users become accustomed to using such technology, privacy advocates are concerned that society has become more willing to tolerate lower levels of privacy in favor of convenience. A recent study by Pew Internet and American Life Project has found that young adults are more likely to take control of their digital identities than their older counterparts. This includes the changing of privacy settings and passwords, restricting access to their data, and removing their names from tagged photographs. However the

FIGURE 9.8 RFID tags are often used as antitheft devices or to track merchandise.

study also found that users across all age levels were paying more attention to privacy-protecting activities than they did in a similar study in 2006.

Radio Frequency Identification The use of radio waves to track a chip or tag placed in or on an object is referred to as **radio frequency identification (RFID).** RFID tags (Figure 9.8) are often used, as an alternative to bar codes, for inventory control in the retail environment. RFID does not require direct contact or line-of-sight scanning. Instead, an antenna using radio frequency waves transmits a signal that activates the transponder, or tag. When activated, the tag transmits data back to the antenna. However, if the tag is not deactivated, the object's movements can continue to be tracked indefinitely. This technology is also used when microchips are inserted in pets and other livestock, and has even been used for people. The RFID chip can include contact information and health records for the individual or animal, or other personal details.

Privacy advocates have been concerned about the use of encrypted, passive RFID

Chip

Processor

RFID label

PASSPORT

Laminate

Person ID

SPECIMEN-ELECTRONIC PASSPORT
USA
Georgeluski
memo/name
oshana jude
address
16/10/2009
xxxxxxx

PASVKGULSKI<<MICHALHTOUIPEI>><<<<

Laminate

Antenna

FIGURE 9.9 The insertion of RFID tags into credit cards and passports has raised suspicion about the ethics of their tracking potential.

Protecting Your Privacy

How should governments protect the privacy of their citizens? Privacy advocates agree that the key lies in giving citizens the right to be informed when personal information is being collected as well as the right to refuse to provide this information. In the European Union (EU), a basic human rights declaration gives all citizens the following privacy rights:

- Consumers must be informed of exactly what information is being collected and how it will be used.

- Consumers must be allowed to choose whether they want to divulge the requested information and how collected information will be used.

- Consumers must be allowed to request that information about themselves be removed from marketing and other databases.

tags in U.S. passports for several years (Figure 9.9). The tag contains the same information included on the actual passport—name, nationality, gender, date of birth, and place of birth of the passport holder, as well as a digitized signature and photograph of that person. The government asserts that the RFID tag does not broadcast a signal and can only be read within close proximity of special scanning devices. However, a new passport card approved in 2008 as part of the Western Hemisphere Travel Initiative for travel to Mexico, Canada, Bermuda, and the Caribbean will use an unencrypted chip that can be read from up to 30 feet away, raising serious concerns that a passport holder's identity could easily be stolen or their location tracked without their consent or awareness.

About 100 million credit cards are now embedded with this technology, replacing the familiar magnetic strip. The new cards seem to make it so much easier that some folks are reading your credit cards before you even take them out of your wallet. These identity thieves use RFID readers to pick the data off your RFID chip as you walk by. Technology has made identity theft quite literally a stroll in the park. Where credit card skimming used to require the thief to have possession of your card, acquiring your personal data is now as easy as passing you on the street. Companies like Identity Stronghold (**www.idstronghold.com/**) offer a line of RFID blocking products like wallets and cell phone cases.

Now that you've read about some of the privacy threats posed by the Internet, let's discuss how you can protect your privacy.

Protecting the privacy rights of U.S. citizens has been a controversial area for years. Most of us agree that our rights should be protected, but our definition of acceptable levels of protection varies widely. Some of the legislation currently in place includes the Fair Credit Reporting Act, which provides limited privacy protection for credit information; the Health Insurance Portability and Privacy Act (HIPAA), which establishes standards for the transmission of electronic health care data and the security and privacy of this information; and the Family Educational Rights and Privacy Act (FERPA), which protects the privacy of student education records. However, there is no comprehensive federal law governing the overall privacy rights of U.S. citizens. Instead, privacy is protected by a patchwork of limited federal and state laws and regulations. Most of these laws regulate what government agencies can do. Except in limited areas covered by these laws, little exists to stop people and companies from acquiring and selling your personal information (Figure 9.10).

Marketing industry spokespeople and lobbyists argue that the U.S. government should not impose laws or regulations to

FIGURE 9.10 Summary of Major U.S. Laws Concerning Privacy Issues

Year	Legislation	Objective
2003	CAN-SPAM Act	Provides the tools to combat Internet spammers
2001	Children's Internet Protection Act (CIPA)	Addresses concerns about access to offensive content over the Internet on school and library computers
1996	Health Insurance Portability and Accountability Act (HIPAA)	Establishes standards for privacy and electronic transmission of health care data
1974	Family Education Rights and Privacy Act (FERPA)	Protects the privacy of student education records
1970	Fair Credit Reporting Act (FCRA)	Provides limited privacy protection for credit information.

protect consumers' privacy. They argue that the industry should regulate itself. Privacy advocates counter that technology has outpaced the industry's capability to regulate itself, as evidenced by the widespread availability of highly personal information on the Internet.

The Direct Marketing Association (DMA) claims to enforce a basic code of ethics among its member organizations. The organization takes steps to ensure that confidential information doesn't fall into the wrong hands and that consumers can opt out of marketing campaigns if they wish. For more information, visit the DMA Web site at **www. the-dma.org/ index.php**.

Be aware that many of the most aggressive Internet-based marketing firms have no ties to or previous experience with the DMA, and several opt-out systems on the Internet are already used for fraudulent purposes. For example, e-mail spammers typically claim that recipients can opt out of mass e-mail marketing campaigns. But recipients who respond

to such messages succeed only in validating their e-mail addresses, and the result is often a major increase in the volume of unsolicited e-mail. A report from the TRACElabs team at M86 Security for the week ending June 6, 2010, revealed that India and the United States (Figure 9.11) were the leaders in relaying **spam**, unsolicited messages sent in bulk over electronic mailing systems, and that messages touting pharmaceutical products accounted for 84.03 percent of all spam sent (Figure 9.12).

In the United States, the CAN-SPAM Act of 2003 provided the tools to combat spammers. The Federal Trade Commission (FTC) and the Department of Justice have primary jurisdiction over spammers, but other agencies, including states and ISPs, can also prosecute them. The legislation has been criticized because it prevents states from enacting tougher laws, prevents individuals from suing spammers, and does not require e-mailers to request permission before sending messages. Additionally, it may be ineffective against foreign spammers who are outside U.S. jurisdiction. Although many contend that the act is just a drop in the bucket, the monetary threat the CAN-SPAM Act poses can't hurt. In 2008, MySpace successfully sued the so-called "Spam King" Sanford Wallace and a business partner for violations of the CAN-SPAM Act. A federal judge awarded MySpace close to $230 million, although it is doubtful the money will ever be collected. At one time, a National Do Not

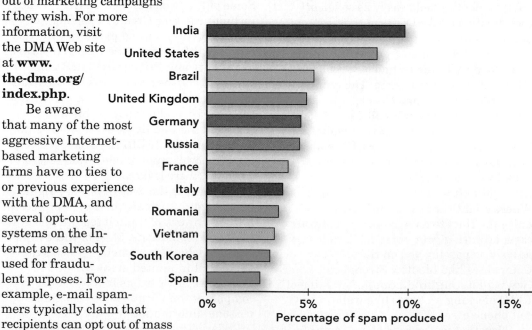

FIGURE 9.11 Over the past year, India and the United States have taken turns occupying the No. 1 position as the weekly leader in relaying spam.

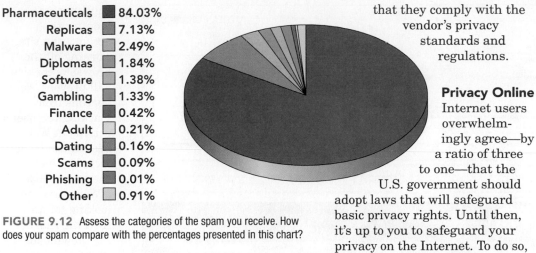

Pharmaceuticals	84.03%
Replicas	7.13%
Malware	2.49%
Diplomas	1.84%
Software	1.38%
Gambling	1.33%
Finance	0.42%
Adult	0.21%
Dating	0.16%
Scams	0.09%
Phishing	0.01%
Other	0.91%

FIGURE 9.12 Assess the categories of the spam you receive. How does your spam compare with the percentages presented in this chart?

Email Registry (similar to the National Do Not Call list to combat telemarketers) was considered but discarded because of the potential for misuse and the inability to provide effective enforcement. States are also enacting their own laws, within the parameters of the CAN-SPAM Act, and other types of legislation, such as the Anti-Phishing Consumer Protection Act of 2008. Such laws are being debated across the country. Private lawsuits have not been effective yet, but they may be a bright spot on the horizon. The threat of monetary penalties may be the only thing that can thwart the growth of the spam industry.

Although some individuals may be discouraged from participating in e-commerce activities because of privacy concerns and fears regarding the use of information collected by Web sites, the Internet retail sector continues to thrive. The Census Bureau records show that, despite economic issues, the estimate of U.S. retail e-commerce sales for the first quarter of 2010 was $38.7 billion, an increase of 1.5 percent from the fourth quarter of 2009.

According to a 2008 survey by the Pew Internet and American Life Project, 66 percent of Americans who use the Internet have made purchases online, despite the fact that 75 percent of online users are concerned about providing personal and financial information online. The survey results also indicate that if privacy concerns were addressed, Internet sales would increase by at least 7 percent. Most popular commercial Web sites have attempted to allay these fears by creating "privacy policy" pages that explain how they collect and use personal information about site visitors. Many also display privacy seals from third-party vendors such as TRUSTe, WebTrust, or the Better Business Bureau as a sign

that they comply with the vendor's privacy standards and regulations.

Privacy Online
Internet users overwhelmingly agree—by a ratio of three to one—that the U.S. government should adopt laws that will safeguard basic privacy rights. Until then, it's up to you to safeguard your privacy on the Internet. To do so, follow these suggestions:

- Surf the Web anonymously by using software products such as Anonymizer's Anonymous Surfing (**www.anonymizer.com**) or devices such as the IronKey Secure USB flash drive (**www.ironkey.com**), which includes special security software to protect your data and encrypt your online communications (Figure 9.13).

- Use a "throwaway" e-mail address from a free Web-based service such as Google's Gmail (www.google.com) for the e-mail address you place on Web pages, mailing lists, chat rooms, or other public Internet spaces that are scanned by e-mail spammers.

- Tell children not to divulge any personal information online without first asking a parent or teacher for permission. Although they seem computer savvy, many children are unaware of the evils that lurk on the Internet. The Children's Internet

FIGURE 9.13 Devices like the IronKey Secure USB flash drive include special security software to allow you to surf the Web privately and securely while protecting your identity and data.

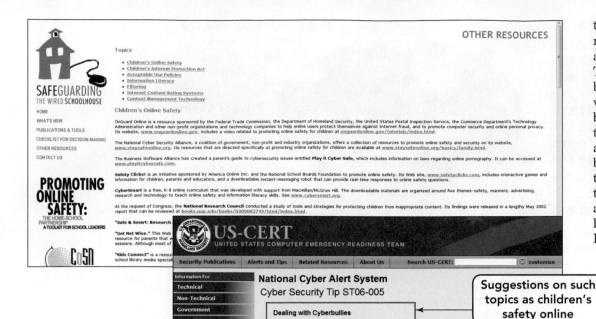

third-party to monitor the activity of a site. Turning off the browser's cookies will prevent Web beacons from tracking the user's activity. A Web beacon can be detected by viewing the source code of a Web page and looking for an IMG tag that downloads from a different server than the rest of the page.

Privacy at Home
Are you aware that all new cell phones in the United States must have GPS awareness? This means that your phone can be located, usually within 30 feet, by law enforcement and emergency services personnel

FIGURE 9.14 These sites act as portals and provide links to government and private sites that are related to Internet security and privacy.

Protection Act (CIPA) of 2001 protects minors from inappropriate content when using computers in schools and libraries. Sites like **www. safewiredschools.org/other.html** and **www.us-cert.gov** provide links to Web pages that contain information on keeping kids safe while on the Web as well as information on Internet privacy and issues of digital security (Figure 9.14).

- Don't fill out site registration forms unless you see a privacy policy statement indicating that the information you supply won't be sold to third parties.

- Turn off cookies in order to prevent the activity of **Web beacons**, transparent graphic images, usually no larger than 1 pixel × 1 pixel, that are placed on a Web site or in an e-mail and used to monitor the behavior of the user visiting the Web site or sending the e-mail. Web beacons are typically used by a

when you dial 911. Some services, such as Where (formerly known as uLocate) and BrickHouse child locator, provide the exact location of a cell phone. This can come in handy when a parent is trying to keep track of a child, but it can be intrusive when an employer uses it to track an employee using a company cell phone.

Some software is so powerful that it will send a notification to the home unit whenever the cell phone leaves a designated geographic area. MIT students recently developed programs using GPS capabilities for the Android mobile OS by Google. One program lets you change your phone's settings as your location changes, so it will be silent in a movie theater or classroom but will ring when you're outdoors. Another program will remind you that you need to pick up milk as you pass by the store! This location-aware tracking software is already in use by the criminal justice system to keep track of offenders who are sentenced to home detention. The subject is fitted with an ankle or wrist bracelet, and then the software is set to trigger an alarm if the wearer strays from the designated area. These bracelets also are being used to keep track of Alzheimer's patients.

As it has evolved, home computing is subject to a decrease in security caused by sharing computing devices and using portable devices in public. A lot of credit card fraud and unauthorized banking access can be traced back to Internet and e-mail use. Some of the security measures you can use on home and portable devices to deter unauthorized access to your accounts include these:

- Create strong logins and passwords for each individual who uses a system. This provides each user with a section to store documents that no other user can see or utilize when logged in. A **strong password** should
  - Be difficult to guess.
  - Be at least 14 characters or more in length.
  - Include uppercase letters, lowercase letters, numbers, and special characters.
  - Not be a recognizable word or phrase.
  - Not be the name of anything or anyone close to you, for example a family member or the name of the family pet.
  - Not be a recognizable string of numbers such as a Social Security number or birth date.

The longer the user login and password, the more time it takes for someone, or some program, to guess it (Figure 9.15). Use online strength testers to evaluate your passwords. The Password Meter at **www.passwordmeter.com** provides guidelines and indicates how including symbols and numbers can improve your score. Microsoft also provides an evaluation site at **www.microsoft.com/ protect/yourself/password/ checker.mspx.**

Using a strong password is a great start toward secure computer use, but there are some additional steps that users can follow to facilitate the privacy and security of their strong password.

- Do not save account numbers or passwords for access to secured sites such as bank accounts and personal e-mail on a shared system.

FIGURE 9.15 Password Length Versus Guess Time

Length of Password Using Mixed Letters, Numerals, and Symbols	Time to Guess (@10,000 Passwords per Second)
2	Instant
4	2.25 hours
6	2.5 years
8	22,875 years

- Do not leave a secured account active on the monitor and walk away. A passerby can easily brush a key and enter a transaction that could be critical.
- Do not leave devices like cell phones and PDAs on tables at restaurants and college facilities. Information left on the screen can easily be read, remembered, and reused. There are many free apps available today for portable devices that automatically lock the system after a brief period without use and require a special password or finger sequence on the touch screen to reopen.
- Turn off services that are not in use, especially Bluetooth.
- Ensure that devices are configured securely and, if necessary, require authentication.

Statistics from the Internet Crime Complaint Center (IC3), a partnership between the FBI, National White Color Crime Center, and the Bureau of Justice Assistance, substantiate that complaints registered on their Web site, **www.ic3. gov**, for Web-related crimes have increased significantly between 2008 and 2009 (Figure 9.16). Financial losses for

FIGURE 9.16
Complaints of Web crimes have been on a constant rise, with a 22.3 percent increase occurring between 2008 and 2009.

4 | Internet Crime Complaint Center

Figure 1: Yearly Comparison of Complaints Received via the IC3 Web site

Year	Complaints
2000	16,838
2001	50,412
2002	75,064
2003	124,515
2004	207,449
2005	231,493
2006	207,492
2007	206,884
2008	275,284
2009	336,655

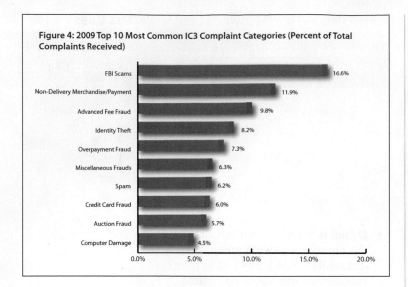

Figure 4: 2009 Top 10 Most Common IC3 Complaint Categories (Percent of Total Complaints Received)

FBI Scams	16.6%
Non-Delivery Merchandise/Payment	11.9%
Advanced Fee Fraud	9.8%
Identity Theft	8.2%
Overpayment Fraud	7.3%
Miscellaneous Frauds	6.3%
Spam	6.2%
Credit Card Fraud	6.0%
Auction Fraud	5.7%
Computer Damage	4.5%

FIGURE 9.17 The main category of complaints to the IC3 was FBI scams.

complaints in 2009 reached an all-time high of $559.7 million, with a median dollar loss of $575. Complaints were received in many different categories of Internet activity, including scams that used the FBI's name (FBI scams), auction fraud, nondelivery of merchandise, credit card fraud, computer intrusion, spam/unsolicited e-mail, and child pornography (Figure 9.17).

Privacy at Work In the United States, more than three-quarters of large employers routinely engage in **employee monitoring**, observing employees' phone calls, e-mails, Web browsing habits, and computer files. One program, Spector, provides employers with a report of everything employees do online by taking hundreds of screen snapshots per hour (Figure 9.18).

About one company in four has fired an employee based on what it has found.

Such monitoring is direct and invasive, but it will continue until laws are passed against it. Why do companies monitor their employees? Companies are concerned about employees who may offer trade secrets to competitors in hopes of landing an attractive job offer. Another concern is sexual harassment lawsuits. Employees who access pornographic Web sites or circulate offensive jokes via e-mail may be creating a hostile environment for other employees—and that could result in a huge lawsuit against the company.

To protect your privacy at work, remember the following rules:

- Unless you have specific permission, don't use your employer's telephone system for personal calls. Make all such calls from a pay phone or from your personal cell phone.

- Never use your e-mail account at work for personal purposes. Send and receive all personal mail from your home computer.

- Be aware of **shoulder surfing**, the attempt by an individual to obtain information from your computer screen by looking over your shoulder.

- When entering a secured area that requires authorized access, be aware of anyone that is attempting to enter with you to avoid using the appropriate check-in or authorization procedure. This act is referred to as **tailgating**. Tailgating was once associated only with the physical entry

FIGURE 9.18
Employers can use Spector, an employee-monitoring program from SpectorSoft, to track everything employees do online.

Click the Screen Snapshots tab to instantly review snapshots of all PC and internet activity.

Easy-to-use VCR-like playback controls. Review like a surveillance tape by pressing PLAY.

Press the green PLAY button to see how screen snapshots playback.

A timeline slider lets you quickly move to the snapshot taken at a specific date and time.

Jump to a snapshot of a specific web site, keyword, or program.

into a restricted zone, but it can also be extended to electronic entry and occurs when a user does not log out of a system and another user sits down and begins to work under the guise of the authorized user instead of logging out and re-logging in as themselves.

- Assume that everything you do while you're at work—whether it's talking on the phone, using your computer, taking a break, or chatting with coworkers—may be monitored and recorded.

Now that you've learned about some important privacy issues, let's take a look at some intentional invasions of your privacy—computer crime.

Computer Crime and Cybercrime

Privacy issues, such as collecting personal information and employee monitoring, should be distinguished from **computer crimes**, computer-based activities that violate state, federal, or international laws. **Cybercrime** describes crimes carried out by means of the Internet. A new legal field—**cyberlaw**—is emerging to track and combat computer-related crime.

In 2006, the United States ratified the Convention on Cybercrime. Developed by the Council of Europe, this is the first international treaty to address the issues and concerns surrounding cybercrime. Its goal is to provide guidelines for consistent cybercrime legislation that is compatible with other member countries and to encourage international cooperation in these areas. Many government agencies, such as the Department of Justice (**www.cybercrime.gov**) and the FBI (**www.fbi.gov/cyberinvest/cyberhome. htm**) have set up special sites to provide information and assistance to help combat cybercrime. The FTC's OnGuard Online site (**http://onguardonline.gov**) has collaborated with government agencies and technology organizations to provide tutorials and activities to educate consumers about the threats and risks posed by cybercriminals (Figure 9.19).

Types of Computer Crime

Anyone who wants to invade or harm a computer system can use a variety of tools and tricks. Pay close attention; you'll learn several facts that could help you avoid becoming a victim.

Identity Theft The phone rings and it's a collection agency demanding immediate payment for a bill for a $5,000 stereo system that's past due. You can't believe what you're hearing—you always pay your bills on time, and you haven't purchased any stereo equipment lately. What's going on?

It's identity theft, one of the fastest growing crimes in the United States and Canada. With **identity theft**, a criminal obtains enough personal information to impersonate you. With a few key pieces of information, such as your address and Social Security number, and possibly a credit card or bank account number, an identity thief can open a credit account, access your bank account, open accounts for utilities or cell phones, or apply for a loan or mortgage—all in your name! Although some laws may limit your liability for fraudulent charges, victims of identity theft have found themselves saddled with years of agony. The bad marks on their credit reports can prevent them from buying homes, obtaining telephone service, and even getting jobs. Although some reports show a slight decline in identity theft in the United States, according to a Javelin Strategy and Research report in 2009, there were 10 million victims of identity theft in 2008 in the United States.

FIGURE 9.19 The FTC's OnGuard Online site provides many resources to help educate the public about various types of cybercrime. Visitors can view tutorials, explore topics, or file a complaint if they've been victims.

Consider the following interesting identity theft statistics:

- Approximately 1.6 million households had their bank accounts or debit cards compromised.
- It can take up to 5,840 hours (the equivalent of working a full-time job for two years) to correct the damage from identity theft, depending on the severity of the case.
- Businesses across the world lose $221 billion a year due to identity theft.
- On average, victims lose between $851 and $1,378 out of pocket trying to resolve identity theft.
- Approximately 70 percent of victims have difficulty removing negative information that resulted from identity theft from their credit reports.
- About 43 percent of victims know the perpetrator.
- In cases of child identity theft, the most common perpetrator is the child's parent.

How do criminals get this information? Most identity theft doesn't even involve computers. Disgruntled employees may physically steal information from their company, thieves may steal your mail or wallet, or they may go through your trash or a company's trash, an act referred to as **dumpster diving**. However, information can also be electronically stolen by criminals if computer data is not properly secured, if you respond to spam or phishing attacks, or if you have malware on your computer. And unfortunately, many Web sites and spammers sell such data to others.

In a **phishing** attack, a "phisher" poses as a legitimate company in an e-mail or on a Web site in an attempt to obtain personal information such as your Social Security number, user name, password, and account numbers. For example, you might receive an e-mail that appears to come from XYZ Company asking you to confirm your e-identity (user name and password). Because the communication looks legitimate, you comply. The phisher can now gain access to your accounts.

Spear phishing, which is similar to phishing, also uses fake e-mails and social engineering to trick recipients into providing personal information to enable identity theft. But rather than being sent randomly, spear phishing attempts are targeted to specific people, such as senior executives or members of a particular organization.

Malware The term **malware** is short for *malicious software* and describes software designed to damage or infiltrate a computer system without the owner's consent or knowledge. Malware is used to commit fraud, send spam, and steal your personal data. It includes spyware and computer viruses, as well as other rogue programs like worms and Trojan horses. A study released by McAfee in early 2010 predicted the following computer-related threats to be key in the coming years:

- Threats to social networking sites such as Facebook will increase.
- E-mail-borne malware will become more sophisticated and will target journalists and corporations, in addition to individual users.
- Popular applications will continue to be the primary targets for cybercriminals.
- Cloud computing will provide a new arena for malware developers to exploit.

The National Cyber Security Alliance (**http://staysafeonline.org**) indicates that fewer than one in four Americans is fully protected against malware. This Web site offers a list tips to keep you safe online.

- Know who you're dealing with online.
- Keep your Web browsers and operating system up to date.
- Back up important files.
- Protect your children online.
- Use security software tools as your first line of defense, and keep them up to date.
- Use strong passwords or strong authentication technology to help protect your personal information.
- Learn what to do if something goes wrong.

> "**Threats** to **social networking** sites such as Facebook will **increase**.... Popular **applications** will continue to be the primary targets for **cybercriminals**."

Malware takes many different forms, the most common of which are discussed in this chapter. Although the United States was the biggest source of malware activity in 2009 (Figure 9.20), the exploits of those in other countries can have equally devastating consequences. Malware, by its nature, has no boundaries.

Spyware is software that collects your personal information, monitors your Web surfing habits, and distributes this information to a third party, often leading to identity theft. Some spyware, such as **adware**, generates pop-up ads and targeted banner ads, and is usually considered a nuisance rather than malicious. However, **keyloggers**, which can record all the keystrokes you type—such as passwords, account numbers, or conversations—and relay them to others, pose a more dangerous security threat.

Spyware is often distributed when you download free software or infected files. File-sharing sites are notorious for this. However, clicking on a pop-up ad can also install spyware, and visiting an infected Web site can trigger a "drive-by" download.

Most spyware is not designed to disable your computer, but you might find that your computer seems sluggish or crashes more frequently. Other signs of infection include an increase in pop-up ads, unauthorized changes to your home or search pages, and the appearance of new browser toolbars.

Your best defense is to do the following:

- Install and use antispyware software and update it frequently. Many experts recommend using at least two products, because one may catch something the other missed.
- Use a firewall, a program or device that allows users to access the Internet but strictly limits the ability of outside users to access local corporate or personal data.
- Avoiding visiting questionable Web sites.
- Never click on pop-up ads.
- Download software only from reputable sources.

Today Internet Explorer (IE) and Mozilla Firefox include pop-up blocking features. Although some pop-ups may be able to evade the browsers, most are blocked and a yellow information bar will appear at the top of the browser

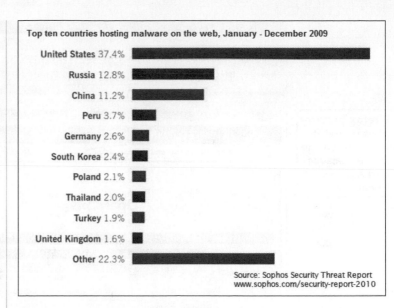

Top ten countries hosting malware on the web, January - December 2009

Country	Percent
United States	37.4%
Russia	12.8%
China	11.2%
Peru	3.7%
Germany	2.6%
South Korea	2.4%
Poland	2.1%
Thailand	2.0%
Turkey	1.9%
United Kingdom	1.6%
Other	22.3%

Source: Sophos Security Threat Report
www.sophos.com/security-report-2010

FIGURE 9.20 Sources of malware span the globe.

(Figure 9.21). It's important to read the message on the information bar. It usually gives you options about how to handle the incident it is reporting. Both browsers also offer built-in antiphishing features to help protect you from a list of known phishing sites that is updated regularly. Firefox will display a warning dialog box when you attempt to access a phishing site, and IE uses a color-coded Security Status bar. IE uses the familiar stoplight color code—green indicates a site that is using a new High Assurance identity verification certificate; yellow indicates a site that may be suspicious; and red is used for known phishing sites or sites whose identification does not match their encryption certificate. A white status bar simply means that no identity information is available. However, the lack of a warning color or dialog box does not guarantee that a site is safe. No matter how efficient these built-in browser features are, it is still important to practice safe surfing methods. Most Internet service providers, for an additional monthly fee, include antivirus software that blocks viruses and worms from infecting your computer.

A **computer virus** is hidden code that attaches itself to a program, file, or e-mail message referred to as a host. Viruses that are attached to program files, like an Excel spreadsheet, are called **file infectors** and spread to other programs or files on the user's hard disk when the file is opened. E-mail viruses travel as attachments to an e-mail message and are spread when the attachment is opened. Some viruses are designed as a prank or to sabotage and damage or destroy the infected file. The dangerous actions the virus performs are referred to as its **payload**. A computer

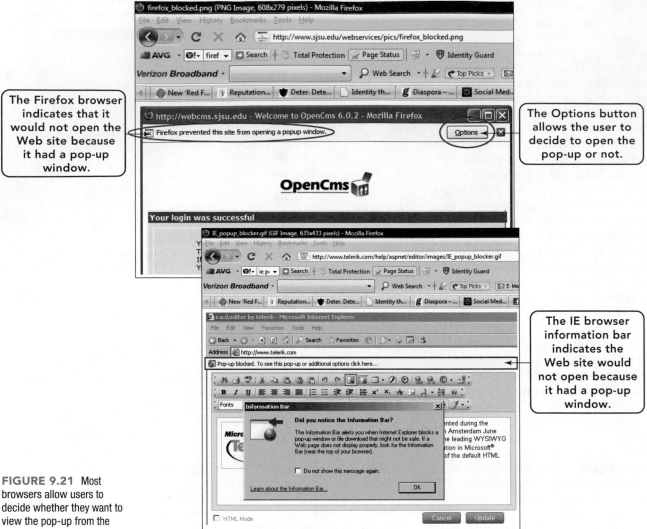

The Firefox browser indicates that it would not open the Web site because it had a pop-up window.

The Options button allows the user to decide to open the pop-up or not.

The IE browser information bar indicates the Web site would not open because it had a pop-up window.

FIGURE 9.21 Most browsers allow users to decide whether they want to view the pop-up from the Web site being accessed.

virus is similar to a human virus in that it requires a host (such as a program, file, or e-mail message) and is designed to duplicate and spread.

The number of viruses sent by e-mail increased by almost 300 percent in July 2009 and was at its highest level of the year, with approximately 12 viruses per customer per hour. The leading sources of these viruses are India (5.2%), Korea (6.2%), Brazil (14.11%), and the United States (16.59%). A virus can be spread on a system by simply opening an infected file or program, but how does a virus spread to another network or system? All a user has to do is simply copy an infected file or program to a USB drive, CD, or DVD and give it to someone. When the storage media with the infected program or file is inserted into the uninfected system, and the infected file is opened, the infection spreads to this system (Figure 9.22).

Many computer viruses are spread by e-mail attachments. When you open an

e-mail, you may see a dialog box asking whether you want to open an attachment. Don't open it unless you're sure the attachment is safe.

Consider the following scenario. A professor with a large lecture section of 100 students receives an e-mail from a former student with an attachment named "Spring Break" that apparently contains a picture from the student's spring break. The professor opens the attachment, which appears to do nothing, and the professor moves on to the next e-mail. The attachment, however, is doing something. It is sending a copy of itself to everyone in the professor's e-mail address box—including each of the 100 students in the class. As students open the attachment, the virus will continue to propagate to the addresses in each of their contact lists. The attachment is received by parents, friends, other professors, and fellow students. Many open the attachment, and the process accelerates very rapidly.

Here are a few simple guidelines for not responding to or not opening an attachment to a message that might contains a virus:

- Never open an e-mail from an unknown sender.
- Never open an attachment unless you first pass it through a virus-checking program.
- Never open an attachment with the file extension of .pif.
- Never trust an e-mail with two "RE" entries in the subject line.

Executable file attachments pose the most serious risk. You can tell an executable file by its extension. In Microsoft Windows, the extension is .exe, but executable files also can be named .vbs, .com, .bin, .scr, or .bat. To make protecting yourself just a little more difficult, these files can be hidden within compressed files that have the extension of .zip. However, you can't be sure that a file is executable by its extension alone. You should also be wary of opening Microsoft Office documents, such as Word, Excel, and Access files. These files can contain **macros**, short segments of executable code, programmed by users, and used to automatically perform repeated tasks. Macros are performed, when needed, with a single command or keyboard stroke. A **macro virus**, takes advantage of the automatic execution. When the infected macro is called into use, the virus activates. The data file that contains the macro is contaminated, and the active virus is able to spread to other files. When these files are shared, the virus is spread and infects other systems. By default, macros are disabled in newer versions of Microsoft Office, but users can adjust security settings to enable them. The best policy is to check any attached file with an antivirus program before opening—no matter who sent the attachment.

Although some viruses are best categorized as nuisances or pranks, others can corrupt or erase data or completely disable a computer. All of them consume system memory and slow the computer's processing speed. In the prank category is the Wazzu macro virus, which randomly relocates a word in a Microsoft Word document and sometimes inserts "wazzu" into the text.

A far more serious type of virus is a boot sector virus. A **boot sector virus** also propagates by an infected program, but it installs itself on the beginning tracks of a hard drive where code is stored that

How Viruses Work

1. The virus arrives on your system, most often through an e-mail attachment.

2. The virus is activated by opening or running the attachment and spreads to other documents on your system.

3. The virus can spread through a network connection, forwarded e-mail, or use of a portable storage device with the other computer.

4. The payload is triggered and performs its programmed activity, which can be a simple joke or the destruction of data on your system.

FIGURE 9.22 Once activated, by opening an e-mail or infected file, a computer virus can be passed automatically from one computer to another by network connections or through portable media such as USB drives, CDs, and DVDs.

automatically executes every time you start the computer. Unlike file infectors, boot sector viruses don't require you to start a specific program to infect your computer; starting your system is sufficient. Boot sector viruses can be very malicious; one called Disk Killer will actually wipe out all of the data on a hard drive.

Malware has spread beyond computers. During the 2007 holiday season, many shoppers found that their new digital photo frames came from the factory with a preinstalled virus. Fortunately, it was an old virus and consumers using up-to-date antivirus software were protected. However, other devices, such as GPS units and digital music players, have had similar experiences. Mobile devices are also at risk.

A spam text message that is sent via a cell phone or Instant messaging service is known as **spim**. In March 2008, a spim message was sent to more than 200 million mobile phone users in China during just one day. Luckily, the spim did not include any malicious code, but it's a very real possibility. And contrary to popular belief, Mac and Linux computers are also vulnerable. Although not as prevalent, malware designed for these systems can also infect them, with the same negative results.

Computer virus authors are trying to "improve" their programs. Some new viruses are self-modifying; each new copy, known as a **variant**, is slightly different from the previous one, making it difficult to protect your computer. Sites such as Snopes.com and Vmyths.com can help you determine whether the latest news about a virus is real or a hoax.

Rogue Programs Spyware and viruses aren't the only types of rogue programs. Other destructive programs include time bombs, worms, zombies, Trojan horses, and botnets.

A **logic bomb** is hidden computer code that sits dormant on a system until a certain event or set of circumstances triggers it into action. That action, or payload, is usually malicious and devastating to the individual or company under attack. An example of a trigger could be the removal of an employee from a database, an action implying that the employee has been terminated. Logic bombs do not try to replicate themselves as a virus does and are often associated with the disgruntled employee syndrome. The reason for this association is that in order to set the trigger, an individual has to have access to the system and thus be an employee.

A **time bomb** is a hidden piece of computer code set to go off on some date and time in the future usually causing a malicious act to occur to the system. Time bombs are less sophisticated than logic bombs, because they are not programmed to be activated by a specific trigger. For example, before leaving a Texas firm, a fired programmer planted a time bomb program that ran two days after he was fired and wiped out 168,000 critical financial records. The only way to prevent permanent loss of data is to perform regular backups on the system.

A **worm** is a program that resembles a computer virus in that it can spread from one computer to another. Unlike a virus, however, a worm can propagate over a computer network and doesn't require an unsuspecting user to execute a program or macro file. It takes control of affected computers and uses their resources to attack other network-connected systems. Some worms, such as Sasser and Slammer, exploit vulnerabilities found in Microsoft Windows and quickly propagate. Newer worms have begun infecting social networking sites such as MySpace and Facebook, retrieving user information and passwords, and directing users to phishing sites. Although patches are usually released quickly, if your computer isn't updated, it remains vulnerable. Even if you don't think your personal information is worth protecting, worms compromise the security of a computer, making it accessible to cybercriminals who can then use it for their own purposes.

Another type of threat is a denial of service attack. With a **denial of service (DoS) attack**, a form of network vandalism, an attacker attempts to make a service unavailable to other users, generally by bombarding the service with meaningless data. Because network administrators can easily block data from specific IP addresses, hackers must commandeer as many computers as possible to launch their attack. When multiple computer systems are involved, it becomes a **distributed denial of service (DDoS) attack**. The commandeered computers form a **botnet** (short for robot network). A **bot** (short for robot), an automated program, connects the individual computers to the controller, usually a server with some type of real time activity like Internet Relay Chat, that is under the power of a botnet controller. These individual computers are called **zombies**, and a group of zombies is called a zombie army. The term is appropriate as the computers do only what the controller tells them to do (Figure 9.23). Criminals also use botnets

FIGURE 9.23 Current botnet attacks are being directed at portable devices like smartphones and GPS units.

1. Bot programs use the Internet to turn ordinary computers into zombies.

2. Bots connect zombies to controllers.

5. The zombies execute the commands, and a DDoS attack is launched or mass spam sent.

4. Commands are sent to the zombies.

3. Control servers are under the direction of botnet controllers.

to send spam, host phishing attacks, and spread viruses and other malware. **Syn flooding** is a form of denial of service attack in which a hostile client repeatedly sends SYN (synchronization) packets to every port on the server, using fake IP addresses, which uses up all the available network connections and locks them up until they time out. This results in a denial of service for legitimate users.

According to a quarterly report from antivirus firm McAfee, botnet criminals took control of almost 12 million new IP addresses between January and May 2009. The number of zombie machines represented a 50 percent increase over 2008, with the largest concentration of botnet-controlled machines in the United States. No one seems safe. In February 2010, the NY Daily News reported that 75,000 computers worldwide, including those of 10 U.S. government agencies, were infected by a virus dubbed the Kneber botnet. The virus, the brainchild of an eastern European group likely selling the information on the black market, compromised 68,000

logins and credentials, several online banking sites, Yahoo, Hotmail, and social networking sites like Facebook.

A **rootkit** is a malicious program that is disguised as a useful program; however, it enables the attacker to gain administrator level access to a computer or network. The primary purpose of a rootkit is to allow an attacker repeated and undetected access to a compromised system. Creating a method to bypass authentication or replacing one or more of the files that run the normal connection processes can help meet this objective. Rootkits often facilitate the creation of a botnet.

A **Trojan horse** is a rogue program disguised as a useful program, but it contains hidden instructions to perform a malicious task instead. Sometimes a Trojan horse is disguised as a game or a utility program that users will find appealing. Then, when users begin running the game, they discover that they have loaded another program entirely. A Trojan horse may erase the data on your hard disk or cause other irreparable damage. More

David versus Goliath—the fight to watch. Four students from New York University's Courant Institute are looking to take on social networking giant Facebook with their software called Diaspora—a distributed, open source social network. The idea is to address the privacy concerns that have recently put Facebook under fire by giving users complete control of their content and who they share it with. How will this be accomplished?

Diaspora will work as a peer-to-peer network in which individual computers will connect with each other instead of a central hub. The software is referred to as the Diaspora "seed" because each computer is considered to be a seed (a node on the Diaspora network) that is owned and hosted by the user. The information posted is stored on the user's computer, and the user can control who is allowed to view the information. Encryption will be used to guarantee the security of information shared over the Diaspora network. If you choose to use Diaspora, the software

will automatically aggregate content from Facebook, Twitter, and Flickr, so you won't miss a single minute of social interaction.

Diaspora founders state that their intention with its development is to avoid storing personal data on a server owned by someone else, which is the way that Facebook and other social networking Web sites operate. Having control of your own data on your own computer allows you to avoid the issues of who accesses or purchases your data and limits possible virus and botnet takeovers. Diaspora seeks to securely share information, pictures, video, and more by making each computer a personal Web server with the Diaspora seed software. Contributions to this venture currently exceed $100,000, allowing the four students to work through the summer of 2010. Their goal is to release the software by the end of the year. Go to **www.joindiaspora.com/project.html** for more information and to view a video introducing the founders.

frequently, Trojan horses are used to install malware or to open a port for easy access by hackers. The Storm Trojan, which is frequently delivered via holiday-themed or weather-related e-mails, has more than 50,000 variants and has infected millions of computers. These infected computers then send out more Storm-infected spam in an endless cycle. At one point, it was responsible for one in every six e-mails that were sent.

Fraud, Theft, and Piracy When computer intruders make off with sensitive personal information, the potential for fraud multiplies. For example, the Hannaford supermarket chain experienced a data breach that exposed credit and debit card numbers for more than 4 million customers, resulting in more than 2,000 cases of fraud.

Physical theft of computer equipment is a growing problem as well (Figure 9.24). An estimated 85 percent of computer thefts are inside jobs, leaving no signs of forced physical entry. In addition, it's difficult to trace components after they've been taken out of a computer and reassembled. Particularly valuable are the microprocessor chips that drive computers. **Memory shaving**, in which knowledgeable thieves remove some of a computer's RAM chips but leave enough to start the computer, is harder to detect. Such a crime might go unnoticed for weeks.

Software piracy is the unauthorized copying or distribution of copyrighted software. This can be done by copying, downloading, sharing, selling, or installing

FIGURE 9.24 To prevent theft, users should lock their doors and turn off their computers. In some cases, it may be wise to secure hardware to desks.

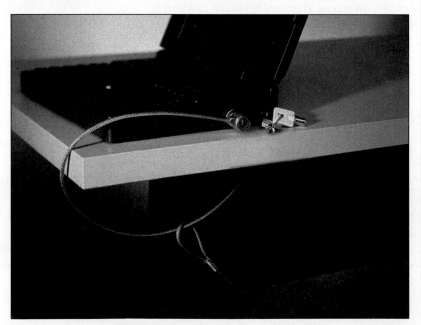

multiple copies onto personal or work computers. What a lot of people don't realize—or don't think about—is that when you purchase software, you are actually purchasing a license to use it, not the actual software. That license is what tells you how many times you can install the software, so be sure you read it. If you make more copies of the software than the license permits, you are pirating software.

Piracy can be intentional or unintentional. Regardless of intention, the Business Software Alliance (BSA), an antipiracy industry group, and the International Data Corporation (IDC), a market research firm, stated that the worldwide piracy rate rose in 2009 by 2 percent over 2008 figures. That means that for every $100 of legitimate software that was sold, $75 of unlicensed software made its way into the market. In dollars, that means that software theft exceeded $51 billion in commercial value in 2009.

Software piracy affects much more than just the global software industry. In the same 2009 study, the IDC predicted that reducing PC software piracy by 10 percent over four years would create as many as 500,000 additional jobs worldwide resulting in the infusion of $140 billion into ailing economies.

Software piracy also increases the risk of cybercrime and security problems. For example, the global spread of the Conficker virus has been attributed in part to the lack of automatic security updates for unlicensed software. An additional side effect of software piracy is that it *lowers tax revenues* at a time of increased fiscal pressures on governments worldwide.

Much software piracy takes place on file-sharing sites like LimeWire or BitTorrent or on online auction sites. It's difficult, but not impossible, to trace the actions of individuals. And when software pirates are found, it is becoming more likely that they will be prosecuted. In fact, the first criminal lawsuit against a member of a piracy group has resulted in a guilty verdict in federal court. Barry Gitarts hosted and maintained a server for the Apocalypse Production Crew that traded hundreds of thousands of pirated copies of movies, music, games, and software. He is facing up to five years in prison for conspiracy to commit criminal copyright infringement, a $250,000 fine, and three years of supervised release—and he must make full restitution. Gitarts may be the first person to go to jail for illegally uploading files to the Internet.

New legislation is being debated that would make piracy penalties even tougher. If passed, the Prioritizing Resources and Organization for Intellectual Property (Pro-IP) Act will strengthen civil and criminal penalties for copyright and trademark infringement, substantially increasing fines and allowing officials to confiscate equipment. What about sharing programs without money changing hands? That's illegal too—and subject to similar penalties: Under the No Electronic Theft (NET) Act, profit does not have to be a motive in cases of criminal copyright infringement.

Cybergaming Crime A large portion of the population today plays some sort of computer-based game. Some choose *Tetris,* others choose *Counter Strike,* and many choose the more virtual and global world of MMORPGs (Massive Multiplayer Online Role Playing Games). In these global battlefields, players can meet other players, become friends, engage in battle, fight shoulder to shoulder against evil, find their virtual destiny—and play, play, play. However, for as much as online virtual gaming is a method of entertainment, virtual evil can become greedy reality. Online games are played by real people,

including thieves and con artists who make real money by stealing other people's "virtual" property. The stolen items are put up for auction (on sites such as ebay.com and other forums), and can be sold to others for virtual or real money. Cybergaming criminals have been known to demand a ransom for the stolen items. Malicious game users can really rake in the money.

FIGURE 9.25 Techniques Used to Obtain Passwords

Password Guessing	Computer users too often choose a password that is easily guessed, such as "password." Other popular passwords are "qwerty" (the first six letters of the keyboard), obscene words, personal names, birthdays, celebrity names, movie characters such as Frodo or Gandalf, and cartoon characters such as Garfield.
Shoulder Surfing	In a crowded computer lab, it's easy to peek over someone's shoulder, look at the keyboard, and obtain his or her password. Watch out for shoulder surfing when using an ATM machine too.
Packet Sniffing	A program called a packet sniffer examines all of the traffic on a section of a network and looks for passwords, credit card numbers, and other valuable information.
Dumpster Diving	Intruders go through an organization's trash hoping to find documents that contain lists of user IDs and even passwords. It's wise to use a shredder!
Social Engineering	This is a form of deception to get people to divulge sensitive information. You might get a call or an e-mail from a person who claims, "We have a problem and need your password right now to save your e-mail." If you comply, you might give an intruder entry to a secure system.
Superuser Status	This enables system administrators to access and modify virtually any file on a network. If intruders gain superuser status, perhaps by using a rootkit, they would then have access to the passwords of everyone using the system.

Tricks for Obtaining Passwords The most publicized computer crimes involve unauthorized access, in which an intruder gains entry to a supposedly secure computer system. Typically, computer systems use some type of authentication technique—usually plaintext passwords—to protect the system from uninvited guests. Many techniques are used to guess or obtain a password (Figure 9.25). Another widely used technique involves exploiting well-known holes in obsolete e-mail programs, which can be manipulated to disclose a user's password.

Salami Shaving and Data Diddling With **salami shaving**, a programmer alters a program to subtract a very small amount of money from an account—say, two cents—and diverts the funds to the embezzler's account. Ideally, the sum is so small that it's never noticed. In a business that handles thousands of accounts, an insider could skim tens of thousands of dollars per year using this method.

With **data diddling**, insiders modify data by altering accounts or database records so that it's difficult or impossible to tell that they've stolen funds or equipment. A Colorado supermarket chain recently discovered it was the victim of data diddling when it found nearly $2 million in unaccounted losses.

Forgery Knowledgeable users can make Internet data appear to come from one place when it's really coming from another. This action is referred to as **forgery**; third-party remailer sites and programs remove the sender's tracking data from a message and then resend the message.

Forged messages and Web pages can cause embarrassment and worse. A university professor in Texas was attacked with thousands of e-mail messages and Usenet postings after someone forged a racist Usenet article in his name. In Beijing, a student almost lost an $18,000 scholarship when a jealous rival forged an e-mail message to the University of Michigan turning down the scholarship. Fortunately, the forgery was discovered and the scholarship was reinstated, but only after a lengthy delay.

Internet Scams Internet auction sites such as eBay attract online versions of the same scams long perpetrated at live auctions. A **shill** is a secret operative who bids on another seller's item to drive up the price. In a recent case, an online jewelry store was charged with illegally bidding on its own merchandise. The store allegedly

FIGURE 9.26 Internet Scams

Scam	Definition	Example
Rip and tear	The action of accepting payment for goods that you have no intention of delivering.	A Seattle man posted ads for Barbie dolls and other goods on eBay, collected more than $32,000 in orders, and never delivered any goods. The swindlers moved to a new state once their activities were uncovered. The perpetrators believed that law enforcement wouldn't be concerned with the relatively small amounts involved in each transaction.
Pumping and dumping	The use of Internet stock trading sites, chat rooms, and e-mail to sing false praises of worthless companies in which an individual holds stock. Once the false hype drives up the share prices, that individual dumps the stocks and makes a hefty profit.	In 2001, Enron participated in an elaborate pump-and-dump scheme by falsely reporting profits and inflating their stock price, then covering the real numbers with questionable accounting practices. More than $1 billion was sold in overvalued stocks.
Bogus goods	The deliberate selling of goods that do not perform the advertised function.	Two Miami residents were indicted on charges of mail and wire fraud after selling hundreds of "Go-boxes," which reportedly turned red traffic lights to green. The boxes, which were actually nothing more than strobe lights, sold for between $69 and $150.

made more than 200,000 bids totaling more than $5 million and drove up auction prices by as much as 20 percent. In a settlement with the New York attorney general's office, the jeweler has agreed to pay $400,000 in restitution and is banned from online auctions for four years. For other types of cons that use the Internet to advertise or hype their scam, refer to Figure 9.26.

Meet the Attackers

A surprising variety of people can cause security problems, ranging from pranksters to hardened criminals. Motives vary too. Some attackers are out for ego gratification and don't intend any harm. Others are out for money or are on a misguided crusade; some are just plain malicious.

Hackers, Crackers, Cybergangs, and Virus Authors To the general public, a hacker is a criminal who illegally accesses computer systems. Within the computing community, several terms are used to describe various types of hacking. However, it is important to note that accessing someone's computer without authorization is illegal, no matter what the motivation might be. The most celebrated intruders are computer hobbyists and computer experts for whom unauthorized access is something of an irresistible intellectual game. **Hackers** are computer hobbyists who enjoy pushing computer systems (and themselves) to their limits. They experiment with programs to try to discover capabilities that aren't mentioned in the software manuals. They modify systems to obtain the maximum possible performance. And sometimes they try to track down all of the weaknesses and loopholes in a system's security with the goal of improving security and closing the gaps. When hackers attempt unauthorized access, they rarely damage data or steal assets. Hackers generally subscribe to an unwritten code of conduct, called the **hacker ethic**, which forbids the destruction of data. **Cybergangs** are groups of hackers or crackers working together to coordinate attacks, post online graffiti, or engage in other malicious conduct. **IP spoofing**, one activity usually associated with hackers, is done by sending a message with an IP address disguised as an incoming message from a trusted source to a computer. The hacker must first locate and modify the message packet headers of a trusted source (called a port) and then manipulate the hacker's own communication so that it appears to come from the trusted port. IP spoofing deceives the message recipient into believing that the sender is a trusted source, and lures that person into responding to a false Web site.

Hacking goes beyond public sites. A few years ago, a 23-year-old hacker known as "RaFa" downloaded about 43 MB of data from a top-security NASA server, including a 15-slide PowerPoint presentation of a future shuttle design. He then sent the plans to a *Computerworld* reporter as proof that the NASA system was not secure. Although NASA didn't experience any direct financial loss from RaFa's activities, many companies do lose money because of hacker attacks—as much as $1 million can be lost from a single security incident.

However, a lot more is at stake than just money. What if terrorists or foreign agents could hack the U.S. government's computers and read, change, or steal sensitive documents? What if hackers could disrupt the networks that support vital national infrastructures such as finance, energy, and transportation? Recognizing the danger, the federal government, through The United States Computer Emergency Readiness Team (US-CERT), has emergency-response teams ready to fend off attacks on critical systems. Internationally, a group of security specialists is using **honeypots**—computers baited with fake data and purposely left vulnerable—to study how intruders operate in order to prepare stronger defenses (Figure 9.27).

Crackers (also called **black hats**) are hackers who become obsessed (often

uncontrollably) with gaining entry to highly secure computer systems. Their intent, however, is to destroy data, steal information, or perform other malicious acts. The frequency and sophistication of their attacks can cause major headaches for system administrators. Many U.S. government sites are constant targets for crackers and hackers, but they are usually able to divert them. However, in June 2007, Chinese crackers were able to breach an unclassified e-mail system in the Department of Defense, affecting more than 1,500 users and shutting down the network for more than a week. An attack on the Epilepsy Foundation's forums caused actual headaches, and much worse, for their viewers. Crackers posted hundreds of pictures and links to flashing animations that caused severe migraines and seizures in some visitors.

Like hackers, crackers are often obsessed with their reputations in the hacking and cracking communities. To document their feats, they often leave calling cards, such as a prank message, on the systems they penetrate. Sometimes these traces enable law enforcement personnel to track them down.

Keep in mind that anyone who tries to gain unauthorized access to a computer system is probably breaking one or more laws. However, more than a few hackers and crackers have turned pro, offering their services to companies hoping to use hacker expertise to shore up their computer systems' defenses. Those who undertake this type of hacking are called **ethical hackers**, or **white hats**.

Computer virus authors create viruses and other types of malware to vandalize computer systems. Originally, authors were usually teenage boys, interested in pushing the boundaries of antivirus software and seeking to prove their authoring skills over those of their competitors. These days, virus authoring has become big business, and many authors are involved with organized crime. If caught and convicted, virus authors face prison and heavy fines. David L. Smith, the 33-year-old programmer who created the Melissa virus, was sentenced to 20 months in jail and a $5,000 fine in 2002, and in 2004 a 19-year-old female cracker known as Gigabyte faced up to three years in jail and almost $200,000 in fines. More recently, Li Jun, the 25-year-old creator of the Fujacks, or Panda, worm, was sentenced by a Chinese court to four years in prison. Hackers and other cyber-criminals can no longer be stereotyped—

FIGURE 9.27 US-CERT provides defense support against cyberattacks and disseminates cybersecurity information to the public.

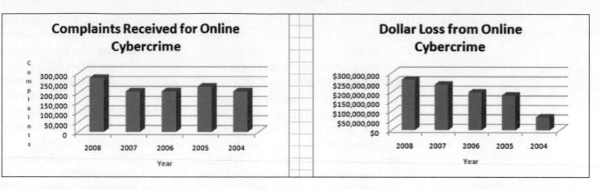

their members include all ages, both sexes, and many nationalities. With a 26.8 percent increase in infected computers around the world, and based on a total of 327,598,028 hacking attempts in the first quarter of 2010, knowing all you can about the current infections and how to prevent them seems essential. For more information on hackers, crackers, current threats, types of vulnerabilities that provide access, and what motivates these individuals, check out Kaspersky Lab's Securelist site at **www.securelist. com/en/**.

Swindlers Swindlers typically perpetuate bogus work-at-home opportunities, illegal pyramid schemes, chain letters, risky business opportunities, bogus franchises, phony goods that won't be delivered, overpriced scholarship searches, and get-rich-quick scams. Today, the distribution media of choice include e-mail, Internet chat rooms, and Web sites.

Estimates of the scope of the problem vary, especially because many cases of fraud are never reported. According to the 2008 Internet Crime Report, consumers reported losses of more than $265 million on a variety of Internet scams, that is 25 million more than in 2007 —and the figure is growing by leaps and bounds (Figure 9.28).

Cyberstalkers, Sexual Predators, and Cyberbullying One of the newest and fastest growing of all crimes is **cyberstalking**, or using the Internet, social networking sites, e-mail, or other electronic communications to repeatedly harass or threaten a person. Cyberstalking, like real-world stalking, is a repeated, unwanted, and disruptive break into the life-world of the victim.

For example, one San Diego university student terrorized five female classmates for more than a year, sending them hundreds of violent and threatening e-mail messages. In another situation, Kathy Sierra was a well-known technology blogger and author who began receiving offensive comments on her blog, Creating Passionate Users. These comments included disturbingly edited images of Sierra and violent, sexual threats that finally escalated to death threats from several sources. The posts also appeared on other blogs. Because of their seriousness, Sierra cancelled plans to make a presentation at a technology conference, claiming she feared for her life, and she eventually suspended her blog. Although several people were linked to the comments, no one was ever prosecuted.

Cyberstalking has one thing in common with traditional stalking: Most perpetrators are men, and most victims are women, particularly women in college. One in every 12 women and one in every 45 men will be stalked, including being watched, phoned, written, or e-mailed in obsessive and frightening ways, during their lifetime.

Concerns about online sexual predators and the risk they pose to children have continued to grow. The Crimes Against Children Research Center (CCRC) reports:

- Approximately 14 percent of 10- to 17-year-olds received some sort of sexual solicitation over the Internet.
- Just over one-third have been exposed to unwanted visually explicit sexual material.

FIGURE 9.28
Complaints concerning online crime in 2008 increased by 33.1 percent over 2007.

- Four percent received a sexual solicitation in which they were asked to meet an individual or where the individual called them on the telephone or sent them money or gifts.
- Of the youth who encountered unwanted sexual material, approximately 1 out of 4 told a parent or guardian, and 4 out of 10 told a parent or guardian if the encounter was defined as distressing or made them feel upset or afraid.

Some online predators may pose as children, but the CCRC reports that many predators admit that they are older and manipulate their victims by appealing to them in other ways. They attempt to develop friendships and often flatter or seduce their victims. Although there have been situations that have ended in kidnapping or murder, violence has occurred in only 5 percent of reported cases. In the majority of cases, the victims have gone with the predator willingly, expected to have a sexual relationship, and often met with the predator on multiple occasions.

Online predators also look for new victims on cyberdating sites. Most cyberdating sites use profiling to match potential mates. The downside is that it is difficult to check someone's cyberidentity against his or her actual identity. Although some sites indicate that they perform background checks, it's doubtful that they are as comprehensive as necessary. Most are based on user-provided information—usually a credit card and birth date. An effective background check would require more detailed information, such as a Social Security number, home address, and possibly fingerprints. And this information would apply only to paying customers—it would not apply to free social networking sites (Figure 9.29).

Cyberbullying involves situations in which one or more individuals harass or threaten another individual less capable of defending himself or herself, using the Internet or other forms of digital technology. Cyberbullying can include sending threatening e-mail or text messages or assuming someone else's online identity for the purpose of humiliating or misrepresenting him or her. In a weird twist of fate, the woman who created a fake MySpace profile of a 16-year-old boy to start an Internet relationship with Megan Meier, the Missouri teen who hung herself after receiving hurtful messages, is now believed to be the victim of a cyberbullying impersonator herself. The online harassment laws that were passed after Meier's death last year now may be used to help the middle-aged woman, who many believe was responsible for the 13-year-old girl's suicide. This isn't an isolated example. The Cyberbullying Research Center noted that 20 percent of the students they surveyed experienced cyberbullying in their lifetime (Figure 9.30).

Preventing cyberbullying can be just as difficult as preventing real-time bullying. In cases that involve school-age children, both the parents and schools need to make students aware of the dangers and provide them with the knowledge and confidence they need to stand up to bullies.

Now that you understand the types of perpetrators who pose a risk to your online privacy and safety, let's look more closely at the growing risks to equipment and data security.

FIGURE 9.29 To protect site users from unscrupulous predators, True.com conducts criminal and marital status checks on its communicating members and requires all site users to agree to a member code of ethics.

Safer Dating

SAFER DATING
WE HAVE BEEN COMMITTED TO
SINCE 2003
WE SCREEN FOR FELONS.

Safer Dating Guidelines

At TRUE, we work to provide a safer dating environment for singles.
Email TRUE about this information

TRUE is committed to safer dating. We can't guarantee that felons, sex offenders and married people won't get on our site, but we can guarantee that they'll be sorry they did.

WE'RE SERIOUS ABOUT YOUR DATING SAFETY
TRUE SCREENS MEMBERS AGAINST A U.S. CRIMINAL DATABASE BEFORE THEY ARE ALLOWED TO COMMUNICATE WITH OTHER MEMBERS.

Before a member is allowed to communicate with other TRUE members, we screen for U.S. felony and sexual offense convictions — using one of the largest criminal records databases on the Internet. Anyone with a felony or sexual offense conviction recorded in these databases is prevented from communicating with TRUE members. Review the current list of covered jurisdictions.

We require that members provide their legal first and last name, as well as their date of birth (they must also certifiy that the information they provide is correct). We also resubmit a member for screening if he or she attempts to communicate with another member and it has been more than 90 days since the last screening.

We turn away tens of thousands of felons, sex offenders and marrieds who, despite our warnings, try to communicate with our TRUE members. At TRUE, we take our members' safety seriously. We don't want felons , sex offenders or marrieds on our website, period.

Remember, though: No system of dating is totally safe, including our online relationship site; YOU HAVE THE FINAL RESPONSIBILITY FOR YOUR OWN SAFETY!

Criminal background screenings are not foolproof:

- They may give members a false sense of security.
- They are not a perfect safety solution.
- Criminals may circumvent even the most sophisticated search technology.
- Not all criminal records are public in all states and not all databases are up to date.
- Only publicly available convictions are included in the screening.
- The screenings do not cover other types of convictions or arrests or any convictions from foreign countries.

Sameer Hinduja and Justin W. Patchin (2010)

Cyberbullying Victimization
N~4000
Random sample of 12-18 year-olds from large school district in the southern U.S.

previous 30 days

Cyberbullying Reseach Center
www.cyberbullying.us

FIGURE 9.30 This survey used a random sample of approximately 4,000 youth between the ages of 12 and 18 from a district in the southern United States. Data was collected in February of 2010 from 41 different schools.

Security

As our entire economy and infrastructure move to networked computer systems, breaches of computer security can be costly. Even when no actual harm has occurred, fixing the breach and checking to ensure that no damage has occurred require time, resources, and money. It's no wonder that security currently accounts for an estimated 10 to 20 percent of all corporate expenditures on computer systems.

Security Risks

Not all of the dangers posed to computer systems are caused by malicious, conscious intent. A **computer security risk** is any event, action, or situation—intentional or not—that could lead to the loss or destruction of computer systems or the data they contain. Some research indicates that security breaches may cost individuals and industry billions of dollars per year because of their impact on customer service, worker productivity, and so on.

Wireless Networks Wireless LANs pose challenges to security, especially hotspots that are designed for open access. Unlike wired networks, which send traffic over private dedicated lines, wireless LANs send their traffic across shared space—airwaves. Because no one owns the space that airwaves travel across, the opportunity for interference from other traffic is great, and the need for additional security is paramount.

To break into a wireless network, you must be within the proximity limits of the wireless signal. In a process called **wardriving**, an individual drives around with a wireless device, such as a notebook computer or smartphone, to look for wireless networks. Some people do this as a hobby and map out different wireless networks, whereas hackers look for wireless networks to break into. It is fairly easy to break into an unsecured wireless network and obtain confidential information (Figure 9.31).

Security methods for wireless networks include **WEP (Wired Equivalent Privacy)**, **WPA (WiFi Protected Access)**, and **WPA2**. WEP was the earliest of the three and has several well-known weaknesses, but it may be the only option for some devices or older equipment. WPA was developed to provide a stronger level of security, and WPA2 improves on WPA's abilities. WPA2 provides confidentiality and data integrity and is far superior to WEP because it uses AES (Advanced Encryption Standard) to provide government-grade security. The need for wireless security is great, and more powerful security systems continue to be developed. Wireless network owners should implement the security that is currently available so their systems are at least protected from the casual hacker.

The newest trend in Internet fraud is **vacation hacking**. Travelers are being targeting by cybercriminals who create phony WiFi hot spots, called **evil twins**, whose names make users believe they are legitimately connected to the airport, hotel, or airline. Users believe that they are using a valid WiFi access point; instead, they're signing onto a fraudulent network. The information being entered is not reaching the desired destination, but is being captured by criminals.

Privacy, Crime, and Security **427**

File Edit View Terminal Tabs Help

```
 Network List--(Autofit)                                        Info
   Name                T W Ch  Packts Flags  IP Range        Size    Ntwrks
 ! RedRover            A N 006   474   T4   66.249.83.19      12k          16
 ! RedRover-Guest      A N 006   505   T4   212.162.69.114    37k     Pckets
 + ! Data Networks     G N 011     6   G    0.0.0.0          288B         2356
 ! RedRover            A N 011    93        0.0.0.0            0B     Cryptd
 + Probe Networks      G N ---    19        0.0.0.0            0B            0
                                                                      Weak
                                                                           0
                                                                      Noise
                                                                          23
                                                                      Discrd
                                                                          23
                                                                      Pkts/s
                                                                          34


                                                                      madwif
                                                                      Ch:   1

                                                                      Elapsd
                                                                      00:02:24
 Status
  Found new probed network "RedRover" bssid 00:18:CE:12:2D:36
  Found new probed network " no ssid " bssid 00:90:96:CA:27:70
  Found IP 128.84.59.16 for RedRover::00:0D:93:85:20:0A via UDP
  Associated probe network "00:18:CE:12:32:E8" with "00:0F:CB:00:14:C9" via probe response.
 Battery: AC 100%
```

The status section of the screen lists the detected networks.

FIGURE 9.31 Wireless network detectors, sniffers, and intrusion detection systems like Kismet will work with any wireless card.

Corporate Espionage Corporate computer systems contain a great deal of information that could be valuable to competitors, including product development plans and specifications, customer contact lists, manufacturing process knowledge, cost data, and strategic plans. According to computer security experts, **corporate espionage**, the unauthorized access of corporate information, usually to the benefit of a competitor, is on the rise—so sharply that it may soon eclipse all other sources of unauthorized access. The perpetrators are often ex-employees who have been hired by a competing firm precisely because of their knowledge of the computer system at their previous place of employment.

According to one estimate, 80 percent of all data loss is caused by company insiders. Unlike intruders, employees have many opportunities to sabotage a company's computer system, often in ways that are difficult to trace. Although incoming e-mail is routinely scanned for threats, outgoing mail is often overlooked, allowing employees to easily transfer data. Similarly, employees can use USB drives, iPods, or other removable storage media to create an unauthorized copy of confidential data, an activity known as **pod slurping**. They may discover or deliberately create security holes called **trap doors** that they can exploit after leaving the firm. They can then divulge the former employer's trade secrets to a competitor or destroy crucial data.

Companies can take a variety of steps to hinder corporate espionage:

- Identify and label sensitive information.
- Protect against data deletion and loss by write- and password-protecting documents and by creating regular backups.
- Make employees aware of security policies and the consequences of violating them.
- Reassess security policies annually or more frequently if needed.
- Perform regular auditing, and random and regular monitoring.
- Install necessary hardware and software to protect systems and data from violations both from inside and outside sources.
- Force password changes every five days or less if data within the organization is highly secure.

The espionage threat goes beyond national borders. Nations bent on acquiring trade secrets and new technologies also are trying to break into corporate, municipal, state, and federal computer systems. According to a recent estimate, the governments of more than 125 countries are actively involved in industrial espionage. Several notable cases include these:

- A disgruntled former employee gained unauthorized access to the voice mail system of Standard Duplicating Machines Corporation (SDMC). The individual in question was found guilty of criminal charges in 1997 and received two years of probation. Through a civil suit, SDMC was awarded $1 million.
- In the mid-1990s a retired Eastman Kodak employee attempted to sell data extracted from confidential documents he had access to while employed. Those approached to buy this information notified the FBI, and the retired employee went to jail for 15 months and paid a $30,000 fine. Kodak additionally sued him in civil court.
- In June of 1997, two naturalized U.S. citizens, on behalf of their employer, the Yuen Foong Paper Manufacturing Co. of Taiwan, attempted to steal the formula for the cancer drug Taxol patented by Bristol-Myers Squibb (BMS). In July of 1997, both were indicted on 11 counts, including the theft of trade secrets.

Congress has attempted to help companies protect themselves with the Economic Espionage Act of 1996. The Act permits legal action regarding "financial, business, scientific, engineering, technical and economic information," if a company can demonstrate it has attempted to keep this information classified and protected. But many companies don't take advantage of the Act except as a last resort. They feel that news of the theft may damage the company's reputation. To view a segment of an award-winning video on industrial espionage titled "The Red Balloon" go to **www.tscmvideo.com/**.

Information Warfare The use of information technologies to corrupt or destroy an enemy's information and industrial infrastructure is called **information warfare**. A concerted enemy attack would include electronic warfare (using electronic devices to destroy or damage computer systems), network warfare (hacker-like attacks on a nation's network infrastructure, including the electronic banking system), and structural sabotage (attacks on computer systems that support transportation, finance, energy, and telecommunications). However, we shouldn't overlook old-fashioned explosives directed at computer centers. According to one expert, a well-coordinated bombing of only 100 key computer installations could bring the U.S. economy to a grinding halt.

According to experts, defenses against such attacks are sorely lacking. In April 2009, the Pentagon issued a statement placing the cost of cyberdefense over a period of six months at $100 million. This figure included the cost of cleanup after several attacks and fixing internal errors. Those advocating an increase in this portion of the budget argue that the emphasis should be on positioning defenses before an attack rather than repairing the system after an attack. A program named "Perfect Citizen" is being launched by the federal government to detect cyberattacks on private and government agencies. The focus of this program will be agencies that control the electrical grid and nuclear power plants that control the country's infrastructure.

A lesson on the damage that a cyberattack can create was made apparent by cyberattacks targeting Estonia in the spring of 2007. Estonia is a small country, but it is on the leading edge of technology, with most of its population relying on the Internet for news, communication, and

> " In April 2009, the **Pentagon** issued a statement placing the cost of **cyberdefense** over a period of six months at $100 million. "

finance. When a Soviet-era war monument was relocated, against the wishes of the Russian government, several days of civil unrest ensued. Once the rioting ended, the cyberattacks began. Estonian sites, including government agencies, ISPs, financial networks, and media outlets, suffered massive DoS attacks originating from botnets controlling nearly 1 million computers. Incoming Internet traffic, primarily from Russia but also from other countries, rose to thousands of times above normal, disrupting commerce and communications for several weeks. Although allegations were made against the Russian government, nothing was ever proven. Many believe the attacks were conducted by activist hackers rather than by a specific government agency. Many also fear that the attack against Estonia was just a test—a way of demonstrating the power of those who control the botnets and a warning to other countries.

In January 2010, Google announced it will no longer censor search results in China. The Chinese government threatened to block the Web site if Google continued to censor the search results. What provoked this action? In mid-December 2009, Google discovered it had a security breach. Quickly it was determined that the hack involved more than just a few workstations. As the investigation progressed, investigators discovered that at least 20 other large companies from a wide range of businesses, including the Internet, finance, technology, media, and chemical sectors, had been similarly targeted. The source of the attack was China. Due to the targeted companies, the fact that the attack focused on Gmail accounts of Chinese human rights activists, and the central location of the source, Google and others believe that the attack was sponsored by Beijing. Google investigated the incident thoroughly for three weeks before coming to its decision to no longer censor search results in China. The U.S. Secretary of State has asked the Chinese government to explain itself.

The U.S. Department of Homeland Security (DHS) reports that in 2007 there was an 81 percent increase in hacking attacks on banks. The U.S. Computer Emergency Readiness Team (US-CERT) is a national cyberwatch and warning center that coordinates activities with the private sector and handled more than 37,000 incidents in 2007. It also oversees EINSTEIN, an early-warning system that looks for malicious or irregular activity on the Internet. Once every two years, the DHS and US-CERT coordinate a national simulation known as Cyber Storm to assess the ability of the United States to identify and respond to a critical cyberattack. Cyber Storm II, held in March 2008, involved 18 government agencies, 5 countries, 9 states, 40 companies, and 10 information-sharing and analysis centers. The exercise simulated an attack on telecommunication centers, the Internet, and control systems. Preliminary results emphasize the need for improved communications between the public and the private sectors before, during, and after an attack (Figure 9.32).

Even if no enemy nation mounts an all-out information war on the United States, information terrorism is increasingly likely. Thanks to the worldwide distribution of powerful but inexpensive microprocessors, virtually anyone can construct electronic warfare weapons from widely available materials. These weapons include high-energy radio frequency (HERF) guns and electromagnetic pulse transformer (EMPT) bombs, which can damage or destroy computer systems up to a quarter mile away.

If this scenario sounds frightening, remember that information technology is a double-edged sword. Information technology gives despots a potent weapon of war, but it also undermines their power by giving citizens a way to organize democratic resistance. In Russia, for example, e-mail and fax machines played a major role in the failure of the 1989 military coup. In the United States, we have learned more about the importance of redundant data backup systems and the resiliency of the U.S. monetary system since the September 11 attacks, but we're still vulnerable and must develop ways to protect our computer systems and infrastructure.

Security Loophole Detection Programs
Intruders can use a variety of programs that automatically search for unprotected or poorly protected computer systems and notify them when a target is found. Such programs include Nessus, a security loophole detection program used by system administrators. In the wrong hands, the program can help an intruder figure out how to get into a poorly secured system.

Public Safety Perhaps the greatest threat posed by security breaches is the threat to human life; computers are increasingly part of safety-critical systems, such as air-traffic control. By paralyzing transportation and power infrastructures, attackers could completely disrupt the distribution of electricity, food, water, and medical supplies.

This threat nearly became a reality when a 14-year-old hacker knocked out phone and radio service to a regional airport's communications tower. Although the hacker didn't realize he had accessed an airport computer and meant no harm, his actions paralyzed the airport's computer system and forced air-traffic controllers to rely on cellular phones and battery-powered radios to direct airplanes until the system was back up and running.

Terrorism Perhaps the brightest spot in the war on terror is the identification of persons of interest by using special security software programs. One program that attempts to find such people is IBM's Real-Time Collaborative Criminal Investigation and Analysis tool. It quickly analyzes data to discover similarities and links among individuals to determine whether they are connected with unsavory characters. The SOMA Terror Organization Portal (STOP) permits analysts to network with other analysts to pool their knowledge and resources about the behavior of terrorist organizations and to forecast potential terrorist behavior. The downside of these

FIGURE 9.32 Cyber Storm II was the second in a series of congressionally mandated exercises that examined the nation's cybersecurity preparedness and response capabilities.

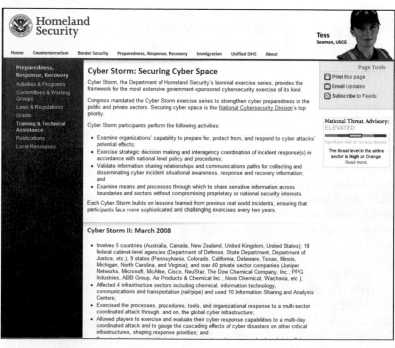

methods is the potential for violating individual privacy rights and mistakenly targeting innocent people.

Protecting Your Computer System

Several measures can safeguard computer systems, but none of them can make a computer system 100 percent secure. A trade-off exists between security and usability: The more restrictions imposed by security tools, the less useful the system becomes.

Power-Related Problems

Power surges, which are often caused by lightning storms or fluctuations in electrical currents, and power outages can destroy sensitive electronic components and carry the threat of data loss. To safeguard your equipment and data, you should always use a surge protector. Additionally, some applications offer an autosave feature that backs up your work at a specified interval (such as every 10 minutes). You can also equip your system with an **uninterruptible power supply (UPS)**, a battery-powered device that provides power to your computer for a limited time when it detects an outage or critical voltage drop (Figure 9.33). Many companies have electric generators to run large-scale computer systems when the power fails.

Controlling Access
Because many security problems originate with purloined passwords, password authentication is crucial to controlling authorized access to computer systems. Typically, users select their own passwords—and that is the source of a serious computer security risk. The use of strong passwords is essential as a first step in preventing an intruder from gaining access to your system and causing problems that appear to have been performed by you.

FIGURE 9.33 A UPS is a battery-powered device that provides power to your computer for a limited time during a power outage.

In addition to password authentication, **know-and-have authentication** requires using tokens, which are handheld electronic devices that generate a logon code. Increasingly popular are smart cards, devices the size of a credit card with their own internal memories. In tandem with a supplied personal identification number (PIN), a smart card can reliably establish that the person trying to gain access has the authorization to do so.

However, when used with digital cash systems, smart cards pose a significant threat to personal privacy. Because every smart card transaction is recorded, regardless of how small a transaction it is, a person's purchases can be assembled and scrutinized. An investigator could put together a list of the magazines and newspapers you purchase and read, where and when you paid bridge tolls and subway fares, and what you had for lunch.

The most secure authentication approach is **biometric authentication**, the use of a physical trait or behavioral characteristic to identify an individual (Figure 9.34). For example, Gateway now offers a built-in biometric fingerprint sensor on its latest notebook that locks access to the computer unless the correct fingerprint is matched. In an experiment in Barcelona, Spain, a soccer club used a database of ticket barcodes matched with

FIGURE 9.34 Biometric authentication devices such as retinal scanners, hand-geometry readers, and fingerprint scanners are often used to provide access to restricted locations.

Retinal scanner   **Hand geometry reader**   **Fingerprint scanner**

Communications leaving a network moves freely.

Internet

Communications entering a network from an outside network must first pass through firewall security options.

FIGURE 9.35 A firewall permits an organization's internal computer users to access the Internet but limits the ability of outsiders to access internal data.

fans' photographs to verify the tickets of more than 100,000 ticket holders as they entered the stadium. If the ticket holder's face did not match the face in the database, the person was not admitted to the stadium.

Firewalls A **firewall** is a computer program or device that permits an organization's internal computer users to access the external Internet but severely limits the ability of outsiders to access internal data (Figure 9.35). A firewall can be implemented through software, hardware, or a combination of both. Firewalls are a necessity, but they provide no protection against insider pilferage. Home users opting for "always on" broadband connections, such as those offered by cable modems or DSL, face a number of computer security risks. Personal firewalls are programs or devices, like routers, that protect home computers from unauthorized access. For information and additional diagrams on how a firewall works or how to choose a firewall for your system, visit **http://computer.howstuffworks.com/firewall.htm** or **www.microsoft.com/security/firewalls/choosing.aspx**. To find out whether your firewall is configured properly, use the free ShieldsUP! service found at **www.grc.com**.

Protecting Yourself

In addition to protecting your system from intrusion or attack, it has become increasingly important to protect your personal data from theft and yourself from a cyberattack. Following the old clichés of the real world, such as "User beware"; "Don't talk to strangers"; and "If something sounds too good to be true, it usually is," will keep you out of trouble in the cyberworld.

Avoiding Scams To avoid being scammed on the Internet, follow these tips:

- Do business with established companies that you know and trust.
- Read the fine print. If you're ordering something, make sure it's in stock and that the company promises to deliver within 30 days.
- Don't provide financial or other personal information or passwords to anyone, even if the request sounds legitimate.
- Be skeptical when somebody in an Internet chat room tells you about a great new company or stock.

Preventing Cyberstalking To protect yourself against cyberstalking, follow these tips:

- Don't share any personal information, such as your real name, in chat rooms. Use a name that is gender- and age-neutral. Do not post a user profile.
- Be extremely cautious about meeting anyone you've contacted online. If you do, meet in a public place and bring friends along.
- If a situation you've encountered online makes you uncomfortable or afraid, contact the police immediately. Save all the communications you've received.

Now that you've learned some ways to protect your security, let's discuss one of the major security measures used to keep information safe on the Internet: encryption.

The Encryption Debate

Cryptography is the study of transforming information into an encoded or scrambled format. Individuals who practice in this field are known as **cryptographers**. **Encryption** refers to a coding or scrambling process that renders a message unreadable by anyone except the intended recipient. Until recently, encryption was used only by intelligence services, banks, and the military.

E-commerce requires strong, unbreakable encryption; otherwise, money could not be safely exchanged over the Internet. But now, powerful encryption software is available to the public, and U.S. law enforcement officials and defense agencies aren't happy about it. Criminals, including drug dealers and terrorists, can use encryption to hide their activities. In the aftermath of the September 11 terrorist attacks, U.S. officials revealed that the terrorist network had used encrypted e-mail to keep their plans and activities secret.

Encryption Basics

To understand encryption, try this simple exercise: Consider a short message such as "I love you." Before it is encrypted, a readable message such as this one is in **plaintext**. To encrypt the message, for each character substitute the letter that is 13 positions to the right in the 26-letter alphabet. (When you reach the end of the alphabet, start counting from the beginning.) This is an example of an **encryption key**, a formula that makes a plaintext message unreadable. After applying the key, you get the coded message, which is now in **ciphertext**. The ciphertext version of the original message looks like this:

```
V YBIR LBH
```

It looks like gibberish, doesn't it? That's the idea. No one who intercepts this message will know what it means. Your intended recipient, however, can tell what the message means if you give him or her the decoding key: in this case, counting 13 characters down (Figure 9.36). When your recipient gets the message and decrypts it, your message reappears:

```
I LOVE YOU
```

With **symmetric key encryption**, the same key is used for encryption and decryption. Some of the keys used by banks and military agencies are so complex that the world's most powerful computer would have to analyze the ciphertext for several hundred years to discover the key. However, there is one way to defeat symmetric key encryption: stealing the key, or **key interception**. Banks deliver decryption keys using trusted courier services; the military uses trusted personnel or agents. These methods provide opportunities for key theft.

Public Key Encryption

Public key encryption is considered one of the greatest (and most troubling) scientific achievements of the 20th century. In brief, **public key encryption (asymmetric key encryption)** is a computer security process in which two different keys—an encryption key (the **public key**) and a decryption key (the **private key**)—are used. The use of two different keys safeguards data and thus provides confidentiality. Additionally it allows a digital signature to be decoded or verified only by individuals that a have access to the sender's public key, thereby proving that the sender is authentic and has access to the private key. The way it works is that people who want to receive secret messages publish their public key, for example, by placing it on a Web page or sending it to those with whom they wish to communicate. When the public key is used to encrypt a message, the message becomes unreadable. The message becomes readable only when the recipient applies his or her private key, which nobody else knows, guaranteeing confidentiality (Figure 9.37).

Public key encryption is essential for e-commerce. When you visit a secure site on the Web, for example, your Web browser provides your public key to the Web server; in turn, the Web server provides the site's public key to your Web browser. Once a secure communication channel has been created, your browser displays a distinctive icon, such as a lock in the address bar, or the address bar may turn green. You can now supply confidential information, such as your credit card number, with a

FIGURE 9.36
Decoding Key for "I Love You"

A	1
B	2
C	3
D	4
E	5
F	6
G	7
H	8
I	9
J	10
K	11
L	12
M	13
N	14
O	15
P	16
Q	17
R	18
S	19
T	20
U	21
V	22
W	23
X	24
Y	25
Z	26

FIGURE 9.37 Krissy uses the public key, provided to her by Mike, to send an encrypted message to Mike. Mike uses his private key to decipher the message. The message would be unreadable to anyone intercepting it.

reasonable degree of confidence that this information will not be intercepted while it is traveling across the Internet.

Digital Signatures and Certificates

Public key encryption can be used to implement **digital signatures**, a technique that guarantees a message has not been tampered with. Digital signatures are important to e-commerce because they enable computers to determine whether a received message or document is authentic and in its original form. A digital signature can be compared to the sealing of an envelope with a personal wax seal. Anyone can open the envelope, but the seal authenticates the sender. So, a digital signature would provide an assurance that an order was authentic and not the result of a hacker who was trying to disrupt a business transaction.

Public key encryption also enables **digital certificates**, a method of validating a user, server, or Web site. For a user, a digital certificate validates identity in a manner similar to showing a driver's license when you cash a check. For example, to protect both merchants and customers from online credit card fraud, Visa, MasterCard, and American Express collaborated to create an online shopping security standard for merchants and customers called **secure electronic transaction (SET)** that uses digital certificates. They enable parties engaged in Internet-mediated transactions to confirm each other's identity. For a server or Web site, a digital certificate validates that the Web server or Web site is authentic, and the user can feel secure that his or her interaction with the Web site has no

eavesdroppers and that the Web site is who it claims to be. This security is important for electronic commerce sites, especially ones that accept credit cards as a form of payment.

Toward a Public Key Infrastructure A **public key infrastructure (PKI)** is a uniform set of encryption standards that specify how public key encryption, digital signatures, and digital certificates should be implemented in computer systems and on the Internet. Although there are numerous contenders, no dominant PKI has emerged.

One reason for the slow development of a PKI involves the fear, shared by many private citizens and businesses alike, that a single, dominant firm will monopolize the PKI and impose unreasonable fees on the public. This was a concern when Microsoft introduced their Windows Live ID system, which implements a Microsoft-developed PKI (Figure 9.38). Originally devised as a single sign-on service for e-commerce sites, consumers and businesses feared it might be used to drive Microsoft's competitors out of business and impose artificially high costs on e-commerce, but Live ID has failed to gain popular acceptance in the marketplace and those fears have proved unfounded. Another concern involving the implementation of a PKI is that governments may step in to regulate public key encryption—or at the extreme, outlaw its use entirely.

Encryption and Public Security Issues

Just one year before the September 11 terrorist attacks on the World Trade Center

FIGURE 9.38 Windows Live ID, an identity and authentication system that permits a single sign-on for multiple sites, hasn't caught on as anticipated, and initial concerns have diminished.

and Pentagon, FBI Director Louis Freeh told the U.S. Congress that "the widespread use of robust unbreakable encryption ultimately will devastate our ability to fight crime and prevent terrorism. Unbreakable encryption will allow drug lords, spies, terrorists, and even violent gangs to communicate about their crimes and their conspiracies with impunity." In light of the terrorists' use of public key encryption—specifically, Pretty Good Privacy (PGP)—Freeh's warning now seems prophetic. Soon after the attacks, there were calls in the U.S. Congress to outlaw public key encryption.

However, recognizing that public key encryption is vital to the electronic economy, U.S. law enforcement and security agencies have not recommended that public key encryption be outlawed entirely. Instead, they advise that the U.S. Congress pass laws requiring a public key algorithm or a PKI that would enable investigators to eavesdrop on encrypted communications. U.S. government agencies have proposed some possibilities.

The government's need to know often conflicts with the public's right to privacy. Recently, the government released a new random-number standard, a critical component of encryption methods. It consisted of four random-number generators, one of which was included at the request of the National Security Agency (NSA). Upon examination, it was discovered that the NSA's random-number generator included a **backdoor**, a method of bypassing normal authentication to secure access to a computer, a vulnerability that could enable someone to crack the code, compromising the security of this encryption tool. Experts are still debating the ramifications of this discovery. In another instance, Sebastian Boucher was arrested on December 17, 2006, at the U.S.–Canada border when his notebook computer was found to contain child pornography. When authorities tried to examine his computer several days later, they found his data was encrypted by PGP and they were unable to access it without the password. The government has tried to force Boucher to reveal the password, but his attorneys successfully argued that this was in violation of his Fifth Amendment rights, which protect him against self-incrimination. On January 22, 2010, Boucher was sentenced to three years in prison and five years of supervised release for the possession of one count of child pornography transported in interstate or foreign commerce. Although Boucher eventually agreed to surrender the password, it was with the stipulation that what was found on the computer could not be used against him for sentencing. Detectives located 2,000 still images and 118 video files depicting sexual assaults on prepubescent children by adults. According to a computer forensics analyst for the Vermont Department of Corrections, the source of the images could not be located, and Boucher's computer had not been used in the production or distribution of the images.

The government doesn't dispute the importance of encrypting data. The theft of a government employee's notebook computer containing the names and Social Security numbers of more than 26.5 million veterans and military personnel resulted in the federal Data at Rest Encryption program, which is mandatory for all military agencies and optional for civilian agencies. The software is available for all notebooks and other portable or handheld devices. It's obvious that there is a fine line between security and privacy, and the debate is far from resolved.

Prosecuting Violators

How is evidence obtained in cases of electronic fraud, cyberstalking, cyberbullying, phishing, or hacking? Likewise, how is data collected electronically in a noncomputer-related crime like hit-and-run or murder? There are two relatively recent areas of study that address these questions: e-discovery and computer forensics.

E-Discovery

E-discovery, an abbreviated term for **electronic discovery**, is the obligation of parties to a lawsuit to exchange documents that exist only in electronic form, including e-mails, voicemails, instant messages, e-calendars, audio files, data on handheld devices, animation, metadata, graphics, photographs, spreadsheets, Web sites, drawings, and other types of digital data. Advances in technology have created an ever-expanding universe of such documents, making e-discovery more expensive, time-consuming, and burdensome than ever before. Consider this: The world sends over 60 billion e-mails daily, and 90 percent of all documents generated today are electronic. A single hard drive can store the equivalent of 40 million pages.

E-discovery is a $2 billion industry, and qualified professionals are in demand. E-discovery professionals use technology to discovery and manage electronic data. The e-discovery professional's knowledge of information technology and legal processes is invaluable to technology-challenged attorneys and clients. E-discovery professionals help identify, collect, process, review, and produce the electronic evidence in court cases.

Computer Forensics

Computer forensics, a complex branch of forensic science, pertains to legal evidence found in computers and digital storage media. It is a field that requires careful preparation and procedural strictness. Because of the scope and technical requirements of this field, there are many subsections such as firewall forensics and mobile device forensics. However, all have the same purposes: to analyze computer systems related to court cases, evaluate a computer after a break in, recover lost data, gather evidence against an employee by an employer, and reverse engineer. Taking the correct actions—in the right order—and recording evidence properly are often as important as having underlying knowledge of the issue being examined. Software developers have fortunately created several forensic tool kits to help in the logical and procedural components of this field (Figure 9.39). These kits spell out proper procedure and contain forms to correctly document every action and event involving a piece of digital evidence, guaranteeing its authenticity, accuracy, and thus its reliability as evidence. This is a current and growing industry that is going to require individuals with organized and logical minds, sharp perception skills, and a strong math and science focus.

FIGURE 9.39 There are many forms in the Computer Forensics Toolkit designed to record actions and observations made on a digital client. This form helps investigators assess hard disk drives.

Users can set some controls over the general level of security at which their system operates and even list specific Web sites from which to either accept or reject cookies.

To set a general level of security:

1. Open Internet Explorer
2. From the menu, select *Tools* and then click *Internet Options*.
3. In the Internet Options dialog box that is displayed, select the *Privacy* tab.
4. In the settings section of the Privacy screen, move the slider bar, located on the left, to the security level you want. For each level, an explanation will appear to its right (Figure 9.40).
5. Click *Apply* and then click *OK*.

FIGURE 9.40 Security settings are located on the Privacy tab of the Internet Options dialog box.

To specifically list individual Web sites from which to accept or reject cookies:

1. Open Internet Explorer
2. From the menu select *Tools* and then click *Internet Options*.
3. In the Internet Options dialog box that appears, select the *Privacy* tab.
4. In the settings section of the Privacy screen, click the *Sites* button.
5. The Per Site Privacy Actions dialog box will open (Figure 9.41).
6. In this area, you can enter the URL of the Web sites from which you want to block cookies and the URL of the Web sites that you want to allow to leave cookies.
7. Repeat step 6 for each Web site you want to allow or block. Then Click *OK*.
8. The Internet Options dialog will still be on the screen to allow you to readjust the slider for your desired level of security. Click *OK* in the Internet Options dialog box.

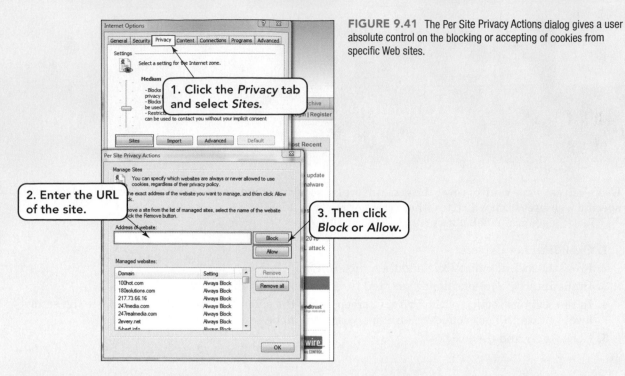

FIGURE 9.41 The Per Site Privacy Actions dialog gives a user absolute control on the blocking or accepting of cookies from specific Web sites.

To adjust control over first and third party cookies:

1. Open Internet Explorer
2. From the menu select *Tools* and then click *Internet Options*.
3. In the Internet Options dialog box that appears, select the *Privacy* tab.
4. In the settings section of the Privacy screen, click the *Advanced* button.
5. The Advanced Privacy Settings dialog box will appear (Figure 9.42). Check the box to the left of the option: *Override automatic cookie handling*.
6. The columns of options below *First-party Cookies* and *Third-party Cookies* will become active, and you can select the options to Accept, Block, or Prompt. Prompt causes a pop-up that asks you to accept or reject the cookie to appear every time a cookie attempts to write to your system.
7. Once your options are selected, click *OK* in the Advanced Privacy Settings dialog box and then click *OK* in the Internet Options dialog box.

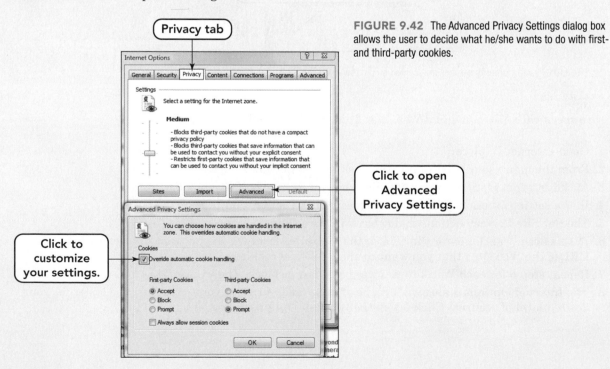

FIGURE 9.42 The Advanced Privacy Settings dialog box allows the user to decide what he/she wants to do with first- and third-party cookies.

Chapter Summary

Privacy, Crime, and Security

- Sensitive personal information such as Social Security numbers and browsing habits can be collected today without informing the owner. Public agencies have always had the ability to collect this data, but today Web pages and online merchants use computerized databases to track information about individuals while cookies and globally unique identifiers (GUIDs) embedded within hardware components and programs are used to track online browsing and shopping habits.

- Examples of computer crime and cybercrime include identity theft; malware, including spyware and viruses; other rogue programs such as time bombs, logic bombs, worms, botnets, zombies, and Trojan horses; fraud and theft; password theft; salami shaving and data diddling; forgery; blackmail; cyberstalking and cyberbullying; and Internet crimes like shilling, rip and tear, pump and dump, and bogus goods.

- These actions are performed by computer criminals that include hackers, crackers, cybergangs, virus authors, swindlers, shills, cyberstalkers, cyberbullies, and sexual predators.

- A computer security risk is any event, action, or situation—intentional or not—that could lead to the loss or destruction of computer systems or the data they contain.

- No computer system is totally secure, but you can do several things to cut down on security risks.

- Safe surfing guides should always be followed in addition to utilizing some software and hardware deterrents, including an uninterruptible power supply (UPS), strong passwords, know-and-have authentication, biometric authentication, encryption of sensitive data, and an installed firewall.

- Encryption, essential for e-commerce and online banking, makes use of encryption keys to encode and decode information traveling over a network. This process guarantees that a message is unreadable by anyone except the intended recipient, who possesses the key to decode the encoded message.

- The U.S. government continues to look for ways to balance the government's need to know with the public's right to privacy. The government recently released a new random-number standard, a critical component of encryption methods. However, a backdoor was discovered that could enable someone to crack the code, compromising the security of this encryption and obtaining confidential information. The U.S. government understands the importance of encryption and the need to collect information, but within the limits of retaining the privacy of its citizens.

- Electronic discovery is the exchange of electronic documents. Computer forensics, a branch of forensic science, examines hardware and software to detect cybercrime. Both facilitate the detection, apprehension, and conviction of cybercriminals.

Key Terms and Concepts

Identification

Identify each of the following types of security risks and electronic inconveniences.

1. _____

Subject: Re: Re: Thanks!
From: mschaus@haverford.edu
    Please have a look at the attached
Attachments: document.pif 29 k

Subject: something for you
From: brendenxcort@hotmail.com
    You are infected. Read the details!
Attachments: old_photos.rtf.scr

3. _____

2. _____

4. _____

5. _____

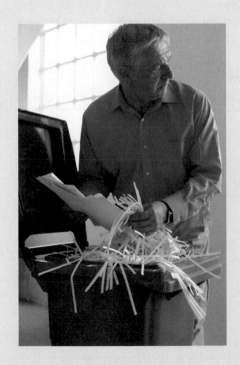

6. _____

Matching

Match each key term in the left column with the most accurate definition in the right column.

_____ 1. cybercrime

_____ 2. banner ad

_____ 3. Web beacon

_____ 4. dumpster diving

_____ 5. RFID

_____ 6. botnet

_____ 7. payload

_____ 8. spim

_____ 9. active badge

_____ 10. cookie

_____ 11. rootkit

_____ 12. shoulder surfing

_____ 13. computer crime

_____ 14. honeypot

_____ 15. salami shaving

a. A group of computers that have been unwillingly commandeered and are under the direction of a controller

b. Uses radio waves to identify lost pets; most recently embedded within passports and driver's licenses

c. Attempting to see private information by strategically positioning yourself to view of the computer screen of an unsuspecting user

d. A device that transmits a unique infrared signal every 5 to 10 seconds, creating an electronic trail of the user's location

e. Activities done on a computer that violate state, federal, or international laws

f. An embezzling technique in which small amounts of money are diverted into another account repeatedly over time, usually by altering a program

g. A text file deposited by a Web site on a Web user's computer system, without consent, that is used to gather data on browsing and shopping habits

h. Illegal activity carried out over the Internet

i. Advertising that appears on a Web page but is not actually part of that page

j. A spam text message

k. The attempt to obtain private information by going through discarded mail and trash

l. A computer baited with fake data and purposely left vulnerable in order to study how intruders operate and to prepare stronger defenses based on results

m. A disguised program that provides unauthorized administrative access to a system

n. The dangerous actions a malicious program performs

o. A transparent graphic image embedded within a Web site or e-mail for the purpose of monitoring the user

Multiple Choice

Circle the correct choice for each of the following:

1. Which is a characteristic of a strong password?
   a. A length of less than 5 characters
   b. A familiar word or the name of a family member or pet
   c. The use of characters, both upper and lower case, numbers, and special characters
   d. The use of an important date like a birth date or anniversary date

2. Which is *not* a benefit of cookies?
   a. They are used by online shopping carts to hold items prior to checkout.
   b. They can hold information like login and password, thus making it easier for individuals to login.
   c. They do not take up much disk space.
   d. They can be used to track a user's browser activity.

3. In public key encryption, which item is kept by the owner of the key?
   a. Public key
   b. Private key
   c. Digital key
   d. Rootkit

4. Who is an individual that deliberately attempts to obtain unauthorized access to a computer or network system with the intent to do harm?
   a. Zombie
   b. Bot
   c. Hacker
   d. Cracker

5. What is the process of observing the behavior of employees, including phone calls, e-mails, and Web browsing habits, with or without the aid of computers?
   a. Phishing
   b. Employee monitoring
   c. Computer forensics
   d. Backdoor

6. Which of the following is an example of malware?
   a. Employee monitoring programs
   b. Globally unique identifiers
   c. Time bombs
   d. Active badges

7. What is a type of software program that records all the keystrokes a user enters—such as passwords, account numbers, or conversations—and relays them to others?
   a. Keylogger
   b. Data diddler
   c. Macro
   d. Time bomb

8. Which is a form of malware that installs itself on the beginning tracks of a hard drive, where stored code is automatically executed every time you start the computer, and spreads the infection by simply starting the system?
   a. Macro virus   b. Rootkit
   c. Boot sector virus   d. Botnet

9. What is the name given to commandeered computers that are often used by botnets to distribute spam and malware?
   a. Zombies
   b. Backdoor
   c. Rootkits
   d. Time bombs

10. Which is an online shopping and security standard for merchants and customers?
   a. 802.11n
   b. WPA
   c. GUID
   d. SET

Fill-In

In the blanks provided, write the correct answer for each of the following:

1. _____ computing is a term used to describe the trend in which individuals interact with multiple devices through an omnipresent network.

2. _____ is a validation method that uses a variety of human features, such as voice recognition, retinal scans, and fingerprints to authenticate a user.

3. _____ is an auction behavior in which an accomplice of the seller drives the price up by bidding for an item he or she has no intention of buying.

4. _____ refers to the ability to send a message without revealing your name or identity.

5. A(n) _____ is an individual who attempts to access computers or network systems without permission, for the purpose of pointing out loopholes and security breaks, but who has no intention of performing any malicious acts on the system.

6. A(n) _____ attack is the flooding of a service with meaningless data in an attempt to make a service unavailable to other users.

7. _____ makes use of fake e-mails and social engineering to trick specific people, such as senior executives or members of a particular organization, into providing personal information, to enable identity theft.

8. A(n) _____ is an identification number that is generated by a hardware component or a program that can be read by Web servers or embedded in various documents, making anonymity difficult.

9. _____ is one of the earliest wireless security standards and may be the only option for older devices, despite known weaknesses.

10. _____ is a condensed term that describes software that is designed to damage and infiltrate a computer system without the owner's consent.

11. A(n) _____ is a method of computer access setup to permit the bypassing of normal authentication procedures.

12. _____ refers to a coding or scrambling process that renders a message unreadable by anyone except the intended recipient.

13. _____ is an activity, usually associated with hackers, which is done by sending an incoming message with a false address in an attempt to fool the receiver into believing that he or she is replying to a valid address.

14. A(n) _____ is a program that permits an organization's computers to use the Internet but places severe limits on the ability of outsiders to access internal data.

15. _____ makes use of both encryption and decryption keys.

Short Answer

1. List three of the rights stated in the "Bill of Rights for Social Network Users" issued by the Electronic Frontier Foundation (EFF).

2. Explain the difference between hackers and crackers.

3. Name and explain three of the laws that protect individual privacy.

4. List the five actions an organization can take to deter corporate espionage.

5. List three techniques used to obtain user passwords without their consent.

Teamwork

1. **Database Security** As a team, develop a list of all the databases members use within a week. Ask each team member to rank his or her login name and password for each database as strong, mild, or weak based on the content of this chapter. Additionally ask when each team member last changed his or her passwords. Collect this information and summarize it in a Word table or Excel spreadsheet. Below your table of data, summarize your findings on the use of databases, strength of passwords, and frequency of password changes. Do you think your findings are representative of your age group and region as a whole?

2. **Electronic Monitoring** Traffic congestion in Hong Kong is a matter of great concern to commuters, environmentalists concerned over air-borne pollution, and the government's Transport Department. Certain areas of the city that draw tourists get extremely congested at peak times during the day. It has been suggested that owners of private cars should be charged for driving in these tourist zones during peak times. The intention is to discourage locals from increasing the congestion and pollution and enable tourists a less harried view of the city. All registered car owners will have to display a scannable chip in the windshield of their car. The chip will be scanned when a vehicle enters a restricted zone, and the individual will be billed. Extensive use of these roads could also result in additional charges for overuse. As a team, consider both the plus side and minus side of this system. Discuss how this system might invade the privacy of a driver. Identify any barriers that might deter this plan. Report your team's stand on the plan in a one-page, double-spaced report.

3. **Clean, Quarantine, or Delete?** As a team, investigate these three choices, which are usually options to apply to infected files when detected by antivirus programs. Investigate at least three antivirus programs, state the options each provides, and explain what each option actually does to the infected file. Determine the type of malware each option is best suited to contain. Present your collective research in a PowerPoint presentation of 5 to 10 slides. Remember to cite your references.

4. **Are Privacy and Social Networking Incompatible?** As a team, investigate the current security issues of Google Buzz and Facebook. Describe the security breaches that occurred and how long it took to identify them. Find statistics on the amount of information that was compromised and the response that the manager of each site issued. As a team, come to a consensus on the initial statement in this question: Are privacy and social networking incompatible? In a one-page, double-spaced paper, respond to the question and cite your references.

5. **Solve the Problem** You are using an antivirus program on your home computer, and a pop-up appears indicating that an infected file has been detected on your system. Your attempt to move the file to quarantine fails. As a team, determine some of the some possible reasons for the quarantine failure. What steps would you need to take?

On the Web

1. **Phishing versus Pharming** Using a search engine and the content of this chapter, explain the difference between phishing and pharming. Locate at least two examples of each. Present your descriptions and examples in a one-page, double-spaced report. Remember to cite your references.

2. **Guilty by Digital Data** Today, an individual can be found guilty of a crime even though no witnesses

were present to verify that that individual actually did the act in question. Digital data and computer forensics are both becoming powerful tools in the courtroom, along with the use of re-enactment software to provide the jury with a virtual crime scene. What used to be circumstantial evidence is now becoming more solid and is not so easily dismissed in court. Cell phone records, GPS tracking, and Web browsing histories are all acceptable evidence in court proceedings and can establish an individual's whereabouts and intent. Using your favorite browser, locate and investigate three instances in which an individual was convicted of a crime when no actual witness could identify him/her, but the digital data proved them guilty. In a one-page, double-spaced paper, present each case, describe the circumstances, and explain how the digital data was used to prove guilt. Remember to cite your references.

3. **Red Flags Rules** Using the Internet and a search engine, locate information on the "Red Flags Rules," which require financial institutions and creditors to develop and implement identity theft programs. Explain the rules, who must comply, and any flexibility that there might be in this policy. Present your findings and cite your references in a one-page, double-spaced report.

4. **Logic Bombs** Using the Internet and your favorite browser, research logic bombs in more detail. The trigger that activates the logic bomb can be a positive trigger or a negative trigger. In a one-page, double-spaced paper, define each type of trigger, and describe two examples in which each type of trigger was used and the payload that each set off.

5. **President's Task Force on Identity** Using the Internet and your favorite browser, identify the year that the President's Task Force on Identity was created. What was the mission of this organization? Who are the members? What has the task force accomplished since its inception? Present your findings in a one-page, double-spaced report, and remember to cite your references.

Acronym Finder

1G first generation

1GL first-generation languages

2G second generation

2GL second-generation languages

3D three-dimensional

3G third-generation

3GL third generation languages

4G fourth generation

4GL fourth-generation languages

AC alternating current

ACCS Alternative Computer Control System

ACM Association for Computing Machinery

ADC analog-to-digital converter

ADSL asymmetric digital subscriber line

AES Advanced Encryption Standard

AFIS Automated Fingerprint Identification System

AGP accelerated graphics port

AIM AOL Instant Messenger

AJAX asynchronous JavaScript and XML

ALU arithmetic logic unit

ARPANET Advanced Research Projects Agency Network

ASCII American Standard Code for Information Interchange

ASIMO Advance Step in Innovative Mobility

ASIS&T American Society for Information Science and Technology

ASP application service provider

ATM asynchronous transfer mode

ATS application tracking system

AUP acceptable use policies

AVI Audio Video Interleave

AWC Association for Women in Computing

B2B business-to-business

B2C business-to-consumer

BCP business continuity plan

BD Blu-ray disc

BDA Blu-ray Disc Association

BD-R Blu-Ray disc-recordable

BD-RE Blu-Ray disc rewritable

BD-ROM Blu-Ray disc ROM

BIOS basic input/output system

BLOB binary large object

BMP Windows Bitmap

BMS Bristol-Myers Squibb

BOINC Berkeley Open Infrastructure for Network Computing

BPM business process management

BPR business process reengineering

Bps bits per second

BRB be right back

BSA Business Software Alliance

BVA Bionic Vision Australia

C2C consumer-to-consumer

CAD computer-aided design

CAN campus area network

CASE computer-aided software engineering

cat-5 category 5

cat-5e category 5 enhanced

cat-6 category 6

CAVE Cave Automated Virtual Environment

CBE computer-based education

CBT computer-based training

CCD charge-coupled device

CCIE Cisco Certified Internetwork Expert

CCNA Cisco Certified Network Associate

CCRC Crimes Against Children Research Center

CDMA code division multiple access

CD-R compact disc-recordable

CD-ROM compact disc ROM

CD-RW compact disc-rewritable

CES Consumer Electronics Show

CIO chief information officer

CIPA Children's Internet Protection Act

CIS computer information systems

CLA Novell Certified Linux Administrator

CMOS complementary metaloxide semiconductor

CO central office

CPSR Computer Professionals for Social Responsibility

CPU central processing unit

CRISP-DM CRoss Industry Standard Process for Data Mining

CRM customer relationship management

CRT cathode ray tube

CS computer science

CSO chief security officers

CSS cascading style sheets

DAC digital-to-analog converter

DARPA Defense Advance Projects Research Agency

DBMS database management system

DBS direct broadcast satellite

DC direct current

DDOS disturbed denial of service attack

DFD data flow diagram

DHS U.S. Department of Homeland Security

DIMM dual inline memory module

DLCI data link control/connection identifier

DLP digital light processing

DMA Direct Marketing Association

DNS domain name service

DoS denial of service attack

DSL digital subscriber line

DSS decision support system

DVD digital video disc

DVD-R digital video disc-recordable

DVD-ROM digital video disc-ROM

DVD-RW digital video disc-rewritable

DVI digital video interface port

DVR digital video recorder

EAI enterprise application integration

EB exabyte

EBCDIC Extended Binary Coded Decimal Interchange Code

ECMA European Computer Manufacturers Association

EDI electronic data exchange

EE electrical engineering

EEPROM electrically erasable programmable ROM

EFF Electronic Frontier Foundation

EIS executive information system

EMPT electromagnetic pulse transformer

EPA Environmental Protection Agency

EPROM electrically programmable ROM

EPS Encapsulated PostScript

ERD entity-relationship diagram

ERP enterprise resource planning

ES expert system

ESS executive support system

EU European Union

f2f face-to-face

FAQ frequently asked questions

FAT file allocation table

FBI Federal Bureau of Investigation

FCC Federal Communications Commission

FCRA Fair Credit Reporting Act

FDIC Federal Reserve System and Federal Deposit Insurance Corporation

FED field-emission display

FERPA Family Educational Rights and Privacy Act

FFIEC U.S. Federal Financial Institutions Examination Council

FiOS fiber-optic service

FOLED flexible OLED displays

fps frames per second

FPU floating point unit

FTC Federal Trade Commission

FTP File Transfer Protocol

FTTH fiber-to-the-home

GB gigabyte

Gbps gigabits per second

GHz gigahertz

GIF Graphics Interchange Format

gigaPOP gigabits per second point of presence

GMSC gateway mobile switching center

gMUD graphical MUD

GPL General Public License

GPS Global Positioning System

GUI graphical user interface

GUID global unique identifier

HAN home area network

HaaS Hardware-as-a-Service

HD high-definition video

HDMI high-definition multimedia interface

HDR high dynamic range

HDSL high bit-rate DSL

HDTV high-definition TV

HERF high-energy radio frequency

HHD hybrid hard drive

HIPAA Health Insurance Portability and Privacy Act

HMD head-mounted display

HP Hewlett-Packard

HTML Hypertext Markup Language

HTTP Hypertext Transfer Protocol

HTTPS Hypertext Transfer Protocol Secure

Hz hertz

IaaS Infrastructure-as-a-Service

IC integrated circuit

IC3 Internet Crime Complaint Center

ICANN Internet Corporation for Assigned Names and Numbers

ICC integrated circuit card

ICCP Institute for Certification of Computing Professionals

ICE Intercity Express

IDC International Data Corporation

IDE integrated development environment

IE Internet Explorer

IEEE Institute of Electrical and Electronics Engineers

IGDA International Game Developers Association

IIS Microsoft's Internet Information Services

IM instant messaging

IMDB Internet Movie Database

I/O input/output

IP Internet Protocol

IPI Institution for Policy Innovation

IR infrared

IRC Internet relay chat

IrDA infrared data association

IRQ interrupt request

IRS Internal Revenue Service

IRU indoor receive unit

IS information systems

ISA Industry standard architecture

ISDN Integrated Services Digital Network

ISO International Organization for Standardization

ISP Internet service provider

IT information technology

ITU indoor transmit unit

JAD joint application development

JPEG Joint Photographic Experts Group

JSON JavaScript Object Notation

KB kilobyte

Kbps kilobits per second or thousand bits per second

KMS knowledge management system

LAN local area network

LCD liquid crystal display

LED light-emitting diode

LOL laughing out loud

MAC media access control

MAN metropolitan area network

MB megabyte

Mbps megabits per second or million bits per second

MCITP Microsoft Certified IT Professional

MCSA Microsoft Certified Systems Administrator

MCSE Microsoft Certified Systems Engineer

MCTS Microsoft Certified Technology Specialist

MIDI Musical Instrument Digital Interface

MIS management information system

MMDS multichannel multipoint distribution service, sometimes called multipoint microwave distribution system

MMPORG massively multiplayer online role-playing game

MMS multimedia messaging service

MPEG Moving Picture Experts Group

MSC mobile switching center

MUD multiuser dungeon

N.O.C. Network Operations Centre

NAP network access point

NAS network attached storage

NET No Electronic Theft Act

NIC network interface card

NOS Network operating system

NSA National Security Agency

NSP network service provider

NTFS new technology file system

OCR optical character recognition

ODBMS object-oriented database management systems

ODC Open Database Connectivity

OLAP online analytical processing

OLPC One Laptop per Child initiative

OMR optical mark reader

OO object-oriented

OOP object-oriented programming

OS operating system

OSI open system interconnection

OSP online service provider

OSS operational support system

P2P peer-to-peer network

PaaS Platform-as-a-Service

PAN personal area network

PARC Xerox Palo Alto Research Center

PB petabyte

PBX private branch exchange

PC personal computer

PCI peripheral component interconnect

PCMCIA Personal Computer Memory Card International Association

PCS personal communication service

PDA personal digital assistant

PDL page-description language

PDLC program development life cycle

PDN public data network

PGP Pretty Good Privacy

PIM personal information manager

PIN personal identification number

PKI public key infrastructure

PNG portable network graphics

PnP plug-and-play

PoP point of presence

POP Post Office Protocol

POS point-of-sale

POST power-on self-test

POTS plain old telephone service

ppm pages per minute

Pro-IP Prioritizing Resources and Organization for Intellectual Property Act

PROM programmable ROM

PSTN public switched telephone network

PUE power usage effectiveness

RAD rapid application development

RAID redundant array of independent disks

RAM random access memory

RDBMS relational database management system

RF radio frequency

RFIC Radio Frequency Integrated Circuit

RFID radio frequency identification device

RFP request for proposal

RFQ request for quotation

RHCE Red Hat Certified Engineer

ROI region of interest or return on investment

RSI repetitive strain injuries

ROM read-only memory

RSS Really Simple Syndication (or Rich Site Summary)

RUN Responsible Use of the Network Working Group

SaaS Software-as-a-Service

SAN storage area network

SATA serial advance technology attachment

SATAIO Serial ATA International Organization

SCJD Sun Certified Java Developer

SCJP Sun Certified Java Programmer

SCSI small computer system interface ports

SD standard definition

SDH synchronous digital hierarchy

SDLC systems development life cycle

SDMC Standard Duplicating Machines Corporation

SDSL symmetrical digital subscriber line

SEC Securities and Exchange Commission

SET secure electronic transfer

SETI Search for Extraterrestrial Intelligence

SFA sales force automation

SIIA Software & Information Industry Association

SIMM single inline memory module

SLC subscriber loop carrier

SLR single-lens reflex digital camera

SMDS switched multimegabit data service

SMIL Synchronized Multimedia Integration Language

SMS short messaging service, better known as text messaging

SOHO small office–home office

SONET synchronous optical network

SOX Sarbanes-Oxley

SPOF single point of failure

SQL structured query language

SSCP Systems Security Certified Practitioner

SSD solid-state drive

STOP SOMA Terror Organization Portal

SVGA super video graphics array

SXGA super extended graphics array

SYN synchronization

TB terabyte

TCO total cost of ownership

TCP Transmission Control Protocol

TCP/IP Transmission Control Protocol/Internet Protocol

TDWI The Data Warehousing Institute

TFT active matrix (thin film transistor)

TLD top-level domain

TPS transaction processing system

UM exchange unified messaging

UML Unified Modeling Language

UPC Universal Product Code

UPS uninterruptable power supply

URL Uniform Resource Locator

USB universal serial bus

US-CERT United States Computer Emergency Readiness Team

USDA Department of Agriculture

UXGA ultra extended graphics array

UV ultraviolet

VAN value-added network

VAR value-added reseller

VB Visual Basic

VDSL very high bit-rate DSL

VGA video graphics array

VM Java virtual machine

VOD video-on-demand

VoIP Voice over Internet Protocol

VPN virtual private network

VR virtual reality

VRML Virtual Reality Modeling Language

W3C World Wide Web Consortium

WAN wide area network

WAP Wireless Application Protocol

WBT Web-based training

WEP Wired Equivalent Privacy

WiMAX worldwide interoperability for microwave access

WITI Women in Technology International

WMA Windows Media Audio

WML Wireless Markup Language

WOW World Organization of Webmasters

WPA WiFi Protected Access

WSXGA+ Widescreen Super Extended Graphics Array Plus

WUXGA Widescreen Ultra Extended Language

WXGA+ Widescreen Extended Graphics Array plus

WWW World Wide Web

XBRL Extensible Business Reporting Language

XGA Extended Graphics Array

XHTML Extensible Hypertext Markup Language

XML Extensible Markup Language

XP Extreme Programming

YB yottabyte

ZB zettabyte

Glossary

1394 port An interface that offers high-speed connections for peripherals. It is ideal for real-time devices like digital video cameras. In an Apple computer, the 1394 port is called the FireWire port.

1G First generation of cellular technology, which used analog signals and allowed callers to make their own calls without operator assistance as they move seamlessly from cell to cell.

2G Second-generation cellular technology that quickly replaced most analog cellular services due to its use of digital signaling. Features of this generation were decreased signal interference, increased reception, better protection from eavesdropping, and increased security features that decreased cell phone fraud.

3G Third-generation cellular technology that offers faster data transmission; greater network capacity; more advanced network services; and transmission of voice, text, images, and video data.

4G Fourth-generation cellular technology, which is currently being rolled out, promises higher data transfer rates, as well as providing voice, data, and high-quality multimedia in real-time (streamed) format all the time from anywhere.

A

Accelerated Graphics Port (AGP) An interface, currently being phased out that is used to transfer graphics from the video card to the motherboard.

acceptable use policy A code of conduct created by colleges or employers that provides guidance for students and employees when dealing with ethical and legal dilemmas.

access time In secondary storage devices, the amount of time it takes a device to access information, from the request for the information to the delivery of that information.

account A record on multiuser systems that consists of a user's name, password, and storage space location, which is called the user's folder or user's directory. Accounts are usually set up and managed by a server/computer administrator.

active badge A small device, worn by an individual, that transmits a unique infrared signal every 5 to 10 seconds. Networked sensors detect these transmissions and the location of the badge—and hence the location of its wearer—allowing e-mail, phone calls, or messages to be forwarded.

active-matrix (thin film transistor [TFT]) A form of LCD display in which electric current drives the display by charging each pixel individually as needed.

address bar (breadcrumb bar) Used for navigation, the address bar displays the route you've taken to get to the current location. It may or may not correspond with a file's path name.

ADSL (asymmetrical digital subscriber line) A transmission technology that separates an ordinary copper telephone line into three separate data channels with different capacities and speeds. The lowest capacity transmits analog voice for telephones; the second, medium capacity, uploads data to the network; and the third, highest capacity, downloads data from the network. This means that ADSL connections upload more slowly than they download.

adware Software similar to spyware, which is usually installed on your computer through the Internet without your knowledge or consent. Adware is created specifically by an advertising agency to collect information about Internet habits or encourage the purchase of a product. It is usually considered a nuisance rather than malicious.

aggregator A Web site that interacts with RSS feeds. It remembers your subscription list, checks each site on a regular basis, alerts you if new information has been published, and organizes the results for you. Many RSS aggregators are available through your browser and are either updated manually, such as the Drudge Report, or through the use of algorithms, as is the case with Google News.

algorithm A series of steps that results in the solution to a problem.

all-in-one computer A compact version of a desktop computer, designed for individual use that combines the system unit and monitor into one component. Its smaller size suits cubicle layouts and apartments.

analog signal Real-world signals, like sound and light, sent via continuous waves that vary in frequency and amplitude. It is the signal sent and received over phone lines.

analog-to-digital converter (ADC) A microchip that contains the circuitry to convert an analog signal into a digital signal.

Android An operating system developed by Google for mobile devices.

animation The technique involved in tricking the eye into seeing continuous motion, which makes static images appear to move.

anonymity The ability to convey a message without disclosing your name or identity.

anonymous FTP An Internet service that enables you to contact a distant computer system to which you have access rights, log on to its public directories, and transfer files from that computer to your own. These sites lack security and should never be used to send sensitive data.

antivirus software Software that protects a computer from computer viruses by using a pattern-matching technique that examines all of the files on a disk, looking for virus code signatures.

application software A set of integrated programs that can be thought of as sitting on top of the operating system and that direct the computer's hardware to perform a task for the user.

application window The area on-screen that encloses and displays a launched application and work in progress.

application workspace The on-screen area that displays the document you are currently working on.

archive A single file that contains two or more files stored in a compressed format. An archive is handy for storage as well as file-exchange purposes because as many as several hundred separate files can be stored in a single, easily handled unit.

argument set In spreadsheet programs, such as Microsoft Excel, the part of a mathematical function that contains the parameters or variables that the function needs in order to perform the calculation. Usually the argument set is placed between parentheses.

arithmetic logic unit (ALU) The portion of the central processing unit that performs arithmetic operations, which return numeric values, and logical operations, which return a value of true or false.

arithmetic operation One of two groups of operations performed by the arithmetic logic unit (ALU). The arithmetic operations are addition, subtraction, multiplication, and division. An arithmetic operation returns the value of the operation.

artificial intelligence A computer science field that tries to improve computers by endowing them with some of the characteristics associated with human intelligence, such as the capability to understand natural language and to reason under conditions of uncertainty.

ASCII (American Standard Code for Information Interchange) A standard and widely used computer character set that makes use of seven bits and can represent 128 different characters. It is used on minicomputers, personal computers, and computers that make information available on the Internet.

aspect ratio A value that determines a monitor's quality and resolution; it is calculated by dividing a monitor's width by its height.

asynchronous communication Communication in which both parties are not necessarily online at the same time, for example, e-mail and text messaging.

Audio Video Interleave (AVI) A Microsoft-created specification for packaging audio and video data into a file. AVI makes no guarantee on the content of the package or the codec used to compress it.

authentication (login) The process that requests a user to enter a user name and password into a dialog box to verify that the user is indeed a person authorized to use the computer; also called login.

automation The replacement of human workers by machines and computer-guided robots.

AutoSave (AutoRecover) A software feature that backs up open documents at a default or user-specified interval; also called AutoRecover.

avatar A virtual representation of a player in a game or a person on a social networking site.

B

backbone In a wide area network (WAN), such as the Internet, a high-speed, high-capacity medium that transfers data over hundreds or thousands of miles. A variety of physical media are used for backbone services, including microwave relay, satellites, and dedicated telephone lines.

backdoor A method of bypassing normal authentication to secure access to a computer.

background application From the user's perspective, the application that appears inactive, as indicated by its appearance behind an active application on the desktop, when more than one application is running.

backup A copy of programs, data, and information created in one secondary storage medium that is duplicated to another.

backup procedure Procedures that protect against loss, change, or damage of an organization's data from natural or other disasters. This process usually involves making copies of data files and storing them in secure location.

backup software Programs that copy data from the computer's hard disk to backup devices, such as CDs or DVDs, an external hard drive, or an online storage location.

bad sector Areas of a hard disk that have become damaged and can no longer reliably hold data.

bandwidth The theoretical maximum amount of data that can be transmitted through a given communications channel, like a network, at one time (usually per second).

banner ad On a Web page, an ad that is not actually part of the Web page itself,

but is supplied separately by an ad network based on analysis of cookies.

bar code reader A handheld or desktop-mounted device that scans bar codes and, with special software, converts the bar code into readable data.

baud The number of signaling elements per second. At slower rates, bauds and bps may be equal, but on higher speed transmissions, more than one bit can be encoded in each signaling element; thus a 4,800 baud may have a transmission rate of 9,600 bps.

BD-R An optical storage media that that can record high-definition video or PC data storage.

BD-RE An optical storage medium that can record and erase high-definition video or PC data storage.

BD-ROM A standard for storing read-only high-definition computer data on optical discs. It is a format used for video or data distribution.

beta version In software testing, a preliminary version of a program that is widely distributed before commercial release to users who test the program by operating it under realistic conditions.

binary digit The digits 0 and 1, which are used to represent the Off/On state of a computer switch, the smallest piece of data that a computer can process. In the Off state, current is not flowing through the switch and is represented by the digit 0. In the On state, current is flowing through the switch and is represented by the digit 1.

binary number Strings of binary digits, 0 and 1, which represent the pattern of Off/On current flowing through switches.

biometric authentication A method of authentication that requires a biological scan of some sort, such as a fingerprint, retinal scan, or voice recognition.

biometric input device A device that uses physical or chemical features of an individual's body to provide a unique method of identification.

BIOS (basic input/output system) A set of programs that are part of the system software, permanently encoded on the computer's ROM memory and executed when the system is powered on. They check and initialize such devices as the keyboard, display screens, and disk drives. Many modern systems have flash BIOS, which is a type of BIOS that makes use of flash memory chips that can be updated by the user if needed.

bit Short for binary digit, a single circuit that either contains a current (represented by the digit 1) or does not contain current (represented by the digit 0). The digits 0 and 1 are the base unit of information in the binary number system. The lowest level of data in a database, the smallest unit of data a computer can store and understand.

bitmapped graphic (raster graphic) An image formed by a pattern of tiny dots, each of which corresponds to a pixel on the computer's display; also called raster graphic.

bitmapped image A representation of an image as a matrix of dots called picture elements (pixels).

block A unit of memory on a flash drive.

blog (Web log) Short for Web log. A Web site that contains an online personal journal with reflections, images, comments, and often hyperlinks provided by the writer.

Bluetooth A trademarked personal area network (PAN) technology, conceived by cell phone giant Ericsson and named after a 10th-century Viking. It uses short-range radio transmission technology to provide automatic and wireless communication among computers, mobile phones, printers, PDAs, and other devices located within 30 feet of each other.

Blu-ray Disc (BD) One of the newest forms of optical storage, Blu-ray technology was developed for the management of high-definition video and for storing large amounts of data.

Boolean search A database or Web search that uses the logical operators AND, OR, and NOT to specify the logical relationship among search words or phrases.

boot disk (emergency disk) A storage device, like a USB drive, CD, DVD, or network device that, in case of an emergency or boot failure, can load a reduced version of the operating system that can be used for troubleshooting purposes; also called an emergency disk.

booting The process of loading the operating system into RAM memory.

boot sector virus A computer virus that copies itself to the beginning tracks of a hard drive where code is stored that automatically executes every time you start the computer. Unlike file infectors, boot sector viruses don't require you to start a specific program to infect your computer; starting your system is sufficient.

Bootstrap Loader A program that locates and loads the operating system into RAM.

bot In a distributed denial of service (DDoS) attack, an automated program that connects the individual computers to the controller, usually a server with some type of real-time activity like Internet Relay Chat, that is under the power of a botnet controller; an abbreviation for robot.

bot herder An individual that controls a botnet.

botnet A set of computers infected with a malicious program that places the computers under the control of a bot herder. Such computers are typically used during a distributed denial of service (DDoS) attack.

bps rate The rate used to measure the exchange of data.

branch prediction A technique used by the central processing unit (CPU) to prevent a pipeline stall. The processor tries to predict what will happen with surprising accuracy.

broadband Refers to any transmission medium that carries several channels at once and thus transports high volumes of data at high speeds, typically greater than 1 Mbps.

browser cache A section of your hard drive in which Web pages visited for the first time are stored. If the user attempts to retrieve the page again, the browser does not go out on the Internet, but instead retrieves the page from the browser's cache. This eliminates excessive roundtrips to the server, brings the page up more quickly on the user's system, and greatly reduces Internet traffic.

buffer An area of RAM memory that temporarily holds data and instruction to make the processing of instructions more fluid.

bug Syntax and logical errors located in a computer program that can cause the program to perform erratically, produce incorrect results, or crash.

business services Services sold to enterprise and business organizations, usually on a subscription basis.

business-to-business e-commerce (B2B) The online exchange or trade of goods, services, or information in which one business provides another business with the materials, services, and/or supplies it needs to conduct its operations.

business-to-consumer e-commerce (B2C) The same experience as shopping at a physical store except the business supplies consumers with services, information, or products online.

bus topology The physical layout of a local area network in which the network cable is a single conduit that forms a bus, or line; every node, whether it is a computer or peripheral device, is attached to that bus. At the ends of the bus, connectors called terminators signify the end of the circuit.

byte A group of eight bits that represents a single character such as the essential numbers (0–9), the basic letters of the alphabet (uppercase and lowercase), and the most common punctuation symbols. Also a unit of capacity for storage devices.

C

cable modem A device that enables a computer to access the Internet by means of a cable TV connection. Cable modems enable two-way communications through the cable system and do not require a phone line. Cable modems enable Internet access speeds from 1.5 Mbps to 6 Mbps, although most users typically experience slower speeds due to network congestion.

cache memory A small unit of ultrafast memory built into or near the processor that stores frequently or recently accessed program instructions and data, increasing the computer's overall performance.

campus area network (CAN) A network that includes several LANs housed in various locations on a college or business campus. Usually smaller than a WAN,

CANs use devices such as switches, hubs, and routers to interconnect.

carpal tunnel syndrome A painful injury caused by repeated motions (such as mouse movements or keystrokes) that damage sensitive nerves in the hands, wrists, and arms. These injuries can become so serious that they may require surgery.

Cat-5 (Category 5) Short for Category 5, it's the fifth generation of twisted-pair data communication cable. Cat-5 cable contains four pairs of copper wire and supports speeds up to 100 Mbps over a maximum distance of 100 m (328 feet).

Cat-5e (Category 5 enhanced) Short for Category 5 enhanced, it uses all four wire pairs, enabling speeds up to 1,000 Mbps (1 Gbps) over a short distance. This enhanced medium is backward compatible with ordinary Cat-5.

Cat-6 (Category 6) Short for Category 6, it is the sixth generation of twisted-pair cable and is backward compatible with Cat-5 and Cat-5e. It contains four pairs of copper wire like that of the previous generation, utilizes all four pairs, supports speeds up to 1 gigabit per second (Gbps), expands available bandwidth from 100 MHz for Cat-5e to 200MHz, and has superior immunity from external noise.

Cave Automated Virtual Environment (CAVE) A virtual reality environment, used primarily by gamers, that replaces headsets with 3D glasses and uses the walls, ceiling, and floor to display projected three-dimensional images.

CD drive A read-only storage device that reads data encoded on CD-ROM media discs and transfers the data to the computer's internal memory.

CD-R (compact disc–recordable) Optical storage media that is a "write-once" technology. The data cannot be erased or written over once it has been saved; they're relatively inexpensive.

CD-ROM (compact disc read-only memory) A standard for storing read-only computer data (it cannot be changed or erased) on optical compact discs (CDs), which can be read by CD-ROM drives and DVD-ROM drives. CD-ROM discs can hold up to 700 MB of data.

CD-RW (compact disc–rewritable) An optical storage media that allows data that has been saved to be erased or written over.

CD-RW drive (burner or CD burner) A compact disc–rewritable storage device that provides full read/write capabilities using erasable CD-RWs.

cell 1. In a spreadsheet, the intersection of a column and row. 2. In telecommunications, a limited geographical area in which a signal can be broadcast.

cell address The column letter and row number that identifies a cell usually in a table or spreadsheet.

cell site In a cellular telephone network, an area in which a transmitting station repeats the system's broadcast signals so that the signal remains strong even though the user may move from one cell site to another.

cellular telephone A radio-based wireless computing device that provides widespread coverage through the use of repeating transmitters placed in zones (called cells). The zones are close enough so that signal strength is maintained throughout the calling area.

central processing unit (CPU; microprocessor or processor) A chip, located on the motherboard within the system unit, that is composed of the control unit and the arithmetic logic unit (ALU). It applies directions received from software to the input data and converts it into information.

channel In Internet Relay Chat (IRC), a chat group in which as many as several dozen people carry on a text-based conversation on a specific topic. This is dated technology that has been replaced by instant messaging, blogging, wikis, and tweeting.

character code An algorithm that translates the numerical language of the computer into keyboard characters readable by humans.

character map A comparison chart or lookup table located in a computer's read-only memory (ROM) on the motherboard. The system uses this table to locate the key that was struck on the keyboard and then notifies the processor of the character corresponding to that matrix location.

charged-coupled device (CCD) A photosensitive computer chip that transforms light patterns into pixels (individual dots). A CCD consists of a grid made up of light-sensitive elements. Each element converts the incoming light into a voltage that is proportional to the light's brightness. The digital camera's picture quality is determined by how many elements the CCD has.

chart A graphical representation of numbers that makes it easier to interpret data.

chipset A collection of chips, located on the motherboard, that act like a traffic controller and work together to provide the switching circuitry needed by the microprocessor to move data throughout the computer via the microprocessor's system bus.

ciphertext The coded message that results from applying an encryption key to a message.

circuit switching One of two fundamental architectures for a wide area network (WAN), in which high-speed electronic switches create a direct connection between two communicating devices. The telephone system is a circuit-switching network.

clickstream The trail of Web links that you have followed to get to a particular site.

click wheel A variation of the touchpad that looks like a circle and uses a circular motion to move through song lists, movie lists, or photos. The click wheel is the method of navigation on the iPod and the iTouch.

client A desktop, notebook, workstation, terminal, or handheld device that is connected to a network and contains the software that enables it to send requests to a server.

client/server network A network system in which individual users, called clients, are connected to each other through a central computer, called a server, which runs special software to enable the network connectivity.

clock speed The speed of the internal clock of a microprocessor that synchronizes and sets the pace of the computer's internal activities, including the movement from one stage of the machine cycle to another.

cloud operating system A specially designed operating system created to run on a cloud provider's datacenter. The OS is delivered to subscribers over the Internet or other network. Windows Azure is a cloud operating system.

cluster On a magnetic disk, a storage unit that consists of two or more sectors.

CMOS (complementary metal-oxide semiconductor) Instructions located in read-only-memory (ROM) that control a variety of actions including starting the power-on self test and verifying that other components of the system are functioning correctly. The CMOS configuration should only be altered by an experienced user.

coaxial cable A broadband transmission medium that consists of a center copper wire surrounded by insulation, which is then surrounded by a layer of braided wire. Data travels through the center wire, and the braided wire provides a shield against electrical interference.

codec Short for compression/decompression standard. A standard for compressing and decompressing video information to reduce the size of digitized multimedia files. Popular codecs include MPEG (an acronym for Motion Picture Experts Group), Apple's QuickTime, and Microsoft's AVI.

code of conduct A set of ethical principles often developed by a professional organization, such as the Association for Computing Machinery (ACM).

cold boot Starting a computer that is not already on.

collaboration software A collection of programs that help people share ideas, create documents, and conduct meetings, regardless of location or time zone, through the use of proprietary networks or the Internet.

collaboration tools Applications that help you work in partnership with team members online.

collision The corruption of network data that results when two or more computers transmit to the same network cable at exactly the same time. Networks have means of detecting and preventing collisions.

column In Microsoft Excel and Word, a block of data presented vertically on the screen.

command-line user interface A method of interacting with an operating system

that requires the user to type, one line at a time, commands using keywords and specific syntax (rules for entering commands) that tell the OS what to do (such as *format* or *copy*).

commerce The selling of goods and services with the expectation of making a reasonable profit.

commercial software Copyrighted software that must be purchased. The current trend is to make such software available as an online download or to give the potential customer a trial period. Once the trial period is over, the user can pay for the program directly on the Web site and download their official copy.

communications The high-speed electronic transfer of data or information within and between computers.

communications channel (link) The transmission media on which the message is sent from one location to the next; also referred to as the link).

communication device A hardware device that is capable of converting data into signals that can travel over a physical (wired) or wireless medium, and moving those signals into or out of the computer. These devices, which include modems, routers, switches, hubs, wireless access points, network interface cards, and other computers, also determine efficient data transfer pathways, boost signal strength, and facilitate overall digital communication.

communications device See communication device.

community cloud An extension of a private cloud in which organizations with similar missions share the infrastructure to reduce cost. This variation of the private cloud disperses cost while providing a high level of conformity and security by allowing access only to trusted users. Google's Gov Cloud is an example of a community cloud.

CompactFlash A popular flash memory storage device that can store up to 128 MB of digital camera images.

composite cloud Evolves when a primary cloud provider offers services that are distributed through another cloud provider.

computer An electronic device that receives data as input, processes that data based on a set of instructions, outputs the results of the processing for the user to review, and stores those results for later use.

computer crime A computer-based activity that violates state, federal, or international laws.

computer ethics A branch of philosophy that deals with computer-related moral dilemmas and defines ethical principles, helping a user to make the morally correct decision in daily computer use.

computer forensics A branch of forensic science that deals with legal evidence found on computers. It is used to find and apprehend criminals.

computer security risk Any event, action, or situation—intentional or not—that could lead to the loss or destruction of computer systems or the data they contain.

computer system A collection of related computer components that have been designed to work together smoothly.

computer virus Hidden code that replicates itself by attaching to other programs, files, or e-mail messages, referred to as hosts, and usually carries out unwanted and sometimes dangerous operations.

congestion In a packet-switching network, a performance interruption that occurs when a segment of the network experiences an overload, too much traffic flooding the same network path.

connectivity The ability to link various media and devices, thereby enhancing communication and improving access to information.

connector A physical receptacle located on the system unit or an expansion card that is visible on the outside of the system unit and enables the connection of a cable to the computer's unit. A male connector contains extended pins or plugs that fit into the corresponding female connector.

consumer-oriented services One of two major categories of Software-as-a-Service (SaaS) that offers features like those supplied by Google Apps and Google Docs to the public, either on a subscription basis or, if supported by advertisement, for no cost.

consumer-to-consumer e-commerce (C2C) The online exchange or trade of goods, services, or information between individual consumers. Often C2C e-commerce involves the use of an intermediate site, such as the popular online auction destination eBay.

content pane (file list) Displayed in the right pane of a Windows Explorer window. It shows the subfolders and files located within the selected folder

contention In a computer network, a problem that arises when two or more computers try to access the network at the same time. Contention can result in collisions, which can destroy data or require frequent and costly retransmissions.

contention management In a computer network, the use of one of several techniques for managing contention and preventing collisions. A common contention-management technique is to abandon any data that could have been corrupted by a collision.

contextual tab In Microsoft Office applications, a tab that is displayed and provides additional options for editing a selected feature, for example, an image.

continuous backup Programs that automatically create a backup, or duplicate, when a change in a system or a data file occurs.

control unit The portion of the central processing unit (CPU) that, under the direction of an embedded program, switches from one stage of the machine cycle to the next and performs the action of that stage.

convergence The merging of disparate objects or ideas (and even people) into new combinations and efficiencies. Within the IT industry, convergence means two things: the combination of various industries (computers, consumer electronics, and telecommunications) and the coming together of products such as PCs and telephones.

cookie A text file that is deposited by a Web site on a Web user's computer system, without the user's knowledge or consent. Mostly used for legitimate purposes, such as implementing "shopping carts," they can also be used to gather data on Web users' browsing and shopping habits.

cooling fan A fan designed to keep the system unit cool. The fan often is part of the power supply, although many systems include auxiliary fans to provide additional cooling.

copy-protected software Computer programs that include some mechanism to prevent users from making or running unauthorized copies.

copyright infringement The act of plagiarizing, using material from a copyrighted source without permission.

copyright protection scheme A method software manufacturers are working to develop to thwart the illegal use of their programs.

corporate espionage The unauthorized accessing of corporate information, usually to the benefit of one of the corporation's competitors.

cracker (black hat) A computer user obsessed with gaining entry into highly secure computer systems; also called a black hat.

cryptographer An individual who specializes in encoding information.

cryptography The study of transforming information into an encoded or scrambled format.

cursor (insertion point) A blinking vertical bar, a horizontal underline character, or a highlighted box located on the monitor that indicates the location in which keystrokes will appear when typed.

cursor-movement keys (arrow keys) A set of four keys clustered together to the left of the number pad that move the cursor up, down, left, or right. The numeric keypad can also move the cursor when in the appropriate mode.

custom software Application software designed by a professional programmer or programming team to meet the specific needs of a company or organization. Custom software is usually very expensive.

cyberbullying A cybercrime that involves situations in which one or more individuals harass or threaten another

individual who is less capable of defending himself or herself, using the Internet or other forms of digital technology. Cyberbullying can include sending threatening e-mail or text messages or assuming someone else's online identity for the purpose of humiliating or misrepresenting him or her.

cybercrime Crime carried out by means of the Internet.

cybergang A group of computer users obsessed with gaining entry into highly secure computer systems.

cyberlaw A new legal field designed to track developments in cybercrime and combat occurrences of such abuses.

cyberspace The reference to the intangible, nonphysical territory that the Internet encompasses.

cyberstalker A person engaging in a form of harassment in which an individual uses the Internet, social networking sites, e-mail, or other electronic communications to repeatedly harass or threaten and disrupt a victim's real life.

cyberstalking A form of harassment in which an individual uses the Internet, social networking sites, e-mail, or other electronic communications to repeatedly harass or threaten a person. Cyberstalking, like real-world stalking, is a repeated, unwanted, and disruptive break into the life-world of the victim.

D

data Raw facts, which can be made up of words, numbers, images, sounds, or a combination of these. The data from the input phase of the information processing cycle is passed to the processing phase.

data bus A set of parallel wires that acts as an electronic highway on which data travels between computer components. It is the medium by which the entire system communicates with the CPU.

data dependency A microprocessor performance problem in which the CPU is slowed in its functioning by the need to wait for the results of one set of instructions before moving on to process another set of instructions.

data diddling A computer crime in which data is modified in accounts or databases to conceal theft or embezzlement.

data set The contents of a table in Access.

data transfer rate 1. In secondary storage devices, the maximum number of bits per second that can be sent from the hard disk to the computer. The rate is determined by the drive interface. 2. The speed, expressed in bits per second (bps), at which a modem can transfer, or is transferring, data over a telephone line.

dead link (broken link) On the World Wide Web, a hyperlink that refers to a resource (such as a sound or a Web page) that has been moved or deleted; also called a broken link.

default In a computer program, the settings that are in effect unless a user deliberately overrides them.

denial of service attack (DoS) A form of network vandalism that attempts to make a service unavailable to other users, generally by flooding the service with meaningless data.

design template A professionally created slide design that can be applied to a presentation and provides coordinated background color, font type, and bullet style.

desktop The screen image that appears after an operating system finishes loading into memory (RAM) and displays pictures (icons) representing files, folders, and windows in the file system. The desktop image can change with the operating system and version, or can be customized by the user.

desktop computer A computer that consists of a system unit, an independent monitor, and a keyboard designed for an individual's use at a desk or fixed location.

details pane Displayed along the bottom of the right pane of a Windows Explorer window. It provides a thumbnail view and information about the selected file or folder; the details vary depending on the object that has been selected.

digital camera A camera that uses digital technology, instead of film, to take and store images in digital format and can input those images directly into your system through a USB or FireWire port.

digital cash system A method for using smart cards and prepaid amounts of electronically stored money to pay for small charges such as parking and tolls.

digital certificate A form of digital identification enabled by public key encryption that serves as a method of validating a user, server, or Web site. For a user, a digital certificate validates identity in a manner similar to showing a driver's license. For a server or Web site, a digital certificate validates that a Web server or Web site is authentic so that the user can feel secure in his or her interaction.

digital divide The age, race, and/or income disparity in computer ownership and Internet access.

digital piracy The unauthorized reproduction and distribution of computer-based media.

digital signal A signal used by digital equipment, like computers, sent via discontinuous pulses, in which the presence or absence of electronic pulses is represented by 1s and 0s.

digital signature A technique enabled by public key encryption that is used to guarantee that a message is authentic, not sent by a hacker, and has not been tampered with.

digital telephony Telephone systems using all-digital protocols and transmission, offering the advantage over analog telephony of noise-free transmission and high-quality audio.

digital video camera (camcorder) A camera that takes and stores videos in digital format, instead of analog, and can input those images directly into your system through a USB or FireWire port.

digital-to-analog converter (DAC) A microchip that contains the circuitry to convert a digital signal to analog.

digitization The transformation of data such as voice, text, graphics, audio, and video into digital form, thereby allowing various technologies to transmit computer data through telephone lines, cables, or air and space. Digitization also allows the data to be shared as files enabling convergence, something difficult to do with analog technologies.

direct broadcast satellite (DBS) A consumer satellite technology that uses an 18- or 21-inch reception dish to receive digital TV signals at microwave frequencies directly from geostationary satellites broadcast at a bandwidth of 12 Mbps. Increasingly, DBS operators offer Internet access as well as digital TV service, but at much lower bandwidth.

disk cache A type of RAM, usually incorporated on the circuit board within the hard drive case, that stores some of the program instructions and data you are working with. When the CPU needs to get information, it looks in the disk cache first. If it doesn't find the information it needs, it retrieves the information from the hard disk.

disk cleanup utility A program that improves system performance and increases storage space by removing files that you no longer need.

disk defragmentation program A utility program used to reorganize data on the disk so that file pieces are reassembled as one chunk of disk space (decreasing disk search time); storage is made more efficient by clustering files into structures more efficiently searched; and the time needed to access files is decreased.

disk scanning program An error-checking program that can detect and resolve a number of physical and logical problems that may occur when your computer stores files on a disk.

distributed denial of service (DDoS) attack A computer attack on multiple systems by a hacker who bombards an Internet server with a huge number of requests so that the server becomes overloaded and unable to respond to requests from valid users.

distributed hypermedia system A network-based content development system in which individuals connected to the network can each make a small contribution by developing content related to their area of expertise. The Web is a distributed hypermedia system.

DLP projector (digital light-processing projector) An output device that projects a computer's display on a screen by projecting light into a chip made of millions of microscopic mirrors to produce a brilliant, sharp image.

document A file created with an application program, such as a word processing or spreadsheet program.

documentation 1. Tutorials, Read Me files, help files, and printed manuals that contain information the software manufacturer believes the user will find helpful. 2. The output of the fifth phase of the Program Development Life Cycle in which in-depth explanations of major program features, reference documentation of all program commands, and a thorough description of the error messages generated by the program are detailed.

domain name On the Internet, a readable computer address, **http://www.microsoft.com**, that gets translated into an IP address and identifies a computer on the network.

domain name registration On the Internet, a process by which individuals and companies can obtain a domain name (such as **www.c34.org**) and link this name to a specific Internet address (IP address).

Domain Name System (DNS) A system used by the Internet to link domain names with their numeric IP address. It functions like a telephone directory for the Internet.

dot-matrix printer (impact printer) Once the most popular type of printer, the dot-matrix printer creates characters by striking pins against an ink ribbon. Each pin makes a dot, and combinations of dots form characters and illustrations.

dot pitch (aperture grill) The distance between the dots (pixels) on a CRT monitor. The lower the dot pitch, the closer the dots are to each other and the sharper the image.

downloading The process of transferring a file from another computer to your computer by means of a computer network.

drive A storage device in which files and folders reside. Drives can be internal (located within the system unit, such as a hard drive) or external (attached to the system unit via a port).

drive activity light The light on the front panel of most computers that signals when the hard drive is accessing data.

drive bay A receptacle or opening into which a hard disk drive, CD or DVD drive, or portable drive can be installed. An internal bay is within the system unit and an external bay is accessed from outside the system unit.

drive imaging software Software that creates a mirror image of the entire hard disk, including the operating system and applications, as well as all files and data. In the event of a hard disk or computer system failure, the drive image can be used to restore the system.

drive letter A letter of the alphabet followed by a colon and a backslash character that identifies the storage devices active on a system.

driver A utility program that contains instructions to make a peripheral device addressable or usable by an operating system.

DSL (digital subscriber line or xDSL) A general term for several technologies that enable high-speed Internet access through twisted-pair telephone lines. Also called xDSL.

DSL modem Similar to a traditional telephone modem in that it modulates and demodulates analog and digital signals for transmission over communications channels, but it does so using signaling methods based on broadband technology for much higher transfer speeds.

dual inline memory module (DIMM) A RAM memory module that fits into special slots on the motherboard that has a 168-pin connector and a 64-bit data transfer rate.

dumpster diving A technique to obtain passwords in which intruders go through an organization's trash hoping to find documents that contain lists of user IDs and passwords.

DVD drive A read-only storage device that reads the data encoded on a DVD-ROM disc and transfers this data to a computer.

DVD+R A recordable format that enables the disc to be written to one time and read many times.

DVD+RW A recordable format that enables the disc to be rewritten to many times.

DVD-R Digital video disc, a recordable optical storage medium that, like CD-R discs, cannot be erased or written over once data has been saved; the disk can be written to only once but read from many times.

DVD-ROM (digital video [or versatile] disc read-only memory) A digital video optical disc format capable of storing up to 17 GB on a single disc, enough for a feature-length movie.

DVD-RW Digital video disc, a recordable optical storage medium on which you can write, erase, and read from many times.

DVI (digital visual interface) port An interface that allows LCD monitors to use digital signals instead of analog signals.

dye sublimation printer A type of thermal-wax transfer printer that uses a heat process to transfer an impression onto paper. Although thermal-transfer printers are the best color printers currently available, they are slow and very expensive.

dynamic A term used to describe Windows Explorer searches that are automatically updated every time you open up a saved search. New files that meet the search criteria are added and ones that no longer meet the criteria are removed.

E

EBCDIC (Extended Binary Coded Decimal Interchange Code) An eight-bit character code used by IBM mainframe computers and some midrange systems that uses a low-to-high code sequence for punctuation, lowercase letters, uppercase letters, and then numbers.

e-book Short for electronic book. A book-sized device that displays e-books. E-book readers may be devices that are built solely for reading e-books or they may be PDAs, handheld devices, or other computing devices that have a processor and display screen. The newest e-book readers are available in a larger size, increasing the ease of reading. Some even boast an auto-rotating screen with a text-to-speech mode.

e-book reader A dedicated reading device dedicated to downloading, displaying, and reading books obtained through an e-bookstore (an electronic book store accessed via the Internet).

e-commerce (electronic commerce) The use of networks or the Internet to carry out business of any type.

e-discovery (electronic discovery) The obligation of parties to a lawsuit to exchange documents that exist only in electronic form, including e-mails, voicemails, instant messages, e-calendars, audio files, data on handheld devices, graphics, photographs, spreadsheets, Web sites, drawings, and other types of digital data.

EEPROM Electrically erasable programmable read-only memory that can be rewritten many times while the chip is in the computer. EEPROM is erased one byte at a time, using an electric field instead of a UV light source, eliminating the need for an erasing window.

e-learning The use of computers and computer programs to replace teachers and the time–place specificity of learning.

electronic mailing list Lists of e-mail addresses that automatically broadcast messages to all individuals on the list. Because the messages are transmitted as e-mail, only individuals who are subscribers to the mailing list receive and view the messages.

e-mail (electronic mail) An Internet service requiring a software application that enables you to send and receive messages though the use of computer networks.

e-mail address A series of characters that provides a unique cyberspace identity for a particular recipient that follows the form myname@somedomain.com and precisely identifies the location of a person's electronic mailbox. On the Internet, e-mail addresses consist of a mailbox name (such as jsmith) followed by an "at" sign (@) and the computer's domain name (as in jsmith@fictitiousschool.edu).

e-mail attachment Any type of computer file—document, photo, audio, or video—that is included with an e-mail message.

embedded operating system Operating systems that are found on ROM chips in the portable or dedicated devices that we use today. They are usually compact and efficient. Embedded operating systems go without some of the features found in nonembedded operating systems.

embedded processor A processor designed and programmed to perform only the tasks intended to be done by the device the processor is implanted within.

emergency disk A storage device, like a USB drive, CD, DVD, or network device

that, in case of an emergency or boot failure, can load a reduced version of the operating system that can be used for troubleshooting purposes; also called a boot disk.

employee monitoring When large employers routinely engage in observing employees' phone calls, e-mails, Web browsing habits, and computer files.

encryption A coding or scrambling process that renders a message unreadable by anyone except the intended recipient.

encryption key A formula that is used to make a plaintext message unreadable.

enhanced keyboard A keyboard containing additional keys, usually positioned above the row of function keys, that consist of media control buttons that adjust speaker volume and access the optical disc drive, and Internet controls that open e-mail, a browser, or a search window, with a single keystroke.

enterprise server Powerful servers that are part of a networked system designed to connect hundreds of thousands of users at the same time. They are usually used in large corporations or government agencies, handle a high volume of data, can fill an entire wall of an average room, and cost from several thousand to millions of dollars.

EPROM Electrically programmable read-only memory is erasable PROM that can be reused many times. Erasure is accomplished using a UV (ultraviolet) light source that shines through a quartz erasing window in the EPROM package. It is used primarily by programmers in the program development process so that errors can be corrected.

ergonomics The field of study that is concerned with the fit between people, their equipment, and their work. It takes into account worker limitations and capabilities in attempting to ensure that the tasks, equipment, and overall environment suit each worker.

e-tailer A Web-based retailer.

Ethernet The most popular LAN standard for large and small businesses. According to International Data Corporation (IDC), approximately 85 percent of all installed networks use various versions of Ethernet.

ethical hacker (white hat) Hackers and crackers who have turned pro, offering their services to companies hoping to use hacker expertise to shore up their computer systems' defenses; also called a white hat.

ethical principle The standards that promote trust, fairness, good behavior, and kindness and are used to justify an act as morally right or morally wrong.

evil twin A phony WiFi hot spot whose name makes users believe it is a legitimate spot. Typically situated in hotels and airports, an evil twin is usually connected to a fraudulent network.

e-waste Obsolete computer equipment.

exabyte A unit of measurement approximately equal to 1 quintillion bytes.

exclusion operator In database and Internet searching, a symbol or a word that tells the software to exclude records or documents containing a certain word or phrase. It is usually denoted as a minus sign (−) in the search statement.

execution cycle (execute, store) In a machine cycle, a phase consisting of the execute and write-back (or store) operations.

exiting Quitting or closing down an application or program.

expansion card (expansion board, adapter card, or adapter) A circuit board that fits into slots on the motherboard and is used to connect computers with various peripherals.

expansion slot Receptacles, usually located on the motherboard, that accept additional circuit boards or expansion cards.

ExpressCard Also referred to as a PC card, a device approximately the size of a credit card that is usually used with notebook computers and that can be inserted or removed from PC card slots while the computer is running. ExpressCards can serve as modems, network adapters, or additional memory.

Extended ASCII A character coding system that uses eight bits and allows representation of 256 characters.

Extended Graphics Array (XGA) The resolution standard for most of today's monitors (1024 × 768).

Extensible Hypertext Markup Language (XHTML) A language that combines the flexibility of HTML with the extensibility of XML by allowing the user to define a tag for clarity across different browsers or create a new markup tag by simply defining it in an XHTML module and using it in a Web page as you would any other HTML tag. This feature makes a page truly compatible with all browsers.

Extensible Markup Language (XML) A language designed to reduce the complexity of HTML.

extension The second part of a file name added after the dot. It is supplied by an application to indicate that the file was created by that application and thus should be reopened with it.

F

Facebook Currently, the largest social networking site, allowing anyone over the age of 13, with a valid e-mail account and residing in a country where it has not been banned, to become a user. Facebook users often join groups set up by region, job, interest, or school and communicate with group members.

facsimile transmission (fax) The sending and receiving of printed pages between two locations using a telephone line and fax devices that digitize the page's image.

fair use An exception to copyright laws that justifies limited uses of copyrighted material without payment to or permission from the copyright holder. This exception limits the selection to no more than 5 percent of the original copyrighted work and only for the purposes of commentary, parody, news reporting, research, and education.

fat client A device that enables a user to connect to a network server but does most data processing in its own system, not on the server.

fax modem A modem that also functions as a fax machine, but unlike a traditional stand-alone fax machine, does everything in a digital way, providing the computer user with the capability of sending word-processing documents and other files as faxes.

fiber-optic cable A broadband transmission medium that consists of thin strands of glass or plastic that carry data by means of pulses of light. Fiber-optic cable carries data at transfer rates of 10 Gbps (gigabits per second) or more, without loss of signal strength and for longer distances than twisted-pair or coaxial cable.

fiber-optic service Fiber-optic lines that run directly to the home and provide users with incredibly fast Internet access, easily surpassing other methods.

file A named unit of related data stored in a computer system.

file compression utility A program that can reduce the size of a file by as much as 80 percent without harming the data, by substituting short codes for lengthy data patterns. The resulting smaller files can be shared more efficiently, particularly over the Internet. Prior to use, compressed files need to be decompressed and converted back to their lengthy form.

file infector A computer virus that attaches to a program file and, when that program is executed, spreads to other program files.

file manager A program that helps you to organize and manage the data stored on your disk.

file name The name that the storage device uses to identify each unique file.

file server In client/server computing, a high-capacity, high-speed computer with a large hard disk set aside (dedicated) to make program and data files available to users on a network.

File Transfer Protocol (FTP) An Internet standard for the exchange of files between two computers connected to the Internet that is especially useful when the files are too large to send by e-mail. Although you can use special FTP client software, such as WS_FTP Home, you can also transfer files to and from an FTP server simply by using your browser or Windows Explorer.

filter In Microsoft Access, a simplified method of locating records that match criteria specified by the user.

firewall A program or device that permits an organization's internal computer users to access the Internet but places severe limits on the ability of outsiders to access internal data.

FireWire (1394 port) FireWire is Apple Computer's name for a 1394 input/output port, an interface that offers high-speed connections for peripherals. It is ideal for real-time devices like digital video cameras.

flame Messages sent through e-mail, chat rooms, instant messaging, and message boards that express an opinion without holding back any emotion and are frequently seen as being confrontational and argumentative.

flash drive A type of storage device that uses solid-state circuitry and has no moving parts, making it a solid-state drive. It retains the data stored in it even if disconnected from its source.

flash EPROM A type of PROM similar to EEPROM except that flash EPROMs are erased in blocks, whereas regular EEPROMs can be erased one byte at a time.

flash memory Nonvolatile memory found on flash drives and memory cards that can be electronically erased and reprogrammed.

flash memory card A wafer-thin, highly portable solid-state storage system that is capable of storing as much as 64 GB of data. Flash memory cards are used with smartphones, MP3 players, digital video cameras, and other portable digital devices.

flash memory reader A slot or compartment into which the flash memory card is inserted.

flexible OLED display (FOLED display) An extremely thin, flexible, and lightweight output display that produces outstanding color, contrast, brightness, and viewing angles. OLED displays are emissive devices, meaning they emit light rather than modulate transmitted or reflected light.

floating point standard A notation standard, created by the Institute of Electrical and Electronics Engineers (IEEE) and used to represent numbers with fractional parts. There is no fixed number of digits before or after the decimal point, so the computer can work with very large and very small numbers.

folder (directory) An organizational tool for grouping files that have something in common.

folder structure (directory structure) An organized set of folders in which to save your files.

footprint The amount of physical space used by a device.

foreground application From the user's perspective, the application that is active (in use), as indicated by its appearance as the topmost image seen on the desktop, when more than one application is running.

forgery The making of Internet data appear to come from one place when it's really coming from another.

form In the Microsoft Access database management system, a template used to enter data into the database in place of the Table entry method.

form factor The specifications for mounting internal components such as the motherboard into the system unit.

formula A combination of numeric constants, cell references, arithmetic operators, and functions that are used to calculate a result.

fragmented A disk that has been used to the point that it becomes a patchwork of files, with portions of files scattered here and there. This placement of sectors slows disk access because the system must look in several locations to find all of a file's segments.

frame In a video or animation, single still images that are flashed on-screen at a rapid rate.

frame rate In a video or animation, a measurement of the number of still images shown per second.

freeware Copyrighted software that can be freely copied but not sold for profit.

full backup The duplicating of all files and data on the entire hard disk as a precaution should the hard disk drive fail.

function In spreadsheet programs such as Microsoft Excel, one of the two basic types of formulas (along with mathematical expressions). A function begins with an equal sign but is then followed by a descriptive name that is predefined in the software (such as SUM to calculate the total of a set of values) and an argument set, which is placed within parentheses and designates the locations of the values that the function needs to utilize in its calculations.

function key A row of keys positioned along the top of the keyboard, labeled F1 through F12. The action performed by each key varies with the program in use.

G

gadget An application that appears as an active icon in the Windows sidebar. Gadgets are selected or downloaded by the user and display photos and current weather conditions, control a multimedia player, or monitor the CPU's performance.

Gantt chart A type of bar chart that facilitates project management by indicating task due dates and project milestones.

General Public License (GPL) A free software license, devised by the Open Software Foundation (OSF), stipulating that anyone may freely copy, use, and modify the software. The modifications must be made available for all users, but no one can sell the software for profit.

general-purpose application A software program used by many people to accomplish frequently performed tasks such as writing (word processing), working with numbers (spreadsheets), and keeping track of information (databases).

gigabits per second (Gbps) A data transfer measurement equivalent to 1 billion bits per second.

gigabyte (GB) A unit of measurement approximately equal to 1 billion bits.

gigahertz (GHz) A unit used to measure a processor's speed in billions of cycles per second.

gigaPOP (gigabits per second point of presence) A point of presence (POP) that provides access to a backbone service capable of data transfer rates exceeding 1 Gbps (1 billion bits per second).

globally unique identifier (GUID) An identification number that is generated by a hardware component or a program. The GUIDs can be read by Web servers or embedded in various documents, detecting which computer is accessing a site and inadvertently making it more difficult to use the Internet anonymously.

Google Docs A free Web-based service that allows project members to share and edit documents and spreadsheets online.

Google Groups A free service provided by Google to help users connect, share information, and communicate effectively over the Internet. Its current version allows group members to collaborate on shared Web pages; set group pictures, colors, and styles; upload and share individually created work; and learn more about other members in the group.

GPS (Global Positioning System) A satellite-based system consisting of a cluster of 27 Earth-orbiting satellites that enables portable GPS receivers to determine their location with an accuracy of 109 yards or less.

graphical MUD (gMUD) A multiuser dungeon (MUD) that uses 3D graphics instead of text to represent the interaction of characters and bring the virtual environment to life.

graphical user interface (GUI) The most popular method of interacting with a computer system. It uses graphics and the point-and-click technology of the mouse to make the operating system and programs easier to use.

grid A combination of several computers or virtual machines that are connected over a network to make them appear and function as one single computer.

grounding bracelet A device that is worn around the wrist with the other end attached to a grounded object. It is worn to avoid discharging static electricity into a system under repair.

grounding strap See grounding bracelet.

group In Microsoft Office, a collection of buttons and commands that appear on tabs within the Ribbon.

H

hacker Traditionally a computer hobbyist who enjoys pushing his or her computer capabilities to the limit, especially by using clever or novel approaches to solving problems.

hacker ethic An unwritten code of conduct subscribed to by hackers that forbids the destruction of data.

handheld computer A computer designed for individual use and portability, it usually fits in the palm of your hand or pocket of your jeans and makes use of a stylus or virtual keyboard.

hard copy Output viewed in printed form.

hard disk controller An electronic circuit board that provides an interface between the CPU and the hard disk's electronics. The controller may be located on the computer's motherboard, on an expansion card, or within the hard disk.

hard disk drive (hard drive) A secondary storage, random access, high-capacity, high-speed device, usually housed in the system unit, that consists of several rapidly rotating disks called platters on which programs, data, and processed results are stored. In almost all modern computers, the hard disk is by far the easiest storage device to access and the most important storage medium.

hardware All the physical components that make up a computer system, including such items as circuit boards, disk drives, printers, and monitors.

Hardware-as-a-Service (HaaS) See Infrastructure-as-a-Service (IaaS).

HDSL (high bit-rate digital subscriber line) The most mature DSL technology, it is a form of SDSL that provides T1 connections over two or three twisted-pair copper lines. Unlike most other forms of DSL, HDSL is not a typical consumer service.

headset (head-mounted display) A wearable output device with twin LCD panels for creating the illusion that an individual is experiencing a three-dimensional, simulated environment.

heat sink A heat-dissipating component that drains heat from a chip. Heat sinks are usually used in combination with cooling fans.

hexadecimal (hex) number A number system, referred to as base-16, that uses the numbers 0 through 9 and the letters A through F to represent a binary string in a shorter, more compact form.

Hibernate mode Used primarily in notebooks to conserve battery life, this mode puts the documents and programs you have opened on your hard disk and then actually turns off your computer. When you restart your system, it is returned to the state prior to hibernation. All windows and programs that were open are restored automatically.

high-definition television (HDTV) A digital television standard found in such televisions as direct-view, plasma, rear screen, and front screen projection that have higher resolutions, typically (1920 × 1080) or better. HDTVs provide extremely high-quality video and audio, enabling the use of your HDTV as a computer monitor.

History list In a Web browser, a window or list that shows all the Web sites that the browser has accessed during a given period, such as the last 30 days.

holographic storage A type of storage that uses two laser beams to create a pattern on photosensitive media, resulting in a three-dimensional image similar to the holograms you can buy in a novelty shop. This 3D approach will enable much higher-density storage capacities and is being promoted for its archiving capabilities.

home and educational program A general-purpose software program for personal finance, home design and landscaping, encyclopedias and other computerized reference information, and games.

home network (home area network or HAN) A personal and specific use of network technology that provides connectivity among users and devices located in or near one residence.

home page (index page) The start page that is automatically displayed when you enter a Web site through its top level; also called an index page.

honeypot A computer baited with fake data and purposely left vulnerable so as to study how intruders operate in order to prepare stronger defenses to thwart attacks.

host A networked computer that has two-way access to other computers; it can receive requests and reply to those requests.

host name The name of the group or institution operating a Web site. It is the first part of the domain portion of a URL. In the URL www.microsoft.com/windows/default.aspx the host portion is Microsoft.

hot spot Usually a public location like an airport, college campus, or coffee shop that provides Internet access for devices fitted with wireless technology.

hot swapping Connecting and disconnecting peripheral devices while your computer is running.

hub A simple, inexpensive broadcast device that joins multiple computers together in a single network but does not manage the traffic between the connections, which usually results in frequent collisions. It is used as the central wiring mechanism in a star topology network layout

hybrid cloud The combination of two or more clouds (private, community, or public) that are unique but are connected by common, standard technology that enables the sharing of applications and data. Its infrastructure can be located both on-site and off the premises, and it can be managed by both the organization and a cloud provider. Users can be trusted and untrusted.

hybrid hard drive (HHD) A hard drive that incorporates flash technology in its design to speed up the boot process.

hybrid network A network that is a combination of both wired and wireless technology.

Hybrid sleep This mode, a combination of Sleep and Hibernate mode, puts open documents and programs in both RAM and on your hard disk, and then places the system in a low-power state so you can quickly resume your work. If power is suddenly terminated, the Hibernate portion of this mode guarantees that your work can be restored. Hybrid sleep is usually turned on by default on most desktops.

hyperlink (link) In a hypertext system, an element in an electronic document that acts as the connector to another place in the same document or to an entirely different document. Typically, you click on the hyperlink to get to the related object. Hyperlinks are the most essential ingredient of the World Wide Web.

hyptertext A system in which objects (text, pictures, music, programs, and so on) can be creatively linked to each other.

Hypertext Markup Language (HTML) A language that uses a tag system of code to create Web pages. This language is interpreted by browsers, which display the page according to the directions specified by the HTML language. HTML includes capabilities that enable authors to insert hyperlinks, which, when clicked, display another HTML document. The agency responsible for standardizing HTML is the World Wide Web Consortium (W3C).

Hypertext Transfer Protocol (HTTP) The Internet standard that supports the exchange of information on the Web by the use of uniform resource locators (URLs).

I

icon A small image that represents a computer resource (such as a program, data file, or network connection).

identity theft A form of fraud in which a thief obtains someone's personal information and then uses this information to impersonate the owner and fraudulently obtain and use the owner's credit.

image editor A sophisticated version of a paint program that is used to edit and transform—but not create—complex bitmapped images, such as photographs. Free programs like Picasa and GIMP, designed for personal and home use, incorporate automated image-processing algorithms to add a variety of special effects, remove blemishes, crop portions, and adjust coloring to photographic images.

inclusion operator In database or Web searching, a symbol or keyword that instructs the search software to make sure that any retrieved records or documents contain a certain word or phrase; it usually is a plus sign (+) in the search statement.

incremental backup Backing up only those files that have been created or changed since the last backup occurred.

information Data that has been converted into a meaningful form.

information kiosk An automated presentation system used for public information or employee training.

information overload A feeling of anxiety and incapacity experienced when people are presented with more information than they can handle.

information processing cycle A sequence of four operations: input, processing, output, and storage. These operations receive data, process it into information, allow it to be outputted for viewing, and save it for future use.

information warfare A military-like strategy that makes use of information technologies to corrupt or destroy an enemy's information and industrial infrastructure.

infrared A wireless data transmission medium, used in TV remote controls, that carries data via beams of light through the air. Transmitting and receiving devices must be in line of sight or the signal is lost.

Infrastructure-as-a-Service (IaaS) The category of cloud services that refers to the outsourcing of hardware, the equipment used to sustain the operations of a company or enterprise; also known as Hardware-as-a-Service (HaaS).

inkjet printer A nonimpact printer, popular for home use, which sprays ionized ink from a series of small jets onto a sheet of paper, creating the desired character shapes. A typical inkjet printer provides a resolution of 300 dots per inch.

input The action of receiving data (raw facts) like a user's login ID number.

input device A hardware component that enables a user to enter data into a computer for processing. The most common input devices are the keyboard and mouse, but other devices include microphones, scanners, digital cameras, and camcorders.

input/output (I/O) bus An electrical pathway that connects the microprocessor to input and output devices via expansion slots.

installing To load and set up a program so that it is ready to function on a given computer system. The installation process may involve creating additional directories, making changes to system files, and other technical tasks. For this reason, most programs come with setup programs that handle the installation process automatically.

instant messaging (IM) A free, real-time method of interaction between computers that enables two or more parties to connect through the use of a buddy list that identifies and restricts the users a person wishes to communicate with.

instruction cycle (fetch, decode) In a machine cycle, a phase consisting of the fetch (retrieve) and decode (determine the action required) operations.

instruction set A list of instructions specific to a given brand and model of processor.

integrated circuit (IC or chip) A circuit that carries an electrical current and contains millions of transistors.

integrated peripheral A device embedded within the system unit case, generally the power supply, cooling fans, memory, CD drive, DVD drive, and internal hard drive.

integrated program A single program that manages an entire business or set of related tasks. It combines the most commonly used functions of many productivity software programs, like word processing, database management, spreadsheet, accounting, and customer service into one application.

intelligent keyboard An onscreen keyboard to which software has been added that provides the user with such features as suggestions for misspelled words and grammar mistakes; magnification of the on-screen text being entered or modified; displaying an enlarged image of each key on the screen, providing visual confirmation of the keystroke; and allowing such features as cut, copy, and paste with the touch of the screen.

internal speaker One of the components inside a computer's system unit, typically useful for emitting beeps and other low-fidelity sounds.

Internet (Net) Thousands of privately and publicly owned computers and networks that grew and interlinked, over time, into one giant network. In short, the Internet is a network of networks.

Internet access provider Companies or businesses that provide access to the Internet free, for a fixed monthly charge, or an itemized per-use fee.

Internet address (IP address) A unique, 32-bit address assigned to every computer that is connected to the Internet. It is represented in four parts, which are separated by periods (such as 128.254.108.7).

Internet backbone The main high-speed routes for Internet data travel.

Internet hard drive Refers to storage space that a computer user pays a subscription fee to access on a remote server via the Internet for a specific period of time; also called remote storage.

Internet Protocol (IP) The lower layer of the TCP/IP suite of protocols that handles the address part of each packet so that it gets to the right recipient.

Internet Protocol address (IP address) A numerical identification and logical address that is assigned to devices participating in a computer network. The IP address consists of four groups of numbers, separated by periods. The value in each group ranges from 0 to 255. As an example, 64.12.245.203 is the IP address for the AOL Web site.

Internet relay chat (IRC) A real-time, Internet, text-based chat service, in which one can find "live" participants from the world over. Today it is mostly the province of specialized communities, such as gamers or programmers.

Internet service A set of standards (protocols) that define how two types of programs—a client, such as a Web browser that runs on the user's computer, and a server—can communicate with each other through the Internet. Examples of Internet services are e-mail, instant messaging, FTP, Usenet, IRC, and VoIP.

Internet service provider (ISP) A company that traditionally provided access to the Internet and no additional services. Today these providers have added features to make them a one-stop source for Internet services. There are both local and national ISPs, each having varied services and pricing, providing Internet access via telephone lines, cable, satellite, or fiber-optic technologies.

Internet telephony The use of the Internet (or of nonpublic networks based on Internet technology) for the transmission of real-time voice communication.

Internet TV The ability to view television shows, videos, and movies over the Internet, for no additional cost via download or streaming video. The benefit of this type of viewing over YouTube is that the content is provided by the original source, so copyright is not an issue; there is no limit on length; the user has a variety of selections from which to choose; and there is no time restriction on when the production needs to be watched.

interoperability The ability of the Internet to exchange data between computers regardless of the brand, model, or operating system the computers are running.

interrupt A signal that informs the operating system that an event has occurred and is in need of immediate attention. For hardware, this can be the user pressing a key, the mouse moving to a new position, or a notice that a document is waiting to be printing.

interrupt handler (interrupt service routine) A miniprogram that immediately responds when an interrupt occurs; also called interrupt service routine

interrupt request (IRQ) The interrupting of an event by an interrupt signal.

interrupt vector table The location that holds the responses to multiple interrupts. The interrupts are processed by the operating system, starting with the ones in the table having the highest priority rating, to the one with the lowest.

intranet A password-protected network controlled by an enterprise and accessed only by employees or authorized users.

IP spoofing The sending of a message with an IP address disguised as an incoming message from a trusted source to a computer. It is an activity usually associated with hackers.

iPad A new, pad-sized portable handheld device for personal use that can download and read e-books, surf the Internet, play movies, view TV shows, make calls, instant/text message, take still photos or video, edit photos and videos, run off battery power for a full day, connect to a TV and play media, and sync its media with a computer.

iPhone OS An operating system developed by Apple for use in mobile devices, specifically the iPhone.

IrDA port A wireless communication device that uses infrared technology to transfer data from your PDA to your desktop or notebook computer or another PDA. The transmitting device must be in line of sight (usually within a few feet) of the port on the receiving device. IrDA ports offer data transfer rates of 4 Mbps.

ISDN (integrated services digital network) A standard for the delivery of digital telephone and data services to homes, schools, and offices using ordinary existing twisted-pair wiring, connections ranging from 56 to 128 Kbps (basic rate ISDN) or 1.5 Mbps (primary rate ISDN).

ISDN adapter (digital modem) An internal or external accessory that enables a computer to connect to remote computer networks or the Internet by means of ISDN lines. (Inaccurately called an ISDN modem.)

J

joystick A pointing device used to move objects easily in any direction on-screen. It employs a vertical rod mounted on a base with one or two buttons. An input device commonly used for games.

jump drive Another name for a USB flash drive.

K

kernel The central part of the operating system that controls the actions that the OS uses most frequently, for example starting applications and managing hardware devices and memory. When the system is booted (started) the computer copies the kernel along with other essential portions of the OS from the hard disk into the computer's RAM memory, where it remains the entire time the computer is powered on and functioning.

keyboard An input device that uses switches and circuits to translate keystrokes into a signal a computer can understand. It makes use of alphabetic, numeric, punctuation, function, arrow, and control keys.

key interception The act of stealing an encryption key.

keylogger Spyware that can record all the keystrokes you type—such as passwords, account numbers, or conversations—and relay them to others.

key matrix A grid of circuits located under the keys of a keypad. When a key is pressed, it completes a circuit on the matrix that provides the identity of the associated character to the system.

keypad A smaller and more compact keyboard, popular on smartphones, on which each key represents multiple letters. The user has to strike a key one to four times to get the desired character entered as input.

keyword Descriptive words matching the qualifications that an employer listed in a job posting. A potential employer will compare applicant skills with these keywords when reviewing resumes.

kilobits per second (Kbps) A data transfer rate of approximately a thousand bits of computer data per second.

kilobyte (KB) A unit of measurement for computer memory and disk capacity, equal to 1,024 bytes or characters.

Kindle 2 A portable reading device that allows the user to scroll though pages of a book, enlarge text size, purchase materials through an e-book store, and use the text-to-speech function.

Kindle DX The newest version of the Kindle portable reading device that boasts a larger display than the Kindle 2, better contrast, and a no-glare screen.

know-and-have authentication A type of computer security that requires using tokens, which are handheld electronic devices that generate a logon code.

L

label In Microsoft Excel, a text entry used to identify or group numeric entries.

labor dumping The flooding of a labor market with foreign workers.

land A flat reflective area on an optical disc that bounces the light back to a light-sensing device, corresponding to a 1 in the computer's binary number system.

laser printer A high-resolution nonimpact printer that uses an electrostatic reproductive technology similar to that used by copiers.

last-mile problem The problems associated with the inability of local area networks that support homes or businesses to access high bandwidth multimedia communications that can accommodate the information superhighway, along with the bottleneck of data on the last mile of twisted-pair phone lines connecting those homes and businesses.

last-mile technologies Digital telecommunications services and standards, such as coaxial cable and ISDN, that serve as interim solutions to the limitations associated with the twisted-pair analog phone wiring still common in many homes and businesses.

latency In a packet-switching network, the delay caused by the examining of a given packet by many routers.

launching Starting an application program.

LCD projector An output device that projects a computer's monitor display on a screen by passing light through three colored panels—red, green, and blue. LCD projectors produce sharp, accurate color images; however, they are subject to pixilation and low contrast.

leased line Sometimes called a dedicated line, leased lines are a connection set up by a telecommunication carrier and are usually a permanent fiber-optic or telephone connection that enables continuous, end-to-end communication between two points.

legacy technology Devices that were once used but are now viewed as obsolete.

Level 1 cache (primary cache) A unit of 4 KB to 16 KB of ultrafast memory included in the microprocessor chip that runs at approximately 10 nanoseconds (one-billionth of a second). This is the fastest memory and is used to store frequently accessed data and improve overall system performance.

Level 2 cache (secondary cache) A unit of up to 512 KB of ultrafast memory that can be located within the microprocessor, but further from the registers than Level 1 cache, or on a separate cache chip located on the motherboard very close to the microprocessor. It runs at 20 to 30 nanoseconds.

Level 3 cache A unit of memory found on some systems with newer microprocessors, like Intel's Xeon processor, that are embedded in some servers and workstations.It is located outside of the processor on a separate cache chip on the motherboard but positioned very close to the microprocessor.

libel The publication of a false statement, in written or faxed form, that injures someone's business or personal reputation.

link rot The "out-of-datedness" that occurs in a search due to the amount of time it takes for spiders to accumulate data from the Web.

Linux A freeware operating system introduced by Linus Torvalds that is based on UNIX but is designed for personal computers. Linux is developed and maintained by volunteer programmers who have willingly donated their time to make sure that Linux's open source code is edited and revised to provide PC users with features similar to those found in commercial versions of UNIX.

liquid crystal display (LCD; flat-panel display) A flat-screen display that uses electrical current that controls the positioning of tiny crystals to either block or allow the current to pass through and form the viewable on-screen images and colors.

load To transfer something from a storage device, such as the hard disk, to RAM memory.

local area network (LAN) A network that uses cables, radio waves, or infrared signals to link computers or peripherals, such as printers, within a small geographic area, such as a building or a group of buildings. LANs are typically owned and managed by a single person or organization.

local exchange switch A telephone system device, based on digital technology and capable of handling thousands of calls, located in the local telephone company's central office.

local loop In the public switched telephone network (PSTN), the region serviced by a subscriber loop carrier (SLC) where analog connections from neighborhood distribution points are converted to digital signals.

location awareness (position awareness) A technology that uses GPS-enabled chips to pinpoint the location of a cell phone (and its user).

logic bomb Hidden computer code that sits dormant on a system until a certain event or set of circumstances triggers it into action. That action, or payload, is usually malicious and devastating to the individual or company under attack.

logical address A unique identifier assigned to a network node by the software in use.

logical operation One of two groups of operations performed by the arithmetic logic unit (ALU). An example of a logical operation is the comparison of data items to determine whether the first number is greater than the second. Logical operations return a value of true or false.

lossless compression In data compression, a method used to reduce the size of a file so it can be decompressed and restored to its original size without any flaws. Most lossless compression techniques reduce file size by replacing lengthy but frequently occurring data sequences with short codes. To decompress the file, the compression software reverses this process and restores the lengthy data sequences to their original form.

lossy compression In data compression, a method of reducing the size of multimedia files by eliminating information that is not normally perceived by human beings.

M

Mac OS An operating system released for the Apple Mac in 1984. It was the first OS to successfully implement the GUI (graphical user interface).

Mac OS X Snow Leopard The current version of Mac OS X released in August 2009. It has a smaller footprint (taking up to 50 percent less storage space than the previous version) and includes a variety of useful features.

machine dependent (hardware dependent) The ability of a computer program to run only on a specific type or brand of computer equipment. With new antitheft features, it also refers to the link created between the program and system ID during the installation process. This link prevents the program from functioning on any other system.

macro In a word processing or spreadsheet program, a saved sequence of commands or keyboard strokes that get recalled later with a single command or keyboard stroke.

macro virus A computer virus that uses the automatic execution capabilities of macros stored within productivity software, like word processing or spreadsheet programs, to spread itself to other files and, in many cases, cause harm to computer data.

magnetic storage device In computer storage systems, any storage device that retains data using a magnetically sensitive material, such as the magnetic coating found on floppy and hard disks.

magnetic stripe card reader A device that can detect and read information stored on magnetic strips that are usually located on the back of credit cards, gift cards, and other cards of similar use.

mainframe (enterprise server) Powerful servers that are part of a networked system designed to handle hundreds of thousands of clients. They are usually used in large corporations or government agencies that handle a high volume of data and can fill an entire wall of an average room.

maintenance release A minor revision to a software program that corrects bugs or adds minor features. Indicated by a decimal in the version number.

malicious network A network, sometimes referred to as an "evil twin" and designed to gather sensitive data such as passwords and credit card numbers, set up by a hacker within the operating area of a legitimate hot spot.

malware Short for malicious software, it describes software designed to damage or infiltrate a computer system without the owner's consent or knowledge. This type of software can wreak havoc on a user's system by deleting files and directory entries; it can also act as spyware, gathering data from a user's system without the user knowing it.

mashup Two or more applications combined into one application, a trend helping in the development of Web 3.0.

massively multiplayer online role-playing game (MMORPG) An online game that permits increasingly larger numbers of players to interact with one another in virtual worlds. These virtual worlds are often hosted and maintained by the software publisher and encourage team building in order to progress to higher levels and continue to progress even when you are not actively playing the game.

mathematical formula In spreadsheet programs such as Microsoft Excel, one of the two basic types of formulas (along with functions) that makes use of numeric constants, cell references, arithmetic operators, or functions and calculates a result by following the mathematical order of operations.

maximize To enlarge a window so that it fits the entire screen.

media Technology used to present information including pictures, sound, and video.

media center PC An all-in-one entertainment device that provides easy access to photos, TV, movies, and the latest in online media, all from the comfort of the couch by using a remote control.

megabits per second (Mbps) A data transfer measurement equivalent to 1 million bits per second.

megabyte (MB) A unit of measurement approximately equal to 1 million bytes.

memory Chips or circuitry, located on the motherboard or within the CPU, that retain instructions and data to be accessed by the central processing unit (CPU).

memory address A number that enables memory locations to be found and accessed in random order.

memory footprint The amount of RAM a program uses while it operates.

memory module (memory card) A small circuit board that holds several memory chips and fits into special slots on the motherboard.

memory shaving A type of computer crime in which knowledgeable thieves remove some of a computer's RAM chips but leave enough to start the computer.

memory stick Another name for a USB flash drive.

menu-driven user interface A user interface that enables the user to avoid memorizing keywords (such as *copy* and *paste*) and syntax (a set of rules for entering commands) by displaying on-screen, text-based menus that show all the options available at a given point.

message board A method of communicating over the Internet that is similar to a newsgroup but is easier to use and does not require a newsreader. Many colleges and universities have switched to message boards for this reason.

metropolitan area network (MAN) A network designed for a city or town. It is usually larger than a LAN but smaller than a WAN. Typically, a MAN is owned by a single government or organization.

MICR reader A device that reduces human data entry by scanning and automatically inputting characters printed with special magnetic ink. Such characters are often located on the bottom of checks and some billing statements so that when they are returned to the creator, the numbers are simply scanned by a MICR reader and inputted into the company's data system; short for magnetic-ink character recognition.

microbrowser A special Web browser that has all of the features of computer-based browsers but is simplified to meet handheld device limitations.

microcomputer Another word for personal computer.

microprocessor (processor) Another name for the central processing unit.

Microsoft Windows The most popular operating system, available in several iterations, and installed on almost all of the personal computers made today.

Microsoft Windows 7 The newest version of the Windows operating system released in 2009. It is more efficient than its predecessor, often performing better on the same hardware, and has resolved the compatibility issues that existed between applications. There are six versions and many new features, including jump list, snap, pin, and Windows Search.

Microsoft Windows Mobile The version of Windows operating system designed for smartphones and PDAs. It includes a simplified user interface and quicker synchronization of mobile devices with corresponding programs on the user's desktop computer.

Microsoft Windows Server 2008 A sophisticated operating system specifically designed to support client/server computing systems in a corporate environment.

Microsoft Windows Vista The version of Windows operating system released in 2007. Its main improvements included a slick new interface, mobile support, increased security features, improved search features and networking tools, integrated speech recognition capabilities, and new multimedia tools such as gadgets.

microwave An electromagnetic radio wave with a very short frequency that travels at speeds of 1 to 10 Mbps and is used to transmit data from a source to a receiving site.

middleware Software that does what its name implies: It sits "in the middle," making the connections among varied applications working on multiple networks being supported by different operating systems. Middleware is essential for scalability as well as interoperability in the cloud.

minicomputer (midrange server) Midsized servers approximately the size of one or several four-drawer file cabinets with the hardware and software to handle computing needs of 4 to 200 client computers in a smaller corporation or organization.

mini-keyboard A keyboard option available on many smartphones and portable devices that has a key for each letter of the alphabet. It is usually is hidden when the phone is held in a vertical position but slides out when the phone is turned horizontally.

minimize To reduce the size of a window so that it appears only as an icon or an item on the taskbar.

minitower case A smaller version of the tower case, used for less complex systems, with a smaller amount of internal room for components.

mobile switching center (MSC) The part of a cellular network that handles communications within a group of cells. Each cell tower reports signal strength to the MSC, which then switches the signal

to whatever cell tower will provide the clearest connection for the conversation.

modeling (what-if analysis) A method by which spreadsheet programs are able to predict future outcomes; also called what-if analysis.

modem Short for modulator/demodulator, a communications device that converts (modulates) data from one form into another, transmits the modulated data, and on the receiving end converts (demodulates) the data for use. It is hardware that enables the computer, a digital device, to access data through nondigital media, such as telephone lines, cable, satellite, and cellular connections.

modifier key A key, like Shift, Alt, or Ctrl, that is pressed to modify the meaning of the next key that is pressed.

modulation protocol In modems, the communications standard or rules that govern how the modem translates between the computer's digital signals and the analog tones used to convey computer data over the Internet so that the message is received and understood by the destination modem regardless of the manufacturer.

module A collection of routines in a program; independently developed modules are combined to create the final program.

monitor (display) A screen that displays data and processed information. This type of output is not permanent.

motherboard The circuit board, located within the system unit, that contains the central processing unit, support chips, random access memory, and expansion slots. It provides the circuitry to connect the central processing unit(s) anchored on the motherboard and other system components.

mouse A palm-sized pointing device designed to move about on a clean, flat surface. As you move the mouse, its movements are mirrored by the on-screen pointer. Actions are initiated by using the mouse buttons.

MUD (multiuser dungeons or dimension) The early name for a genre of role-playing games in which multiple players could use their imaginations to construct a persona and build their environment. Players interacted in a text-based environment through text chatting.

multifunction device A device that combines printing, scanning, faxing, and copying.

multimedia An application that involves two or more media, such as audio, graphics, or video. Multisensory stimulators that stimulate our senses of sight, sound, touch, smell, or taste.

multimedia and graphics software A general category of software programs for professional desktop publishing, image editing, three-dimensional rendering, and audio and video editing

multiplexing A technique that enables more than one signal to be conveyed on a physical transmission medium.

multitasking A process by which the CPU gives the user the illusion of performing instructions from multiple programs at once when in reality the CPU is rapidly switching between the programs and instructions.

multitasking operating system A descriptive phrase applied to personal computer operating systems that enable multiple applications to run at the same time.

N

name The first part of a file name.

nanosecond One-billionth of a second.

native application A program that is compatible with a given processor and therefore capable of running on that processor.

navigation pane The pane that appears on the left side of a Windows Explorer window. It allows a user to navigate directly to a specific folder listed in the content pane (file list), access a prior search that was saved by clicking on a desired folder, and add a shortcut to a frequently used folder by dragging the folder into the Favorite Links area of the navigation pane.

nesting A process of embedding control structures within one another.

netbook A handheld computing device with a relatively small hard drive that is used primarily for Web browsing, e-mail, and cloud computing.

netiquette A lengthy series of specific behavior guidelines, developed by Internet and computer users, that provide specific pointers on how to show respect for others—and for yourself—while you're online.

network A group of two or more computer systems linked together to exchange data and share resources, including expensive peripherals such as high-performance laser printers.

network access point (NAP) A special communications device that sends and receives data between computers that contain wireless adapters. 2. The location where equipment from one network service provider connects with equipment from another provider.

network administrator Computer professionals who install, maintain, and support computer networks, interact with users, handle security, and troubleshoot problems. Also called a network engineer.

network architecture The collection of protocol suites that specify how the network functions.

network attached storage (NAS) High-performance devices that offer little more than data and file sharing to clients and other servers on a network. An NAS is comprised primarily of hard drives or other media used for data storage and is attached directly to a network.

network interface card (NIC) An expansion board that fits into a computer's expansion slots, or an adapter built into the motherboard, that provides the electronic

components to make the connection between a computer and a network. This can be either wired or wireless.

network layers Separate divisions within the network architecture with specific functions and protocols. Each layer's protocol precisely defines how that layer passes data to another layer. Because of this distinction between layers, it's possible to make changes within one layer without having to rebuild the entire network.

network operating system (NOS) An operating system designed to enable data transfer and application usage among computers and other devices connected to a local area network.

network service provider (NSP) A company or organization that maintains the Internet backbone.

network topology The physical layout of a network, which provides a solution to the problem of contention. Typical topologies include bus, star, and ring.

newsgroup In Usenet, a discussion group devoted to a single topic that typically requires participants to use a program called a news reader. Those reading the discussion send reply messages to the author individually or post replies that can be read by the group as a whole.

node Any device connected to a network. A node can be any computer, peripheral (such as a printer or scanner), or communication device (such as a modem).

nonvolatile memory Memory, like ROM, that is not easily edited and keeps its content even when the system powers off. It's used primarily to hold programs essential to system start up.

notebook computer A computer, designed for individual use, approximately the size of a spiral bound notebook and popular with individuals that travel and students.

NTFS (new technology file system) A file allocation table that contains the name of each file and the file's exact location on the disk for Windows NT, 2000, XP, Vista, and Windows 7. It provides improved security and encryption ability.

O

offshoring The transfer of labor from workers in one country to workers in other countries.

OLED (organic light-emitting diode) display An emissive output device that displays images by emitting light rather than modulating transmitted or reflected light. These displays are extremely thin and lightweight, and produce outstanding color, contrast, brightness, and viewing angles.

onboard video Video circuitry that is built into the motherboard.

online service provider A for-profit firm that provides a proprietary network offering special services that are available only to subscribers. Members may participate in chat rooms and discussions and take advantage of fee-based content, such as magazines and newspapers.

online workshop A structured, interactive Web-based session that is assisted by an electronic meeting system, a set of tools that enable discussion, brainstorming, voting, and categorization.

Open Cloud Manifesto A document published in March 2009 to provided some guides and business practices for cloud providers in an attempt to guarantee subscribers the freedom of choice, flexibility, and openness they need in order to take full advantage of the benefits of cloud computing.

open source software Software whose source code (the code of the program itself) is available for all to see and use. Users of open source software are invited to scrutinize the source code for errors and to share their discoveries with the software's publisher. Linux is an open source operating system.

operating system (OS) The most important type of system software. It integrates and controls the computer's internal functions and provides the connectivity for the user to interact with the computer's hardware. Common operating systems include Microsoft Windows 7, Microsoft Vista, Microsoft Windows XP, Linux, and Mac OS X Snow Leopard.

optical character recognition (OCR) Software that automatically decodes imaged content into text. Most scanners come with OCR software.

optical mark reader (OMR) A device that scans the magnetized marks from a no. 2 pencil, or other device that produces such marks, to determine which responses were made. The response is compared against a provided key with the correct answers. OMR devices facilitate the tabulation of responses to large surveys.

optical mouse A palm-sized pointing device that makes use of an LED (light-emitting diode) light, located on the underside of the mouse, and a small camera that takes continuous images of the changes in the surface under the mouse as it is moved. The differences are compared and the direction and speed of the mouse movement are recognized and the on-screen pointer shifted accordingly.

optical storage device A computer storage device that retains data in microscopic patterns, pits and lands, which are encoded on the surface of plastic discs and detected by a laser beam.

option Choices made by a user to specify how that user wants the program to operate.

output The display of the results (information) of the processing operation.

output device A monitor, printer, speaker, or other device that enables people to see, hear, and—with some newer inventions—feel the results of processing operations.

outsourcing The subcontracting of portions of a job to a third party to reduce cost, time, and energy consumption.

P

packaged software Aimed at a mass market that includes both home and business users, packaged software can be customized, but its appeal lies in the fact that is ready to use off the shelf. Synonymous with commercial off-the-shelf software (COTS) and shrink-wrapped software.

packet In a packet-switching network, a unit of data of a fixed size—not exceeding the network's maximum transmission unit (MTU) size—that has been prepared for network transmission. Each packet contains a header that indicates its origin and its destination.

packet switching One of two fundamental architectures for a wide area network (WAN); the other is a circuit-switching network. In a packet-switching network, such as the Internet, no effort is made to establish a single electrical circuit between two computing devices; instead, the sending computer divides a message into packets, each of which contains the address of the destination computer, and dumps them onto the network. They are intercepted by devices called routers, which send the packets in the appropriate direction. The receiving computer assembles the packets, puts them in order, and delivers the received message to the appropriate application. Packet-switching networks are highly reliable and efficient, but they are not suited to the delivery of real-time voice and video.

page In virtual memory, a unit of fixed size into which program instructions and data are divided.

paging Transferring of files from the hard disk to RAM and back, as needed.

Palm OS A mobile operating system initially developed in 1996 by Palm Inc. for personal digital assistants (PDAs). It's designed for use with a touch screen, uses graphical user interfaces and natural gestures, and comes with a suite of personal information management applications.

parallel port Considered legacy technology, these ports were commonly used to connect a printer to a PC but have been replaced by USB and Ethernet ports.

parallel processing The use of more than one processor to run two or more portions of a program at the same time.

partition A section of a hard disk set aside as if it were a physically separate disk. Partitions are required if a system is going to give the user an option of running more than one operating system.

passive-matrix (dual scan) Technology that creates the content of a display or monitor by charging groups of pixels, either in a row or column, at once. The screen brightens and fades as the current moves from group to group. Appliances, toys, remote controls, and home medical products use this type of display.

path The sequence of directories that the user must follow to locate a file.

payload The actions, most often malicious and devastating, performed by rogue programs like spyware and viruses to the individual or company under attack.

PC card (PCMCIA card) A credit card–sized accessory, typically used to enhance the abilities of notebook computers, designed to fit into a compatible PC card slot located on or within the computer's case. Some PC cards are modems, others are network adapters, and still others provide additional memory or storage capacity.

PCI (peripheral component interconnect) bus An input/output bus that connects devices like hard drives and sound cards to the faster microprocessor system bus usually through expansion slots.

PCI Express An interface currently in use that transfers graphics from the video card to the motherboard. Most current video cards from manufacturers like ATI and NVIDIA use PCI Express.

PCI Express Base 2.1 The most current version of the PCI express interface.

PCS (personal communication service) A group of related digital cellular technologies that are rapidly replacing analog cellular services.

peer-to-peer (P2P) network A computer network design in which all the computers on the network are equals or peers. There is no file server. File sharing is decided by each computer user. A user may choose to share a few files, an entire directory, or even an entire disk. They also can choose to share peripherals, such as printers and scanners. P2P is best used for home networks or small businesses connecting fewer than ten computers and does not require a network operating system (NOS).

peripheral device Computer components located outside the system unit housing that are connected physically or wirelessly to the system unit and motherboard, such as keyboards, monitors, speakers, and external storage devices.

personal area network (PAN) A network created among an individual's own personal devices, usually within a range of 32 feet. Such networks involve wireless technology.

personal computer (PC or microcomputer) A computer designed to meet the computing needs of an individual or, when connected to a network, to be used by a contributor in a collaborative project. The two most commonly used types of personal computers are Apple's Macintosh, referred to as a Mac, and the more numerous IBM-compatible systems referred to as PCs.

personal digital assistant (PDA) A small handheld personal computing device that usually uses a stylus or virtual keyboard to interface with built-in software to manage contacts, use e-mail, and schedule appointments.

petabyte A unit of measurement approximately equal to 1 quadrillion bytes.

petaflop A unit of measurement for computer processing speed that is the equivalent of one quadrillion calculations per second, approximately 150,000 calculations for every human being on the planet per second.

phishing Posing as a legitimate company in an e-mail or on a Web site in an attempt to learn personal information such as Social Security numbers, user names, passwords, and account numbers.

photo-editing program A program that enables a person to enhance, edit, crop, or resize the images.

photo printer An inkjet or laser printer that makes use of special inks and good-quality photo paper to produce pictures that are as good as those generated by commercial photo processors. Many permit bypassing a computer and printing directly from a digital camera or memory card.

phrase searching In database and Web searching, the placing of a phrase between quotation marks so the search retrieves only documents that contain the entire phrase.

physical address Also called the data link control address, data link control/connection identifier (DLCI), or media access control (MAC) address; a unique numeric identifier built into the hardware of a network node and used to identify the node.

picture messaging (MMS) A mobile service that allows you to send full-color pictures, backgrounds, and even picture caller IDs on your cell phone.

piggybacking The use of a network without permission.

pipelining A processing technique used in CPUs built with superscalar architecture. It feeds a new instruction into the processor at every step of the processing cycle so that four or more instructions are worked on simultaneously, increasing the speed at which instructions are performed.

pit A microscopic indentation in the surface of an optical disc that scatters the laser's light so that the drive's light-sensing device receives no light from these areas and sends a signal to the computer that corresponds to a 0 in the computer's binary numbering system.

plagiarism The use of someone else's intellectual property, ideas, or written work, as one's own or without permission.

plaintext A readable message before it is encrypted.

platform The combination of microprocessor chip and operating system used by a distinct type of computer, such as a Mac or a PC.

Platform-as-a-Service (PaaS) The category of cloud services that permits subscribers to have remote access to application development, interface development, database development, storage, and testing to facilitate the creation and testing of subscriber-developed programs and interfaces, using a cloud provider's hardware and development environment.

platter The fixed, high-capacity, rapidly rotating, storage medium in a hard drive that is coated with a magnetically sensitive material. High-capacity hard drives typically have two or more platters.

plotter An output device that produces high-quality images by moving ink pens over the surface of the paper.

plug-and-play (PnP) Refers to a set of standards, jointly developed by Intel Corporation and Microsoft, which enable a computer to automatically detect the brand, model, and characteristics of a device when you plug it in and configure the system accordingly.

plug-in An additional software program, located on the user's computer, that is activated by a Web page to enhance the ability of the browser, usually to enable multimedia features such as sound or video.

podcast A blend of the words *iPod* and *broadcast*. It has come to mean a program (of music or talk) that is made available in digital format for automatic download over the Internet. Such files contain audio, images, and videos and are released periodically by means of Web syndication.

podcatcher Applications, such as Apple Inc.'s iTunes or Nullsoft's Winamp, that can automatically identify and retrieve new files in a given series and make them available through a centrally maintained Web site.

pod slurping An activity in which employees use USB drives, iPods, or other removable storage media to create an unauthorized copy of confidential data.

point-and-shoot digital camera A camera that includes automatic focus, automatic exposure, built-in automatic electronic flash with red-eye reduction, and optical zoom lenses with digital enhancement. Sometimes called a compact camera.

pointer An on-screen symbol, usually an arrow, that shows the current location of on-the-screen activity.

pointing device An input device that allows you to control the movements of the on-screen pointer.

pointing stick A pointing device that looks like a pencil eraser located between the G, H, and B keys. It is pressure sensitive and is pressed and moved in various directions with the forefinger.

point of presence (POP) A wired or wireless access connection point in a wide area network. ISPs that provide connectivity to the largest WAN, the Internet, are likely to have POPs in many cities and towns; however, rural areas may not be so lucky.

pop-up A small window that suddenly appears ("pops up") in the foreground of the current window.

port An electronically defined pathway or interface for getting information into and out of the computer.

portable storage (removable storage) A popular, removable, compact storage device that is easy to carry around, simple to use, and can be quickly plugged into any computer with the correct connector. Examples are USB flash drives, also known as memory sticks, thumb drives, or jump drives.

portal A Web page that acts as a gateway to a lot of diverse sources and presents those sources in an organized way and enables a user to locate fast-breaking news, local weather, stock quotes, sports scores, and e-mail with the click of a mouse. Portal sites usually use indexes and lists of links to provide a jumping-off point for your search. Sites such as MSNBC, AOL, iGoogle, and Yahoo! are examples of portals.

positioning performance A measure of how much time elapses from the initiation of drive activity until the hard disk has positioned the read/write head so that it can begin transferring data.

POST (power-on self test) A program, stored in ROM memory, that conducts a series of tests during system startup after the BIOS instructions are loaded into memory. It checks the circuitry, making sure that the computer and circuitry are working correctly, and marks any RAM locations that are defective so that they do not get used.

postimplementation system review A process of ongoing evaluation that determines whether a system has met its goals.

power-on light The light, located on the front panel of most computers, that signals whether the power is on.

power-on self-test (POST) A series of tests conducted during a system boot, after the BIOS instructions are loaded into memory, to make sure that the computer and associated peripherals are operating correctly.

preemptive multitasking An environment in which programs that are running receive a recurring slice of time from the CPU. Depending on the operating system, the time slice may be the same for all programs or it may be adjustable to meet the various program and user demands. This method of multitasking ensures that all applications have fair access to the CPU and prevents one program from monopolizing it at the expense of the others.

printer An output device that produces a permanent version, or hard copy, of the contents on a computer's display screen.

privacy An individual's ability to restrict or eliminate the collection, use, and sale of confidential personal information.

private cloud Operated for a single organization and its authorized users. The infrastructure can exist on-site or off-site and is controlled by either the organization or a contracted third party.

private key A decryption key associated with a public key in a public key encryption scheme.

processing The actions performed on data (input) to convert it into information.

processing cycle (machine cycle) A four-step process performed in the central processing unit (CPU) that involves the fetch, decode, execute, and store operations.

productivity program A program that helps individuals work more efficiently and effectively on both personal and business-related documents. The value of a productivity program is that it performs its functions regardless of the subject matter. Productivity software includes word processors, spreadsheets, databases, presentation, project management, and a personal information management programs.

product registration key An alphanumeric code that is unique and specific to a particular copy of a program. It is necessary to enter this key after installation in order to validate authenticity and activate the program. The key may be necessary later to download upgrades, patches, or templates.

professional workstation High-end desktop computers with system units equipped with more powerful CPUs, extra RAM, additional graphics power, and multitasking capabilities for handling technical or scientific applications that require exceptionally powerful processing and output capabilities.

profile A record of a specific user's preferences for the desktop theme, icons, and menu styles.

program A set of instructions that tells the hardware how to perform an operation on the inputted data.

PROM Programmable read-only memory that can be written on only once, but requires a special writing device.

property A setting that provides information on a file such as its date of creation, size, and the date it was last modified.

proprietary file A file whose format is patented or copyright protected and controlled by a single company. The extent of restriction depends on the company and its policies.

protocol In data communications and networking, the standard or set of rules that enable network-connected devices to communicate with each other.

protocol stack In a computer network, a means of conceptualizing network architecture as vertical layers, connected by protocols that move the data down the stack from its initial level, or transmitting node, to the lowest, physical hardware level that sends it over the network. When the data arrives at its destination, it moves back up the stack through the layers in reverse order, eventually arriving at the receiving node.

protocol suite In a computer network, the collection of network protocols, or rules, that defines the network's functionality.

PS/2 port Considered legacy technology, these ports were typically used for mice and keyboards, but were not interchangeable. Today most mice and keyboards connect via USB connectors.

public cloud Available to the general public, large organizations, or a group of organizations, the public cloud offers the most risk because it is accessed by users that have not been authenticated or established as trusted. The infrastructure is owned and operated by a cloud provider and is located off site.

public domain software Noncopyrighted, free programs that can be used, copied, modified, or sold without restriction or acknowledging the source.

public key In public key cryptography, the encoding key, which you make public so that others can send you encrypted messages. The message can be encoded with the public key, but it cannot be decoded without the private key, which you alone possess.

public key encryption (asymmetric key encryption) A computer security process in which an encryption (or public) key and a decryption (or private) key are used to safeguard data and thus provide confidentiality. This system allows a digital signature to be verified by anyone who has access to the sender's public key, thereby proving that the sender is authentic and has access to the private key; also called asymmetric key encryption.

public key infrastructure (PKI) A uniform set of encryption standards that specifies how public key encryption, digital signatures, and digital certificates should be implemented in computer systems and on the Internet.

public switched telephone network (PSTN) The global telephone system, a massive network used for data as well as voice communications, comprising various transmission media ranging from twisted-pair wire to fiber-optic cable.

Q

Quick Access Toolbar Located above the Ribbon in the Windows environment. This customizable toolbar displays a series of buttons used to perform common tasks, such as saving a document and undoing or redoing the last action performed.

R

racetrack memory A type of memory under development that uses the spin of electrons to store information. This technology will greatly increase the speeds for transferring and retrieving data.

radio frequency identification (RFID) A tracking device, replacing bar codes, which does not require direct contact or line-of-sight scanning. Instead, an antenna using radio frequency waves transmits a signal that activates the transponder, or tag. When activated, the tag transmits data back to the antenna.

radio transmission Data in a variety of forms (music, voice conversations, and photos) travels through the air as radio frequency (RF) signals or radio waves via a transmitting device and a receiving device.

random access memory (RAM) Memory chips, located on the motherboard, which temporarily store the programs and data being used and accessed by the central processing unit through a high-speed data bus. RAM is also referred to as primary memory or temporary memory. The designation of temporary comes from the fact that the information located in this memory in not permanent and is lost when the computer is turned off.

random access storage device A storage device that can begin reading data without having to go through a lengthy linear search.

range In Microsoft Excel, a range consists of two or more contiguous cells and is identified by the addresses of first cell (the top left) and last cell (bottom right) separated by a colon. For example, the range from cell A1 to cell D5 would be represented as A1:D5.

ray tracing A 3D rendering technique in which color intensity on a graphic object is varied to simulate light falling on the object from multiple directions.

read/write head An electromagnet located within magnetic storage devices, such as a hard disk drive, that moves across the surface of a disk and records information by transforming electrical impulses into a varying magnetic field. When reading, the read/write head senses the recorded pattern and transforms this pattern into electrical impulses that are decoded into text characters.

read-only memory (ROM) Nonvolatile memory that does not lose its content when power is shut off. It contains essential prerecorded computer start up instructions that cannot be erased or changed by the computer without user initiation.

Really Simple Syndication (RSS) A way to keep abreast of updates on news, weather, and sports in our fast-moving and informative world. Once a user sets up a connection to a Web site that has an RSS feed, he or she will receive constant updates over the Internet from that site without any further involvement.

receiving device A component of communication that accepts a transmission and responds.

register Temporary memory located in the microprocessor that is used to store values and external memory addresses while the processor performs arithmetic and logical operations on them.

registration fee The amount of money paid to an author of a piece of software to continue to use it beyond the duration of the evaluation period.

registry In Microsoft Windows, the name of the database in which configuration information about installed peripherals and software is stored.

remote storage Sometimes referred to as an Internet hard drive, this is a type of storage space on a server, accessible from the Internet, and usually requires the user to pay a subscription free.

report A database feature that displays information from tables, queries, or a combination of both in a professionally styled manner.

resolution Refers to the sharpness of an image and is controlled by the number of pixels on the screen. The higher the resolution number, the sharper the image.

restore down A mode that, if the window is full screen, will cause the window to revert to a smaller size.

RFID reader A device used to detect radio signals being emitted from a radio frequency identification tag placed on an item.

Ribbon A band located across the top of the application window and below the title bar in Office 2007 and Office 2010 applications. It consists of tabs with icons assembled into groups based on their function. Each application has a Ribbon with tab options that match the activities performed by that application.

ring topology The physical layout of a local network in which all nodes are attached in a circle, without a central host computer. This topology, which is no longer used frequently, employs a unit of data called a *token* that travels around the ring. A node can transmit only when it possesses the token, thus avoiding collisions.

risk management The process of analyzing exposure to risk and determining how to best handle it within the tolerance level set by the enterprise.

ROM (read-only memory) The part of a computer's primary storage that contains essential computer start-up instructions and doesn't lose its contents when the power is turned off. Information in read-only memory cannot be erased by the computer without initiation by the user.

rootkit A malicious program that is disguised as a useful program that enables the attacker to gain administrator level access to a computer or network. The primary purpose of a rootkit is to allow an attacker repeated and undetected access to a compromised system.

router A complex device, or in some cases software, used to connect two or more networks. Routers have the capability to determine the best path to route data and locate alternative pathways so that the data reaches its destination.

row In Microsoft Excel and Word, a block of data presented horizontally across the screen.

RSS (Really Simple Syndication or Rich Site Summary) A technology that publishes content to you and lets you know when Web content has been updated or news events are taking place.

Safe Mode An operating mode in which Windows loads a minimal set of drivers that are known to function correctly. Within Safe Mode, the user can use the Control Panel to determine which devices are causing a configuration problem that may occur after adding a new peripheral device such as an external hard drive or new printer to the system.

salami shaving A computer crime in which a program is altered so that it transfers a small amount of money from a large number of accounts to make a large profit.

Sarbanes-Oxley (SOX) An act administered by the Securities and Exchange Commission (SEC) that specifies the type of business records that need to be stored and how long they must be kept, but leaves the method of storage up to the business.

SATA (serial advance technology attachment) An interface developed by the Serial ATA International Organization (SATA IO) as a replacement for legacy ports that greatly increases the data transfer rate between the motherboard and storage devices like hard drives and optical drives. The user benefits from greater speed, simpler upgradable storage devices, and easier configuration.

satellite In data communications, a communication device placed in a geosynchronous (stationary) orbit that transmits data by sending and receiving microwave signals to and from Earth-based stations.

satellite radio A type of communications technology that broadcasts radio signals back and forth between satellites orbiting more than 22,000 miles above the Earth and radio receivers on Earth.

saving The process of transferring a file from the computer's temporary memory, or RAM, to a permanent storage device, such as a hard disk.

scanner A device that copies anything that is printed on a sheet of paper, including artwork, handwriting, and typed or printed documents, and converts the input into a graphical image for the computer. The scanner does not recognize or differentiate the type of material it is scanning and converts everything into a graphic bitmapped image.

scroll arrows An arrow appearing within the scroll bar that enables the user to scroll up or down (or, in a horizontal scroll bar, left and right) by small increments.

scroll bar A vertical or horizontal bar that contains scroll arrows and a scroll box. The scroll bar enables the user to navigate though content, revealing hidden portions of a document in the application workspace.

SCSI (small computer system interface) port Considered legacy technology, a type of parallel interface that enabled users to connect up to 15 SCSI-compatible devices, such as printers, scanners, and digital cameras, in a daisy-chain series.

Search box A Windows Explorer input box that allows the user to locate files. Select one of the main folders and begin typing a search term in the search input box. As you are typing, Windows Explorer searches the contents of the folders and subfolders of your selected main folder and immediately filters the view to display any files that match your search input.

search engine Any program that locates needed information in a database, or on an Internet-accessible search service (such as Google or Ask) that enables you to search for information on the Internet.

search operator In a database or a Web search engine, a word or a symbol that enables you to specify your search with precision.

search utility A program that enables you to search an entire hard disk and any indexed network storage device for a file by querying single or multiple specifics about the file such as the name, date, and/or size.

secondary cache An additional location for memory storage located on the processor's architecture or very close to it, allowing for quick access; also known as L2 cache.

secondary storage (fixed storage) Hardware that retains the programs and data even when power is disrupted or turned off. Examples include hard disks, USB flash drives, CDs, and DVDs.

sector A pie-shaped wedge of the concentric tracks encoded on a disk during formatting (set up). Two or more sectors combine to form a cluster.

secure electronic transaction (SET) An online shopping security standard for merchants and customers that uses digital certificates.

seek time In a secondary storage device, the time it takes for the read/write head to locate the data on the disk before reading begins.

semiconductor The material that transistors are made out of that conducts electrical current or blocks the current's passage through the circuit.

sending device A component of communication that initiates a transmission.

serial port Considered legacy technology, it is an interface that was used with dial-up modems to achieve two-way communication. Although they are still in use on servers, many new computers no longer include serial ports, opting to use USB ports instead.

server A computer that ranges in size from a two-drawer file cabinet to a four-drawer file cabinet and is equipped with the hardware and software to manage network resources like files, e-mail, printers, and databases, and that makes the programs and data it manages available to people who are connected via a network.

server operating system An operating system used in client/server network environments.

setup program A program located in the computer system's BIOS that contains settings that control the computer's hardware.

sexting A combination of sex and texting. Sending sexually explicit messages or photos electronically, primarily between cell phones.

shareware Copyrighted programs that may be used or copied, without cost, during the specified trial period. Once the trial period has expired, a registration fee must be paid or the software must be deleted from your computer.

shill In an auction, an accomplice of the seller who drives up prices by bidding for an item that the accomplice has no intention of buying.

shoulder surfing The attempt by an individual to obtain information from your computer screen by looking over your shoulder.

sidebar An invisible vertical strip located on the right side of the desktop in a graphical user interface where the user can place and arrange applications referred to as gadgets.

single inline memory module (SIMM) A RAM memory module that fits into special slots on the motherboard; it preceded the dual inline memory modules in use today, used a 72-pin connector, and had a 32-bit data transfer rate.

single-lens reflex (SLR) digital camera A digital camera that uses a mechanical mirror system to direct light from the lens to an optical viewfinder on the back of the camera. Such cameras offer the features that professional photographers demand, such as interchangeable lenses, through-the-lens image previewing, and the ability to override the automatic focus and exposure settings.

single point of failure (SPOF) Any system component, such as hardware or software, that causes the entire system to malfunction when it fails.

single-tasking operating system An operating system that could run only one application at a time, which was often inconvenient. To switch between applications, you had to quit one application before you could start the second.

site license A contract with the software publisher that allows an organization to install copies of a program on a specified number of computers at a reduced price per unit.

Sleep mode A power-saving feature that transfers the current state of your computer to RAM, turns off all unneeded functions, and places the system in a low-power state. Returning from Sleep mode is faster than returning from Hibernate due to the state of the computer being held in RAM not stored on the hard drive.

slide In a presentation graphics program, the equivalent of a canvas, sized in proportion to a 35 mm slide, on which the user organizes text boxes and graphics to represent ideas or points.

smart card (chip card, integrated circuit card [ICC]) A credit card–sized device that combines flash memory with a tiny microprocessor, enabling the card to process as well as store information. It is viewed as a replacement for magnetic stripe cards, from which data is eventually lost.

smartphone Mobile devices that fit in the palm of your hand or pocket of your jeans. Designed primarily for use as a mobile phone but can be enabled with Web access. The added features and downloadable applications for these devices are making the line between the smartphones and handheld computers more difficult to distinguish.

social network site Web sites like Facebook, MySpace, LinkedIn, or Twitter, where users join groups set up by region, job, school, or family and communicate through postings, instant messaging, and e-mail.

social networking A method of creating and expanding online communities. For example, sites such as Facebook, MySpace, and LinkedIn allow users to create online profiles, post images, and invite friends and acquaintances to join their network. Many view it as a substitute for e-mail.

soft copy Output displayed on a monitor or played through speakers.

soft keyboard (virtual keyboard, on-screen keyboard) Also known as a virtual or on-screen keyboard. A keyboard that appears on a touch-sensitive screen. Tapping the key on the screen with a stylus or finger is the same as pressing a key on a traditional keyboard.

software One of two basic components of a computer system (the other is hardware). It is a collection of programs, and associated documentation, that directs the operation of the computer to complete a desired end result. There are two categories of software: system software and application software.

software license An agreement included with most commercial software that defines what the user may and may not do with the software.

software piracy The unauthorized copying or distribution of copyrighted software, an act that is a federal offense in the United States.

software suite (office suite) A collection of individual, full-featured, stand-alone programs, usually possessing a similar interface and sharing a common command structure, that are bundled and sold together; sometimes called an office suite.

software upgrading The process of keeping a version of an application current with the marketplace, whether through patches, service releases, or new versions.

Software-as-a-Service (SaaS) 1. The most widely used and widely known form of cloud computing, it enables software to be deployed from a cloud provider, delivered over the Internet, and accessed by a subscriber through a browser.

2. Provides software-based services and solutions to companies that want to outsource some of their information technology needs.

solid-state drive (SSD) A drive with no moving parts; another name for a flash drive.

solid-state storage device A device that consists of nonvolatile memory chips, which retain the data stored in them even if disconnected from their source. Solid-state storage devices are small, lightweight, highly reliable, and portable. See flash drives.

SONET (synchronous optical network) A standard for high-performance networks using optical fiber with data transfer rates of 52 Mbps to higher levels of approximately 20 Gbps.

sound file A file containing digitized data in the form of digital audio waveforms (recorded live sounds or music), which are saved in one of several standardized sound formats. These formats specify how sounds should be digitally represented and generally include some type of data compression that reduces the size of the file. The file can be played back if a computer is equipped with multimedia.

spam Unsolicited e-mail or newsgroup advertising.

sparklines In an Excel spreadsheet, tiny charts embedded into the background of a cell that help users visualize and detect trends in their data more easily.

spear phishing Behavior similar to phishing, in that it uses fake e-mails and social engineering to trick recipients into providing personal information to enable identity theft. Rather than being sent randomly, spear phishing attempts are targeted to specific people, such as senior executives or members of a particular organization.

specialized search engines Web location programs, like Infoplease, that index particular types of information, such as job advertisements, newspaper articles, or quotations.

speculative execution A technique used by advanced CPUs to prevent a pipeline stall. The processor executes and temporarily stores the next instruction in case it proves useful.

speech recognition (voice recognition) The conversion of spoken words into computer text. The spoken word is first digitized and then matched against a dictionary of coded voice waves. The matches are converted into text as if the words were typed on the keyboard.

spider A computer program used by search engines to roam the World Wide Web via the Internet, visit sites and databases, and keep the search engine's database of Web pages up to date. They obtain new pages, update known pages, and delete obsolete ones. Their findings are then integrated into the search engine's database.

spim A spam text message.

spimming Sending unsolicited messages (spam) as an instant message.

spyware Internet software that is installed on your computer without your knowledge or consent. It may monitor your computer or online activity, relay information about you to the spyware's source, or allow others to take control of your computer. Spyware usually enters your system through the Internet.

stand-alone operating system An operating system designed to be used by a single user on a desktop computer, notebook, or any portable computing device. The name *stand-alone* comes from the fact that it does not need to be connected to any other system or computer in order to run.

stand-alone program An application sold individually.

star topology The physical layout of a local network in which a central wiring device, which can be a hub, switch, or computer, manages the network. A new user is added by simply running a cable to the hub or switch and plugging the new user into a vacant connector.

status bar An area within a typical application's window that displays information about the application and the document.

storage (mass storage, auxiliary storage, secondary storage) The operation in which information generated during processing is stored for later use.

storage device A general term for hardware that holds programs and data.

streaming A transmission method that enables the ability to hear or see content while it is being downloaded from a Web site instead of waiting till the download is complete.

strong password A strong password should be difficult to guess; be at least 14 characters or more in length; include uppercase letters, lowercase letters, numbers, and special characters; not be a recognizable word or phrase; not be the name of anything or anyone close to you; and not be a recognizable string of numbers such as a Social Security number or birth date.

structural unemployment Unemployment caused by advancing technology that makes an entire job category obsolete.

stylus A device that looks like an ordinary pen except that the tip is dry and semi-blunt. It is commonly used as an alternative to fingers on touch-screen devices.

subfolder A folder positioned within another folder that enables you to organize your files even further.

subject guide On the World Wide Web, a search site that contains hyperlinks classified by subjects in broad categories like business, news, or travel, and multiple levels of subcategories.

subnotebook A portable computer that omits some components, such as a DVD drive, and usually has a smaller screen and weighs less than a notebook. It is used by individuals that like full application features but not all the peripheral devices.

subscriber loop carrier (SLC) A small, waist-high, curbside installation of the public switched telephone network that transforms local home and business analog calls into digital signals and routes them through high-capacity cables to the local exchange switch.

Super Extended Graphics Array (SXGA) A resolution of 1280 × 1024, typically found on standard 17- and 19-inch monitors.

supercomputer An ultrafast system, stored in a special secure room that has a controlled climate. It processes a few sets of instructions as fast as possible and is used primarily to handle large amounts of scientific data, often to search for underlying patterns. A supercomputer can be a single computer or a series of computers working in parallel as a single computer.

superscalar architecture The design of the fastest CPUs today that enables them to execute more than one instruction per clock cycle.

swap file A hard disk file that serves as a temporary storage space for pages, the bits and bytes that the operating system will access as the user works.

swindler An individual that perpetrates bogus work-at-home opportunities, illegal pyramid schemes, chain letters, risky business opportunities, bogus franchises, phony goods that won't be delivered, overpriced scholarship searches, and get-rich-quick scams.

switch A device that filters and forwards data between computers, printers, and other nodes on the same network, enabling them to talk to each other. It is more intelligent than a hub and actually inspects the source and destination of a data packet to facilitate its delivery, an activity that condenses bandwidth and improves network performance.

Symbian OS An open industry standard operating system for data-enabled mobile phones that powers devices at the lower end of the smartphone price spectrum.

symmetric key encryption An encryption technique that uses the same key for encryption and decryption.

syn flooding A form of denial of service attack in which a hostile client repeatedly sends SYN (synchronization) packets to every port on the server, using fake IP addresses, which uses up all the available network connections and locks them up until they time out. This results in a denial of service.

Synchronized Multimedia Integration Language (SMIL) A simple multimedia scripting language designed for Web pages. SMIL enables Internet users to view multimedia without having to download plug-ins.

synchronous communication Communication in which both parties are online at the time and have a coherent conversation, as in instant messaging.

system clock An electronic circuit in the computer that emits pulses at regular intervals, enabling the computer's internal components to operate in synchrony.

system requirements The minimum level of equipment that a program needs to run.

system software The collection of programs written and configured to provide the infrastructure, basic services, and hardware control that enables other programs to function smoothly. It includes the operating system and utility programs.

system unit The base unit of the computer made up of the plastic or metal enclosure, the motherboard, and the integrated peripherals. It provides a sturdy frame for mounting and protecting internal devices, connectors, and drives.

system utilities (utility programs) Programs that work in tandem with the operating system and are considered essential to the effective management of a computer system. They perform such functions as system backup, antivirus protection, file search and management, system scans, disk and file defragmentation, and file compression; also called utility programs.

systems analyst A problem-solving computer professional who works with users and management to determine an organization's information system needs.

T

T1 line A high-bandwidth telephone trunk line made of fiber-optic (or specially conditioned copper) cables that can handle 24 digitized voice channels or transferring computer data at a rate of up to 1.544 megabits per second (Mbps).

T2 line A high-bandwidth telephone trunk line made of fiber-optic cable that can handle up to 44.7 Mbps of computer data.

T3 line A high-bandwidth telephone trunk line made of fiber-optic cable that can handle up to 44.7 Mbps of computer data. T3 lines can cost approximately $3,000 per month. Internet service providers, financial institutions, and large corporations that move a large amount of data find these lines critical to their operations. One T3 line is equivalent to having 28 T1 lines.

tab A segment of the Ribbon that contains category titles of tasks you can accomplish within an application. Several advanced tabs, such as Add-Ins and Developer, which are not visible by default, can be turned on.

tabbed browsing A feature on most Internet browsers today that makes use of tabs located at the top of the browsers window, allowing the user to have several Web pages open at once and switch quickly between them. You can customize your home page by adding tabs for sites that you frequently access.

table A series of columns (fields) and rows (records) that compose the content of a data set.

tablet PC A type of notebook computer whose LCD screen swivels and can be made to lie flat over the keyboard, allowing the user to input data in handwritten form with a stylus. Recognition software converts it to digital text.

tag A marker that identifies various elements within markup language codes. Tags usually come in pairs. The actual text to be displayed is enclosed by an opening tag and a closing tag.

tailgating The entry of someone into a restricted area that requires authorization, by simply sticking close behind the approved individual. Tailgating was once associated only with the physical entry into a restricted zone, but it can also be extended to electronic entry and occurs when a user does not log out of a system and another user sits down and begins to work under the guise of the authorized user instead of logging out and re-logging in as him- or herself.

tailor-made application A piece of software designed for specialized fields or the consumer market, such as a program to handle the billing needs of medical offices, manage restaurants, and track occupational injuries.

TCP/IP (Transmission Control Protocol/Internet Protocol) The standard suite of methods used to package and transmit information on the Internet. TCP/IP employs a two-layer communication design. The TCP layer, Transmission Control Protocol, manages the assembling of a message or file into smaller packets that are transmitted over the Internet and received by a TCP layer on the destination computer that reassembles the packets into the original message. The lower layer, the Internet Protocol, handles the address part of each packet so that it gets to the right destination.

terabyte (TB) A unit of measurement approximately equal to 1 trillion bytes.

terminal An input/output device made up of a keyboard and video display, used as an inexpensive means to connect to a server.

terminator A special connector that signifies the end of a circuit in the bus topology.

text messaging (SMS) A mobile service, similar to using your phone for instant messaging or as a receiver and transmitter for brief e-mail messages.

texting A quick communication that might include text, images, video, and/or sound content that is generally delivered using a cell phone.

thermal-transfer printer A printer that uses a heat process to transfer colored dyes or inks to the paper's surface. Although thermal-transfer printers are the best color printers currently available, they are very expensive.

thrashing The excessive transfer of files from the hard disk to RAM and back (paging).

thread In Usenet, a series of articles that offer a continuing commentary on the same specific subject.

throughput The actual amount of data that can be sent through a specific transmission medium at one time (usually per second). Throughput is almost always lower than bandwidth, especially with wireless communications.

thumb drive Another name for a USB flash drive.

thumbscrew Small screws that are usually attached to the plug and are used to secure the plug to the system unit or expansion card extender to prevent an accidental disconnect.

time bomb A hidden piece of computer code set to go off on some date and time in the future, usually causing a malicious act to occur to the system. Time bombs are less sophisticated than logic bombs, because they are not programmed to be activated by a specific trigger.

time-limited trial version A commercial program offered over the Internet that can be used on a trial basis for a period of time, after which the software is unusable.

title bar In a graphical user interface (GUI), the top bar of an application window. The title bar typically contains the name of the application, the name of the document, and window controls.

toggle key A key on a keyboard that has two states: on and off. When pressed, the function is turned on, and when pressed again, the function is turned off. The Caps Lock key is an example of a toggle key.

token A special unit of data that travels around the ring in a ring topology layout of a network. A node can transmit only when it possesses the token, thus preventing collisions.

top-level domain (TLD) name The last part of the domain portion of a URL. For computers located in the United States, it indicates the type of organization in which the computer is located, such as commercial businesses (.com), educational institutions (.edu), and government agencies (.gov).

top-level folder The folder at the beginning of the folder structure; in a path, it is directly after the drive letter indicator. It is the starting point of an organization strategy to place files with common or related content in the same location.

touch screen A touch-sensitive display that enables users to input choices by touching a region of the screen.

touchpad (trackpad) A stationary, pressure-sensitive, pointing device that provides a small, flat surface on which you slide your finger, using the same movements as you would with a mouse. An area is set aside along the right and bottom edges of the pad to accommodate vertical or horizontal scroll operations. Commands are issued through one of the touchpad keys located near the edge of the pad or by tapping on the pad's surface.

tower case A tall and deep vertical system unit container designed to sit on the floor next to a desk and to easily accommodate add-on components.

track One of several concentric circular bands on computer disks where data is recorded. Tracks are created during formatting (set up) and are divided into sectors.

trackball A stationary pointing device that contains a movable ball held in a cradle. The on-screen cursor is moved by rotating the ball with the fingers or palm. From one to three keys can be located in various positions, depending on the unit, to perform the equivalent of mouse actions like a click and right-click.

transfer performance A measure of how quickly read/write heads are able to transfer data from a hard disk to RAM.

transistor An electronic switch (or gate) that controls the flow of electrical signals through the circuit. Due to their small size, reduced power consumption, and lower heat output, transistors replaced vacuum tubes in the second generation of computers.

transition In a presentation graphics program, it is the visual movement and effects that appear as one slide exits the presentation and another enters.

Transmission Control Protocol (TCP) Part of the TCP/IP suite of protocols that regulate packaging and transmitting information over the Internet. TCP is the higher layer of the standard of transmission that permits two Internet-connected computers to establish a reliable connection. It is responsible for managing the assembling of a message or file into smaller packets that are transmitted over the Internet and received by a TCP layer on the destination computer that reassembles the packets into the original message.

trap door In computer security, a security hole created on purpose that can be exploited at a later time.

travel mouse A pointing device half the size of a normal mouse, but with all the same capabilities.

Trojan horse A rogue program that contains instructions to perform a malicious task that is disguised as a useful program.

truncation In using a search engine, the action of inserting wildcard symbols such as ? and *, also called truncation symbols, to search for various word endings and spellings simultaneously.

tweet A posting on a Twitter account that cannot exceed 140 characters.

twisted-pair An inexpensive copper cable used for telephone and data communications. The term *twisted-pair* refers to the interweaving of the paired wires, a practice that reduces interference from electrical fields.

Twitter A free, real-time social messaging utility that allows postings of up to 140 characters.

U

ubiquitous computing A scenario for future computing that foresees an emerging trend in which individuals no longer interact with one computer at a time but instead interact with multiple devices connected through an omnipresent network, enabling technology to become virtually embedded and invisible in every aspect of our lives.

Unicode A character coding system that uses 16 bits and can represent over 65,000 characters and symbolize all the world's written languages. The first 128 codes in the Unicode system represent the same characters as the first 128 in the ASCII system.

uninstalling The act of removing a program from a computer system by using a special utility.

uninterruptible power supply (UPS) A device that provides power to a computer system for a short time if electrical power is lost.

UNIX An operating system developed by Bell Laboratories in 1969. It was the first operating system written in the C language. It is a free OS installed primarily on workstations and features preemptive multitasking.

uploading Transferring a file from your computer to another computer by means of a computer network.

URL (Uniform Resource Locator) On the World Wide Web, a string of characters that precisely identifies an Internet resource's type and location. For example, the fictitious URL http://www.wolverine.virginia.edu/~toros/winerefs/merlot.html identifies a World Wide Web document (http://), indicates the domain name of the computer on which it is stored (www.wolverine.virginia.edu), fully describes the document's location in the directory structure (~toros/winerefs/), and includes the document's name and extension (merlot.html).

USB dongle A device that is inserted into a USB port and adds additional features to the base system, such as enabling network connectivity, increasing RAM memory, and permitting Bluetooth communication.

USB flash drive An average user's choice of portable storage that is about the size of an adult's thumb and can hold up to 64 GB of data; also referred to as a flash drive or solid-state drive.

USB hub A device that plugs into an existing USB port and contains four or more additional ports.

USB (universal serial bus) port An external bus architecture designed to replace older parallel and serial ports that became popular in 1998 with the release of the iMac. It connects keyboards, mice, digital cameras, and many other peripheral devices. A single USB port can connect up to 127 peripheral devices, eliminating the need for special ports that work only with specific devices.

USB wireless network adapter A communication device that plugs into a USB port and usually provides an intuitive graphical user interface (GUI) for easy configuration. It supports data encryption for secure wireless communication and is perfect for the traveler and notebook user.

Usenet A worldwide computer-based discussion system that uses the Internet and other networks for transmission media. Discussion is channeled into thousands of topically named newsgroups, which contain original contributions called articles, as well as commentaries on these articles called follow-up posts. As follow-up posts continue to appear on a given subject, a thread of discussion emerges.

user interface The part of the operating system that the user sees, interacts with, and uses to communicate with programs.

utility programs Programs that work in tandem with the operating system and are considered essential to the effective management of a computer system. They perform such functions as system backup, antivirus protection, file search and management, system scans, disk and file defragmentation, and file compression; also called system utilities.

V

vacation hacking Usually occurs in hotels and airports, where an unsuspected traveler accesses a rogue WiFi access point, called an evil twin, on a fraudulent network. The information the traveler enters is not reaching the desired destination but is being captured by criminals running the fraudulent network.

validate After purchasing a software program, it is the process of providing a special code or product key before you can use it. Validation proves that you are using a legal copy, not a pirated version.

variant A copy of a self-modifying virus. Each new copy is slightly different from the previous one, making it difficult to protect your computer.

VDSL (very high bit-rate digital subscriber line) The next generation of DSL transmission technology providing super-accelerated rates of 52 Mbps for downloads and 12 Mbps for uploads. It will provide services like HDTV and Video-on-Demand along with Internet access.

vector graphic An image composed of distinct objects, such as lines, shapes, or any element created by a mathematical equation. Thus, the final image is described by a complex mathematical formula that can be edited quite easily to accommodate a change in size, location, or shape.

vendor A company that sells goods or services. In this context, it refers to a company that develops software and sells it to other firms.

VGA (video graphics array) connector A 15-pin male connector that works with standard monitor cables. VGA connectors transmit analog video signals and are used for legacy technology cathode ray tube (CRT) monitors.

video card Video circuitry that fits into an expansion bus and determines the quality of the display and resolution of your monitor.

video editor A program that enables you to modify digitized videos by cutting segments, resequencing frames, adding transitions, and compressing a file, as well as determining a video's frame rate and saving the digitized video file in several video file formats.

Video Graphics Array (VGA) The lowest resolution standard for color graphics displays (640 × 480).

videoconferencing (Web conferencing) The use of digital video technology to transmit sound and video images to facilitate online, virtual meetings through which two or more people can have a face-to-face meeting even though they're geographically separated; also called Web conferencing.

virtualization The process of running multiple virtual machines on one physical machine, which means that the applications and infrastructure are separate, a feature critical to the category of cloud service referred to as Infrastructure-as-a-Service (IaaS).

virtual laser keyboard A keyboard image generated by a device about the size of a small cellular phone that displays a light projection of a full-sized computer keyboard on almost any surface. Its adaptable technology studies the user's finger movements to interpret and record keystrokes.

virtual machine Not an actual physical machine, but a software-created segment of a hard drive that contains its own operating system and applications, which makes it behave as a separate physical machine in the eyes of the user.

virtual memory A term used to refer to a portion of the hard drive that the operating system treats as a portion of RAM when RAM is full.

virtual private network (VPN) A network that operates as a private network over a public network, usually the Internet, using exclusive leased lines, that makes data accessible to authorized users in remote locations through the use of secure, encrypted connections and special software.

vlog (video log) Short for video log. A series of personal reflective videos that are usually created simply by talking to a webcam and uploading the video. Many vloggers post their vlogs on YouTube.

vodcast (video podcast) Short for video podcast. A term used for the online delivery of video clips on demand.

VoIP (Voice over Internet Protocol) A type of Internet telephony that uses the Internet for real-time voice communication.

volatile memory Storage that is very fast but that is erased when the power goes off. RAM is volatile memory.

W

WAP (Wireless Application Protocol) A standard that specifies how users can access the Web securely using pagers, smartphones, PDAs, and other wireless handheld devices.

wardriving A process in which an individual drives around with a wireless device, such as a notebook or smartphone, to look for wireless networks to break into.

warm boot (restart) Restarting a computer that is already on.

Web 1.0 A set of techniques that were used in the early years of the Web for developing static Web pages that included no interactivity other than hyperlinks.

Web 2.0 A set of techniques currently in use that collectively provides an upgraded presentation and usefulness for the World Wide Web. It provides even more opportunities for individuals to collaborate, interact with one another, and create new content by using applications such as blogs, wikis, and podcasts.

Web 3.0 The future generation of the Web. Many experts believe that the Web 3.0 browser will act like a personal assistant, learning what you are interested in as you browse.

Web beacon A transparent graphic image, usually no larger than 1 pixel × 1 pixel, that is placed on a Web site or in an e-mail and used to monitor the behavior of the user visiting the Web site or sending the e-mail. One common use is to alert a sender when a message has been opened.

Web browser A program on the user's computer that displays a Web document by interpreting the HTML or XHTML format, enabling the user to view Web pages and activate hyperlinks embedded within those pages.

webcam An inexpensive camera attached to the computer, can be used to hold live chat sessions and make video phone calls. In most newer systems, a Webcam is standard equipment.

Web-enabled device Any device that can connect to the Internet and display and respond to the codes in markup languages, such as HTML (Hypertext Markup Language) or XML (Extensible Markup Language). Web-enabled devices include PDAs, smartphones, and notebook PCs.

Web-hosted technology A new wave of office suites that, for application software, provides the capability to upload files to an online site so the documents can be viewed and edited from another location. This technology makes file sharing and collaboration easier. Windows Office Live and Google Docs are two examples of online services that offer these capabilities.

Web page A document or resource on a Web site, transported over the Internet, created using the established standards, and made viewable to a user through a program called a browser.

Web server A computer on the Web running server software that accepts inputted information and makes that information available to an Internet user when requested.

Web site A collection of related Web pages.

WEP (Wired Equivalent Privacy) One of the earliest security methods for wireless networks, WEP has several well-known weaknesses, but it may be the only option for some devices or older equipment.

wheel mouse A type of mouse that has a rotating wheel that is used to scroll text vertically within a document or on a Web page.

whiteboard A separate area of a videoconferencing screen that enables participants to create a shared workspace. Participants can write or draw in this space as if they were using a chalkboard in a meeting.

wide area network (WAN) A network that uses long-distance transmission media, including microwave relay, satellites, and phone lines, to link computers separated by a few miles or several thousand miles. A WAN is a geographically dispersed collection of LANs. The Internet is the largest WAN. A WAN is not owned by a single organization; it has a collective ownership or management, like the Internet.

Widescreen Extended Graphics Array plus (WXGA+) A resolution of 1440 × 900, typically found in 19-inch monitors.

Widescreen Super Extended Graphics Array plus (WSXGA+) A resolution of 1680 × 1050, typically found in 20-inch monitors.

Widescreen Ultra Extended Graphics Array (WUXGA) A resolution of 1920 × 1200, typically found in 24-inch monitors.

WiFi A wireless LAN standard used for home networks that offers Ethernet speeds through the use of radio signals instead of wires.

wiki A collection of Web pages designed to let anyone with access contribute or modify content. Wikis are often used to create collaborative or community Web sites.

wildcard (truncation symbol) A symbol that stands for any character or any group of characters. Common wildcards are the ? for a single character and * for multiple characters; also called a truncation symbol.

WiMAX A wireless up-and-coming digital communication system designed to deliver high-speed access over long distances, either point to point (both sender and receiver are stationary) or through mobile access (sender or receiver is moving).

window border A thick line that encloses the window and can be manipulated to resize the window larger or smaller.

window control buttons In a graphical user interface (GUI), a group of window management tools, located on the right side of the title bar, that enable the user to minimize, maximize, restore, or close the window.

Windows CE One of the early embedded operating systems, first introduced in 1996, with upgrades made available in 1997. It is used by consumer electronic devices like handheld PCs, video game players, and digital cameras, and by industrial products like barcode readers. Its primary features include a low overhead device driver and a built-in power manager.

Windows Update A free operating system update service designed to keep your Windows operating system up to date with fixes (service patches) or protections against external environment changes.

wireless access point (AP or WAP) A node on a network that acts as a receiver and transmitter of wireless radio signals between other nodes on a network. A WAP can also act as a bridge connecting wireless clients to a wired network.

wireless Internet service provider An Internet access provider that can be a local or national company that provides wireless Internet access to computers and other mobile devices, such as notebooks and smartphones. Some familiar providers are AT&T, T-Mobile, and Verizon Wireless.

wireless keyboard A keyboard that connects to the computer through infrared (IR), radio frequency (RF), or Bluetooth connections instead of a cable.

wireless LAN A local area network that connects its nodes though the use of radio signals spread over a seemingly random series of frequencies for greater security.

wireless memory card A card that has all the storage features of a regular flash memory card and combines it with wireless circuitry. It can connect with your PC via a wireless network or send pictures directly from your digital camera to your favorite online photo site.

wireless mouse (cordless mouse) A mouse with no cord that transmits infrared or radio signals (RF) to a base station receiver. Wireless mice eliminate the cord tangling associated with the corded variety. The infrared type requires line of sight to the receiver, whereas the RF variety uses radio waves that transmit in a wider pattern.

wireless PC card adapter A device, approximately the size of a credit card, that is inserted into a slot on the side of most notebooks and netbooks. It has a built-in

WiFi antenna that provides wireless capability and LED lights that indicate whether the computer is connected.

wiring closet A central location that extends through all floors of the building in which the appropriate wiring is housed to support most types of data transfer that the individuals or companies that occupy the building might want to access.

word size The maximum number of bits the central processing unit (CPU) can work with at once.

workbook In a spreadsheet program such as Microsoft Excel, a file that can contain two or more spreadsheets, each of which has its own tab in the workbook.

worksheet In a spreadsheet program such as Microsoft Excel, a single tab of a workbook.

World Wide Web (Web or WWW) The portion of the Internet that contains billions of documents. The Web uses the Internet as its transport mechanism but is a separate entity. The Web is an information resource that enables millions of Internet users to research products, get medical advice, read about current events, and much more.

worm A program resembling a computer virus that can spread over networks without the user executing an infected file.

WPA (WiFi Protected Access) A security method for wireless networks that was developed to provide stronger security than WEP.

WPA2 A security method for wireless networks that improves on WPA's abilities. WPA2 provides confidentiality and data integrity and is far superior to WEP, because it uses AES (Advanced Encryption Standard) to provide government-grade security.

X

X.25 A packet-switching network protocol optimized for use on noisy analog telephone lines.

xD Picture Card A type of flash memory card used in digital cameras. It is available in capacities of 64 MB to 32 GB of digital data.

Y

yottabyte A unit of measurement approximately equal to 1 septillion bytes.

Z

zettabyte A unit of measurement approximately equal to 1 sextillion bytes.

zombie A single computer commandeered during a denial of service (DoS) attack.

Illustration Credits

Chapter 1

Fig. 00-01 JGI/Tom Grill/Blend Images/ Corbis Fig. 01-02 iStockphoto Fig. 01-03 U.P.images_ photo/Shutterstock Fig. 01-04 Studio 37/Shutterstock Fig. 01-04c Courtesy of Apple Fig. 01-04d Courtesy of Research In Motion (RIM). Research In Motion, the RIM logo, BlackBerry, the BlackBerry logo and SureType are registered with the U.S. Patent and Trademark Office and may be pending or registered in other countries - these and other marks of Research In Motion Limited are used under license. Fig. 01-05 Jason Stitt/Shutterstock Fig. 01-06 jcwait/Shutterstock Fig. 01-06a © Dell, Inc. All Rights Reserved. The Dell logo is a trademark of Dell Inc. Fig. 01-06b Michael Jarrett/Gateway Inc. Fig. 01-06j Susan Van Etten/PhotoEdit Inc. Fig. 01-06k Motorola, Inc. Fig. 01-06l © Greg Nicholas/ Courtesy of www.istockphoto.com Fig. 01-06m Courtesy of Cisco Fig. 01-07 Photographer's Choice/Superstock Royalty Free Fig. 01-07a Courtesy of Apple Fig. 01-08a Shutterstock Fig. 01-08b iStockphoto Fig. 01-09 Shutterstock Fig. 01-10 Microsoft product screen shot(s) reprinted with permission from Microsoft Corporation. Fig. 01-11 Shutterstock Fig. 01-12a Eyewire, Inc./Getty Images Fig. 01-12b Alan Klehr/Churchill & Klehr Photography Fig. 01-12c Shutterstock Fig. 01-13a Zefa Collection/CORBIS- NY Fig. 01-13b Courtesy of Intel Corporation Fig. 01-13c jossnat/Shutterstock Fig. 01-13d Nick Koudis/Getty Images, Inc.- Photodisc./ Royalty Free Fig. 01-14a Shutterstock Fig. 01-14b iStockphoto Fig. 01-14c Apple Computer, Inc. Fig. 01-14d Realimage/ Alamy Images Fig. 01-14e Shutterstock Fig. 01-15a francesco riccard iacomino/ Shutterstock Fig. 01-15b Apple Computer, Inc. Fig. 01-15c Anatoliy Samara/ Shutterstock Fig. 01-15d Henrik Andersen/ Shutterstock Fig. 01-16 iStockphoto Fig. 01-17 iStockphoto Fig. 01-18 Shutterstock Fig. 01-19 Shutterstock Fig. 01-20 iStockphoto Fig. 01-25 iStockphoto Fig. 01-27 Photodisc/Getty Images Fig. 01-29 iStockphoto Fig. 01-30 iStockphoto Fig. 01-32 Shutterstock Fig. 01-33 Gravitonus, Inc. Fig. 01-34 iStockphoto Fig. 01-35 Alan Howden/Alamy Images Fig. 01-36 michael ledray/Shutterstock Fig. 01-aa A1Stock/Shutterstock Fig. 01-bb Pedro Tavares/Shutterstock Fig. 01-cc Lomaney/Shutterstock Fig. 01-dd juliengrondin/Shutterstock Fig. 01-ee Shutterstock Fig. 01-ff Shutterstock Fig. 01-gg Shutterstock Fig. 01-hh Shutterstock

Spotlight 1

Fig. SP01-CO iStockphoto Fig. SP01-A Shutterstock Fig. SP01-B Reprinted with permission. Fig. SP01-C Mikael Damkier/Shutterstock Fig. SP01-E AmyWalters/Shutterstock Fig. SP01-F beerkoff/Shutterstock Fig. SP01-G Reprinted with permission. Fig. SP01-H The Software & Information Industry Association Fig. SP01-I Source: Rhapsody

Chapter 2

Fig. 02-13a Lenovo, Inc. Fig. 02-13b Lenovo, Inc. Fig. 02-14 Alan Evans/ Diane M. Coyle Fig. 02-16a Kingston Technology Co., Inc. Fig. 02-16b © Creative Technology Ltd. Fig. 02-16c © US Robotics Fig. 02-16d Replace on Revision Fig. 02-16e Manic Photos/Alamy Images Fig. 02-17a thumb/iStockphoto.com Fig. 02-17b ranplett/iStockphoto.com Fig. 02-17c gdpozzi/iStockphoto.com Fig. 02-17d Zocha_K/iStockphoto.com Fig. 02-17e zoomstudio/iStockphoto.com Fig. 02-17f maelms/iStockphoto.com Fig. 02-17g Pannonia/iStockphoto.com Fig. 02-17h Norman Chan/Shutterstock Fig. 02-24 Courtesy of Intel Corporation Fig. 02-27 Fotosearch.com, LLC Fig. 02-28 © Carolina K. Smith, M.D. / Courtesy of www.istockphoto.com Fig. 02-29 David A. Tietz Fig. 02-30 Phil Burton/Alamy Images Fig. 02-31 Lewis - Global Public Relations Fig. 02-32 Goodshot/Corbis RF

Photodisc./Royalty Free Fig. 03-44 ExpressCard - PCMCIA Fig. 03-45a SanDisk Corporation Fig. 03-45b SanDisk Corporation Fig. 03-45c Lexar Media Fig. 03-46 SanDisk Corporation Fig. 03-47 © William Whitehurst/CORBIS All Rights Reserved Fig. 03-ID01 Alamy Fig. 03-ID02 Alamy Fig. 03-ID03 Alamy Fig. 03-ID04 Alamy Fig. 03-ID05 Shutterstock Fig. 03-ID06 Shutterstock Fig. 03-ID07 AFP Photo/Sony Corporation/HO Fig. 03-ID08 Alamy

Spotlight 2

Fig. SP02-CO iStockphoto

Chapter 4

Fig. 04-11b Thomas Brummett/Getty Images Inc. - PhotoDisc Figs. 04-14–04-16 Source: Google Fig. 04-19 Aurora Photos/ Alamy Fig. 04-24 Source: Ubuntu Fig. 04-25 One Laptop per Child Fig. 04-27a robophobic/Shutterstock Fig. 04-27b Alex Segre/Alamy Images Fig. 04-27c Wave Royalty Free/Alamy Images Royalty Free Fig. 04-28 Newscom Fig. 04-29 HTCAmerica Fig. 04-30 PRNewsFoto/ VerizonWireless Fig. 04-31 Courtesy of Apple Fig. 04-40 Computers Are Your Future is an independent publication and has not been authorized, sponsored, or otherwise approved by Apple Inc.

Spotlight 3

Fig. SP03-A1 jossnat/Shutterstock Fig. SP03-A2 goory/Shutterstock Fig. SP03-A3 Dmitry Melnikov/Shutterstock Fig. SP03-Ba Xebeche/Shutterstock Fig. SP03-Bb iStockphoto.com Fig. SP03-Bc iStockphoto.com Fig. SP03-C Shutterstock Fig. SP03-D Reprinted with permission. Fig. SP03-E Pioneer Electronics (USA) Inc. Fig. SP03-F Advanced Micro Devices Fig. SP03-G1 Ximagination/Shutterstock Fig. SP03-G2 Reprinted with permission from Microsoft Corporation. Fig. SP03-H American Power Conversion Corporation Fig. SP03-I Targus, Inc. Fig. SP03-J Peter Cade/Image Bank/Getty Images Fig. SP03-L Falk Kienas/Shutterstock Fig. SP03-M Natalia Siverina/Shutterstock

Spotlight 4

Fig. SP04-C Reprinted with permission. Fig. SP04-G Source: Twitter Fig. SP04-J Thinkstock Fig. SP04-L Khromov Alexey/ Shutterstock

Chapter 6

Fig. 06-04 Shutterstock Fig. 06-05a © Andres Stapff / CORBIS All Rights Reserved Fig. 06-05 Shutterstock Fig. 06-06 Reprinted with permission by Microsoft. All rights reserved. Fig. 06-09 W3C® is a trademark (registered in numerous countries) of the World Wide Web Consortium; marks of W3C are registered and held by its host institutions MIT, ERCIM, and Keio. Fig. 06-22 Reprinted with permission by Microsoft. All rights reserved. Fig. 06-23 Reproduced with permission from the ipl2 Consortium, copyright 2010 by the ipl2 Consortium (http://www.ipl.org). All rights reserved. Fig. 06-24 Reprinted with permission by Yahoo! All rights reserved. Fig. 06-38 Reprinted with permission by Amazon. All rights reserved. Fig. 06-39 Reprinted with permission by Shopzilla. All rights reserved. Fig. 06-42 Source: Travelocity Fig. 06-44 Source: Net Nanny

Spotlight 5

Fig. CO-SP05 Ye/Shutterstock

Chapter 8

Fig. 08-05A, D Shutterstock Fig. 08-07 Zhu Difeng/Shutterstock Fig. 08-09 © David A. Tietz/Editorial Image, LLC Fig. 08-10 Zwola Fasola/Shutterstock Fig. 08-12 Undergroundarts.co.uk/Shutterstock Fig. 08-14 Cables Unlimited Fig. 08-15 © Bluetooth SIG 2008 Fig. 08-17 Chris Curtis/Shutterstock Fig. 08-18 Kawish/ Shutterstock Fig. 08-19a Dgbomb/Shutterstock Fig. 08-19b Skyline/Shutterstock Fig. 08-19c HHF/Shutterstock Fig. 08-19d Bart J/ Shutterstock Fig. 08-19e GDM/Shutterstock Fig. 08-20a Courtesy of IBM Archives. Unauthorized use not permitted. Fig. 08-20b D-Link Systems, Inc. Fig. 08-20c MOTOROLA, stylized M Logo, and SURFboard are registered in the US Patent & Trademark Office. All other product or service names are the property of their respective owners. © Motorola, Inc. 2008. All

Spotlight 6

Chapter 9

Index

GPS (Global Positioning System), 4, 373–374, 376, 410
graphical MUDs (gMUDs), 212
graphical user interfaces (GUIs), 138, 139
Graphics Interchange Format (GIF), 199, 204
graphics software, 196–208
graphics tablet, 82
Green Maven, 268
GreenDisk, 215
grids, 296, 297
grounding bracelets, 55, 180
groups, 190
GUIDs. *See* global unique identifiers (GUIDs)
GUIs. *See* graphical user interfaces (GUIs)

H

hacker ethic, 423
hackers, 423–425
handheld computers, 13, 15
HANs. *See* home networks
hard copy, 94
hard disk controllers, 100
hard drives, 57, 173–174
  external, 11, 107, 173–174
  internal, 10–11, 100–102, 173–174
hardware, 7, 22–23
Hardware-as-a-Service (HaaS). *See* Infrastructure-as-a-Service (IaaS)
HDSL (high bit-rate digital subscriber line), 359, 360
headsets, 9, 393–394
Health Insurance Portability and Privacy Act (HIPAA), 407
heat sinks, 57, 58
hexadecimal (hex) numbers, 52
hibernate mode, 132, 160–161
high-definition televisions (HDTVs), 95
high-definition video (HD), 104–105
high-energy radio frequency (HERF) guns, 430
history list, 263
holographic storage, 106
home and educational programs, 211–213
home networks, 329–338
  future of, 336
  maintenance and support, 335–336
  setting up, 333–338
  wired, 330–331, 334–335
  wireless, 331–333, 335
home pages, 256

honeypots, 424
host name, 261–262
hosts, 248
hot spots, 252, 324, 377
hot swapping, 69
howstuffworks.com, 180
HTC Droid, 388
HTML. *See* Hypertext Markup Language (HTML)
HTTP. *See* Hypertext Transfer Protocol (HTTP)
HTTPS. *See* Hypertext Transfer Protocol Secure (HTTPS)
hubs, 311
HughesNet, 375
hybrid cloud, 299
hybrid hard drives (HHDs), 102
hybrid network, 330
hybrid power mode, 160–161
hybrid sleep mode, 132
hyperlinks, 256, 262
hypertext, 256–258
Hypertext Markup Language (HTML), 232, 256
Hypertext Transfer Protocol (HTTP), 261
Hypertext Transfer Protocol Secure (HTTPS), 261

I

iAds, 198
IBM-compatible computers, 13. *See also* personal computers (PCs)
IBM Lotus SmartSuite, 214
IBM Roadrunner, 17
icons, 138
identity theft, 234, 283–284, 400, 407, 413–414
iGoogle, 231, 265
iLife, 208
image editors, 202–203
iMovie, 207
inclusion operator, 268
incremental backup, 152
Indeed, 267
index pages. *See* home pages
Infoplease, 267
information, 10
information kiosks, 387
information overload, 21
information processing cycle (IPOS), 7–13
information warfare, 429–430
infrared, 354
Infrastructure-as-a-Service (IaaS), 296
inkjet printers, 96–97, 174–175

input
  in information processing cycle, 7, 9–10, 12
  and the operating system, 137–138
input devices, 81, 82–93
  biometric input devices, 93
  digital camcorders, 9, 93
  digital cameras, 9, 93
  drivers for, 137–138
  graphics tablet, 82
  keyboards. *See* keyboards
  magnetic stripe readers, 82, 93
  mice. *See* mice
  MICR readers, 93
  microphones, 9, 82
  pointing devices, 87–89
  RFID readers, 93
  scanners, 9, 92
  webcams, 82, 93
input/output (I/O) bus, 63
insertion point. *See* cursor
installing software, 219–220
instant messaging (IM), 19, 39, 238–239, 276
Institute for Certification of Computing Professionals (ICCP), 41
Institute of Electrical and Electronics Engineers (IEEE), 52
instruction cycle, 59
instruction set, 58
integrated circuit cards (ICCs). *See* smart cards
integrated circuits (IC), 57
integrated peripherals, 7–8
integrated programs, 214
Intel microprocessors, 62–63, 171
intellectual property, 41–43, 270
intelligent keyboards, 85
interactivity, 196
internal speakers, 56
Internet, 4
  access to, 248, 251–254
    4 Mbps download target, 327
    cable, 253, 360–361
    dial-up, 253
    DSL, 253, 350, 359–360, 361
    fiber-optic service (FiOS), 254, 350
    MMDS, 362
    satellite, 253–254, 357, 374–375
  backbones, 249, 324–325
  children's safety on the, 284–285, 409–410, 425–426
  connecting to, 12
  defined, 248
  ethics, 6
  gaming, 211–212

Nessus, 430
nesting, 269
Net. *See* Internet
Net Nanny, 285
netbooks, 7, 13, 15, 84, 169–170
netiquette, 38–39, 242, 283, 366
Netscape Navigator, 258
Netware, 148
network access points (NAPs), 249, 332, 357
network administrators, 313
network architecture, 320–321
network-attached storage (NAS), 102
network connector (Ethernet/RJ-45), 70
network interface cards (NICs), 9, 12, 56, 57, 175, 308, 331
network layers, 321
network operating system (NOS), 312
network service providers (NSPs), 249
networks, 11–12
   advantages and disadvantages of, 314
   CANs, 308, 310
   client/server, 16, 316–318, 332
   communication devices, 308–313
   defined, 308
   Ethernet, 322
   fundamentals, 308–313
   home, 329–338
   LANs, 308, 309, 314–324
   MANs, 308, 310
   PANs, 308
   peer-to-peer (P2P), 315–316, 332
   protocols, 320–324
   security issues and, 314
   topologies, 319–320
   virtual private networks (VPNs), 319
   WANs, 308, 309, 324–329
   Wi-Fi, 322–324, 331–333
newsgroups, 277–278
NexTag, 280
NICs. *See* network interface cards (NICs)
9/11, 434–435
Ning, 237–238, 277
Nintendo Wii, 393
No Electronic Theft (NET) Act, 421
nodes, 308
nonvolatile memory, 133
Nook, 15, 389
Norton, Richard, 403
notebook computers, 7, 13, 14, 54, 56, 169–170
   bags for, 169
   connectors on, 69
   cooling pads for, 176
   keyboard, 84

Novell SUSE, 312
NTFS (new technology file system), 101

O

office suites. *See* software suites
Ogg Vorbis, 206
OLED (organic light emitting diode) displays, 96
on-screen keyboards. *See* virtual keyboards
onboard video, 70
One Laptop per Child (OLPC), 146
1394 port, 70
OnGuard Online, 413
online banking, 4, 282
online business, building an, 280–282
online classes, 4
online dating, 426
online discussion forums, 39, 241–242, 277–278
online service providers (OSPs), 252
online shopping, 280, 409
online stock trading, 282
online travel reservations, 282
OnStar, 373–374, 406
Open Cloud Manifesto, 302
open source software, 144–145, 150–151
Opera, 258
operating systems (OS), 8, 129–151
   embedded, 141, 148–150, 368–369
   functions
      coordinating tasks, 137–138
      managing applications, 134–135
      managing memory, 135–137
      starting the computer, 130–134
      user interfaces, 138–141
   Linux, 144–146, 148, 151
   Mac OS, 142–144
   Microsoft Windows. *See* Windows operating systems
   multitasking operating systems, 135
   server, 141, 148
   single-tasking operating systems, 135
   stand-alone, 141–147
   UNIX, 144, 148
operations per cycle, 60–61
optical character recognition (OCR), 92
optical mark readers (OMRs), 92
optical mouse, 88
optical storage devices, 103–104
options, 221
OQO model 2+, 363
Oracle SaaS, 297

O'Reilly, Tim, 231
organizations
   computers for, 16–17
   ethics for, 40–41
ORNL's Jaguar, 17
Outlook 2010, 186, 187, 195–196
output, 94
   in information processing cycle, 7, 10, 13
   and the operating system, 137–138
output devices, 81, 93–98
   data projectors, 98
   drivers for, 137–138
   faxes, 98
   monitors. *See* monitors
   printers. *See* printers
   speakers, 9, 10, 98
outsourcing, 27–28

P

packaged software, 213–214
packet switching, 327–329
packets, 322
page-description languages (PDLs), 200
pages, 136
paging, 136
paint programs, 199–200
Palm OS, 148, 150, 368
Palm Pre, 392
PANs (personal area networks), 308, 355
parallel ports, 71
parallel processing, 61
parental controls, 285
Parkin, Stuart, 107
partitions, 101
passive-matrix LCDs, 95
PassMark Software, 171–172
Password Meter, 411
passwords, 134, 422, 431
   strong, 411
path, 117, 262
payload, 415
PayPal, 281–282, 285
PBworks, 232
PC card slots, 70
PC cards. *See* ExpressCards
PCI Express, 174
PCI Express Base 2.1, 174
PCI (peripheral component interconnect) bus, 63
PCI standards, 402
pcmag.com, 170, 180
PCMCIA cards. *See* ExpressCards
PCs. *See* personal computers (PCs)
PCS (personal communication service), 366–368